THE ORIENTAL INSTITUTE OF THE UNIVERSITY OF CHICAGO

ORIENTAL INSTITUTE COMMUNICATIONS · NO. 24

AMERICAN EXPEDITION TO IDALION, CYPRUS 1973-1980

LAWRENCE E. STAGER

ANITA M. WALKER

Project Directors and

General Editors

THE ORIENTAL INSTITUTE OF THE UNIVERSITY OF CHICAGO

ORIENTAL INSTITUTE COMMUNICATIONS · NO. 24

Chicago • Illinois

Library of Congress Catalog Card Number: 87-60773

ISBN: 0-918986-52-4
ISSN: 0146-678X

The Oriental Institute, Chicago

© 1989 by *The University of Chicago. All rights reserved
Published 1989. Printed in the United States of America*

A version of the article, "Ancient Mining and Mineral Dressing on Cyprus," by Frank L. Koucky and Arthur Steinberg, appeared in Smithsonian publication *Early Pyrotechnology: The Evolution of the First Fire-Using Industries*, eds. T. A. Wertime and S. F. Wertime, Washington, DC: Smithsonian Institution Press, 1982, pp. 149-180.

Cover design: Idalion Object 712/A516, WNW 9/18.045 (Pit 10)

Bearded male terracotta figurine, pointed cap, flared base, holding shield (?) in left hand; base and right arm broken; red and black painted bands. Ht: 9 cm.

IN MEMORIAM

G. Ernest Wright
1909-1974

Multas per gentes et multa per aequora vectus
    Advenio has miseras, frater, ad inferias,
Ut te postremo donarem munere mortis
    Et mutam nequiquam adloquerer cinerem,
Quandoquidem fortuna mihi tete abstulit ipsum,
    Heu miser indigne frater adempte mihi.
Nunc tamen interea haec, prisco quae more parentum
    Tradita sunt tristi munere ad inferias,
Accipe fraterno multum manantia fletu
    Atque in perpetuum, frater, ave atque vale.

                                     Catullus

TABLE OF CONTENTS

Dedication v
List of Illustration ix
List of Tables xv
Acknowledgments xix
Staff, 1973-1980 xxi
List of Abbreviations xxiii

INTRODUCTION 1

PART I. EXCAVATIONS AT IDALION, 1973-1980

    A. West Terrace Excavations
    L. Stager and A. Walker with P. Gaber and A. Graham
    Palace 5
    West Terrace Fortifications 13
    B. Lower City Excavations
        1. Fortifications   *A. Walker* 45
            a. A Greek Geometric Kantharos (Object 595)   *P. Ålin* 58
            b. A Reconstructed Archaic Bronze Fibula
               (Object 548)   *S. Brown* 62
        2. West Lower City Domestic Precinct
           A. Walker and P. Gaber with L. Stager 66
            a. Selected Pottery Groups from the West Lower City
               Domestic Precinct   *P. Ålin* 83
    C. A Late Cypriot II C Tomb: Idalion Tomb 1.76
        1. Introduction and Skeletal Remains   *C. Schulte-Campbell* 119
        2. Artifactual Remains with Some Historical Observations
           C. Adelman 138

PART II. EXCAVATIONS AT DHALI-AGRIDHI: 1972, 1974, 1976

    A. Dhali-Agridhi: The Neolithic by the River   *Y. Lehavy* 203
    B. Fauna from the 1976 Season   *P. Carter* 244
    C. A Reconsideration of Fauna from the 1972 Season   *P. Croft* 259

PART III. METALLURGICAL STUDIES

    A. Ancient Mining and Mineral Dressing on Cyprus
    F. Koucky and A. Steinberg 275
    B. Metalwork from Idalion, 1971-1980   *J. Waldbaum* 328

PART IV. REGIONAL STUDIES

    A. Neutron Activation Analysis of Cypriot Pottery   *A. Bieber* 357
    B. Regional Styles in Cypriot Limestone Sculpture   *P. Gaber* 398

PART V. ETHNOARCHAEOLOGY AND ETHNOGRAPHY

    A. Ethnoarchaeological Investigations, 1976   *J. Sallade* 407
    B. Dhali: A Traditional Community in Transition   *P. Allen* 425

PART VI. NUMISMATICS

   Catalogue, Idalion 1970-1977   *I. Nicolaou* 447

PART VII. SUMMARY   *A. Walker and L. Stager* 459

BIBLIOGRAPHY 469

General Index 495
Author Index 507
Place Name Index 513

LIST OF ILLUSTRATIONS

INTRODUCTION

1. Upper Yalias Drainage Basin, Cyprus, 1973-1976 Survey 3
2. Idalion contour plan, showing areas of excavation, 1971-1980 4

PART I. EXCAVATIONS AT IDALION, 1973-1980

A. West Terrace Excavations
    Figures
        1. Idalion West Terrace, Areas C and D 21
        2. Idalion West Terrace, Area C Enlarged 22
        3. Idalion WSW Section (B-B) 23
        4. Idalion WSW Section (C-C) 24
        5. Idalion WSW Section (D-D) 25
        6. Pottery from Idalion WSW 8/15 (Area D) 27
        7. Pottery from Idalion WSW 11/16 (Area D) and 10/9, 11/9 (Area C) 29
        8. Idalion West Terrace Citadel Wall 30
        9. Idalion WSW Section (A-A) Citadel Wall 31
    Plates
        1. Area C 32
        2. Street 33
        3. Northern Facade 34
        4. Area C Chamber and Area D Room 35
        5. Area D Room and Area C Roofing 36
        6. Inscriptions, Phase 4 of Area D Room 37
        7. Inscriptions, Phase 4 of Area D Room and Backfill of Robber Trench 38
        8. East Face of Citadel Wall 021 39
        9. Walls 038 and 039 40
      10. Citadel Wall 021 41
      11. Citadel Wall 021 (Phase 5) 42
      12. Citadel Wall 021 43
      13. Wall 006 44

B. Lower City Excavations
  1. Fortifications
    Figures
        1. Plan of Idalion West Lower City Wall 49
        2. Idalion WNW Section (A-A^1) West Lower City Wall 50
        3. Idalion WNW Section (B-B^1) West Lower City Wall 51
        4. Idalion WNW Section (C-C^1) West Lower City Wall 52
        5. Idalion WNW Section (D-D^1) West Lower City Wall 53
    Plates
        1. City Wall 54
        2. Pit and Probe east of City Wall 55
        3. Lower City Fortifications 56
        4. Ashlar Facing (Wall 010) 57

    a. A Greek Geometric Kantharos
      Figure
        1. Greek Geometric Kantharos (Object no. 595) 60

Plate
    1. Greek Geometric Kantharos (Object no. 595).. 61
  b. A Reconstructed Archaic Bronze Fibula
    Figure
      1. Archaic Bronze Fibula (Object no. 548).. 65

2. West Lower City Domestic Precinct
  Figures
    1. West Lower City Domestic Precinct Plan 73
    2. Sequence Diagram of West Lower City Domestic Precinct 74
    3. Idalion WNW 9/18 South Section... 75
  Plates
    1. Pits 14 and 10 76
    2. Pits 9 and 10 77
    3. Pits 10 and 4 78
    4. Pit 14 and Buildings A and B.. 79
    5. Building A 80
    6. Buildings A and B 81
    7. Building B and Modern Vernacular Architecture 82

  a. Selected Pottery Groups from the West Lower City Domestic Precinct
    Figures
      1. Pottery from Idalion WNW 9/18 Locus 045 (Pit 10) 99
      2. Pottery from Idalion WNW 9/18 Locus 045 (Pit 10) 101
      3. Pottery from Idalion WNW 9/18 Locus 045 (Pit 10) 103
      4. Pottery from Idalion WNW 9/18 Locus 045 (Pit 10) 105
      5. Pottery (1-14) from Idalion WNW 9/18 Locus 045 (Pit 10)............................. 107
      5. Pottery (15-28) from Idalion WNW 9/18 Locus 045 (Pit 10) (*cont.*)............ 109
      6. Pottery (1-13) from Idalion WNW 9/18 Locus 045 (Pit 10)............................. 111
      6. Pottery (14-21) from Idalion WNW 9/18 Locus 045 (Pit 10) (*cont.*) 113
    Plates
      1. Pottery Sherds from Idalion WNW 10/18 114
      2. Pottery Sherds from Idalion WNW 9/18 115
      3. Pottery Sherds from Idalion WNW 9/18 116
      4. Pottery Sherds from Idalion WNW 9/18 117
      5. Pottery Sherds from Idalion WNW 9/19 118

C. A Late Cypriot IIC Tomb: Idalion Tomb 1.76
  1. Introduction and Skeletal Remains
    Figure
      1. Idalion Tomb 1.76.. 135
    Plates
      1. Cranial Remains.. 136
      2. Cranial and Post-cranial Remains 137

  2. Artifactual Remains with Some Historical Observations
    Figures
      1. Cat. nos. 1 (Jug), 2 (Bowl), and 3 (Jug).. 168
      2. Cat. nos. 5 (Bowl) and 6 (Tankard)... 170
      3. Cat. nos. 7 (Bowl) and 8 (Lentoid Flask).. 172
      4. Cat. nos. 9-13 (Fragmentary Jugs) 174
      5. Cat. nos. 14 and 15 (Jugs) 176
      6. Cat. nos. 19-22 (Fragmentary Jugs) and 23 (Inscribed Body Sherd) 178
      7. Cat. no. 24 (Jug) 180
      8. Cat. nos. 25 and 26 (Bowls), 28 (Jug), and 29 (Fragment of Tray?) 182
      9. Cat. nos. 30-33 (Bowls) 184
     10. Cat. nos. 34-36 (Bowls) and 37 (Fragments of Side-spouted Juglet) 186
     11. Cat. nos. 38 (Bowl), 39 (Cup), 40, 41 (Three-handled Jars), and 42
         (Three-handled or False-necked Jar).. 188

12. Cat. no. 43 (False-necked Jar) 190
13. Cat. nos. 44-46 (Jugs) 192
14. Sherd Profiles a-ii 194
15. Cat. nos. 47 (Bronze Ring), 48 (Perforated Disk), and 49 (Fragment of Animal Figurine) 196
16. Cat. nos. 50 (Glyptic Cylinder Seal), 51 (Perforated Flat Ivory Disk), 52 (Perforated Plano-convex Ivory Disk), 53 (Ivory Button?), and 54-56 (Perforated Ivory Buttons?) 198
17. Cat. nos. 57-61 (Cylindrical Ivory Rods) and 62-65 (Fragments of Ivory Bowls) 200

Plates
1. Cat. nos. 1-4 169
2. Cat. nos. 5 and 6 171
3. Cat. nos. 7 and 8 173
4. Cat. nos. 9-13 175
5. Cat. nos. 14-17 177
6. Cat. nos. 19-23 179
7. Cat. no. 24 181
8. Cat. nos. 25-29 183
9. Cat. nos. 30-33 185
10. Cat. nos. 34-37 187
11. Cat. nos. 38-42 189
12. Cat. no. 43 and Levanto-Mycenaean Sherds a-m 191
13. Cat. nos. 44-46 193
14. Iron Age Sherds a-jj 195
15. Cat. nos. 47-49 197
16. Cat. nos. 50-56 199
17. Cat. nos. 57-65 201

PART II. EXCAVATIONS AT DHALI-AGRIDHI: 1972, 1974, 1976

A. Dhali-Agridhi: The Neolithic by the River
Figures
1. Dhali-Agridhi, General Area of Excavation 217
2. Map of Cyprus, Showing Selected Neolithic Sites 218
3. Dhali-Agridhi, Final Top Plan; Seasons 1972, 1974, and 1976 219
4. Dhali-Agridhi, Area 1A, North and East Sections 220
5. Dhali-Agridhi, Areas of Excavations as of 1976 221
6. Dhali-Agridhi, Site E, 1976 222
7. Dhali-Agridhi, Site E, 1976 223
8. Lithics 224
9. Stone Bowls 225
10. Stone Bowls or Mortars 226
11. Stone Pounders or Hammers 227
12. Stone Hammer 228
13. Bone Implements 229
14. Ceramics, Dark-faced Burnished Ware 231
15. Ceramics, Horseshoe-shaped Vessel 233

Plates
1. Site before Excavation Started in the Summer of 1972 234
2. Dhali-Agridhi, Area 2 and Site E 235
3. Dhali-Agridhi, Site E 236
4. Stone Bowls 237
5. Stone Bowls or Mortars 238
6. Stone Pounders or Hammers 239
7. Stone Objects 240
8. Bone Implements 241
9. Ceramics, Dark-faced Burnished Ware 242
10. Ceramics, Horseshoe-shaped Vessel 243

B. Fauna from the 1976 Season
   Figures
   1. Pig, Maximum Distal Width of Humeri 252
   2. Pig, Length of Third Lower Molar 253
   3. *Dama dama mesopotamica*, Proximal Epiphyseal Width of Radius 254
   4. *Dama dama mesopotamica*, Astragalus Length 255
   5. *Dama dama mesopotamica*, Distal Epiphyseal Width of Humerus 256
   6. *Dama dama mesopotamica*, Proximal Epiphyseal Width of Radius 257
   7. Specimen 708. Horn Core and Section of *Ovis orientalis orientalis* 258

C. A Reconsideration of Fauna from the 1972 Season
   Figures
   1. Graph Showing Mean Total Body Weights of Southern English Male
      Fallow Deer (*Dama dama*) Killed during their First through Fourth
      Years of Life 271
   2. Graph Showing Distal Breadth of Humeri of *Dama mesopotamica*
      from Dhali-Agridhi Plotted against Medial Height of Trochlea 272
   3. Graph Showing Frequency Distribution of Distal Breadth Measurements
      on the Humerus of *Dama mesopotamica* from Dhali-Agridhi, Kissonerga-
      Mylouthkia, and Lemba-Lakkous Area II 273
   4. Diagram Showing Ranges and Means of Breadth of *Dama mesopotamica*
      Distal Humerus 274

PART III. METALLURGICAL STUDIES

A. Ancient Mining and Mineral Dressing on Cyprus
   Figures
   1. Mine Location Map for Cyprus 305
   2. Bulk Analyses of Cypriot Slags 306
   3. Temperature-composition Diagram for the System: SiO_2-FeO 307
   4. Diagram of Mineral Deposit Being Altered by Weathering 308
   5. Classification of Cypriot Slags 309
   6. Map of Teredhia Area 310
   7. The Teredhia Furnace 311
   8. Deeply Buried Massive Sulfide Deposits Having Very Little
      Alteration or Secondary Enrichment Mineralization 312
   9. Massive Sulfide Deposit Exposed by Erosion 313
   10. Deeply Weathered Massive Sulfide Ore Deposit 314
   11. Possible Flow Chart for Obtaining Copper from Sulfide Ores by
       Roasting 315
   12. Possible Flow Chart for Obtaining Copper from Sulfide Ores by
       Hydrometallurgy 316
   13. Sketch of an Ancient Heap Leaching Pile 317
   14. Sketch of Ancient Heap Leaching Galleries 318
   15. Sketch of an Active Leach Pile Showing Biological Leaching Zones 319
   16. Elements Enriched in Secondary Zones 320
   Plates
   1. Slag Heap North of Polis 321
   2. West Wall of the Platies Mine, Kalavasos District 322
   3. Slags from Petra and Skouriotissa Slag Piles 323
   4. Slags from Spilli and the Skouriotissa Slag Pile 324
   5. Pits of the Skouriotissa and South Mathiati Mines 325
   6. Rio Tinto and Mavri Sykia Mines 326
   7. A "False Gossan" in the Kalavasos District 327

B. Metalwork from Idalion, 1971-1980
   Figures
   1. Arrowheads (a-i) and Sling Bullets (j-p) 350
   2. Utilitarian Objects and Jewelry 351

Plates
1. Weapons and Armor (Cat. nos. 1-21 and 23-26) 352
2. Utilitarian Objects (Cat. nos. 27-40, 42, and 43) 353
3. Utilitarian Objects (Cat. nos. 44-50 and 52-62) and Jewelry (Cat. nos. 63-65) 354
4. Jewelry (Cat. nos. 66-73, 75, 76, and 78-86) 355

PART IV. REGIONAL STUDIES

B. Regional Styles in Cypriot Limestone Sculpture
Plates
1. Sculptures from Idalion 402
2. Sculptures from Idalion, Pyla, and Vouni 403
3. Sculptures from Vouni, Mersinaki, and Idalion 404
4. Sculptures from Idalion 405

PART V. ETHNOARCHAEOLOGY AND ETHNOGRAPHY

A. Ethnoarchaeological Investigations, 1976
Figures
1. Map of the Alambra Area 418
2. Map of Alambra Village 419
3. Map of Compound 70, Alambra 420
4. Plot Map Illustrating the Rest Locations of All Movable Objects in Compound 70 that Were Used among the Ten Analyzed Activities 421
5. Plot Map Illustrating the Rest Locations of All Analyzed Movable Objects in Compound 70 422

Plates
1. Compound 70 423
2. Compound 70 424

B. Dhali: A Traditional Community in Transition
Figure
1. Settlement Expansion in Dhali, 1923-1974 442

Plates
1. Examples of Dhali Continuities 443
2. Ayios Sozomenos Architecture 444
3. Architectural Styles from Ayios Sozomenos and Dhali 444
4. Agricultural Activities in Dhali 446

PART VI. NUMISMATICS

Catalogue, Idalion 1970-1977
Plates
1. Coins (a-s) 457
2. Coins (a-q) 458

LIST OF TABLES

PART I. EXCAVATIONS AT IDALION, 1973-1980

A. West Terrace Excavations
1. Types of Cement Mortar 8
2. Area C Phasing Summary 9
3. Area D Phasing Summary 11
4. West Terrace Fortifications Phasing Summary 20

B. Lower City Excavations
      1b. A Reconstructed Archaic Bronze Fibula (Object 548)
         1. Fibulae Close in Date and Appearance to Latest Idalion Examples 64

2. West Lower City Domestic Precinct
    1. Key to West Lower City Domestic Precinct Loci 68

    a. Selected Pottery Groups from the West Lower City Domestic Precinct
        1. Loci Discussed, by Square 84
        2. Loci Discussed, by Phase 85
        3. Number of Sherds from the Different Loci According to Type and Ware 94
        4. Number of Type V Sherds According to Subperiod 95

C. A Late Cypriot IIC Tomb: Idalion Tomb 1.76
1. Introduction and Skeletal Remains
    1. Analysis of Adult Individual Teeth 123
    2. Analysis of Deciduous Individual Teeth 123
    3. Results of Analysis of All Adult Dentition 127
    4. Wear Categories by Tooth Type 127
    5. Number of Persons Represented 127
    6. Description of Radius Fragments 130
    7. Description of Ulna Fragments 130
    8. Description of Humerus Fragments 130
    9. Description of Femur Fragments 131
    10. Description of Fibula Fragments 131
    11. Description of Tibia Fragments 131
    12. Measurements and Pairing of Patellae 132
    13. Description of Clavicle Fragments 132
    14. Description of Pelvic Ischium Fragments 132

2. Artifactual Remains with Some Historical Observations
    1. Summary of Pottery Vessels 154
    2. Summary of Sherds and Chips 155
    3. Summary of Other Finds 156
    4. Concordance of Catalogue, Drawing, and Registration Numbers for Idalion Tomb 1 167

PART II. EXCAVATIONS AT DHALI-AGRIDHI: 1972, 1974, 1976

A. Dhali-Agridhi: The Neolithic by the River
1. Dhali-Agridhi Obsidian Cross Reference Numbers 213
2. Dhali-Agridhi Area Study of Rock Fragments from Cobble Floor that Show Definite Usage by Man 213

3. Dhali-Agridhi Area Study of Rock Fragments from Cobble Floor
   that Do Not Show Definite Usage by Man 214
4. Stone Object Classification Based on Raw Material 215
5. Bone and Ivory Implements 215
6. Radiocarbon Dates from Dhali-Agridhi 216

B. Fauna from the 1976 Season
1. Number of Identified Postcranial Fragments of Caprovines 245
2. Number of Identified Postcranial Fragments of *Sus scrofa* 245
3. Number of Identified Postcranial Fragments of *Dama dama
   mesopotamica* 246
4. Number of Fragments Identified to the Species Level 247
5. Number of Shed and Unshed Antler Fragments at Dhali-Agridhi and
   Khirokitia 248
6. Number of Fused and Nonfused Bones of *Dama dama mesopotamica* 248

C. A Reconsideration of Fauna from the 1972 Season
1. Number of Identified Fragments 259
2. Minimum Number of Individuals 260
3. Number of Identified Fragments of Pig 262
4. Number of Identified Fragments of Caprine 263
5. Number of Identified Fragments of *Dama mesopotamica* 266
6. *Dama mesopotamica* Epiphyseal Fusion Data and Age Structure 267
7. A Metrical Comparison of Selected Skeletal Elements of *Dama
   mesopotamica* from Dhali-Agridhi (D-A) 1972 (ca. 5500-4000 B.C.)
   and Ain Mallaha (A-M) (ca. 10,000 B.C.) 268
8. Comparison of Mean Values of Three Measured Dimensions of Some
   Prehistoric Cypriot *Dama* 269

PART III. METALLURGICAL STUDIES

A. Ancient Mining and Mineral Dressing on Cyprus
1. Tentative Dating of Cypriot Slag Types 283
2. Contradictions between Current Metallurgical Concepts and Field
   Observations 294
3. Nature and Properties of Blue Vitriol, $CuSO_4 \cdot 5H_2O$ 296
4. Interpretation of Ancient Mineralogy Based on Agricola's
   De Natura Fossilium (1546) 297
5. Generalized Composition of Cypriot Massive Sulfide Ore 301

B. Metalwork from Idalion, 1971-1980
1. Concordance of Metal Objects by Find Spot 348

PART IV: REGIONAL STUDIES

A. Neutron Activation Analysis of Cypriot Pottery
1. Chemical Elements Determined by Neutron Activation Analysis in
   This Study, with the Isotope Produced, Its Half-life, and the
   Approximate Energy of the Gamma Rays Used 362
2. Chemical and Geographic Data on Clay Specimens 372
3. Archaeological Data on Samples Analyzed 377
4. Archaeological Data on Compositional Groups 389

PART V: ETHNOARCHAEOLOGY AND ETHNOGRAPHY

A. Ethnoarchaeological Investigations, 1976
1. Locational Predictability at Rest and Frequency of Object Use in
   a Single Activity for Movable Objects in Alambra Compound 70 417

B. Dhali: A Traditional Community in Transition
1. Populations of Dhali and Cyprus, 1881-1973 439
2. Births and Deaths in Dhali, 1881-1970 440
3. Population of Dhali, 1881-1973 440
4. A Comparison of Some Critical Statistics from Dhali for the Years
   1946 and 1970 441

PART VII. SUMMARY

1. Summary of Phasing, West Terrace and West Lower City 467

ACKNOWLEDGMENTS

We gratefully acknowledge the unfailingly generous and cooperative help of Dr. Vassos Karageorghis, Director of the Department of Antiquities; of the late Dr. Kyriakos Nicolaou, former Curator of the Cyprus Museum; of Mr. Michael Louloupis, the present Curator; of Dr. Ino Nicolaou, Assistant Curator of the Cyprus Museum; and of the staffs of the Department of Antiquities and the Museum. The Department has kindly undertaken the consolidation of excavated remains at Idalion. We would also like to extend our thanks to the hospitable people of Dhali, most especially to George Demosthenous, who acted as our liaison for so many years, and to Anastasis Savvas, who went to considerable trouble to continue feeding "his Americans" during the 1974 troubles.

A very special word of thanks is due to Helen Dates, without whose dedication to archaeology and knowledge of computers this volume would not have been completed.

STAFF, 1973-80

Project Directors

G. E. Wright (1971-1974)
L. E. Stager and A. M. Walker (1974-1980)

Field Directors

L. E. Stager and A. M. Walker (1971-1974)

Associate Director

Pamela Gaber (1977-1979)

Specialists

Charles Adelman, Ceramic Typologist; Per Ålin, Ceramic Typologist; Peter Allen, Anthropologist; Alan Bieber, Neutron Activation Analyst; Patrick Carter, Faunal Analyst; Paul Croft, Faunal Analyst; Frank M. Cross, Epigraphist; Robert Johnston, Ceramic Technologist; Frank Koucky, Geologist, Metallurgist; Ino Nicolaou, Numismatist; Jane Sallade, Ethnoarchaeologist; Carola Schulte-Campbell, Physical Anthropologist; Arthur Steinberg, Metals Historian; Robert Stewart, Botanist; and Jane Waldbaum, Metals Historian.

Administrative Staff

George Demosthenous, Faith Richardson, and H. Neil Richardson.

Field Supervisors

Michael Coogan (1974), Ralph Doermann (1974), Pamela Gaber (1976), Alan Graham (1980), Yechiel Lehavy (1974, 1976), Miranda Marvin (1973), John Matthers (1974), and Glenn Rose (1974).

Area Supervisors

Gösta Ahlström (1974), Jean Aigner (1975, 1976), John Betlyon (1974), Elizabeth Bloch (1980), Janet Dackendorf (1977, 1978), Douglas Esse (1977), Valerie Fargo (1974), Bruce Fullem (1973), Pamela Gaber (1973-1975), Patty Gerstenblith (1974), Joseph Green (1977, 1978), Lawrence Ingalls (1974, 1977, 1980), Peter Jenkins (1974), Burton MacDonald (1974), Kathleen McVey (1978), Ellen Messer (1974), Thomas Parker (1974), Gary Pratico (1977), Bruce Redford (1973-1974, 1976), David Reece (1973), Diane L. Saltz (1974), Carola Schulte-Campbell (1976), Elmo Scoggin (1974), Anna D. Sophocles (1974), Jane Waldbaum (1973, 1974, 1976, 1978), and David Yesner (1973).

Registrars

1973-74, 1980	Dorothy Ingalls
1976	Betsy King
1977-78	Eileen Caves

Conservator

1974, 1976   Frances Vassiliades

Photographers

1973	John Hansen
1974	Christine Helms
1975	A. M. Walker and Jean Aigner
1976	Cheryl Amand
1977	Graydon Wood
1978	P. L. Carter
1980	L. E. Stager

Draftspersons

1973	Betsy King
1974	F. Johnson and T. Schaub
1975	A. M. Walker and P. Gaber
1976	Odile Le Brun, A. M. Walker, and P. Gaber
1977-78	Charles Schumacher, Shelby Brown, and Noelle Soren
1980	Alan Graham

Additional Drafting

Christine Begg
Anne Dowd
Carlene Friedman
John Sanders

LIST OF ABBREVIATIONS

Babelon	Babelon, E. *Traité des monnaies grecques et romaines*. Vol. 2. Paris: 1910.
BASOR	*Bulletin of the American Schools of Oriental Research*
BCH	*Bulletin de Correspondance Hellénique*
BMC Cyprus	Hill, G. F. *A Catalogue of the Greek Coins in the British Museum, Greek Coins of Cyprus*. London: 1904.
BMC Ptolemies	Poole, R. S. *A Catalogue of the Greek Coins in the British Museum, The Ptolemies Kings of Egypt*. London: 1883.
CDP	Newell, E. T. *The Coinages of Demetrius Poliorcetes*. London: 1927.
IBC	Wroth, W. *Imperial Byzantine Coins in the British Museum*. Vols. 1 and 2. London: 1908.
Idalion 1	Stager, L. E.; Walker, A.; and Wright, G. E. *American Expedition to Idalion, Cyprus. First Preliminary Report: Seasons of 1971 and 1972*. *BASOR* Supplement 18. Cambridge, Massachusetts: 1974.
Lambros	Lambros, P. Athens: 1876.
Longuet	Longuet, H. *Introduction à la numismatique byzantine*. London: 1961.
Müller	Müller, L. *Numismatique d'Alexandre le Grand*. Reprint, Chicago: 1981, from original edition, Copenhagen: 1855.
NC	Newell, E. T. Some Cypriote "Alexanders." *Numismatic Chronicle*, 4th series, 15:294-322.
RDAC	*Report of the Department of Antiquities, Cyprus*
RIC 4/3	Mattingly, H.; Sydenham, E.; and Sutherland, C. *The Roman Imperial Coinage in the British Museum*. Vol. 4, pt. 3. London: Spink, 1949.
RIC 7	Sutherland, C. and Carson, R. *The Roman Imperial Coinage in the British Museum*. Vol. 7. London: Spink, 1966.
RIC 9	Mattingly, H.; Sutherland, C.; and Carson, R. *The Roman Imperial Coinage in the British Museum*. Vol. 9. London: Spink, 1951.
SCE I-III	Gjerstad, E.; Lindros, J.; Sjöqvist, E.; and Westholm, A. *The Swedish Cyprus Expedition: Finds and Results of the Excavations in Cyprus 1927-1931*. Vol. I-III. Stockholm: 1934, 1935, and 1937.
SCE IV/1A	Dikaios, P. and Stewart, J. R. *The Swedish Cyprus Expedition*. Vol. IV, part 1A. *The Stone Age and the Early Bronze Age in Cyprus*. Lund: 1962.
SCE IV/1B	Åström, P. *The Swedish Cyprus Expedition*. Vol. IV, part 1B. *The Middle Cypriot Bronze Age*. Lund: 1972.
SCE IV/1C	Åström, P. *The Swedish Cyprus Expedition*. Vol. IV, part 1C. *The Late Cypriot Bronze Age: Architecture and Pottery*. Lund: 1972.
SCE IV/1D	Åström, P. and Åström, L. *The Swedish Cyprus Expedition*. Vol. IV, part 1D. *The Late Cypriot Bronze Age: Other Arts and Crafts*. Lund: 1972.
SCE IV/2	Gjerstad, E. *The Swedish Cyprus Expedition*. Vol. IV, part 2. *The Cypro-Geometric, Cypro-Archaic and Cypro-Classical Periods*. Stockholm: 1948.
SCE IV/3	Vessberg, O. and Westholm, A. *The Swedish Cyprus Expedition*. Vol. IV, part 3. *The Hellenistic and Roman Periods in Cyprus*. Stockholm: 1956.
Schlumberger	Schlumberger, G. L. *Numismatique de l'Orient latin*. Graz, Austria: 1954.
Svoronos	Svoronos, J. Athens: 1904.
SNG Cop. The Ptolemies	Kromann, A. and Mørkholm, O. *Sylloge Nummorum Graecorum*. The Royal Collection of Coins and Medals, Danish National Museum. *Egypt, The Ptolemies*. Copenhagen: 1977.

INTRODUCTION

The Dhali region lies about fifteen miles southeast of Nicosia, in the shallow valley formed by the Yalias River as it runs out of the foothills of the Troodos Mountains toward the east coast of the island. In 1971, under the general direction of G. Ernest Wright, with the authors as field directors, we began a project of archaeological investigation. Our broad objective was to study the variability of settlement pattern and type with economic system within the Dhali region (an area of about 65 square kilometers), and changes within these variables over time. Within the scope of these broad aims, we have also been concerned with intrasite variability, both synchronically and diachronically. We have used three approaches: excavation, survey, and area studies. In 1971 we undertook a pilot study, with trial excavations at the major urban site of Idalion and excavated in all three topographic divisions of the site. In addition, we began excavation in 1972 at Dhali-Agridhi, a Neolithic site on the banks of the Yalias River, and undertook a number of area studies. Preliminary results of these two seasons appear in *Idalion 1*. For a full statement of the objectives of the project the reader is referred to chapter 1, "Objectives and Procedures," of that volume.

The current volume presents the results of some of the project's work from 1973-1980. In 1973 we did an intensive survey of land within a mile radius of Idalion, and excavation in the Lower City of the urban site. In 1974 we began a survey of sites in the vicinity of the Ayios Sozomenos plateau, a center of Bronze Age settlement in the region, expanded our excavation at Idalion proper, and continued work at Dhali-Agridhi. In 1975 we began a survey of the copper-mining areas on the southwestern periphery of the region, and made soundings at a late medieval smelting site, Teredhia, near Lythrodonda. In 1976 we finished the survey of the mining area, continued soundings at Teredhia, and renewed excavation in the central Lower City of Idalion and at Dhali-Agridhi. In 1977 we continued work in the central Lower City of Idalion and expanded excavation on the West Terrace. Excavation on the West Terrace continued in 1978 and 1980. Figure 1 shows the Dhali region with the major sites of excavation and survey. Figure 2 shows our areas of excavation at Idalion proper. During the years 1973-77 additional work was also done on ethnoarchaeology and traditional village economies. This volume presents the results of excavation at Idalion and Dhali-Agridhi, together with some of the area studies. A detailed treatment of the artifacts, together with an analysis of excavation and survey not included here, will be presented in a final volume.[1]

Since 1972 a number of changes have taken place in the organization and scope of the project. In August 1974 the project director, G. Ernest Wright, died, and, following this sad event, the authors became co-directors. Gaber was associate director from 1977-1979. Walker supervised fieldwork for the 1973, 1975, and 1976 seasons, and Stager and Walker jointly supervised the 1974 and 1977 seasons. Gaber was acting field director in 1978 assisting Walker. Fieldwork was resumed under Stager's supervision in 1980.

The project was adversely affected by the 1974 war and its aftermath. Since August 1974 the Turks have held the old main road from Nicosia to Larnaca, in a salient that includes the Turkish village of Louroujina, just south of ancient Idalion. When the area of no-man's-land between the current cease-fire line is included, access is precluded to about one third of our original area of interest in the Dhali region. Due to the proximity of Idalion and the Dhali region to the lines, there has also been a large Cypriot military presence in the area since 1974. The strategic location of ancient Idalion has meant that parts of the site itself, including the East Acropolis, the West Acropolis, and the East Terrace, have been placed off limits for further excavation, and we are no longer permitted to take photographs other than those of our trenches. Our survey area has been likewise curtailed, both because of Cypriot military

---

[1] Almost all the articles in this volume were completed by 1980 and have not been revised. Publication has been delayed because of other commitments of L. E. Stager.

restrictions and because of the presence of minefields in the area. We have thus been obliged to redefine and limit the scope of our investigations and to abandon, at least for the present, several of our most promising areas of excavation at Idalion proper.

Our excavation methods at Idalion from 1973 to 1980 followed basically the same procedures as those in 1971 and 1972, except that from 1974 onward we ceased to float our soil from central Lower City, because the proximity of the archaeological deposit to the modern surface was not conducive to the preservation of seeds, despite careful use of the Legge froth-flotation machine. However all soils except plow soil continued to be dry-sieved in a 1/4-inch mesh screen. Procedures at Dhali-Agridhi in 1974 and 1976 were the same as in 1972, with the addition of the use of the Legge froth-flotation machine (Jarman, Legge, and Charles 1972).

The overall sponsor of the project was the American Schools of Oriental Research. Subsidiary sponsors were the University of Connecticut, the Oriental Institute of the University of Chicago, the Semitic Museum of Harvard University, and the State University of New York at Albany. The project was funded in 1973 and 1974 by grants from the National Endowment for the Humanities and the University of Connecticut; in 1975 and 1976 by grants from the University of Connecticut; in 1977 by grants from the Oriental Institute at the University of Chicago, the University of Connecticut, and by aid to refugee workers from the Cyprus Department of Antiquities; and in 1978 and 1980 by grants from the National Endowment for the Humanities and the Oriental Institute, as well as by private donations.[2]

A.M.W. and L.E.S.

---

[2] NEH grant numbers: 1972-73, H-7117; 1973-74, H-9381; 1974-75, RO-2070000-74; 1979-81, RO-23812-79-0081.

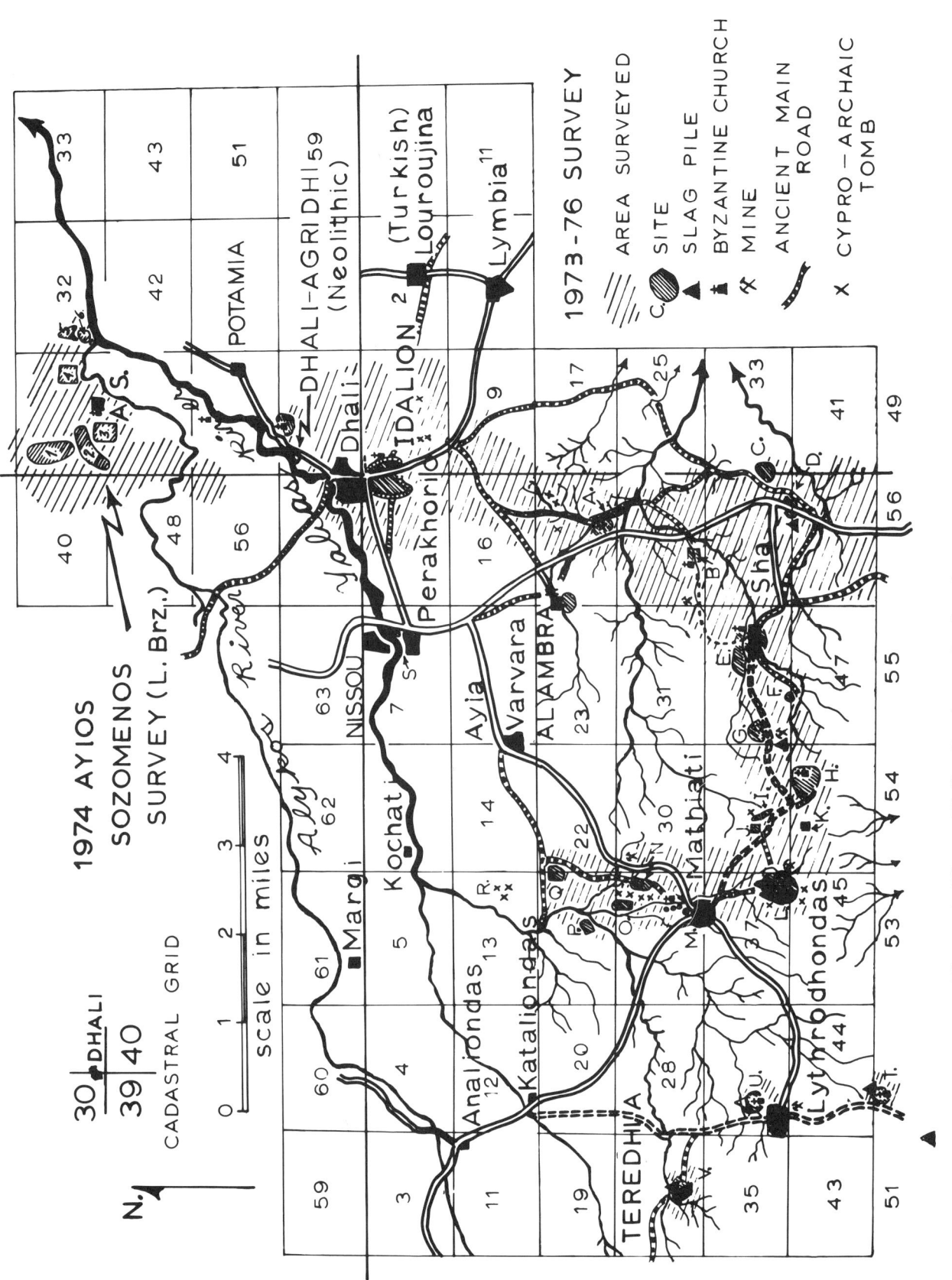

Figure 1. Upper Yalias Drainage Basin, Cyprus, 1973-1976 Survey.

4   AMERICAN EXPEDITION TO IDALION, CYPRUS, 1973-1980

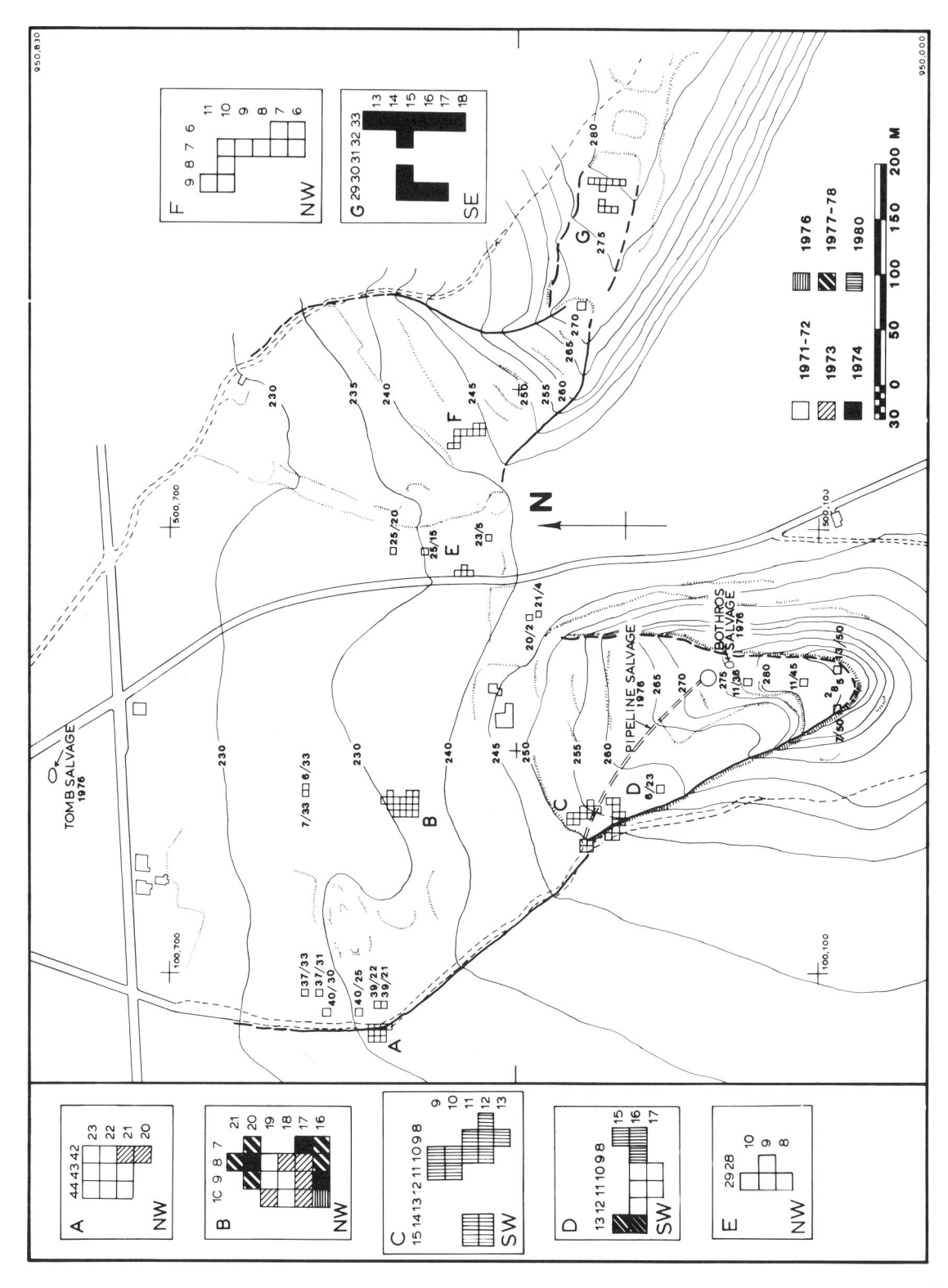

Figure 2. Idalion Contour Plan, Showing Areas of Excavation, 1971-1980.

I. EXCAVATIONS AT IDALION, 1973-1980
A. WEST TERRACE EXCAVATIONS

*Lawrence E. Stager**
*Anita M. Walker***

*with Pamela Gaber****
Alan Graham

PALACE

Objectives

The West Terrace occupies a rectangular plot, ca. 2 ha in size (ca 120.00 m [north-south] x 160.00 m [east-west]), and sits at an intermediate level some 25.00 m below the summit of the West Acropolis to the south, on which the Temple of Athena stood, and some 15.00 m above the Lower City to the north, where the residential quarters lay.

During the final days of the Swedish Cyprus Expedition to Idalion, Gjerstad and his team cut a narrow exploratory trench across the West Terrace. From the size and quality of a few ashlars in this "pipeline" trench, Gjerstad surmised that a "Palace" lay buried there. It was our purpose to locate monumental architecture. This was done through two soundings in what is now designated Area C on the north and Area D on the south of the West Terrace (Stager, Walker, and Wright 1974:50-58). Then our task was to date the small exposures of sandstone and limestone walls and later to expand these soundings in order to retrieve the plan of this complex of "public" buildings, perhaps a Palace.

Strategy

By 1974 it was evident that the techniques of sandstone ashlar masonry and gypsum mortar/plaster used in West Terrace walls (see fig. 5, Section D-D) resembled those used in the Lower City fortifications, particularly Bastion Id WNW 44/22 Loc 016 (see below), which was dated to the Cypro-Classical period. Work resumed on the West Terrace structures during the 1977-78 seasons in Squares 10/9, 11/9, 10/10, and 11/10; i.e., north and south of the Northern Facade in Area C (fig. 1) and in Squares 8/15 and 9/16; i.e., the Room in Area D. Because of the size of these structures, some still standing to a height of 3.00 m, and the depth of debris above floor levels, in places 3.00 m or more, it became clear that large-scale exposures were needed and could be recorded more efficiently using a larger module of excavation. In 1980 deposits and features were recorded by Area designations C and D, which included several contiguous Squares from previous seasons as well as those excavated for the first time (see fig. 2 in Introduction). During 1980 our strategy consisted of excavating the backfill from trenches dug from the modern surface by stone robbers in order to remove the more accessible well-cut blocks of sandstone and limestone used in the monumental buildings. In this way we would gain a negative plan of parts of the building complex before excavating the preserved architecture and related stratigraphic deposits. This strategy worked well for delineating the Eastern Facade in Area C (pl. 1a, b) and the Room in Area D (pl. 4b). However, it would require several more seasons of such backfill removal before a comprehensive plan of the

---

[*] Harvard University, The Semitic Museum, Cambridge, Massachusetts

[**] Departments of History and Anthropology, University of Connecticut, Storrs, Connecticut

[***] University of New Hampshire at Manchester, New Hampshire

buildings could be drawn. Only within the Area D Room and in the Area C Street (pls. 1c, 2b) did we excavate undisturbed deposits, which provide a date for the later use phases of these features. Prior to the revised strategy of 1980, a "triangular" probe was made between the south section of Id WSW 8/15 and the north wall of the Area D Room (pl. 5a). That, too, provided very limited evidence for the earlier use of this building (cf. fig. 6:20-32).

Results

A north-south alignment of four massive piers forms the Eastern Facade of a monumental building (figs. 1-2, Piers 041, 040, 037, and 053; pl. 1a, b, c), which extends to the west, perhaps as much as 30.00 m, where possibly it incorporates the sandstone segment labeled Citadel Wall 006 (fig. 1; see below). The southern extent of the sandstone building complex is not known beyond the 20.00 m line of the Eastern Facade. However, the solitary (as yet) Room in Area D, with sandstone foundations, is part of the overall organizational scheme of what seems to be a large building complex, which we, following Gjerstad's lead, would identify as a Palace and date to the Cypro-Classical period.

Area C (see table 2)

Phase 5. The earliest architectural components of this long-lived and frequently renovated complex consisted of the alignment of four sandstone piers. Perhaps Pier 053 and sandstone Wall 031 formed the northeast corner of the earliest building. If so, there would have been a 3.00 m-wide doorway flanked by Piers 053 and 037, which was entered from the east (fig. 1). Because of the very limited exposure of this large complex and the fact that the founding levels of the earliest sandstone structures have not yet been reached, our interpretation of the relationships of the Phase 5 piers remains only a conjecture.

We can be more certain of the construction techniques used in building the piers themselves, especially Pier 037, the best preserved of the lot. Its overall dimensions are ca. 2.00 m x 4.00 m. At its highest point it stands 2.50 m (253.50 m asl) above the Phase 4 Street level to the north (pls. 1a, 1c-2b). At Street level (ca. 251.00 m asl; cf. fig. 3, Section B-B), Pier 053 was set on a large gypsum slab, 0.20 m thick and 1.60 m long. During Phase 4 a curbstone made of a fine sandstone block (0.60 m high), coated with a thick layer of cement (0.10-0.20 m) containing river pebbles, was added to the northeast corner of Pier 053. A shallow probe beneath the Street indicated, however, that the sandstone ashlars continued downward for at least another course or more (founding level not yet established). Above the gypsum slab, five courses of ashlar sandstone blocks were neatly laid and tuck-pointed with gypsum cement or mortar (Type 1, see table 1). Each course was ca. 0.50 m thick, the largest ashlars being 0.50 x 1.25 x 0.50 m (pls. 1a, 1c, 2a).

The overall dimensions of this pier and the size of individual sandstone ashlar blocks were comparable to those of Pier 041, which unfortunately had most of its courses robbed out, down to ca. 251.75 m asl, as had smaller Pier 040 (ca. 2.00 x 2.00 m). This robbing did have the benefit of providing us with a look at the interior construction of the piers. They were formed from a rectangular or square shell of sandstone ashlars (one row wide), which was filled with sandstone rubble and gypsum cement.

The meter-wide "gaps" between Piers 037, 040, and 041 remain an enigma. The gap to the south has not been excavated below the robber trench. The one to the north had a single ashlar placed on edge with marl and limestone rubble packed behind it. If this filling was a later addition, perhaps some form of arched doorway should be reconstructed over the piers of the Eastern Facade. If the packing was original, then a variant of ashlar pier-and-rubble masonry was in use. This technique was well known along the Phoenician coast during the Persian period and used in Phoenician colonies in the western Mediterranean (Stager 1985:12-13; Stern 1977; Elayi 1980; and Van Beek and Van Beek 1981).

The northern end of the Eastern Facade seems to have terminated with Pier 053 (1.20 x 1.60 x 1.50 m), the east face of which was true to the line of the three piers to the south. Pier

053 was, however, part of a much larger and probably multiphase complex of walls, which have yet to be conclusively sorted out (cf. pl. 3a, fig. 5, Section D-D for numerous repairs and rebuildings on the north side of Pier 053). The main wall line runs east-west on both sides of Pier 053 and was not at perfect right angles to the north-south pier alignment. Wall 050/051, the eastern extension, is, like limestone Wall 030 to the west of Pier 053, a Phase 4 addition. But below Wall 030, two courses of sandstone ashlar Wall 031 (fig. 3, Section B-B) were interlocked with Pier 053 to form what seems to be the interior sandstone northeast corner of the original Phase 5 building.

Direct evidence for dating this phase of construction and use must await further excavation. In the meantime, comparisons with sandstone masonry from firmly dated structures, such as the fortification wall in the Lower City, and the overall architectural scheme of the West Terrace in relation to its Citadel Wall, built ca. 500-475 B.C. (see below), suggest that the foundations of the Palace were probably laid at that time as well.

Phase 4. A 5.00 m wide Street, flanked on the north by Wall 030/031 and on the south by Wall 033/034/038 (fig. 3, Section B-B), separated the Northern Facade of the Phase 5 structure from the Eastern Facade. The curbstone was added to the northeast corner of Pier 037 to protect it from wheeled vehicles, such as carts or chariots.

The building south of the Street consisted of the Eastern Facade (minus Pier 053), behind which a range of rooms had been added. These rooms were ca. 4.00 m wide; their length (along the east-west axis), has not yet been determined. Wall 046 was mortared to the west face of Pier 040 and served as an east-west partition shared in common by the rooms to the north and the south. The south side of the southern room was demarcated by the line of an east-west robber trench (unexcavated), dug at a right angle to the west face of Pier 041. Wall 046 was built of reddish-brown unbaked mudbricks, preserved 12 courses high (1.25 m) and 0.75 m wide. It was built on a stone footing (Loc 047) of cemented limestone boulders (1.00 m high). Stone Footing 047 was founded at ca. 251.00 m asl on a sandstone footing which seemed to belong to a lower extended "course" of Pier 040 to the west.

Wall 034/038, ca. 1.30 m wide, formed the northern wall of the Phase 4 building complex south of the Street. Although Wall 038 was built of sandstone blocks, rising three courses high (1.00 m) above the Street level (pls. 1c-2b and fig. 3), it was not asssigned to Phase 5 because it abutted the west side of Pier 037 at a straight vertical joint (unlike Wall 031 and Pier 053 to the north) and bore none of the gypsum tuck-pointing noted on the north face of Pier 037. Wall 034, ca. 1.20 m wide, sat directly on Wall 038. The former was built of well-laid slabs of tabular limestone (0.60 m long and 0.20 m thick). Finally, a poorly preserved limestone Wall (or core) 033 was built above Wall 034, bringing the height of the wall (033/034/038) to nearly 3.00 m above Street level. It is possible that "Wall" 033 represents the exposed core of Wall 034 after the tabular limestone face had collapsed into the Street (fig. 3, Section B-B; cf. east face of Citadel Wall in Id WSW 11-12/16).

A series of Street surfaces (Loc 026-028) have been partially excavated, continuous up to Phase 3, when the walls of the Area C buildings collapsed (pls. 1c-2b; fig. 3, Section B-B; fig. 4, Section C-C). As yet, there has been no material excavated from levels associated with the construction phase of this Street and adjoining buildings. The three Street surfaces that have been excavated were composed of indurated marl, containing charcoal flecks and a few flat-lying potsherds, all of which dated to the Cypro-Classical II period. Surface 027 produced a Black Glazed bowl fragment with signs of rouletting on the interior. This would suggest a 4th century B.C. date, sometime after 390 B.C., for the deposit.

Pier 053 and remnants of Wall 031 (Phase 5) formed the core of the east-west wall which flanked the Street on the north. Limestone and rubble Wall 030 was built on the ruins of sandstone Wall 031. This rebuild was contemporary with the addition of two walls running northward, Loc 057 and 058 (figs. 1-2; pls. 3a-4a), and perhaps with the extension of the east-west wall line by Walls 050/051 to the east of Pier 053. Thus north of the Street a new range of rooms was built just inside the northern limits of the West Terrace. (The northern Citadel Wall has not been located.)

Table 1. Types of Cement Mortar
(F. L. Koucky)

Type 1   Coarse crushed gypsum mortar. Low density, porous; fine pores (mixed sizes); few rounded sand grains; crushed gypsum binder (0.25 cm) including broken limestone fossil fragments and rare charcoal fragments; Hardness = 2 (Moh) [H = hardness].

Examples:
Id WNW 44/22, Ashlar Wall 010 from Lower City
Id WSW 11/16, plaster on Citadel Wall 021
Id WSW 10/9, plaster (Loc 011) from Northern Facade

Type 1   (Variant)   Very coarse crushed gypsum mortar. Low density; much coarser gypsum binder, both white and gray (up to 2 cm) with more charcoal.

Example:
Id WSW 10/9, Wall 006/058

Type 2   Very fine crushed gypsum mortar. Low density, extremely fine pores; pure gypsum; very few sand grains and charcoal fragments; H = 2.

Example:
Id WSW 8/15, plaster from robbed East Wall of Room

Type 3   True concrete with subsurface of river pebbles embedded in gypsum matrix.

a (top)--flat pale yellow brown surface layer. True concrete finish. High carbonate material; minor gypsum, mainly a crushed and heated material (oxidized fragments of Fe_2O_3 and charcoal): fossil fragments. H = 3+.
b (middle)--layer of igneous river pebbles set in 3c matrix; oxidized limestone chips; mixed size (up to 2 cm).
c (bottom)--white layer of higher density gypsum fragments; compact with low porosity; rare limestone or slate fragments.

Example:
Id WSW 10/9, Plaster Floor 009

The earliest floor level excavated in the northern complex was a meter below Street level (251.00 m asl). It consisted of a flagstone floor (Id WSW 10/9.008) over which a thin layer of true concrete (Type 3, table 1) had been spread (D.005 = WSW 10/9.009; pl. 3a). Occupational debris within the room had accumulated to a depth of 0.25-0.40 m above the concrete and slab floor (Id WSW 11/9.040-046; 10/9.017-019), its pottery dating to the Cypro-Classical period. Near the top of the floor buildup was a heavy concentration of carbonized olive pits. Part of a large pithos was found crushed in the marly occupational debris (pl. 4a). Since the top of the pithos was nearly 0.50 m above the base, the jar had probably been sunk into the marl buildup and used for storing or processing olive oil. Perhaps the large rotary crushing wheel of an olive press, found in the Phase 3 collapse in WSW 11/9, had originally been part of this pressing installation.

The marl buildup in this north room probably occurred about the same time as the traffic accumulations in the Street (Loc 026-028).

Table 2. Area C Phasing Summary

Phase	Area C	11/9	10/9	10/10	Period
1 Colluvium and robber trenches	001-004	002, 006	004		Hellenistic to Modern
2 Marl mudbrick wash and puddling	005, 011, 014-015				Hellenistic
3 Collapse and destruction debris of Palace	008-009 019 016 012-013 024-025 010	009 008=032 018 020 031-035 039	007.1	008 018 022 019 021	Late 4th century B.C.
4 Street; buildings north and south of Street = Palace	026-028 057 058 050 051 034 030 038 046/047	043-046 010=D.057	006=D.058 007.2 007.3 009 008 015-019		Mid-5th and 4th centuries B.C.
5 Sandstone piers; North and East Facades = Palace	031-053 037 040 041			024=D.053 011=D.037	ca. 500-450 B.C.

Phase 3. Everywhere in Area C there was evidence that the Palace collapsed in the latter part of the 4th century B.C. Walls had collapsed into the Street, creating an avalanche of architectural debris from 1.25-2.00 m deep (pls. 1c, 2b). Destruction debris reached even greater depths in the rooms to the north. Sections B-B and C-C (figs. 3, 4) indicate that the sandstone and limestone walls on the south side collapsed first into the Street. The limestone facing blocks (Loc 016) from Wall 033/034 lay at the top of the heap of building rubble.

Throughout the destruction debris there were bits and pieces of evidence for the superstructure of the nearby buildings: segments of fallen mudbrick walls (Id WSW 11/9.009), roofing and ceiling fragments made of gypsum plaster applied to a matrix of cane (pl. 5b), and wall plaster painted with red ochre. In the collapse above the Street (Loc 009) a bronze cheekpiece from a Cypriot(?) helmet was found (Waldbaum, catalogue no. 25). It had been pierced by an arrow. The pottery from the collapse in Id WSW 11/9.031-035 was predominately

Plain White Ware VI-VII, or Cypro-Classical II; there were also a few sherds of 4th century B.C. Black Glazed Ware (cf. fig. 7:41) and a fragment of late Red Figured Ware.

Phase 2. Directly above the building collapse were patches of indurated marl (Loc 015) followed by puddling (Loc 014). During this period of abandonment a meter-thick layer of marl brick detritus washed over the collapsed rubble (Loc 011, 005; fig. 4, Section C-C). Pottery in Loc 005 ranged in date from the Cypro-Archaic through Hellenistic I periods.

Phase 1. Colluvium and rubble backfill from modern stone robbing operations (Loc 003, 004) concluded activity in Area C.

Area D (see table 3)

The most prominent feature excavated east of the Citadel Wall in Area D is the Room (Id WSW 8/15, 9/16) formed in Phase 4 when an east wall was added to the three sides of a pre-existing Building (Phase 5). The Room is 7.50 m x 4.00 m. The north, south, and west walls were originally 1.25 m wide; however, robber trenching had removed most of the sandstone ashlar blocks which formed the external face of the Building, exposing the rough limestone and cement interior of the walls (pls. 4b, 5a). The robber trench at the northwest corner of the Building revealed the rubble interior of the west wall, standing ca. 2.50 m high, with ashlar sandstone facing blocks preserved at the bottom (founding level not yet reached).

Phase 5. Inside the Building, prior to the construction of the Phase 4 partition wall, there was abundant evidence that a mudbrick superstructure with well rendered plastered surfaces and features had collapsed to produce over a meter of debris. The surface on which the superstructure fell has not been reached at a depth of 254.60 m asl. Probably when reached, it will correspond to Surface 021, outside the Building to the west at 254.50 m asl. This surface could be traced in the south section of the robber trench and was composed of indurated marl, with thick patches of charcoal as well as sandstone fragments and pieces of concrete lying on it. Surface 021 corresponds in elevation and perhaps in date to the surface which seals the foundation trench of the Citadel Wall (Id WSW 11/16), 15.00 m to the west. Probably the Phase 5 Building was constructed at the same time that the Citadel Wall was built.

Inside the Building the Phase 5 destruction debris consisted of a large segment of mudbrick wall (once thought to be a "platform" or "bench" [8/15.023]), which had toppled just inside the (once) ashlar-faced sandstone and limestone foundations of the north wall. Some of the reddish-brown bricks still had their gray mortar lines preserved (pl. 5a). Beside the mudbrick segment of wall, large slabs of concrete had pitched vertically (pl. 5a). Near the top of the debris (D.020) four small pieces of gypsum wall plaster bore traces of red and light brown paint: clues to the decorative scheme of the interior. Crushed marl and mudbrick detritus was mixed throughout the collapse. Pottery joins were made between several loci (Id WSW 8/15.021, 022, 024, and 026), comprising the upper 0.70 m of the debris. The deepest probe into the collapse (8/15.028) revealed a similar jumble of mudbrick detritus, concrete fragments, heavy concentrations of bone, charcoal, and some partially restorable pottery of Plain Whitelain White IV-V (fig. 6:14-32).

From top to bottom within the meter of building debris, slabs of concrete, often as much as 0.05-0.10 m thick, appeared (pl. 5a). It had once been used as flooring or walling. The thick concrete had a smooth upper surface. Several specimens had pithos fragments adhering to the underside. This must have been flooring made by pouring cement over a bed of flat-lying body sherds from storage jars.

The ingredients for this portland-like cement were locally retrieved, suggesting that somewhere on or near the site, lime kilns should be found. Local marls of various colors--gray, yellow, pink, and tan--produced cement of different hues. According to staff geologist Frank Koucky, gray marl produced the strongest cement; red, the weakest. Sorted river pebbles served as "temper" in the concretes. These pebbles included mainly diabase, some pillow lava and chert; rarely, limestone and gypsum fragments provided the temper. The tempering material was gathered from the bed of the Yalias River. Some of the batches of concrete with poorly sorted fill included not only small river pebbles but also larger ones along with sand.

Specimens of these cements are being tested at the Smithsonian Institution. Preliminary results, reported by Koucky, confirm that the Idalion samples are true concrete: a most surprising result since the technology for making concrete of this quality was usually thought to be known no earlier than Roman times.

According to Koucky, the local marls, when calcined, form a natural portland-like cement mixture (silica clay and limestone). Thus conditions were right for early experimentation in concretes. Perhaps the abnormally thick concretes reflect some uncertainty about the strength of the product in the early stages of this pyrotechnology. Nevertheless, the fine technical quality of most of the concretes found in the buildings on the West Terrace leave little doubt that the Idalion builders were well advanced in the techniques of concrete production for floors and walls by the Cypro-Classical period.

Table 3. Area D Phasing Summary

Phase	Area D	8/15	9/16	Period
1 Colluvium and robber trenches	001	001 003/006/011 007/012/019	003 004	Hellenistic to Modern
2 Copper metallurgy	002	--- 009	011	Late 4th century B.C.
3 Latest use of Room; river cobble surface	004* 009 (upper)	005	008	Late 4th century B.C.
4 4A Room collapse (Phoenician and Cypro-syllabic inscriptions)	009 (lower) 010 014	008 009 012		Mid-5th to mid-4th centuries B.C.
4B Building partitioned to form Room	013	016		
5 Building collapse prior to partitioned Room	020	018-030		Late 6th to mid-5th centuries B.C.

*Underlined Locus Numbers = Building/Room interior

Phase 4. The east wall was added to partition the earlier Phase 5 Building into a Room. The base of east wall was founded directly on top of Phase 5 destruction debris at ca. 255.80 m asl. Debris, with a random distribution of mudbricks and architectural fragments, reached a depth of ca. 0.50 m. Indurated earthern "floors" at the bottom of the debris (D.013) provided the prepared surface on which concrete flooring had once been laid. None of the flooring was *in situ*. Concrete fragments were abundant (seven bucketsful), however, amid the mudbrick detritus and disaggregated pebbles from decomposed flooring. Obviously the flooring had been torn up, leaving us with small flat pieces of portland-like cement, usually less than 0.05 m^2 in size, smoothed on one side and distributed throughout the mudbrick matrix. Some of the pieces had rounded contours, suggesting their use as wall plaster. In the upper part of the debris several pieces of cement were found lying with smooth face down, perhaps remnants of ceiling material.

Within the debris a few ostraca with ink inscriptions in either Phoenician or Cyprosyllabic script appeared (pls. 6-7). In a preliminary palaeographic study, Frank Moore Cross, staff epigraphist, has dated the Phoenician inscriptions to the fourth century B.C. They will be published in detail in his forthcoming article.

Black Glazed pottery and the inscriptions provide a date in the latter part of the 5th century B.C. for the construction and use phase of this Room. The presence of Phoenician ostraca suggests that the remodeling of the building took place after the Phoenicians from Kition took over Idalion in the period 450-425 B.C., when ᶜOzibaᶜal, the Phoenician king of Kition, added Idalion to his kingdom, as indicated by Phoenician coinage and other inscriptions.

Phase 3. The preservation of wall plaster above the "floor" level of Phase 3 indicates that the Room was still being used but perhaps for purposes quite different from those of the earlier phases. The latest floor within the structure was composed of river cobbles held in place within a compact earthen matrix. This surface was further delineated by flat-lying pottery consisting mostly of Plain White VI-VII, alongside restorable cooking pots, a mortarium fragment, and Black Glazed sherds. Pieces of "wall" plaster (0.05 m^2 and 0.05 m thick), lying face down on the floor, provides further evidence that the Room was still in use. But for what purpose? Mixed throughout the river cobbles and occupational debris were numerous sheep or goat teeth, several still set in jawbones.

Phase 2. The Room had definitely gone out of use by Hellenistic I times, late in the 4th century B.C., when copper metallurgy had become the leading activity on the West Terrace (see Stager, Walker, and Wright 1974:50-56). Between Id WSW 8/15 and 11/16, a distance of more than 30.00 m, slag heaps were piled everywhere. Inside the then defunct Room evidence for copper metallurgy consisted of charcoal deposits, slag, at least fourteen bowl-shaped crucible fragments, and hard-fired terracotta lining perhaps for metallurgical furnaces.

Phase 1. Colluvium and modern trenching for sandstone blocks characterized the final phase.

Discussion (Areas C and D)

The structures east of the Citadel Wall represent the most massive and monumental architecture yet found at Idalion. What few alignments we have suggest that the West Terrace structures were designed and built as a single, coherent architectural unit. The contrast with contemporary construction in the residential quarters of the Lower City (see below) compels us to designate the West Terrace structures as "public" architecture. Gjerstad's immediate impression of this site as the palatial precincts of Idalion has been reinforced, if not completely confirmed, by our excavations. The style of sandstone ashlar masonry used in the Palace foundations resonates with that used in the Citadel Wall and Lower City fortifications, built at the end of the Cypro-Archaic II period (ca. 475 B.C.; see below). Although in our limited exposures on the West Terrace we have not reached the founding levels of the Palace, the earliest use phases excavated (Area D Building, Phase 5) date to the first half of the 5th century B.C. During this period the Northern and Eastern Facades as well as Citadel Wall 006 (the

Western Facade?) probably formed a single palatial complex which was then divided into separate units by the Street during Phase 4. At the same time the Area D Building was subdivided to form the Room in which both Phoenician and Cypro-syllabic ostraca were recovered (Phase 4). The fact that nearly all of the inscriptions (mainly ostraca) found came from the West Terrace excavations further indicates that this was the administrative center of Idalion in the 5th-4th centuries B.C.

After a long period of use and reuse (cf. the several renovations in the Northern Facade), the buildings and fortification walls of the West Terrace completely collapsed, or more likely, were destroyed by an invading army, late in the 4th century B.C., and were never rebuilt. By that time the West Terrace was not solely an administrative area. In the south (Area D), part of the site had been converted into an industrial zone for metallurgy (Phase 2), which was then sealed under tons of collapsed mudbricks, probably from the fallen superstructure of the Citadel Wall or Bastion (see below). In the north (Area C), what remained of the Palace was reduced to a pile of stone building rubble and mudbrick debris, in places 2.00-3.00 m deep.

In its heyday the Palace of Idalion must have resembled that of Vouni (5th century B.C.). Although too little of the Idalion complex is known to allow comparison of its overall plan with that of the Vouni Palace, there are many similarities in the selection of building materials and in their execution for walls, floors, and ceilings, which we can detail. For example, neither the roofs of Vouni or Idalion were covered with terracotta tiles, but rather with a plaster "matting of reeds ceiled with earth and lime. . . " (*SCE* III, p. 153; cf. pl. 5b). Floors were made of slabs or poured concrete mixed with gravel. The most common floor inside Vouni Palace was made of "thick, blue-grey lime-cement with a coat of white plaster" (*SCE* III, p. 151). The walls of Vouni Palace were mainly built with ashlar foundations and mudbrick superstructures. Well-dressed ashlar blocks ("orthostatic construction") formed a "double-faced shell wall" which encased a "core of chips of stone and much hard lime-mortar." The joints between ashlars were "bound with hard lime-mortar and the face [of the ashlar wall was] partly covered with a calcareous plaster" (*SCE* III, p. 124).

WEST TERRACE FORTIFICATIONS

Objectives.

One of the objectives in our examination of Idalion proper was to understand the system of defenses during the history of the city. We wanted to know when the city was first fortified, the method of construction of the fortifications, their extent, the location of gates, the history of usage of the fortifications, their relationship to other structures and the date at which the fortifications went out of use.

Strategy.

Our strategy for fulfilling these objectives was to open a section which would intersect with the line of any fortification in three areas of the site. These were on the West Terrace, in the west Lower City and on the East Acropolis. The East Acropolis section was opened for a very short time in 1974. We were unable to resume work on the East Acropolis for military security reasons.

It is clear from the excavations of the Swedish Cyprus Expedition that the hilly part of Idalion known locally as Ambeleri in the southwest of the site was from the first one of the most important areas of settlement. It comprises an acropolis area (West Acropolis, contours 285-270 m asl) and a lower plateau or terrace (West Terrace, contours 270-250 m asl). Soundings in 1971 had indicated a substantial depth of deposit on the West Terrace, much of it colluvium or slope wash from the acropolis above. This in turn suggested that something had retained the material on the West Terrace and prevented it from creeping down into the Lower City. The most likely explanation was the presence of a retaining wall, which served most probably as a continuation of the City Wall in Lower City (see Stager, Walker, and Wright

1974:44-48 and see below) and possibly also enclosed the West Terrace and Acropolis area, forming a citadel. Accordingly in 1972, a line of squares (Id WSW 12/16-8/16, Area D, see figs. 1 and 8) was laid out in an east-west direction cutting across the 255 m asl contour (see Stager, Walker, and Wright, 1974:50-56). In 1977, when the extant top of the City Wall was uncovered, work in 11/16 was restricted to a rectangle 2.50 x 1.25 m along the south balk, in order to be able to attain a trench to bedrock. In 13/16, for similar considerations, excavation along the outer (west) face of the wall was also restricted to a probe trench 2.00 x 1.50 m. In 1978, in order to obtain a larger expanse of the wall, excavation was undertaken in the remainder of 12/16 and 13/16 and extended northward into 12/15 and 13/15 and westward into 11/16 until it intersected with the modern military road. In 1980 in Id WSW 14/11-12 and 15/11-12 (Area CW, see fig. 1) a probe 6.75 x 8 m was opened parallel to the military road in order to find the northward continuation of the fortification wall in Area D and to locate a city-gate or entrance to the West Terrace.

Results

In Area D we located the Citadel Wall of Idalion and obtained a section to bedrock along its inner (east) face (see pl. 8; figs. 8 and 9). In the westward extension of our probe in WSW 14/16 we reached bedrock from the military road eastward into WSW 13/16 but were unable to reach it along the outer (west) face of the City Wall. However, in Area CW we located the northward continuation of the fortification and obtained a section to bedrock along its outer (west) face.

A sequence of eight phases of occupation can be posited from our small probe against the inner face of the wall in WSW 11/16. On top of the wall in Area D and along the outer face of the wall in Areas D and CW extensive modern trenching and stone-robbing activity had destroyed any ancient stratigraphy down to bedrock except in the deepest part of the probe against the outer face of the wall in WSW 13/16.

Phase 8 (see fig. 9, Section A-A). In the probe in WSW 11/16 bedrock was reached at approximately 248.00 m asl. Even in this small exposure bedrock showed signs of artificial deformation or cutting, probably the result of quarrying to obtain limestone blocks. Immediately above bedrock was a sandy matrix of decayed bedrock and limestone chips (WSW 11/16 Loc 047). Above this chippy layer was a build-up of hard limestone angular fragments (WSW 11/16 Loc 046), with patchy use surfaces (WSW 11/16 Loc 043 and 044). These loci contained sherds as well as pockets of mudbrick and ash. Pl. 9a shows sherds embedded in the top of Loc 043-046.

Phase 7B. Over this earliest phase of occupation was constructed Wall 039. Pl. 9a shows the top of Loc 043-046 at the lowest course of Wall 039 which appears north-south in the right hand side of the picture. Wall 039 was constructed of rough ashlar limestone blocks chinked with limestone cobbles. Only one row appeared but there were four courses, totaling 0.85 m. Wall 039 runs north-south, but on a slightly different orientation from the Citadel Wall above it and its face extended further eastward into the probe trench. Even in our small exposure it was apparent that Wall 039 was monumental. It may thus represent the inner face of the first defensive fortifications of Idalion. Associated with the initial use of Wall 039 were a hard compacted layer with chunks of marl and cobblestones (WSW 11/16 Loc 042) and an indurated gray soil with a high clay and ash content, probably a use-surface (WSW 11/16 Loc 041). The top of Loc 041 is a layer of ash 2-3 cm thick (WSW Loc 037).

Phase 7A. A second wall (WSW 11/16 Loc 038) running E-W intersects at a 90° angle with Wall 039 with its base on a level with ashy layer 11/16 Loc 037, partway up the first course of Wall 039. Wall 038 was roughly five courses high, two rows wide, and survived to a height of 0.62 m. The top two courses were constructed of massive rough-cut ashlar limestone blocks with limestone cobble chinking, while the lower courses were limestone field-stone cobbles packed with limestone chips. It was not bonded to Wall 039 but abutted it (see pls. 9b, c). Although Wall 038 was built at a later date than Wall 039, they were in use together, as is attested by occupation debris stratigraphically associated with both walls (WSW 11/16 Loc 036 and 035). Loc 036 was composed of fragments of reddish mudbrick and abundant charcoal overlying ashy Loc 037, and Loc 035 was an ashy surface which ran up to the top of the extant uppermost courses of both Walls 039 and 038. Surmounting Wall 038 was 0.65 m of irregular limestone boulders and cobbles, pieces of sandstone and marl-brick detritus and several preserved articulated rectangular greenish marl-bricks each a 0.30 x 0.15 m (WSW Loc 034, pl. 10a). The top of Loc 034 was marked by 0.03 m of unevenly deposited ash and charcoal. The disposition of the components of Loc 034, with boulders on the bottom and segments of fallen mudbricks above, would be consonant with wall-fall from Walls 039 and 038, assuming that either or both originally had a mudbrick superstructure. One large boulder in the south balk protruded over the outer edge of the top extant course of Wall 039, which indicates that Wall 039 was destroyed down to this level.

Phase 6. Above the ash at the top of Loc 034 was 0.95 m of cobbles and boulders (some cracked) in a clay and mudbrick matrix (Loc 033). Incorporated into this matrix were concrete architectural fragments with plaster facing, including a corner piece. Above Loc 033 was a further 1.15 m of hard-packed mudbrick detritus with large pieces of charcoal and much bone and sherds (Loc 031). These two loci seem also to have been formed from the destruction of some large structure.

Phase 5. This is the construction phase of the Citadel Wall, although it is likely there will be intervening phases between 6-5 when the build-up of material beneath the surface of the foundation trench in the east section of WSW 11/16 is excavated. In WSW 11/16 the construction of the City Wall is marked by a huge foundation trench 4 m wide and 4.50 m deep (see fig. 9, Section A-A). It is funnel-shaped in section, broadly flared for the top 2 m, constricting sharply at 252 m and becoming narrower and narrower for the last 2.5 m (see pl. 10b). The founding courses of the Citadel Wall's outer face were not reached in WSW 13/16, but in Area C the outer face of the wall was completely excavated and proved to have been founded directly on bedrock. We may thus infer that this was probably also the case in WSW 13/16. The following sequence can be posited for the construction of the Citadel Wall.

On the west slope of the West Terrace the builders cleared earlier occupation down to bedrock to found the outside of the wall. They cut back the debris roughly vertically to the level of the top of Loc 031 in WSW 11/16. In doing so, they uncovered the top extant course of Wall 039 in WSW 11/16. They incorporated this wall into their own fortification, accommodating a large boulder protruding from WSW 11/16 Loc 034 into their inner face by stepping back their first course above Wall 039 in the south balk. Between the destruction of Wall 039 and the construction of Citadel Wall 021 some structure must have served to retain the 4 m accumulation of debris between Loc 034 and the top of the foundation in the east of WSW 11/16. This putative second wall may be hidden in the core of Citadel Wall 021 but only a section through the Citadel Wall will show whetherthis hypothesis is correct. Having prepared an L-shaped wall-bed, the builders then constructed their fortifications. In WSW 11-13/16 the wall consisted of an inner and an outer facing of coursed ashlar limestone blocks, with a core of tabular limestone rubble, the whole totally 10.75 m in thickness with a maximum extant height of 7.80 m.

Inner Face (pls. 8, 10c)

The inner face of the Citadel Wall is preserved to a height of eighteen courses plus the four courses of Wall 039, standing to an extant height of 5.10 m. It is composed of ashlar limestone blocks. The first ten courses above Wall 039 were irregularly cut, dry-laid with chinking of angular limestone chips. The roughness of the coursing suggests that up to the top of the tenth course, which is level with the top of the narrow area of the foundation trench, the builders constructed their wall from the west. At the height of the tenth course on the inner face (251.675 m asl) the foundation trench broadens out. The narrow trench between the Citadel Wall and earlier debris was back-filled. Three distinct layers could be distinguished in this fall. WSW 11/16 Loc 032 and 032 at the base of the trench were layers of angular limestone chips. Above this, Loc 029 contained much decayed mudbrick. The upper surface of Loc 029 and the broad slope of the rest of the foundation trench were extremely indurated suggesting heavy use. The remaining eight extant courses of the inner face of ashlar limestones were carefully dressed, some showing diagonal chisel marks, and tightly fitted with chinking limestone cobbles, suggesting that the upper part of the inner face was built from the east, using the sloping surface of the broadened foundation trench as a working platform.

The two uppermost extant courses of the inner face were tuck-pointed with coarse crushed gypsum mortar (Koucky's Type 1). Pl. 10c shows this tuck-pointing. The limestone facing is here two rows wide (2.25 m) and abuts the east face of the rubble core (see pl. 11a). Adhering to the mortar of the top course, outside row of limestone ashlars were fragments of sandstone. From impressions in the upper surfaces of the mortar, these were originally sandstone blocks 0.50 m x 0.90 m, laid in header-stretcher fashion. The sandstones have been robbed out but must have formed a continuation of the inner facing. The foundation trench was back-filled (WSW 11/16 Loci 023, 028) and sealed by the lowest surface of WSW 11/16 Loc 020 (Loc 020.3). The modern robber trench which was dug to rob out the sandstone blocks has cut through the association of surface Loc 020 and the projected continuation of the Citadel Wall, but it can be inferred that all the limestone ashlars were intended to be below ground and sandstone ashlars formed the visible above ground inner face.

Rubble Core.

Between the inner and outer sheathing of the Citadel Wall was a core of very friable tabular limestone rubble 6.25 m thick. The inner face of this rubble core (WSW 12/16 Loc 007), where it abutted the ashlar sheathing was very roughly coursed, with a pronounced batter. Pl. 8 shows the rough rubble coursing in the right hand side of the picture. This edge of the rubble core survives to a maximum height of 1.5 m. It is likely that it also bore a mudbrick superstructure which later collapsed into WSW 11/16 to form Loc 005. An expanse of the rubble core twelve meters long was uncovered in 12-13/15 and WSW 12-13/16. The rubble core is much decayed from exposure to the elements. Plate 11b, c, and d show what remains of it.

Outer Face.

Area D. Because it was not concealed and protected by the back fill of the foundation trench, the outer (west) face of the Citadel Wall has not survived as well as the inner face. In WSW 13/16 the west face consisted of two outer rows of ashlar limestones, plastered on their outer faces (pls. 11d, 12a, b). There appear to be six courses thus far excavated, but the plastering on the outer face makes it difficult to be certain. The outer face stands 1.70 m high; the founding course was not reached at 247.50 m asl. Bedrock probably lies just a few centimeters below this level, but danger from falling rubble made further excavation in this narrow trench impracticable. A third row of ashlar limestones set in Type 1 coarse crushed gypsum plaster survived for an additional four courses (ca. 1 m) above the two outer rows, separated from them by 0.65 m of cobble-sized rubble (pls. 12a, b).

Traces of another wall (WSW 13/16 Loc 015) were found immediately outside the Citadel Wall, running N-S parallel to it at a depth of 248.45 m asl (pl. 12c). Wall 015 was constructed of limestone fieldstones, dry-laid, 4-5 courses preserved to a height of 0.85 m. Only the east face was excavated. Wall 015 was in use with later phases of the Citadel Wall, since WSW 13/16 Loc 017 and 018 ran up against both walls. Loc 017 consisted of occupational debris, including small amounts of slag, and Loc 018 beneath it was a use-surface. However, the foundation of Wall 015 postdates the construction of the Citadel Wall since Loc 019 runs under the founding course of Wall 015 (see table 4).

Although chunks of sandstone were found in the backfill of later excavation and robber trenches along the outer face of the Citadel Wall, there was no direct evidence to show that in this part of the outer face the ashlar limestones were ever surmounted by sandstone upper coursing, but since the outer face was robbed out completely to a depth more than 3 m below the point at which traces of sandstone occur on the inner face, this negative evidence is inconclusive.

Area CW. In Area CW, 28 m north of the Citadel Wall in Area D, the lowest courses of the outer face of a massive wall (WSW CW Loc 006) were found (see pl. 13a). This wall is on the same N-S alignment as the outer face of the Citadel Wall and formed the northward continuation of it. Its construction, however, resembles that of the monumental facades of Area C (see above) and it may thus have also functioned as part of that public building. Wall 006 has been excavated for a length of 8 m and an additional meter or more of this wall has been exposed to the north by weathering since these excavations. Wall 006 is founded directly on bedrock and its outer face is constructed of massive ashlar sandstone blocks 1 m. x 0.75 m x 0.5 m, laid header and stretcher, leveled up with limestone cobbles and consolidated with Type 1 gypsum plaster. These sandstone blocks have been robbed out almost to founding level. The builders built their wall to conform to the irregular configurations of bedrock, so that most of Wall 006 is preserved only 2 courses high, but where bedrock dips it is 3 courses (see pl. 13a). Two rows of sandstone ashlars form the outer face; behind this facade, and bonded into it, two crosswalls built of coursed limestone extend eastward. The crosswalls are separated by a two-meter gap (pl. 13a, b). The south crosswall (WSW CW Loc 002) was preserved 7 courses high (2.95 m); the bottom course was built of larger and more carefully drafted ashlars. Its width is not known but 2.5 m were exposed of its west side. Since this part of Area CW had been robbed out down to the founding courses on bedrock, there were no sealed layers associated with the construction or use of Wall CW 006.

Phase 4. The best indication for the history of the Citadel Wall after its construction and initial use comes from the deep probe in WSW 11/16. Here, above the initial surface (WSW 11/16 Loc 020) sealing the foundation trench, the wall continued in use with surface buildup WSW 11/16 Loc 015. On top of these 015 surfaces were the slag-heaps of Loci 009 and 007 (see Stager, Walker, and Wright 1974:50-52).

Phase 3. This is the phase in which the Citadel Wall went out of use. It is marked by a thick layer of toppled marl-bricks (WSW 11/16 Loc 005 and 004) which probably resulted from the collapse of the mudbrick superstructure of the Citadel Wall (see Stager, Walker, and Wright 1974:56).

Phase 2. This phase comprises WSW 11/16 Loc 003, the colluvium which formed over the phase 3 mudbricks.

Phase 1. This last phase represents a complex history of recent excavation and stone-robbing. First trenching took place along the inner face of the Citadel Wall down to the level of the ashlars, across the top of the wall core and along the entire outer face of the wall down to bedrock, except in a pocket immediately against the outer face in WSW 13/16. After this initial trenching and excavation was backfilled, a second trenching operation took place for the purpose of robbing-out the valuable sandstone and limestone ashlars along the inner and outer faces of the wall, cutting through the earlier backfill. This narrow robber trench can be clearly seen in outline in the north balk of WSW 13/16 (pl. 11c).

Dating.

Phase 8. The pottery associated with this earliest phase of occupation on the West Terrace dates from the Cypro-Geometric III-Cypro-Archaic I periods.

Phase 7. The pottery of this phase dates to the Cypro-Archaic I-II (see fig. 7, nos. 33-34).

Phase 6. The majority of the sherds from Loci 033 and 031 belong typologically to Cypro-Archaic II and Cypro-Classical I. Examples of Plain White V bowls, which Ålin considers to show a tendency towards angular body and out-turned rim, are illustrated in fig. 7, nos. 7-10, and 15. Ålin further comments that the neck and rim (fig. 7, no. 5) belong to a jug or amphora in Bichrome Red Ware, while the rim and shoulder fragment (fig. 7, no. 11) comes from a jar in Plain White V ware (*SCE* IV:2, fig. L11:4) and rim (fig. 7, no. 13) is Black-on-Red III (V) and belongs to the Type V bowl with off-set rim (*SCE* IV:2, fig. L11:2).

Phase 5. The best evidence for dating the construction of the Citadel Wall comes from the massive fills in the foundation trench, represented by WSW 11/16 Loci 023, 025, 028, 029, 030 and 032. The mass of the pottery uncovered belongs to the end of the Cypro-Archaic and the beginning of the Cypro-Classical periods, with nothing later represented. Figure 7, nos. 2, 16, 17, and 23 belong to Plain White Type V while fig. 7, nos. 21 and 27 could also be Type IV.

Phase 4. The use phase of the Citadel Wall in WSW 11/15 and 11/16 Slagheaps 007 and 009 contained ceramics with a spread throughout the Cypro-Classical period and down to the end of the 4th century B.C. (see Stager, Walker, and Wright 1974:51-52).

Phase 3. The destruction phase of the Citadel Wall belongs to the second half of the 4th century B.C., on the basis of the pottery and palaeographic evidence from an ostracon found in WSW 11/16 Loc 005 (see Stager, Walker, and Wright 1974:77-81).

Phases 2-1. These are the highly disturbed strata post-dating the collapse of the Citadel Wall. From the finding of a galvanized steel tag in the earliest trenching operation in WSW 12/15 it seems likely that one of Idalion's late 19th or early 20th century excavations trenched into the center of the wall, believing that the decayed limestone rubble core was wall fall lying against the face of the fortification. Fragments of shell casings above the core of the wall show that at least that part of the Citadel Wall lay exposed when an ammunition dump was exploded in the 1950's some 25 m to the north.

Discussion (see table 4).

Although our exposure is extremely small and our evidence very sparse, the first occupation of this part of the site, as elsewhere in Lower City (see below) seems to have been in the late Cypro-Geometric period. The first defensive system of Idalion was probably that represented by Wall 039 which dates to the Cypro-Archaic I. Since no wall of comparable date has so far been found in Lower City (see below), it seems likely that only the citadel area (West Terrace and West Acropolis) was enclosed by a fortification wall at this time. This earliest citadel wall continued in use down to the Cypro-Archaic II period, when it was destroyed and presumably replaced by a second citadel wall, whose existence can so far only be inferred from the 4 m of deposit separating the destruction of Wall 039 from the construction of the main Citadel Wall.

At the end of the Cypro-Archaic and beginning of Cypro-Classical I the fortification system on the West Terrace was radically reorganized (and the Lower City enclosed for the first time, see below). The earlier debris was cut back and a huge foundation trench dug to construct a massive wall with a limestone rubble core and inner and outer facings of ashlar blocks. In Area D the inner facing consisted of limestone ashlars for twenty-two below ground courses and we infer the addition of sandstone ashlars to an unknown height above ground. The outer facing in Area D for at least 3.2 m consisted of limestone ashlars plastered over. In Area CW, however, where the wall was founded directly on bedrock, the outer facing consisted of sandstone ashlars. The dissimilarity of construction of the wall between Areas D and CW and the similarity in the use of sandstone ashlars between CW and the facades of the Palace suggest that the wall in Area CW functioned both as part of the Palace and the northward continuation of the Citadel Wall, although the founding levels of the Palace have not been reached. The maximum extant height of the wall in Area D, from the lowest course of limestone ashlars reached on the outer face to the top of the rubble core is 7.80 m, and it is likely that in addition the Citadel Wall in both Areas D and CW carried a mudbrick superstructure of unknown height. The thickness of the wall (10.75 m) is truly astounding and unprecedented in Cyprus at this early period, although Gjerstad mentions that the Palace of

Vouni (ca. 500-380 B.C.) was surrounded by a rampart (*SCE* III:77-79). It is hard to believe the whole West Terrace and Acropolis were surrounded by a wall of this thickness. It is more plausible that our stratigraphic trench has serendipitously come down upon a specially thickened or strengthened section of the wall, perhaps a bastion or pier (see Lower City Fortifications, below). We have no indication so far of the location of a gate or entrance to the West Terrace citadel. It is possible that in fact there was no entrance to the West Terrace along the western perimeter, but that instead access was through a gate somewhere along the north perimeter of the West Terrace, that is from inside the city proper. This situation would be somewhat analogous to the relationship between medieval motte and bailey, with the West Terrace and Acropolis corresponding to a kind of motte and the Lower City to the bailey.

On the basis of ceramic dating, the person responsible for the construction of the massive fortification was one of the kings of independent Idalion prior to its conquest by Kition sometime between 450-425 B.C.

The fortification continued in use down to the end of the fourth century B.C., when it was destroyed, if our interpretation of the fallen mudbricks in 11/16 Loc 005 as the collapsed superstructure of the Citadel Wall is correct.

Table 4. West Terrace Fortifications Phasing Summary

Phase	Area						Period
1	11/16	12/16	13/16	12/15	13/15	CW	
Robber trenches	011; 001,002	-----------	-----------	-----------	-----------		Modern
2 Colluvium	003						Hellenistic to Modern
3 Destruction of Citadel Wall	004,005						End of 4th century, (312 B.C.)
4 Use of Citadel Wall	007,009 015,020.1 020.2		015? 017 018				
5 Construction of Citadel Wall	020.3, 021 (inner face) 023,025, 028,029, 030,032 (foundation trench)	007 (core)---	----------- 019 009 (outer face)			008 (core) 006 (outer face) 002	ca. 475 B.C.
6 Mudbrick detritus and architectural fragments	031,033						Cypro-Archaic II to Cypro-Classical I
7 1st Fortification Wall	034-039						Cypro-Archaic I-II
8 Earliest occupation above bedrock	043-047						Cypro-Geometric III to Cypro-Archaic I

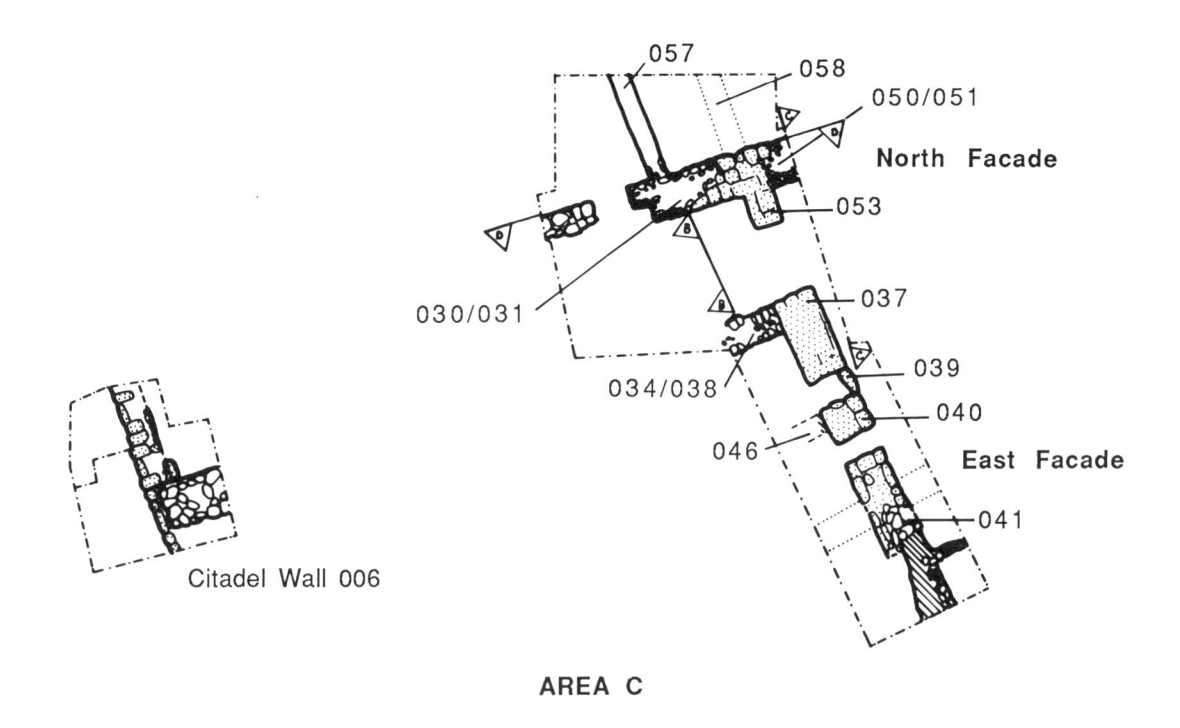

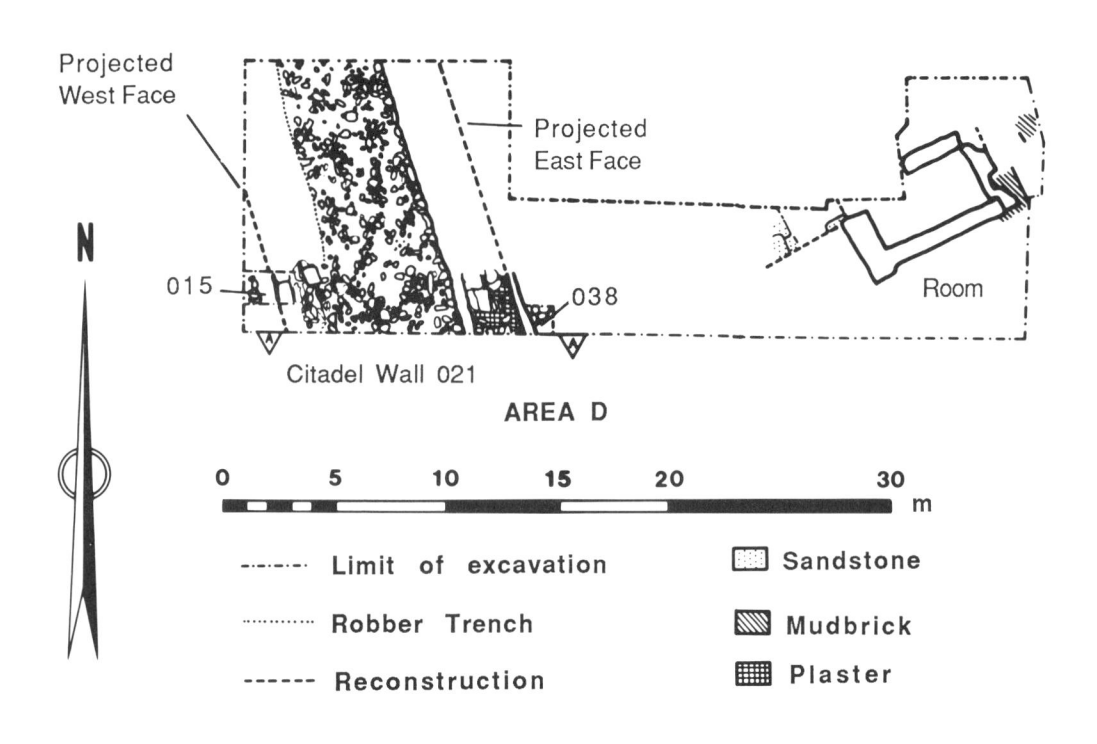

Figure 1. Idalion West Terrace, Areas C and D.

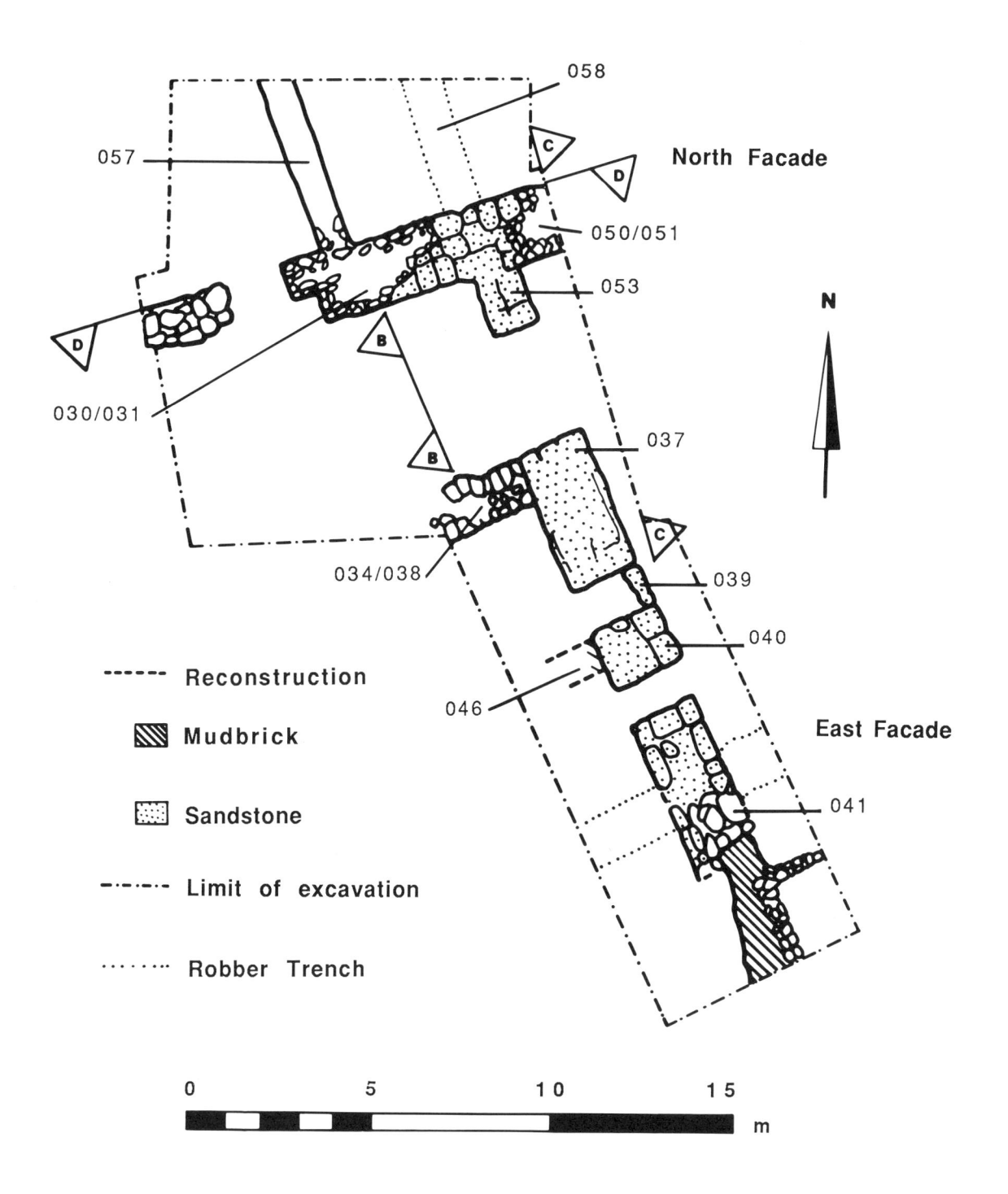

Figure 2. Idalion West Terrace, Area C enlarged.

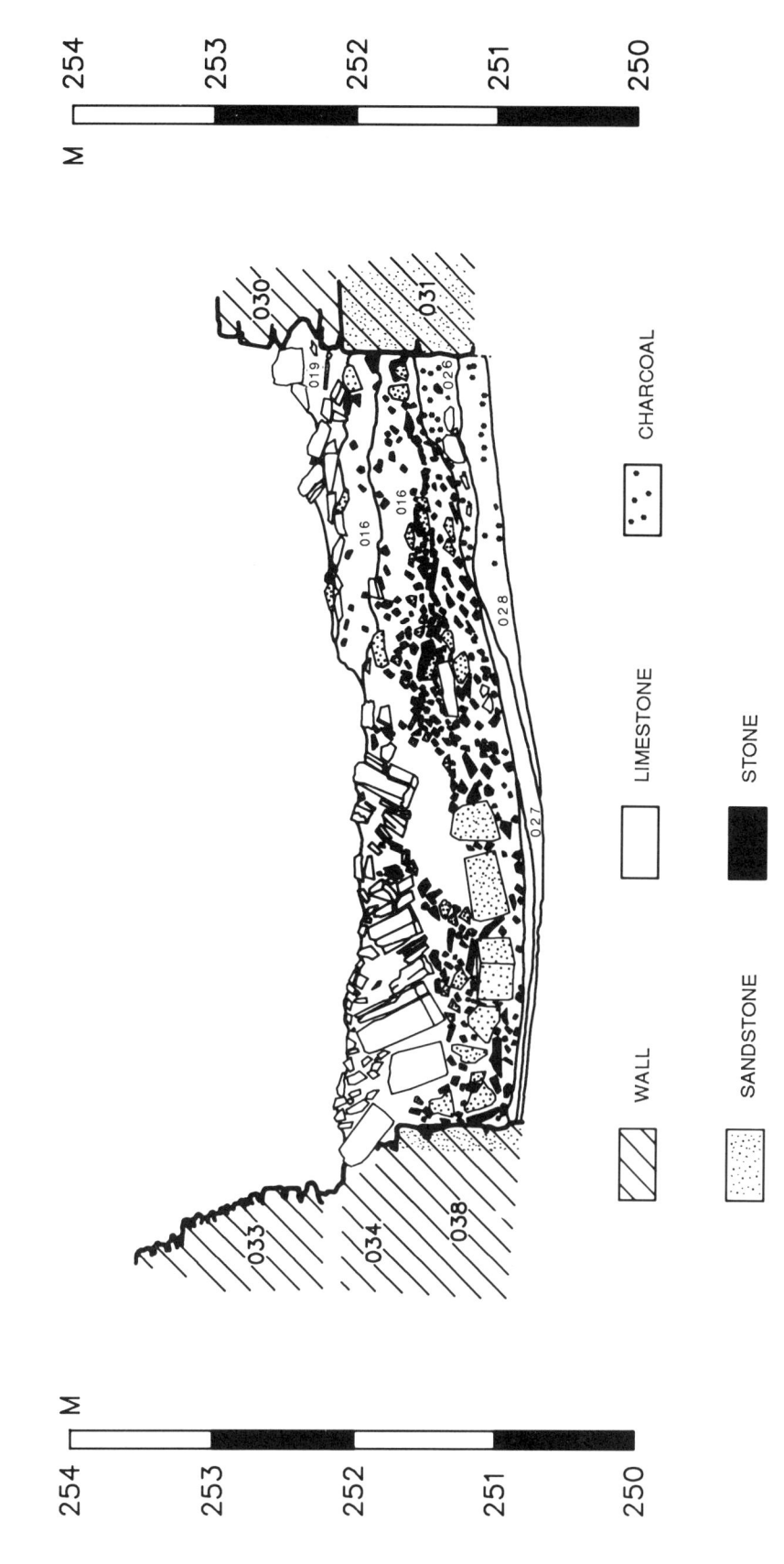

Figure 3. Idalion WSW Section (B-B). Key: 016, 019, Wall collapse of sandstone and limestone blocks in gray brown marl matrix of disintegrated mudbricks; 026, 027, 028, Street surfaces of indurated marl.

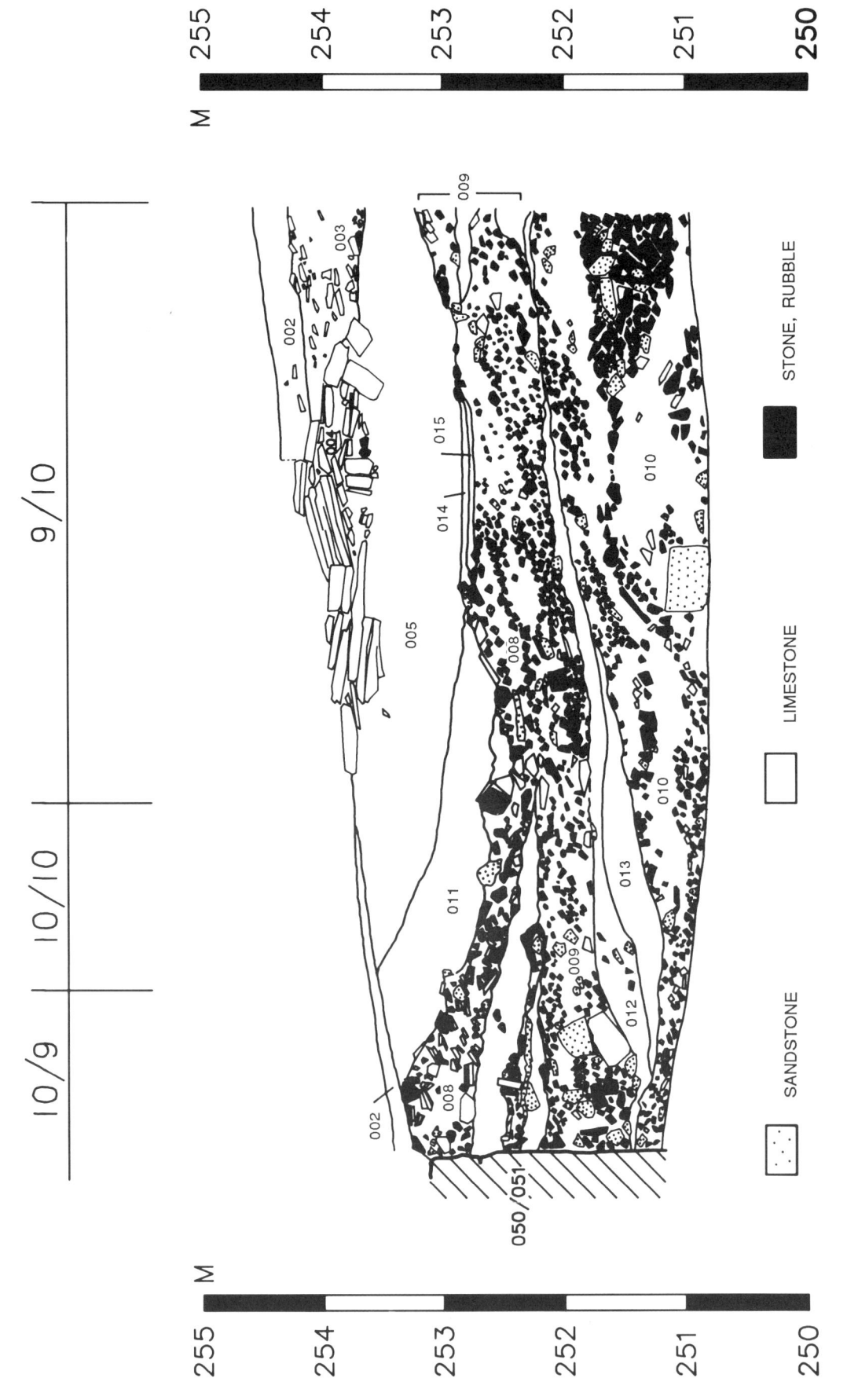

Figure 4. Idalion WSW Section (C-C). Key: 002, Gray brown marl; 003, Gray brown marl, sandstone rubble; 004, Sandstone; 005, Fine compact gray brown marl; 008, Gray brown compact marl, mixed rubble; 009, Fine gray green marl; 010, Loose fine rubble; 011, Very fine compact gray green marl; 014, Horizontally banded brown marl; 015, Very compact pale gray green marl.

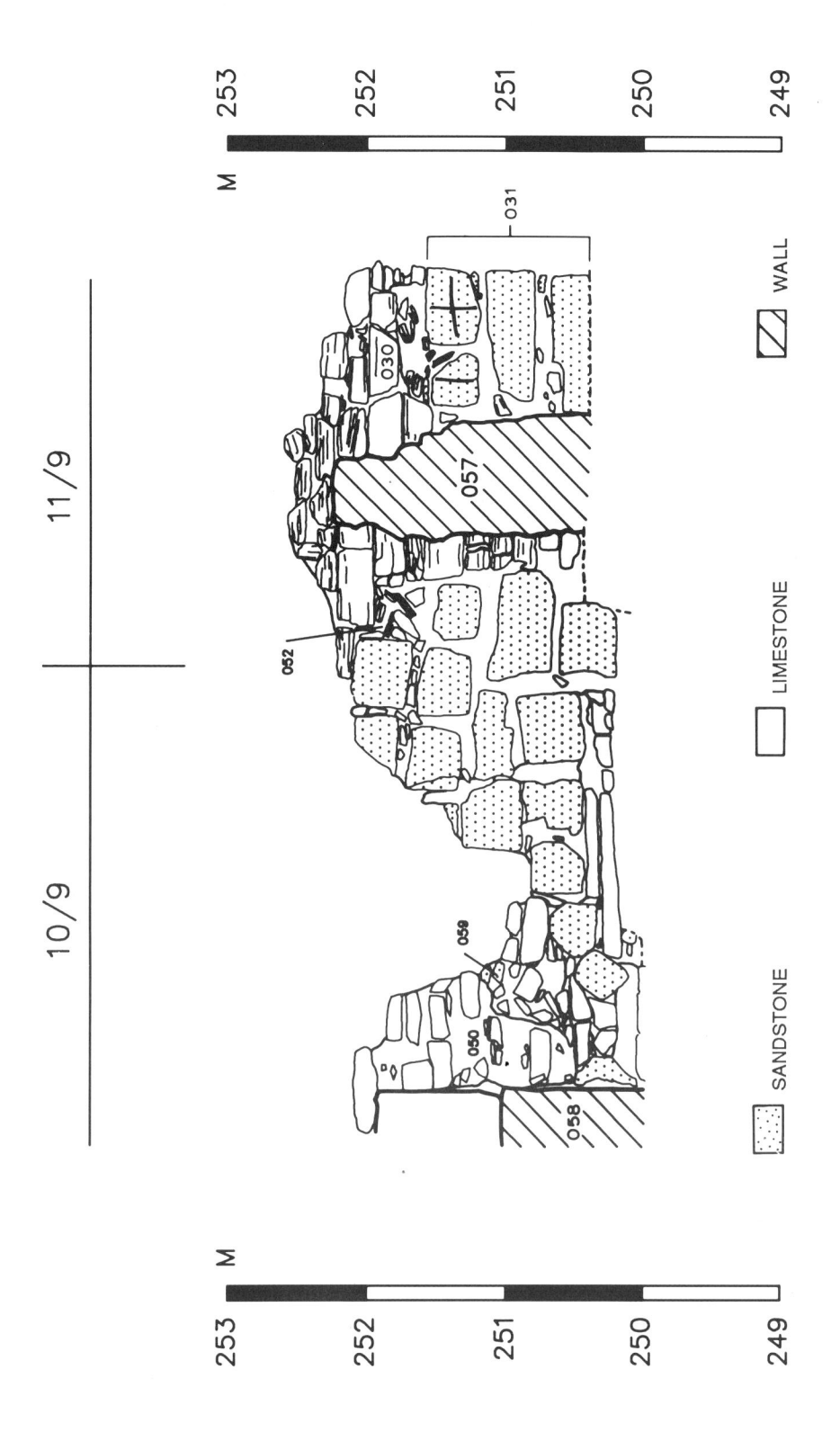

Figure 5. Idalion WSW Section (D-D).

Figure 6. Pottery from Idalion WSW 8/15 (Area D)

	Phase	Locus	Registration no.	Description
1.	5	021	77.923	Ware: 10 YR 7/3 (very pale brown).
2.	5	022	77.937	Ware: 7.5 YR 6/4 (light brown).
3.	5	022	77.947	Charred; ware: 10 YR 7/2 (light gray); core: 10 YR 4/1 (dark gray).
4.	5	022	77.935	Ware: 10 YR 8/3 (very pale brown).
5.	5	024	77.1227	Ware: 10 YR 8/3 (very pale brown).
6.	5	024	77.1053	Ware: 10 YR 7/4 (very pale brown).
7.	5	024	77.951	Ware: 10 YR 6/4 (light yellowish brown).
8.	5	024	77.953	Ware: 2.5 YR 6/4 (light reddish brown).
9.	5	024	77.954	Ware: 5 YR 6/4 (light reddish brown).
10.	5	024	77.1232	Ware: 2.5 Y 7/2 (light gray).
11.	5	026	77.1242	Slipped; ware: 10 YR 8/3 (very pale brown); slip: 7.5 YR 8/2 (pinkish white).
12.	5	026	77.1235	Ware: 10 YR 8/3 (very pale brown).
13.	5	028	77.1255	Painted; ware: 7.5 YR 7/4 (pink): paint: 7.5 YR N3/ (very dark gray).
14.	5	028	77.1270	Ware: 10 YR 8/4 (very pale brown).
15.	5	028	77.1285	Slipped; ware: 10 YR 7/3 (very pale brown); slip: 2.5 YR 5/6 (red).
16.	5	028	77.1299	Ware: 10 YR 7/4 (very pale brown).
17.	5	028	77.1280	Ware: 10 YR 7/4 (very pale brown).
18.	5	028	77.1288	Ware: 5 YR 6/6 (reddish yellow).
19.	5	028	77.1290	Ware: 7.5 YR 6/4 (light brown).
20.	5	028	77.1257	Ware: 10 YR 7/3 (very pale brown).
21.	5	028	77.1294	Ware: 7.5 YR 7/4 (pink).
22.	5	028	77.1275	Ware: 7.5 YR 7/6 (reddish yellow).
23.	5	028	77.1265	Ware: 10 YR 7/1 (light gray).
24.	5	028	77.1281	Ware: 10 YR 7/4 (very pale brown).
25.	5	028	77.1256	Ware: 7.5 YR 7/4 (pink).
26.	5	028	77.1262	Ware: 10 YR 6/4 (light yellowish brown).
27.	5	028	77.1252	Ware: 10 YR 7/4 (very pale brown).
28.	5	028	77.1258	Ware: 5 YR 7/4 (pink).
29.	5	028	77.1263	Ware: 7.5 YR 7/6 (reddish yellow).
30.	5	028	77.1296	Ware: 10 YR 7/1 (light gray).
31.	5	028	77.1279	Ware: 7.5 YR 6/4 (light brown).
32.	5	028	77.1277	Ware: 5 Y 8/3 (pale yellow).

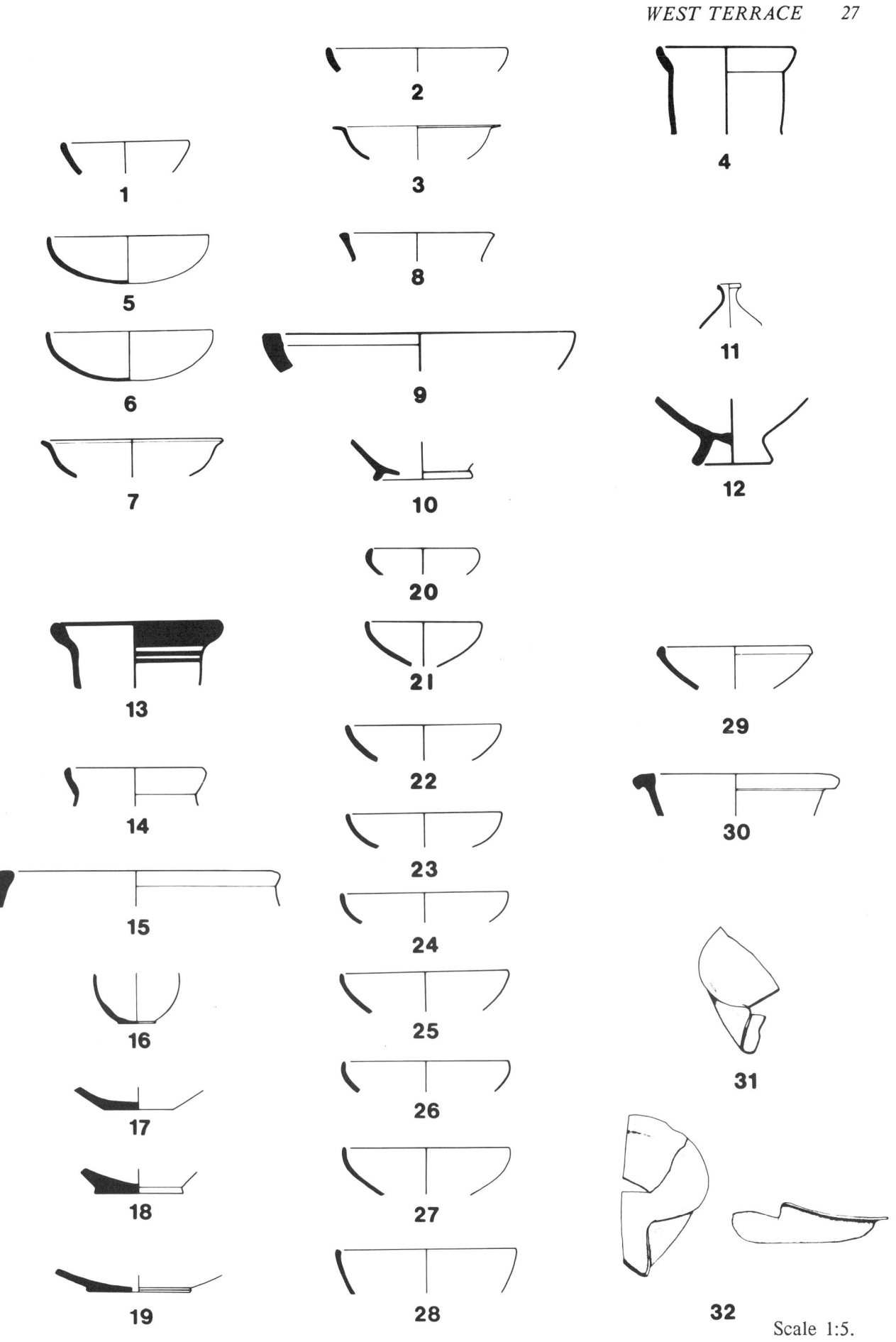

Figure 6. Pottery from Idalion WSW 8/15 (Area D). Scale 1:5.

Figure 7. Pottery from Idalion WSW 11/16 (Area D)
and 10/9, 11/9 (Area C)

	Phase	Locus	Registration no.	Description
1.	5	023	77.990	Ware: 5 YR 6/6 (reddish yellow).
2.	5	023	77.1021	Ware: 10 YR 7/3 (very pale brown).
3.	5	025	77.1313	Ware: 5 Y 8/2 (white).
4.	6	031	77.1682	Ware: 10 YR 7/3 (very pale brown).
5.	6	031	77.1692	Slipped and painted; ware: 10 YR 8/3 (very pale brown); slip: 2.5 YR 5/4 (reddish brown); paint: 2.5 YR N3/ (very dark gray).
6.	6	031	77.1699	Ware: 10 YR 7/2 (light gray).
7.	6	031	77.1584	Ware: 10 YR 7/2 (light gray).
8.	6	031	77.1697	Ware: 2.5 YR 7/2 (light gray).
9.	6	031	77.1698	Ware: 5 YR 7/6 (reddish yellow).
10.	6	031	77.1679	Ware: 10 YR 8/4 (very pale brown).
11.	6	031	77.1676	Charred; ware: 2.5 YR 3/4 (dark reddish brown).
12.	6	031	77.1687	Ware: 10 YR 7/3 (very pale brown).
13.	6	031	77.1782	Painted; ware: 2.5 YR 6/4 (light reddish brown); paint: 2.5 YR N2.5/ (black).
14.	6	031	77.1695	Ware: 10 YR 7/4 (very pale brown).
15.	6	031	77.1678	Surface: 7.5 YR 7/4 (pink); core: 7.5 YR N6/ (gray).
16.	5	028	77.1205	Surface: 7.5 YR 7/4 (pink); core: 7.5 YR N6/ (gray).
17.	5	028	77.1523	Surface: 7.5 YR 8/4 (pink); core: 10 YR 5/2 (grayish brown).
18.	5	029	77.1673	Ware: 5 YR 7/6 (reddish yellow).
19.	5	030	77.171(?)	Ware: 7.5 YR 6/4 (light brown).
20.	5	030	77.1725	Ware: 5 YR 6/4 (light reddish brown).
21.	5	030	77.1722	Ware: 10 YR 7/3 (very pale brown).
22.	5	032	77.1827	Ware: 2.5 Y 8/4 (pale yellow).
23.	5	032	77.1784	Ware: 10 YR 7/3 (very pale brown).
24.	5	032	77.1824	Ware: 10 YR 7/3 (very pale brown).
25.	5	032	77.1829	Ware: 10 YR 7/3 (very pale brown).
26.	5	032	77.1776	Ware: 10 YR 7/3 (very pale brown).
27.	5	032	77.1782	Ware: 10 YR 7/3 (very pale brown).
28.	6	031	77.1852	Painted; ware: 5 YR 7/4 (pink); paint: 5 YR 2.5/1 (black).
29.	6	031	77.1743	Ware: 10 YR 7/2 (light gray).
30.	6	031	77.1751	Ware: 7.5 YR 7/6 (reddish yellow).
31.	6	033	77.1810	Ware: 7.5 YR 7/4 (pink).
32.	6	033	7711814	Ware: 2.5 YR 6/4 (light reddish brown).
33.	7	034	77.1940	Ware: 10 YR 6/2 (light brownish gray).
34.	7	035	77.1941	Ware: 7.5 YR 6/4 (light brown).
35.	3	10/9 007.1	77.834	Painted and slipped; ware: 10 YR 7/3 (very pale brown); slip: 5 YR 7/4 (pink); paint: 5 YR 2.5/1 (black).
36.	3	11/9 032	77.477	Charred; ware: 7.5 YR 2.5/ (black).
37.	3	11/9 033	77.972	Ware: 5 YR 7/4 (pink).
38.	3	11/9 039	77.1361	Ware: 5 YR 7/6 (reddish yellow).
39.	3	11/9 033	77.974	Ware: 10 YR 7/3 (very pale brown).
40.	3	11/9 033	77.973	Ware: 10 YR 7/3 (very pale brown).
41.	3	11/9 035		Black Glazed Ware
42.	3	11/9 039.1	77.1495	Ware: 2.5 YR 7/2 (light gray).

WEST TERRACE 29

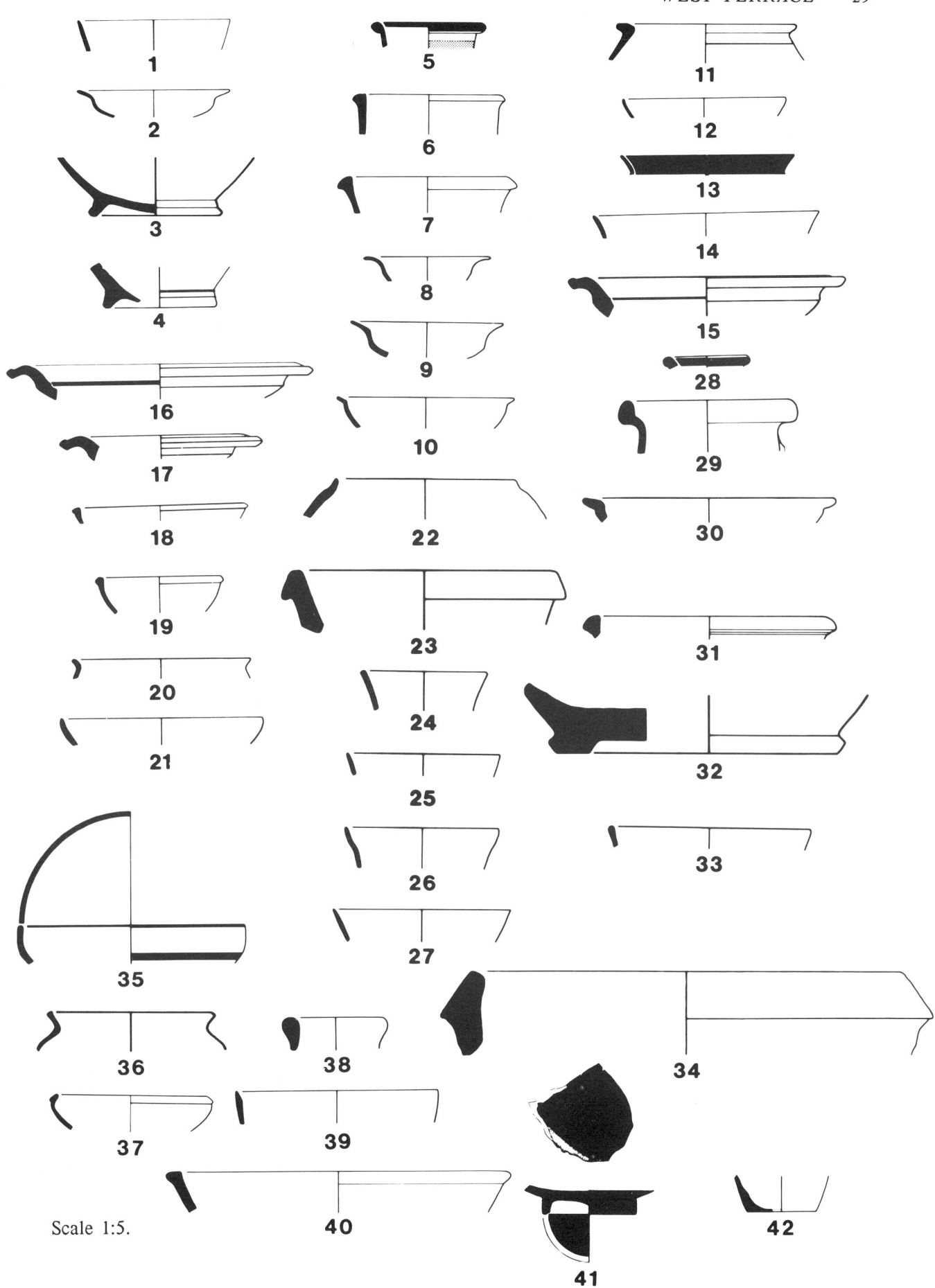

Figure 7. Pottery from Idalion WSW 11/16 (Area D) and 10/9, 11/9 (Area C).

Scale 1:5.

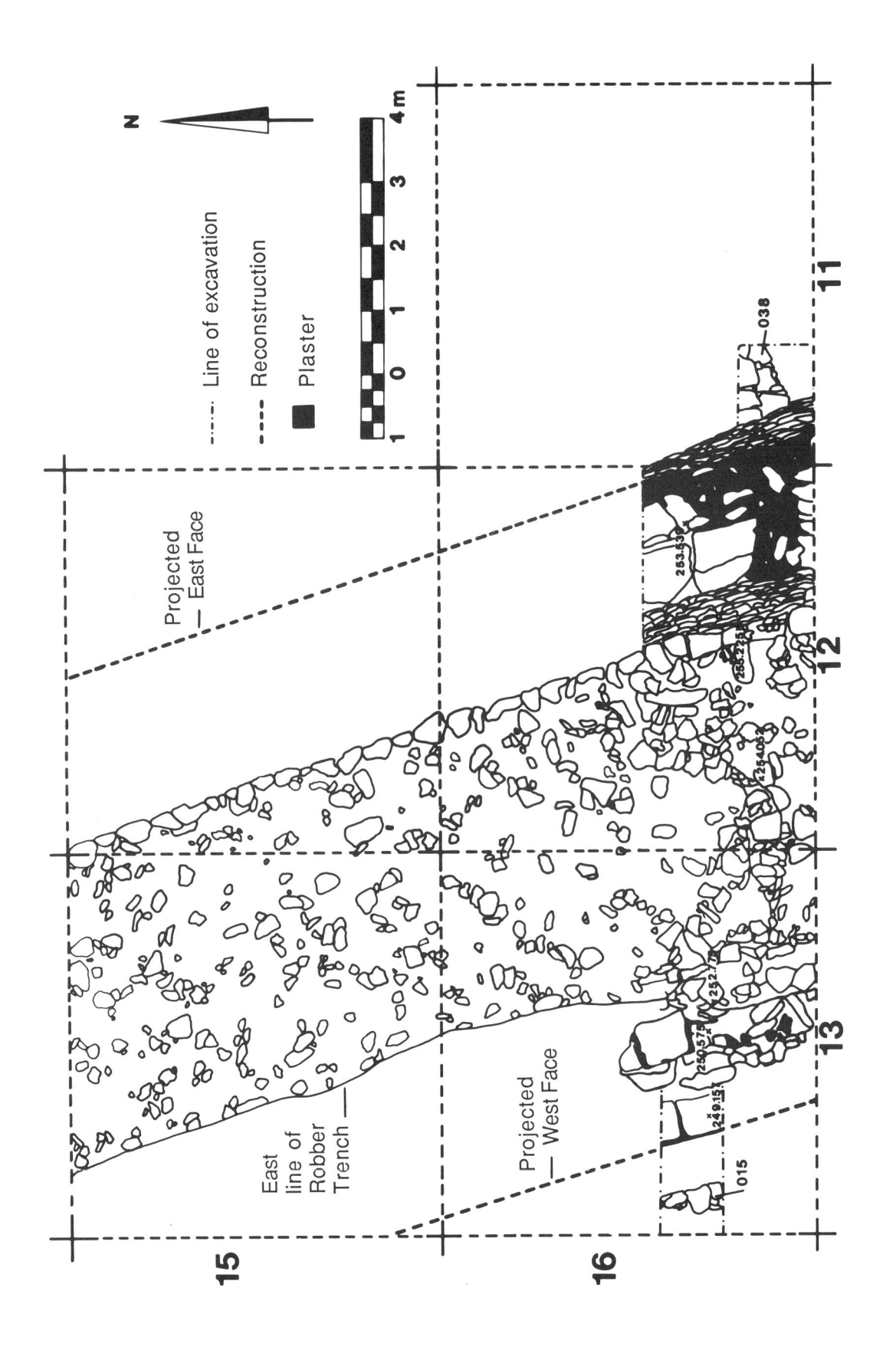

Figure 8. Idalion West Terrace Citadel Wall.

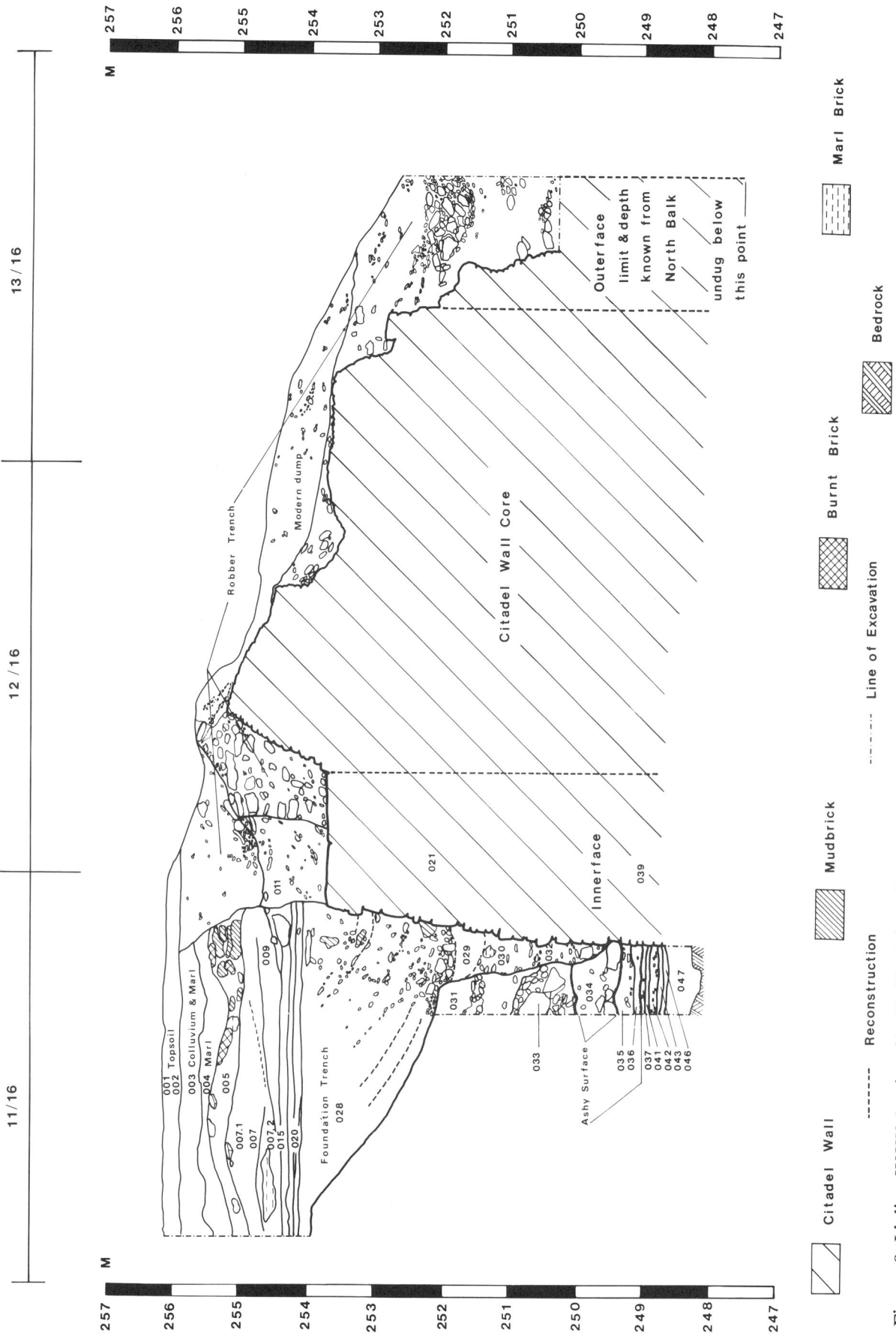

Figure 9. Idalion WSW Section (A-A) Citadel Wall. Key: 001, 002 topsoil, 003 colluvium and marl, 004 marl, 905 mudbricks, 007, 009 slag heaps, 011 robber trench, 015 surface buildup, 020 surface, 021 citadel wall, 028, 029, 030, 032 foundation trench, 031 mudbrick detritus, 033 cobbles and boulders, 034 limestone boulders, 035 ashy surface, 036 mudbrick and charcoal, 037 ash, 039 wall, 041 surface, 042 marl and cobbles, 043 surface, 046 angular limestone, 047 decayed bedrock.

PLATE 1

Area C. a. Eastern Facade of "Palace," looking south. Pier 037 in center. b. Eastern Facade, looking north. Village of Dhali in background. c. Building collapse into Street (10/10, Loc 016), upper level, looking west. Pier 053 on right; Pier 037 and Wall 034/038 on left.

PLATE 2

Street. a. Looking east. Note curbstone built into Pier 037 on south side of Street. b. Building collapse into Street, lower level, looking west.

PLATE 3

Northern Facade. a. North face. North arrow sits on Wall 057/010; horizontal meter stick (foreground), on robbed-out paving. b. Looking east at Walls 057/010 (foreground) and 058/006 (partially robbed, with meter sticks on it), jutting north of Northern Facade.

PLATE 4

Area C Chamber and Area D Room. a. Looking west at chamber between Walls 057/010 (background) and 058/006 (foreground). Crushed Cypro-Classical pithos lies on floor, marked by charring and olive pits. b. Area D Room, looking west inside room. Upper surface (D.020= 8/15.023) with triangular probe beneath, including destruction debris from 8/15.021-030.

PLATE 5

a

b

Area D Room and Area C Roofing. a. Area D Room, looking west at collapse inside north part of room. Meter stick lies on mudbrick superstructure collapse (8/15.023), next to "triangle" of concrete slabs from floor or wall destruction (8/15.024), with other destruction debris to left (8/15.021). b. Roofing material with river reed impressions from Cypro-Classical construction.

PLATE 6

Inscriptions, Phase 4 of Area D Room. a. Phoenician, D.009.19 (lower) (Obj. no. 931);
b. Phoenician, D.010.28 (Obj. no. 933); c. Incised sherd, D.010.28 (Obj. no. 934).

PLATE 7

Inscriptions, Phase 4 of Area D Room (a, b) and Backfill of Robber Trench (c). a. Cyprosyllabic inscription, D.010.31 (Obj. no. 935); b. Phoenician letter *mem*, D.010.35 (Obj. no. 937); and c. Phoenician inscription, D.011.34 (Obj. no. 938).

PLATE 8

East Face of Citadel Wall 021. North arrow rests on remnants of ashlar sandstone interior face (robbed out), behind which lies core of small limestone boulders and rubble fill.

PLATE 9

Walls 038 and 039. a. Phase 8 sherds embedded in upper surface of Loci 043-046. Wall 039 runs north-south in right hand side of picture. b. Wall 038 intersecting at 90° angle to Wall 039. Citadel Wall is built onto top course of Wall 039. c. Near bottom of probe trench, looking northwest at Wall 038 (running east-west), which extends under or is bonded into Wall 039.

PLATE 10

Citadel Wall 021. a. Foundation trench above and right of meter stick, looking south. At bottom of probe, marl bricks (Loc 034) can be seen in center.

b. Meter stick stands in foundation trench for Wall 039, which lies under Wall 021, whose foundation trench (Loc 032) appears filled with limestone chips in the south section behind meter stick.

c. East face of Wall 021. Robbed out sandstone courses above top of meter stick. Below robber trench, courses of tabular limestone with diagonal chisel marks. Upper course has "tuck pointing" of gypsum mortar.

PLATE 11

Citadel Wall 021 (Phase 5). a. Detail of limestone facing with mortar attached abutting east face of rubble core. b. Citadel Wall looking southeast from 13/15. Expanse of limestone rubble core; rubble against south balk of 12/16 consolidated by Department of Antiquities. c. Detail of Citadel Wall core looking north. Note rough coursed inner (east) face of core. In extreme left hand side of picture robber trench can be seen in north balk of 13/15. d. Rubble core of Citadel Wall looking northeast. Outer (west) face visible in right of picture. Note line of emptied robber trench along core in left and center.

PLATE 12

Citadel Wall 021. a. Looking east from west face (below lowest meter stick) across rubble core (consolidated at top) of Wall 021. b. Close up of outer (west) face of Citadel Wall, showing outer rows of ashlar limestones below, inner row above. Note line of emptied robber trench on left. c. Detail of outer (west) face showing plastering. Wall 015 appears running north-south in bottom of picture.

a

b

c

PLATE 13

a

b

Wall 006. a. Looking east at sandstone facade founded on bedrock, probably continuation of Citadel Wall 021. b. Looking south. Meter stick stands in "drain" cut into bedrock.

B. LOWER CITY EXCAVATIONS

1. FORTIFICATIONS

Anita M. Walker

Objectives

Parts of the fortification system that enclosed ancient Idalion can still be seen even today (see Introduction, fig. 2). In 1972 we decided to cut a section across the city wall at a point where a modern dirt track runs along the top of the old wall (fig. 1). The objective was to find the date and method of construction of the fortification system and the period of its use. Excavation that season uncovered the wall, but a section against its inner face failed to produce satisfactory evidence of the date of its construction or unequivocal data about the period of its use. This was due in part to the fact that along most of the face of the wall in the areas excavated, a robber trench of unknown date had cut off, below the founding levels of the wall, associations with layers and features within the wall's perimeter. Nor did the outer face present a clear picture. The thickened section of the outer face (Bastion Id WNW 44/22 Locus [hereafter abbreviated "Loc"] 016), while well defined along its western edge, disappeared within a confused mass of rubble along its northern edge, and its junction with the western outer face of the city wall proper was also ill defined. In 1973 and 1974, therefore, the objective was to clarify further the phasing of the city wall, the nature of Bastion Loc 016, and its relationship to the wall proper.

Strategy

The strategy consisted in cutting a series of probe trenches at right angles to the inner and outer faces of the wall (see fig. 1 and Sections A-A^1 to D-D^1, figs. 2-5). The placing of these probe trenches was determined by several factors. Along the inner face of the wall, in Id WNW 43/23, probe trench Loc 021 (fig. 3, Section B-B^1) was sited against the north balk because this seemed to offer the best chance of uncovering a section linking the small buildings inside the city wall to the wall itself, without interruption by the robber trench. Later a second probe trench, Loc 022 (fig. 4, Section C-C^1), was opened in the same square, not only to provide a confirmatory stratigraphic section between the city wall and Wall 008, but to recover more pottery, particularly for dating purposes, since the yield of probe Loc 021, despite assiduous dry-sieving, was very sparse. Further south, along the inner face of the city wall, in Id WNW 43/22 and 42/22, we cut a section between the city wall and Wall 003--(fig. 5, Section D-D^1). These cross sections were subsequently joined up by the removal of the intervening balks, after the drawings had been made. Another probe was opened in Id WNW 42/22 (fig. 5, continuation of Section D-D^1), along the west balk, since the steep slope of bedrock in the area offered sufficient depth of deposit to yield datable material. In 1973 a probe was opened along the outer face of the city wall, along the north balk of Id WNW 44/22 (Probe 005), to take in the junction of Bastion 016 with the outer face of the city wall. In 1974 sections were excavated along the bastion. Expansion southward also began in the adjacent square, Id WNW 43/20, with a small sondage to find the southern contour of the bastion, when work was interrupted by the troubles of 1974.

Results

A series of sections was obtained against the inside of the city wall and one against the outside. The results were complicated, however, by several factors. The total area available for excavation immediately inside the wall was quite small and fragmented by later disturbances. Conclusions about occupation prior to the building of the city wall are thus based on a very small sample. The bedrock slopes down steeply both to the south and to the west. As a result, the earliest strata of occupation east of the city wall are preserved only in deep pockets in the south of our field. Furthermore, because of a ridge of bedrock to the west, the builders of the city wall were able to contour the founding courses of their wall to the bedrock on the outside, west face. This effectively caused the pre-city wall stratum west of the wall to be separated from the strata east of the city wall by a ridge of bedrock, making correlation of the occupation east and west of the city wall before its construction stratigraphically tentative. Nevertheless, it is possible to posit the following stratigraphic sequence:

Phase 4. West of the city wall, in the section cut through the northern edge of Bastion 016 and lying just above bedrock, were traces of occupation stratigraphically earlier than the fortification system. Although the exposure was small, three distinct soil layers (Id WNW 44/22 Loc 013-015) were found overlying bedrock and cut into by later Phase 2 and 1 materials (see fig. 2, Section A-A[1]). One of these layers was a use-surface (Loc 014), which appears in plate 1a. On it were lying a number of fine Cypro-Archaic II sherds.

Phase 3. Inside the city wall the stratification is a little more complex.

Phase 3B. Immediately overlying bedrock, in a deep pocket in Id WNW 43/22 and along the east balk of Id WNW 42/22, was a layer of C-zone soil with sand and gravel, surmounted by a layer of occupation debris containing some pottery and charcoal flecks (fig. 4, Section C-C[1] 43/23 Loc 022, Layer 7; fig. 5, Section D-D[1] 43/22 Loc 023). Above that was a use-surface with abundant sherds, including (in Id WNW 43/22 Loc 022) most of a Greek Geometric bowl, or kantharos (Object 595, fig. 5, Section D-D[1] 43/22 Loc 022) and fragments of a fibula (Object 548 in Id WNW 42/22 Loc 011, Layer 9 = 43/22 Loc 022).

Phase 3A. The base of Phase 3A is marked by a layer composed partly of limestone cobbles, partly of tamped soil, which is found throughout most the area excavated between the city wall and Walls 003 and 008 (fig. 5, Section D-D[1] 43/22 Loc 020; fig. 4, Section C-C[1] 43/23 Loc 022, Layer 6; and pl. 1b). Above the cobble layer, which seems to be a use-surface, possibly a roadbed, is a layer of occupation debris (fig. 5, Section D-D[1] 43/22 Loc 019; fig. 4, Section C-C[1] 43/23 Loc 022, Layer 5; fig. 3, Section B-B[1] 43/23 Loc 021, Layer 5). One of the small puzzles in this field is a curious installation along the east balk of Id WNW 42/23 and 42/22. This is a semicircular pit (as far as has been excavated), about 1.75 m in diameter (pl. 2a, Loc 013). This pit was cut into bedrock, and modern disturbances have obliterated all soil layers between bedrock and the present road surface, so it is not possible to relate the contents of this pit to loci in the squares. It is partly filled by a rubble wall (Id WNW 42/22 Loc 012) about 1.30 m high, running north-south--a wall that does not seem to be aligned with other walls inside the city wall. The rest of the interior of the pit is filled with mudbricks and mudbrick detritus (pl. 2a). The function of this peculiar installation is totally obscure, although the same phenomenon of building walls across pits can be observed in West Lower City. Stratigraphically, however, it remains an orphan and could be assigned to either Phase 3A or Phase 2.

Phase 2. Phase 2 represents the construction and use phase of the city wall (see pls. 3a, b). Where possible, the builders seem to have tried to found the outer face of the wall along a ridge of bedrock. (Plate 1 shows a section along the north balk between Id WNW 44/22 and 43/22). In it the bedrock can be seen immediately underlying the outer face of the city wall. The inner parts of the wall, where the bedrock is deeply indented, are founded upon earlier occupation levels. Plate 2b illustrates this quite clearly. The builders do not seem to have dug a foundation trench for the city wall proper through these earlier strata, but to have erected their wall to conform with the extant surfaces and then filled in behind the inner face with a thick layer of tabular limestone rubble, which was found all along the inner face of the wall (pl. 2b and fig. 3, Section B-B[1] Loc 021, Layer 3; fig. 4, Section C-C[1] Loc 022, Layer 3; fig. 5, Section D-D[1] Loc 018). In places, a thin layer of pebble and gravel rubble underlay the larger cobble and boulder fill (fig. 3, Section B-B[1] Loc 021, Layer 4; fig. 4, Section C-C[1] Loc 022, Layer 4 and pl. 2b). The sections linking the city wall and Walls 003 and 008 also showed that this complex of small rubble walls was contemporary in construction and use with the city wall (Sections B-B[1], C-C[1], and D-D[1]). Wall 003, like the city wall, was built to conform to the contours of the bedrock, varying in extant height from 0.60 m in parts of its west face (see Section D-D¹) to a mere 0.25 m on its east face, where the bedrock rises sharply. Throughout Id WNW 43/23, 43/22, and 42/22, between the city wall and the walls east of it, a layer of mudbrick detritus of varying thickness overlay the rubble layer (fig. 3, Section B-B¹ Loc 021, Layer 2; fig. 4, Section C-C¹ Loc 022, Layer 2; fig. 5, Section D-D¹ Loc 017). This was also probably part of the constructional fill laid down by the builders. Traces of a use-surface associated with the city wall and the structures inside it were found throughout (fig. 3, Section B-B¹ Loc 009; fig. 4, Section C-C¹ Loc 009; fig. 5, Section D-D¹ Loc 016). Wall 008 may be slightly later in date than Wall 003 and the city wall, since the use-surface runs right up to its founding course.

The most interesting aspect of our continued investigation of this section of the city wall was undoubtedly the complexity of construction on the outer face of the wall in Id WNW 44/22 and 44/21. In 1972 we uncovered a feature in Id WNW 44/22 Loc 016, which was interpreted as a rubble bastion. Plates 3a and 3b show general views of Bastion 016 looking north. In sectioning this rubble bastion in 1973, a two-row wall of ashlar sandstone blocks was found (pl. 7, Id WNW 44/22 Loc 010). There is only one course extant but there are clear traces of footings of gypsum plaster (see West Terrace table 1, type 1) to receive further courses. Figure 2, Section A-A¹ and plates 1a and 4a, b show Loc 010. Like the city wall, Loc 010 is founded in part directly on bedrock (at its junction with the city wall), where the underside of one of the ashlar blocks seems to have been carefully shaped to follow the contour of the bedrock. Elsewhere it is founded on earlier strata (Phase 4), with traces of a small foundation trench along its north face (see pl. 1a). In 1973 it was thought that Loc 010 antedated Bastion 016, but further investigation in 1974 showed that in fact both Loc 010 and Bastion 016 represent a single structure built against the city wall, comprising a rubble core (Bastion 016) that was originally contained and faced by an ashlar facade (Loc 010). Id WNW 44/22 Loc 009 (see fig. 2, Section A-A¹), a layer composed mainly of lumps of decomposed mudbrick, may represent the brick superstructure of the bastion. In 1974 a small sondage was undertaken in Id WNW 43/20 in order to find the southward extension of the city wall and the southern limits of Bastion 016. We had just located what appeared to be not merely the southern edge of Bastion 016 but also a gap in the city wall, the troubles began and the work had to stop. When excavation resumed in 1975 the Cypriot National Guard had filled in the trench in Id WNW 43/20 with gravel and built a sentry box over it.

Phase 1. This is the destruction phase of the city-wall complex, and includes the mudbrick detritus Loc 004 in Id WNW 43/22 and 42/22 (see fig. 5, Section D-D¹), and Loc 004 in Id WNW 43/23 (see fig. 3, Section B-B¹). In Id WNW 44/22, in the northeast part of the square, a large irregularly shaped pit (Loc 006) was dug, presumably to rob out the ashlar blocks of Loc 010 down to their present level (see fig. 2, Section A-A¹ Loc 006 and pl. 1a). It was the removal of this protective ashlar facing that caused the confused northward slump of the rubble core Loc 016.

Dating

West of the city wall in Id WNW 44/22 (Loc 013-015) the pottery is exclusively Cypro-Archaic II in date, and thus Phase 4 represents the earliest occupation in this vicinity of Idalion. East of the city wall, although the mass of pottery recovered from Phase 3 is Cypro-Archaic II (including a few even earlier pieces, such as the Greek Geometric bowl), the presence of two pieces of Cypro-Classical pottery, even in Phase 3B, leads to the conclusion that Phase 3B must date to the end of Cypro-Archaic II and the beginning of Cypro-Classical I. The increasing number of Cypro-Classical sherds in Phase 3A suggests a date close to the beginning of the fifth century B.C. for the construction of this section of the city wall (Phase 2). This is confirmed by the absence from the rubble fills against the base of the wall of sherds datable later than Cypro-Classical I, although the total number of sherds recovered from these fills is very small. Phase 1 loci contain many Hellenistic sherds but nothing later, which suggests that at least this part of the fortification system may have remained in use down to the Hellenistic period.

Discussion

It can now be said with some confidence that in this sector of the fortification system of Idalion there is a bastion that is constructed with a solid rubble core and an outer facing of dressed sandstone blocks, built against the outer face of the city wall. It is also possible, from a sondage in Id WNW 43/20, that this bastion may have formed the north side of a city gate (suggested by the gap in the city wall). If that is so, since this is the western part of the city, such a gate may be the "Tamassian Gate" mentioned in Ostracon T 54/308, found on the West Terrace in 1972 (see *Idalion* 1:77-81). The interpretation of Bastion 016 as part of a gateway would further suggest that the small buildings inside the city wall functioned as guardhouses.

Although there are traces of thin use-surfaces, occupation debris, and a possible roadbed, datable to earlier periods, the absence of any architectural remains (except possibly Pit 013 and Wall 012) in this area of Idalion prior to the construction of the city wall suggests that the town of Idalion did not extend this far west before about 500 B.C., and that the beginning of the Cypro-Classical I period represents an expansion of settlement, at least on the western perimeter of the town. This expansion was probably correlated with the growing economic prosperity of Idalion, which eventually attracted the attention of the Persians and the Kitionites.

LOWER CITY FORTIFICATIONS 49

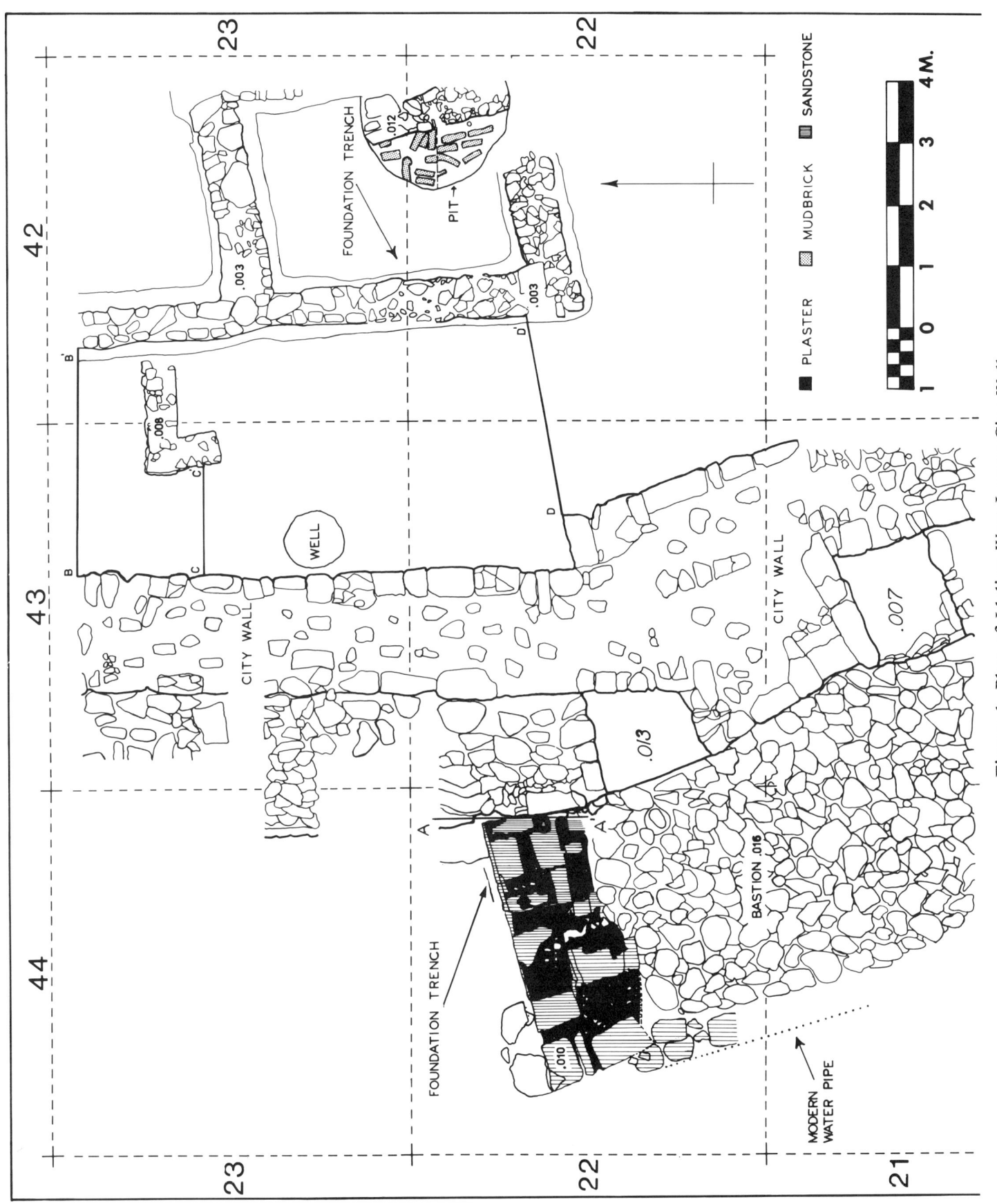

Figure 1. Plan of Idalion West Lower City Wall.

LOCUS	DESCRIPTION	PHASE
001	colluvium	1
006	robber trench	1
009	decomposed mudbrick	1
010	ashlar facing wall	2
011	surface of rain-washed soil	3?

LOCUS	DESCRIPTION	PHASE
012	fine gravel	3?
013	occupational debris	4
014	surface	4
015	occupational debris, charcoal flecks	4
016	bastion	2

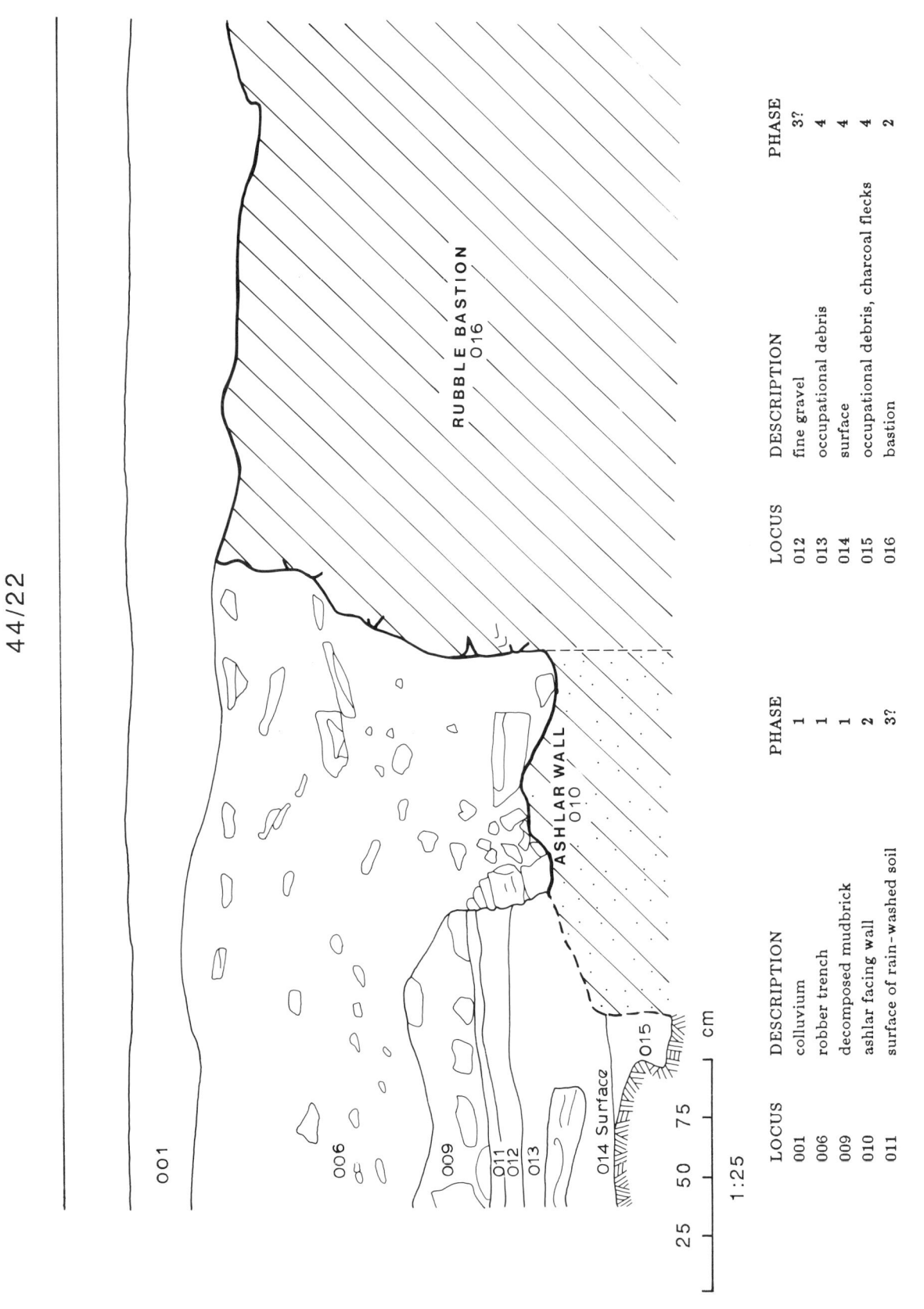

Figure 2. Idalion WNW Section (A-A¹) West Lower City Wall.

LOWER CITY FORTIFICATIONS   51

LOCUS		DESCRIPTION	PHASE
004		colluvium	1
009		surface	2
021	layer 2	mudbrick detritus	2
	layer 3	tabular limestone rubble	2
	layer 4	pebbly fill with chalk chips	2
	layer 5	occupational debris	3A

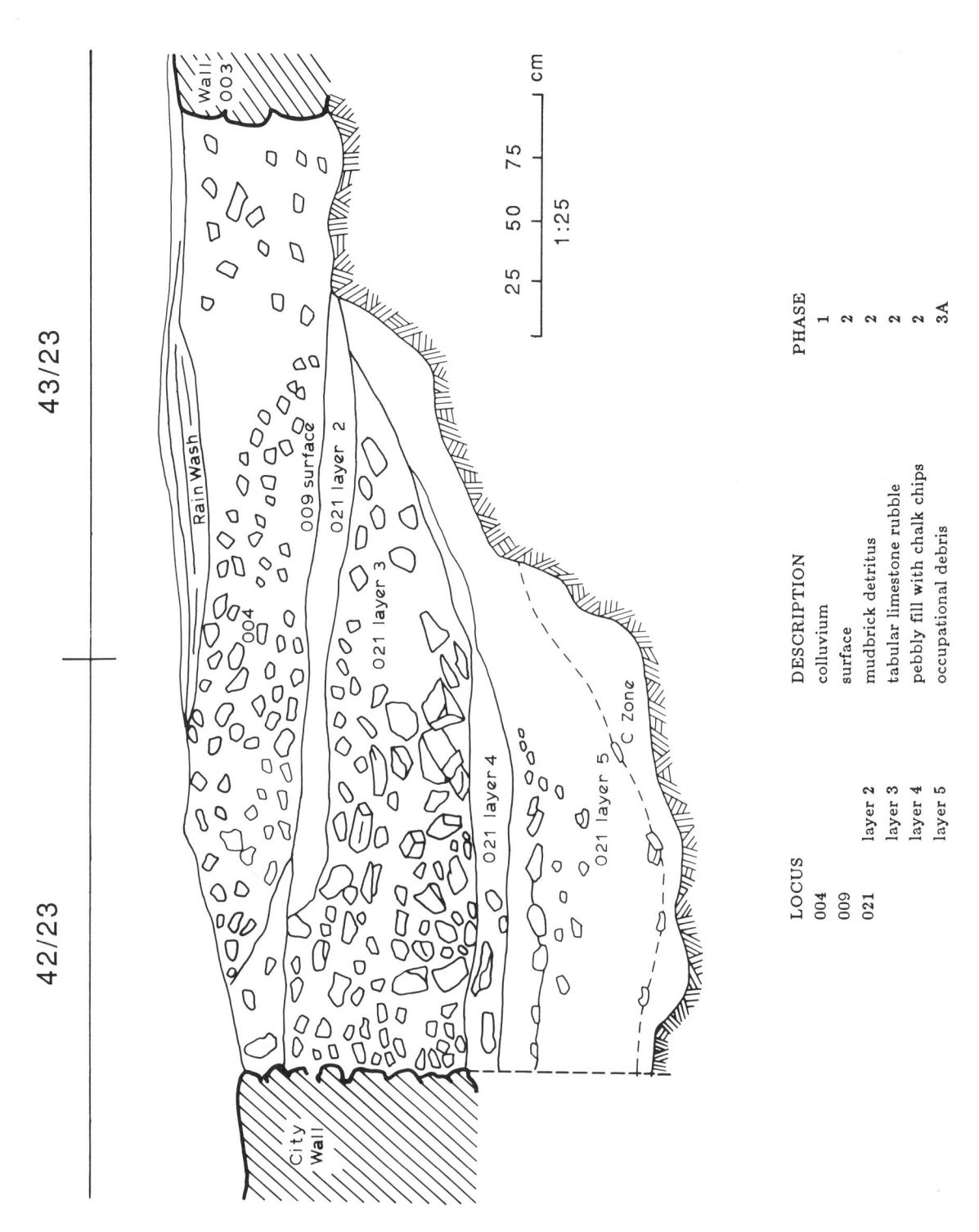

Figure 3. Idalion WNW Section (B-B^1) West Lower City Wall.

43/23

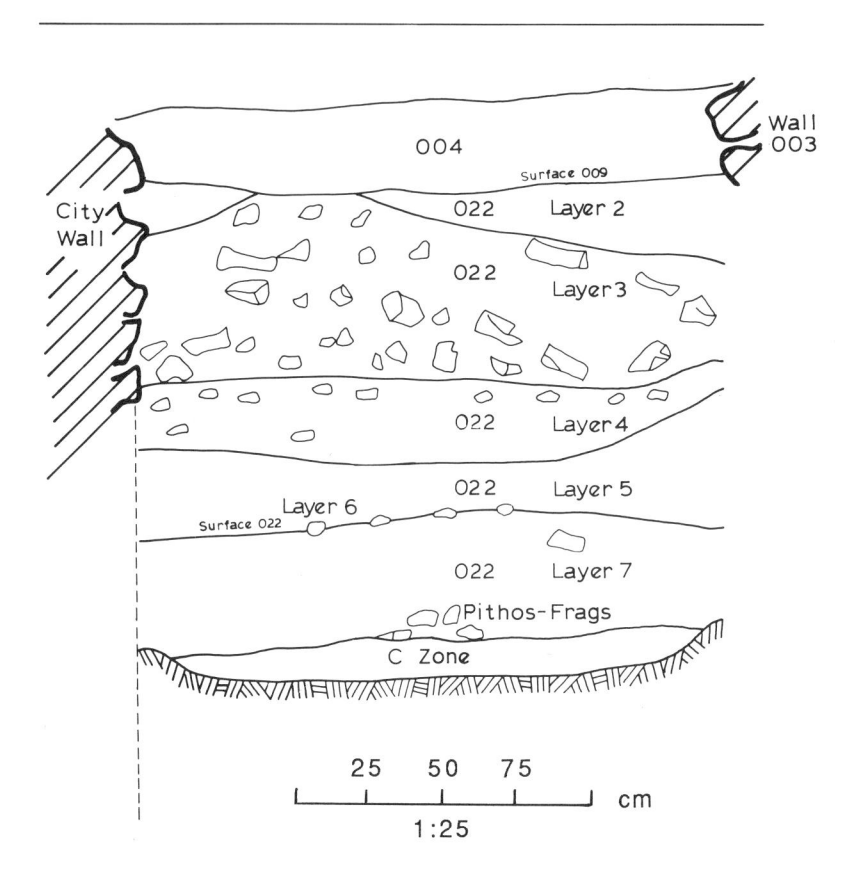

LOCUS		DESCRIPTION	PHASE
004		colluvium	1
009		surface	2
022	layer 2	mudbrick detritus	2
	layer 3	tabular limestone rubble	2
	layer 4	limestone pebbly fill	2
	layer 5	occupational debris	3A
	layer 6	cobble surface	3A
	layer 7	occupational debris, some limestone and diabase cobbles	3B

Figure 4. Idalion WNW Section (C-C¹) West Lower City Wall.

LOWER CITY FORTIFICATIONS 53

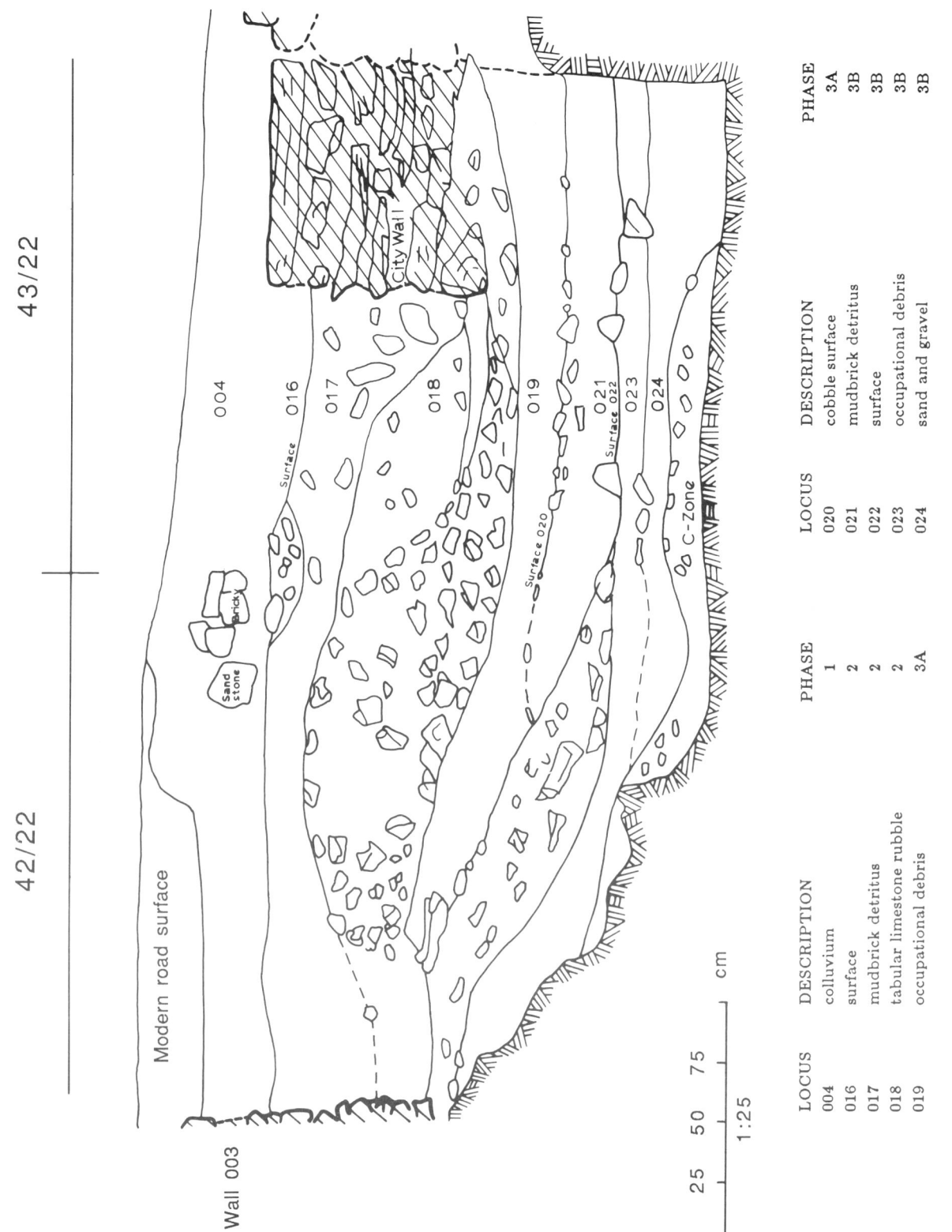

Figure 5. Idalion WNW Section (D-D¹) West Lower City Wall.

LOCUS	DESCRIPTION	PHASE
004	colluvium	1
016	surface	2
017	mudbrick detritus	2
018	tabular limestone rubble	2
019	occupational debris	3A

LOCUS	DESCRIPTION	PHASE
020	cobble surface	3A
021	mudbrick detritus	3B
022	surface	3B
023	occupational debris	3B
024	sand and gravel	3B

PLATE 1

City Wall. a. Probe west of wall. The meter stick is resting on the Phase 4 use-surface (44/22 Loc 014). Above the stick is the foundation trench for the ashlar facing wall (44/22 Loc 010). The City Wall fills the center and left of the picture. Robber trench (44/22 Loc 006) is visible along the upper left edge of the picture. b. East of the City Wall, a surface of limestone cobbles, possibly a roadbed, of Phase 3B.

PLATE 2

Pit and Probe east of City Wall. a. Pit (Loc 013) in east balk of 42/43 and 42/22, showing rubble wall built into it and mudbrick detritus. b. Probe against inner east face of City Wall, which appears on left with rubble filled in behind it. Earlier occupation underlies both rubble fill and City Wall.

PLATE 3

a

b

Lower City Fortifications. a. Overall view, looking north. b. Bastion 016 of City Wall with ashlar facing (Wall 010) visible along north edge.

PLATE 4

Ashlar Facing (Wall 010). a. Bounding Bastion 016. b. Looking west.

a. A Greek Geometric Kantharos (Object 595)

Find Spot: WNW 43/22 Loc 022, Phase 3B

(See above, "Lower City Fortifications")

Per Ålin[*]

During the excavations of 1973 at the western section of the city wall of ancient Idalion considerable amounts of pottery were found at a level earlier than the Classical wall. Provisionally this was dated early Cypro-Archaic, some of it even earlier. Among this unusually interesting pottery were also some imported sherds, one of them Proto-Corinthian and the rest belonging to a Greek Geometric kantharos (fig. 1, and pl. 1), the pieces of which have been glued together. The following remarks will be devoted to this fragmentary vase.

Less than half of the vase was found, but all of the pieces join and there is enough to establish its dimensions and most of its characteristics. Diameter of rim 12 cm, of body 12.7 cm, of base 5.4 cm; height 7 cm. The color of the clay is brown, with a very pale brown slip and dark reddish brown paint (Munsell nos. of clay 7.5 YR 5/4, of slip 10 YR 8/3, of paint 5 YR 2.5/2). The rim portion leans outward somewhat and has a smooth transition to the slightly outward-bulging body, which is offset only a little from the flat base. The one preserved handle base shows that the vase had vertical strap handles, which establishes that it is a kantharos. It is covered with a thin slip and has a very smooth surface. On the inside the bowl is painted with the dark brown paint, which is quite worn and remains mainly as horizontal streaks corresponding to the wheelmarks. The inside bottom seems to have been left unpainted. The inside of the rim is decorated with four lines of varying thickness; on the outside there is a band of concave vertical chevrons between lines. The chevrons are rather clumsily painted and could also be interpreted as degenerated sigmas (Coldstream 1968:397, with references; idem, 1979:258-59, fig. 1b). The handle zone design consists of hatched meanders with flanking vertical strokes and three horizontal lines below. The bottom field is painted solid. On the whole, the vase is well produced, and the few irregularities do not detract from the general impression that this was the work of a skilled and rapidly working craftsman.

The rather rare kantharos is closely related to the skyphos, which was quite common in the Aegean as well as the eastern Mediterranean areas during Geometric times and is therefore useful for comparative purposes. Many imported skyphoi have been found on Cyprus, where they influenced the local pottery in both shape and decoration. Both imports and their local derivatives have in recent years been discussed by Gjerstad, Coldstream, and others (Coldstream 1979; Gjerstad et al. 1977). The differences between imports and local products are so substantial that it is clear that the Idalion vase must be an import from the Aegean area.

In attempting to date the vase, a few features are significant. The shape is characterized by the absence of a well-defined border line between rim and body, and by the comparatively small bulge in the latter. Such details of shape, which are more or less pronounced in many other examples, seem to belong to the Middle or early Late Geometric periods. Although the various elements of the decoration belong to the standard repertoire that is to be found on all kinds of Geometric vases, the particular combination and execution of the patterns are also characteristic of this time (Coldstream 1968, passim).

In its general conception the Idalion vase seems to stand fairly close to several of the skyphoi found in the Salamis tombs (Dikaios 1963, cols. 126-98, with appendix by Coldstream,

---

[*]History Department, State University of New York at Stony Brook, New York

The research for this study was made possible by a grant from the American Council of Learned Societies, which enabled me to participate in the Idalion campaign of 1973 during which the vase was found.

cols. 199-204; *BCH* 89, 1965:249, fig. 27; Calvet and Yon, "La céramique des îles de l'Egée," in Gjerstad et al. 1977:12-13, pl. IV:32). These, with parallels in Attic Middle Geometric, date to the middle of the eighth century B.C. The Cypriot pottery found with them belongs to Types III and IV. There are, of course, other parallels from Cyprus, among which a skyphos from Ayia Irini deserves particular mention because of the close similarity in the execution of the rim decoration (*BCH* 97, 1973:667, fig. 103; Coldstream 1979:259, fig. 1b), and also a skyphos in the Hadjiprodromou collection in Famagusta with a similar feature (these two references communicated by Dr. Charles Adelman). In spite of variations in details of composition, for which there are innumerable possibilities, these and other similar vases resemble each other so closely in general execution that they must be considered contemporary.

Since the production of the Idalion kantharos should thus be dated to about the middle of the eighth century B.C., its appearance in a Cypriot context with mainly Type IV but also Type III pottery would seem to support the argument by Coldstream (1979:267) that places the beginning of Cypro-Archaic I around 750 B.C., about half a century earlier than generally assumed. The vase and its context obviously belong to Idalion Period 4 as established by the Swedish Cyprus Expedition in its excavations on the West Acropolis (*SCE* II, pp. 460-628), where also some imported Geometric pottery was found, as is exemplified by a fragment of a Late Geometric vase (*Opuscula Atheniensia* 12, 1978:105, fig. 15:8).

Figure 1. Greek Geometric Kantharos (Obj. no. 595).

PLATE 1

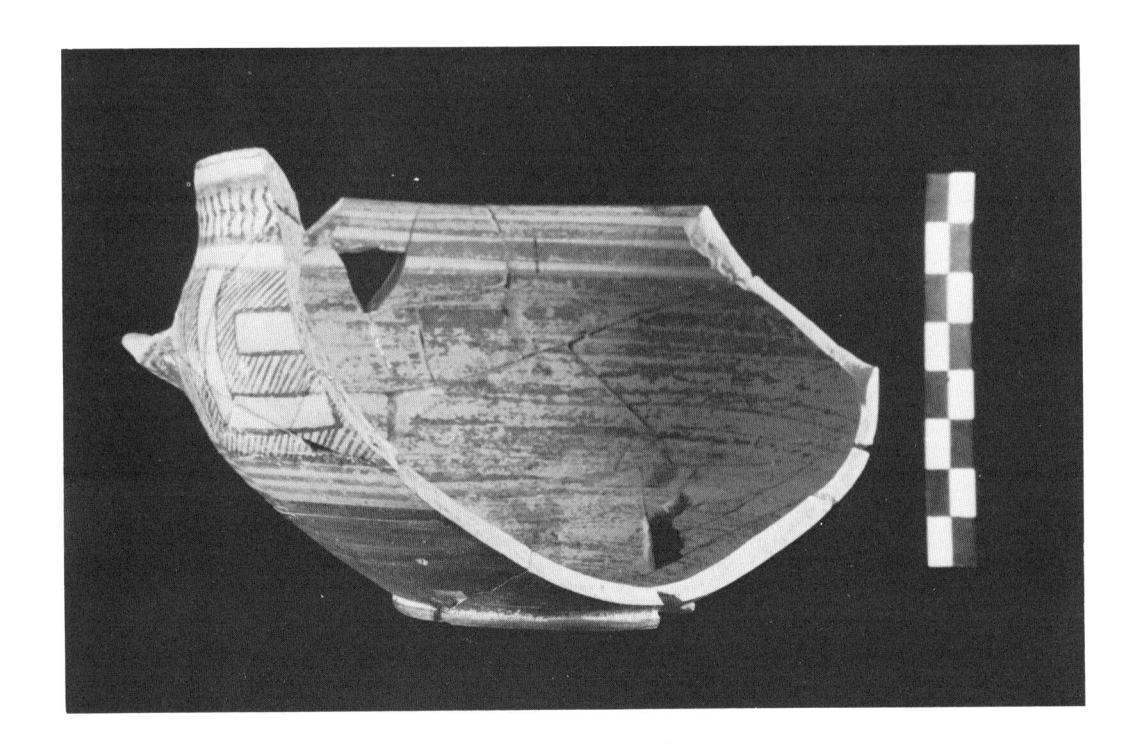

Greek Geometric Kantharos (Obj. no. 595). Find Spot: WNW 43/22 Loc 022.

b. A Reconstructed Archaic Bronze Fibula (Object 548)

Find Spot: WNW 42/22 Loc O11, Layer 9, Phase 3B

(See above, "Lower City Fortifications")

Shelby Brown [*]

In 1973, in the course of excavation along the inner face of the Lower City west wall, two fragments of a bronze fibula were found (fig. 1). The fibula was discovered in a sealed locus, a probe below the stone pavement contemporary with the wall, in occupational debris immediately above bedrock. Associated pottery was exclusively Cypro-Archaic. Other probes below the pavement along the inner wall contained some Cypro-Classical pottery as well; none contained earlier sherds. A full discussion of the context of the fibula is given by Dr. Anita Walker.

The two preserved fragments, which do not join, are the central, molded arc of a roughly semicircular bow, and the catch for the pin. The bow fragment appears to have been cast in one piece. It is corroded and broken at one end. At the other end a socket is preserved into which the spring of the pin was originally inserted. The catch is less badly corroded than the bow, cleanly broken off into a U-shaped section, and rounded at the front. It is incised with three vertical parallel grooves suggesting a paw or hand.

The bow fragment is 0.043 m long, round in section, and decorated with spherical beads and slightly convex disks.[1] In the center, a large disk is flanked by two smaller ones; at each end a large spherical bead is closely bordered by a small disk on the outside. The disk at the socket end of the bow is broken and badly corroded; at the other end, it is intact although corroded with a small irregular section of the continuing shaft of the bow preserved beyond it. Another small disk lies between the central disks and the bead at each end, closer to the ends than to the center. These disks are tilted inward at the bottom, the right one inclining at a sharper angle toward the center than the left. The clear separation of beads and disks is unusual on such molded fibulae, on which the disks usually form closely set collars for the beads.

The three central disks must have been located at approximately the apex of the bow, since they are positioned at right angles to the shaft, while the disks closer to the ends are angled in toward the central disks. The bead at the catch end of the bow is lower than the other bead, and the overall placement of the decoration is slightly asymmetrical. Bead and disk moldings are often placed slightly to one side of the bow, toward either the catch or the spring of the pin.

Although it is possible that another molding had decorated the shaft toward the catch, it is more likely that the preserved section of the arc was the only decorated part of the bow. The socket at the end toward the spring of the pin indicates the termination of moldings on that side. The thick end of the pin was inserted into the socket and served for a short distance as a continuation of the bow shaft, then looped around and narrowed to form the straight horizontal pin for the catch. The socket is unusually high on the bow, so that a reconstruction allowing for additional moldings on the catch end would produce an uncommon degree of asymmetry. Our example fits a customary pattern in which three molded units, often beads with collars, are placed slightly off center at the apex of a fibula.

---

[*] Department of Classics, Dartmouth College, Hanover, New Hampshire

[1] The usual term for such moldings is "bead-and-collar," which implies that the main function of the disks is to frame the beads. On this fibula, however, the disks are separate decorative units.

Fibulae of fairly similar type have been found in Cyprus both at Idalion and elsewhere, in both tomb and settlement contexts.[2] They fall into Chr. Blinkenberg's Cypriot type XIII;7 (Blinkenberg 1926:239). The type is characterized by a roughly semicircular slightly asymmetrical bow with molded decoration at the top of the arc: three closely set roughly spherical beads alternating with single disks or disk pairs. Similar fibulae have been found in Rhodes as temple dedications (Blinkenberg and Kinch 1931:89) and in Delos, in a settlement context (Deonna 1938:289). In all cases the contexts indicate dates not conclusively earlier than the seventh century, and no later than the sixth (Blinkenberg 1926:239; Blinkenberg and Kinch 1931:75-76; Ohnefalsch-Richter 1899:341, 343; *SCE* III, pp. 403-4; *SCE* IV:2, pp. 215-16). The new Idalion fibula, however, is the only example of this type found in a closed Archaic context.

A peculiarity of many of these fibulae is the separate manufacture of bow and pin, the pin being inserted into a socket in the bow (as on the latest Idalion fibula) or twined around the end of the bow in a loop. This is characteristic of Palestinian and Syrian (and other Near Eastern) fibulae of contemporary and earlier date (Petrie 1928:11, pl. XCII; *SCE* IV:2, p. 382; Stronach 1959:185). The technique was not used in Europe.[3]

Although the latest Idalion fibula is similar to other Cypro-Archaic examples with thickly molded semicircular bows, some differences are apparent. The moldings are not closely set, and the central unit is not a bead with collars but a disk with collars. The separation of apex moldings on semicircular bows is more common in Syria and Palestine; there, however, the tripartite division is not retained and the number of units is usually greater. A further association of our fibula with Syrian types is afforded by the catch resembling a hand, common on the mainland along with the technique of separate bow and pin manufacture (Deonna 1938:290).

Blinkenberg believed that his fibulae of Type XIII:7 were Cypriot products, and that similar molded types with both semicircular and slightly angular bows from Syria and Palestine were imports from Cyprus (Blinkenberg 1926:230-31). E. Gjerstad first pointed out the greater likelihood that it was the Cypriot fibulae that were influenced by the Syrian (*SCE* IV:2, pp. 216, 415), rather than the other way around. In the eighth century B.C. the use of fibulae increased all over Syria and Palestine, and molded semicircular and angled bows developed side by side. In the seventh century semicircular bows with simple and convex beaded moldings were common throughout the Near East (Stronach 1959:185-88). The Archaic bead-and-disk fibulae found on Cyprus were strongly influenced by Near Eastern examples, but the emphasis on the apex of the bow and the choice of a tripartite division of molded decoration are both peculiarly Cypriot elements. The newest Idalion fibula has especially strong ties with the Levant but retains these distinguishing Cypriot characteristics.

Table 1 lists fibulae close in date and similar in appearance to this latest Idalion example. Sites within Cyprus are noted first. Reference is made to context as well as to published illustrations, descriptions, and relevant discussions.

---

[2] In addition to the examples listed at the end, there are several fibulae of this type in the Cyprus Museum that I did not have the opportunity to examine (Birmingham 1963a:99).

[3] For general discussion of the development and distribution of Cypriot semicircular and molded fibulae and related Near Eastern types see Stronach 1959:181-206, and Birmingham 1963a:80-112).

Table 1. Fibulae Close in Date and Appearance to Latest Idalion Examples

Site	Context	Illustrations	Descriptions and discussions
Idalion, Cyprus	Tomb	Blinkenberg 1926:239, fig. 278, XIII 7c; Ohnefalsch-Richter 1899: 340, fig. XXV, 14	Blinkenberg 1926:239; Ohnefalsch-Richter 1899:341, 343
Idalion, Cyprus	Settlement	SCE II, pl. LXXVII, 6; Birmingham 1963a:98, fig. 9	SCE II, pp. 540, 580, 601; 1948:144, 215-16, 382-84, 415
Idalion, Cyprus	Settlement	None	SCE II, pp. 560, 580, 601; 1948:144, 215-16, 382-84, 415
Soli, Cyprus	Settlement	SCE III, pl. CLXXX, 8	SCE III, pp. 403-4, 414
Kutrafa Nikitari, Cyprus	Tomb	Ohnefalsch-Richter 1899:340, fig. XXV, 13	Ohnefalsch-Richter 1899:341, 343; Blinkenberg 1926:239
Marion, Cyprus	Tomb	None	Ohnefalsch-Richter 1899:343
Tamassos, Cyprus	Tomb	Ohnefalsch-Richter 1899: 340, fig. XXV, 13	Ohnefalsch-Richter 1899:341, 343; Blinkenberg 1926:239
Rhodes	Temple dedication (10 examples)	Blinkenberg 1926:239, fig. 279, XIII 7d;	Blinkenberg 1926:239; 1931:75-76
Delos	Settlement	Deonna 1938:pl. CXXXVI, 735	Deonna 1938:289
Gezer	Tomb	Macalister 1912:vol. 3, pl. LXXXIX, 10; Stronach 1959:188, fig. 4:3	Macalister 1912:vol. 1, pp. xxi, 334-35; vol. 2, p. 211
Megiddo	Settlement (Stratum III)	Lamon and Shipton 1939: pl. 79, 13	Lamon and Shipton 1939:82, 87, 132

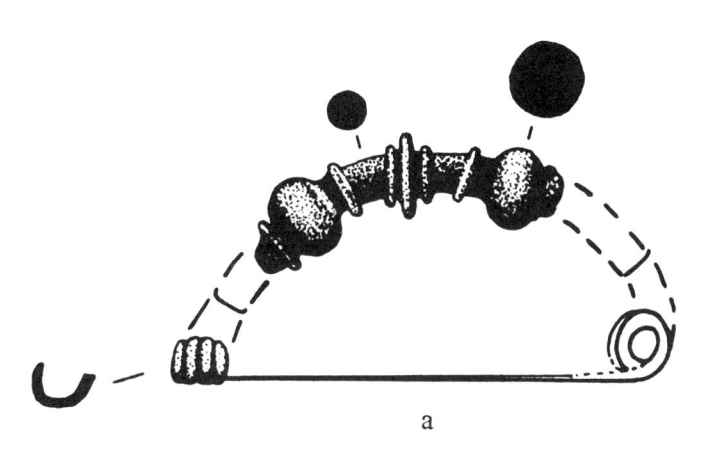

Figure 1. Archaic Bronze Fibula (Obj. no. 548). a. Reconstructed. b. As found.

2. WEST LOWER CITY DOMESTIC PRECINCT

Anita Walker and Pamela Gaber

with Lawrence E. Stager

Objectives

In 1971, when investigations began at Idalion proper, one of the objectives was to excavate a domestic precinct of the city, preferably one that reflected occupation earlier rather than later in the history of the site. Aerial photographs suggested substantial architectural remains flanking a street in this general vicinity. Systematic surface survey indicated occupation in this area, mainly from the Cypro-Archaic and Cypro-Classical periods, and coring with a soil auger showed that the remains lay very close to the modern surface. With these factors in mind, three squares were opened in 1972: Id WNW 10/18, 9/18, and 9/19 (see fig. 1). Parts of two buildings separated by a metaled corridor or street were uncovered. The original construction phase of these buildings was tentatively assigned to a time from the middle of the Cypro-Archaic II to the beginning of the Cypro-Classical I periods on the basis of the pottery recovered from the founding levels of Building A (formerly Building 1). Since 1973 research has centered upon discovering whether this area of Lower City was continuously occupied; whether occupation was purely domestic in character or contained both workshops and houses; and in investigating the internal organization of houses of the Cypro-Archaic II-Cypro-Classical I periods, about which relatively little is known, to see whether differences in the use of space or differences in status between buildings could be distinguished.

Strategy

The preservation of remains in West Lower City is influenced by the slope of the land westward toward the drainage basin in the western sector of the site. There has been considerable runoff and erosion north and west of the first three excavated squares. In addition, modern deep plowing each season until 1976 (when the field which contains West Lower City was purchased by the Department of the Antiquities) continued to remove the architectural remains. As a result, the most northwesterly squares have the worst preserved and most disturbed deposits. There the undisturbed archaeological zone between the plow soil and the virgin marl is only a few centimeters thick. Consequently it was decided to expand mainly to the east and south. In 1973 areas Id WNW 10/19, 10/17, 9/17, 8/18, and 8/19 were opened. Other areas added included 9/16, 7/17, and 8/20 (1974); 10/16 (1976); and 7/18, 8/16, 8/21, and 9/20 (1977) making a total of seventeen squares, although these most recently opened squares have not been excavated to any depth. Before 1974 excavations were 5 m squares with 1 m balks; the balks were removed down to the level of excavation after the sections had been drawn. Since 1974 the excavations were in 6 m squares, with the rolling-balk system, as this method is better suited to preserving the coherence of the architecture while continuing to maintain vertical and horizontal control. It was clear from the beginning that the excavated material represented more than one cultural period. The Department of Antiquities is most interested in preserving the remains of Phase 3, and therefore, in those areas where the remains antedating Phase 3 stratigraphically and chronologically have been investigated, the stones were carefully set aside so that later the holes could be refilled and the Phase 3 architecture restored (for instance in Id WNW 9/18). Conversely, where there were remains overlying Phase 3 that were stratigraphically and chronologically later (for instance in Id WNW 8/18), the post-Phase 3 installations were removed in order to investigate and preserve the Phase 3 occupation.

Results

In the report on the 1971-72 seasons in West Lower City (*Idalion* 1:42-44) the material was subdivided into four phases: Phase 4--occupation layers underlying Phases 3-2; Phases 3-

2--building phases; and Phase 1--a series of pits whose original associated surfaces had been plowed off. The subsequent expanded investigations in this vicinity have caused some modification of the original attributions, although the division into four phases has been preserved. Buildings 1 and 2 have also been renamed Buildings A and B respectively. Because of the complex and fragmentary nature of occupation in these squares, the following aids are included: a plan of the West Lower City domestic precinct (fig. 1), a sequence diagram (fig. 2), a key to loci in both the sequence diagram and the plan (table 1), and a section drawing (fig. 3).

The stratigraphic sequence in West Lower City is as follows:

Phase 4: The earliest archaeological deposit in West Lower City is represented mainly by a series of pits (Pits 1, 2, 3, 4, 6, 7, 8, 9, 10, 11, 12, 13, 14, 15, 16, and 19). In places these pits were sited beneath later building phases and their stratigraphic attribution is unequivocal (for instance Pits 3, 4, 6, 9, 10, 14, and 15). Elsewhere, the occupation layers from which some of the pits were dug, as well as some of the subsequent deposits, have been shaved off by plowing, so that their attribution must remain stratigraphically uncertain (for instance Pits 1, 2, 7, 8, 11, 12, 13 and 17). These pits were dug into the virgin red marl, which bakes to a cement-like hardness. They were roughly circular in plan, with sides splaying gently outward toward the top, providing a slightly convex profile and varying in depth from a few centimeters (Pit 7) to 1.25 m (Pit 14). The larger pits, where completely excavated, were flat bottomed (Pits 3, 10, 14); the smaller ones, mere rounded scoops out of the marl (Pits 7, 8). Plate 1a shows the shape of Pit 14; plate 1b of Pit 10; plate 2a of Pit 9. The original function of these pits is not clear. In the bottom of Pit 14 was a circular patch of charcoal and ash, which suggests that at least this pit had been fumigated by fire and might have been used to store grain, but the absence of similar deposits at the base of other pits and the convex profiles of the pits argue against such an interpretation. In the excavated section of Pit 9 there was one course of a wall of fieldstones (Id WNW 9/17, Loc 023) and a tamped-earth surface (Id WNW 9/17 Loc 004, Layer 5), which suggests as an alternative hypothesis that at least the larger pits were used as semisubterranean dwellings (see pl. 2a). Whatever their original function, the history of these pits was quite complex. Some of them were cut into earlier pits (e.g., Pit 6 into Pit 4). Even more intriguing, some pits were definitely filled in prior to the construction of Phase 3 buildings (Pits 4, 9, 10) while others stood open (Pits 3, 14). This is particularly plain in the cases of Pits 10 and 14. Plates 1b and 2b show Pit 10. Pit 10 was used eventually as a rubbish dump (whether or not that was its original function), and was stuffed with restorable pottery, fragments of stone bowls, and figurines (see cover and pl. 2b). After it had filled up, a surface with a band of charcoal (A1S) was laid down over it, and use caused this surface to sink down into the less densely packed pit fill (pl. 3a). Above this very clearly defined surface, which represents the construction and early use phase of Building A, a thick layer of occupation debris built up. Above this debris can be seen Wall A4 of Building A (pl. 3a). Pit 10 was thus completely sealed by surface A1S. Pits 3, 4, 6, and 9 were also filled up by the time the Phase 3 Building A was constructed. Pits 6 and 9 run right under Wall A9. In the case of Pit 4 (one of the largest pits in the field, full of sherds, charcoal, rubble, and mudbrick detritus), Walls A11 and A13 run right across it and would clearly never have stood had this pit not been completely filled at the time of their construction. Plate 3b shows Wall A11 built across the western perimeter of Pit 4. On the other hand, Pits 3 and 14 (and probably also 15) stood open and empty when other parts of Building A were erected. This is best illustrated by Pit 14. In plates 1a and 4a it can be seen that the builders of Building A were forced to contour their Walls A2 and A7 to accommodate Pit 14. Thus, within the pit, Wall A2 is fourteen rough courses high, while its southwest extension outside the pit is only three rough courses high. Pit 14 must therefore have stood open at the time Wall A2 was constructed.

Phase 3 (pls. 4b, 5a, 6a, b, 7a): The initial investigation in 1972 identified part of a building with a rounded corner (Building A, formerly Building 1), and a street or corridor outside its eastern boundary wall. At that time it was thought that the long wall bounding the street on the side opposite Building A was a second building (Building B, formerly Building 2; see pl. 4b). Continued excavation in these areas and expanded excavation in adjacent areas have confirmed these suppositions.

Table 1. Key to West Lower City Domestic Precinct Loci

Id WNW

Building A

Walls

A1	=9/17 Loc 025, 9/18 Loc 011, 9/19 Loc 013
A2	=10/18 Loc 004, 9/19 Loc 006
A3	=9/18 Loc 010
A4	=9/18 Loc 006
A5	=10/18 Loc 008
A6	=10/18 Loc 007
A7	=10/18 Loc 017, 10/19 Loc 006
A8	=9/19 Loc 013
A9	=10/18 Loc 003, 9/17 Loc 005
A10	=9/17 Loc 024
A11	=10/17 Loc 011
A12	=9/117 Loc 008
A13	=10/17 Loc 018
A14	=10/17 Loc 010
A15	=10/16 Loc 008, 9/16 Loc 008
A16	=9/16 Loc 005, 9/17 Loc 009
A17	=9/17 Loc 009
A18	=9/17 Loc 010

Use-Surfaces

A1	=9/17 Loc 004.3, 9/18 Loc 039, 9/18 Loc 040
A2	=9/17 Loc 004.2, 9/18 Loc 026, 9/18 Loc 016.1
A3	=9/17 Loc 004.1, 9/17 Loc 015, 9/18 Loc 044, 10/18 Loc 011
A4	=9/17 Loc 014, 9/18 Loc 043, 10/18 Loc 010
A5	=9/18 Loc 023
A6	=9/17 Loc 011
A7	=10/17 Loc 029.1

Building B

Walls

B1	=9/19 Loc 003
B2	=8/19 Loc 006
B3	=8/20 Loc 007
B4	=8/20 Loc 011
B5	=8/20 Loc 012
B6	=8/20 Loc 013
B7	=8/20 Loc 014, 9/20 Loc 010, 9/20 Loc 016.2
B8	=9/20 Loc 006
B9	=9/20 Loc 005
B10	=9/20 Loc 007
B11	=9/20 Loc 014
B12	=9/19 Loc 003

Use-Surface

B1	=8/19 Loc 011

Table 1. Key to West Lower City Domestic Precinct Loci (*cont.*)

Building C

    Walls

        C1   = 8/18 Loc 002.3, 8/18 Loc 012
        C2   = 7/17 Loc 004, 7/17 Loc 005, 8/17 Loc 011
        C3   = 7/17 Loc 011
        C4   = 8/17 Loc 010

    Use-Surfaces

        C1   = 7/17 Loc 013, 8/17 Loc 015
        C2   = 8/18 Loc 008

Building D

    Wall

        D1   = 10/16 Loc 017, 10/16 Loc 020, 10/16 Loc 021, 9/16 Loc 012, 9/16 Loc 013, 9/16 Loc 014, 9/16 Loc 017

    Surface

        D1   = 10/16 Loc 023

Street

    8/19 Loc 003.3, 8/19 Loc 012, 9/16 Loc 016.2, 9/16 Loc 011, 9/16 Loc 003, 9/17 Loc 007, 9/17 Loc 018, 9/18 Loc 020, 9/18 Loc 022, 9/18 Loc 025, 9/18 Loc 035.1, 9/18 Loc 041, 9/18 Loc 042, 9/18 Loc 047, 9/18 Loc 048, 9/19 Loc 009, 9/19 Loc 010, 9/19 Loc 011

Drain

    9/18 Loc 035.2, 9/19 Loc 012, 9/19 Loc 016

Wells

        1   = 10/17 Loc 015
        2   = 8/21 Loc 004

Silo = 8/18 Loc 006

Bin = 10/16 Loc 011, 10/16 Loc 016

Pits

        P1   = 10/16 Loc 018
        P2   = 10/16 Loc 004
        P3   = 10/17 Loc 020.1
        P4   = 10/17 Loc 031
        P5   = 10/17 Loc 030
        P6   = 10/17 Loc 026.2
        P7   = 10/17 Loc 019

Table 1. Key to West Lower City Domestic Precinct Loci (*cont.*)

```
P8   = 10/17 Loc 013
P9   = 9/17 Loc 004.4 (Surface 9/17 Loc 004.5, Wall 9/17 Loc 023)
P10  = 9/18 Loc 045
P11  = 10/18 Loc 006
P12  = 10/18 Loc 009
P13  = 10/18 Loc 012
P14  = 10/18 Loc 016, 10/19 Loc 003, 9/18 Loc 052
P15  = 10/19 Loc 008, 9/18 Loc 053, 9/19 Loc 017
P16  = 10/19 Loc 004
P17  = 8/19 Loc 013, 8/20 Loc 006, 9/19 Loc 007, 9/20 Loc 003
P18  = 8/19 Loc 010
P19  = 8/21 Loc 005, 8/21 Loc 006
P20  = 8/18 Loc 018
```

Phase 3B: In the western half of the field, Building A extends southward up the slope. As indicated above, in some places, the builders of Building A erected their structure over the filled pits of Phase 4, while in others they built their walls across the floors of the pits. In the case of Wall A2, built in Pit 14, it was presumably structurally sounder to build a deeper wall inside the empty pit than to build a wall designed to carry a great deal of weight over an unstable fill. There are no traces of any foundation trenches for these walls, other than a small depression along the inside row of Wall A1. Instead the walls are laid directly on the virgin marl or on earlier occupation. The walls themselves are built of pillow lavas and undressed fieldstones set in mud mortar, surmounted in one or two places fronting the street with large blocks of dressed limestone. In general, except in the pits, the walls survive to an extant height of only about 0.25-0.35 m. This may be because deep plowing has dislodged higher courses. However there is still observable in Dhali today, a technique of building whereby a substructure of small undressed stones is surmounted by a row of large dressed blocks, which in turn form a level footing for a mudbrick superstructure. It may be that a similar technique was used here; the mudbrick superstructure has collapsed, the good dressed stones have almost all been robbed out, and all that is left are the founding courses of undressed pillows lavas and fieldstones. Building A is irregularly shaped. In the northernmost squares, its outside, east wall seems to have accommodated to a bend in the street (pl. 5a). Its west wall has three small masonry spurs of equal length (Walls A6, A7, and A8), extending northwest at right angles to Wall A2, such as can be found in village architecture in Dhali even today (pl. 5b). The entrance to this part of Building A was presumably from the street, running over earlier Pit 9. South of this entrance, another entrance, also from the street with a small stand of undressed fieldstones just inside it, led to a room formed by Walls A15, A16, A17, and A12, which in turn led into another square enclosure with a well (Well 1; see pl. 6a) in the southwest corner. Much of the area in the center of this enclosure was taken up with earlier pits and their fills (Pits 3, 4, and 6). In this phase a later pit (Pit 5) was dug into Pit 4. The well was dug through the fill of Pit 4 and in its upper levels was faced with stones to prevent the collapse of the pit fill into it. The presence of the well, together with the nature of the debris in the enclosure, which consisted of a large quantity of animal bone (including *Ovis*, *Capra*, *Bos*, *Sus*, *Equus cabalis*, *Equus asinus* and *Canis familiaris*), led us to interpret the function of this enclosure as a courtyard, and to conclude that it had not been roofed. This enclosure is assigned to the Building A compound although, in fact, there was no direct access from the courtyard to the northern part of Building A. South of the courtyard the architecture is very much disturbed. There is a boundary wall fronting the street (Wall D1) and behind it a small, flagstoned bin or manger laid down on the virgin marl. Stratigraphically these remains seem to belong to Phase 3, but they are separated from the Building A compound by an open space and probably belong to a separate compound (possibly Building D). The surfaces associated with Building A are complex. Not only are they patchy, but they do not extend throughout the whole compound. There appears to have been a much heavier buildup of surfaces and occupation layers in the northern part of Building A (i.e., north of Wall A9 and running up to it) than in the courtyard south of Wall 9, although Wall A9 was clearly in use with both sets of surfaces. The heaviest build up was in the room formed by Walls A5, A3, and A1, (see fig. 3), where there were no less than four superimposed floors during the period of the building's use. Outside Buildings A and D a long narrow street runs roughly N-S, with a bend to the left in Id WNW 9/19. The street may also have opened out into a plaza or another wider street in Id WNW 8/18. It was composed of fieldstones and pillow lavas in the pebble and cobble ranges, in a matrix of sherds and silt. There are traces of a V-shaped drain cut into the virgin marl in 9/18. It was stuffed with pottery that had been carried down the street by rainwash.

Northeast of the street lay Building B (pl. 6b, 7a), whose presence was suspected in 1972 from Wall B1. The construction of Building B is similar to that of Building A, with walls composed mostly of pillow lavas and undressed limestone in the large cobble range, set in mud mortar and standing about 0.25 m high, except that Wall B1 has an additional course of well-cut ashlar limestone blocks. Building B itself is more regular in plan than Building A and so far consists of one large rectangular room fronting the street, with a possible entrance to the north, and at least three more smaller rectangular rooms off it. It is not yet clear whether a well (Well 2) in Id WNW 8/21 also belongs to the Building B compound. To date, only one use surface (surface B1) has been found associated with this building. a cache of cooking-pot sherds in the big rectangular room in the corner formed by Walls B5 and B7 suggests that this area was used for cooking, and Pit 18 seems to be a trash pit cut into the use surface.

Phase 3A: Building A underwent some structural modification. Wall A4 of Building A is not bonded to Wall A3 in its lower course, but only in its upper course, and surfaces A1 and A2 run under this wall. The same is true of the northward spur of Wall A10 (see fig. 3). These walls therefore represent a later building phase of Phase 3. Plate 3a illustrates wall A4 overlying the earlier surfaces of Building A.

All the artifacts found in Buildings A and B suggest domestic use, but there is nothing to differentiate function between rooms other than the courtyard of Building A and the cooking and trash pit area of Building B.

Phase 2: After Buildings A and B and part of the street went out of use, another building, Building C, was put up in the eastern part of the field. The plow has carried off most of the stones from this building, so that our plan is very incomplete. The construction technique and materials are similar to those of Phase 3, but most of the walls survive only one course high. Building C was oriented NE/SW. It was probably rectangular in overall outline. In Id WNW 8/18, the Building C wall overlay the Phase 3 street. This part of the building (in Id WNW 8/18) had a tamped-earth use-surface preserved over most of the square, with a small fire pit (Pit 20) and a clay-lined, bottle-shaped pit 1.50 m deep, which is interpreted as a silo. This part of the structure was probably an open-air courtyard. South of Building C there are walls that suggest other buildings belonging to this phase, but these have only just begun to be uncovered.

Phase 1: The latest phase is represented by one large pit (Pit 17) full of pebble- to cobble-sized fieldstones, dug from a surface now obliterated by the plow. Other loci assigned to this phase are colluvium washed down from the acropolis above Lower City, and surface loci, all very disturbed.

Dating

Phase 4: The best evidence for dating Phase 4 comes from Pit 10 which represents a sealed locus. The majority of the pottery that filled the pit was Cypro-Archaic I, with a few sherds probably Cypro-Archaic II and nothing later. This suggests at least the latest date at which the pit went out of use. The digging of the pit should probably therefore be dated to the Cypro-Archaic I period (seventh century B.C.).

Phase 3B-A: The dating of this Phase is based on field readings of all pottery by Per Ålin and on the pottery analyzed by him in more detail (see below, "Selected Pottery Groups"). He suggests that Building A was constructed some time during the third quarter of the sixth century B.C., and that the building had a life-span of about one hundred years. After Building A went out of use, Well 1 functioned as a rubbish dump down to the Hellenistic period, as is indicated by the finding of a Ptolemaic coin (H49/553) in its upper levels.

Phase 2: The pottery and other evidence indicate that Phase 2 should be dated to the Hellenistic period. A number of coins that come from the loci of Building C corroborate this dating. The most important of these are H 97/767 and H 98/768 which I. Nicolaou has dated to Evagoras II (361-351 B.C.) and Ptolemy X Alexander I (110 B.C.) (see Coin Catalogue). These coins come from the founding levels of Wall C1, and would thus indicate a date late in the second century B.C. for the construction of Building C. Such a date would confirm Per Ålin's hypothesis, based on ceramic analysis, that settlement in this part of the site declined for a period of time after the fifth century B.C.

Phase 1: Since the Phase 1 loci are very disturbed and in some cases are clearly secondary deposits resulting from slope wash, it is not possible to assign to Phase 1 a date more definite than post-Hellenistic.

Discussion

The exposure in West Lower City is still quite small and as yet the two buildings are incomplete, so any conclusions must remain tentative. There is no trace of occupation in West Lower City earlier than the Cypro-Archaic and nothing other than some stray coins and a few sherds later than the Hellenistic. The picture of intrasite settlement in Lower City, as it is gradually developing, suggests that by contrast with the West Acropolis, settlement in this part of Idalion was sparse down to the middle of Cypro-Archaic II. There was apparently a sharp expansion of settlement at the end of the Cypro-Archaic and the beginning of the Cypro-Classical period, that is during the first part of the fifth century B.C., which lasted for about one hundred years, after which settlement in West Lower City declined until the second century B.C. Thus this area of Lower City does not appear to have been continuously occupied. There is no evidence that the occupation during the Cypro-Archaic, Cypro-Classical, and Hellenistic periods was ever other than purely domestic in character. In our small sample of houses excavated so far, we find no evidence of workshops. As for the internal organization of the few buildings excavated to date, they appear to be rambling compounds that include a courtyard with its own water supply, and a number of small interconnecting rooms (see Allen's description of traditional Dhali architecture, below). The analogy of modern buttresses, already mentioned, may explain the masonry spurs of Building A. The small subdivisions of Building A may be analogous in use to other modern vernacular architecture. In the mountain village of Kakopetria, the traditional houses are organized with only animal keeping and storage on the ground floor, and human occupation on the upper story (see pl. 7b). The buttresses would thus make sense as supports for a second story. Plate 7c shows a street in Kakopetria with a drainage channel and composition similar to that of the street in West Lower City.

The absence of any remains later than Hellenistic fits in well with the evidence elsewhere in Idalion, but the absence of anything earlier than the Cypro-Archaic here and in the West City Wall does not accord with the traditional dating for the urbanization of the site, nor with the evidence of the Swedish Cyprus Expedition on the West Acropolis (*SCE* II). Nothing that has been found so far in West Lower City, or in Lower City as a whole, suggests that Lower City was incorporated into a town site much before the seventh century B.C. This suggests that Idalion was perhaps more restricted in its area prior to the sixth century than has previously been thought to be the case, and that it underwent rapid expansion in the late Cypro-Archaic and Cypro-Classical periods.

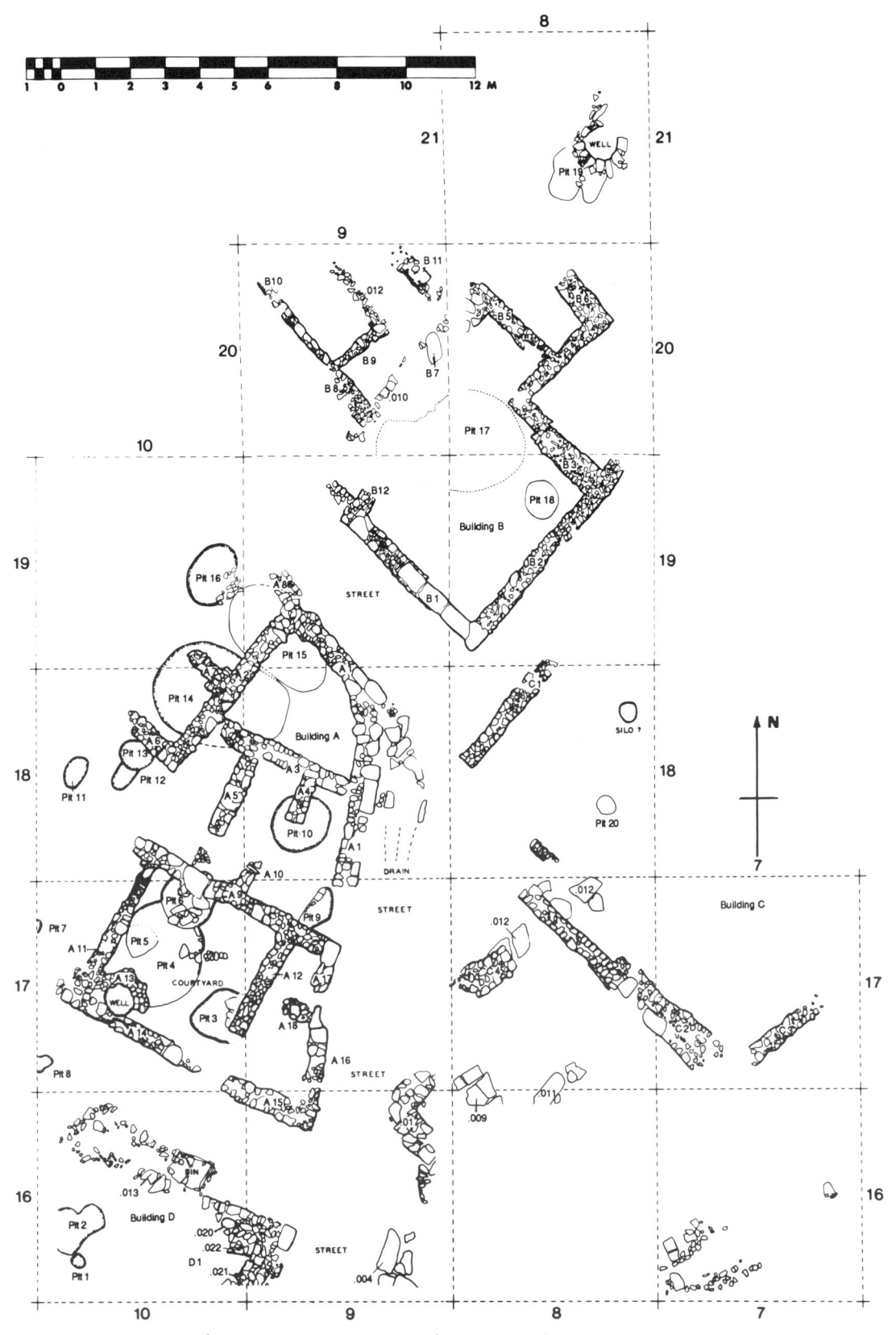

Figure 1. West Lower City Domestic Precinct Plan.

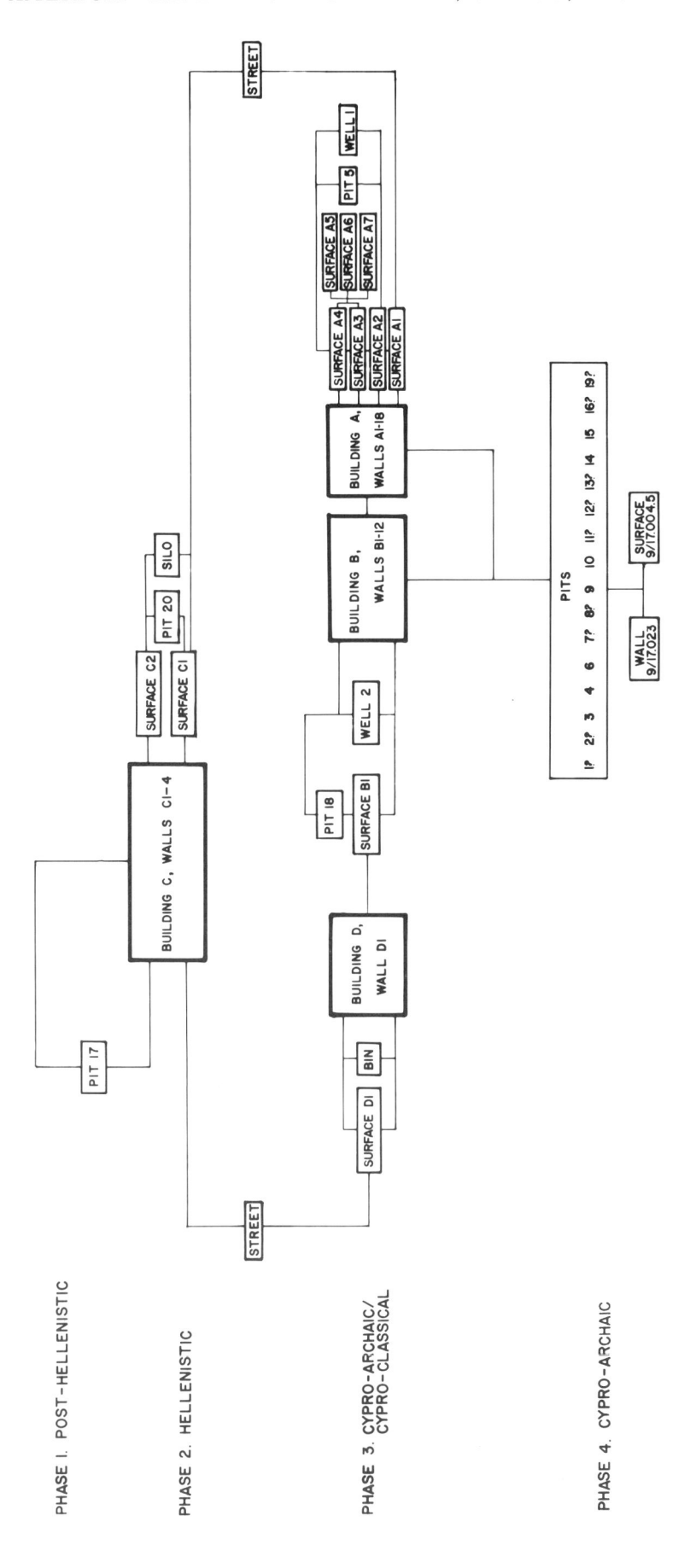

74 AMERICAN EXPEDITION TO IDALION, CYPRUS, 1973-1980

Figure 2. Sequence Diagram of West Lower City Domestic Precinct.

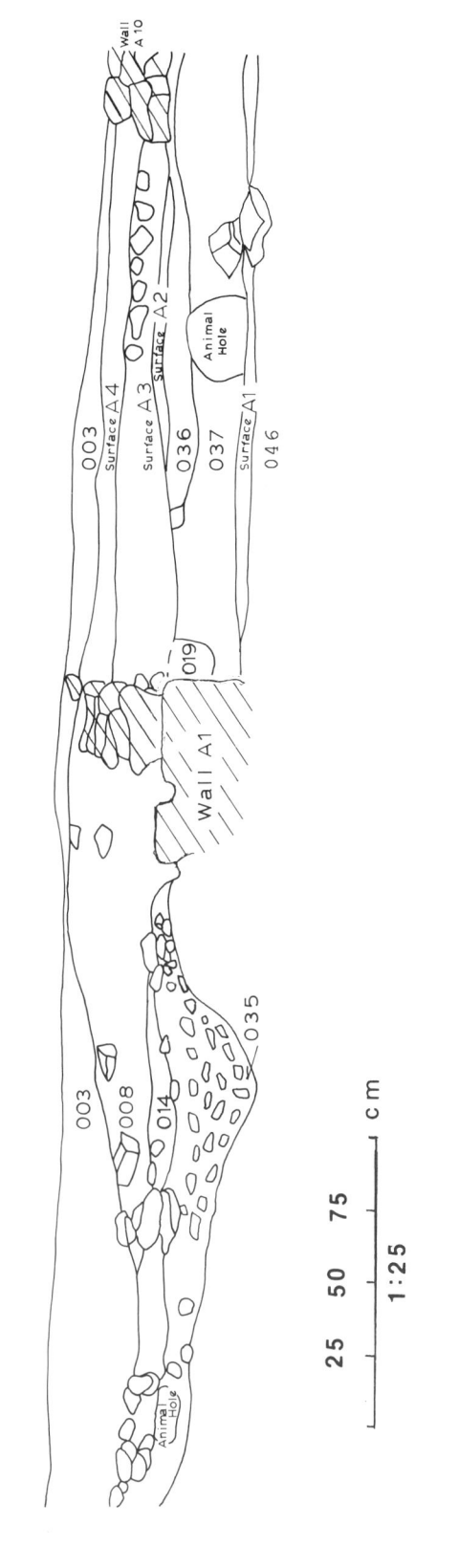

LOCUS	DESCRIPTION	PHASE
003	colluvium	1
008	wall fall	1/2
Wall A1		3
Wall A10		3A
014	occupation debris, plaster and cobbles	2/3
019	rain wash	3B
Street		2/3

LOCUS	DESCRIPTION	PHASE
035	drain	2/3
036	mudbrick detritus	3B
037	occupation debris	3B
Surface A1		3B
Surface A2		3B
Surface A3		3A
Surface A4		3A
046	virgin marl	

Figure 3. Idalion WNW 9/18 South Section.

PLATE 1

a

b

Pits 14 and 10. a. Pit 14, bisected by Wall A2. Within the excavated half of the pit is buttress Wall A7. b. Pit 10, underlying Building A.

PLATE 2

Pits 9 and 10. a. Pit 9, underlying Building A. At the base of the excavated section of the Pit are visible tamped earth surface 9/17 Loc 004.5 and wall 9/17 Loc 023. b. Pit 10 in course of excavation showing its contents.

PLATE 3

Pits 10 and 4. a. Pit 10 in course of excavation. Surface A1 is visible sealing the pit; above it, later surfaces and occupational build-up associated with Phase 3B. At the top center is Wall A4 (Phase 3A). b. Wall A11 built across western perimeter of Pit 4.

PLATE 4

a

b

Pit 14 and Buildings A and B. a. Pit 14, showing Wall A2 built across it. b. Overall shot of Buildings A and B, divided by the street, looking northeast.

PLATE 5

Building A. a. Building A, north half, showing curved wall bounding street, looking northeast (note masonry spurs, lower left). b. Exterior buttress wall or arch springer in modern Dhali.

PLATE 6

Buildings A and B. a. Building A, courtyard with Well 1. b. Building B, with Well 2 in foreground, looking southwest.

PLATE 7

a

b

c

Building B and Modern Vernacular Architecture. a. Building B, looking northeast. b. Vernacular architecture at Kakopetria, showing ground level storage, with wooden staircase to living story. c. Street with drainage channel in Kakopetria.

a. Selected Pottery Groups from the West Lower City Domestic Precinct

*Per Ålin**

During the excavations of 1972 in the West Lower City remains of houses were found in three adjacent squares. The preliminary study of the pottery indicated that these houses were of Archaic date, from which period very little domestic architecture has been found on Cyprus as yet. The houses were therefore of particular interest and the pottery from these squares was brought to the United States for study. The stratigraphy and plans were published and discussed by Dr. Anita Walker in *Idalion* 1 (pp. 42-45, figs. 35-38) and some profiles were illustrated and described (pp. 86-87, pl. II).

This paper is based on a study of some of the sherds excavated in 1972 from these three squares. As will be seen, there are some discrepancies between the dates given in *Idalion* 1 and the dates suggested here. The responsibility for these discrepancies is mine, but they may perhaps be excused in view of the pressures and lack of time during the excavations, and also my inexperience with Cypriot pottery at the time.

First a description of selected and illustrated sherds, and a brief characterization of the remaining material in each pottery bucket will be given, arranged by square and locus. Table 1 gives a list of loci discussed by square; table 2, by phase. This will be followed by a general discussion. The study concludes with a summary of the results.

In addition to the pottery from these selected groups, I include a note on the pottery from Id WNW 9/18.045 (Pit 10). My study of this material is preliminary and I may modify my opinions about this pottery upon more detailed analysis. This material is not included in tables 3 and 4.

The use of the term "Type" (with or without capital T) refers to pottery with a certain "Ware" number as listed in *SCE* IV:2. For example, White Painted V Ware, Bichrome V Ware, and so forth, all belong to Type V.

Remarks about fabrics usually attempt to describe only certain characteristics of appearance, which may or may not have been intentionally produced by the potter. Even if only accidentally produced, such characteristics are nonetheless often a great help in classifying the pottery, which after all must be related to the commonly accepted terminology. Since I did not have access to the material itself, I have not included relevant pottery that was illustrated and described very precisely in *Idalion* 1 (ibid.). The abbreviation "PB" will be used to designate "Pottery Bucket."

---

[*]The present study was greatly aided by a grant from the American Council of Learned Societies, which enabled me to spend another summer on Cyprus and at Idalion studying and sorting Cypro-Archaic and Cypro-Classical pottery. Without this opportunity I would be far less familiar with the material than I am now. I also wish to thank Mrs. Andrea Green for her assistance during my study of the pottery at Stony Brook.

Table 1. Loci Discussed, by Square

Locus	Description	Phase
Id WNW 10/18		
005	Mudbrick detritus	2/3
010	Use-surface A4	3
006	Pit 11	4(?)
009	Pit 12	4(?)
012	Pit 13	4(?)
015	Compact mudbrick detritus overlying virgin soil	4
Id WNW 9/18		
012	Cobbles and pottery in silt matrix	3
017	Silt and limestone chips	2/3
018	Sand and pebbles overlying Surface A5	3
019	Clay and cobbles above Loc 027	3
020	Street	2/3
022	Street	2/3
023	Use-surface A5	3
026	Use-surface A2	3
027	Circular patch of large pebbles	3
029	Occupation debris	3
031	Gray ashy soil probably occupation debris below Surface A5	4
045	Pit 10	4
Id WNW 9/19		
009	Street	2/3
010	Street	2/3
011	Street	2/3
015	Occupation debris associated with Building B	2/3

Table 2. Loci Discussed, by Phase

Phase	Square		
	Id WNW 10/18	Id WNW 9/18	Id WNW 9/19
4	006, Pit 11(?) 009, Pit 12(?) 012, Pit 13(?) 015, mudbrick detritus	031, gray ashy soil 045, Pit 10	
3	010, Use-surface A4	012, cobbles and pottery 018, sand and pebbles overlying Surface A5 019, clay and cobbles above Loc 027 023, Use-surface A5 026, Use-surface A2 027, large pebbles 029, occupation debris	
2/3	005, mudbrick detritus	017, silt and limestone chips 020, Street 022, Street	009, Street 010, Street 011, Street 015, occupation debris associated with Building B

Catalogue of Sherds

Square WNW 10/18

Plate 1a

Loc 005, PB nos. 5 and 7; Phase 2/3 (mudbrick detritus); Loc 010, PB no. 24; Phase 3 (use-surface A4)

Sherd no. 1 is part of a vertical handle with three ridges; probably Plain White VI Ware. No. 2 is a shoulder fragment from a closed vase in fine red buff clay with a whitish buff slip; probably Plain White V, very close to Type VI fabric. No. 3 is another shoulder fragment, but in coarse Ware. No. 4 is part of a vertical ribbon handle of soft smooth buff clay with a whitish slip; Plain White VI. No. 5 belonged to an open vase of soft reddish clay with a slip on both sides, shifting from red to dark brown; probably Red Slip III(V). No. 6 is a shoulder fragment from a large amphora in brown red rather soft clay with buff slip that is decorated with a wiggly line; White Painted IV-V. Finally, nos. 7 and 8 are shoulder fragments from a closed vase in clay similar to no. 5 but with no slip; Plain White V.

The remaining sherds (not illustrated) from these loci are for Loc 010, PB no. 24: 15 sherds of Plain White V, and 1 Red Slip III(V), the latter probably belonging to a bowl; for Loc 005, PB nos. 5, 5, 7, and 12: 78 sherds, of which 54 appear to be Plain White V, 1 White Painted V, and 2 Red Slip III(V), one of which belonged to a closed vase in rather gritty clay with a red brown slip and is probably an early Type V. The remaining sherds consist of 19 fragments of cooking pots and 2 Hellenistic sherds.

Loc 006, PB no. 9; Phase 4(?), (Pit 11)

This pottery bucket contained 2 White Painted V sherds, one of which was a shoulder and neck fragment from a jug in buff clay with a whitish buff slip and wavy-line decoration (cf. *SCE* IV:2, fig. 57:15). There were also 85 sherds of Plain White V Ware, very few of which could be considered early Type V. Three sherds may be labeled transitional Plain White V-VI, and 10 belong to cooking pots and Coarse Ware. The contents of this pit should thus be placed in the middle to second half of Type V pottery.

Plate 1b

Loc 009, PB nos. 15 and 18; Phase 4(?), (Pit 12)

Sherds nos. 1-3 are shoulder fragments from a jug in thin reddish fabric with green white slip. There are grooves around the base of the neck. Probably several of the sherds in this locus, PB nos. 15, 18, and 19, come from the same vase; Plain White V (cf. *SCE* IV:2, fig. 57:14 or a similar vessel). Nos. 4 and 5 belong to a jug of thin greenish clay with no slip. The jug has grooves around the base of the neck and clay "rivets" at the handle base, imitating metal prototypes; Plain White V. No. 6 is part of a vertical handle; probably Plain White V Ware. No. 7 is a shoulder fragment from a closed vase in hard-fired gray buff clay with no slip. This fabric is typical of the bulk of the pottery from this locus; Plain White V. No. 8 comes from the shoulder of a closed vase and has a rather smooth greenish fabric. This fabric should perhaps be considered a late development of an earlier coarser and grittier fabric that was fairly common and can be followed all the way back to the latest Bronze Age pottery at Idalion. No. 8 is also Plain White V. No. 9, the base of a vertical handle, is of the same ware as no. 8. Nos. 10-13 are handle fragments of the double rope type, probably from a jug, in very fine gray fabric; Gray and Black Polished III(V) Ware (for the handle type cf. *SCE* IV:2, fig. 54:1-12). No. 14 is a fragment of a Black Glazed cup with the base for a horizontal handle. The paint covers it both inside and outside, and it should fit as an import into this generally late Type V context. No. 15 belonged to the shoulder of a closed vase in red brown unslipped clay decorated with a wiggly line; White Painted IV. Nos. 16 and 17 come from a Hellenistic bowl and are made in fine buff fabric and dip-painted in dark brown, with stack marks from the firing. No. 18 is a handle fragment from a jug in Coarse Ware made of hard-fired reddish clay. No. 19 belonged to a vertical ribbon handle and should probably be assigned to Plain White VI. No. 20 is a handle fragment from a closed vase with slightly sandy surface and a groove at the base. No. 21 is a rim fragment from a bowl in reddish clay with brown red slip, probably a coarse Red Slip bowl in Type II(IV) Ware. No. 22 comes from a cooking pot.

This locus also contained 435 large and small fragments, mostly from closed vases belonging to Plain White V. Of these, only a few sherds seem to be early. The fabric of most should place them in the middle to later part of Type V pottery. Two sherds may be considered Plain White VI, but if so they are very close to V. There were also 5 White Painted V sherds, 1 Black Polished III(V) handle fragment, 2 Red Slip III(V) sherds, and 50 fragments belonging to cooking pots and Coarse Ware.

Loc 012, PB nos. 16 and 20; Phase 4(?), (Pit 13)

These buckets contained 27 sherds of Plain White V vases, most of these in varieties of the greenish fabric mentioned above. Some were very thin and hard; others were thicker and smoother. One of these may belong to a late Type V vase, as do two or three of the others. Most of the sherds, however, are middle Type V and belonged to a few vases only, although there were no joining pieces. The locus also contained 9 sherds from cooking pots.

Loc 015, PB no. 22; Phase 4, (mudbrick detritus)

PB no. 22 contained 1 White Painted V and 34 Plain White V sherds. The latter probably come from only a few vases, some of which were large amphorae. The clay was in most cases rather soft and reddish brown. The majority should probably be assigned to the middle of Type V. There were also 3 sherds from cooking pots.

Square WNW 9/18

Plate 2a

Loc 012, PB no. 25; Phase 3, (cobbles and pottery)

No. 1 is a handle and shoulder fragment of what was probably a point-based amphora, in hard-fired red, rather uneven clay with wheelmarks and no slip; Plain White VI-VII (cf. *SCE* IV:2, figs. 62:3 and 67:25). No. 2 is a body fragment, probably from the same vase as no. 1. No. 3 is a vertical jug handle with double straps in greenish white clay; Plain White V.

Plate 2b

Loc 017, PB no. 30; Phase 2/3, (silt and limestone chips)

No. 1 is a shoulder fragment from an amphora in brown clay, with gray core and yellow slip, decorated with horizontal bands in brown color; White Painted V. No. 2 comes from a closed vase, probably an amphora, in hard sandy brown black clay covered with a whitish slip and decorated with dark brown and red brown bands and lines; Bichrome V. No. 3 comes from a closed vase and is in reddish clay with a green white slip and brown decoration consisting of large vertical concentric circle lines. It must have been a jug of the barrel-shaped or oinochoe type and belongs to White Painted IV-V (cf. *SCE* IV:2, fig. 46:7). No. 4 is a fragment from a closed vase in the gritty greenish fabric, with brown black decoration; White Painted V. No. 5 belongs to a White Painted V vase. Finally, nos. 6-8 are fragments of a Black Glazed cup with horizontal handles. All of the Cypriot sherds just described appear to belong to the earlier part of Type V.

Plate 2c

Loc 018, PB no. 45; Phase 3, (sand and pebbles overlying Surface A5)

No. 1 is a handle in Coarse Ware, probably from an amphora or a cooking pot (cf. *SCE* IV:2, fig. 71:2 or 7). No. 2 is a fragment from a large closed shape in reddish clay; Plain White V-VI. No. 3 also comes from a closed shape, is in red clay, and belongs to Plain White VI. No. 4 is a fragment in reddish clay that has been stroke-polished inside and covered with a dark red brown slip outside; probably Red Slip III(V), from late in the Type V development. No. 5 is a White Painted V fragment with horizontal bands. No. 6 belonged to a closed shape, is hard fired, and should probably be assigned to Plain White VI. No. 7 comes from the lower part of a body and is probably a late Plain White V. Finally, no. 8 is a fragment of a closed vase in Coarse Ware.

Eighty-two sherds of Plain White V remain from this locus, almost half of which are very late, and difficult to distinguish from early Type VI. Most of the rest seem to belong to middle Type V. Plain White VI is represented by 15 sherds, most of which seem to be early. Only about four are well advanced into Type VI Ware. There are also 6 White Painted V sherds, 1 Black-on-Red III(V), and 38 fragments from cooking pots and Coarse Ware.

Loc 019 PB no. 35; Phase 3, (clay and cobbles above Loc 027)

Only 5 sherds were contained in this bucket. They consisted of Plain White V and 2 Coarse Ware sherds.

Loc 020, PB nos. 50 and 53; Phase 2/3, (Street)

These buckets contained 117 sherds in Plain White V, most of which were hard fired and probably rather late; 1 Plain White VI; 1 White Painted V fragment from a closed vase in hard gritty clay with green gray slip; and, finally, 5 sherds from cooking pots and Coarse Ware.

Plate 3a

Loc 022, Layer 1, PB no. 39; Phase 2/3, (Street)

No. 1 is a shoulder fragment from an amphora or jug in gritty green fabric. The decoration consists of wide dark bands enclosing thin lines; early White Painted V. No. 2 is also a shoulder fragment from an amphora or jug, in a greenish fabric; White Painted V, but probably later than the previous sherd. No. 3 is a fragment from a closed vase in red clay with gray core. The decoration consists of the usual bands and thin lines; White Painted V. No. 4 belonged to a closed vase in green clay, with decoration similar to the previous sherd; White Painted V. No. 5 is a White Painted V sherd in greenish clay. No. 6 should probably be labeled Black-on-Red III(V). No. 7 is a fragment in reddish clay; Plain White V Ware. With the exception of nos. 4 and 7, all of these sherds should be early Type V.

Plate 3b

Loc 022, Layer 1, PB no. 39; Phase 2/3, (Street)

No. 1 is a shoulder fragment of a closed vase in a commonly occurring reddish gritty clay with no slip, decorated with wide, badly worn brown bands; White Painted IV. No. 2 comes from a closed vase in slightly gritty reddish clay that is covered with a dark red slip; Red Slip III(V). No. 3 is a shoulder fragment from a closed vase in hard, yellow buff clay, with the decoration consisting of wide bands enclosing thin lines; White Painted V. No. 4 belonged to the shoulder of a closed vase in fine, very hard-fired dark clay, covered with a brown slip and decorated in darker shades of brown; it should be assigned to Type VI, probably white Painted VI, but perhaps Bichrome Red III(VI). No. 5 is a body fragment from a closed vase in fine greenish clay that should be considered a late Plain White V. No. 6 is part of a cooking-pot handle. No. 7 is White Painted VI, a shoulder fragment in fine hard gray buff clay. No. 8 comes from a closed vase in a rather smooth clay, greenish gray at the surface, and decorated with a brown line; White Painted V. No. 9 belonged to the shoulder of a closed vase in reddish smooth clay; Plain White VI. No. 10 is a base fragment from a cooking pot. Nos. 11 and 12 are fragments of vertical handles from Hellenistic vases; the former has only traces of reddish paint; the latter is covered with brown paint. Nos. 13 and 14 belonged to Hellenistic I cups or plates, covered on both sides with brown and red brown paint. Nos. 15-18 are also fragments of Hellenistic I vases; nos. 17 and 18 are covered with brown black paint on both sides.

The remaining sherds consist of 51 Plain White V, mostly very late, although one or two are early; 43 Plain White VI, some of which may be early; 5 White Painted V; 1 Red Slip III(V); 20 small Hellenistic sherds, mostly from cups; and 25 small sherds from cooking pots and Coarse Ware. One small fragment in Type V fabric was probably part of a lamp spout. Most of the sherds in this group seem to belong to closed shapes and may be considered borderline cases between Types V and VI.

Plate 4a

Loc 022, Layer 3, PB no. 42; Phase 2/3, (Street)

No. 1 is a fragment of the upper half of the neck of a handle-ridge jug in greenish gray, rather coarse clay with no slip. Its decoration consists of black bands, with wider bands at the ridge and rim; White Painted IV. No. 2 is a shoulder fragment from a closed vase in reddish clay with wide and narrow black bands as decoration; probably White Painted V. Nos.

3, 4, and 6 seem to be transitional White Painted IV-V; their decoration consists of horizontal bands. Nos. 5 and 7, which also have horizontal bands, are White Painted V. No. 8 is a shoulder fragment of an amphora with encircling bands and a row of small concentric circles below these; white Painted V. No. 9 comes from the extreme point of the body of a barrel-shaped jug in red clay with no slip and with the usual vertical concentric circle decoration; White Painted IV. No. 10 is also a fragment of a barrel-shaped jug, similar to no. 9, but with a whitish slip; White Painted IV. No. 11 is a shoulder fragment from a closed vase, decorated in unusually thin lines with concentric circles or what may have been intended as a spiral; it is probably transitional White Painted IV-V. Nos. 12, 14, 15, 17, 19, 24, 25, 27, and 31 mostly belong to vases with decoration similar to the one above; they are probably to be considered transitional White Painted IV-V or cannot be clearly assigned to either type. No. 12 differs from the others in that it has a thin-line spiral decoration. Nos. 22 and 28 are White Painted IV sherds. Nos. 21, 26, and 30 belong to White Painted V Ware. No. 26 seems to have a concentric circle touching the band decoration. Nos. 13 and 16 are Bichrome V. Nos. 18, 20, and 29 are probably to be considered Bichrome Red II(V). No. 23 is a fragment of a cup or bowl with no decoration on the outside, which may belong to Black-on-Red III(V) Ware.

Plate 4b

Loc 022, Layer 3, PB no. 42; Phase 2/3, (Street)

No. 1 is a bowl fragment in fine buff clay with brown black worn paint on both sides; Hellenistic I. No. 2 comes from a jug in red buff clay with worn red brown paint on both sides; Hellenistic I. Nos. 3-5 are likewise jug or bowl fragments; also Hellenistic I. No. 6 probably belonged to a closed shape. It is made of a very fine red buff clay with worn paint on the outside; Hellenistic I. No. 7 is from the same period, in fine greenish clay with brown black paint on both sides. No. 8, a fragment in red buff clay with red brown paint on both sides, is again Hellenistic I. No. 9, in similar clay but with Black Glazed decoration, is slightly earlier. No. 10 is a shoulder fragment from a closed vase in buff clay; Plain White V-VI. No. 11 is also from the shoulder of a closed vase, but in red buff clay with a whitish slip; perhaps early Plain White VI. Nos. 12 and 13 are in greenish fine and hard clay; the former is a shoulder fragment from a closed vase; they should be assigned to Plain White VI or possibly late V Ware, and may be considered a late development of the greenish, formerly gritty fabric mentioned above. No. 14 is a base fragment in Plain White Ware. No. 15 comes from a large vase in reddish clay with a buff slip; Plain White VI. No. 16 belonged to a closed vase in very hard-fired Plain White Ware. No. 17 is a fragment of a closed vase in gritty red buff clay with brown red slip, which makes it Red Slip II(IV). No. 18 is a neck fragment in coarse reddish clay with buff slip, decorated with mat brown lines; White Painted IV. No. 19 belonged to the shoulder of a closed vase in thin brown red clay with no slip and a decoration of concentric circles in gray, touching a wide band in dark brown color; Bichrome IV. No. 20 is a shoulder fragment of a closed vase with a zone of thin lines surrounding the neck; White Painted IV. No. 21 comes from a shoulder and is in reddish gritty clay with no slip, a fabric common for Type IV pottery. It has a circumcurrent field with dark border bands enclosing thin lines and a red brown band, the last feature making it Bichrome IV. No. 22 should probably be assigned to White Painted V. No. 23 is a handle fragment from a closed vase in rather gritty red buff clay with a whitish slip; probably Plain White V. No. 24 comes from a double rope handle in red buff clay with greenish-white slip; Plain White V.

Of the 135 remaining sherds 3 are Plain White IV, 67 Plain White V, 18 Plain White VI, 3 White Painted V, and 44 were part of cooking pots and Coarse Ware. Many of the Type V and VI sherds seem to be borderline cases; most of the former belong to late Type V, and a few of the latter to early Type VI.

As will be noticed, the pottery contained in this bucket of Loc 022 has generally been given an earlier type designation than other buckets from later layers of the same locus. This attribution is based on fabric characteristics: rather coarse and gritty, sometimes green, sometimes brown reddish in color, and also rather thick, light, and soft. This fabric makes this group clearly distinguishable from the pottery of the later part of Type V, when harder and smoother fabrics become common or dominant. This tendency toward harder and smoother fabrics culminates in Type VI and VII fabrics. As a whole this group should thus be considered transitional Type IV-V, and seems to correspond rather well with pottery found in the wells excavated in the same area. It is of course also related to the pottery found on top of the Acropolis by both the Swedish and American excavations, although it generally seems to be of higher quality than much of the acropolis pottery (*SCE* II, pp. 514, 596-97, pls. 162, 163, 166-168).

The remaining buckets from this locus (not illustrated) are as follows:

Loc 022, Layer 1, PB no. 37 contains a fragment from a closed vase in what is probably Black Slip III-IV, and a sherd in Red Slip II(IV).

Loc 022, Layer 2, PB no. 41 has 47 Plain White V, mostly very small sherds, a few in the greenish variety but most in brown clay with pinkish surface; they should be attributed to middle-to-late Type V. The rest of this bucket consists of 2 White Painted V and 4 cooking pot sherds and one fragment from a large storage vase.

Loc 022, Layer 4, PB no. 44 has 99 Plain White V, a few of these early, but most of them middle Type V; and 16 White Painted V, two of which belong to the gritty green variety. One of the decorated sherds may be a Type IV, a few of them are probably early Type V, and the remainder belong to middle Type V. There were also 2 Red Slip III(V) sherds and 35 sherds from cooking pots and Coarse Ware.

A comparison between Layers 3 and 4 of this locus shows that sherds of Type VI or close to it are present in Layer 3, but generally absent in Layer 4.

Loc 023, PB no. 49; Phase 3 (Use-surface A5)

This locus contained 6 sherds in White Painted V Ware with insignificant decoration. Of the 62 sherds in Plain White V, some seem to be early and some late, but most of them belong around the middle of the period. These were made in a hard-fired pink to brownish clay with a smooth surface, and come from both large and small vases. One rim fragment from a bowl made in unslipped red brown clay, has a parallel in *SCE* IV:2, fig. 56:20; it belongs to what may be defined as the soft and light fabrics of Cypro-Archaic pottery. This locus also contained 17 sherds from cooking pots and Coarse Ware, and a fragment from a figurine of a horse and rider, as well.

Plate 3c

Loc 026, PB no. 43; Phase 3, (Use-surface A2)

No. 1 is a fragment of a horizontal handle in gritty clay, painted in black; White Painted V, probably close to IV. No. 2 belonged to a large amphora in yellow green smooth clay; White Painted V. No. 3 is also from an amphora, similar to the preceding, and is in green clay decorated with brown bands; White Painted V. No. 4 probably comes from a neck and is in gritty green clay, with brown decoration consisting of wide bands enclosing thin lines; White Painted V. No. 5 was part of a closed vessel in green rather smooth clay, decorated with brown black lines; White Painted V. No. 6 is a body fragment from a closed vase in red buff clay with a greenish surface and lines in brown violet. A slight trace of a broad reddish band, in addition to the usual thin lines, may qualify this as Bichrome V, rather than the White Painted variety.

This locus also contained 29 sherds of Plain White V Ware, some in the gritty green fabric, mostly small in size; others in red brown clay with buff-to-pinkish surface; most of these should probably be placed around the middle of Type V, but a few are in the later part. There were also 15 sherds of cooking pots and Coarse Ware.

Loc 027, PB no. 48; Phase 3 (large pebbles)

This locus contained 3 sherds of Plain White V Ware that were part of one or more large closed vases in reddish clay with a sandy yellow white slip, and one White Painted V sherd in reddish rather soft clay with green white slip and brown black lines.

Loc 029, PB nos. 51 and 53A; Phase 3 (occupational debris)

These buckets contained 30 sherds of Plain White V Ware. Only a very few of these were close to Type VI; most of them evidently belong to the middle of Type V. Seven Plain White sherds seem to have been close to V. Three sherds that come from closed shapes are of White Painted V Ware. One fragment of a large closed vase, in hard-fired rather gritty clay with red brown slip and the worn remains of two large concentric circles, is to be classified as Black-on-Red III(V). Finally, 2 sherds are Red Slip III(V) and 15 belong to cooking pots and Coarse Ware.

Loc 031, PB no. 56; Phase 4 (gray ashy soil)

This locus contained 12 sherds of Plain White V, all of which seem to be middle to late; there were also 3 Plain White VI and 2 Coarse Ware sherds.

Square WNW 9/19

Loc 009, PB no. 19; Phase 2/3 (Street)

This bucket contained 38 Plain White V sherds, probably mostly middle to late; 6 sherds that should probably be considered Plain White IV-V; 1 White Painted V, probably early; 1 Red Slip II(IV); 1 Red Slip III(V); and 1 possibly Bichrome Red IV-V. Finally, 12 sherds were part of cooking pots or Coarse Ware.

Loc 010, PB no. 12; Phase 2/3 (Street)

This bucket contained 59 Plain White V sherds, four of which came from the same large vase. Most of these sherds belong to the middle of Type V, although some are late and a few may be close to Plain White IV, to which another of the sherds seems to belong. Three sherds are Plain White VI, one is Hellenistic, and 9 come from cooking pots.

Plate 5a

Loc 011, PB no. 13; Phase 2/3, (Street)

No. 1 consists of five fragments that belong to a closed vase, most probably a jug. The placing of the upper and lower parts may not be correct, but it does show the pattern. The fine buff-to-reddish clay is decorated in brown paint with rows of concentric circles and multiple hooks between parallel lines. The body shape is probably comparable to *SCE* IV;2, fig. 46:16, and the pattern comparable for example, to that of fig. 48:10. The fine quality of this vase suggests an early White Painted V, since the decoration indicates proximity to Type IV pottery. Nos. 2 and 3 are a body and a neck fragment, possibly from the same vase, similar to no. 1 in fabric and decoration. The body shape was probably like *SCE* IV:2, fig. 52:9. This should also be a borderline case, White Painted IV-V.

The following three sherds are not illustrated: one that may derive from the same as no. 1; one fragment from a closed vase in gritty green fabric, that should probably be assigned to early White Painted V; and one bowl fragment in thick reddish, slightly coarser fabric than the two others. Unlike the first two, this third fragment is covered with a greenish white slip. The decoration consists of broad black horizontal and vertical bands on the outside and a field of narrow bands inside. The bowl type may be similar to *SCE* IV:2, fig. 52:2. Although the fabric seems close to that typical of White Painted VI Ware, the bowl shape is more common in Type IV pottery. It probably belongs to White Painted V.

Plate 5b

Loc 011, PB no. 13; Phase 2/3, (Street)

Nos. 1-3 are shoulder fragments of the same type of small amphora as found in large numbers at the Idalion excavations of the Swedish Cyprus Expedition, particularly among the so-called Idalion Deposit material (*SCE* II, pp. 514, 596-97; pls. 162, 163, 166-68). The fabric is the characteristic rather soft and reddish sort, with no slip and with decoration in brown red and black paint, which makes the sherds Bichrome IV. No. 4 is a shoulder fragment of an amphora in a rather coarse reddish clay, with the neck painted inside; Black-on-Red II(IV). No. 5 is a rim fragment of an amphora with red slip on the buff clay, probably Bichrome Red Slip Type IV. No. 6 is a fragment of a closed vase, in clay similar to that of no. 4, but with no slip and decorated with a circumcurrent field of thin lines bordered by thick bands; White Painted IV. No. 7 is a fragment of a vertical handle in buff rather coarse clay decorated with brown stripes; White Painted IV. No. 8 is a shoulder fragment from a jug, probably of the handle-ridge type, in buff thin and hard clay, decorated with concentric circles and vertical fields of circumcurrent lines. These details and the colors used indicate Bichrome of Type IV. No. 9 is also a Bichrome IV shoulder fragment, but in gritty green fabric. No. 10 is a shoulder fragment, probably from a jug, in green, but in this case in smooth and soft clay. It should be assigned to White Painted IV or possibly early Type V. No. 11 is a jug or amphora fragment in the hard, thin, gritty, green clay; Bichrome IV. Nos. 12 and 13 both belonged to closed vases of smooth green clay, and seem to be borderline Bichrome IV-V. No. 14 probably comes from a jug, and is in a thin, gritty, green clay; two lighter lines on either side surround a darker brown band, which should make it a Bichrome IV. No. 15 is a shoulder fragment from a closed vase in a light green, rather gritty clay, decorated with brown black and red brown lines; Bichrome IV. No. 16 is a fragment from a closed vase in reddish clay; Bichrome IV. No. 17 is a White Painted IV sherd in gritty green clay. No. 18 is a shoulder fragment in buff clay with brown decoration that is probably a late White Painted IV or early V. No. 19 belonged to a closed vase in gritty green clay; Bichrome IV. No. 20 is a shoulder fragment from a jug in White Painted IV. No. 21, a neck fragment from a large amphora in coarse red clay, is decorated with a hatched hourglass pattern within vertical lines and horizontal bands in a panel arrangement. Both its shape and decoration were probably rather similar to the amphora shown in *SCE* IV:2, fig. 20:2. Since this sherd must be assigned to White Painted III ware, it should be the earliest of the sherds found in this square. No. 22 is a sherd in smooth greenish clay with brown black decoration, possibly a White Painted V. No. 23 belonged to the body of a handle-ridge or barrel-shaped jug in greenish clay that should belong to White Painted IV. No. 24 is a fragment of a jug in hard, thin, gritty, green clay; White Painted IV. No. 25 belonged to a jug in thick smooth brown-to-reddish clay and should perhaps be assigned to Bichrome V. No. 26 comes from a closed vase in White Painted IV Ware.

Not illustrated but also among the rich finds in this locus and bucket were 62 sherds that belong to White Painted and Bichrome IV, except for a few probably of Type V. There were also 1 Black Glazed, 12 Plain White V, and 1 White Painted V, 9 Hellenistic, and 10 sherds of cooking pots and Coarse Ware.

Loc 015, PB no. 20; Phase 2/3 (occupation debris)

This bucket contained 20 sherds of Plain White V, 1 Plain White VI fragment from a large closed vase, 1 White Painted V, 1 double-string handle fragment in Red Slip III(V), 2 Hellenistic sherds from open vases, and 9 cooking-pot and Coarse Ware sherds.

Discussion of selected groups

The catalogue of the pottery found in these squares has shown that we are dealing here with the generally plain and simple repertoire of shapes and decorative styles that can be expected in the average settlement. This becomes quite clear in table 3, in which all of the material is summarized and arranged according to square, locus, and type.

The almost complete dominance of Plain White Ware and Type V is the most obvious information found in the table. Even though many of the Plain White sherds were fragments of White Painted pots, most of the pottery by far must have been still undecorated. Since most of the pottery has been so badly broken, it is difficult to make conclusions regarding the more detailed characteristics of the vases. It is often sufficient to identify sherds as having belonged to open or closed vases. A rough comparison between the approximate numbers of one or the other type of shape shows that the closed shapes outnumber the open ones by a ratio of about four to one. Many of the open ones, moreover, are Hellenistic, and thus only marginally relevant in the present context. Although this predominance may be explained to some extent by the generally larger size of the closed vases, the disproportion is still substantial. Open shapes, mainly in the form of small cups or bowls, such as were found here, are very common in Hellenistic contexts, but this does not seem to have been the case a few centuries earlier at the same site.

The few decorated sherds show the simple patterns typical for the era under discussion: wide and narrow bands on the shoulder and body fragments; small concentric circles in the shoulder zone; and large circles on the handle-ridge jugs. However in the context of the bulk of the pottery, these and other examples of decoration would be regarded as survivals. As was pointed out above, plain wares predominate, and most of the pottery discussed here stands close to the end of a development that leads from the often richly decorated but rather coarse Type IV wares to its culmination in Type VI, with generally excellent plain ware.

From the *Idalion* 1 excavation report it seems clear that few of the loci should be considered sealed. In any one of them a certain chronological spread in the types represented may thus be expected, even if a locus is dominated by one type. In this connection, one problem naturally, is to define the boundaries between different types. As is well known, the development of Cypriot pottery during the Iron Age should be regarded, with few exceptions, as an ongoing process, with only gradual changes. To complicate matters, in only a small percentage of the present material does decoration give any help in assigning sherds to one or another type. There are some indicators, however, particularly in the fabric, that make it possible to assign sherds to Type V with a fair degree of certainty in most cases. As seen above, the vast majority of sherds with this label belong to the middle-to-late stages in the development of this type. This judgement is supported by the clearly recognizable differences between this pottery and the decorated Type IV pottery found here, and most notably in the wells in the same general area of Idalion. In defining what would be considered Type VI, fabric was the only available criterion in most cases, which means that late Type V-early Type VI was often treated as one transitional stage.

The development outlined above is further supported by the statistical analysis of Type V sherds given in table 4. This table shows the approximate number of sherds that can be considered early, middle, or late Type V. "No record" includes the Type V sherds that could not be assigned to any one of the three groups. Sherds other than White Painted and Plain White were disregarded, since they were found in such insignificant numbers. Even if the figures given in table 4 should be regarded as only approximate, they do indicate the decline of White Painted Ware and the predominance of later Type V pottery in this area.

Table 3. Number of Sherds from the Different Loci
According to Type and Ware

Square	WNW 10/18						WNW 9/18				
Locus	005	006	009	010	012	015	012	017	018	019	020
Phase	2/3	4?	4?	3	4	4	3	2/3	3	3	2/3

TYPE											
WP III											
WP IV			1					1			
WP IV-Bi IV											
Bi IV											
BoR II(IV)											
RS II(IV)			1								
BS III-IV											
PW IV											
WP V	2	2	5			1		10	7		1
Bi V								1			
BoR III(V)									1		
RS III(V)	3		2	1					1		
BiR II(V)											
BP III(V)			5								
PW V	55	85	443	17	27	34	1	34	84	3	17
WP VI											
PW VI	2	3	3	1			2	11	17		1
BG			1					1			
Hellenistic	2		2								
Cooking Pots and Coarse Ware	20	10	51	3	9	3		23	40	2	5
Total	84	100	514	22	36	38	3	81	150	5	24

Table 3. Number of Sherds from the Different Loci
According to Type and Ware (*cont.*)

Square	WNW 9/18						WNW 9/19				
Locus	022	023	026	027	029	031	009	010	011	015	*Total*
Phase	2/3	3	3	3	3	4	2/3	2/3	2/3	2/3	
TYPE											
WP III									1		1
WP IV	8								6		16
WP IV–Bi IV									62		62
Bi IV	2								10		12
BoR II(IV)									1		1
RS II(IV)	2						1		1		5
BS III–IV	1										1
PW IV	3										3
WP V	54	6	6	1	3		1		13	1	113
Bi V	2		1						3		7
BoR III(V)	2				1						4
RS III(V)	4				2		1			1	15
BiR II(V)	3						1				4
BP III(V)											5
PW V	269	62	29	3	30	12	44	59	12	20	1340
WP VI	2										2
PW VI	66				7	3		3		1	120
BG									1		3
Hellenistic	37							1	9	2	53
Cooking Pots and Coarse Ware	111	17	15		15	2		9	10	9	354
Total	566	85	51	4	58	17	48	72	129	34	2121

Table 4. Number of Type V Sherds According to Subperiod

	Early	*Middle*	*Late*	*No record*
White Painted V	33	3	10	108
Plain White V	34	738	310	101

A note on the Pottery of Pit 10

Square WNW 9/18

Figures 1-6

Locus 045, Phase 4, (Pit 10)

The pottery from Locus 045 (Pit 10), which is shown on figures 1-6 with accompanying fabric descriptions, exemplifies with few exceptions the more common closed and open shapes of the earlier Cypro-Archaic period.

The amphoras on figures 1, 3, and 4 are mostly in Bichrome Ware. Figure 1 nos. 2 and 3 and figure 4 nos. 5-7 are examples of the smaller amphoras of which so many were found on the western acropolis by the Swedish Cyprus Expedition. This parallel is particularly well seen in the lotus and the reserved rosette patterns on figure 1 no. 3, and also in the concentric circles and the red wavy lines on shoulders and necks (*SCE* II, pl. CLXIII, CLXVI, CLXVII; *SCE* IV:2, fig. XXXVI:5). These vases belong to Type IV. Of particular indicative value is the neck fragment, figure 4 no. 4, with its group of small concentric circles and a paneled pattern. The latter of course has contemporary parallels (e.g., *SCE* IV:2, fig. XXXVIII:1), but really refers to a long Cypro-Geometric tradition.

Figure 1 no. 4, and probably also no. 5, are neck and rim fragments from handle-ridge jugs, which are still frequent in the early Cypro-Archaic period, although the ridge has a tendency to disappear more and more. This is seen in an example of a similar jug from the Swedish Cyprus Expedition excavations that belongs to Idalion Period 5 (*Opuscula Atheniensia* 12, 1978:107, fig. 19). The Bichrome jugs, figure 2 nos. 1 and 2, both show slight traces of the handle ridge.

The White Painted and Bichrome jugs, figure 2 nos. 3-5 and figure 3 no. 4, are of the round-bodied shape with the high narrow neck and the characteristic heavy use of concentric circle decoration so popular at this stage. These are good examples of the innumerable variations possible. The double-strap handles of figure 2 nos. 4 and 5 are also common at this time. The two small decorated sherds, figure 6 nos. 6 and 8, probably belonged to the extremely fine small handle-ridge jugs in Black-on-Red II(IV) Ware known from many sites and also from Idalion.

Of the jars with horizontal handles on figure 3, nos. 2 and 3, the latter one, in Bichrome, is particularly valuable because an almost exact parallel to its profile, with the slightly angular turn from body to shoulder, is found in a Bichrome IV jar (*SCE* IV:2, fig. XXI:8). The side-spouted jug or feeding bottle, figure 3 no. 7, is probably similar to the one depicted in *SCE* IV:2, fig. XXXV:7.

Figure 5 contains bowls and plates, whose profiles and decorative features in most cases can be identified as Type IV. Many of these simple vases are Plain White, most of the decorated ones are White Painted, no. 5 is Bichrome, and nos. 12, 14, and 15 seem to be Black-on-Red. Of particular interest here are nos. 9-11, which continue the Cypro-Geometric tradition of rather shallow bowls with horizontal strap handles at the rim and a variety of concentric circle designs inside and out. These bowls constitute another good indicator, since both in the shallow and the more rounded variety and in what may be called their decorative intention they refer back in time and are actually gone by the time of Type V pottery (*SCE* IV:2, fig. XXX:13 ff., *Opuscula Atheniensia* 12, 1978:104, fig. 14).

Some of the several fragments of undecorated vases on figure 6 may be identified as Type IV, for example, probably the point-based amphora no. 2 and jars no. 18-20. However both on this figure and in the case of a few fragments mentioned earlier there are some that should probably be dated later.

Summary of Results

As mentioned earlier, the excavators recognized two occupation phases in connection with Building A (formerly Building 1). Many of the loci mentioned in the description of the various features of the building remains in *Idalion* 1 are those in which the above pottery was discovered. Among these we should mention the Street WNW9/18 (Loc 022) and WNW 9/19 (Loc 011), both of which contained a wide range of pottery, including a considerable number of Type IV, as well as of Hellenistic sherds. These and other stray finds in other loci show that the area was occupied much earlier than the present building remains seem to indicate. Although the one White Painted III amphora fragment in WNW 9/19 (Loc 011) does not prove occupation in Cypro-Geometric III, other finds of similar type in the vicinity show that this must have been the case.

Phase 4, the earliest occupation phase is represented in the present material by only three sealed loci (see table 2). Of these, Id WNW 10/18.015 and Id WNW 9/18.031, although not of great diagnostic value, seem to belong mainly to the middle part of Type V. The pottery in Locus 045 generally appears with fair consistency to represent the Type IV stage. It includes good indicators of Type IV and shows a conspicuous absence of pottery that should be expected had the previous or the following periods been represented in any major way. Thus it seems fairly safe to assume that the pottery in this locus represents settlement in the Cypro-Archaic I period. There are also some stratigraphically uncertain pits. One of them in particular, WNW 10/18 Loc 009, contained large numbers of sherds mostly belonging to the later part of Type V. It seems clear, therefore, that the use of these pits must have already begun during Phase 3 or even earlier in Phase 4, and that they may have continued to receive broken pottery occasionally over a considerable length of time.

Phase 3 was the most important one, and the major share of the Phase 3B remains and pottery come from five loci. Disregarding a few earlier and later stray sherds, these all belong to Type V, most of it evidently from the middle, but some also from the later part. This was followed by Phase 3A (formerly Phase 2), represented by two loci, one of which WNW 9/18 Loc 018, contained a considerable number of sherds. About half of the Type V sherds are very late, and many belong to Type VI. With Phase 3A the remains directly connected with Building A seem to come to an end.

The pottery studied here thus shows that settlement in this area must date back to at least Cypro-Archaic I, or the seventh century B.C. Most of the pottery belongs to the Cypro-Archaic II period, mainly its middle and later parts. This is the time of the erection of Building A, which should probably be dated to about the third quarter of the sixth century B.C. The existence of this and other structures in the area from this time onward, explains the richness of the finds from late Cypro-Archaic into early Cypro-Classical times. The two occupation phases of Building A should bring the period of its use down into the second quarter of the fifth century B.C., which gives us somewhat less than a century to accommodate the various phases of the building--a quite adequate time. Due to the disturbed surface conditions, the subsequent occupation of the area is less clear. The virtual absence of later Classical as well as the presence of some Hellenistic pottery, however, seem to indicate that settlement in this particular area of ancient Idalion must have declined, at least for a time.

Figure 1. Pottery from Idalion WNW 9/18 Locus 045 (Pit 10)

	Phase	Locus	Registration no.	Description
1.	4	045	73.2930 = 2117	Wheelmade; fine sand inclusions; ware: 5 YR 6/4 (light reddish brown); paint: broad bands and wavy lines 2.5 YR 4/2 (weak red), thin bands 2.5 YR N3/ (very dark gray).
2.	4	045	75.4602	Wheelmade; fine sand, some grog inclusions; ware: 10 YR 7/4 (very pale brown); paint: wavy lines below circles 2.5 YR 4/4 (reddish brown), circles and bands 10 R 3/1 (dark reddish gray).
3.	4	045	75.33	Wheelmade; very fine paste, thin section, no visible inclusions; ware: 10 YR 7/4 (very pale brown); paint: pendant flowers and trellis pattern under rim 5 YR 4/4 (reddish brown), bands, rosettes 2.5 YR N3/ (very dark gray).
4.	4	045	75.654 = 1197	Wheelmade; some finely ground grog inclusions; ware: 7.5 YR 6/2 (pinkish gray); overall slip: 10 YR 8/2 (white); paint: 10 YR 3/1 (very dark gray).
5.	4	045	73.9988	Wheelmade; medium to coarse grog and carbonate inclusions; ware: 5 YR 7/4 (pink); paint: 5 YR 4/1 (dark gray).
6.	4	045	75.2858	Wheelmade; fine sand and carbonate inclusions; ware: 5 YR 7/4 (pink); applique band on exterior; paint (very faint): 5 YR 4/1 (dark gray).
7.	4	045	75.1915 = 2224	Wheelmade; fine sand and carbonate inclusions; ware: 5 YR 6/6 (reddish yellow); paint: bands 5 YR 3/1 (very dark gray), wavy lines 5 YR 4/4 (reddish brown).
8.	4	045	75.4087	Wheelmade; fine sand and carbonate inclusions; ware: 10 YR 8/4 (very pale brown); paint: 7.5 YR N/3 (very dark gray).
9.	4	045	no number	Wheelmade; fine paste (PB 112) carbonate and grog inclusions; ware: 10 YR 7/4 (very pale brown); paint: 10 YR 2.5/ (black); small hole pierced in neck.
10.	4	045	75.14	Wheelmade; composition: raw alluvial clay with nothing added; porous; contains rounded fine pebbles of mixed types: chert, limestone, microfossils, etc.; local clay from marl soils; ware: 10 YR 7/4 (very pale brown); paint: 2.5 YR 5/4 (reddish brown) and 5 YR 3/1 (very dark gray).

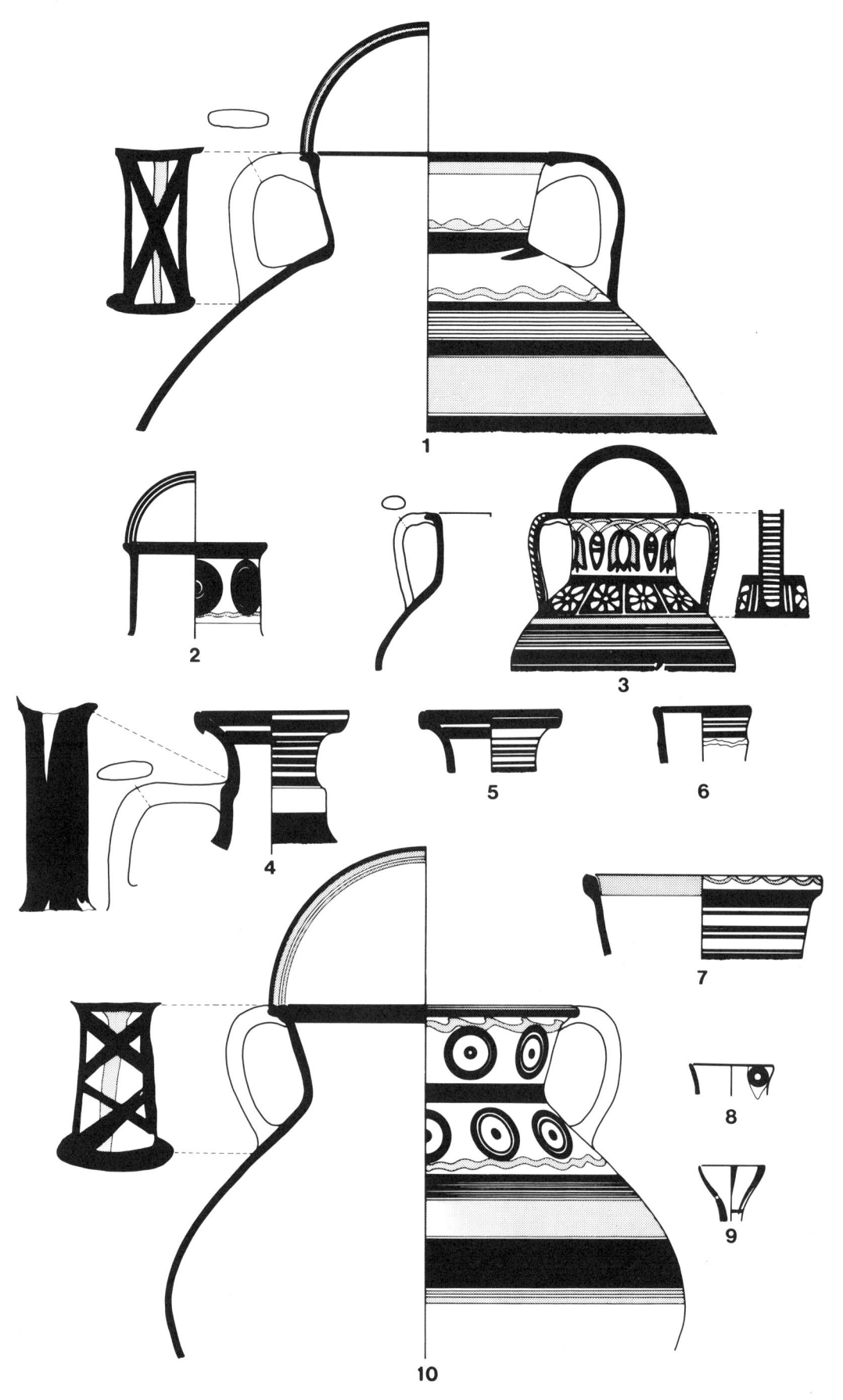

Figure 1. Pottery from Idalion WNW 9/18 Locus 045 (Pit 10). Scale 1:5.

Figure 2. Pottery from Idalion WNW 9/18 Locus 045 (Pit 10)

	Phase	Locus	Registration no.	Description
1.	4	045	75.494	Wheelmade; pure clay, very fine; nothing added; inclusions of grog (accidental); coarser material removed; ware: 7.5 YR 7/4 (pink); paint: 2.5 YR 4/4 (reddish brown) and 2.5 YR 2.5/2 (very dusky red).
2.	4	045	75.3958	Wheelmade; gray firing; clay soil, sand-sized mixed grains of chert, diabase quartz; no microfossils noted; source: possibly soil derived from pillow lavas; ware: 10 YR 7/3 (very pale brown); paint: 10 YR 3/2 (very dark grayish brown) and 2.5 YR 3/4 (dark reddish brown).
3.	4	045	73.9845	Wheelmade; grog and sand added; slipped and painted exterior; ware: 5 YR 6/6 (reddish yellow); slip: 10 YR 7/4 (very pale brown); paint: 5 YR 2.5/2 (dark reddish brown).
4.	4	045	73.9842	Wheelmade; very fine clay, few carbonates; ware: 2.5 Y 7/4 (pale yellow); paint: 5 YR 4/4 (reddish brown) and 5 YR 2.5/2 (dark reddish brown).
5.	4	045	73.3382	Wheelmade; grog, carbonate and some fine sand inclusions; ware: 7.5 YR 7/4 (pink); paint: 10 YR 3/1 (very dark gray).

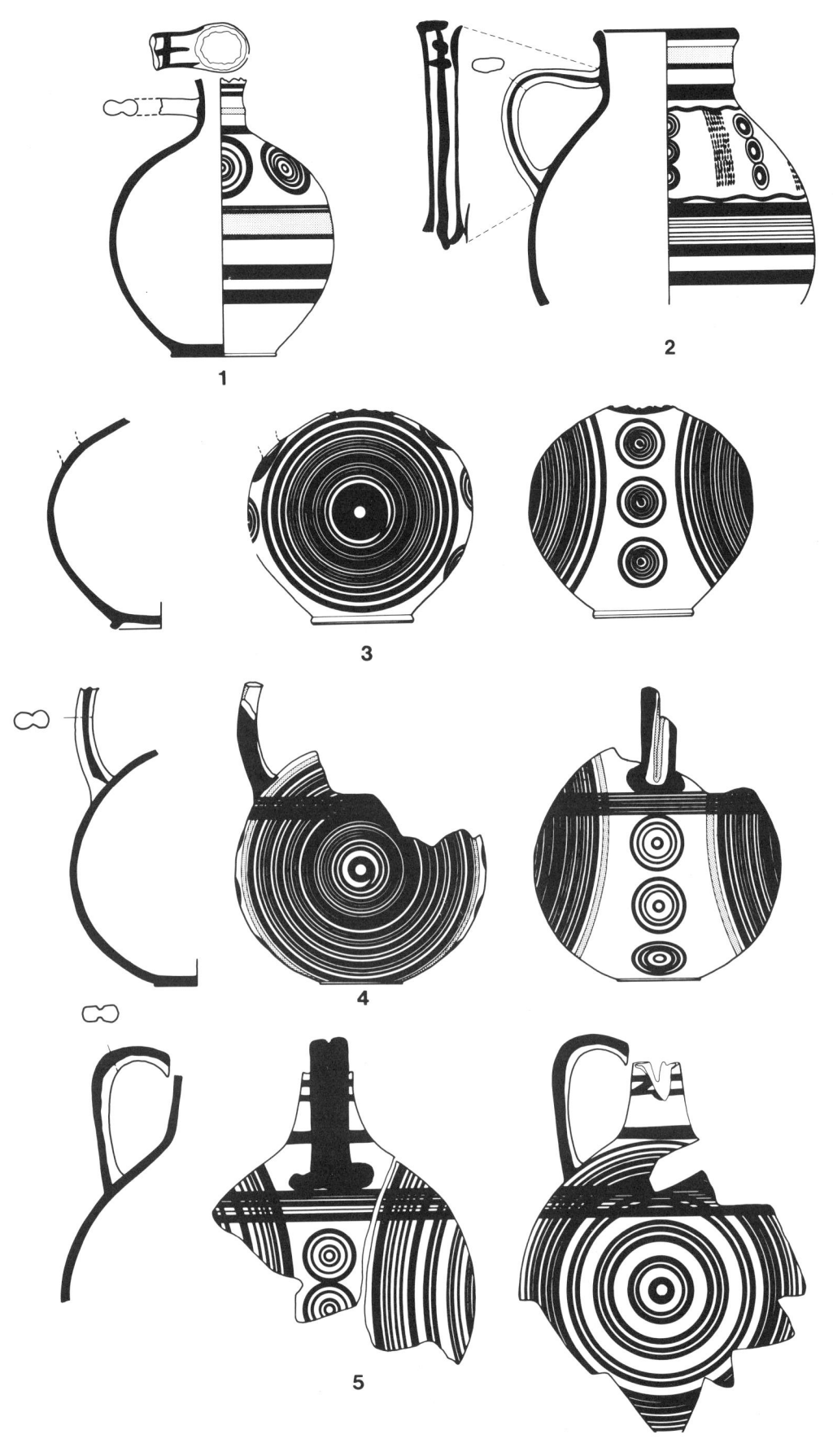

POTTERY GROUPS, WEST LOWER CITY DOMESTIC PRECINCT 101

Figure 2. Pottery from Idalion WNW 9/18 Locus 045 (Pit 10). Scale 1:5.

Figure 3. Pottery from Idalion WNW 9/18 Locus 045 (Pit 10)

	Phase	Locus	Registration no.	Description
1.	4	045	73.41	Wheelmade; medium grog and carbonate inclusions; ware: 7.5 YR 6/4 (light brown); paint: over most of body and thick band on rim 5 YR 5/4 (reddish brown) varying to 5 YR 3/2 (dark reddish brown), paint on handle and rest of rim 5 YR 2.5/1 (black).
2.	4	045	75.641	Wheelmade; very sandy mixed low carbonate content; ware: 5 YR 6/4 (light reddish brown); slip: 2.5 YR 4/6 (red); paint: 2.5 YR 2.5/2 (very dusky red).
3.	4	045	73.9772	Wheelmade; fine carbonate inclusions; ware: 5 YR 7/3 (pink); exterior slip: 10 YR 8/2 (white); paint: rim, bars on handle and bands on neck 5 YR 5/4 (reddish brown), circles and bands 10 R 3/1 (dark reddish gray).
4.	4	045	73.9765	Wheelmade; very fine sand and carbonate inclusions; ware: 10 YR 8/3 (very pale brown); paint: inner bands 2.5 YR 3/2 (dusky red), circles and outer bands 2.5 YR N 3/ (very dark gray).
5.	4	045	75.4140	Wheelmade; grog and sand marl clay; ware: 5 YR 6/4 (light reddish brown); paint: 5 YR 2.5/2 (dark reddish brown).
6.	4	045	73.9955	Wheelmade; medium grog and carbonate inclusions; ware: 7.5 YR 6/4 (light brown); paint over most of body and thick band on rim: 5 YR 5/4 (reddish brown) varying to 5 YR 3/2 (dark reddish brown), paint on handle and rest of rim 5 YR 2.5/1 (black).
7.	4	045	75.180	Wheelmade; coarse sand inclusions; ware: 5 Y 8/2 (white); paint: on spout 10 YR 3/1 (very dark gray), circles and bands 10 YR 5/1 (gray).

Figure 3. Pottery from Idalion WNW 9/18 Locus 045 (Pit 10). Scale 1:5.

Figure 4. Pottery from Idalion WNW 9/18 Locus 045 (Pit 10)

	Phase	Locus	Registration no.	Description
1.	4	045	75.380	Wheelmade; fine sand and carbonate inclusions; ware; 5 YR 6/6 (reddish yellow); exterior slip: 5 YR 8/2 (pinkish white); paint: 5 YR 3/3 (dark reddish brown).
2.	4	045	73.9993	Wheelmade; carbonate inclusions; ware: 5 Y 8/3 (pale yellow); paint: 7.5 YR 3/2 (dark brown).
3.	4	045	73.9768	Wheelmade; fine carbonate inclusions; ware: 10 YR 8/3 (very pale brown); exterior and inside rim slip: 2 YR 6/4 (light reddish brown); paint: thick bands and thin bands 10 YR 8/2 (white), medium bands: 10 YR 2.5/1 (black).
4.	4	045	75.11	Wheelmade; grog inclusions; ware: 10 YR 7/4 (very pale brown); paint: 7.5 YR 3/0 (very dark gray).
5.	4	045	75.2430	Wheelmade; fine sand and carbonate inclusions; ware: 7.5 YR 6/4 (light brown); exterior slip: 2.5 Y 8/2 (white); paint: circles and thick bands, 10 YR 3/1 (very dark gray), thin bands and wavy lines 2.5 YR 3/6 (dark red).
6.	4	045	73.9991	Wheelmade.
7.	4	045	73.7204	Wheelmade; few large grog inclusions; ware: 5 YR 7/6 (reddish yellow); paint: circle and band on body and innermost and outer-most bands on rim 7.5 YR N 4/ (dark gray), very faded, three inner bands on rim 10 YR 4/6 (red).
8.	4	045	73.9805	Wheelmade; grog and sand inclusions; ware: 5 Y 7/2 (light gray); paint: 10 YR 3/1 (very dark gray).
9.	4	045	75.2875	Wheelmade.
10.	4	045	75.158	Wheelmade; fine sand and grog inclusions; ware: 5 Y 7/2 (light gray); paint: thin bands 2.5 YR 4/2 (weak red), thick bands 5 YR 3/1 (very dark gray).
11.	4	045	75.652	Wheelmade; fine carbonate and sand, coarse grog inclusions; ware: 10 YR 7/4 (very pale brown); interior and exterior slip: 2.5 YR 7/4 (pale yellow); paint: thick bands on rim 5 YR 3/1 (very dark gray), thin bands on rim and thick band below rim 2.5 YR 3/4 (dark reddish brown).

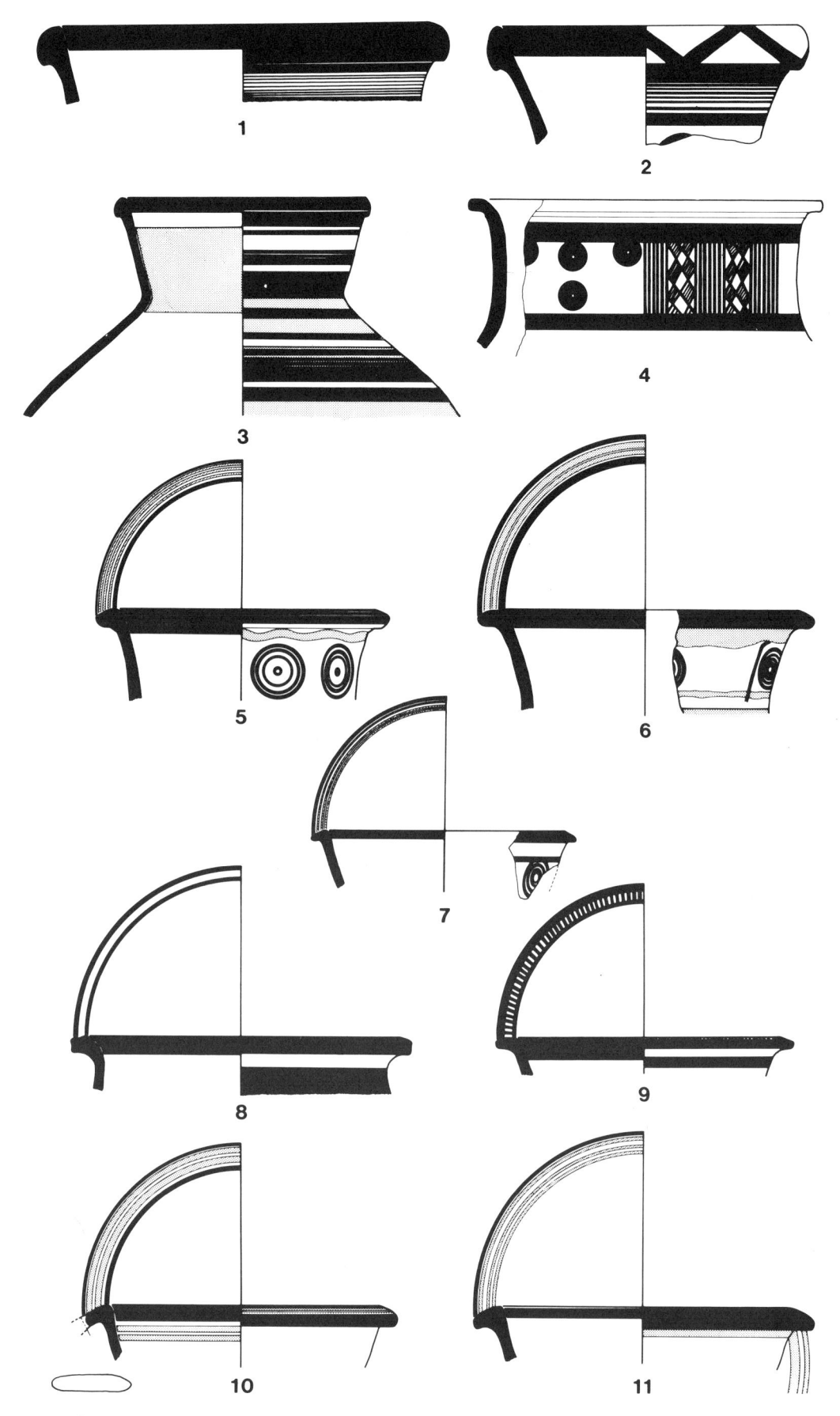

Figure 4. Pottery from Idalion WNW 9/18 Locus 045 (Pit 10). Scale 1:5.

Figure 5. Pottery from Idalion WNW 9/18 Locus 045 (Pit 10)

	Phase	Locus	Registration no.	Description
1.	4	045	75.2358	Wheelmade; very gritty paste, many fine sand and carbonate inclusions; ware: 10 YR (7/3 (very pale brown).
2.	4	045	73.9791	Wheelmade; gritty paste with fine sand inclusions; ware: 5 Y 8/2 (white); paint: 10 YR 3/1 (very dark gray).
3.	4	045	73.9811	Wheelmade.
4.	4	045	73.9935	Wheelmade.
5.	4	045	75.22(?)1	Wheelmade; fine carbonate inclusions; ware; 5 YR 7/6 (reddish yellow); slipped and burnished interior and exterior: 10 R 5/6 (red); paint: 2.5 YR N 2.5/ (black).
6.	4	045	75.857	Wheelmade; fine sand, grog and carbonate inclusions; ware: 10 YR 7.5 8/3 (very pale brown); paint: 7.5 YR N 3/ (very dark gray); 2 string holes.
7.	4	045	75.1364	Wheelmade; few fine carbonate inclusions; ware: 7.5 YR 7/6 (reddish yellow); slipped interior and exterior: 10 YR 8/3 (very pale brown); paint; 5 YR 3/3 (dark reddish brown).
8.	4	045	75.708	Wheelmade; gritty paste, many fine carbonate inclusions; ware: 5 Y 7/2 (light gray); exterior slip: 2.5 Y 7/6 (yellow); paint: 10 YR 3/1 (very dark gray).
9.	4	045	75.227	Wheelmade; sand and carbonate inclusions; ware; 10 YR 8/3 (very pale brown); paint: 5 YR 3/1 (very dark gray).
10.	4	045	75.204	Wheelmade; fine to medium sand and grog inclusions; ware; 7.5 YR 6/4 (light brown); exterior slip: 7.5 YR 8/2 (pinkish white); paint: 5 YR 3/1 (very dark gray).
11.	4	045	75.2198	Wheelmade; ware; 5 YR 6/4 (light reddish brown); slip over body: 2.5 Y 8/4 (pale yellow); paint: thin bands on rim and inside 5 YR 4/1 (dark gray), thick band 10 R 5/4 (weak red).
12.	4	045	75.4534	Wheelmade; gritty paste with many fine sand and carbonate inclusions; ware; 10 YR 6/3 (pale brown); paint: 5 YR 3/1 (very dark gray).
13.	4	045	75.811	Wheelmade; mainly fine sand, few coarse carbonate inclusions; ware: 10 YR 8/3 (very pale brown); paint: 10 YR 3/1 (very dark gray).
14.	4	045	75.202	Wheelmade; fine carbonate inclusions; ware: 10 YR 7/4 (very pale brown); interior slip: 2.5 YR 6/4 (light reddish brown); paint: interior band 2.5 YR 3/4 (dark reddish brown), exterior bands 5 YR 3/1 (very dark gray).

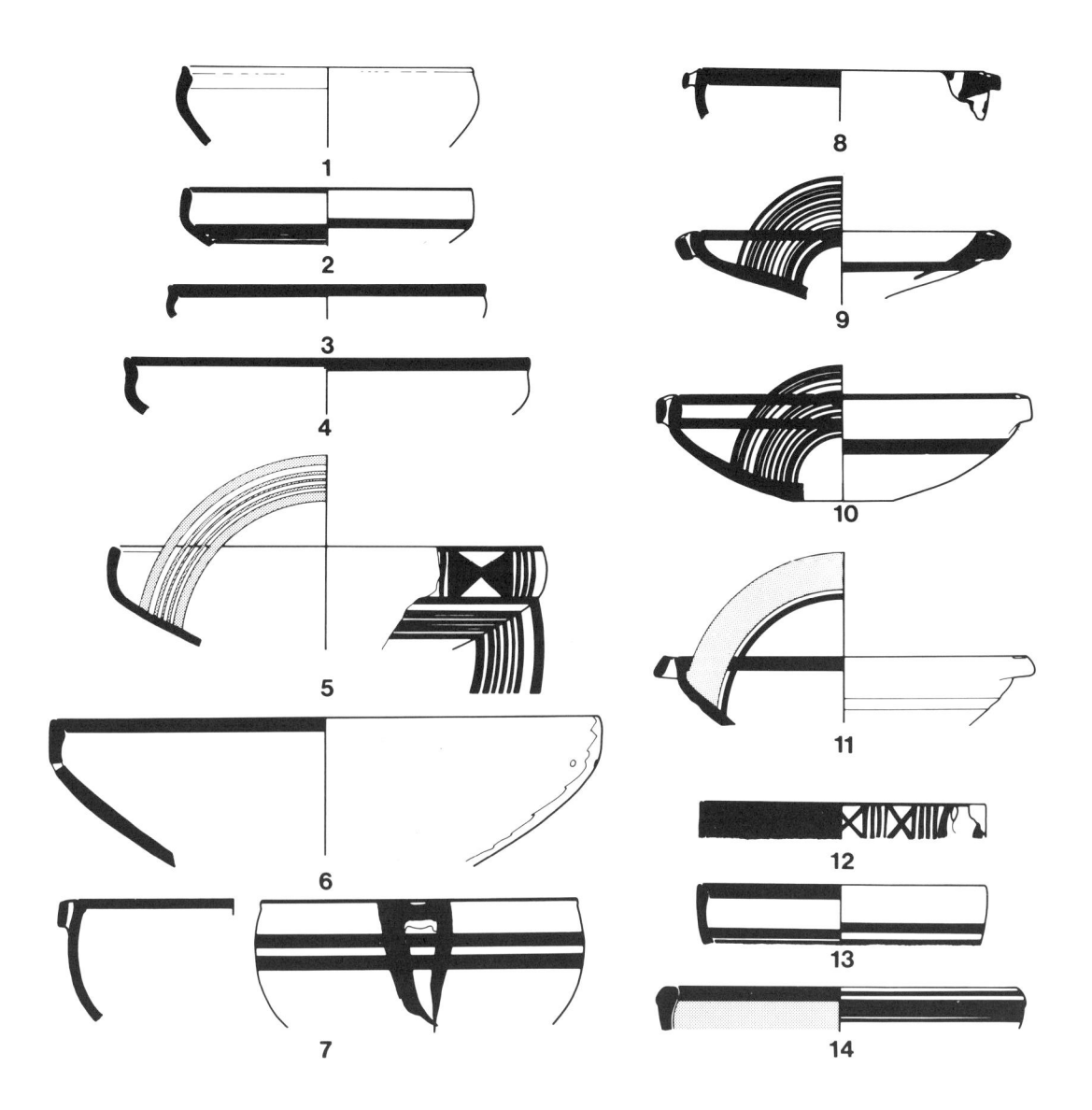

Figure 5. Pottery from Idalion WNW 9/18 Locus 045 (Pit 10). Scale 1:5.

Figure 5. Pottery from Idalion WNW 9/18 Locus 045 (Pit 10) (*cont.*)

	Phase	Locus	Registration no.	Description
15.	4	045	73.9893	Wheelmade; medium to coarse grog and carbonate inclusions; ware: 10 YR 7/4 (very pale brown); paint: 7.5 YR N 4/ (dark gray).
16.	4	045	73.9877	Wheelmade; carbonate and grog inclusions; ware; 10 YR 7/3 (very pale brown).
17.	4	045	75.2513	Wheelmade; fine sand and grog inclusions; ware: 5 YR 7/4 (pink).
18.	4	045	75.144	Wheelmade; fine to coarse carbonate inclusions; ware: 2.5 YR 6/4 (light reddish brown).
19.	4	045	73.9927	Wheelmade; fine sand and grog inclusions; ware; 5 YR 7/6 (reddish yellow); exterior slip: 10 YR 8/3 (very pale brown).
20.	4	045	75.1360	Wheelmade; medium grog and carbonate inclusions; ware: 10 YR 8/3 (very pale brown).
21.	4	045	75.2155	Wheelmade; fine sand inclusions; ware; 10 YR 8/4 (very pale brown).
22.	4	045	75.4138	Wheelmade; extremely fine sand inclusions; ware: 2.5 Y 8/6 (yellow).
23.	4	045	75.2311	Wheelmade; very fine paste; ware; 5 YR 7/6 (reddish yellow); slip inside bowl and on rim: 10 R 5/6 (red).
24.	4	045	75.2702	Wheelmade.
25.	4	045	75.2448	Wheelmade; fine clay with dense rounded gray inclusions; ware: 5 YR 6/2 (pinkish gray), fired 10 R 6/3 (pale red); self slip 5 YR 7/4 (pink).
26.	4	045	75.741	Wheelmade; fine sand and grog inclusions, few large carbonates; ware; 5 YR 6/4 (light reddish brown); exterior slip: 5 YR 8/3 (pink).
27.	4	045	73.9939	Wheelmade; coarse grog and fine sand inclusions; ware; 10 YR 8/4 (very pale brown).
28.	4	045	75.7403	Wheelmade; medium to coarse grog inclusions; ware: 5 YR 6/6 (reddish yellow).

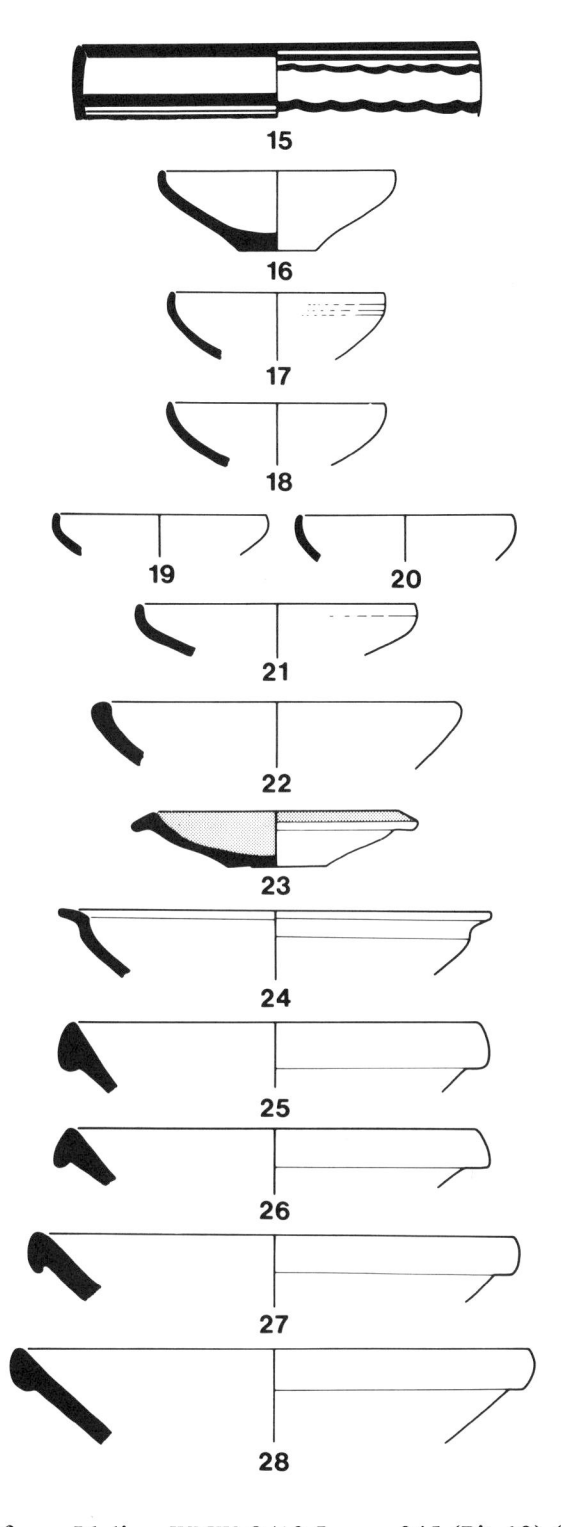

Figure 5. Pottery from Idalion WNW 9/18 Locus 045 (Pit 10) (*cont.*). Scale 1:5.

Figure 6. Pottery from Idalion WNW 9/18 Locus 045 (Pit 10)

	Phase	Locus	Registration no.	Description
1.	4	045	73.9811 = 9963	Handmade; many coarse carbonate inclusions; ware; 10 YR 4/1 (dark gray).
2.	4	045	75.2860	Handmade; fine sand, some coarse carbonate inclusions; ware: 5 YR 6/8 (reddish yellow); exterior possibly slipped: 5 YR 8/4 (pink).
3.	4	045	75.3169	Wheelmade; coarse grog and carbonate inclusions; ware: 5 YR 6/6 (reddish yellow).
4.	4	045	73.9959/1	Handmade; coarse grog inclusions; ware: 5 YR 5/4 (reddish brown); vessel partly darkened by smoke.
5.	4	045	75.674	Wheelmade; many coarse inclusions of carbonate and diabase; ware: 5 Y 6/3 (pale olive).
6.	4	045	75.9848	Wheelmade; extremely fine paste, no visible inclusions; very delicate hard-fired ware: 7.5 YR 6/4 (light brown); exterior slip: 10 YR 7/4 (very pale brown); paint: 10 YR 3/1 (very dark gray).
7.	4	045	75.87	Wheelmade; carbonate and grog inclusions; ware: 2.5 YR 6/8 (light red); paint: circles and thin bands 2.5 YR N 3/ (very dark gray), thick band 10 R 5/6 (red).
8.	4	045	75.4035	Wheelmade; extremely fine paste, no visible inclusions; very delicate hard-fired ware: 7.5 YR 7/6 (reddish yellow); paint: 5 YR 3/2 (dark reddish brown).
9.	4	045	73.10,009	Handmade; very fine paste, no visible inclusions; ware; 2.5 YR 6/6 (light red); overall slip: 10 YR 8/3 (white); lamp spout fragment.
10.	4	045	73.9880	Handmade; very fine paste, no visible inclusions; ware: 5 YR 6/6 (reddish yellow); fugitive overall slip: 2.5 Y 8/2 (white); lamp spout fragment.
11.	4	045	75.1857	Wheelmade; very fine paste, fine carbonate inclusions; ware: 5 YR 6/4 (light reddish brown); paint: rim and 3rd band 2.5 YR 5/6 (red), 2nd and 4th band pale turquoise.
12.	4	045	75.4047	Wheelmade; fine carbonate inclusions; ware: 7.5 YR 7/4 (pink); paint: diagonals 7.5 YR N4/ (dark gray), traces of paint above diagonals 2.5 YR 5/4 (reddish brown).
13.	4	045	73.10,007	Wheelmade; very fine paste with very small carbonate inclusions; ware: 5 YR 7/3 (pink); slip inside and out: 10 YR 8/2 (white); paint: thin bands 2.5 YR N 3/ (very dark gray), thick band 2.5 YR 5/4 (reddish brown).

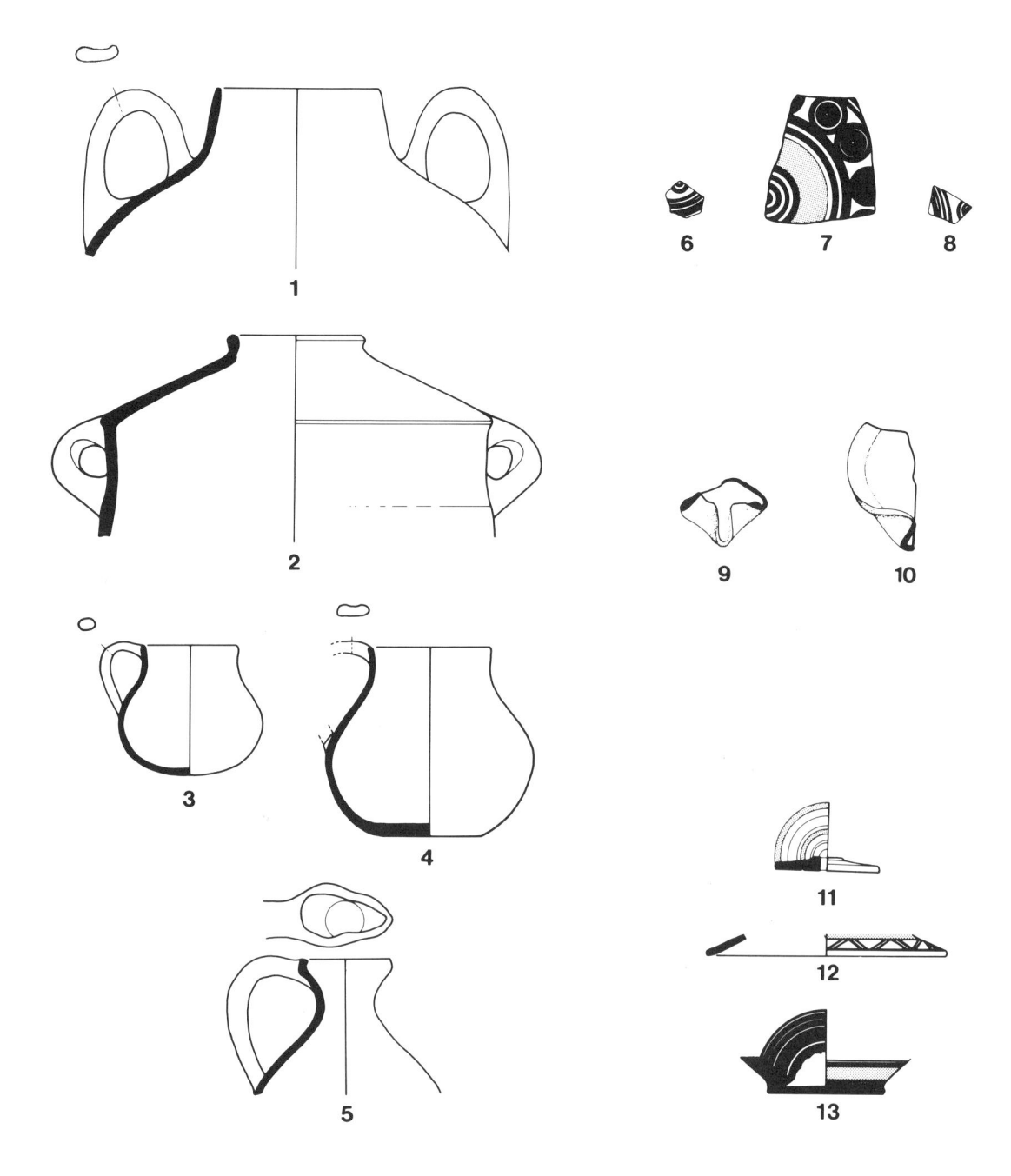

Figure 6. Pottery from Idalion WNW 9/18 Locus 045 (Pit 10). Scale 1:5

Figure 6. Pottery from Idalion WNW 9/18 Locus 045 (Pit 10) (*cont.*)

	Phase	Locus	Registration no.	Description
14.	4	045	75.1082	Wheelmade; fine carbonate inclusions; ware: 5 YR 7/4 (pink); overall slip: 2.5 Y 7/4 (pale yellow).
15.	4	045	75.5	Wheelmade; grog and quartz inclusions; ware: 2.5 YR 5/4 (reddish brown).
16.	4	045	75.510	Wheelmade; fine carbonate and grog inclusions; ware: 5 YR 6/4 (light reddish brown).
17.	4	045	75.2967	Wheelmade; no visible inclusions; ware: 10 YR 7/4 (very pale brown).
18.	4	045	75.825	Wheelmade; coarse carbonate and fine grog inclusions; ware: 5 YR 6/3 (light reddish brown); core: 5 YR 6/1 (gray).
19.	4	045	75.8251	Wheelmade.
20.	4	045	75.9800	Wheelmade; many fine carbonate inclusions; ware: 7 YR 6/4 (light brown); exterior slip: 2.5 Y 8/2 (white).
21.	4	045	73.9768	Wheelmade; many coarse carbonate inclusions; ware; 10 YR 7/3 (very pale brown); overall exterior slip: 5 YR 6/6 (reddish yellow); paint: thin bands and handles 5 YR 3/2 (dark reddish brown), thin bands 10 YR 8/2 (white).

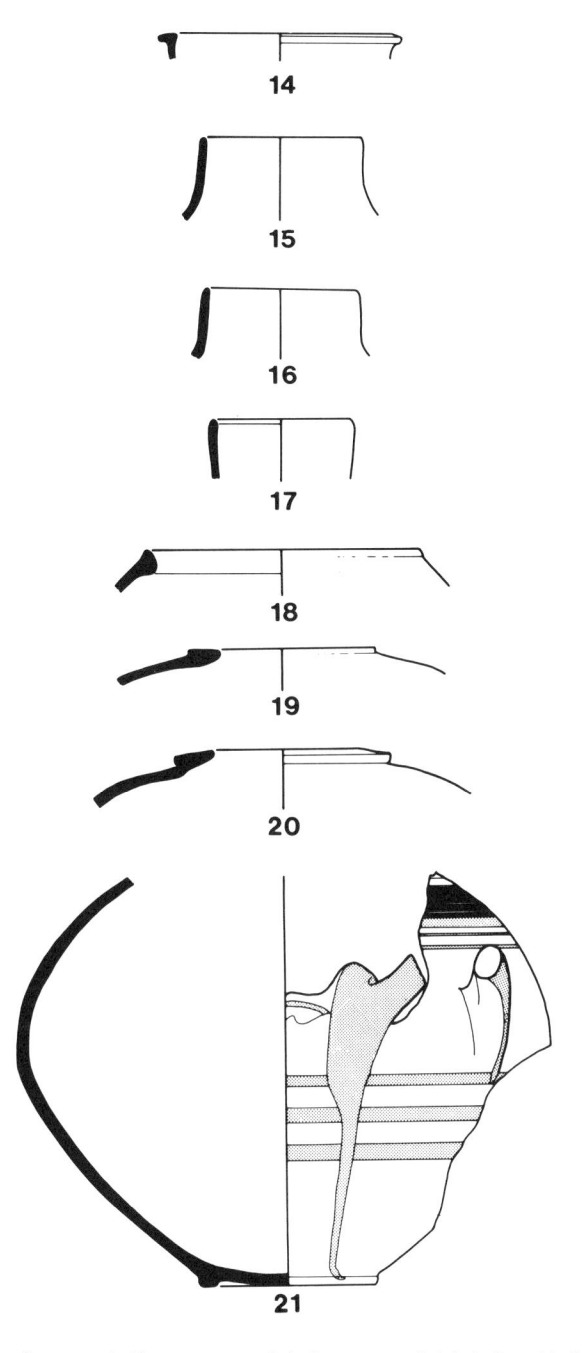

Figure 6. Pottery from Idalion WNW 9/18 Locus 045 (Pit 10) (*cont.*). Scale 1:5.

PLATE 1

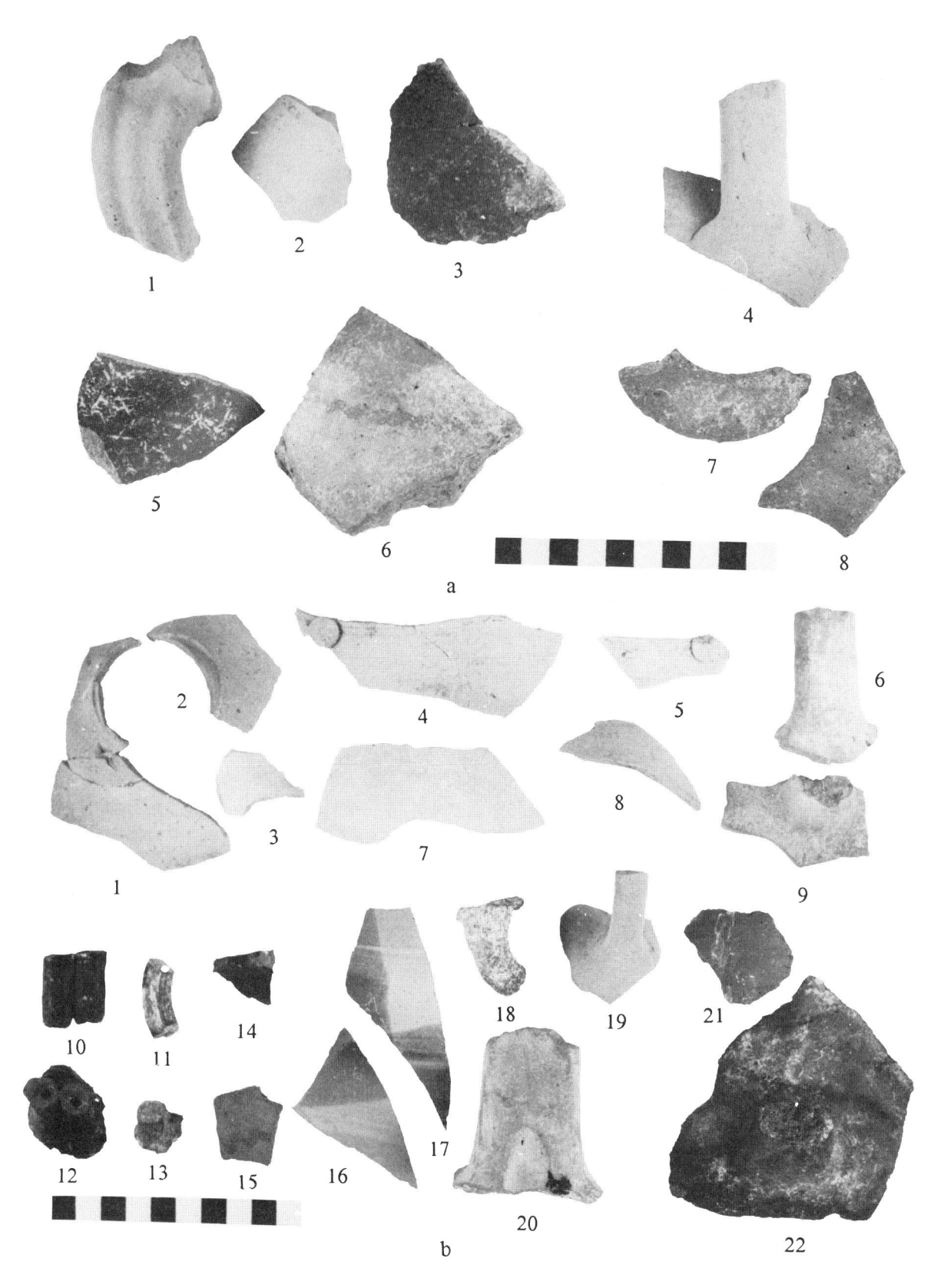

Pottery Sherds from Idalion WNW 10/18. a. 1-3, Locus 005, PB 5; 5-6, Locus 005, PB 7; 4, 7-8, Locus 010, PB 24. b. 1-9, Locus 009, PB 15; 10-22, Locus 009, PB 18.

PLATE 2

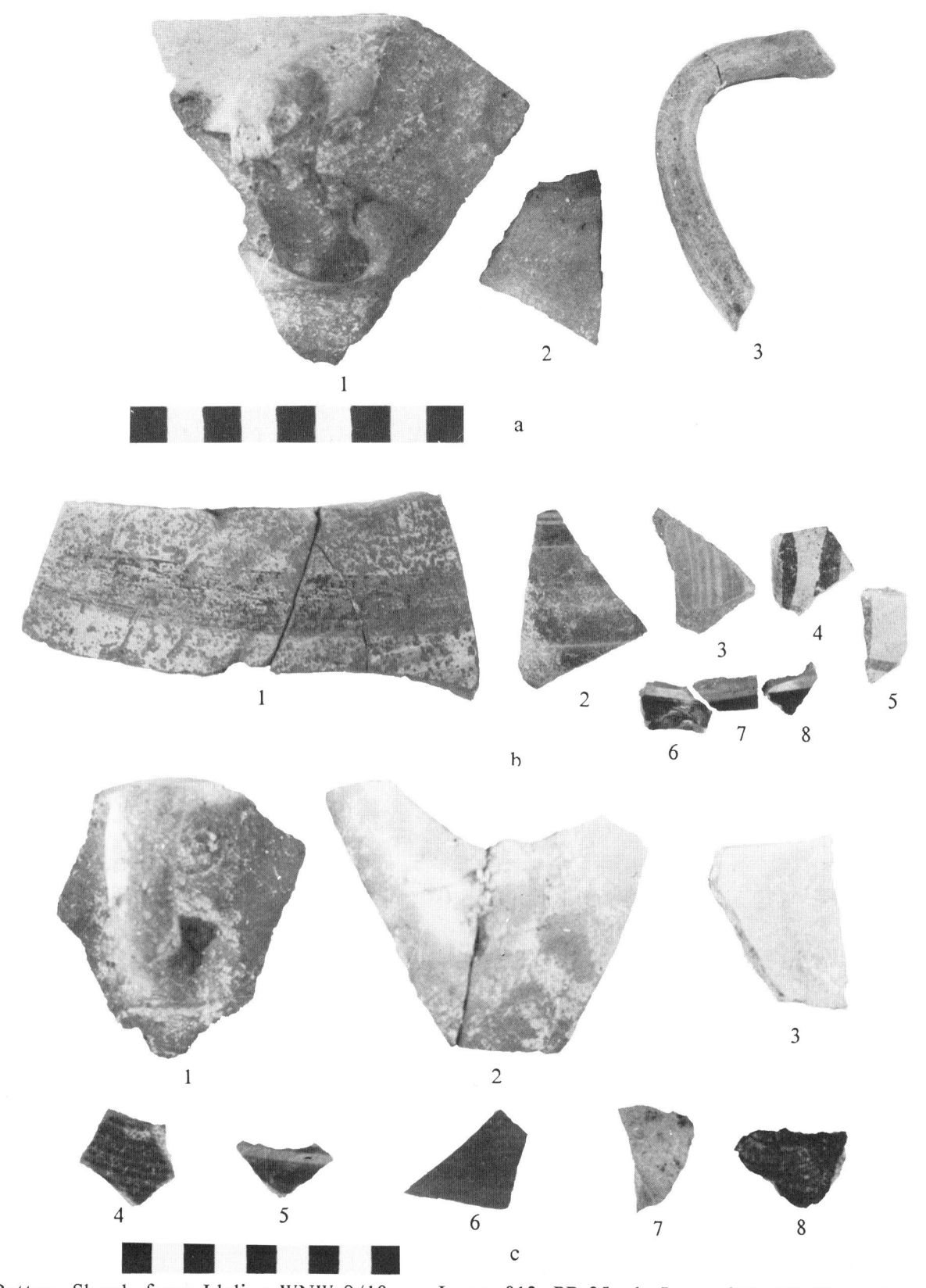

Pottery Sherds from Idalion WNW 9/18. a. Locus 012, PB 25. b. Locus 017, PB 30. c. Locus 018, PB 45.

PLATE 3

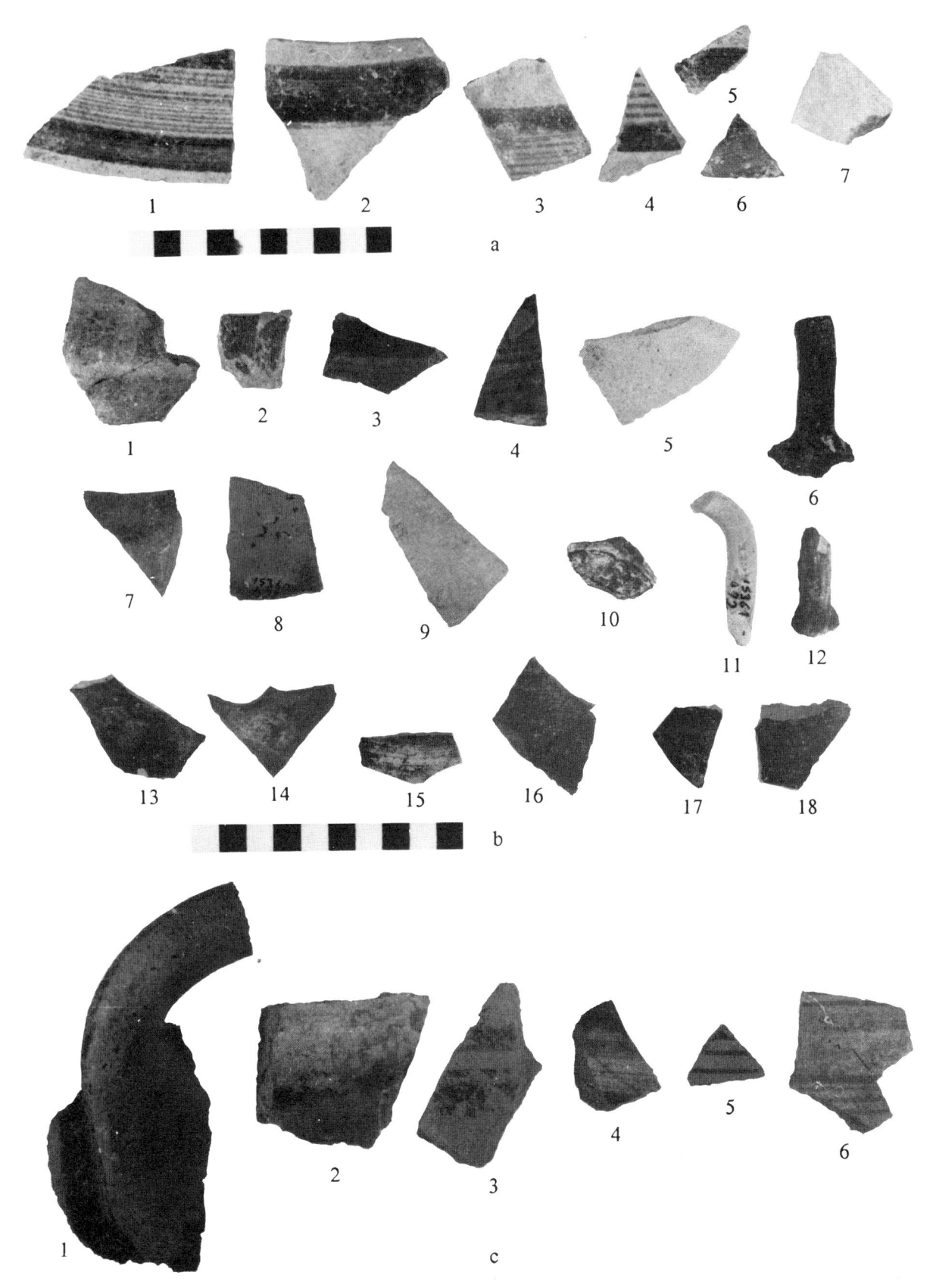

Pottery Sherds from Idalion WNW 9/18. a. and b. Locus 022, Layer 1, PB 39. c. Locus 026, PB 43.

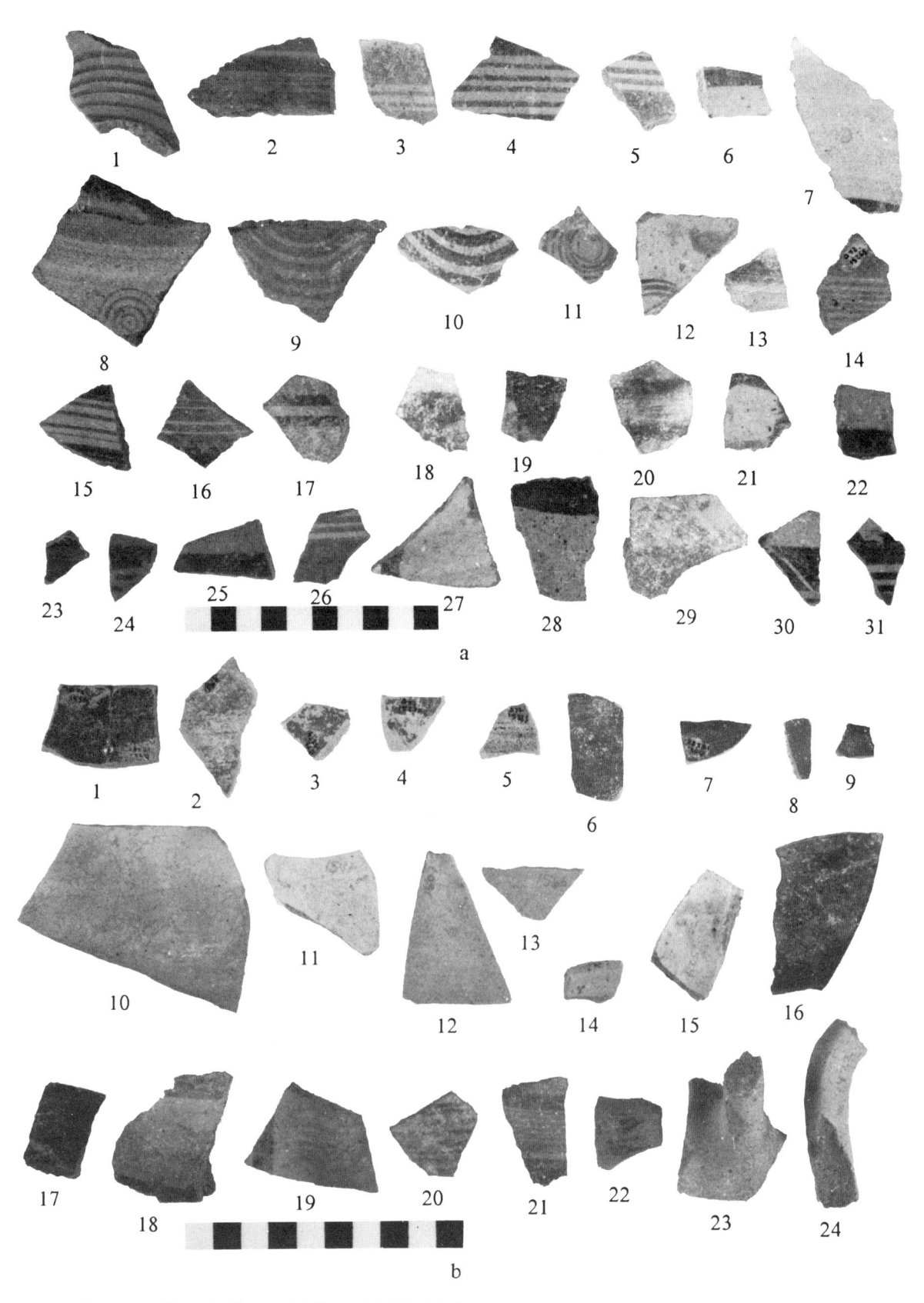

PLATE 4

Pottery Sherds from Idalion WNW 9/18. a. and b. Locus 022, Layer 3, PB 42.

PLATE 5

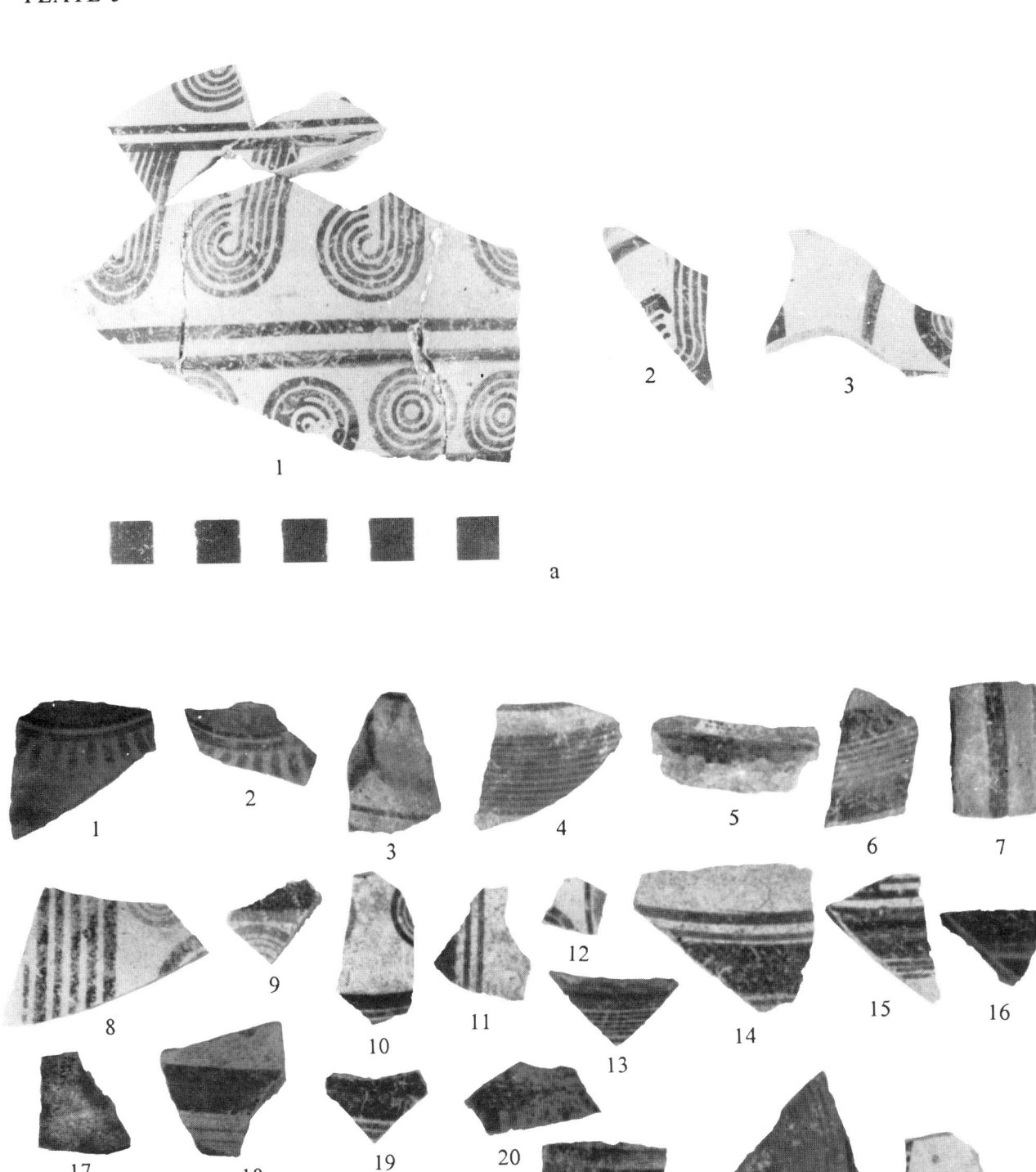

Pottery Sherds from Idalion WNW 9/19. a. and b. Locus 011, PB 13.

C. A LATE CYPRIOT IIC TOMB: IDALION TOMB 1.76

1. INTRODUCTION AND SKELETAL REMAINS

*Carola C. Schulte-Campbell**

Introduction

During the 1976 field season, at the request of the Department of Antiquities of Cyprus, the Idalion Expedition undertook several salvage projects. One of these was a Late Cypriot II tomb, designated Id Tomb 1.76. The tomb was discovered when a Dhali resident found a hole leading to a subterranean structure in an open lot. Recognizing its archaeological significance, he reported it to Dr. V. Karageorghis, who identified the structure as a tomb.

Idalion Tomb 1.76 is the oldest feature excavated to date by the American Idalion Project. It was also the first tomb found at the site which had not been looted by Cesnola, although unfortunately the fragmented state of the bones and associated grave goods give evidence that it had been plundered in antiquity. Despite the poor condition of the skeletal material, it is an important find, as it represents the only surviving human remains at Idalion.

Methodology

The hole that led to the discovery of the tomb broke through what appears to have been the ceiling of the chamber. This tiny hole was only 43 cm in diameter. The fill within the tomb lay approximately 25 cm below the opening, and in this small space the slope of the tomb ceiling was visible. It slanted gently away from the opening, suggesting that there was a fair-sized chamber below. The first step was to lay out the lines of north/south and east/west vertical sections, dividing the tomb into quadrants. Excavation was then begun, but at a depth of 50 cm it was necessary to enlarge the opening in order to permit further access to the tomb. The southeast quadrant fill was removed to a depth of approximately 50 cm to expose the north/south and east/west profiles.

At this point we stopped, recorded the vertical sections, and proceeded to remove the southwest quadrant to the same level. We continued with this procedure in the south half, until we reached the bottom of the chamber. After completion of the east/west section drawing, the fill in the north side of the tomb was removed in the same manner.

Tomb Description

The Idalion tomb was located on the southern rampart of the village proper. It lay northwest of the intersection of the Larnaca-Nicosia Road with the road leading to the center of Dhali. Ohnefalsch-Richter (1893:344) reported twenty-six tombs in this area. He noted that these were "older than Idalion," by which he probably meant that they dated to the Late Cypriot period. The existence of these other tombs makes it logical to assume that Id Tomb 1.76 was once part of a cemetery, although its association with a settlement is still unknown.

The tomb was relatively small and simple. It consisted of an entrance passage and a circular chamber cut into occupation debris and marl bedrock (see fig. 1). The symmetry of the chamber was the only aspect of tomb construction that showed care. It had no internal structures and the walls had no plaster facing. The tomb's maximum measurements were 2.60 m north to south and 2.38 m east to west, and approximately 1.5 m in depth from the original ground surface from which it was dug. The Idalion tomb appears to be neither one of the

---

*Anthropology Department, University of Connecticut, Storrs, Connecticut

larger and more elaborate chamber tombs, nor one of the simple pit or shaft tombs--the two basic types found during this period. Two other tombs of this intermediate form have been reported, Tombs 2 and 3 at Akhera (Karageorghis 1965).

During the looting processes the tomb fill was mixed. However it was possible, on the basis of content, to define four loci. These are described as follows:

Locus 001 included all the occupation debris, both that into which the tomb had been dug and that which had developed outside its limits after its construction. This debris consisted of a hard and compact sand that could be removed only with the aid of a handpick. The Munsell color reading was 10YR 6/4. The cultural material in this fill differed from that found in the other loci in that it represented settlement debris, including animal bones, utilitarian pottery, charcoal, and so forth.

Locus 002 was the uppermost layer found within the tomb. The soil was less compact than the occupation debris. The Munsell reading was the same--10YR 6/4. This was the smallest of the loci, measuring 0.47 m in depth. The east/west dimension at maximum was 1.38 m. It was difficult to evaluate its north/south dimension as the section had been placed arbitrarily at the outset of the excavation, and fell somewhat off center. The maximum measurement we obtained was 1.62 m.

Locus 002 contained a high concentration of cultural material, including 10 pottery buckets, 9 bone bags, several ivory fragments, and 5 metal fragments.[1] The ceramics and the skeletal material in this locus were extremely fragmented, more so than in the lower layers. Only one long bone, a femur found in the northwest corner, was in reasonably good condition.

Locus 003 was the second layer found in the tomb. This locus was 0.58 m deep and measured 1.75 m maximum east to west. In the plane of the arbitrary north/south section the maximum width was 2 m. The soil in this layer was the same as in the previous one, a moderately compacted sand, with a 10YR 6/4 Munsell color reading. The cultural material contained in Locus 003, however, differed greatly from that in Locus 002. In all, 10 pottery buckets were recovered. There was a smaller quantity of less fragmentary ceramics. The skeletal material was also less concentrated, and was better preserved. Fifteen bone buckets were recorded for Locus 003 (5 or 6 of these contained only a few fragments or a single large bone fragment that had to be packed separately). A number of large crania and long bone pieces were found, adhering to the southern wall of the tomb. The northern half of the tomb had a lower concentration of osteological material. The only other cultural material found was 7 metal fragments.

Locus 004 was the largest layer, measuring 0.72 m in depth and 2.25 m east to west. This bottom layer of tomb fill consisted of loose sand and contained a large number of pillow lavas. The fill was a shade darker than that in the previous loci. The condition and percentage of cultural material was similar to that of 003; 22 pottery buckets and 18 bone bags were recorded. Crania and long bone fragments were again found along the southern wall, but these were fewer than in the previous layer. Many objects were found in this lower layer, including a bronze ring (pls. 29 and 30), a cylinder seal (see Adelman, figs. 15, 16; pls. 15, 16), a black amphora juglet, several ivory fragments, and 9 pieces of metal, 8 of which were extremely fragmentary.

The pillow lavas in Locus 004 presented the most unusual problem in the tomb stratigraphy. This stone is usually used in construction, as pillow lavas are uniform and oval in shape. There seems to be no logical reason why there should have been such rockfall in the bottom layer of the tomb, since the tomb was a cut and not a built tomb, and there was no internal construction in it.

---

[1] Ten-quart buckets and 12-quart ceramics bags were used in the analysis of pottery and bone. The actual quantity in each unit, however, varied according to the size and shape of the material collected.

The major differences between the loci were differences of content, due to the disturbances caused by looting. It was not possible, however, to discern whether these content differences indicated temporal sequences. It was not possible to determine stratigraphically whether the burials were all contemporary, or whether this tomb was used for a succession of interments.

The condition of the contents of each locus gives some indication of the possible looting practices. Locus 002 was more disturbed than the others, and the skeletal and ceramic material was more fragmented. This may indicate that the top fill was removed during the plundering. Once some of the dirt was removed, it would have been possible to search the remainder by shifting it within the tomb. Under these circumstances, the area around the walls would have been the least accessible, and, indeed, it was found that in the Idalion tomb the bones and grave goods were least fragmentary around the south and west walls. Such looting techniques would have expended less time and energy than the removal and redisposition of all the fill. They would not have allowed for thorough examination of the tomb contents, however, nor made possible complete recovery of valuable items. The Idalion tomb supports this hypothesis concerning looting practices, for various goods were left behind--such goods as ivory fragments, a copper(?) ring, a cylinder seal, metal fragments, and imported ceramics.

Analysis of the human remains indicated that there were at least 21 persons interred in the tomb. This number included nine children and twelve adults, ranging in age from newborn through middle or old age. It is hypothesized that both males and females were represented in the group. The results of the study of this skeletal material will be presented in greater detail below.

Skeletal Remains

Idalion Tomb 1.76 was the first to be excavated by the American Dhali project. The skeletal remains contained therein are the only human remains recovered by this expedition at urban Idalion thus far. Because these provide our first knowledge of the Late Cypriot population, these fragmentary osteological materials have assumed an importance they might otherwise not have had.[2]

Material and Methods

The excavation recovered many thousands of bone fragments, but only those that were identifiable as part of a specific bone have been used in this analysis. In the final phases of this study, less than 25 percent of the 5,000 such identifiable bones were found to be informative.

Though the skeletal material had been churned up and broken, climatic and other natural factors of preservation were favorable, so that the osteological fabric remained in excellent condition. As it was not possible to distinguish individual skeletons, the analysis was made and will be presented by bone type. It should be noted that, due to the fragmented state of the bones, systematic anthropometric measurements could not be taken.

Human Dentition

The dental remains were the best preserved of the skeletal material. As a result of careful excavation techniques, over 400 teeth were recovered, both individually and in their bone sockets. The dental evidence played the primary role in determining the number and relative ages of the tomb's population.

---

[2] I should like to acknowledge the help of Dr. W. S. Laughlin, who kindly provided me with laboratory facilities and access to a large comparative skeletal collection.

The study of the dentition entailed several different analyses. Initially, the teeth were separated from the jaw fragments and subdivided into age groups: deciduous, adult, and in the case of certain individual teeth, unerupted. Each group was then analyzed for the following variables: 1) tooth type, 2) tooth location (maxillary or mandibular), 3) amount of wear, and 4) recognizable pathologies or anomalies.

The use of tooth wear in the aging of skeletons has been much debated. The major problem in using this technique is that it is highly population specific. Brothwell (1963:69) established age classifications for premedieval British molars. No such standards have been set for the Late Bronze populations in Cyprus. Thus, the present study employed tooth wear as a very relative and supplementary aging technique that allowed for some differentiation between individuals. The amount of wear was rated on a scale of one to three as follows:

Grade 1)   Enamel on the occlusal surface of the tooth showed either no wear or only slight use, with minor pitting.
Grade 2)   Enamel was increasingly pitted and cusps showed definite wear.
Grade 3)   Dentine was exposed, with the enamel very worn or gone. The cusps were very worn, in extreme cases down to the gum line, almost to the neck where the roots began.

Results of Analysis of Individual Teeth

The results of the analyses of adult teeth are presented in table 1. In cases where the condition of the tooth made it impossible to determine whether it was mandibular or maxillary, it was classified as miscellaneous. For all tooth types except canines, the ratio of upper to lower teeth was correct. The results of the wear analysis indicated that the largest number of teeth of each type were in the Grade 1 group, with varying representation in the other wear categories. For example, incisors and canines were more numerous in Grade 2 than in Grade 3: molars and premolars were more numerous in Grade 3 than in Grade 2.

In studying the individual teeth, it was possible to identify two persons on the basis of unusual wear patterns. The first, characterized by very large and very worn teeth, was represented by a premolar (miscellaneous) and 3 molars (2 maxillary and 1 mandibular). Although tooth size is not usually used to determine sex, the extremely large size of these teeth makes it probable that this individual was male. The second individual was characterized by small, very worn teeth with an uneven wear pattern. This individual was represented by 2 premolars (miscellaneous) and 2 molars (1 maxillary and the other mandibular). A number of teeth were found not yet fully developed. These unerupted teeth, which had probably been removed from their crypts during the looting process, were not counted in the total, since they may have not yet replaced their deciduous counterparts. Counting them would have given an inaccurate estimate of the number of individuals present in the tomb. The following list identifies the unerupted teeth found separated from their mandibular or maxillary crypts:

    Incisors   7
    Premolars   6
    Canines   0
    Molars   19

The results of the analyses of the children's teeth are presented in table 2. For two reasons no attempt was made to establish the number of children on the basis of individual teeth. First, inasmuch as tooth eruption occurs at different ages, not all the infants and children would have had all of their teeth. Thus, it would be impossible to tell where the limits of our collection of deciduous teeth left off and eruption had not yet occurred. Secondly, no maxillary fragments from children were recovered from the tomb, which explains why the vast majority of the individual teeth found were identified as maxillary. For the number and ages of the children we were therefore forced to rely upon the mandibular fragments.

Table 1. Analysis of Adult Individual Teeth

	Grade	1	2	3
Incisors				
Maxillary		20	8	14
Mandibular		17	9	9
Miscellaneous		8	6	2
Canines				
Maxillary		14	7	3
Mandibular		6	3	4
Miscellaneous		4	3	1
Premolars				
Maxillary		21	2	2
Mandibular		16	5	8
Miscellaneous		5	5	13
Molars				
Maxillary		27	5	12
Mandibular		21	13	15
Miscellaneous		3	1	2

Table 2. Analysis of Deciduous Individual Teeth

	Incisors	*Canines*	*Molars*
Maxillary	9	5	15
Mandibular	0	0	11
Miscellaneous	0	0	3

Analysis of Mandibular and Maxillary Fragments

This section will list and discuss the mandibular and maxillary fragments found in the tomb. A brief description will be given, along with the age and sex of the individual, based on these dental studies.[3] Each fragment was closely compared with other fragments, not only for reconstruction, but also for determining whether any of them came from the same individual. Due to fragmentation, however, it was not always possible to determine whether the adult maxillary and mandibular fragments matched.

---

[3] The analysis employed the tooth eruption standards of Schlour (1941).

A. Adult maxillary fragments

1. A maxilla found in two parts was reconstructed. It contains the dental arcade ranging from M1 on the right side to M2 on the left. Only the second premolars and first molars are present. There is very little wear on the teeth (Grade 1 on the attrition scale). The maxilla is very gracile. It represents a young adult, perhaps female, between late teens and mid-twenties in age (pl. 1a).

2. A right fragment was found with PM1, M1, and M2. There is little tooth wear (Grade 1) and the third molar does not appear to have erupted. The individual was probably between 15 and 25 years of age.

B. Adult mandibular fragments

1. A right mandible fragment was found containing PM2, M1, and M2. The M3 is just beginning to erupt. The mandible is of an intermediate size. The individual was probably between 17 and 20 years of age.

2. A right mandible fragment has M1 and M2, with M3 erupted but missing. The ramus is large and rugged and the teeth are very well worn (about Grade 3). This fragment represents an individual who was in mid-adult years and perhaps male.

3. A worn central and left mandible has no teeth remaining in the sockets. The preservation of the alveolar surface is so poor that it is impossible to tell whether the teeth were lost before or after death. The area around the second premolar seems to show some resorption, as if lost premortem. The incisor sockets seem better defined, which would indicate that their loss was postmortem. The ramus seems more gracile than in the previous specimen; however, it is impossible to determine whether this was a male or female.

4. A right mandible fragment has PM2 and M1. The teeth are somewhat worn (Grade 2), and no third molar socket is present. The ramus is small and gracile. The fragment represents an adult, perhaps female, in the mid-adult years.

5. Two mandible fragments

    (a) A right mandible fragment has the three molars in place. The teeth are in excellent condition; the M1 shows some tooth wear, but both the M2 and M3 have very little wear.

    (b) This left mandible fragment matches (a) in mandible width, tooth wear, and cusp pattern. It was therefore assumed to have come from the same individual as (a). This fragment contains the I2, C, PM1, PM2, and M1. The teeth show Grade 1 wear. The individual was probably a young adult in the late teens to mid-twenties.

6. A left fragment contains PM1, PM2, M1, and M2. The third molar has erupted, but was split off from the mandible fragment. The teeth show Grade 2 wear. The individual was in mid-adult years.

7. A right fragment contains the M1 and M2, which show Grade 2 wear. This represents an individual who was in mid-adult years.

8. A small left fragment has M2 and M3. The teeth are both small and worn; the second molar has Grade 2 wear and the third molar Grade 1 wear. On the basis of mandible and tooth size, this fragment is interpreted as representing a woman in mid-adult years.

9. A dental arcade ranges from the ramus on the left side through M1 on the right. It is a rugged mandible with large teeth. The M1 has definite wear (Grade 2), the M2 has some wear (Grade 1), and the M3 is only slightly worn (Grade 1). This represents an individual in the late teens to mid-twenties, perhaps male (pl. 1b).

C. Children's mandibular fragments

1. A left mandible was of a newborn or late fetal infant (pl. 1c).

2. A right infant mandible was found. No teeth had erupted, but the tooth sockets are developed. This may represent a child between 3 and 6 months of age.

3. A child's mandible contains almost the whole dental arcade. The M1 was just beginning to erupt, and the m2 is present. The child was approximately 5 years of age.

4. Two mandible fragments

    (a) A left mandible and ramus has all deciduous dentition. The M1 has not yet erupted.

    (b) A central area of a child's mandible has no teeth intact. The size indicates a child about 3 to 5 years of age. It was determined that (a) and (b) came from the same individual.

5. Two mandible fragments

    (a) A left and central mandibular fragment has its deciduous dentition. The permanent incisors, still in the crypts, have developed the cusp, but there are no roots. The child was approximately 6 or 7 years of age.

    (b) A small right central mandible fragment contains adult incisors that have not yet erupted and were in the same general state of eruption as that of the above fragment. It is likely that these two fragments came from the same individual.

6. Two mandible fragments

    (a) A left mandible fragment has the m2. The six-year molar (M1) was just about to erupt or had just erupted.

    (b) This central fragment contains the developing central and lateral incisors. The cusps are formed but no roots had grown, and it was not near the time of eruption. This would indicate a 6-year-old child, and may belong to the fragment.

7. A left mandible fragment of an infant was found. The cap of the m2 fragment was just beginning to develop, but was nowhere near the time of eruption. This infant was approximately 6 to 12 months old.

8. Two mandible fragments

    (a) A right fragment with the m1 is a mandible fairly well developed in size. The child was approximately 4 to 5 years of age.

    (b) A left central area of a child's mandible has the m1 intact. The deciduous incisors are missing, but the developing permanent ones can be seen. The cap of the incisor had not fully developed. The child was between 4 and 6 years of age, and it is likely that these two fragments are from the same individual.

9. The central and left part of a child's mandible was found with no teeth intact. The six-year-old molar socket is enlarged, and contained either a fully developed cap or a newly erupted tooth. This child was between 4 and 6 years old.

General Description of Teeth

A. Caries

For the most part the teeth were in excellent condition and very few carious lesions were found. The number of carious teeth for adults and children combined is as follows:

Incisors	2
Premolars	7
Canines	1
Molars	11

Twenty-one carious teeth out of 387 erupted teeth yields a 5.43 percent occurrence rate of carious lesions.

Healthy teeth seem to be characteristic of Cypriot populations. Angel (1953:424) indicates with regard to the Neolithic peoples at Khirokitia that "The good condition and relatively little worn state of the teeth may speculatively be brought back to genetic factors, as well as the major factor of diet and food preparation." The Late Bronze group at Bamboula confirms this, averaging only 0.1 carious lesion per individual (Angel 1972).

B. Carabelli's cusps

Three adult molars exhibited Carabelli's cusps. Carabelli's cusp, known also as tuberaculum anomale, is a lateral tubercle located on the anterior surface of a first or second maxillary molar (Bass 1971:230). It occurs in varying proportions in different populations (higher in Caucasian groups) and is believed to be essentially nonfunctional. Carabelli's cusps have also been observed in the Late Bronze Age population at Kition (2 individuals); however, none were found at Hala Sultan Tekke, Akhera, or Pendayia (Schwartz 1974c:160). Carabelli's cusps were found in only 2.5 percent of the 121 adult molars from Id Tomb 1.76.

Summary of Tooth Analysis

In order to determine the number of individuals in this tomb, and, where possible, their age and sex, it was necessary to synthesize all the data from the individual teeth and bone frag-

Table 3. Results of Analysis of All Adult Dentition

Grade	1	2	3
Incisors			
Maxillary	20	8	14
Mandibular	18	9	9
Miscellaneous	8	6	2
Canines			
Maxillary	14	7	3
Mandibular	7	3	4
Miscellaneous	4	3	1
Premolars			
Maxillary	24	2	2
Mandibular	19	8	8
Miscellaneous	5	5	13
Molars			
Maxillary	31	5	12
Mandibular	30	21	17
Miscellaneous	3	1	2

Table 4. Wear Categories by Tooth Type

Grade	1	2	3
Incisors	46	23	25
Canines	25	13	8
Premolars	48	15	23
Molars	64	27	31

Table 5. Number of Persons Represented

Grade	1	2	3
Incisors	5.75	2.875	3.125
Canines	6.25	3.25	2.0
Premolars	6.0	1.875	2.875
Molars	6.4	2.7	3.1
Average	6	3	3

ments. Table 3 gives the total number of teeth in each category. To estimate the number of persons present, the maxillary, mandibular, and miscellaneous classifications were pooled (table 4). These figures were then divided by the number of teeth of each type to be found in an adult, except for the molar category. Third molars, which erupt late in maturation, are unpredictable, and two or even all four may not be present. Due to their genetic instability and late eruption, we assigned an average of 2 third molars, or a total of 10 molars, per person. The resulting number of individuals deduced from this tooth analysis is found in table 5. In determining the approximate number of people represented in each wear category, an average was taken of the number of individuals in each tooth type. Where a type was very poorly represented, however (e.g., the premolars in wear Grade 2, and the canines in Grade 3), the figures were omitted from the average. The estimates in table 5 represent the minimum number of individuals present in the tomb.

Listed below are the age and sex descriptions of the persons interred in the tomb, made on the basis of the analysis of mandibular and maxillary fragments and of individual teeth. The descriptions are grouped according to the wear grade into which they fit best.

Adults:

Grade 1

1. Young adult, 17 to 20 years
2. Young adult, late teens to mid-twenties
3. Young adult (male?), late teens to mid-twenties
4. Mature adult (female?), late teens to twenties or older
5. No description (recognized only from individual teeth)
6. No description (recognized only from individual teeth)

Grade 2

1. Mature adult (female?), twenty years or older
2. Mature adult, twenty years or older
3. Mature adult, twenty years or older

Grade 3

1. Mature adult (male?), middle age or older
2. Mature adult (male?), middle age or older (recognized from distinctive wear pattern on individual teeth)
3. Mature adult, middle age or older (recognized from distinctive wear pattern on individual teeth)

Children:

1. Infant, late fetal to newborn
2. Infant, 3 to 6 months
3. Infant, 6 months to 1 year
4. Child, 3 to 5 years
5. Child, 5 years
6. Child, 4 to 6 years
7. Child, 4 to 6 years
8. Child, 6 years
9. Child, 6 to 7 years

The analysis of the dental material has indicated that the tomb population consisted of no fewer than 21 persons, ranging in age from infancy to old age.

Osteological Analysis

As we shall see, the cranial and postcranial studies do not entirely correspond to the population size deduced from the dental material, although they do give a similar age range.

Crania

The crania were extremely fragmented as a result of looting and reburial practices. Whether the destruction of the skulls was intentional cannot be determined at this time. During the excavation several large skullcap fragments were recovered, but unfortunately these were broken in shipment from Cyprus. Reconstruction of old and new breaks was carried out during the analysis. Although cranial material was not well represented, it was possible to make the following descriptions:

1. The largest fragment consists of an occipital with parts of the right and left parietal bones. This fragment has been reconstructed from 5 separate smaller fragments. It was not possible to make an age estimate of the skullcap because of the damage incurred during shipment (pl. 1d).

2. A partial frontal bone with left orbital was excavated. This frontal bone is of particular importance because it has a metopic suture (pl. 2a). At this time it is not known what the presence of metopism implies. This is an inherited trait that has often been found in Cypriot Neolithic and Late Bronze Age populations. Metopic sutures were found in 17 percent of a sample of 71 at Neolithic Khirokitia. They were also found in 11 percent of the Late Bronze Age population at Hala Sultan Tekke, and 20 percent of the populations at Bamboula or Pendayia (Schwartz 1974c:161). The presence of metopism in some Late Bronze Age populations may link them to earlier Neolithic groups, whereas populations that do not have the trait may represent new immigrants. It is of interest that this Idalion frontal does exhibit metopism, though the rate of occurrence in the population cannot be determined until more data are available.

3. A portion of an occipital bone belonging to an infant 4 to 7 years of age was also found in the tomb.

The paucity of cranial material, combined with the poor condition of what little material was available, made it impossible to analyze the collection for the two important features of thalassemia and cranial deformation. Thalassemia is an inherited anemia, fatal to individuals homozygous for the gene. It is believed to have persisted in Mediterranean populations because the heterozygotes are immune to malaria. Osteologically, this is recognizable primarily in the skull, when there is a porosity and inflammation of cranial diploe and the development of holes in the outer table of the skull vault. Angel (1972:156) recognized two cases of thalassemia at Bamboula, among the nine children in the sample. Although it is very probably that some of the children represented in the Idalion tomb died of thalassemia, there is no evidence to verify this hypothesis.

Deliberate cranial deformation, which originated in Neolithic times, was widely practiced during the Late Bronze Age. It has been found in crania from the sites of Bamboula, Kition, Hala Sultan Tekke, Akhera, and Enkomi. Unfortunately it is not possible to determine the existence or type of cranial deformation in the Idalion group.

Postcranial Skeletal Material

The postcranial bones were found in thousands of fragments. One of the first steps in the analysis of these bones was to separate the material according to bone categories: long bones, foot and hand bones, vertebrae, ribs, and so forth. Due to the immense number of these fragments, it was impossible to study all of the bone types in detail. Thus, the hand and foot bones, ribs, and vertebrae were identified, but were not studied further.

Table 6. Description of Radius Fragments

4 left proximal ends, sutures closed
1 small left proximal end, sutures recently closed
2 right proximal ends, sutures closed
1 small right proximal end, sutures closed
3 proximal ends, sides undetermined, sutures closed
1 right distal end, sutures closed
1 distal end, side undetermined, sutures closed
1 shaft, sutures not closed, adult size
1 shaft, infant (newborn)

Table 7. Description of Ulna Fragments

1 right olecranon process, sutures newly closed
2 small right olecranon processes, sutures closed
2 right olecranon processes, sutures closed
1 large left olecranon process, sutures closed
1 small olecranon process, sutures closed
2 left olecranon processes, sutures closed
1 left proximal end, sutures closed
1 left proximal end, sutures closed
1 olecranon process, broken, side undetermined
1 proximal end, side undetermined, sutures closed
1 large right distal end, sutures closed
1 right distal end, sutures closed
1 right proximal end, small infant (0 to 6 months)
1 left olecranon process, large child (8 to 10 years)

Table 8. Description of Humerus Fragments

3 right proximal ends, adult
1 small right proximal end
1 left proximal end, adult
1 small right distal end (does not match small right proximal end)
2 right distal ends, adult
1 left distal end, sutures not closed, adult size
4 left distal ends, sutures closed
1 distal end, side undetermined, adult
1 small distal end, side undetermined, adult
3 distal ends, side undetermined
1 distal end, newborn
1 distal end, infant (less than 6 months)
1 distal end, child (2 to 4 years)
1 proximal end, child (4 to 6 years)
1 head humerus, large child (7 to 10 years)
1 head humerus, child (6 to 10 years)
1 head humerus, infant (less than 6 months)
1 whole humerus, infant at birth
1 right distal shaft, child (4 to 6 years)

Table 9. Description of Femur Fragments

1 right proximal end, sutures closed
1 right proximal end, sutures not closed, adult
2 left proximal ends, sutures closed
3 undetermined sides, sutures closed
1 shaft, adult
1 small shaft, adult
1 large shaft, adult
2 heads of femur, child (4 to 7 years)
1 head of femur, child (1 to 3 years)
1 proximal end of shaft, infant (0 to 6 months)
1 right femur, infant (0 to 6 months)
1 distal end, newborn
1 distal end, infant (0 to 6 months)
1 distal end, child (3 to 7 years)
2 distal ends, child (2 to 4 years)
1 left distal end, child (4 to 7 years)

Table 10. Description of Fibula Fragments

1 left proximal end
1 small left proximal end, sutures recently closed
3 right proximal ends, adult
5 left distal ends, adult
1 right distal end, adult
1 large right distal end
3 distal ends, adult
1 distal end, child (less than 4 years)

Table 11. Description of Tibia Fragments

1 large left proximal end
2 left proximal ends
1 left proximal end, sutures not closed, adult size
1 small left proximal end, adult
1 right proximal end, sutures just closed
1 right proximal end, sutures not closed, adult size
1 right proximal end
1 left distal end
1 small left distal end
1 right distal end
1 condyle, sutures not closed, child (3 to 5 years)
1 condyle, sutures not closed, child (7 to 10 years)
1 right proximal end, infant (less than 1 year)
1 proximal end, child (less than 4 years)
1 proximal end, child (5 to 7 years)

Table 12. Measurements and Pairing of Patellae*

Right			Left	
Width (cm)	Height (cm)		Width (cm)	Height (cm)
4	3.9		?	3.9
4.8	4.4		No match	
3.7	?		3.6	3.7
3.9	3.6		3.8	3.6
No match			3.9	3.9
No match			4.3	4.0
No match			3.5	3.7
No match			?	4.1

*There were six unmeasurable patellae.

Table 13. Description of Clavicle Fragments

2 right conoid tubercles
1 right conoid fragment
3 left conoid tubercles
1 left, newborn
1 left, child (5 to 10 years)
1 right, child (5 to 10 years)

Table 14. Description of Pelvic Ischium Fragments

1 right ischium, child (3 to 5 years)
1 left ischium, child (4 to 5 years)
1 left ischium, child (6 to 8 years)
1 left ischium, child (8 to 12 years)

The postcranial study focused primarily on the long bones and other bone types from which age and sex interpretations could be made. Each fragment was studied for level of maturity, size, and side (right or left). Maturity designations were made on the basis of epiphyseal fusion.[4] The size categories for adults were designated small, medium, and large. They were used only to identify individuals and, where possible, to determine their sex. Since the material was so fragmented and not uniformly represented, we were unable to take systematic measurements. The few measurements that were possible are presented below. A summary of the results of the postcranial studies by bone type is given in tables 6-14. These tables list the osteological data and also give size and age descriptions.

Several of the postcranial bones were found to be measurable as follows:

1. A right femur was recovered with 3/4 of the shaft present, but missing the distal condyles (pl. 2b). The subtrochanteric transverse and sagittal diameters were measured. These are

---

[4] The age standards were those of Krogman (1973).

the width and breadth measurements of the shaft just below the lesser trochanter on the femur. The subtrochanter transverse diameter was 3.2 cm and the sagittal diameter 2.6 cm. It is possible to determine the platymeric index of the bone by dividing the sagittal diameter by the transverse diameter and multiplying by 100. The result in this case was 84.4 percent, which indicates that the specimen is on the borderline between having a platymeric- and a eurymeric-shaped shaft. The values for the platymeric index are:

Platymeric or flattened	X-84.9%
Eurymeric or moderate	85-99%
Stenomeric or rounded	100-X% (Krogman 1973:322)

Angel (1946:76) noted that among the ancient Greeks there was flattening of the femur and tibia. He attributes this to muscular stress connected with posture.

2. One large left pubic symphysis was well enough preserved for analysis (pl. 2c). The pubic symphysis is the most reliable bone in the human skeleton for aging adults. McKern and Stewart (1957) did a study of the aging of pubic symphyses and developed a technique that employs three separate components, each with five developmental stages. Each stage is measured by a point system. Later Gilbert and McKern (1973) established that there is definite sexual dimorphism in the age changes that occur in this bone. Studies that had employed only the male standards had systematically underestimated the ages of females. Because the sex of this Idalion individual was not known, both male and female standards were figured. The comparative collections used were the Suchey and the Miles Gilbert series (female) and the McKern and Steward series (male). If the Idalion individual was a female, the result of the analysis was a score of 12.0 points, indicating an age between 32 and 52 years, with a mean age of 39 (Krogman 1973:106). If the individual was a male, the result was a score of 11.5 points, indicating an age between 23 and 49 years, with a mean age of 28.18. Because the Idalion symphysis was larger than that of any females represented in either the Suchey or the Miles Gilbert series, it is postulated that the individual was probably male.

3. A large number of patellae were found to be measurable (see table 12). These measurements made it possible to match the patellae to individuals.

Summary of Cranial and Postcranial Analyses

The following list presents the number and characteristics of the persons represented in the cranial and postcranial study. This analysis was concerned with determining the most reliable and therefore the smallest possible number of persons interred in the tomb. It was necessary to collapse overlapping age margins in the case of children and adolescents to insure that no individual was represented twice. For example, a tibia designated as belonging to a 14 to 17 year old and an ulna designated as belonging to a 15 to 17 year old were assumed to have been from the same individual.

Adults	Children
1. 15 to 19 years	1. Newborn
2. 12 to 16 years	2. 0 to 6 months
3. 17 to 19 years, small adult (female?)	3. Less than 1 year
4. Large adult (male?)	4. 2 to 4 years
5. Small adult (female?)	5. 3 to 5 years
6. Mature adult	6. 7 to 12 years
7. Mature adult	7. 5 to 10 years

Conclusions of Osteological Analysis

The postcranial analysis tended to confirm the findings of the study of dentition. Only two new items of information resulted: 1) identification of an adolescent between the ages of 12 and 16, and 2) identification of a child between the ages of 7 and 12. This evidence would suggest that two of the age estimates based on dental age may have been incomplete or inaccurate. One of the unidentified young adults may, in fact, be the adolescent between 12 and 16 years of age. The child between 7 and 12 may have been misjudged to be 6 to 7 because the mandibular fragments were small and incomplete. It is also possible that no dental evidence whatever was recovered from the tomb for one of both of these individuals, who would then constitute additional persons. In conclusion, the population description of the individuals interred in Idalion Tomb 1.76, on the basis of the dental, cranial, and postcranial evidence, is as follows:

Children--9

1. Newborn or late fetal
2. 0 to 6 months old
3. Less than 1 year
4. 3 to 5 years
5. 4 to 6 years
6. 4 to 6 years
7. 4 to 6 years
8. 6 to 7 years
9. 7 to 12 years

Adults--12

1. Male(?), middle age or older
2. Female(?), 20 years or older
3. Male(?), middle age or older
4. Adult, middle age or older
5. Female(?), 20 years or older
6. Adolescent, 12 to 16 years
7. Young adult, 17 to 20 years
8. Young adult (male?), late teens to mid-twenties
9. Young adult, late teens to mid-twenties
10. Adult, 20 years or older
11. Adult, 20 years or older
12. Adult

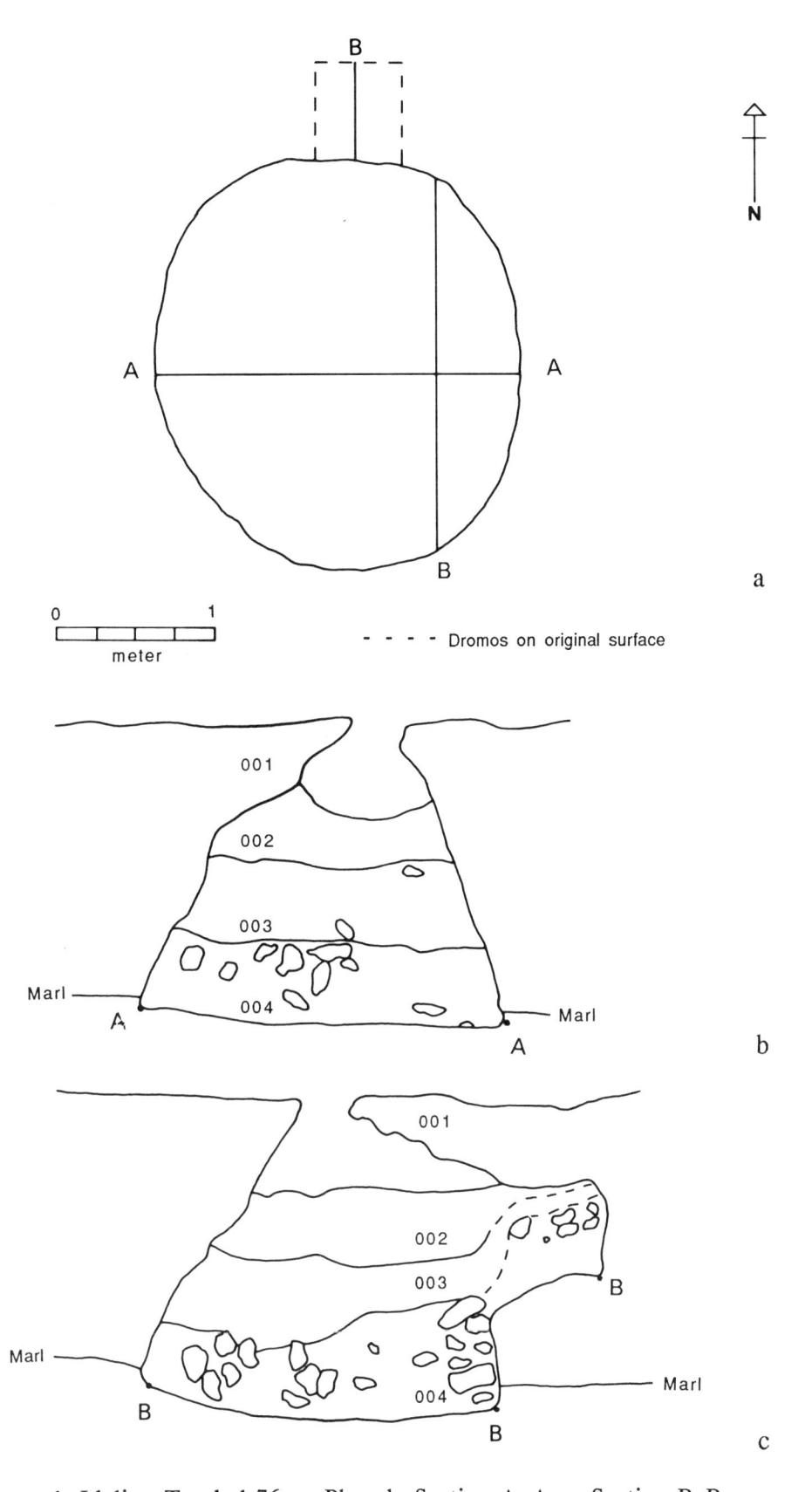

Figure 1. Idalion Tomb 1.76. a. Plan, b. Section A-A, c. Section B-B

PLATE 1

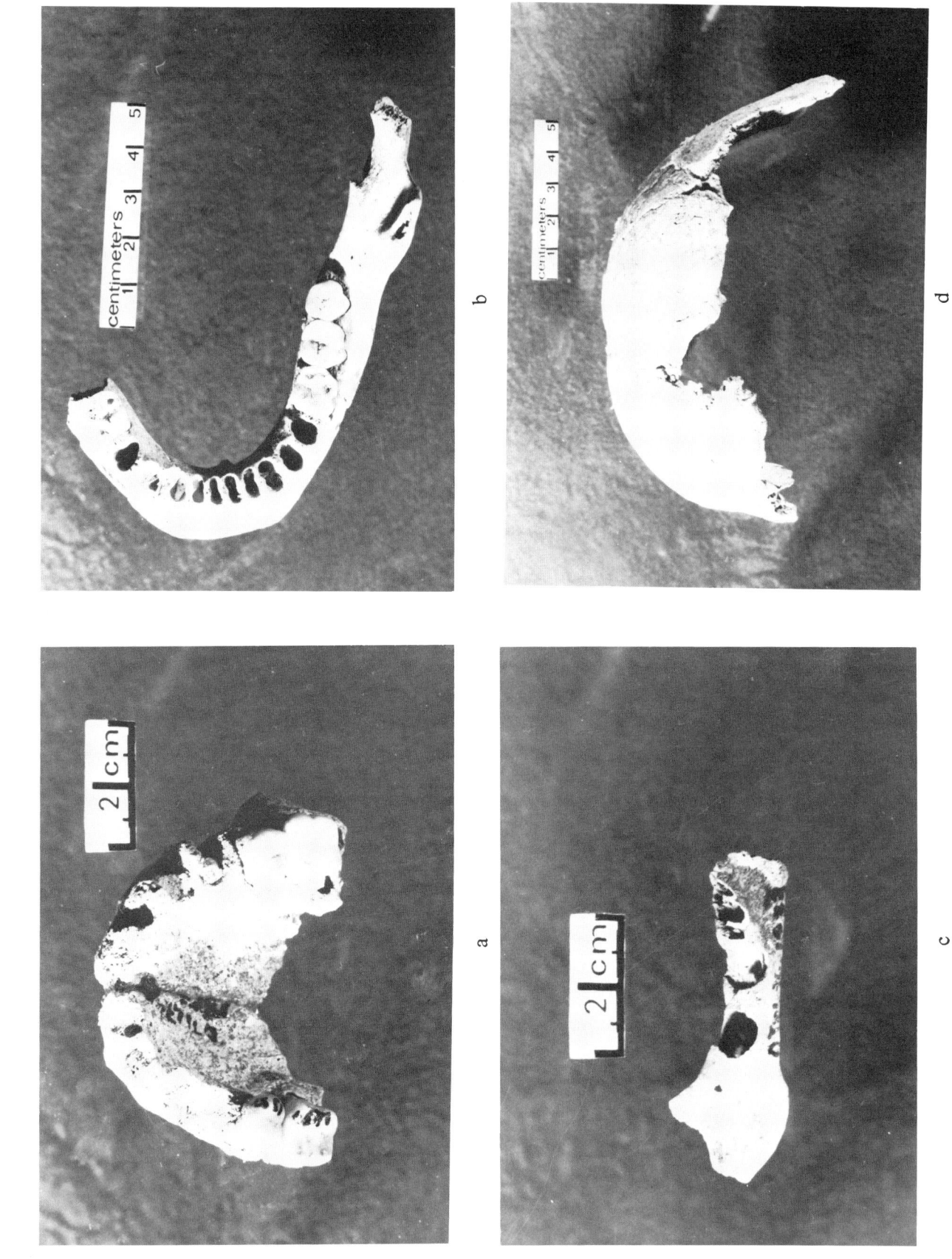

Cranial Remains. a. Adult maxilla, b. Mandible fragment, c. Newborn or late fetal infant mandible fragment, d. Occipital fragment.

PLATE 2

Cranial and Post-cranial Remains. a. Frontal bone with metopic suture, b. Right femur, c. Pubic symphysis.

2. ARTIFACTUAL REMAINS WITH SOME HISTORICAL OBSERVATIONS

Charles Martin Adelman *

Introduction

The remains from Idalion Tomb Id 1.76 were in a very fragmented state and included Bronze and Iron Age wares. Work on the material, however (which did not begin until several months after the regular season), showed that the tomb was, in fact, a Bronze Age one. Of the thousands of sherds and chips, only Bronze Age material proved mendable; at most, only a few Iron Age sherds joined. The sherds were sorted, mended, drawn, and photographed in the excavation house (tables 4 and 5).[1]

By the time that work on the pottery began, the tomb was being used as a local rubbish pit. That, together with the autumn rains, caused the sides of the tomb to collapse, exposing two angled sections of wall in the southeast portion. These walls probably had originally extended to form a corner over the tomb (or dromos). Whether these walls belonged to a Bronze Age construction contemporary with the tomb or to a later, Iron Age, construction, is a question that may be answered upon further excavation. If the walls were indeed later, this may account in part for the fragmented state of the finds.

Catalogue of Finds

1. Jug (fragmentary, now desurfaced). Black Slip IV, handmade. Biconical body with rounded carination at midbody; concave neck with pinched mouth ending in rounded lip; nearly flat base; thrust-through handle from shoulder to lip; vertical paring (shaving) on neck; on interior, deep finger impressions, vertical from base to midbody, horizontal from midbody to shoulder. Fabric soft, porous, friable (like White Shaved); contains some black grits; pink (7.5 YR 8/4) to very pale brown (10 YR 8/3) at surface. Traces of black slip (on exterior and interior). Includes D.76.720 (handle).

---

*Department of Art, University of Northern Iowa, Cedar Falls, Iowa

I would like to thank Dr. V. Karageorghis, Director of Antiquities; Drs. K. and I. Nicolaou and the staff of the Cyprus Museum; and Mrs. Frances Vassiliades, whose useful suggestions and able assistance in the conservation and drawing of the small objects (nos. 47, 48, 51-65) greatly aided my task.

[1] The drawings and photographs of the artifacts are listed sequentially according to catalogue number on the figures and plates. In drawing the fragmented vessels, the reconstructed profile continues the curves of the existing fragments. Munsell Color notations are used throughout. The following abbreviations are used: d. - diameter; ht. - height; ht.max.d. - height of maximum diameter; d.b. - diameter of base; d.r. - diameter of rim; est. - estimated; pres. - preserved; w. - width; l. - length; th. - thickness; w/o - without. The Greek delta is the symbol used by the Idalion excavation for the registered sherds. In this text, however, the letter D has been substituted for the Greek symbol. All measurements are in centimeters. Those sherds that received registration numbers during the regular season (e.g., .76.392) are listed under their respective sherd categories or with the vessels to which they belong.

The standard SCE terms and spelling used in the original manuscript of this paper have been changed by the editor to conform with the rest of the volume, which departs from the SCE in using the spelling "Cypriot" rather the "Cypriote"; using no hyphen in terms like "Base Ring," "Black Glazed"; and writing as one word, not hyphenated, terms like "Wheelmade," "Handmade," etc.

est.d.	10.0
ht.	14.7
ht.max.d.	6.5
d.b.	5.2

(fig. 1, pl. 1)

2. Bowl (fragmentary). (Coarse?) Monochrome, handmade. Hemispherical bowl with slightly flattened base and slightly inturned blunt lip with shallow groove below lip on interior; scratch marks on eroded surface. Fabric contains black and red grit, calcium carbonate, clear quartz crystal slivers; dark reddish brown (2.5 YR 3/4), core gray in thicker sections (but not in base). Slip reddish brown (2.5 YR 4/4).

d.	12.0
ht.	5.1
ht.max.d.	4.6
d.b.	ca. 4.0

(fig. 1, pl. 1)

3. Jug (fragmentary). Coarse Monochrome, handmade. Globular body, tapering neck everted slightly to round mouth with swollen lip, base slightly flattened (circular scrape marks on interior delineate area); thrust-through handle (covered with blob of clay on interior) from shoulder to lip (widening slightly at lip); triangular ridge on handle center; neck attached to body with slight overfold of clay. Vessel burnished leather dry to low luster on most areas--vertical strokes on neck, horizontal/oblique strokes on body. Fabric porous; contains black and red grit, grog, calcium carbonate; red (7.5 R 5/6). Slip red (10 R 7/6) with patches of dark mottling. Includes D.76.378, .5609, .5674, .5724 (bodies).

d.	22.2
ht.	27.2
ht.max.d.	11.0
d.b.	ca. 3.5

(fig. 1, pl. 1)

4. Jug fragments. Coarse Monochrome, handmade. Nearly identical to no. 3, with preserved fragments of same dimension and profile but handle slightly more oblique. Vessel burnishe☺ while wet but no luster--vertical strokes on neck, horizontal/oblique strokes on body. Fabric porous; contains black and some red grit, small pebbles; red (7.5 R 5/6) with gray core. Slip weak red (7.5 R 4/2) to gray (7/5 R N4).

pres.ht.	14.5
pres.w. ca.	12.0

(pl. 1)

5. Bowl (fragmentary). Painted Monochrome, handmade. Rounded body (lopsided) incurving slightly to flattened lip, with groove below lip on interior; spreading base ring; one horizontal loop handle from body. Decoration in matt white paint; on exterior, below lip, horizontal bands, wavy line, horizontal bands; in lower zone, seven sets of vertical lines with sets of short oblique strokes in the interstices; on lip, groups of short strokes; on handle, above, groups of strokes; below, painted band; underside of foot, on edge, painted band. Fabric contains black grit, small and large bits of calcium carbonate; red (2.5 YR 5/6) with gray core. Slip mottled from red (2.5 YR 5/6) to reddish brown (2.5 YR 5/4) probably as result of stacking in firing (upper area is generally lighter). Includes D.76.371 (lip).

d.	ca. 16.1
ht.	7.3-8.2
ht.max.d.	ca. 7.0
d.b.	6.4

(fig. 2, pl. 2)

6. Tankard fragments. White Slip II, handmade. (Restoration drawing from three nonjoining fragments.) Bulging body (probably lopsided), concave neck to triangular rim; flaring base ring; vertical strap handle from shoulder to rim(?); at join of neck and body, thickening of section, with horizontal paring marks and deep curve below neck on interior. Decoration in black paint; on rim, band of swags (drawn continuously); edges of rim painted; on neck (from rim), band of dotted scales (drawn continuously with slant from upper left to lower right), three lines, double band of dotted scales, three lines, double band of dotted scales; on body (below handle root), two framed crosshatched horizontal bands (ladder bands) framing a hooked chain; below handle, two framed crosshatched vertical bands linked by horizontal bar framing vertical ladder band; vertical twisted lines in the interstices; handle barred; on foot, two horizontal bands and sets of short vertical strokes; on underside of foot, four sets of two parallel lines radiating from central circle; circles in interstices. Fabric friable; contains grog; light gray (5 Y 7/1). Slip light gray to white (5 Y 7/1-8/1). Includes D.76.370 (base).

est.d.	14.1
est.ht.	19.6
est.ht.max.d.	9.5-10.0 (below rim)
d.b.	7.6
d.r.	10.1

(fig. 2, pl. 2)

7. Bowl (fragmentary). Base Ring II, handmade. Warped; sharp carination below lip, rounded carination at midbody, furrow above foot; low base ring; wishbone handle composed of two elements; lower part of foot possibly finished on wheel; parallel lines for ca. 1 cm above base in furrow (see detail, pl. 3). Fabric contains some fine black grit, calcium carbonate; red (10 R 7/6) with gray core. Slip mottled red (10 R 7/6), gray and black.

d.	17.2
d.r.	16.8
ht.	7.0-7.8
ht.max.d.	5.6-6.5
d.b.	5.4

(fig. 3, pl. 3)

8. Lentoid flask (fragmentary). Base Ring II, handmade. (Erroneously described as "black amphora" on registration card.) Body composed of two more or less hemispherical sections joined at vertical carination; thrust-through vertical strap handle from shoulder to neck; cylindrical neck tapers slightly to (funnel?) mouth, now missing; on the body of the vessel, opposite the handle, is a circular pierced area, later filled by overlap of clay (see drawing, fig. 3; possibly used in the manufacture of the vessel for the insertion of the neck and handle). Decoration in matt white paint; on body, two sets of five oblique lines arranged as chevrons in respect to carination; on neck, five horizontal lines. Fabric contains grog and much calcium carbonate; light red (2.5 YR 6/8) at surface with gray core. Slip black. Includes D.76.401 (body).

frontal w.	7.9
lateral w.	5.9
ht.	10.9
ht.max.d.	ca. 4.0

(fig. 3, pl. 3)

9. Jug (fragmentary). Plain White Handmade. Biconical body with slightly rounded carination at ca. 11 cm above slightly concave base; concave neck with pinched mouth (mostly missing) ending in rounded lip with deep wide furrow beneath; handle from lip to shoulder; heavy grit on base. Fabric slightly porous; contains black, gray, and red grit, large black organic (seed?) inclusions; reddish yellow (5 YR 7/6) with pink (7.5 YR 8/4) core. Slip white (2.5 Y 8/2) with patches of pink mottling.

d.	14.9
ht.	19.6
ht.max.d.	8.5
d.b.	7.0

(fig. 4, pl. 4)

10. Jug fragments. Plain White Handmade. Biconvex body with rounded carination at 12.7 cm below lip; flat base (nonjoining); concave flaring neck to swollen delineated lip; mouth pinched to form spout; vertical strap handle from upper body to lip; neck attached to body with overlap of clay; wall thickness varies. (Upper body and base probably from same vessel, although resulting restoration is slightly squatter than usual, d.:ht. 77%). Fabric porous; contains black and red grit, calcium carbonate; reddish yellow (5 YR 6/6). Slip very pale brown (10 YR 7/4).

Upper body:		Base:	
d.	15.9		
pres.ht.	13.6	pres.ht.	4.7
est.ht.	20.8	d.b.	9.6
ht.max.d.	12.7 below lip		
est.ht.max.d.	8.2 above base		

(fig. 4, pl. 4)

11. Jug (fragmentary). Plain White Handmade. Globular body; flat base; incision at neck root; neck flaring slightly to rounded lip; mouth pinched to form spout; handle from lip to upper body (body join missing); lip/handle fragment probably joins lip, but small chip missing; heavy grit on base. Fabric porous; contains black and red grit; very pale brown (10 YR 7/4). Slip white (2.5 Y 8/2); black stains on parts of surface. Includes D.76.389 (base), .350 (handle).

d.	17.8
ht.	22.4
ht.max.d.	13.5
d.b.	10.2

(fig. 4, pl. 4)

12. Fragments of jug with inscribed handle. Plain White Handmade. (Restoration from three nonjoining but clearly recognizable fragments.) Biconical body; concave to rounded base; slightly flaring neck to swollen lip (diameter of mouth varies, suggesting mouth was probably pinched to form spout); handle from upper body to lip with shallow incisions on

upper surface--line crossed by two converging lines (see detail, fig. 4; pl. 4); neck attached to body with overlap of clay; heavy grit on base. Fabric friable (very recognizable), porous; contains black and red grit, grog, calcium carbonate; very pale brown (10 YR 7/4). Slip very pale brown (10 YR 8/4). Includes D.76.379, .388 (neck roots).

est.d.	16.1
est.ht.	22.6
est.ht.max.d.	11.5
d.b.	8.3

(fig. 4, pl. 4)

13. Fragments of jug with inscribed handle. Plain White Handmade. (Restoration from two nonjoining fragments.) Biconvex body with rounded carination at ca. 14.5 cm below rim; flat base; ridge at neck root; slightly flaring neck to thickened, delineated rim pinched to form spout; handle from shoulder to rim with deep incision on upper surface--one thick and two thin parallel lines crossed by a thick line (see detail, fig. 4; pl. 4); heavy grit on base. Fabric porous; contains black and red grit, calcium carbonate; light red (2.5 YR 6/6). Slip very pale brown (10 YR 8/3); black flecks on body and base. Includes D.76.717 (rim).

est.d.	19.1
pres.ht.	17.8
est.ht.	26.7
est.ht.max.d.	10.8 (16.1 below rim)
d.b.	9.0

(fig. 4, pl. 4)

14. Jug (fragmentary). Plain White Handmade. Biconical body with rounded carination at join of upper and lower body (concavity on inner wall at join); flat base; ridge at neck root; flaring neck to rounded lip pinched to form spout; handle from shoulder to lip (lip join missing); neck attached to body with overlap of clay; deep finger marks on interior upper body; marks from scraping tool on exterior body with paring marks at carination; finger impressions on pinched mouth; heavy grit on base. Fabric slightly porous; contains black grit, grog, calcium carbonate, and small pebbles; reddish yellow (5 YR 7/6). Slip very pale brown (10 YR 8/3).

d.	20.6
ht.	28.4
ht.max.d.	12.5
d.b.	9.6

(fig. 5, pl. 5)

15. Jug (fragmentary). Plain White Handmade. Biconical to globular body; flat base; ridge at neck root; flaring neck pinched to form spout; handle from upper body to lip; heavy grit on base; uneven firing on body. Fabric contains black and red grit, calcium carbonate, and sparse mica (or silicate); pink (7.5 YR 7/4). Slip very pale brown (10 YR 7/3); old breaks coated black. Includes D.76.710 (lip).

d.	21.3
ht.	29.1
ht.max.d.	12.0
d.b.	8.8

(fig. 5, pl. 5)

16. Fragments of jug. Plain White Handmade. (Base and upper body nonjoining, with many nonjoining sherds.) Biconvex body with rounded carination; flat to slightly convex base; shallow ridge at neck root; slightly flaring neck to swollen delineated lip; mouth pinched to form spout; handle from upper body to lip (body join missing). Fabric porous, brittle; contains much black and red grit, grog; pale yellow (5 Y 7/3). Slip white (2.5 Y 8/2). Includes D.76.5649 (body).

ht. neck	6.2
length of mouth through spout	ca. 8.0
d.b.	7.4

(pl. 5)

17. Fragments of jug. Plain White Handmade. (Three nonjoining fragments.) Globular body; flat base; ridge at neck root; slightly flaring neck to blunt lip (mouth probably pinched to form spout); handle from upper body to lip; neck joined to body with overlap of clay. Fabric porous; contains much large and small black and red grit; pink (7.5 YR 7/4). Slip pink (7.5 YR 7/4). Surface eroded and pockmarked.

d.	ca. 16.0
pres.ht.	20.0
d.b.	ca. 6.5

(pl. 5)

18. Fragments of jug. Plain White Handmade. (Base and handle sherds nonjoining.) Convex body; flat base; handle from upper body to (missing) lip (mouth probably pinched to form spout); heavy grit on base. Fabric porous; contains black and red grit, calcium carbonate; reddish yellow (5 YR 6/8). Slip (mostly missing) pink (5 YR 7/4).

d.	ca. 20.0
pres.ht.	9.5
d.b.	9.0

(not illustrated)

19. Jug (fragmentary). Plain White Handmade. (Lower body and base missing.) Biconical body with rounded carination at 12 cm below lip (carination not consistent); deep finger marks just below carination; shallow groove at neck root; concave neck terminating in rounded lip; round mouth; handle from shoulder (now missing) to neck just below lip; vertical paring marks on neck. Fabric slightly porous; contains much black, gray, and some red grit, bits of quartz crystal or silicate; light gray (2.5 Y 7/2). Slip very pale brown (10 YR 8/3). Includes D.76.713 (body).

pres.d.	15.0
est.d.	17.5
est.ht.	ca. 27.0
ht.max.d.	12.0-13.0 below lip

(fig. 6, pl. 6)

20. Jug (fragmentary). Plain White Handmade. Biconvex body with rounded carination at midbody; flat base; ridge at neck root; nearly vertical neck to thickened lip; round mouth; handle from shoulder to neck just below lip. On interior, scrape marks; below neck root, finger impressions; heavy grit on base. Fabric contains much black and brown grit, brown and red grog (grit and grog in equal quantities), calcium carbonate, organic forms

(shells), pebbles; reddish yellow (5 YR 7/6). Slip very pale brown (10 YR 8/3); uneven firing.

d.	21.6
ht.	27.7
ht.max.d.	12.5
d.b.	9.5

(fig. 6, pl. 6)

21. Fragments of jug. Plain White Handmade. (Lower body, base, and nonjoining neck fragment.) Biconvex body with rounded carination at ca. 12 cm.; flat, slightly concave, uneven base; nonjoining neck fragment with ridge at neck root; neck flaring to rounded lip; mouth pinched to form spout; handle now missing. Fabric contains black and red grit; reddish yellow (5 YR 6/6). Slip very pale brown (10 YR 7/4). Includes D.76.702 (body).

d.	22.0
ht.	19.3
ht.max.d.	13.0
d.b.	11.1
ht. neck	9.0

(fig. 6, pl. 6; neck fragment not illustrated)

22. Fragment of jug. Plain White Handmade. (Neck and handle missing.) Squat flat body; neck root preserved on side opposite handle; handle from upper body; dark band on interior (vessel tilted in tomb, leaving stain of liquid contents?). Fabric porous; contains black and red grit, grog, calcium carbonate; yellowish red (5 YR 5/6). Slip white (2.5 Y 8/2); patches of black on exterior.

d.	27.0
pres.ht.	22.0
ht.max.d.	13.8
d.b.	16.2-16.5

(fig. 6, pl. 6)

23. Fragment of inscribed body sherd from closed vessel. Plain White Handmade. Fabric porous, containing black and red grit, grog, calcium carbonate; very pale brown (10 YR 8/4). Slip very pale brown (10 YR 8/3).

l.	3.5
w.	2.7
th.	0.7

(fig. 6, pl. 6)

24. Jug (fragmentary). Anomaly of Plain White Handmade, with red slip and white paint. Globular body; shallow ridge at neck root; nearly straight neck to rounded lip; mouth pinched to form spout; handle from shoulder to lip (handle root missing); neck joined to body with overlap of clay. Decoration in matt white paint on red slip (mostly effaced); on neck, below spout, "S"; on body, chains of loops pendant from neck. Fabric contains black and red grit, grog, calcium carbonate; reddish yellow (5 YR 6/6). Slip dusky red (7.5 R 3/4) where preserved. Fabric and shape identical to Plain White Handmade (compare no. 13 for shape). (N.B. Treatment with Calgon removed some traces of white paint.)

d.	15.4
pres.ht.	15.4
ht.max.d.	13.0 below lip

(fig. 7, pl. 7)

25. Bowl (fragmentary). Plain White Wheelmade. Rounded body incurving to rounded lip; slightly concave flat base; one horizontal loop handle from curve of upper body (left handle root lower than right); on exterior, shallow furrow 2.2 cm below lip. Fabric somewhat porous; contains some black grit, grog, much calcium carbonate; reddish yellow (5 YR 6/6). Slip very pale brown (10 YR 8/4). Includes D.76.729 (lip/handle), .730 (base).

d.	15.0
ht.	6.8-7.0
ht.max.d.	5.5-6.0
d.b.	6.0

(fig. 8, pl. 8)

26. Bowl (fragmentary). Plain White Wheelmade. Rounded body incurving slightly to flattened lip with concavity below inner edge; slightly concave everted disk base; one horizontal triangular loop handle from lip; exterior, upper body shaved on wheel (see detail, pl. 8). Fabric contains black grit, calcium carbonate, pockmarks from burnt-out organic matter; pink (7.5 YR 7/4). Slip white (2.5 Y 8/2); no traces of paint. Includes D.76.392 (base).

d.	17.9
ht.	6.3
ht.max.d.	5.5
d.b.	6.8

(fig. 8, pl. 8)

27. Fragment of closed vessel. Plain White Wheelmade. Thick-walled flat base with convex interior floor split from firing. Fabric porous; contains grit, grog; light brown (7.5 YR 6/4). Surface coated.

pres.ht.	5.5
d.b.	14.0
th. of wall	1.6

(pl. 8)

28. Fragments of jug. Plain White Wheelmade II. (Three sherds from separate areas of vessel, but giving complete profile for restoration drawing.) Ovoid body; ridge at neck root; concave neck to everted rounded lip; high spreading molded base ring with slight demarcation line at join of body and two shallow ridges above flaring foot; central-channeled strap handle from upper body to lip(?), now missing; small clay pellet on handle at handle root (imitating rivet); on interior, strong wheelmarks. Fabric somewhat porous; contains black grit, grog, calcium carbonate; light red (2.5 YR 6/6). Slip white (2.5 Y 8/2) on surface and on interior neck. Includes D.76.372 (body).

d.	16.2
ht.	31.0
ht.max.d.	13.5
d.b.	8.8

(fig. 8, pl. 8)

29. Fragment of tray(?) or rim(?). Coarse Ware. Flat base; slight tapering of wall in horizontal section. Fabric contains large grit, pebbles, burnt-out organic matter; pink (5 YR 3/4).

pres.ht.	5.5
pres.w.	4.5
depth	6.0
th. of wall	1.5

(fig. 8, pl. 8)

30. Fragments of bowl. White Painted Wheelmade III (Quasi Mycenaean IIIB Linear Ware). Rounded body incurving to rounded lip; on exterior, shallow groove below lip; low base ring; slight convexity on floor and underside of base at center; paring marks on lower body; no extant handles, but handle(s) possible adjacent to painted pendant arc at lip. Decoration in diluted matt red paint (7.5 R 5/6); on exterior, band at lip and curve of body; pendant, solid-filled arc below lip (perhaps a second arc opposite, below lip, now missing); on interior, band at lip and curve of body; at center, spiral issuing from central blob. Fabric porous; contains a few black grits, calcium carbonate; very pale brown (10 YR 7/4). Slip white to pale yellow (2.5 Y 8/2-8/4).

d.	14.4
ht.	7.2
ht.max.d.	5.5
d.b.	5.4

(fig. 9, pl. 9)

31. Bowl (fragmentary). White Painted Wheelmade III (Quasi Mycenaean IIIB Linear Ware). Rounded body incurving slightly to rounded lip; on exterior, three shallow furrows below lip (made on wheel) and shallow indentation at ca. 2 cm.; low base ring; one horizontal handle at lip with two finger-made depressions creating three blunt projections. Decoration in matt red paint (7.5R 4/6); on exterior, band below handle; on interior, band at curve of body; at center, spiral issuing from central dot and enclosed by thick band. Fabric contains black grit, grog, calcium carbonate; light reddish brown (2.5 YR 6/4). Slip very pale brown (10 YR 8/3).

d.	13.3
ht.	6.8
ht.max.d.	5.5
d.b.	5.5

(fig. 9, pl. 9)

32. Fragment of bowl. White Painted Wheelmade III (Quasi Mycenaean IIIB Linear Ware). Rounded body to blunt lip; low base ring; no handles preserved; on exterior, groove at base root; shaving on lower body. Decoration in matt black paint; on exterior, band at midbody; on interior, band (at lip?), two bands below lip; at center, spiral issuing from dot. Fabric porous; contains fine black and red grit, grog(?); pale brown (10 YR 6/3). Slip light gray (10 YR 7/2). Includes D.76.719 (nonjoining lip).

d.	11.8
ht.	5.5
ht.max.d.	5.4
d.b.	5.3

(fig. 9, pl. 9)

IDALION TOMB 1.76: ARTIFACTUAL REMAINS 147

33. Bowl (fragmentary). White Painted Wheelmade III (Quasi Mycenaean IIIB Linear Ware). Slightly flattened (ca. 3 cm below lip), rounded body incurving slightly to rounded lip; slightly concave disk base; two opposing horizontal triangular loop handles (one nonjoining) at lip; left handle root higher than right; on interior, slight concavity just below lip. Decoration in matt black paint diluted to brown (7.5 YR 5/4); on exterior, band below handle, two bands above base; on interior, four concentric bands; rim and handles painted. Fabric porous; contains black grit, grog; very pale brown (10 YR 7/4). Slip very pale brown (10 YR 7/4). Includes D.76.374 (handle), .385, .5643 (bodies), .5601 (base), .377 (nonjoining lip).

d.	15.0
ht.	5.9
ht.max.d.	5.5
d.b.	6.1

(fig. 9, pl. 9)

34. Bowl (fragmentary). White Painted Wheelmade III (Quasi Mycenaean IIIB Linear Ware). Rounded body with slight angularity below lip incurving to slightly thickened rounded lip; slightly concave disk base; one horizontal loop handle (nonjoining) at lip (probably a second opposite, now missing). Decoration in matt weak red paint (7.5 R 4/4); on exterior, three bands, one below angle, one at midbody, one above base; on interior, two bands just below curve of body; three concentric bands at center; lip and handle(s?) painted. Fabric porous; contains black and red grit, grog, calcium carbonate; reddish yellow. Slip very pale brown (10 YR 8/3). (Slip is this light color only on upper body, probably as result of stacking in firing.)

d.	17.2
ht.	6.1
ht.max.d.	5.6
d.b.	7.0

(fig. 10, pl. 10)

35. Fragments of bowl. White Painted Wheelmade III (Quasi Mycenaean IIIB Linear Ware). (Two nonjoining fragments. The restoration drawing may be incorrect; the height of the base could be reduced by ca. 0.5 cm.) Slightly rounded body incurving to slightly thickened rounded lip; very shallow depression below lip on exterior; no handles preserved but very similar to no. 34, with two opposing handles (probably same manufacturer). Decoration in matt weak red point (7.5 R 4/4); on exterior, three bands, one below angle, two above base; on interior, two bands at curve of base; one band preserved at center (probably there had been more). (Similar in shape to no. 33, but differs in fabric and paint.) Fabric porous; contains black grit, grog, calcium carbonate; reddish yellow (7.5 YR 6/6). Slip very pale brown (10 YR 7/3).

est.d.	15.0 or greater
pres.ht.	5.7
est.ht.	6.0-6.5 (as drawn)
ht.max.d.	0.8 below lip
est.d.b.	6.0

(fig. 10, pl. 10)

36. Bowl (fragmentary). White Painted Wheelmade III (Quasi Mycenaean IIIB Linear Ware). Angular body with rounded carination below nearly vertical upper body; everted lip; low base ring. Two opposing horizontal loop handles just below lip; body warped. Decoration in matt black paint (mostly missing, but traces and ghost-remains); on exterior, two bands,

one just below carination, one at midpoint of lower body; on interior, bands, one at lip, one below lip, one at curve of lower body, one at midpoint of lower body; spiral at center; handles painted. Fabric porous; contains a few black grits, calcium carbonate, pockmarks; yellowish red (5 YR 5/6). Slip very pale brown (10 YR 7/3). Includes D.76.707 (lip/handle).

d.	16.0-17.0
ht.	5.2-5.5
ht.max.d.	5.0-5.3
d.b.	ca. 4.7

(fig. 10, pl. 10)

37. Fragments of side-spouted juglet with basket handle. White Painted Wheelmade III (Quasi Mycenaean IIIB Linear Ware). (Nonjoining rim/handle and spout fragments.) Concave neck to beveled flaring rim; basket handle from edge of rim; conical spout. Decoration in matt red paint (7.5 R 5/6); band ca. 1.5 cm. below rim; rim painted; handle barred (or solid?); on spout, four longitudinal bands from root to tip. Fabric contains some black and red grit, grog; reddish yellow (5 YR 5/6). Slip pink (7.5 YR 7/4).

pres.d.	5.5
ht. w/o handle	2.6

(fig. 10, pl. 10)

38. Fragments of bowl. Levanto-Mycenaean IIIB (Wheelmade). Slightly curving body with rounded carination below handle; everted flattened lip; two opposing horizontal loop handles (one missing) at rim. Decoration in lustrous black to red (2.5 YR 5/8) paint; on exterior, band at curve of body, thin and thick band at base; on interior, band below lip; at curve of body, band with transverse groups of more or less zigzag lines painted on it; at center, a spiral enclosed by thick band; lip and handle(s) painted. Fabric well levigated; contains scattered black grit (ca. 1 mm.), some calcium carbonate; pink (7.5 YR 7/4). Slip contains mica; very pale brown (10 YR 8/4).

d.	18.0
ht.	5.0
ht.max.d.	5.0
d.b.	4.5

(fig. 11, pl. 11)

39. Fragments of cup. Levanto-Mycenaean IIIB (Wheelmade). Slightly concave body to flaring everted lip; sharp carination and inturn at cup base (interior has smoother curve); floor fragment (nonjoining) with downturning edge (to base? or foot?); vertical strap handle from body just above carination to midpoint of body. Decoration in lustrous black to red (2.5 YR 4/8) paint; on exterior, bands and lines below lip, above carination, and below carination on floor fragment; in handle zone, deep wavy line (like octopus tentacle); on interior, band at lip; handle painted. Fabric well levigated; contains sparse grog; reddish yellow (5 YR 7/6). Slip contains mica; pink (7.5 YR 7/4) interior and exterior. Includes D.76.5608 (lip/handle).

d.	8.0
pres.ht.	6.0

(fig. 11, pl. 11)

40. Three-handled jar (fragmentary). Levanto-Mycenaean IIIA2/IIIB (Wheelmade). Piriform body; flaring hollow foot; three horizontal loop handles (two missing) on shoulder;

nonjoining neck fragment with everted triangular rim (possibly not belonging to this vessel). Decoration on vessel in lustrous red paint (2.5 YR 4/8); on neck in matt red paint (2.5 YR 4/8); bands at curve of body and on foot; in handle zone, parallel oblique lines-- to left of handle, leaning right; to right of handle, leaning left; handles painted; surface burnished. Fabric somewhat porous; contains sparse grit; pink (7.5 YR 7/4). Slip pink (7.5 YR 7/4). Includes D.76.402 (body).

d.	10.4
pres.ht.	9.7
est.ht.	11.7
ht.max.d.	7.5
d.b.	3.4

(fig. 11, pl. 11)

41. Three-handled jar (fragmentary). Levanto-Mycenaean IIIA2/IIIB (Wheelmade). Piriform body to flaring neck and triangular rim; low base ring; three horizontal loop handles on shoulder (two missing). Decoration in lustrous black paint diluted brown; on exterior, solid band on neck and upper shoulder; in handle zone, groups of "concentric" right angles; below handles, spiraling line enclosed by thick bands; on foot, spiraling line; on rim, spiraling line; on interior, band below rim; handles painted. Fabric well levigated; contains some fine black grit, grog; very pale brown (10 YR 7/4). Slip very pale brown (10 YR 7/4). Includes D.76.709, .724, .735 (bodies).

d.	11.3
ht.	13.2-13.5
ht.max.d.	8.5
d.b.	4.3

(fig. 11, pl. 11)

42. Three-handled or false-necked jar (fragmentary). Levanto-Mycenaean IIIA2/IIIB (Wheelmade). Piriform body; slightly flaring foot with slight delineation of base ring; preserved to shoulder with handle root at 12.1 cm; strong wheelmarks inside shoulder from 12.3 cm. Decoration in lustrous black to red (2.5 YR 4/8) paint; in handle zone, three "concentric" concave-sided triangles (the smallest solid filled) framed by hatched bands; as lower border to handle zone, thick bands framing thin lines; on foot, traces of bands and lines. Fabric slightly porous; contains a few fine black grits; reddish yellow (7.5 YR 7/6). Slip pink (7.5 YR 7/4).

pres.d.	13.0
ht.	14.2
ht.max.d.	9.0
d.b.	4.9

(fig. 11, pl. 11)

43. Fragments of false-necked jar. Levanto-Mycenaean IIIA2/IIIB (Wheelmade). (Restoration from nonjoining body and handle/false-spout fragments.) Biconical body to neck root; nonjoining vertical strap handle; low base ring. (One handle, false spout, and spout missing.) Decoration in lustrous red paint (10R 5/8); band at neck root; bands framing thin lines at curve of body; bands framing thin spiraling lines near base; in handle zone, band of parallel chevrons and, in opposing direction, two parallel arcs as ending motif. Handle(s) painted. Fabric well levigated; light red (2.5 YR 6/6). Slip reddish yellow (5 YR 7/6). Includes D.76.714 (neck root).

d.	5.1
ht.	5.5
ht.max.d.	2.5
d.b.	3.0

(fig. 12, pl. 12)

44. Jug (fragmentary). Bucchero Handmade. Biconical body; ridge at neck root; slightly flaring neck to outturned lip; round mouth; modeled base ring; vertical strap handle from shoulder to lip (shoulder root and handle missing); vertical channeling from below shoulder to above foot. Body, mouth interior, and complete base decorated with thick black slip; some yellow incrustation on body. Fabric hard fired; contains sparse black grit, calcium carbonate; red (2.5 YR 5/8) with gray core. Slip black. Includes D.76.380, .396 (bodies), .386 (neck root), .393 (neck).

d.	13.8
ht.	18.5
ht.max.d.	8.5
d.b.	7.0

(fig. 13, pl. 13)

45. Fragments of jug. Bucchero Handmade. (Neck and body possibly not related.) Body ovoid with flattened shoulder (rather sharply bent on interior); body ends in rounded base with flaring base ring attached secondarily; vertical channels from shoulder to foot; neck cylindrical with flaring rim cut to form molding; handle from rim; neck fragment of slightly better clay, perhaps made separately. Body and neck decorated with black slip. Fabric of neck well levigated; contains black and red grit, calcium carbonate; light red (2.5 YR 6/8) with thin gray core. Slip of neck very dark gray (2.5 YR N3). Fabric of body similar but more porous and containing more inclusions; light red (2.5 YR 6/8). Slip of body very dark gray (2.5 YR N3). Includes D.76.700 (plus nonjoining .384, .722, .723 bases), .678 (body).

Body:

d.	13.6
pres.ht.	12.5
est.ht.	19.1
ht.max.d.	13.0
d.b.	ca. 6.0

Neck:

d.r.	3.4
pres.ht.	4.9

(fig. 13, pl. 13)

46. Jug (fragmentary). Bucchero Wheelmade. (With vertical strap handle, nonjoining but probably belonging.) Ovoid body with slightly flattened shoulder; ridge at neck root; flaring base ring with shallow furrow on foot; vertical strap handle (from shoulder); deep wide (ca. 1 cm) channels from shoulder to foot; on interior, rather strong wheelmarks near shoulder. Decorated with black slip on exterior and beneath foot. Fabric contains black, red, and amber grit; light red (2.5 YR 6/6) near interior, light gray (10 YR 7/2) near exterior. Slip black. Includes D.76.6701, .699, .732 (bodies), .703 (neck root).

d.	14.7
pres.ht.	15.1
ht.max.d.	9.5
w. handle	2.2

(fig. 13, pl. 13)

47. Fragments of bronze ring, consisting of two joined wires.

d.	1.7
th. wire	0.225
(two wires	0.45)

   (fig. 15, pl. 15)

48. Perforated terracotta disk (fragmentary). Bronze Age. Fabric porous; contains grit and large (ca. 1 cm) pebbles; reddish brown (2.5 YR 5/4); traces of burning on one side.

d.	5.3
th.	2.3
weight	61.5 grams
	(ca. 63 grams if complete)

   (fig. 15, pl. 15)

49. Fragment of terracotta animal figurine. Cypro-Archaic. (Probably neck and upper legs of horse.) Decorated in Bichrome technique (red and black paint). Fabric contains sparse mica; light red (2.5 YR 6/6).

pres.ht.	3.3
w.	ca. 2.0
depth	2.3

   (fig. 15, pl. 15)

50. Glyptic cylinder seal (frit? with chip missing). Much worn; pierced longitudinally. Decoration with drilled holes and lines. Two long-necked quadrupeds, with dotted rosette heads and pendant, dotted necklaces, moving right; the one quadruped is shown in quiet movement, with legs (indicated by straight lines) striding; the other is shown in more rapid movement, with legs (indicated by dots) flung apart. Two birds with outstretched wings (and horned heads?) alight on the quadrupeds' backs. Chip missing between the two quadrupeds. Fabric (seen in chipped area) yellow (10 YR 8/6). Surface white.

l.	2.8
d.	1.05
d. pierced hole	0.04

   (fig. 16, pl. 16)

51. Fragment of perforated flat ivory disk. No decoration.

est.d.	2.5
ht.	0.3

   (fig. 16, pl. 16)

52. Fragment of perforated plano-convex ivory disk with incised decoration. On upper surface near edge, incised lines.

est.d.	2.6
ht.	0.4

   (fig. 16, pl. 16)

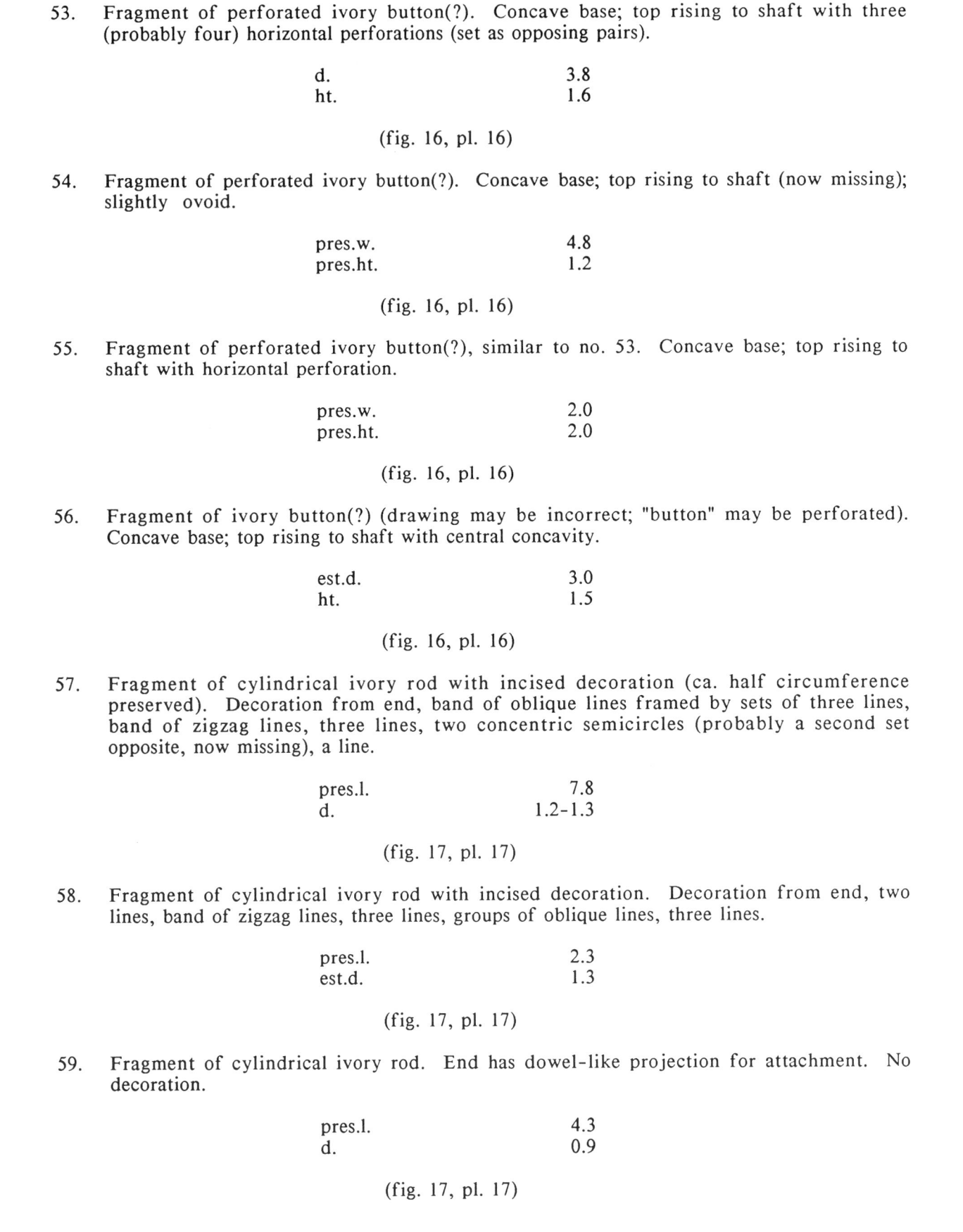

52 AMERICAN EXPEDITION TO IDALION, CYPRUS, 1973-1980

53. Fragment of perforated ivory button(?). Concave base; top rising to shaft with three (probably four) horizontal perforations (set as opposing pairs).

        d.   3.8
        ht.   1.6

(fig. 16, pl. 16)

54. Fragment of perforated ivory button(?). Concave base; top rising to shaft (now missing); slightly ovoid.

        pres.w.   4.8
        pres.ht.   1.2

(fig. 16, pl. 16)

55. Fragment of perforated ivory button(?), similar to no. 53. Concave base; top rising to shaft with horizontal perforation.

        pres.w.   2.0
        pres.ht.   2.0

(fig. 16, pl. 16)

56. Fragment of ivory button(?) (drawing may be incorrect; "button" may be perforated). Concave base; top rising to shaft with central concavity.

        est.d.   3.0
        ht.   1.5

(fig. 16, pl. 16)

57. Fragment of cylindrical ivory rod with incised decoration (ca. half circumference preserved). Decoration from end, band of oblique lines framed by sets of three lines, band of zigzag lines, three lines, two concentric semicircles (probably a second set opposite, now missing), a line.

        pres.l.   7.8
        d.   1.2-1.3

(fig. 17, pl. 17)

58. Fragment of cylindrical ivory rod with incised decoration. Decoration from end, two lines, band of zigzag lines, three lines, groups of oblique lines, three lines.

        pres.l.   2.3
        est.d.   1.3

(fig. 17, pl. 17)

59. Fragment of cylindrical ivory rod. End has dowel-like projection for attachment. No decoration.

        pres.l.   4.3
        d.   0.9

(fig. 17, pl. 17)

60. Fragment of cylindrical ivory rod. No decoration.

        pres.l.   5.3
        d.   1.3

    (fig. 17, pl. 17)

61. Fragment of cylindrical ivory rod. No decoration.

        pres.l.   2.5
        d.   0.9

    (fig. 17, pl. 17)

62. Fragment of ivory bowl with incised decoration. Rounded profile to inturned flattened rim. Decoration with incised lines; on rim, encircling lines framing short transverse lines; on floor, encircling lines; on exterior below floor, encircling lines and set of two oblique lines (probably forming a zigzag pattern).

        pres.w.   2.1
        pres.ht.   1.6

    (fig. 17, pl. 17)

63. Fragment of ivory bowl with incised decoration, similar to no. 62. Rounded profile to inturned flattened rim; floor not preserved. Decoration with incised lines; on rim, encircling lines framing short transverse lines; on exterior below floor, encircling lines.

        pres.w.   1.8
        pres.ht.   1.5

    (fig. 17, pl. 17)

64. Fragment of ivory bowl with incised decoration. At rim, encircling lines and sets of two oblique lines forming zigzag pattern; on exterior below floor, encircling lines and zigzag lines.

        pres.w.   2.5
        pres.ht.   1.6

    (fig. 17, pl. 17)

65. Fragment of ivory bowl(?). No decoration.

        pres.l.   2.2
        pres.w.   0.5

    (fig. 17, pl. 17)

Summary Tables

Table 1. Summary of Pottery Vessels

Ware	BLACK SLIP IV	MONOCHROME	COARSE MONOCHROME	PAINTED MONOCHROME	WHITE SLIP II	BASE RING II	PLAIN WHITE HANDMADE	PLAIN WHITE WHEELMADE	PLAIN WHITE WHEELMADE II	COARSE	WHITE PAINTED WHEELMADE III	LEVANTO-MYCENAEAN (IIIA2/IIIB)	BUCCHERO HANDMADE	BUCCHERO WHEELMADE
	1	2	3 4	5	6	7 8	9 10 11 12 13 14 15 16 17 18 19 20 21 22 23 24(?)	25 26 27	28	29	30 31 32 33 34 35 36 37	38 39 40 41 42 43	44 45	46
Total	1	1	2	1	1	2	15 (+1?)	3	1	1	8	6	2	1

Table 2. Summary of Sherds and Chips

Wares	Sherds	Chips
BRONZE AGE WARES		
Monochrome	51[a]	220[b]
Plain White Handmade: "red"[c]	175[d]	1600±[e]
"light"[f]	60[g]	
Pithos	12	
White Painted Wheelmade III	41[h]	
Fine wares:[i] decorated	20	
undecorated	64[j]	184[k]
Bucchero: Handmade	16	
Wheelmade	13[l]	
IRON AGE (and later) WARES		
Plain White: normal	87[m]	36[n]
with mica	22	
White Painted	34[o]	
Bichrome	5	
Red Slip	2	
Black-on-Red	3	
Hellenistic Glazed	9	
Medieval 14th-15th century	1	
UNASSIGNED	76	49
Total	691	2089±

[a]Includes the following registered sherds: .5616, .5700, .5703, .5788.

[b]Includes: .5626, .5635, .5659, .5660, .5708, .5714, .5739, .5742, .5748, .5757.

[c]"Red"=reddish yellow (5YR 7/6).

[d]Includes: .5604, .5605, 5607, .5610, 5629, .5664?, .5705.

[e]Contains some Iron Age wares. Includes: .5617, .5618, .5622, .5627, .5628, .5630, .5631, .5633, .5634, .5639, .5641, .5642, .5644, .5645, .5647, .5651, .5652, .5653, .5654, .5657, .5658, .5661, .5666, .5669, .5670, .5671, .5673, .5675, .5677, .5699; .5704, .5707, .5709, .5710, .5711, .5713, .5718, .5719, .5721, .5722, .5723, .5725, .5726, .5736, .5740, .5741, .5744, .5746, .5748, .5750, .5751, .5752, .5755, .5756, .5758, .5759, 5760, .5761, .5763, .5765, .5767, .5768.

[f]"Light"=light yellowish brown (10YR 6/4) and light gray (10YR 7/2).

[g]Includes: .5603, .5618.

[h]Includes: .5391, .5718, .5735.

[i]Primarily Levanto-Mycenaean but includes a few Iron Age wares.

[j]Includes: .5382, .5390, .5612, .5702, .5711, .5716.

[k]Includes: .5664, .5717.

[l]Includes: .5640, .5725.

[m]Includes: .5602, .5615, .5695, .5701, .5705, .5706, 5734, .5999.

[n]Includes: .5624, .5655, .5718, .5745.

[o]Includes: .5656, .5698.

Table 3. Summary of Other Finds

	Bronze	Terracotta	Glyptic	Ivory
	47	48	50	51
		49		52
				53
				54
				55
				56
				57
				58
				59
				60
				61
				62
				63
				64
				65
Total	1	2	1	15

Discussion

Pottery

The discussion includes all the catalogued vessels (nos. 1-46; see table 1) and all sherds and chips (see table 2).

1. *Black Slip IV Ware*

Black Slip IV is represented by only one fragmentary jug (no. 1), with biconical body, pinched mouth, and thrust-through handle. Although the vessel is now nearly completely desurfaced of its slip (apparently common for this ware), the ware is easily distinguishable from Plain White Handmade by the fabric (soft, porous, and friable) and by the deep finger impressions on the interior and the paring marks on the exterior; the ware is, in fact, more similar to White Shaved.[2]

2. *Monochrome Ware*

Monochrome is represented by one bowl (no. 2) of common shape and a number of sherds and chips. The fabric of the bowl is very similar to that of the Coarse Monochrome vessels (nos. 3, 4), but the walls are very much thinner in section; we have used this difference as the determining characteristic in making the classification.[3]

---

[2] Cf. SCE IV:1C for ware and disappearance of slip, pp. 74-75; for shape (Type V.A.2), p. 77, fig. XLII; for thrust-through handle, fig. XLII.7. Fragments of this ware are reported from Period 1 on the acropolis at Idalion by Ålin (1978:94).

[3] Cf. SCE IV:1C, pp. 90-103 (Type I); fig. XLV.1 (notwithstanding the questionable absence of a handle on no. 2).

3. Coarse Monochrome Ware

Coarse Monochrome (also referred to as "Apliki Ware") is represented by two jugs (nos. 3, 4) of common type, with globular body, tapering neck, round mouth, and thrust-through handle (with central ridge) from shoulder to rim; the vessels are stroke-burnished.[4]

4. Painted Monochrome Ware

Painted Monochrome, a less common ware (also referred to as "Apliki Ware") is represented by one bowl (no. 5), with rounded body, base ring, and horizontal loop handle. The vessel has obvious affinities with both White Slip II and Base Ring II. The shape is like that of the White Slip II hemispherical bowls, with the addition of the base ring. The decoration, typical of Painted Monochrome, is applied in matt white paint (common to Base Ring) and consists of elements (horizontal and pendant parallel lines, a horizontal wavy line, and sets of short oblique strokes) which surely derive from the more popular White Slip II.[5]

5. White Slip II Ware

White Slip II is represented by one fragmentary tankard (no. 6) of known shape and decoration.[6]

6. Base Ring II Ware

Base Ring II is represented by a bowl (no. 7)[7] and a lentoid flask (no. 8),[8] both of common shape, the latter with common decoration. Both vessels show aspects of production techniques. For the bowl, the parallel horizontal lines on the exterior of the foot suggest that the foot, at least, was finished on the wheel.[9] For the flask, it appears that the thrust-through handle and neck were attached to the interior wall by means of entry (by finger?) through the circular opening opposite the handle, which was subsequently covered.

---

[4] Cf. SCE IV:1C for ware, terminology, pp. 103-4; for shape (Type VII.B.1) and occurrence, p. 106. For parallel from Level IIB at Enkomi cf. Dikaios 1969b, pl. 62:14 (2715.21).

[5] Cf. SCE IV:1C for ware, terminology, shape (Type I.A.a), and occurrence, pp. 110-11; Åström notes that the similarly shaped vessel from Apliki (Taylor 1952, fig. 11:12) may be Base Ring II, and lists it in both categories. For Base Ring II (Type I.D.c) cf. SCE IV:1C, pp. 173-75. Dikaios discovered similar vessels in Level IIB at Enkomi (cf. Dikaios 1969b, pl. 62:25 [1696/2]), and in the Late Cypriot (LC) II tomb at Pyla-Verghi (Tomb 1, idem 1971, pl. 298:3 [65]; p. 914); for discussion of ware cf. ibid., p. 828.

[6] Cf. SCE IV:1C for shape, fig. 55:2, 3 (p. 451); fig. LXXXV:5, 6; for decoration (called "dotted scale pattern" by Popham), p. 455; fig. 55:4, 5 (p. 451); fig. 56:7 (p. 452); figs. LXXXIV:9, LXXXV:2; for "hooked chain," p. 454. For "dotted scale pattern" from Enkomi Level IIB cf. Dikaios 1969b, pl. 63:10 (6007/9B). For chronology of ware (with reference to Idalion) cf. SCE IV:1D, p. 704.

[7] Cf. SCE IV:1C for ware, pp. 173-74; for shape, Base Ring II (Type I.F.b) and occurrence, p. 176 and fig. LII:4; for Base Ring Wheelmade (Type I.a), pp. 197-98 and fig. LII:6.

[8] Cf. SCE IV:1C for shape (Type XIII) and occurrence, pp. 189-90 and fig. LIII:11, 13.

[9] Åström notes a vessel that is only partly wheelmade (ibid., p. 197). For a Base Ring Wheelmade bowl from Enkomi Level IIB similar in shape cf. Dikaios 1969b, pl. 62:21 (1670); for occurrence of Base Ring Wheelmade bowls in Enkomi Level IIB contexts (LC IIC), Dikaios 1971:451 (table). A vessel similar to the Enkomi example was found at Sinda in a disturbed deposit; it is classified by Furumark as Base Ring III (Furumark and Adelman, forthcoming), but by Åström as Base Ring Wheelmade (SCE IV:1C, p. 198). Base Ring III Ware at Sinda, however, has a characteristic yellowish red color (5YR 5/6).

7. *Plain White Handmade Ware*

Plain White Handmade is represented by ten pinched-mouth jugs (nos. 9-18),[10] two round-mouth jugs (nos. 19, 20),[11] two base fragments from jugs (nos. 21, 22), a body sherd with inscribed sign (no. 23),[12] and a large number of sherds and chips. The vessels are all of known shape, though at other contemporary sites often wheelmade.[13] Also included in this group is the anomaly (no. 24); although it is decorated with a red slip and white paint, the shape and fabric of no. 24 are so similar to other vessels of Plain White Handmade that we have included it in this group.[14] In general, the fabric of these vessels is either "red" (in the range of reddish yellow [5 YR 7/6]) or "light" (in the range of light yellowish brown [10 YR 6/4] and light gray[10 YR 7/2]).[15] All of the vessels have a flat base, usually with heavy grit, suggesting that they were set to dry base down on a bed of grit. Where the neck and body are preserved, the join is made with a slight overfold of clay on the interior and a shallow ridge on the exterior at the neck root. The vessels with pinched mouth have handles from shoulder to rim; those with round mouth have handles from shoulder to just below rim. The uniformity of production technique and the apparently strict adherence to shape differences (representing function) suggest a strong local tradition (probably workshops) for the manufacture of these vessels. As to the decoration of no. 24, we have found no close parallel; it seems that a producer of Plain White Handmade wares, perhaps on a whim, was inspired by the decorative elements of White Painted Wheelmade II and White Slip II and the surface of Red Slip to create this anomaly.[16] Inscribed signs occur on the upper handle of jugs no. 12 and no. 13, and on body sherd no. 23.

8. *Plain White Wheelmade Ware*

Plain White Wheelmade is represented by two bowls (nos. 25, 26) and a base fragment of a closed vessel (no. 27), all of known type. Bowl no. 25 has an encircling horizontal furrow below the handle; no. 26 has its exterior upper body shaved on the wheel. The interior floor of no. 27 was split in firing. The ware and technique of these vessels is quite different from the very distinctive ware of no. 28 (Plain White Wheelmade II), with its strong wheelmarks and white slip. No. 25 has close parallels in bowls of Plain White Wheelmade I;[17] no. 27 has parallels in jugs of this same ware.[18] No. 26, however, has less close parallels in Plain White

---

[10] Cf. SCE IV:1C for Plain White Handmade (Type IX.C.2) shape and occurrence, p. 228 and fig. LXXII:1; for Plain White Wheelmade I (Type VIII.C.2) shape and occurrence, pp. 245-47 and fig. LXVII.

[11] Ibid., for Plain White Handmade (Type IX.D.1) shape and occurrence, p. 229; for Plain White Wheelmade I (Type VIII.D.1) shape and occurrence, pp. 247-48 and fig. LXVIII.

[12] Ibid., pp. 250-52, for listing of pot marks on Plain White Handmade and Plain White Wheelmade I.

[13] Ibid., for Plain White Handmade, p. 225; for Plain White Wheelmade I, p. 232. According to Åström even in Period 1 of the Swedish Cyprus Expedition excavations on the acropolis at Idalion (which corresponds to LC IIIA and postdates Idalion Tomb 1), Plain White Handmade and Coarse Ware constituted 45 percent of all sherds (ibid., pp. 693-94).

[14] Shape, fabric, and color nearly identical to no. 13.

[15] For distinction of two Plain White fabrics at Idalion (a "pink" and a "greenish gray") cf. Ålin 1978:93.

[16] For White Painted Wheelmade II cf. SCE IV:1C, pp. 274-75 and fig. LXXV; for White Slip motif, fig. 53:3 (p. 449) and p. 454.

[17] Cf. SCE IV:1C, fig. LX:4, 5.

[18] Ibid., fig. LXVIII:8.

Wheelmade I, and in shape, closer parallels to White Painted Wheelmade III.[19] Karageorghis has had similar difficulties in classifying undecorated bowls of this type from Kition, and has included them under his classification of "Late Mycenaean IIIB ware," comparing them to Plain White Wheelmade I.[20] No. 26 has no traces of paint (and no indication that there had ever been any decoration), but it is very similar in shape and fabric to White Painted Wheelmade III bowl no. 34;[21] rather than classify it as undecorated White Painted Wheelmade III, we have included it in this more general classification.

9. *Plain White Wheelmade II Ware*

Plain White Wheelmade II is represented by a very elegant jug (no. 28), with ovoid body, high foot with ridged profile, and clay pellet imitating metal rivet near the handle root. A rather similar vessel was discovered in the Period 1 level at Idalion by the Swedish Cyprus Expedition;[22] no. 28 differs from it in having a central-channeled handle (the handle was probably less swung) and a high, vertical-sided foot, spreading just below the two shallow ridges.

10. *Coarse Ware*

Coarse Ware is represented by one fragment of a tray(?) or rim(?) (no. 29).[23]

11. *Pithos Ware*

Pithos Ware is represented only by body sherds, including one that is perforated.

12. *White Painted Wheelmade III Ware* (Quasi Mycenaean IIIB Linear Ware)

White Painted Wheelmade III is represented by seven bowls (nos. 30-36) and one fragmentary juglet (no. 37). We have followed the *SCE* classification for these vessels as White Painted Wheelmade III to stress the Cypriot aspect, but have included, in parentheses, Furumark's classification "Quasi Mycenaean IIIB Linear Ware" to stress the dependence on the corresponding Mycenaean ware and the chronological relationship to it.[24] Concomitantly, these objects are quite distinct from those classified below as Levanto-Mycenaean, even ones that are similarly shaped. These latter imitate more closely the "true" Mycenaean shapes and other characteristics, and/or are of superior manufacture. In the catalogue, the bowls have been ordered according to the relationship between height and diameter (h.:d. nos. 30 - 50%; 31 -

---

[19] Compare ibid., fig. LX:10, 11 (Plain White Wheelmade I) and fig. LXXVI:3 (White Painted Wheelmade III).

[20] Karageorghis 1974:86.

[21] Notwithstanding the more vertical base of no. 34. The relationship height:diameter of no. 26 is 35 percent; see discussion of White Painted Wheelmade III.

[22] SCE III, pl. CLXIV:7 = SCE IV:1C, fig. LXX:8. For shape (Type VI.C.1) and occurrence see ibid., p. 256. Compare bronze jugs SCE IV:1D, p. 493, fig. 64 (p. 494) and p. 564.

[23] Cf. SCE IV:1D, p. 519 for basin.

[24] For extensive discussions of this ware, particularly the bowls, see Karageorghis 1965:158-84 (Kouklia-Mantissa); Dikaios 1971:841-43; Karageorghis 1974:39, 41 (Tombs 4 and 5), 86-87 (Tomb 9, upper burial); SCE IV:1C, p. 276. The dating used here follows the evidence from Enkomi, where the "Late Mycenaean IIIB dishes" appear prior to the beginning of Level IIIA, which is dated to about 1200 B.C. This dating is corroborated by the finds from Sinda, where the equivalent "Quasi Mycenaean IIIB Linear Ware" (Sinda Ware P) dates to Sinda Period I, corresponding to LC IIC (P 30, P 74, P 75, Px 34, with a few finds from disturbed Period I/II contexts); see Furumark and Adelman, forthcoming.

49%; 32 - 47%; 33 - 39%; 34 - 34%; fragment 35 - 30-43%; 36 - 31%), which puts them into groups that more or less correspond to Karageorghis' divisions for the bowls from Kouklia.[25] The Idalion bowls are of relatively common shapes and decoration (the latter consisting of encircling bands and spirals).[26] There are, however, certain variations: no. 30, with rounded body, has a slightly incurving lip with a groove below it on the exterior; the painted, pendant, solid-filled arc below the lip on the exterior possibly marked the join of a handle. No. 31, with more angular profile, has three wheelmade horizontal furrows below the lip; the horizontal handle at the lip has two finger-made depressions that create three blunt projections.[27] Nos. 34 and 35 are surely of the same manufacturer; we have mentioned the general similarity in shape and fabric between no. 34 and no. 26 (Plain White Wheelmade). The juglet fragments (no. 37) are of a common type, with the basket handle transverse to the axis of the spout.[28]

13. *Levanto-Mycenaean IIIA2/IIIB (Wheelmade Ware)*[29]

Levanto-Mycenaean IIIA2/IIIB Ware is represented in the repertoire from this tomb by each of the following vessels: a bowl (no. 38[30]), a cup (or kylix?, no. 39[31]), three jars (nos. 40,[32]

---

[25] Karageorghis 1965:158-84.

[26] Ibid.; no. 30 is similar to Type A4, fig. 38; no. 31 is similar to Type A6 with handle, fig. 39:18; no. 32 is similar to Type A3, fig. 38:36; nos. 33-35 similar to Type A7, fig. 39; no. 36 similar to Type A9, figs. 42, 43. For ware, type, and occurrence cf. SCE IV:1C, pp. 276-89 and fig. LXXVI:3, 4.

[27] Compare Karageorghis 1965, fig. 39:18 and Dikaios 1971:841; a metal prototype for the similar but pierced handle from Kouklia is suggested.

[28] Cf. SCE IV:1C, fig. LXXVI:8; for shape (Type X) and occurrence see pp. 286-87. Our drawing of no. 37 (fig. 10) is meant to help visualize the general shape; the sherds are not place in the correct positions.

[29] For discussion of Levanto- and Cypro-Mycenaean see Karageorghis 1965, chap. 5 ("Sur quelques formes de vases particulières à la céramique Chypro-Mycénienne"), pp. 201-30; Furumark 1941:66; Dikaios 1971:835-79 ("Stylistical Observations on the Mycenaean and Derivative Pottery"); SCE IV:1C, pp. 289-403.

[30] For classification see Furumark Type 296 (Furumark 1941:52-54, fig. 15), classified as Levanto-Mycenaean; SCE IV:1C, fig. LXXVII:6, classified as White Painted Wheelmade III (Type III.a) (for occurrence see p. 281), and as Mycenaean Type 296 dated IIIB (for occurrence see pp. 378-80); Karageorghis (1965:213, 215, fig. 50:1, 2), classified as Cypro-Mycenaean dated IIIA2/IIIB (NB: line 17 should read "Type 296," not "Type 196"); Schachermeyr (1976:281-83), classified as IIIB; Dikaios 1971:841-43 ("Classification and General Chronology of Late Mycenaean IIIB Shallow Bowls or Dishes"), 865-66 ("Notes on the Mycenaean IIIB Shallow Bowls or Dishes"). For parallels see Dikaios 1969b, pl. 66:10 (1980/2 from level IIB = pl. 111; Karageorghis 1974, pl. XXXI.133 (from Tombs 4 and 5 dated Mycenaean IIIB).

[31] Cf. SCE IV:1C, variation of White Painted Wheelmade III cup, with handle from carination to body below lip (Type VIII.d = Furumark Type 229), fig. 46 (p. 277); for classification to "Cypro-Mycenaean" dated Mycenaean IIIB and occurrence see p. 362. Compare Karageorghis 1976, fig. 32 (IIIB kylix) and idem 1965:208-10, pl. XIX:5, fig. 49:1, 2, and pp. 208-10 (Cypro-Mycenaean type). For decoration compare Furumark motif 53:14 (wavy line: deep waves, curtailed cuttlefish) dated to IIIB (Furumark 1941:373, fig. 65); especially Dikaios 1971, pl. 306:110, pp. 844, 858 (tentacles of stylized octopus = Furumark motif 21:8) dated Late Minoan (LM) IIIB from Level B; also pl. 311:368, called LM IIIB style; for wavy line on shoulder of three-handled jar dated IIIA2 see ibid., pl. 196:33 (Tomb 3.178). For dotted octopus tentacle cf. Karageorghis 1974, pl. XXIV:163. For Type 220 with solid-painted interior (as a determining Minoan characteristic) cf. SCE IV:1C, p. 407.

[32] Furumark Type 45 in Furumark 1941, fig. 4 (p. 23) and p. 27; SCE IV:1C, p. 301; for occurrence, ibid., pp. 297-301. For nearly exact parallels see Benson 1972, pl. 32 (B 1107) from Tomb 19 dated LC IIA-B; Dikaios 1969b, pl. 208:12, 14 (Tomb 10:272, 271, third burial layer dated to the early part of Enkomi Level IIB, Dikaios 1969a:391); Hennessy 1963, pl. XXVII:25 (from Tomb 4A dated LC IIA-B, p. 12).

41,[33] 42[34]), a false-necked jar (no. 43[35]), a number of uncatalogued sherds illustrated on plate 12 (see descriptions below), and a number of the Fine Ware sherds listed in table 2. Inasmuch as the points of origin of these Mycenaean-type vessels are still in dispute, all of them have been included in this category, those usually classified as Levanto- (or Cypro-)Mycenaean as well as those usually classified as Mycenaean and Late Minoan. The use of lustrous red, black, or diluted brown paint distinguishes these wares from the local Cypriot decorated wares. The fabric and slip vary: one sort has well-levigated clay fired pink or reddish yellow, and a very pale brown micaceous slip; a second sort, that has well-levigated clay fired very pale brown or light red, lacks mica in the pink or reddish yellow slip; a third sort, similar to the native Cypriot, has a porous, pink or reddish yellow fabric, and pink slip with no mica; and a fourth sort has a very pale brown fabric and a light, burnished surface without mica. Interestingly, it is the first sort, with the micaceous slip (quite unlike any local wares found in the tomb), that includes two vessels normally classified as Levanto- (or Cypro-)Mycenaean shapes (nos. 38 and 39, with variation of handle). The second sort includes a vessel of Mycenaean shape (no. 41) and one of Levanto-Mycenaean shape (no. 43). The third sort includes vessels of Mycenaean (no. 40) and Minoan (no. 42) shapes, and sherd m (pl. 12). The fourth includes sherds a-e and f-g (pl. 12). All of the vessels are of common shape and decoration except for the cup (no. 39) and the jar (no. 42), which show Minoan influence. The cup differs from most cups in the placement of its handle--from carination to midbody. The decoration of deep wavy line or stylized octopus tentacles suggests the Minoan sphere, but the interior of the vessel is not painted solid. This vessel is similar enough to a stemmed Mycenaean IIIB kylix from Kition (albeit without a handle) to suggest that it, too, may be a kylix (see note 31). The jar (no. 42), either three-handled or false-necked, is decorated with a variation of an elaborate triangle. Elaborate triangle motifs are common to Crete, but the particular example cited by Furumark that seems similar to this one is from a vessel of non-Mycenaean shape of IIIA2 date found in Maroni Tomb 1 (see note 34.)

14. *Description of Levanto-Mycenaean Sherds Illustrated on Plate 12*

a-e. Fragments of a IIIA2/IIIB jar, including ring base, globular body sherds, neck root. Decorated with lustrous orange paint; encircling lines and bands on body; in shoulder zone, band of arcs closed by opposing arcs. Fabric and slip white (2.5Y 8/2); surface lustrous.

f-g. Fragments of a IIIA2/IIIB closed vessel (similar to a-e), including body and ring base. Decorated with lustrous red paint; encircling bands and lines on body. Fabric pink. Slip very pale brown (10 YR 8/3); surface lustrous.

---

[33] Furumark Type 45 in Furumark 1941, fig. 4 (p. 23) and p. 27; SCE IV:1C, p. 301; for occurrence, ibid., pp. 297-301. Compare Karageorghis 1965, fig. 31 (p. 113) (Tomb 2:17) for shape; for description see p. 119; for Furumark motif 19:20 (multistem and tongue pattern) dated IIIA:2 Late and occurrence (on Types 45, 220) see Furumark 1941, fig. 47 (p. 299) and p. 301. For parallel see Karageorghis 1974, pl. XLIV:103 (from Tomb 9, lower burial). Contrast Dikaios 1971, pl. 299:3 (Pyla-Verghi Tomb 1:7.)

[34] For shape compare SCE IV:1C, fig. 46f (p. 414, Type 166a, false-necked jar), and for IIIA2 dating and occurrence, pp. 337-38; Karageorghis 1974, pl. CXXIV and pp. 27, 39 (LM IIIA stirrup jar from Tombs 4 and 5:161) and for three-handled jar, Furumark Type 45 (see note 33, above). For Furumark motif 71:c (elaborate triangle) dated to LM IIIA1 see Furumark 1941, fig. 71 (p. 411) and p. 407. Furumark notes that these motifs are common to LM III false-necked jars (ibid.), and that "only on one [Mycenaean] IIIA:2 jar, belonging to the early part of this period [Mycenaean IIIA-B], are there ornaments of the triangular class in the quadrantal fields. These ornaments are similar to c left), the only difference being that the interior filling has a rounded top as in b. The vase in question [166:17 from Maroni Tomb 1] is somewhat un-Mycenaean in shape, and the decoration of the semicircular field has a close LM IIIA:2 parallel."

[35] Furumark Type 191 in Furumark 1941, fig. 6 (p. 31); SCE IV:1C, fig. LXXVII:11 (Levanto-/Cypro-Mycenaean); for shape (Type 191) and occurrence (dating to IIIA2b-IIIB), ibid., pp. 352-53; for Furumark motif 58 (parallel chevrons), see Furumark 1941, fig. 67 (p. 383). For motif cf. Dikaios 1969b, pl. 65:27 (5942/1 from Level IIB).

h. Mouth fragment of a juglet (possibly White Painted Wheelmade III). Everted flattened lip. Decorated with nonlustrous paint; bands and dots. Fabric very pale brown. D. ca. 3.0.

i. Fragment of a false-necked jar (handle root and disk). Decorated with black paint (traces only). Fabric white.

j. Fragment of a IIIA2/IIIB juglet (neck, and handle from neck).[36] Decorated with black paint (traces inside mouth). Fabric white.

k-l. Handle fragments from IIIA2/IIIB juglets.[37] Decorated with lustrous black paint. Fabric very pale brown.

m. IIIB (rude style?) body sherd. Decorated with red paint (2.5 YR 5/8); band of crosshatched lozenges. Fabric reddish yellow (5 YR 6/6).

14. *Bucchero Handmade Ware*

Bucchero Handmade Ware, which is related to Base Ring II,[38] is represented by two jugs (nos. 44,[39] 45[40]), and a number of sherds. Both jugs are of common type. In fact, similar vessels were found on the Acropolis at Idalion by the Swedish Cyprus Expedition.[41]

15. *Bucchero Wheelmade Ware*

Bucchero Wheelmade Ware is very similar to Bucchero Handmade found at the site; it, too, is related to Base Ring II.[42] The ware is represented here by a jug of common type (no.

---

[36] Furumark Type 191 in Furumark 1941, fig. 6 (p. 31); SCE IV:1C, fig. LXXVII:11 (Levanto-Mycenaean) and fig. 46e (p. 413, 191d2 bis); for occurrence, ibid., p. 352 (Type 191).

[37] Cf. Benson 1972, pl. 33 (B 1177).

[38] SCE IV:1C, p. 425. Compare Base Ring II jugs (ibid., fig. LII:10-12) from Lapithos Tomb 702 (dated to LC IIIA1, SCE IV:1D, p. 831).

[39] Compare SCE IV:1C, fig. LXXVIII:2 for proportions, 11 for base.

[40] Compare ibid., fig. LXXVIII:5 for shape. NB: the drawing of no. 45 on pl. 25 should have a ridge indicated at the neck root, whether or not the two fragments belong to the same vessel.

[41] SCE II, pl. CLXIV:1 (I.475, Bucchero Handmade = SCE IV:1C, fig. LXVIII:11), 2 (I.884, Bucchero Handmade), 4 (I.423, Bucchero Wheelmade), 5 (I.451, Black Slip Wheelmade = SCE IV:1C, fig. LXXVIII:12).

[42] SCE IV:1C, p. 425. There has been confusion as to the dating of the Bucchero Handmade and Wheelmade. Sjöqvist considered Bucchero Wheelmade an indicator of LC III (SCE I, p. 538 re Enkomi Tomb 15, which contained two Bucchero Handmade [15.2, 15.3] and one Bucchero Wheelmade [15.1], as well as an ivory box [15.4]), and assigned the earth tomb to that date. Åström refers to the handmade Enkomi jug 15.3 (SCE IV:1C, and fig. LXXVIII:4, p. 427, Type I.B.e) as belonging to the earlier variety (i.e., similar to Base Ring II). He lists Bucchero Wheelmade in LC II contexts (SCE IV:1D, pp. 689-93) and notes (p. 770) that "Bucchero Ware appears on the scene in Late Cypriote IIB as a ribbed or fluted variety of Base-ring II Ware, but is more common in Late Cypriote III." Compare a Bucchero jug from Apliki (Taylor 1952, fig. 5:17 [p. 137], from House A Room 4 [p. 140] dated LC IIC-III [p. 144], dated LC IIC in SCE IV:1D [p. 689]) and a Base Ring jug from Apliki (Taylor 1952, pl. XXVI:4, from House B III, Pit 2); note on Bucchero, p. 159. For a Bucchero jug similar to no. 46, from a LC IIC context at Kouklia-Mantissa see Karageorghis 1965, fig. 45:39 (p. 173) and pp. 166, 180, 184. See also idem 1974, pl. XXVIII, p. 86, for eight Bucchero Wheelmade vessels from Kition Tomb 9 (upper burial), dated LC IIC. Bucchero Wheelmade is therefore attested in LC IIC contexts, and there is no problem in assigning no. 46 to this period. No. 46 is of the earlier fabric related to Base Ring II (a ware phased out by LC IIIA1; cf. chart SCE IV:1D, pp. 700-701).

46[43]) and by a number of sherds.

16. *Iron Age (and later)*

The Iron Age and later periods are represented only by very scanty remains, ranging in date from Cypro-Geometric (CG) III/Cypro-Archaic (CA) I to modern times. The more informative sherds are illustrated on figure 14 and plate 14 (see descriptions below); the others are included in table 2.

Description of Iron Age (and later) Sherds Illustrated on Figure 14 and Plate 14

a.	White Painted rim, CG III/CA I
b-g.	White Painted body sherds, CG III/CA I
h.	White Painted rim, CG III/CA I
i.	White Painted handle, CG III/CA I
j.	Bichrome rim
h.	Black-on-Red rim
l.	Black-on-Red neck fragment, slightly lustrous
m.	Black-on-Red jug fragment, polished
n.	Black-on-Red body sherd, matt, rough surface
o.	White Painted jug body fragment
p.	Bichrome III offset rim fragment (bowl)
q.	Black-on-Red rim fragment (bowl)
r.	White Painted rim fragment (bowl)
s.	White Painted (III-IV) base decorated with concentric circles or spirals
t.	Neck fragment (traces of paint?), green fabric (CA)
u.	Hellenistic glazed bowl fragment
v.	Hellenistic handle
w.	East Greek body fragment; contains mica; fabric pink (7.5 YR 7/4)
x-y.	East Greek base (x) and body (y) fragment; contains mica; fabric light reddish brown (5 YR 6/4)
z.	Plain White bowl fragment (Cypro-Classical [CC]?)
aa.	Plain White Rim
bb.	Plain White neck fragment (CA-CC)
cc-ff.	Attic Black Glaze: cc rim; dd rim; ee body with black parallel polish lines; ff ring base
gg.	Roof tile (modern?)
hh.	Glaze ware rim, white celadon (late)
ii.	Glaze ware rim, brown (17th-18th century)
jj.	Glaze ware sherds, celadon (14th-15th century)

Other Finds (see tables 3 and 4)

1. *Bronze*

Bronze is represented by one fragmentary, much corroded finger ring of simple form (no. 47).[44] Similar rings are common to all Late Cypriot periods.[45]

---

[43] Compare SCE IV:1C, fig. LXXVIII:4 (E.15.3), Bucchero Handmade jug for shape.

[44] The ring consists of either two plain closed hoops joined, or a spiral with overlapping ends.

[45] Cf. SCE IV:1D, pp. 489-90 and fig. 63:13 (p. 490, finger ring Type 2 and ring Type 3); for chronology see p. 563. For "double" ring cf. Karageorghis 1974, pl. XCII (from Tomb 9, upper burial). For spiral cf. Dikaios 1969b, pl. 157:14 (1519 from Level IIB).

2. Terracotta

Terracotta is represented by a perforated flat disk (a loom weight?, no. 48)[46] of common Late Cypriot type, and a fragmentary Cypro-Archaic animal figurine (no. 49)[47] of common type. In fact, fragments of such figurines have been found as surface finds in the fields surrounding the tomb.

3. Glyptic

Glyptic is represented by a cylinder seal (frit? no. 50).[48] Although we have found no exact parallel for this cylinder, there are parallels for its iconographic and compositional elements. The simple and economical rendering with drilled holes and lines suggests local Cypriot manufacture early in the thirteenth century B.C., in imitation of seals in the Mitannian style with more intricate naturalistic scenes.[49] The much worn condition of no. 50 suggests that it was already old and much used at the time of its deposition in the tomb. Quadrupeds in file--one with straight legs, striding, one with dotted legs, in more rapid movement--with birds alighting on the quadrupeds' backs appear on a seal from Stephania in a LC I context.[50] Dotted rosettes (which are used on no. 50 as heads) are found on local cylinders from Kourion.[51] Rosettes and pendant necklaces are to be found on a cylinder from Kition Tomb 9 (lower burial) dated by Porada to the first half of the thirteenth century.[52] A cylinder in the Larnaca Museum, Cyprus (1960.VI.2717) depicts a sphinx on a table, with a necklace hanging from its mouth; a bird flying left; a bird flying downward; and bucrania.[53]

---

[46] Cf. SCE IV:1D, fig. 65:50 (p. 509) and p. 517, loom weight (Type 3) dating from LC IIC. For nearly exact parallels cf. Karageorghis 1974, pls. LXXXIX, CLXIII and pp. 64, 93, Tomb 9 (upper burial):23, 24, 25; compare pl. CXXXIII, Tombs 4 and 5:224, 225, of smaller diameter.

[47] Similar figurines have been found by the Swedish Cyprus Expedition excavations at Idalion; cf. SCE II, pl. CLXXXII:4 (I.1130). Also cf. SCE IV:2.

[48] For discussion of Cypriot seals cf. Porada 1948:179-98 and idem, "Seals" (Appendix V), in Dikaios 1971:783-810.

[49] For Mitannian influence cf. ibid., especially pp. 786-95. For use of lines cf. Karageorghis 1965, pl. X:3 (Akhera Tomb 3:29 dating to LC II and attributed by Porada to Cypriot [possibly of Kourion] manufacture; ibid., p. 152).

[50] Cf. Hennessy 1963, pl. VIII.e and p. 40, dated by Buchanan to ca. 15th century B.C.; tomb dated to LC I, p. 44. For birds with outstretched wings above quadrupeds on seal of Cypriot origin and showing Mitannian influence cf. Poursat 1977, pl. XXII and p. 245.

[51] For rosette cf. Benson 1972, pl. 38 (B 1625), attributed to local manufacture by Porada, ibid., pp. 141-44. Also cf. Dikaios 1969b, pl. 180:4 and discussion by Porada, ibid., vol. 2, p. 787.

[52] In Karageorghis 1974:164-66 (cylinder seal 2, Kition Tomb 9/16, lower burial), fig. 2.

[53] The combination of quadruped, bird, and pendant necklace on no. 50 suggests a relationship to the winged griffins or sphinxes that were characteristic of earlier seals. Perhaps the composition on no. 50 is based on some seal-cutter's misunderstanding of these earlier seals, or perhaps the two compositions run parallel. For griffins cf. Porada in Dikaios 1971:791.

IDALION TOMB 1.76: ARTIFACTUAL REMAINS   165

4. *Ivory*

a. Disks. There are two disks (nos. 51,[54] 52[55]) of known type. No. 52 is decorated with incised encircling lines.

b. Buttons(?). There are four buttons(?) (nos. 53, 54, 55, 56[56]) of known type. (No. 54 may be a whorl.) Nos. 53 and 55 have horizontal perforations in addition to the central vertical perforation; no. 56 is not completely perforated.

c. Rods. There are five rod fragments (nos. 57, 58,[57] 59, 60, 61) of known type. Nos. 57 and 58 are decorated with incised lines; no. 59 has a dowel-like projection for attachment.

d. Bowls. There are four(?) bowl fragments (nos. 62, 63, 64, 65, the last merely a sliver) of uncommon type. Nos. 62 and 63 (which probably come from the same vessel) and no. 64 are decorated on both surfaces with incised lines. The motifs are common to the Late Cypriot period.[58]

Chronology and General Remarks

As stated above, the excavation of Idalion Tomb 1, which is located in the fields below the West Acropolis just south of the modern village of Dhali, was conducted as an emergency salvage operation. The remains, which included Bronze and Iron Age and later wares, were in a very fragmented state (testifying to a plundering in antiquity).

The Iron Age materials proved to be very scanty, with hardly more than a single sherd per vessel. The earliest Iron Age sherd may belong to the Late Cypro-Geometric period (CG III), but most belong to the Archaic period; there are also several splintered sherds of East Greek origin, with high mica content; some fragments of Attic Black Glaze; and a few chips of Medieval fabric.

The bulk of the material (including all the catalogued objects with the exception of the fragmentary Cypro-Archaic terracotta figurine, no. 49) dates to the Late Cypriot IIC period. There are strong similarities between the finds from Idalion Tomb 1 and the LC II tombs at Kition[59] and Enkomi,[60] as well as the contemporaneous Level IIB at Enkomi and Period I at

---

[54] For shape compare Dikaios 1969b, pl. 156:37 (1285b), ivory disk from Level IIB.

[55] Compare ibid., pl. 156:40 (1743), ivory disk from Level IIB. Also cf. SCE IV:1D, fig. 74 (p. 551).

[56] Cf. Karageorghis 1965, fig. 33:42 (p. 117) for ivory button with three horizontal perforations and central concavity, from Akhera Tomb 2, dated LC IIC, p. 137.

[57] For similarly incised rods cf. Karageorghis 1974, pls. LXXXVIII, CLXX (nos. 60-62 et al. from Tomb 9, upper burial), CXLIX:139 (Tomb 9, lower burial).

[58] Cf. SCE IV:1D, p. 553. An ivory vessel from Sinda (I 2, from Tomb 1 E.C.5, dating from Period I/II) is decorated on the rim with similar encircling lines framing a double zigzag (see Furumark and Adelman, forthcoming). Other objects have motifs similar to those of nos. 62-64: a lid from Kition has short transverse strokes between encircling lines (cf. Karageorghis 1974, pl. CXXXIII:235 from Tombs 4 and 5); and a disk with similar decoration from Enkomi Tomb 3:84 (SCE IV:1D, fig. 74:19 [p.551]).

[59] Cf. Karageorghis 1974, Tombs 4 and 5, 9, pp. 16-94.

[60] Cf. Dikaios 1969b for, e.g., Tomb 10, pls. 208-12; idem 1969a:357-94; for Level IIB, idem 1971:451-57.

Sinda.[61] Yet the fact that twenty-seven of the forty-six pottery objects are handmade points to a degree of provincialism (or conservatism) at the site. Even so, the local potters, although they retained the handmade technique, appear to have kept abreast of the current trends, for the Plain White Handmade vessels (which form the bulk of this group) follow closely the shapes of the Plain White Wheelmade vessels common to the other sites.[62] The latest material is the White Painted Wheelmade III pottery; concomitantly, the absence of any Mycenaean IIIC:1b ware allows us a terminal date toward the end of Late Cypriot IIC.[63]

Although only a few precious objects were found in Idalion Tomb 1, the presence of the bronze finger ring, the scraps of ivory, the cylinder, and the better quality Levanto-Mycenaean vessels suggests that the tomb was richly furnished at the time that it was plundered.[64]

Idalion Tomb 1 bears witness to the presence of a contemporaneous Late Cypriot IIC community in its vicinity, in the unprotected open fields below the hill of what later became the West Acropolis site.[65] The location of this earlier community suggests a peaceful life, and the wealth of the tomb suggests a degree of comfort among the inhabitants of the community. Subsequently, at the beginning of Late Cypriot III, when their security was threatened by the events and peoples associated with Mycenaean IIIC:1b wares, they, and perhaps other neighboring communities including Kafkalia, retreated to the hill at Idalion and established the fortified West Acropolis settlement.[66]

---

[61] Cf. Furumark 1965, and Furumark and Adelman (forthcoming). For chronological table of wares cf. SCE IV.1D, pp. 700-701.

[62] Of interest are the incised signs on Plain White Handmade vessels nos. 12, 13, 23. For incised signs at Enkomi cf. Dikaios 1969b, pl. 160.

[63] For absolute chronology cf. SCE IV:1D, p. 762; for relative chronology of pottery see ibid., pp. 689-93; for historical conclusions, ibid., pp. 769-75. For chronology see also Karageorghis 1976:173; Schachermeyr 1976:277-303. NB: in Tomb 9 (upper burial) at Kition (Karageorghis 1974, pl. LXXII:339, 138) were found two bowls with antithetic spirals in imitation of IIIC1 bowls, suggesting that the Kition tomb postdates Idalion Tomb 1. Cf. above, "Pottery, 12. White Painted Wheelmade III."

[64] See above, Carola C. Schulte-Campbell, "A Late Cypriot IIC Tomb: Idalion Tomb 1.76, 1. Introduction and Skeletal Remains."

[65] It has been postulated that populations from north of the Yalias River were responsible for the founding of the acropolis site at the beginning of LC IIIA. Cf. Ålin 1978:91-92, 108-9.

[66] Cf. SCE II, pp. 626-27; SCE IV:1C, pp. 4-5, 11-14, 35-38; SCE IV:1D, pp. 693-94.

Table 4. Concordance of Catalogue, Drawing*, and Registration Numbers for Idalion Tomb 1

Catalogue	Drawing	Registration	Bucket	Locus	Catalogue	Drawing	Registration	Bucket	Locus
1	25	T 146/863			34	27	T 167/885		
2	18				35	28			
3	38	T 147/864			36	7	T 168/886		
4	38 bis				37	29			
5	1	T 148/865			38	10	T 170/888		
6	26				39	12	T 171/889		
7	20	T 149/866			40	13	T 172/890		
8	30	T 122/746	36	004	41	2	T 173/891		
9	23	T 150/867			42	19	T 174/892		
10	45a+b	T 151/868			43	11	T 175/893		
11	46	T 152/869			44	9	T 176/894		
12	47				45	44a+b	T 177/895		
13	42	T 153/870			46	21	T 178/896		
14	15	T 154/871			47	33	F 557/846	32	004
15	14	T 155/872			48	32	A 539/776	41	004
16	50				49	55			
17	51				50	40	B 897/743	35	004
18	52				51	36:3	I.004/772a	37	004
19	22				52	36:2	see no. 51		
20	5a	T 156/873			53	36:4	see no. 51		
21	43	T 157/874			54	37	I.005/773a	16	003
22	41	T 158/875			55	36:5	see no. 51		
23	31	T 125/833	36	004	56	36:6	see no. 51		
24	39	T 159/876			57	34	I.001/769a	20	004
25	6	T 160/877			58	35:4	I.003/771a		003
26	4	T 161/878			59	35:2	see no. 58		
27	53	T 162/879			60	35:1	see no. 58		
28	24	T 163/881			61	36:1	see no. 51		
29	54				62	36:7	see no. 51	35	002
30	16	T 164/882			63	35:5	I.002/770a		
31	3	T 165/883			64	36:8	see no. 51		
32	17				65	35:3	see no. 58		
33	8	T 166/884							

*These are the drawing numbers assigned to the finds in the field, before the catalogue numbers were assigned to them.

1
Scale 2:5

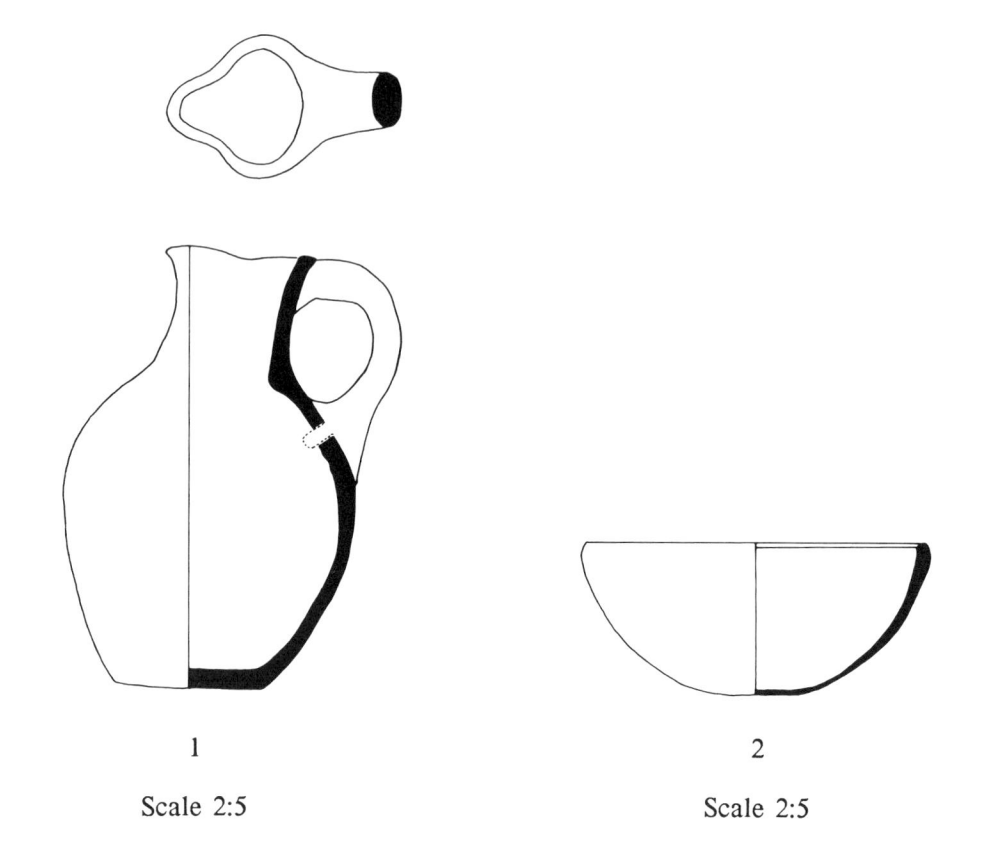

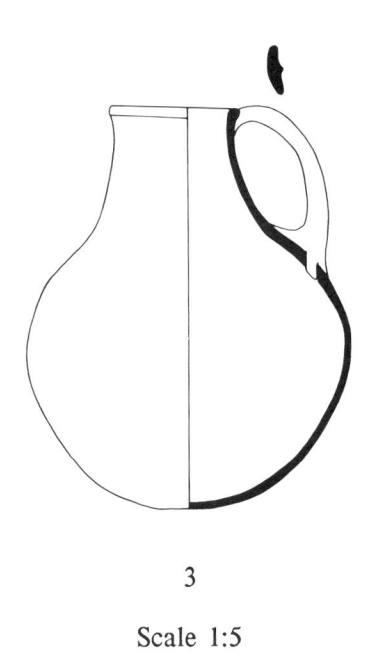

2
Scale 2:5

3
Scale 1:5

Figure 1. Cat. nos. 1 (Jug), 2 (Bowl), and 3 (Jug).

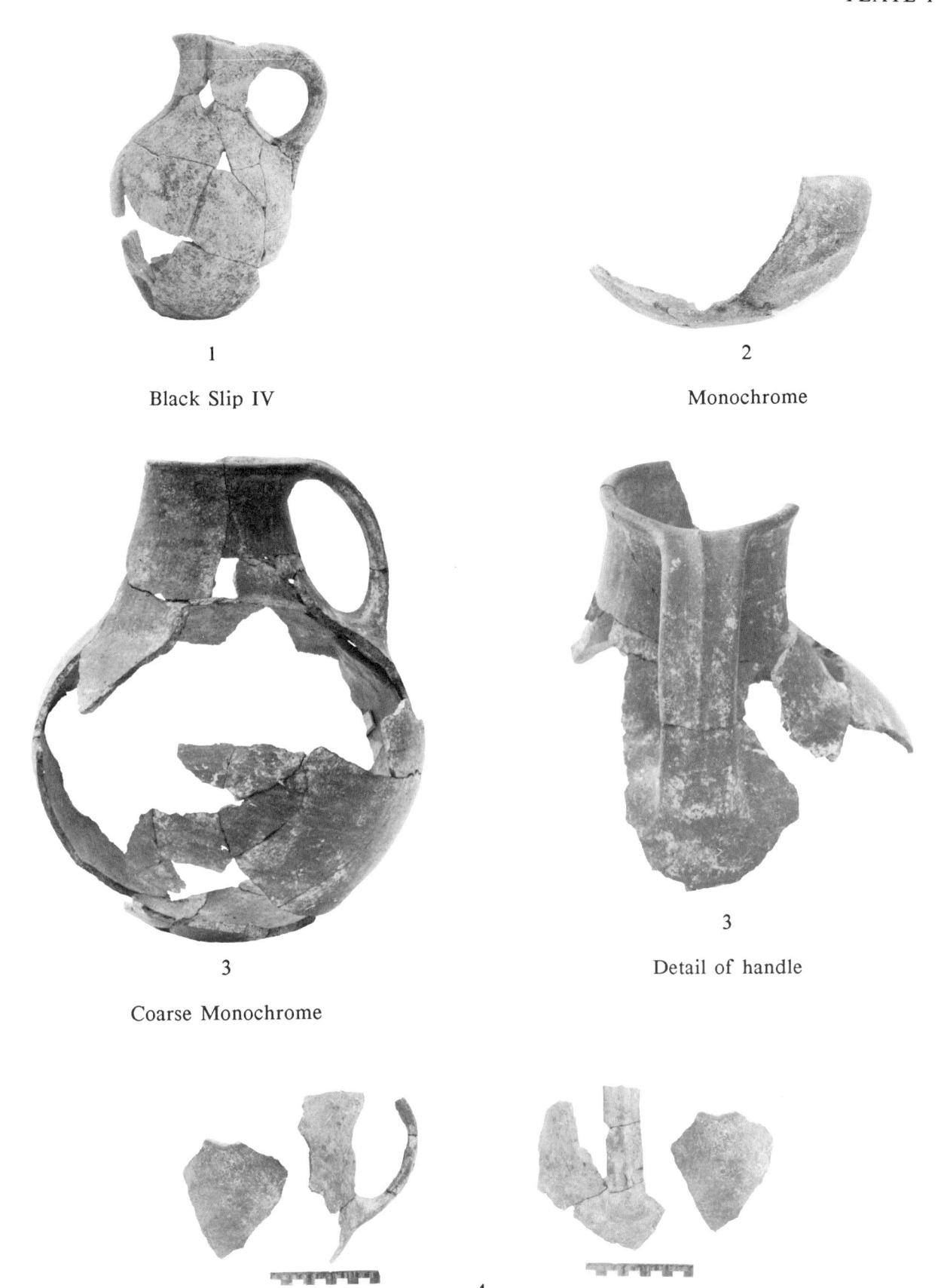

PLATE 1

1
Black Slip IV

2
Monochrome

3
Coarse Monochrome

3
Detail of handle

4
Coarse Monochrome

5

Scale 2:5

Sketch   6   Sketch

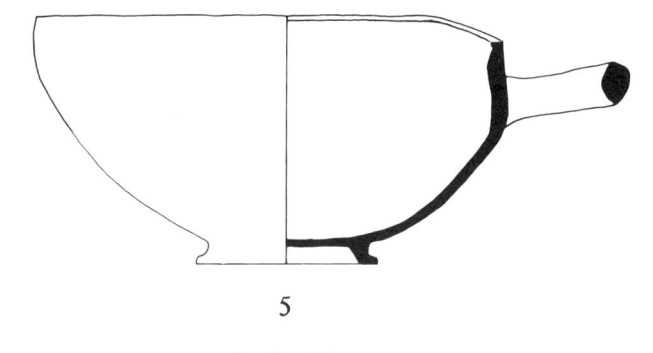

Scale 2:5

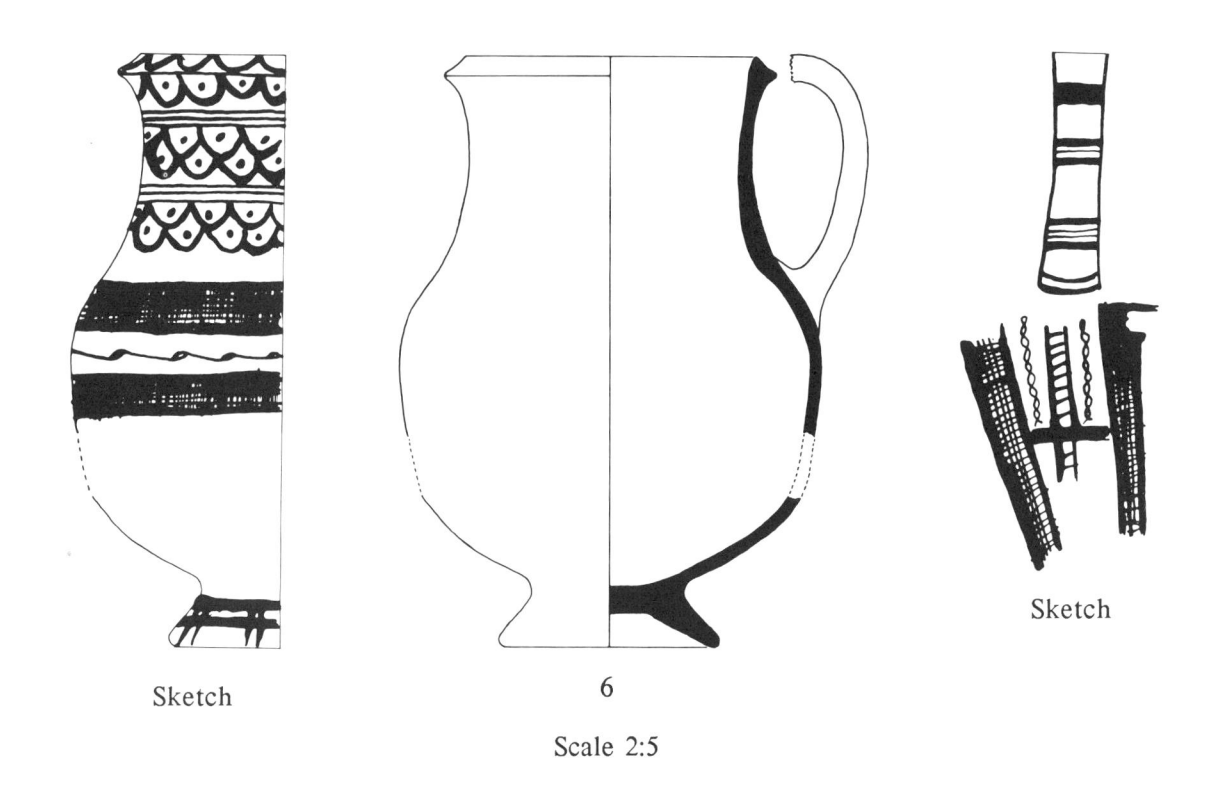

Figure 2. Cat. nos. 5 (Bowl) and 6 (Tankard).

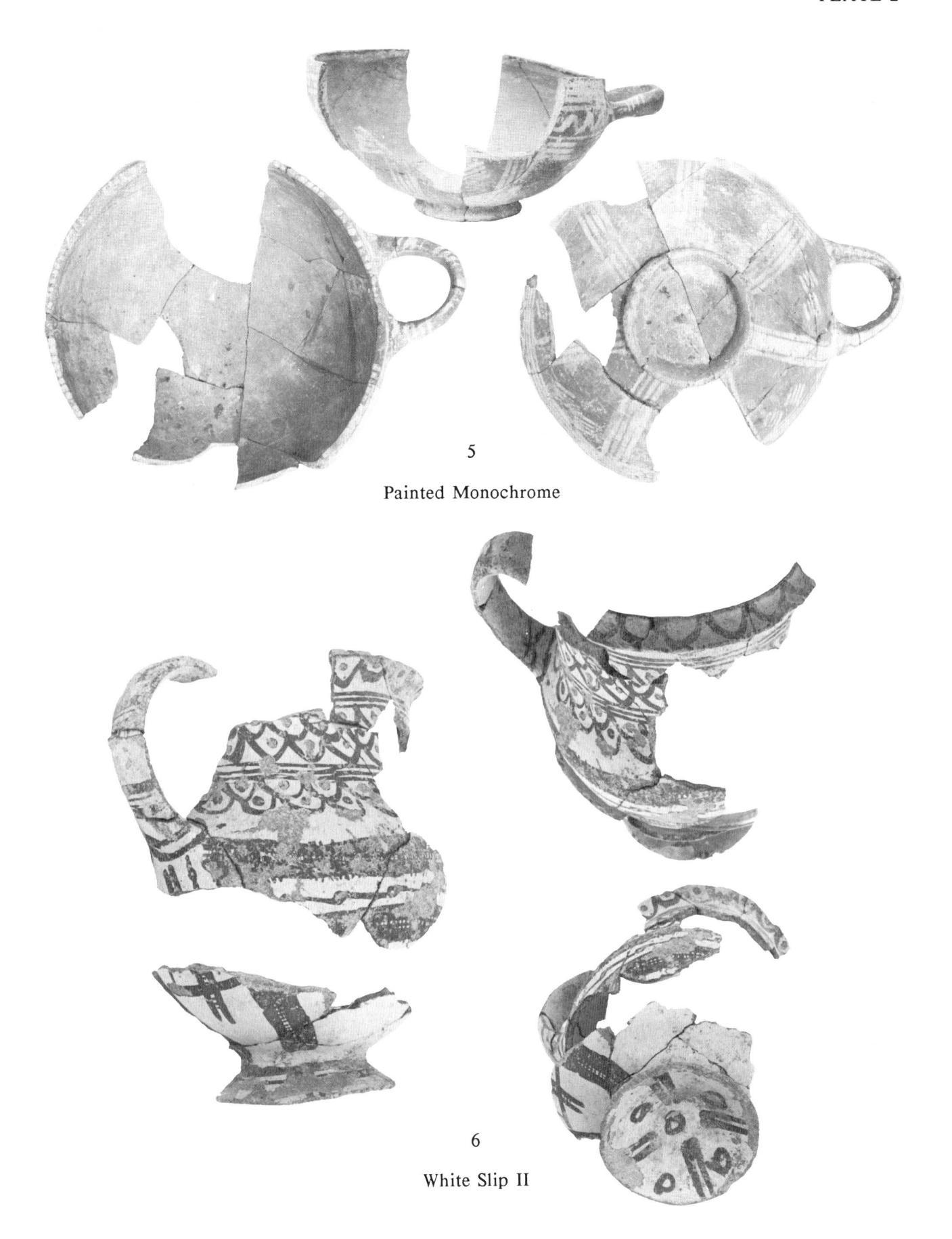

PLATE 2

5
Painted Monochrome

6
White Slip II

7

Scale 2:5

8

Scale 2:5

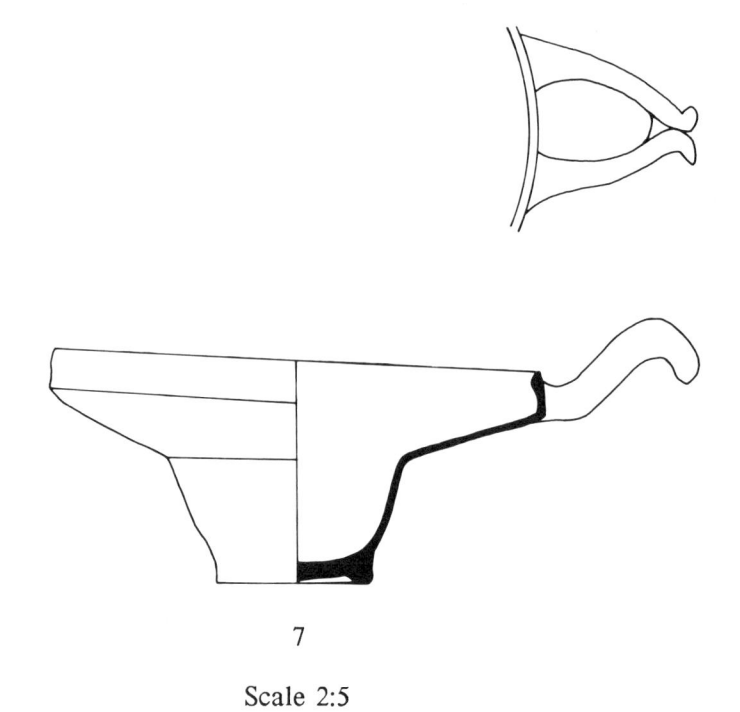

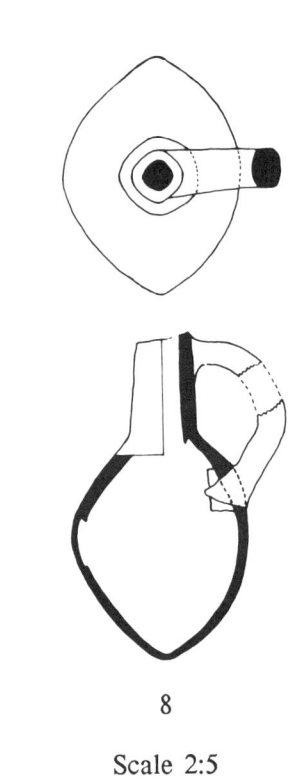

Figure 3. Cat. nos. 7 (Bowl) and 8 (Lentoid Flask).

PLATE 3

7

Base Ring II

8

Base Ring II

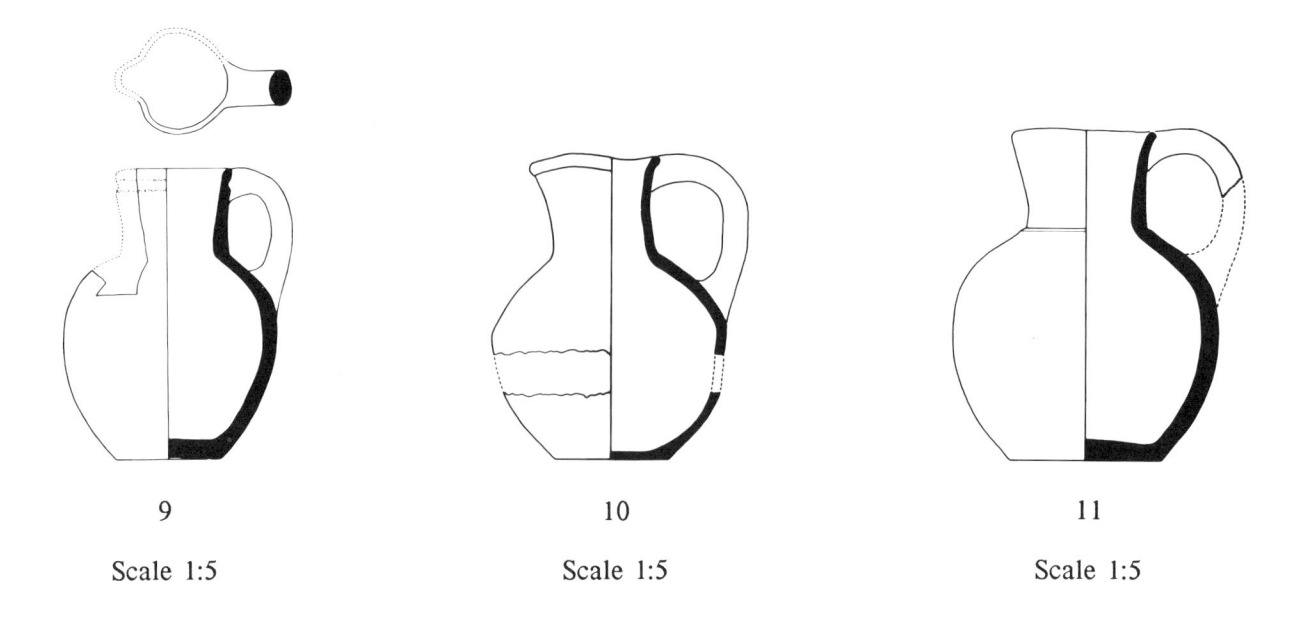

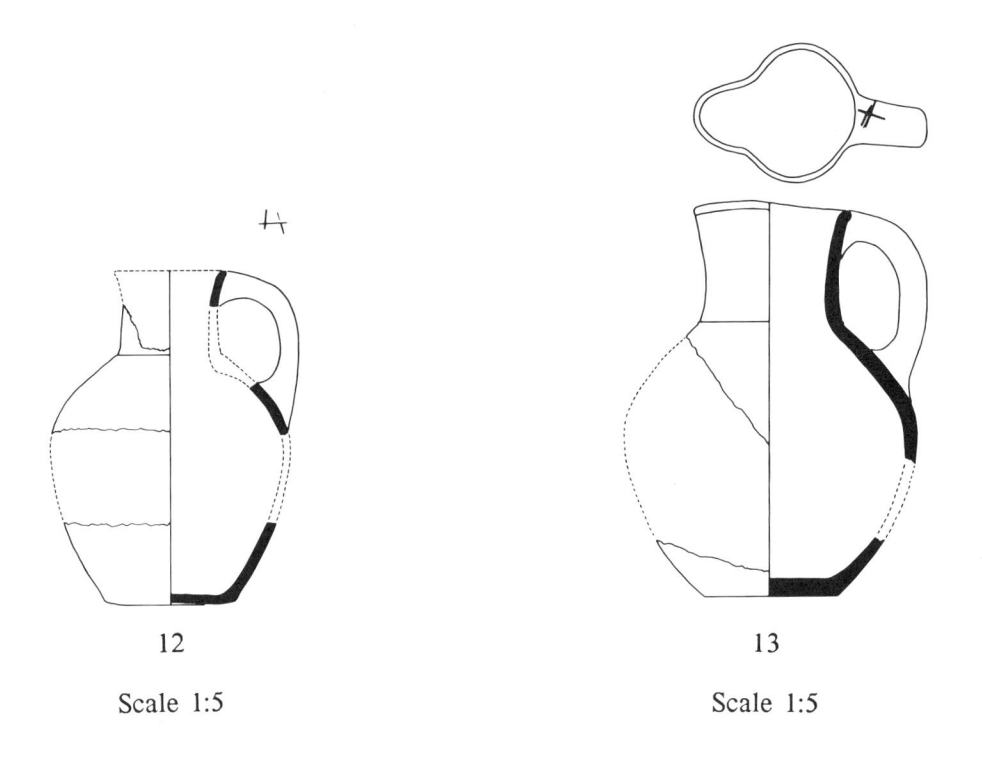

Figure 4. Cat. nos. 9-13 (Fragmentary Jugs).

PLATE 4

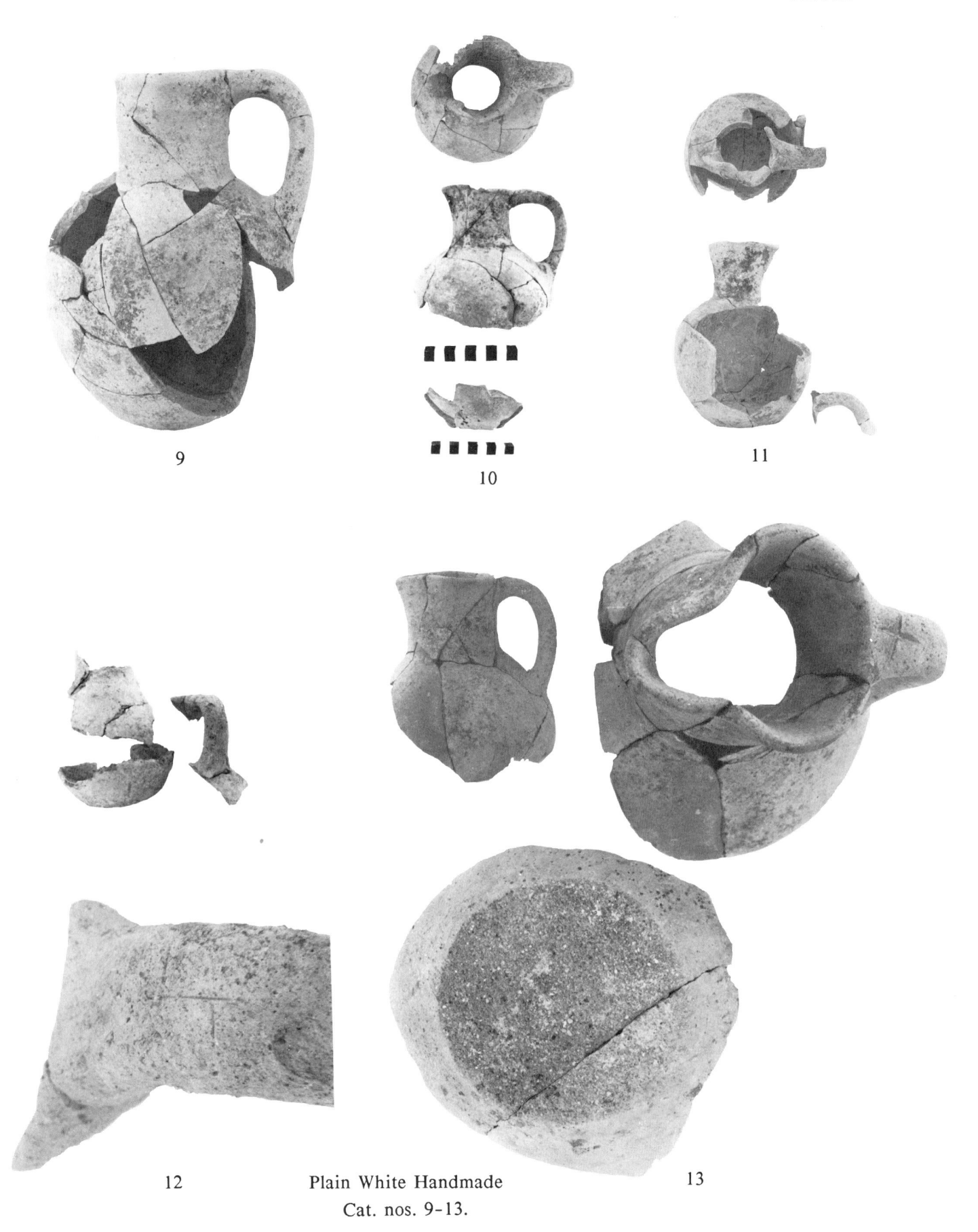

9

10

11

12 Plain White Handmade 13
Cat. nos. 9-13.

14

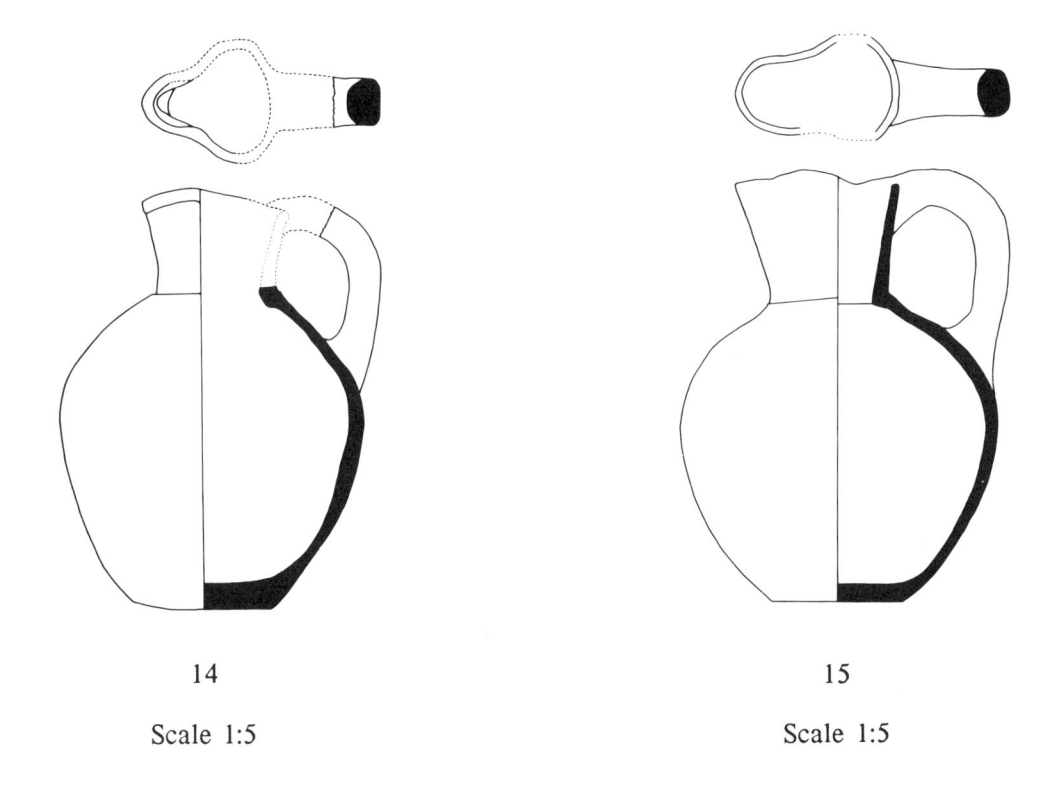

Scale 1:5

15

Scale 1:5

Figure 5. Cat. nos. 14 and 15 (Jugs).

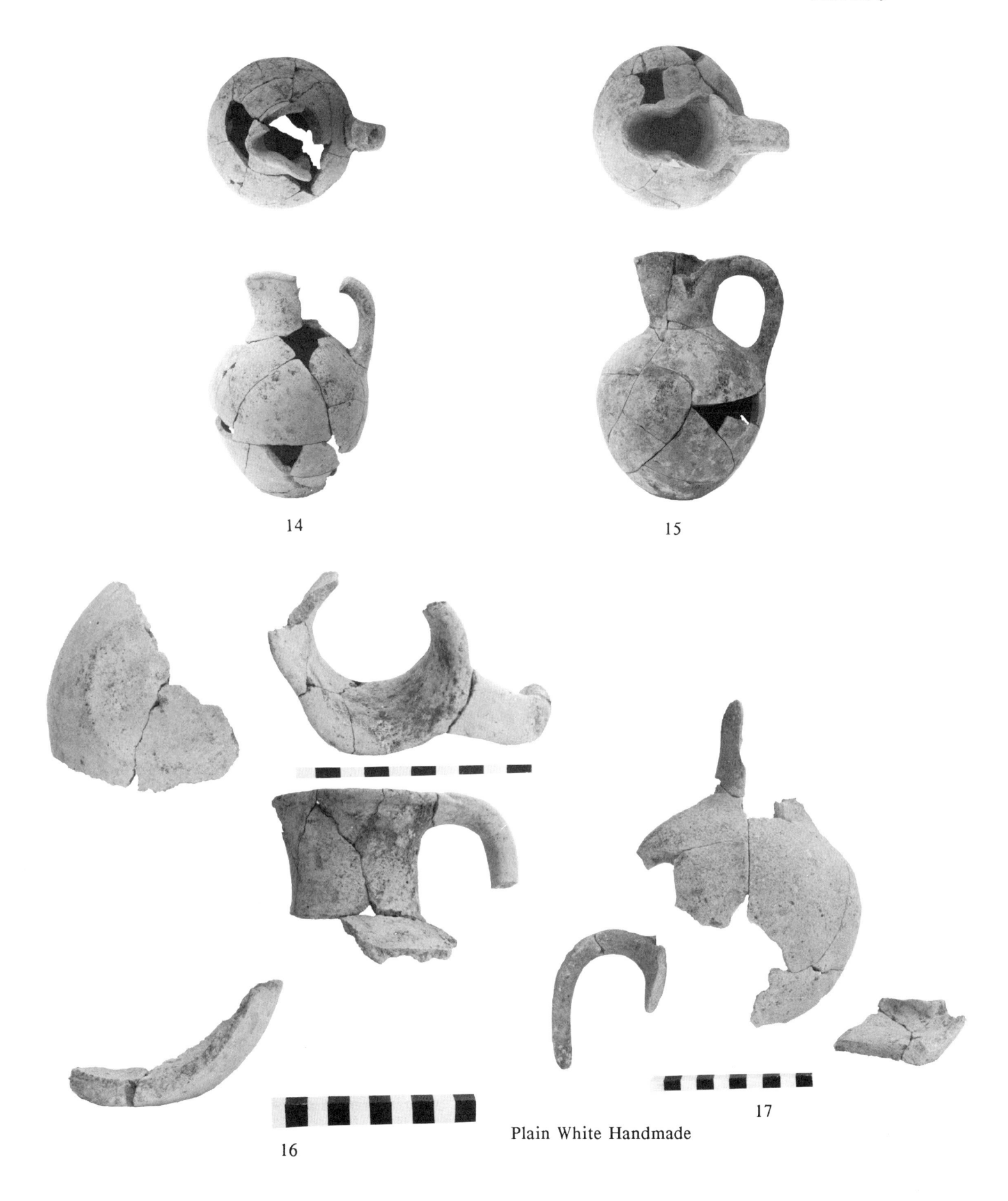

PLATE 5

14

15

16

Plain White Handmade

17

19

Scale 1:5

20

Scale 1:5

21

Scale 1:5

22

Scale 1:5

23

Scale 4:5

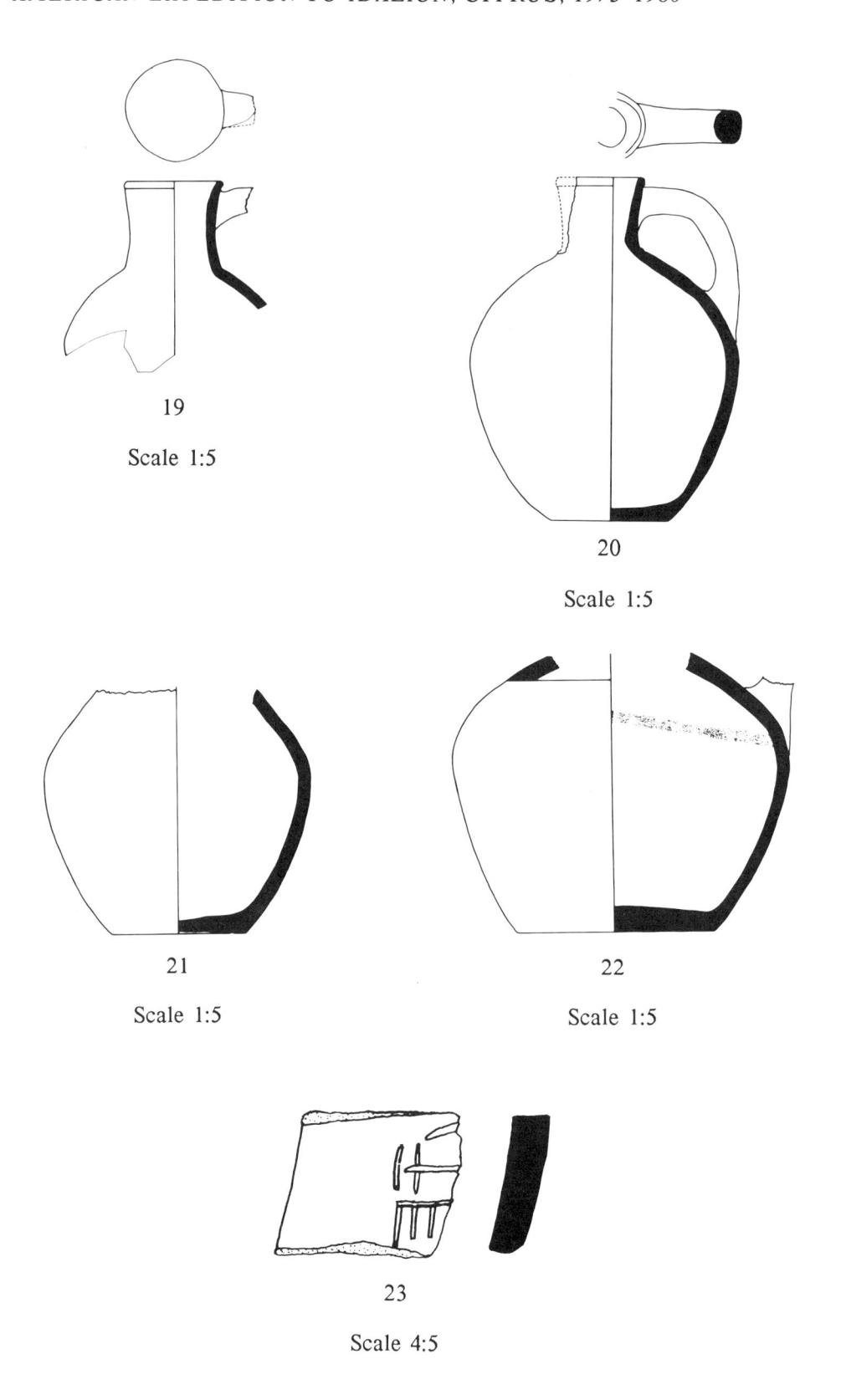

Figure 6. Cat. nos. 19-22 (Fragmentary Jugs) and 23 (Inscribed Body Sherd).

PLATE 6

19

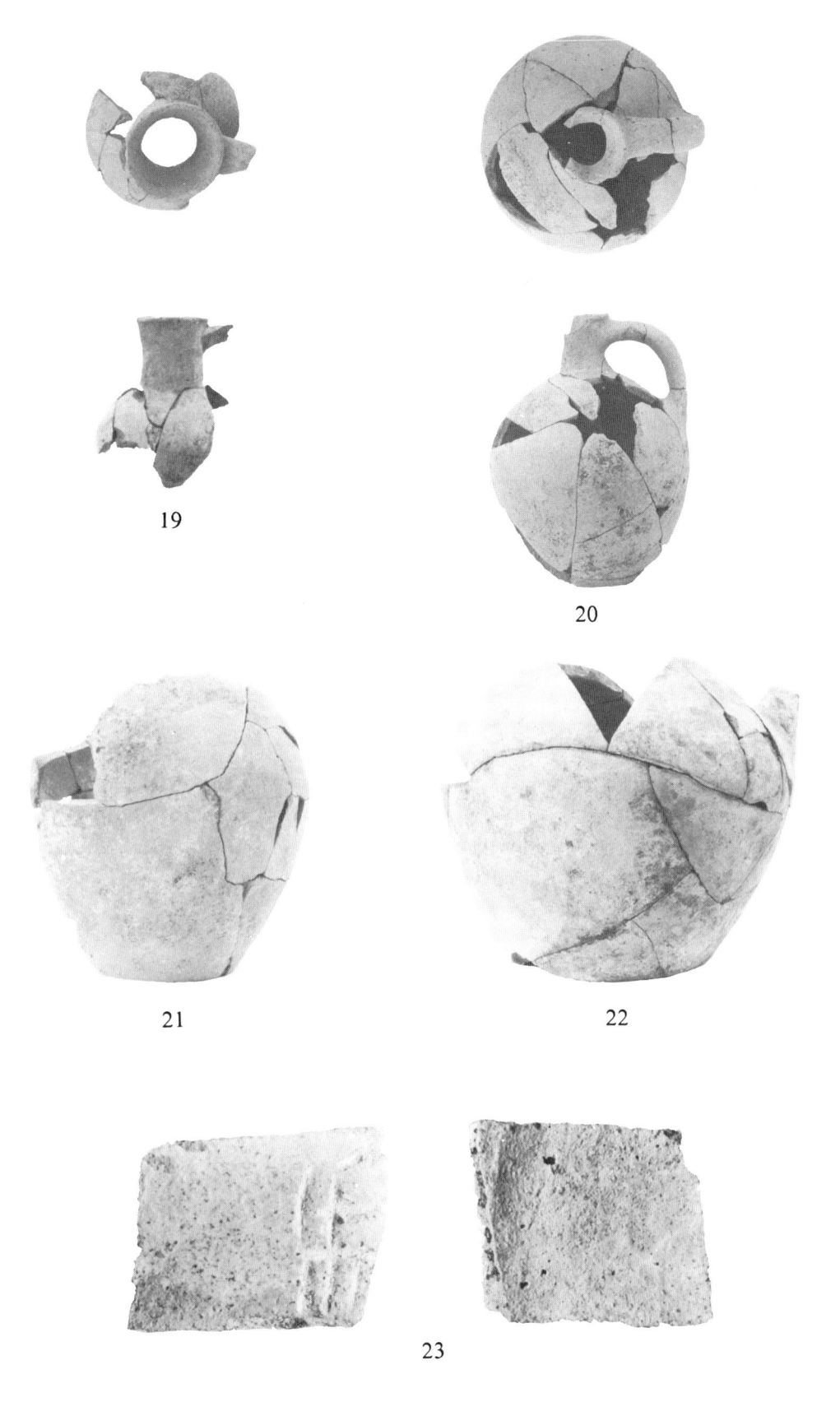

20

21

22

23

Plain White Handmade
Cat. nos. 19-23.

24

Scale 2:5

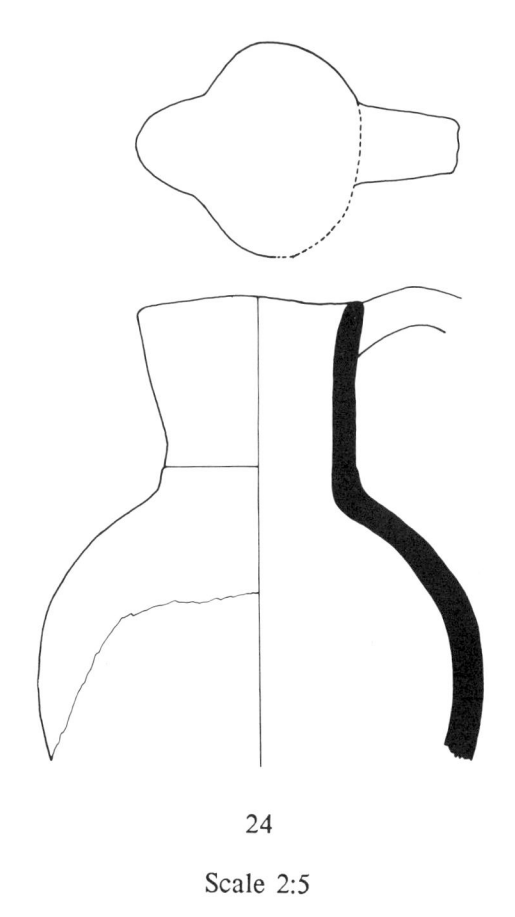

Figure 7. Cat. no. 24 (Jug).

PLATE 7

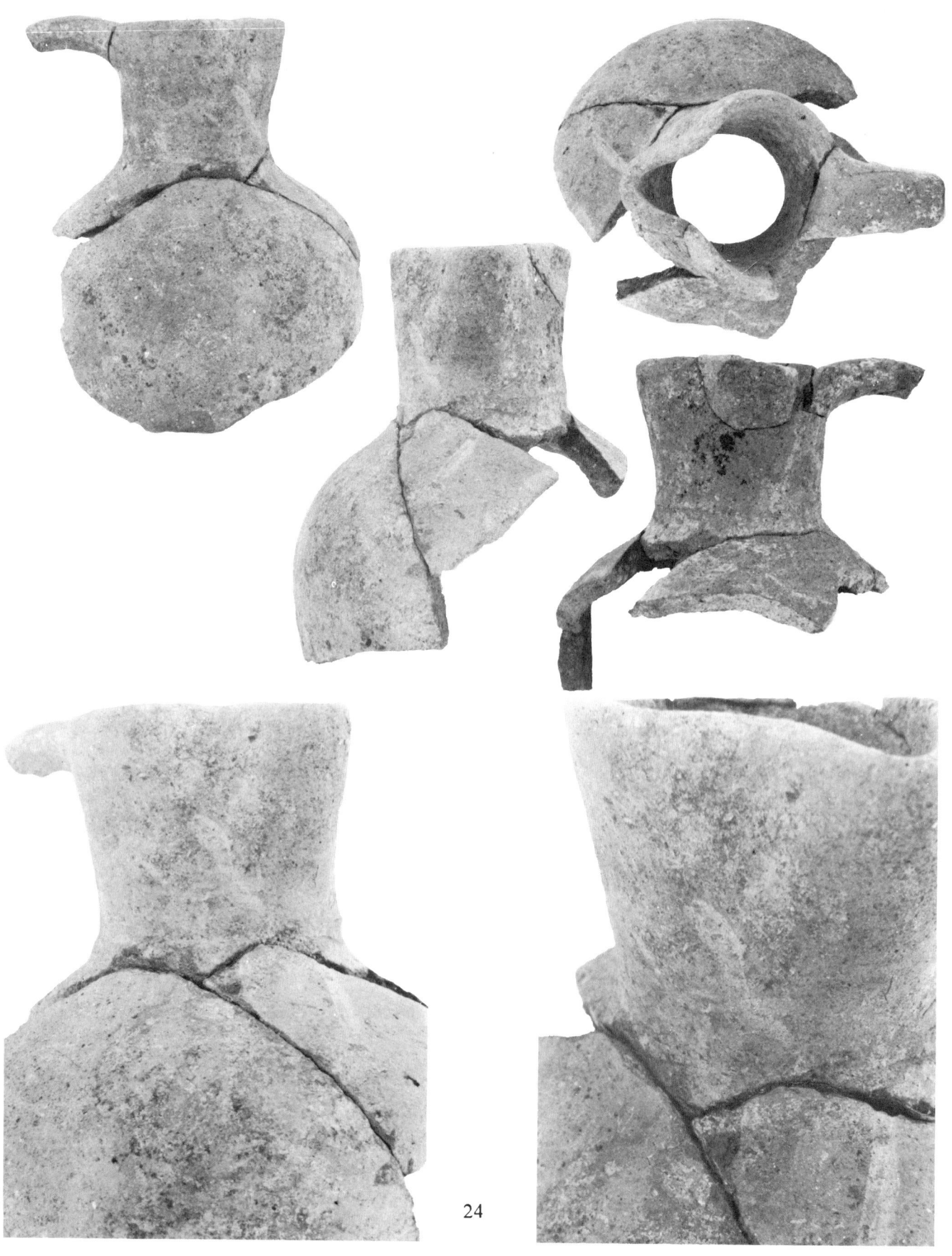

24

Plain White Handmade
Cat. no. 24.

25

Scale 2:5

26

Scale 2:5

28

Scale 2:5

29

Scale 2:5

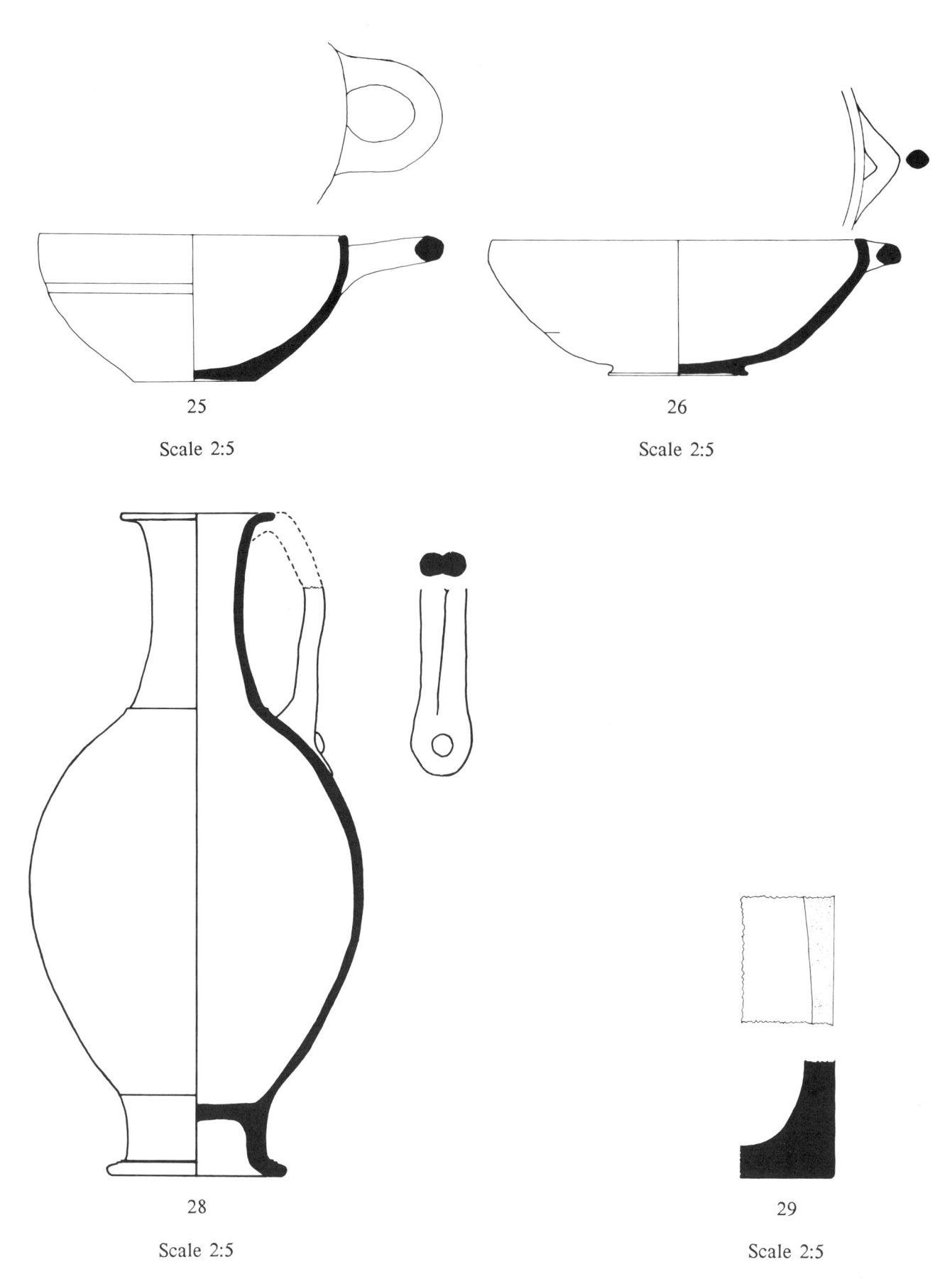

Figure 8. Cat. nos. 25 and 26 (Bowls), 28 (Jug), and 29 (Fragment of Tray?).

PLATE 8

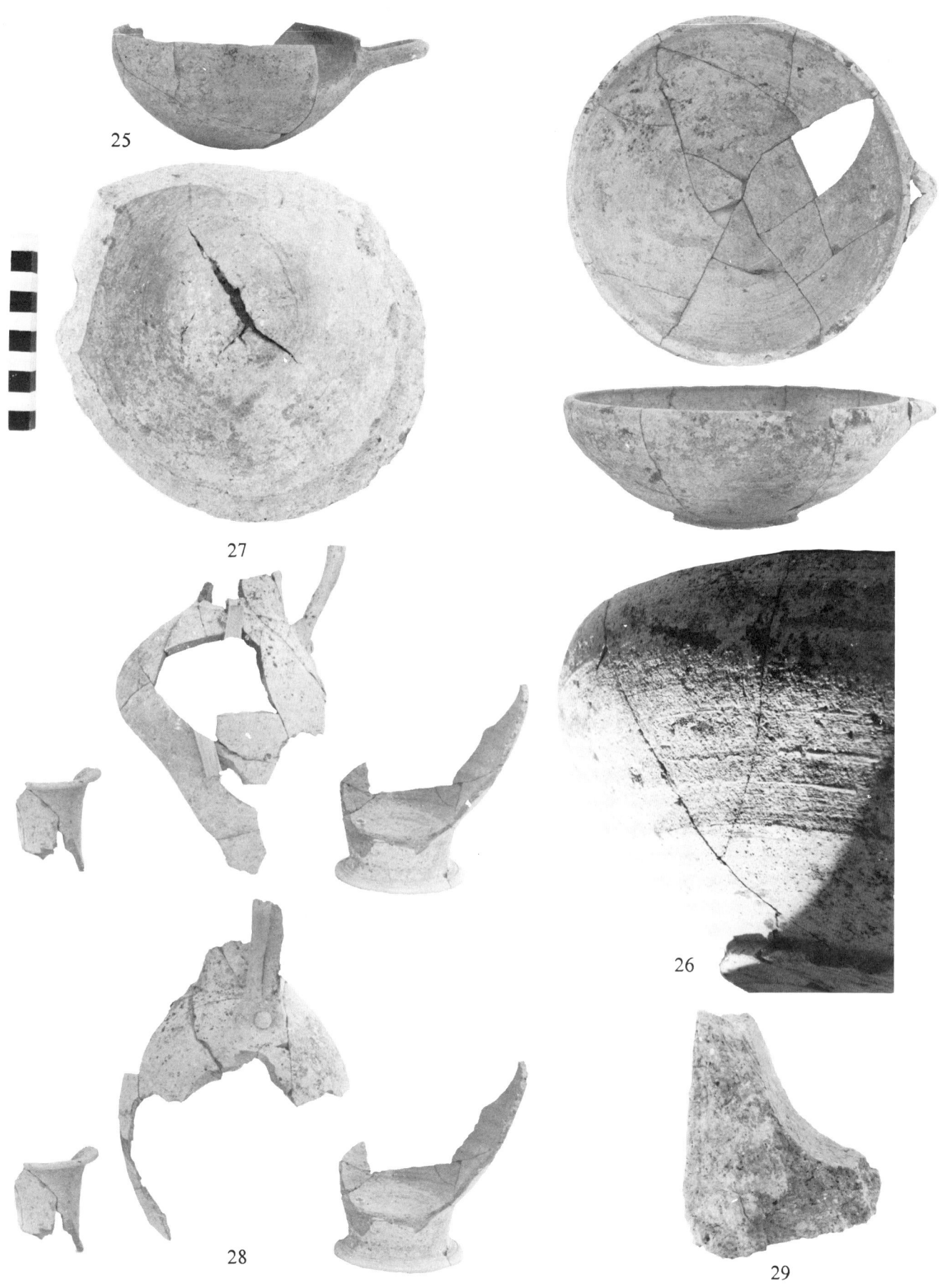

25-27 Plain White Wheelmade; 28 Plain White Wheelmade II; 29 Coarse.

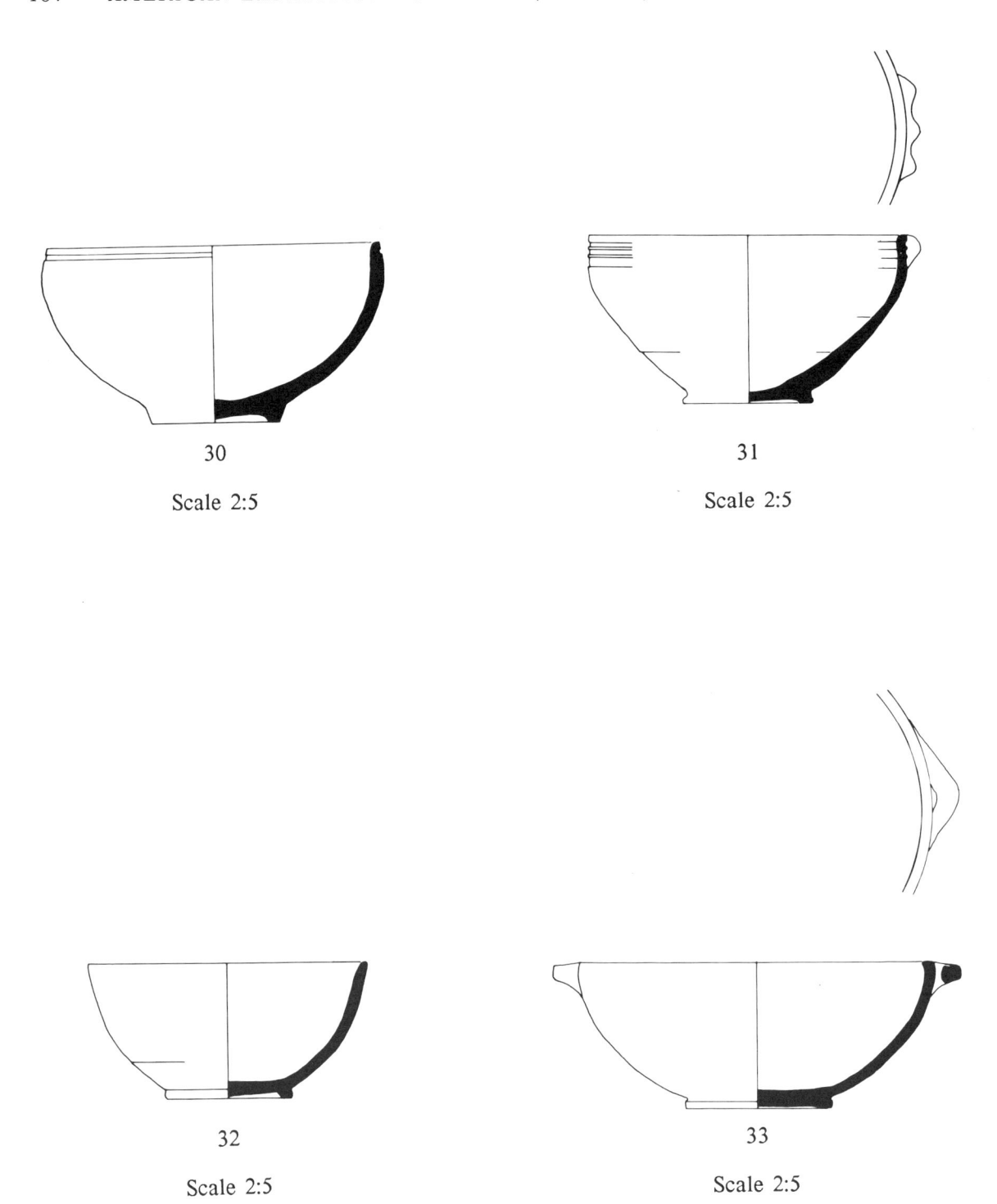

Figure 9. Cat. nos. 30-33 (Bowls).

PLATE 9

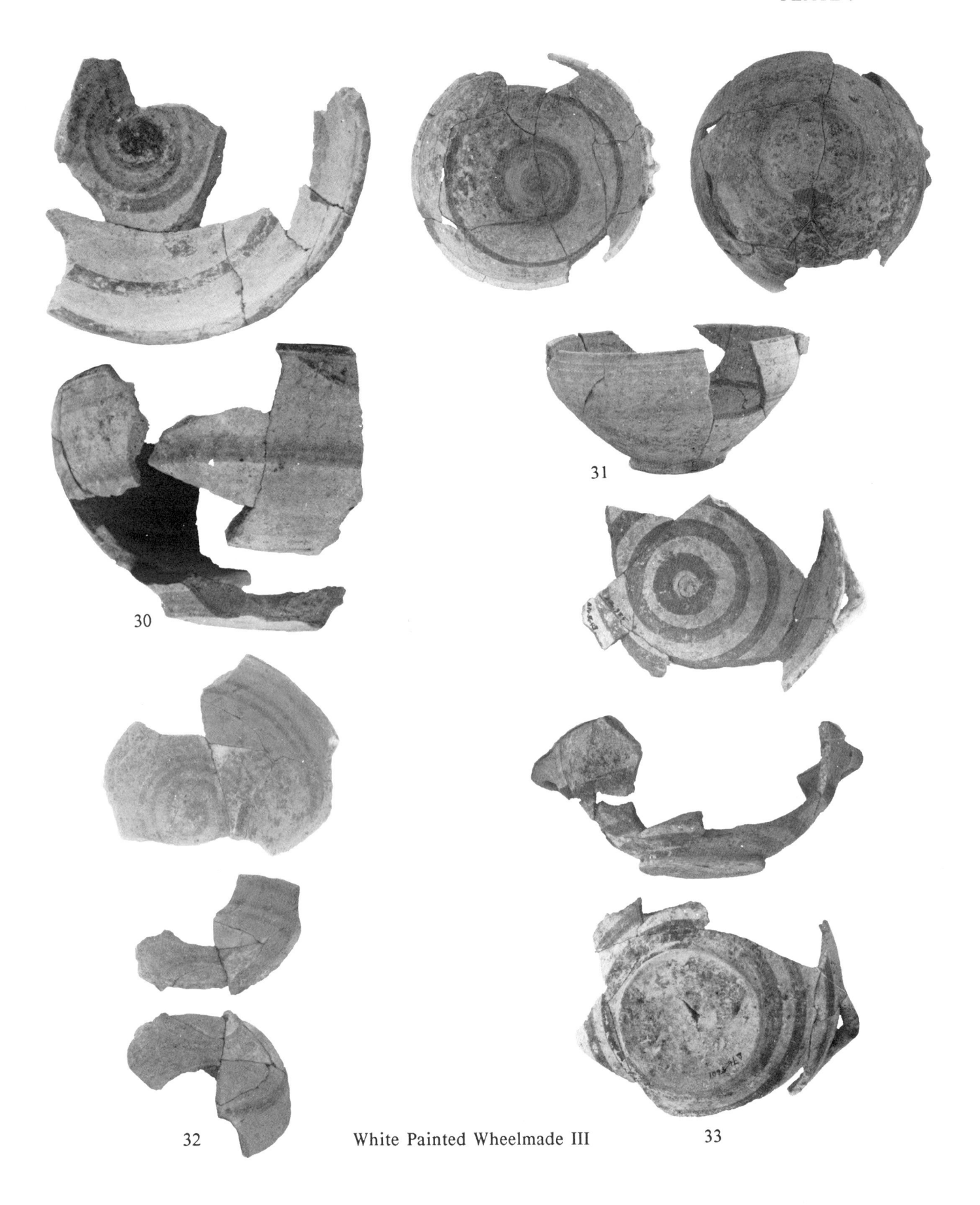

30

31

32

White Painted Wheelmade III

33

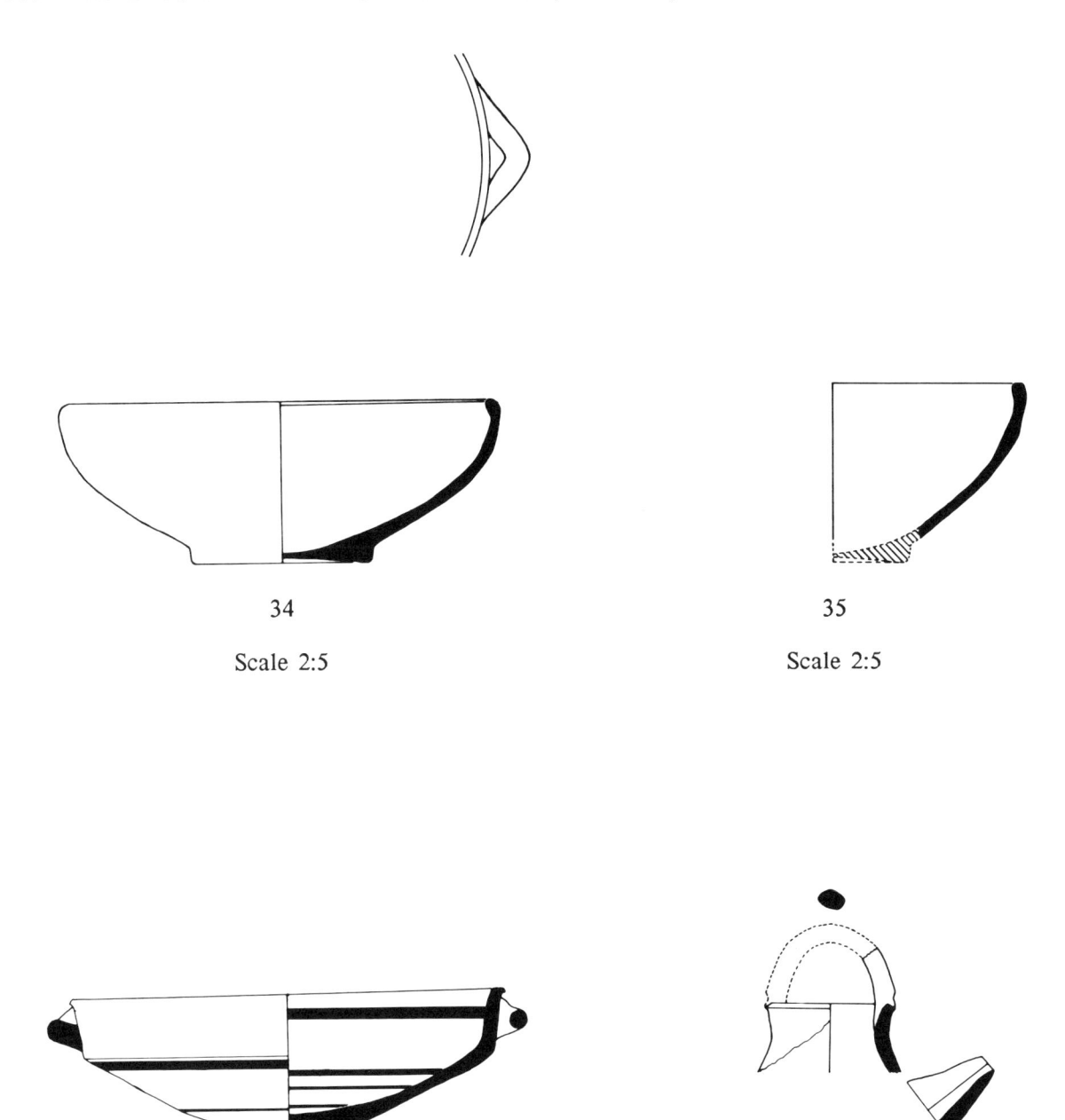

Figure 10. Cat. nos. 34-36 (Bowls) and 37 (Fragments of Side-spouted Juglet).

PLATE 10

34

35

36

37

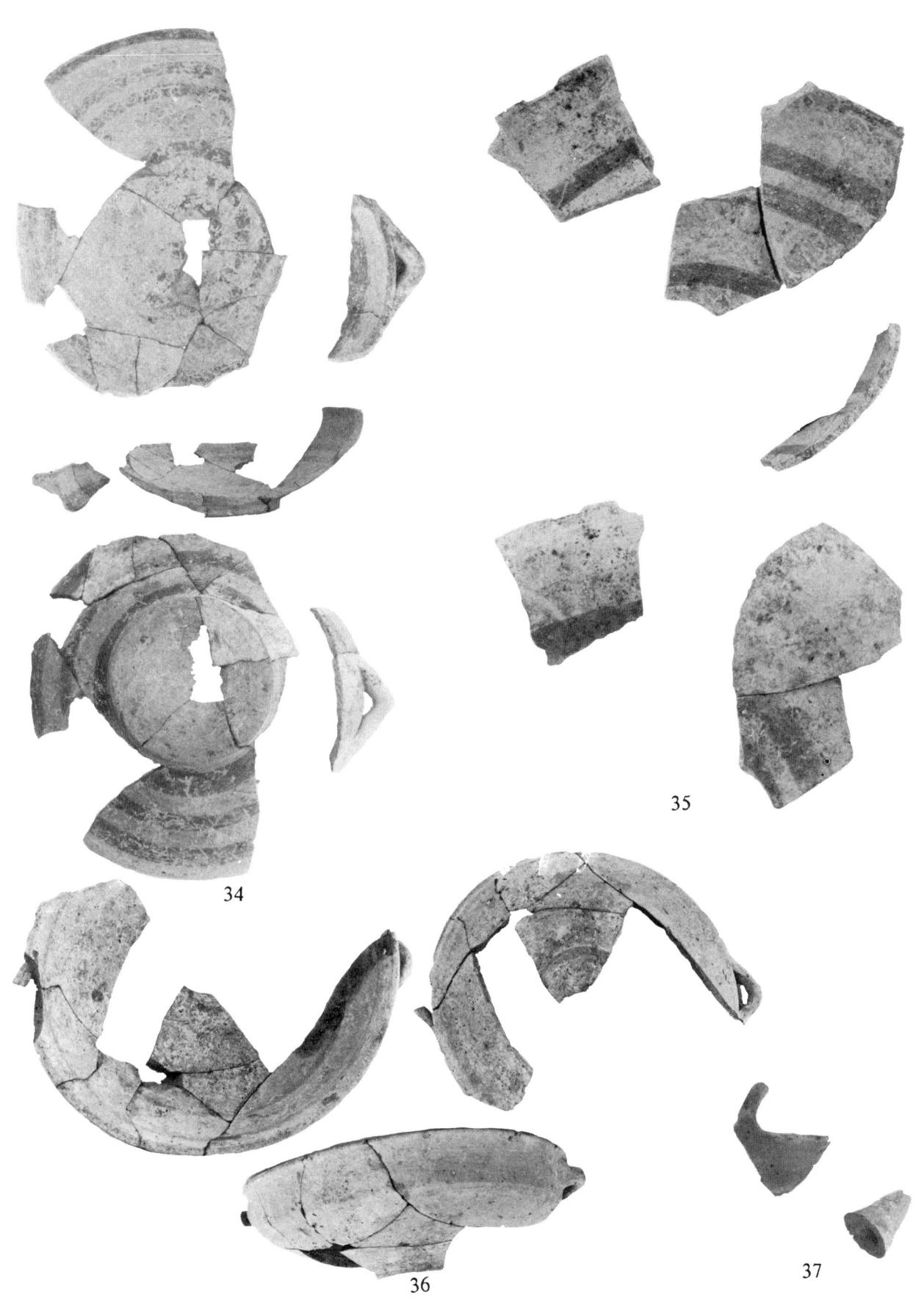

White Painted Wheelmade III

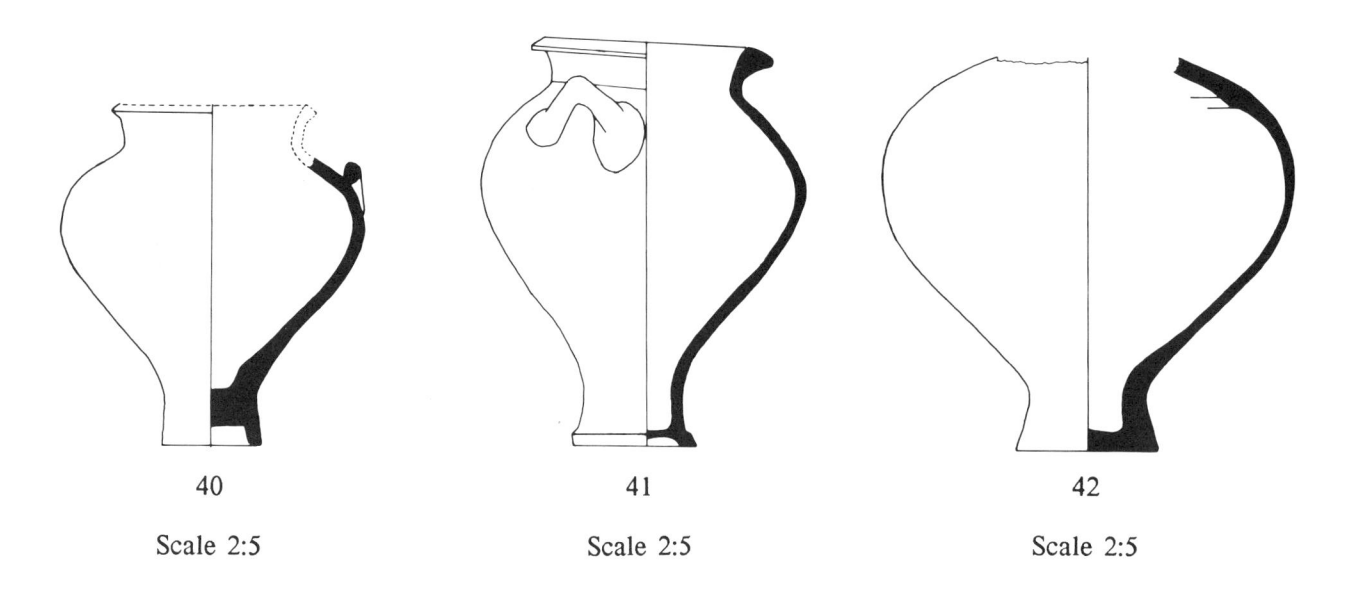

Figure 11. Cat. nos. 38 (Bowl), 39 (Cup), 40, 41 (Three-handled Jars), and 42 (Three-handled or False-necked Jar).

PLATE 11

38

39

40

41

42

Levanto-Mycenaean
Cat. nos. 38-42.

43

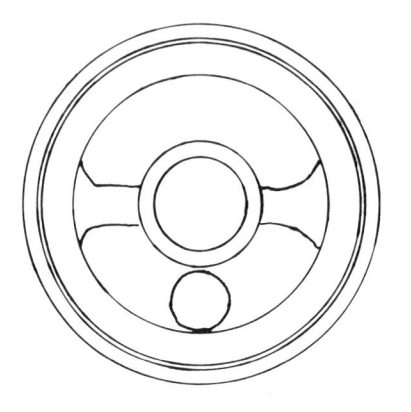

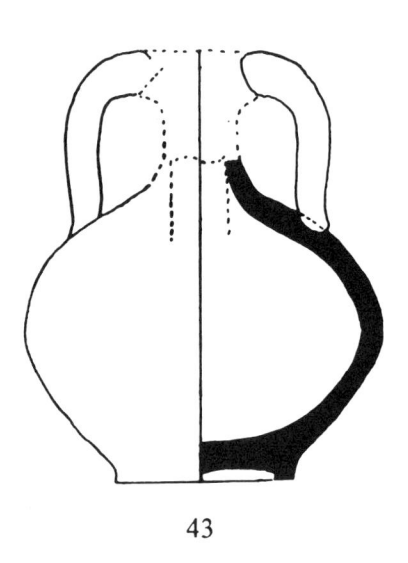

Scale 4:5

Figure 12. Cat. no. 43 (False-necked Jar).

PLATE 12

43

Levanto-Mycenaean

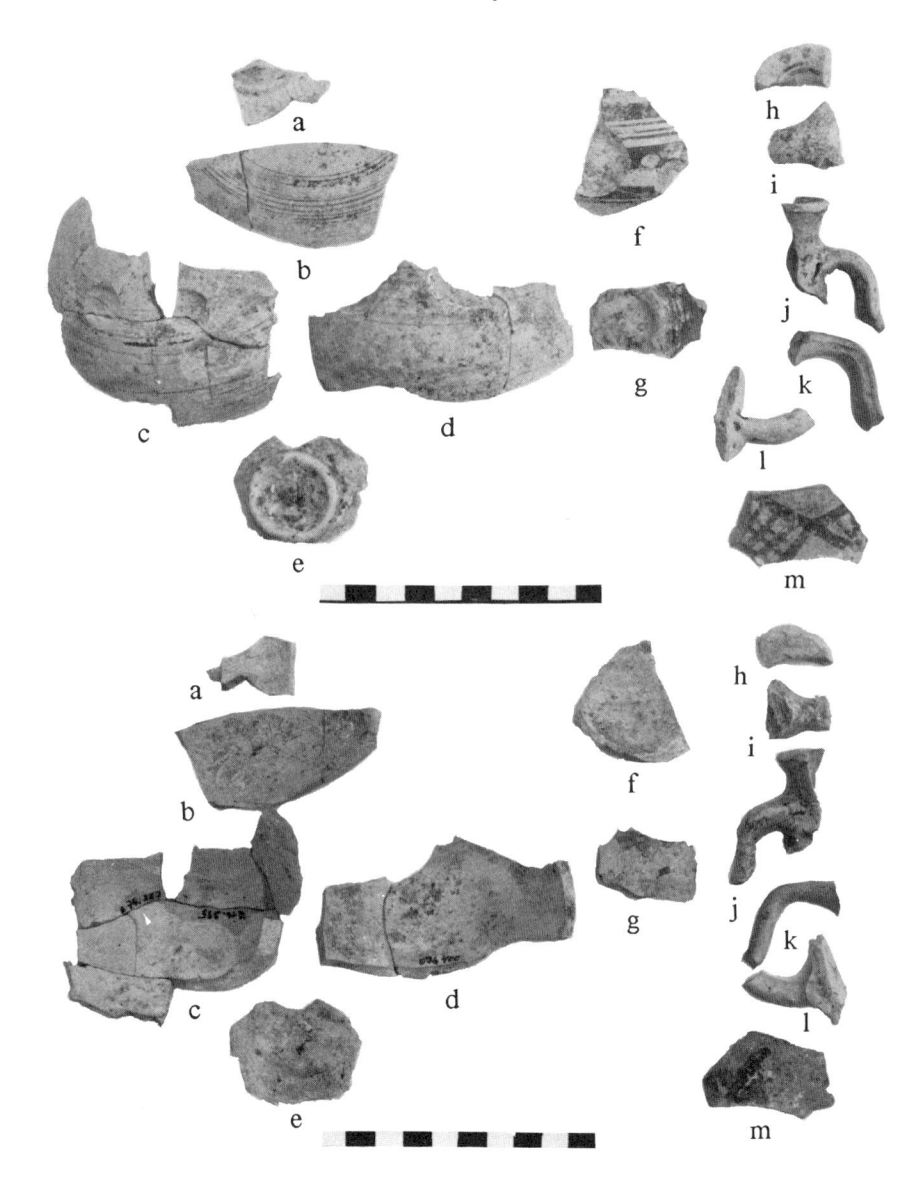

192   AMERICAN EXPEDITION TO IDALION, CYPRUS, 1973-1980

44
Scale 2:5

45
Scale 2:5

46
Scale 2:5

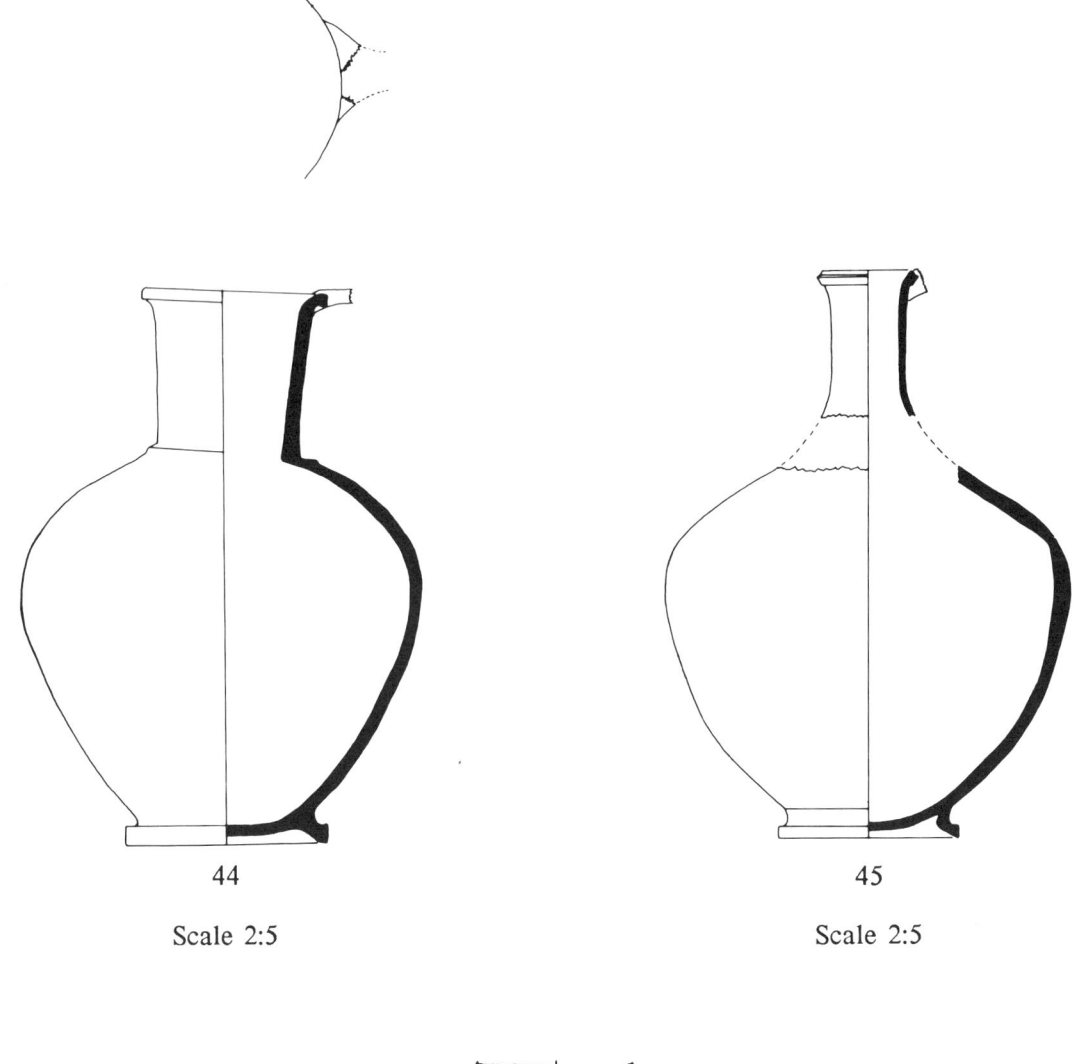

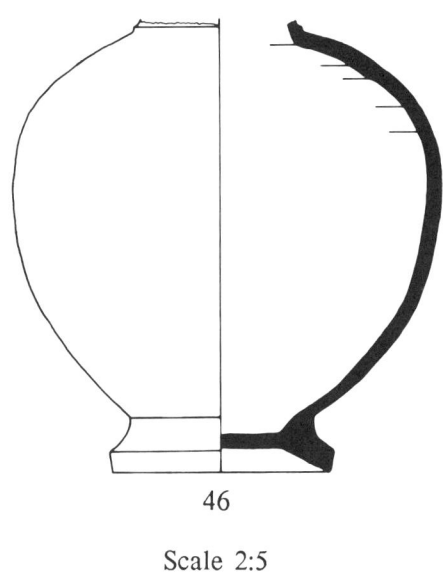

Figure 13. Cat. nos. 44-46 (Jugs).

PLATE 13

44 45

Bucchero Handmade

46

Bucchero Wheelmade
Cat. nos. 44-46.

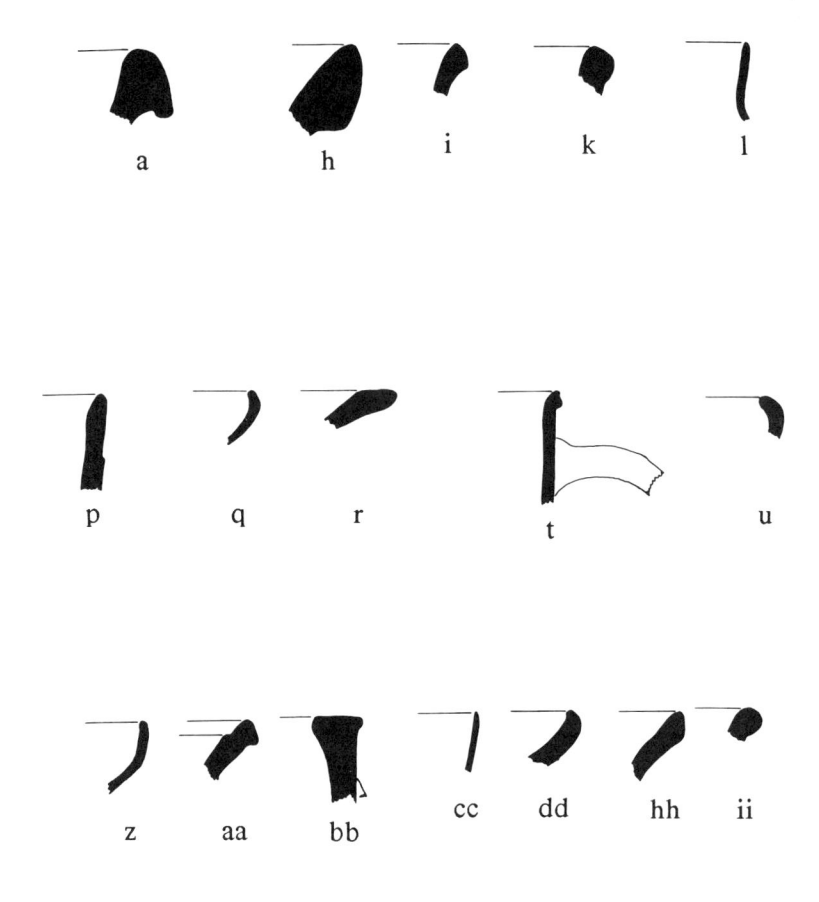

Scale 2:5

Figure 14. Sherd Profiles a-ii.

PLATE 14

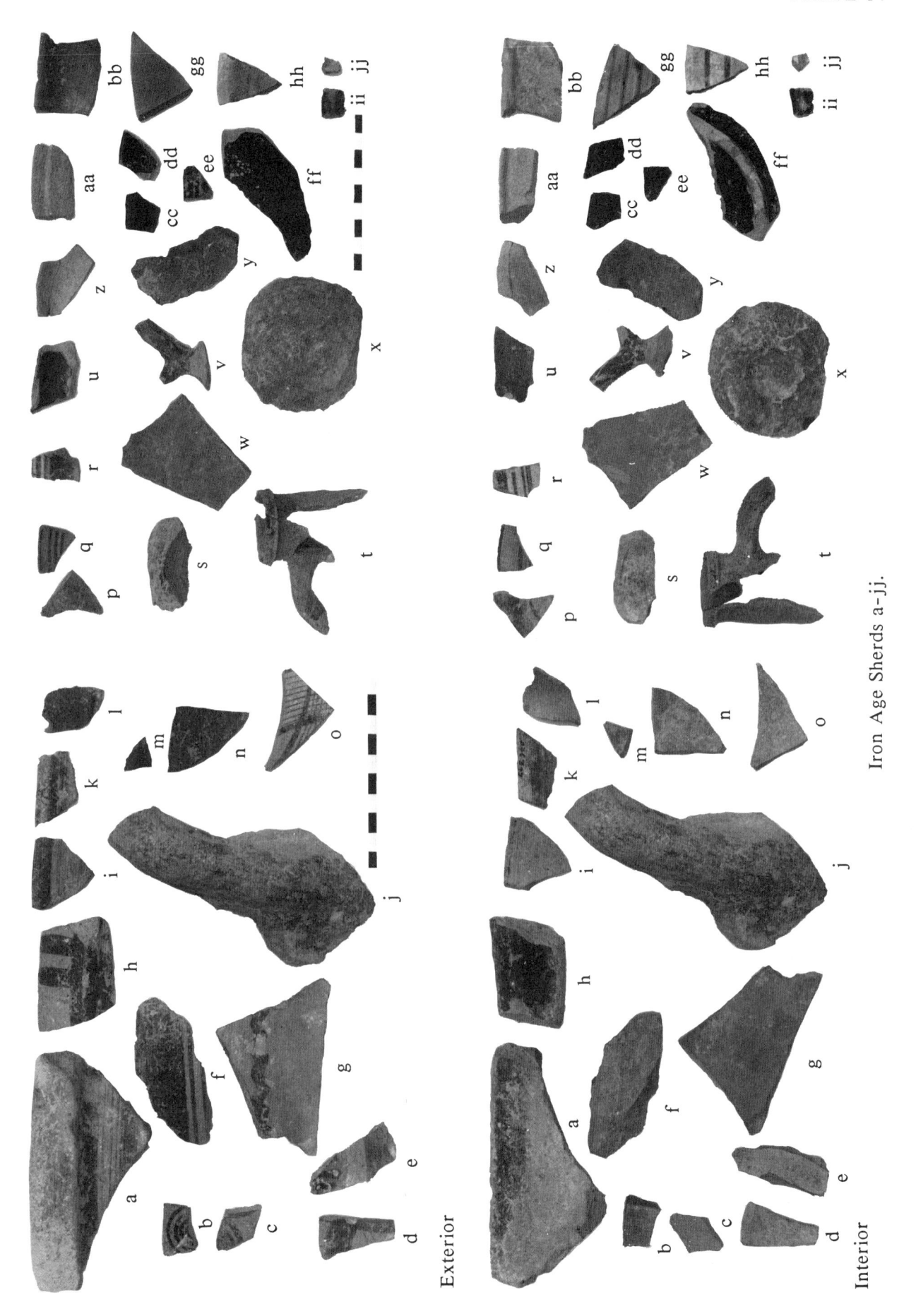

Exterior

Interior

Iron Age Sherds a–jj.

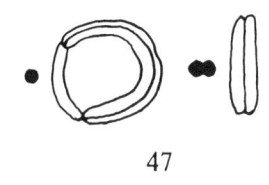

47

Scale 4:5

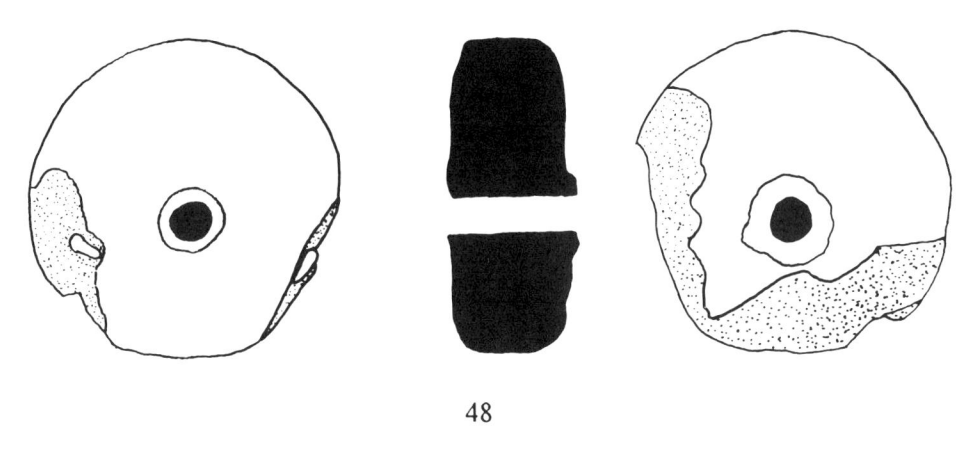

48

Scale 4:5

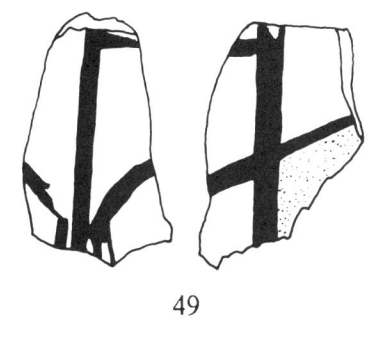

49

Scale 2:5

Figure 15. Cat. nos. 47 (Bronze Ring), 48 (Perforated Disk), and 49 (Fragment of Animal Figurine).

PLATE 15

47
Bronze

48
Terracotta

Top   Side
49
Terracotta
Cat. nos. 47-49.

50

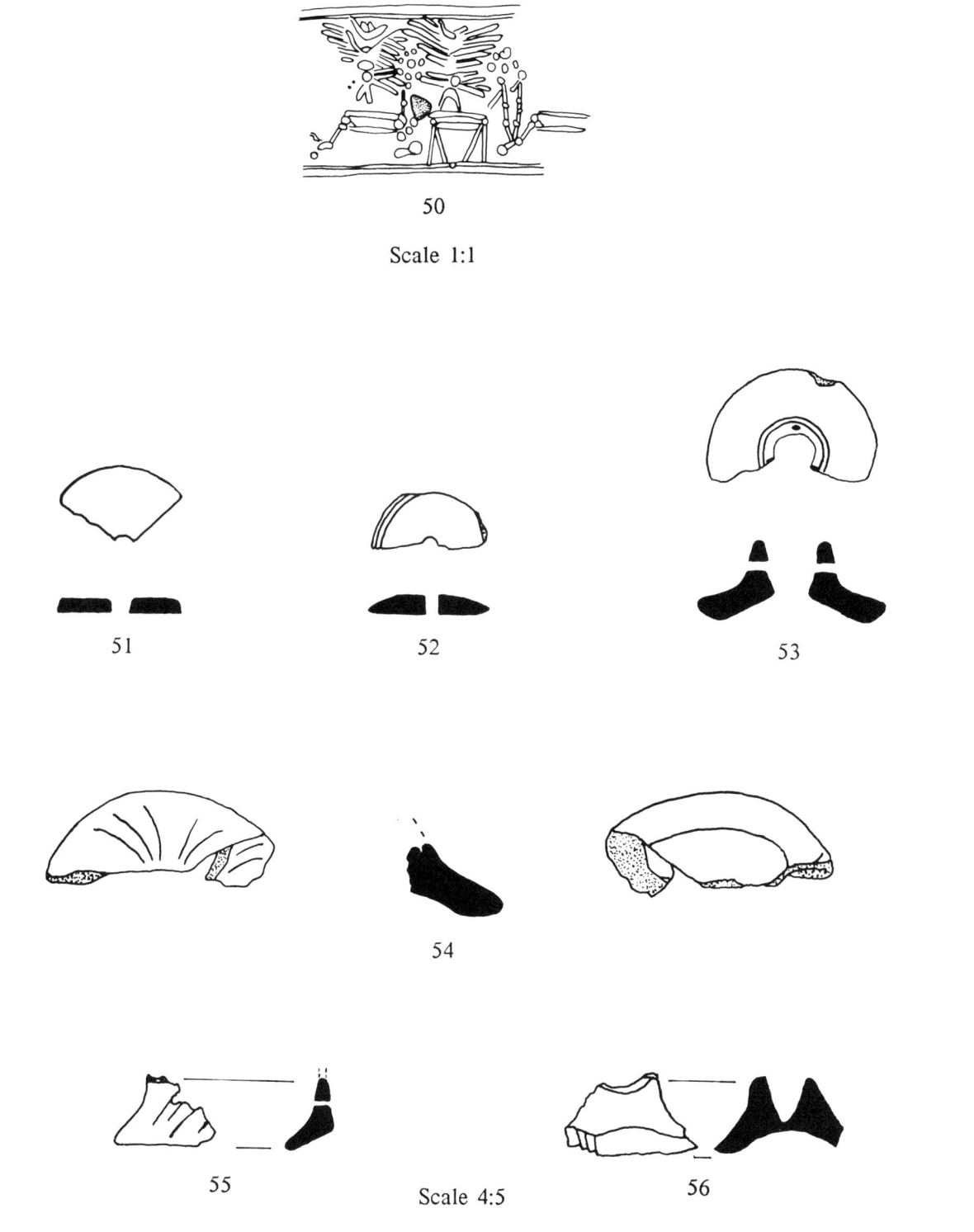

Scale 1:1

51 52 53

54

55 Scale 4:5 56

Figure 16. Cat. nos. 50 (Glyptic Cylinder Seal), 51 (Perforated Flat Ivory Disk), 52 (Perforated Plano-convex Ivory Disk), 53 (Ivory Button?), and 54-56 (Perforated Ivory Buttons?).

PLATE 16

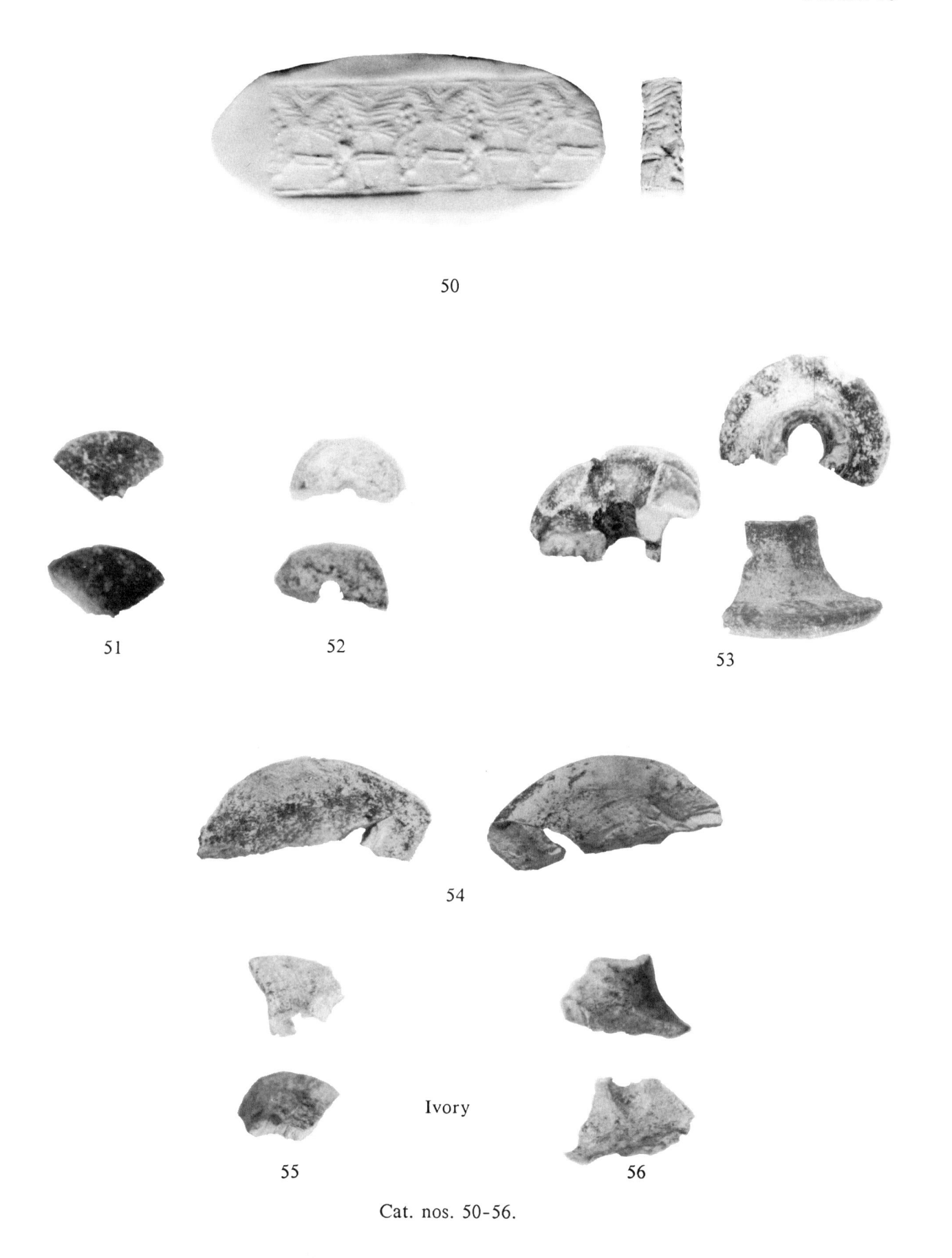

50

51 52 53

54

Ivory

55 56

Cat. nos. 50-56.

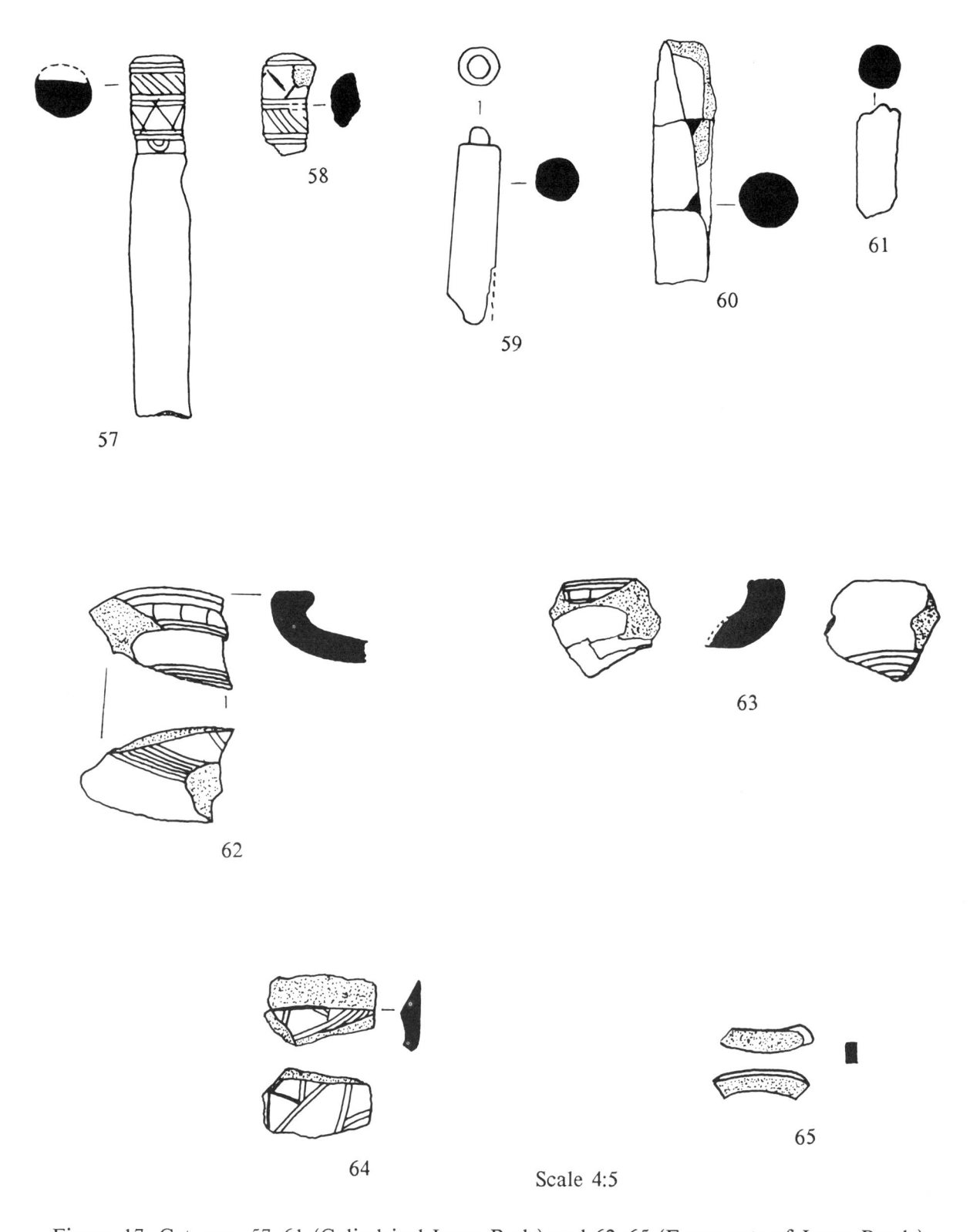

Figure 17. Cat. nos. 57-61 (Cylindrical Ivory Rods) and 62-65 (Fragments of Ivory Bowls).

PLATE 17

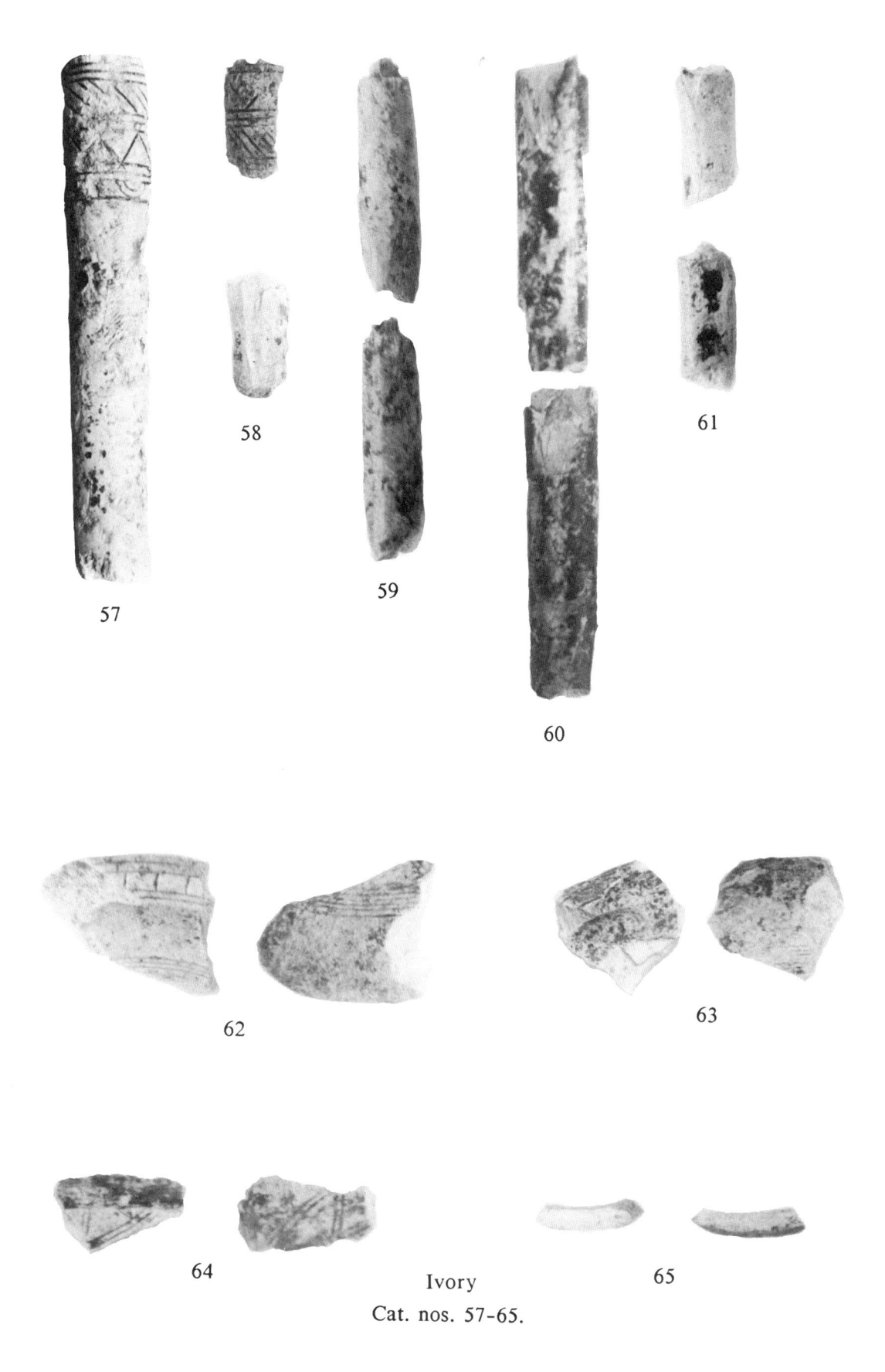

Ivory
Cat. nos. 57-65.

II. EXCAVATIONS AT DHALI-AGRIDHI: 1972, 1974, 1976
A. DHALI-AGRIDHI: THE NEOLITHIC BY THE RIVER

Yechiel M. Lehavy *

The Dhali-Agridhi site[1] lies on the southern bank of the Yalias River on the road to Potamia in the Agridhi section of Dhali north of the village of Dhali proper (fig. 1 and pl. 1a, b). Three seasons of excavations (1972, 1974, and 1976) have revealed Neolithic remains dating to both aceramic and ceramic periods (fig. 2). However the 1974 season had to be halted prematurely; because of the military and political situation in Cyprus work was not resumed until 1976.

A preliminary report of the 1972 season has already appeared (Lehavy 1974) which gives the background and principal objectives of the Dhali-Agridhi excavation and also explains how this connects with the long-range goals of the Idalion expedition. The following brief summary of the 1972 season highlights the most important discoveries and gives the reasons for continued research at the site.

The 1972 season yielded C^{14} dates belonging to both aceramic and ceramic periods. One of the most important discoveries of this season was the earliest Neolithic pottery found in Cyprus, dated by C^{14} to the fifth millennium B.C. [4465±310 B.C. (GX2847 A)]. This date, moreover, falls within a period that had previously been thought to constitute an occupational hiatus on the island. The surface color of the pottery varies--it may be black, brown, red brown, or orange buff. Comparable pottery has been found in the excavation of Philia-Drakos A and described as Dark-faced Burnished Ware (DFBW) (Watkins 1970:5-6). The date proposed for this type of pottery was the fifth millennium B.C. (Watkins 1972:170-71), and typologically it has been compared with the Amuq ceramic sequence (Watkins 1973:50). This date is plausible when compared with the Dhali-Agridhi C^{14} ceramic date.[2]

The Dhali-Agridhi aceramic deposit, dated to 5340±465 B.C. (GX 2848 A), is contemporary with Khirokitia. Although this C^{14} sample has a large margin of error, when compared with other C^{14} dates it does fall within a plausible mean date pattern (Stanley Price 1977a:66-89).

The area excavated in 1972 was confined to a 5.0 x 5.0 m square, located near Dikaios' earlier discoveries (Lehavy 1974:94-95). Since the loci that were tentatively identified as aceramic and ceramic were immediately adjacent to, rather than superimposed on, each other, and since the margin or error in the C^{14} dates of the two deposits left room for the possibility that these occupations had in fact been contemporary (ibid., p. 98), one of the major objectives of the 1974 season was to determine whether the aceramic and ceramic deposits could be sequenced stratigraphically. Areas adjacent to that of the 1972 season were therefore opened-- Area 1A and Area 2 (figs. 3 and 5). Area 1A (1.25 x 5.0 m) north of Area 1, was opened mainly for the retrieval of faunal and floral remains. Because of the high summer temperature

---

*Atlantic Community College, Mays Landing, New Jersey

The excavations of the site were assisted in 1972 by Nicholas Stanley Price and in 1976 by Jean S. Aigner.

[1] Not to be confused with the Neolithic site Dhali, discovered early in the 1930s by Dikaios (1953:1-2).

[2] Dr. Watkins kindly gave me permission to study the Philia-Drakos A sherds stored in the Cyprus Museum, Nicosia, for which I am grateful.

in Cyprus, there was a rapid dehydration of the newly exposed soil during the 1972 season, which resulted in damage to the faunal and floral remains uncovered. In order to eliminate a repeat of such damage in the subsequent season Area 1A was kept narrow. Area 2 (5.0 x 5.0 m), east of Area 1, was opened in order to enlarge the excavation so that the nature of the 1972 Concentrations A and B could be further investigated. Due to the shortness of the 1974 season (two weeks of excavation) only the top soil was removed from Area 2. However, virgin soil was reached in Area 1A.

Two new areas, Area 11 (2.5 x 2.5 m) and Area 12 (2.5 x 5.0 m), were opened in 1976 to meet two objectives: first, to increase horizontal exposure and investigate further the nature of 1972 Concentrations A and B; and second, to determine the extent of the settlement. To these same ends, test trenches Area 21 and Area 31 were opened later in the season (fig. 5). Furthermore the field was probed with a soil auger in the proposed areas of 41, 51, and 031, 041 (fig. 5).

In searching for a promising location to excavate in 1972, two sites were located, one near Dikaios' initial site (Dhali-Agridhi proper), the other about 200 m due southwest. Toward the end of the 1976 season this second location, designated Site E, was probed (fig. 1). The site was chosen because the outcrop revealed unmistakable cultural remains. Site E actually consists of two sections cut along the upper terrace of the Yalias River.

As previously mentioned in the preliminary report of the 1972 season, it was impossible to excavate the cultural deposits according to natural layers. The soil showed a remarkable variety of inseparable colors. However while excavation was in progress it was noticed that there were two main concentrations of debris. The difference in the nature of the concentrations was observed almost immediately upon excavation of the Neolithic levels. Both concentrations are separated by their horizontal locations (pl. 2a). The four northeast subsquares (NE I, NE II, NE III, and NE IV) and the northern margins of subsquares SE I and SE II became Concentration A (tentatively identified as ceramic Neolithic), while the rest of the excavated area became Concentration B (tentatively identified as aceramic Neolithic) (see Lehavy 1974, figs. 81-84). C^{14} dates from both concentrations in the 1972 and 1976 seasons supported the horizontal separation observed. Subsequent to the 1972 season, sixteen subsquares were used as controls to avoid contamination between the two concentrations.

The methods of investigation and excavation during the 1974 and 1976 seasons were the same as those used in 1972, with the exception of retrieval methods for paleobotanical remains: in 1974 a different kind of water-sieving and flotation device was used (Jarman, Legge, and Charles 1972); this was supplemented in 1976 by the French machine (French 1971). All soil removed from the excavation was floated. In the 1976 season four of every five buckets of excavated soil (80 percent) were processed by water-sieving and flotation; the remaining 20 percent of soil was processed by froth flotation. The percentage of carbonized seeds retrieved was the same, regardless of which method was used.

Nearly total retrieval of the cultural remains was attempted during these excavations. Among other things, all chipped stones were kept, regardless of size or shape. All material retrieved by flotation, including small flint or chert chips, was also retained.

General Stratigraphic Discussion

Dhali-Agridhi Proper

The horizontal stratigraphic separation between the aceramic and ceramic deposits posited in 1972 was confirmed in 1974 (figs. 3 and 4 and pl. 2a). Typologically the 1974 ceramic deposit was the same as the adjacent 1972 deposit, and many of the sherds could in fact be joined. The more or less circular shape of 1972 Concentration A (fig. 3) was also confirmed. The nature of the aceramic deposit was identical in composition and content to 1972 Concentration B; in addition, it yielded a broken obsidian blade and some lentil seeds.

The aceramic deposit contained at least three different indicators of cultural activities: a workshop, a garbage area with a large number of animal bones (Concentration B of 1972), and two pits. One of the pits was uncovered in Locus 008, Area 12. The other was located in Locus 004, Area 11, but extended through the balk into Area 1. Domestic structures relating to the aceramic deposit have yet to be located.

The ceramic Neolithic area excavated was too small to permit the identification of areas of different cultural activity. It was suggested earlier that Concentration A might represent a dwelling area (Lehavy 1974:98). Despite the disturbance of this area by a post-Neolithic pit (Loci 017, 018, and 019 of Area 2, 1976) (see fig. 3), which substantially reduced the area of this ceramic Neolithic deposit, this interpretation still holds.

The natural layers in Area 31 (a test trench 2.50 x 1.25 m, opened in 1976) were easily separable. Both the top soil, which was approximately a half meter deep, and a thick layer (35 cm) of sterile soil containing caliche were removed. The latter sealed the aceramic Neolithic deposit below. Excavation in this test trench was halted at the end of the 1976 season before sterile soil had been reached. Nevertheless Area 31 yielded large quantities of cultural debris, such as two obsidian blades, fragments of stone bowls, stone implements, flint tools, and a large number of animal bones.

Site E

Site E is located about 200 m due southwest of Dhali-Agridhi proper (see fig. 1). Because modern terracing revealed Neolithic cultural remains, the site was probed toward the end of the 1976 season. The probes consisted of two sections, each 2.50 m long and 0.75 m wide (see figs. 6 and 7). Both probes were cut along the upper terrace of the Yalias River. No ceramic remains were found in Site E.

Aceramic Deposit

Dhali-Agridhi Proper

The aceramic deposit included parts of Areas 1A and 2 and extended into Areas 11 and 12. No material remains relating to the ceramic period were found in Areas 11 and 12. Areas 21 and 31 were opened to investigate the extent of the settlement (fig. 5). They were test trenches, measuring 2.50 x 1.25 m. Area 21 was sterile, while 31 yielded typical aceramic remains, including two obsidian pieces, at a depth of 1.10 m below top soil. An additional part of the field was tested, using a soil auger. The site was found to be much more extensive than had been thought previously. Below the top soil, at a depth of 1.00 to 1.25 m, there appeared bone fragments, decayed organic matter, and other indicators of occupation. Since Area 31, and proposed areas 41, 51, and 031 and 041 all yielded Neolithic remains, these have been designated for future excavation (see fig. 5).

Site E

The natural layers in Site E sections were easily separable (pl. 2b). Loci 001 and 002 represent the top soil. The former locus consisted of soil dug from the chain of wells and laid over the soil in the latter locus. Locus 003 consisted of post-Neolithic debris. Locus 004 was sterile soil which had a large content of caliche very similar in composition to Locus 002 of Area 31, 1976. In the NE-SW probe a stone pavement overlay a mud-packed layer--Locus 005. Locus 005, as well as Loci 006 and 007, consisted of aceramic cultural remains, while Loci 008, 009, and 010 were sterile. These loci were river-laid sediments mixed wih caliche (see fig. 6).

In the northeast-southwest section the Neolithic layer was sealed or paved by a stone floor. In both sections a sterile soil layer was situated above the bone-rich Neolithic layer. The depth of the deposit ranged from 0.25 to 0.70 m. The top of the sterile soil below the Neolithic deposit was uneven, similar to that in Concentration B at Dhali-Agridhi proper. The Neolithic layer consisted of a mixture of bones (some of them charred), stone bowl fragments, other stone implements, flint tools, and carbonized seeds. It would seem that this part of the site had functioned as a dump. Such an interpretation is strongly suggested by the disarticulation of the bones and the mixture of burnt and unburnt bones, the flint tools lying in a vertical position as though they had been discarded, and the assemblage of stone bowl fragments. Apparently when the area began to fill up, the top in the north-south section was burnt, while in the northeast-southwest section it was paved with cobbles and fragments of stone implements.

The cobble floor, paved with rock fragments, is itself an enigma (pl. 3a, b). As yet only a small section of the floor has been uncovered--1.8 x 0.6 m. The floor consisted of a total of 232 cobble fragments. This collection of cobbles, however, is much different from the normal Yalias River assemblage, where pillow lavas and diabase predominate. Moreover, 29 fragments (12 percent of the collection) show definite usage by man. An additional 70 fragments (30 percent of the collection) may have been used by man, and the remaining 133 fragments (58 percent of the collection) show no evidence of use. Twenty-four of the rocks in the latter category must have been imported to the site from either across the river or even from as far away as the mines of Mathiati and Sha. The question then arises, if the rocks were never used, why were they imported? Two of the rocks were initially classified as "unused" because they were not fragments of stone implements. After closer examination, however, it was found that these stones had obviously been used as grinders. Tables 2 and 3 give the full analysis of the cobble-paved floor. Obviously at this point it would be premature to speculate on the purpose of the pavement. Only further excavation can throw light on the puzzle of this floor in Site E.

Site E yielded a large number of bones together with a large number of chipped stones, chiefly flints. The whole assemblage very closely resembles the aceramic deposit of Dhali-Agridhi proper. A C^{14} sample to determine the date of the site was also secured (see table 6).

Paleobotanical Remains

The amount of seeds retrieved by flotation in the aceramic deposit was too small to permit any quantitative comparison. Three kinds of seeds have been identified: *wild lentil* (*Lens orientalis*), *wild einkorn* (*Triticum boeoticum* var. *aeglopoides»*), and wild pistachio (*Pistacia atlantica»*). Size was the criterion used to determine whether the lentils were a wild form.[3] The seeds were about 2.5 mm in diameter; Robert Stewart was inclined to call them *Lens orientalis*, following the classification of Zohary and Hopf (1973:890-92).[4] The wild einkorn determination was based on the size and compressed lateral faces of the kernel. To be absolutely sure, one would need to examine the spikelet fragments, but Stewart feels quite confident that the einkorn is wild. The pistachio is *Pistacia atlantica»*, which, of course, has never been cultivated, but which is found regularly in Middle Eastern sites and appears to have been a source of oil. (For faunal analysis, see below, Carter and Croft.)

Lithics

A large number of chipped stones, chiefly siliceous and breakable ones, were recovered from the aceramic deposit. As yet this material has not been studied. At some time in the future the aceramic chipped-stone tool kit will be compared with the ceramic deposit collection, with special attention to the study of cultural continuity in the tradition of chipped-stone tools.

Area 1A of 1974 yielded a broken obsidian blade (Obj. 880; fig. 8a), which came from the aceramic deposit of Concentration B. Another broken piece of obsidian blade was found in

---

[3] According to this interpretation, Lens orientalis would have the wild progenitor of the domesticated lentil, Lens culinaris. Renfrew, on the other hand (1973:113), suggests that the wild progenitor of domesticated lentils is Lens nigricans.

[4] Personal communication, Robert Stewart.

Area 2 aceramic deposit of 1976. In the investigation of the extent of the Neolithic settlement of Dhali-Agridhi Area 31 yielded two additional broken obsidian blades in association with typical aceramic remains. These obsidian pieces were subjected to neutron activation analysis.[5] All four pieces were found to correspond to Renfrew's Group 2b, Çiftlik, Anatolia. Table 1 presents the object registration number, field number, and analytical results for each piece.

The results of this analysis, showing that all of the Dhali-Agridhi samples belong to Renfrew's Group 2b, Çiftlik, Anatolia, are consistent with all previous work. It seems that all of the material thus far examined from Cyprus (including Khirokitia) comes from this source in Anatolia.[6]

Over one hundred fragments of stone bowls (including two with handles), stone hammers, grinders, a very large stone bowl or trough(?), and other stone implements were recovered from the aceramic deposit.[7] In the initial identification of Dhali-Agridhi by the Cyprus Survey the site was listed as a hunting station. Judging from the stone vessels and implements inventory, it would appear that the occupation of Dhali-Agridhi represents more than a mere hunting station; perhaps it was a permanent settlement. As noted above, during the 1976 season it was discovered that the site was much more extensive than had previously been thought, but only workshops, pits, and garbage deposits have thus far been uncovered. The dwelling area remains to be found.

In addition to vessels and implements, the workshops yielded raw material in the form of two large boulders, one of flint, and the other of red ochre. Some of the grinding stones found in the workshops had traces of ochre on them. Two pits excavated next to the workshops yielded fragments of stone bowls, hammerstones, a flint core, broken flint blades, charred bones, and bits of charcoal. The trough(?) mentioned above came from one of these pits. The raw material for the lithic remains (both the chipped tools and stone implements) is to be found in the general area of the Dhali region. Six different types of siliceous flints or cherts have been identified: white lime chert, brown and black chert, gray chert, translucent chalcedony, green prase or green chalcedony, and red agate. All can be found in the vicinity of the site. The farthest source--that of the green prase--is about six miles away from Dhali-Agridhi. The practice of complete retrieval has proved very rewarding. Many flakes that at first appeared to be unused turned out after examination to be flint tools, with at least one used sharp edge. The flint tool assemblages from both the aceramic and ceramic deposits are now being subjected to a thorough microwear analysis. To date, at least two types of wear have been identified.

<u>Description and Analysis of the Aceramic Objects</u>

Stone Objects

Basically the collection of stone objects included the following types: stone bowls, mortars, hammerstones, grinding stones, platters, and miscellaneous objects, of which the functions of three remain unidentified (table 4). The following description and analysis includes objects from both Dhali-Agridhi proper and Site E.[8]

---

[5] The analysis was conducted by Stanley Warren of the University of Bradford, Bradford, England.

[6] Personal communication, Renfrew. The complete Dhali-Agridhi obsidian analysis, together with other Middle Eastern obsidian analyses, will be published by Renfrew and his associates.

[7] I wish to thank Mr. M. Loulloupis of the Cyprus Survey, who assisted me with my study of the Neolithic remains stored in Nicosia.

[8] I wish to thank Dr. Jack Lee of the St. John Fisher College who assisted me with the photography of the stone objects in the summer of 1978.

The objects were made from the following raw material: limestone (coarse or fine), gabbro (coarse or fine), pillow lava, sandstone, and flint or chert. Some of the raw materials were imported to the site either from the vicinity of the river bed or from across the river from a distance of 0.8 km. Other raw materials were imported from as far away as the mines of Mathiati and Sha, approximately 13 km distant from Dhali-Agridhi. In Site E, some sandstone was recovered that was probably imported from the Nicosia area. This sandstone was used for the manufacture of grinders.

The stone bowls are usually deep and large or shallow and small. Two stone bowls have handles (Object no. 724, fig. 9a, pl. 4a, and Object no. 745, fig. 9b, pl. 4b), and there is one stone bowl with a negative handle (Object no. 762, fig. 9c, pl. 4c). One small shallow stone bowl fragment (Site E), with a flat base and slightly convex sides, has an engraved pattern of single straight vertical lines alternating with single oblique lines arranged diagonally between the straight ones. A hole (spout?) is located just below the bowl's rim (Object no. 774, fig. 9d, pl. 4d). The engraved pattern of this bowl is very similar to a diabase bowl fragment found at Khirokitia (Dikaios 1953, pls. XLVI and CIX, Object no. 103).

Other stone vessels may be classified as either bowls or mortars (Objects no. 727, 762, 763, pl. 5b; 784, fig. 10a, pl. 5a; and 801, fig. 10b, pl. 5c). For example, Object no. 784 is called a "small bowl," while Object no. 801 is labeled a "mortar." Perhaps these stone vessels served a dual function during their lifetime, first as mortars (Objects no. 794 (pl. 5d), 797 (pl. 5e), and 800), and then, as the depression became deeper and the walls thinner, as bowls. This may have been the case with Object no. 762. To some of these mortar/bowl objects a spout was added. Table 2 illustrates that there is a very close relationship between the raw material employed for the manufacture of the stone implements and the function of the objects themselves. Almost all of the bowls that may be definitely classified as such were made of limestone. Two were manufactured of sandstone (Objects no. 795 and 763). Most of the platters and the trough(?) were also made of limestone. All the mortar/bowls were made of pillow lava. One engraved and decorated small bowl was made of fine-grained gabbro. Hammers, querns, grinders, and pounders were almost all made of either gabbro or diabase, a hard igneous stone. However there is one grinder (Object no. 782, pl. 7b) and one quern (Object no. 796) made of limestone. These two artifacts may have been used for grinding cereals, since they resemble tools that are used for this purpose today.

Pounders are simply either pebbles or boulders, picked up in all probability from the adjacent river bed and used accordingly (Object no. 740, fig. 11a, pl. 6a; Objects no. 751, 753, 789, fig. 11b, pl. 6b; and Object 791). Stone hammers were most probably used for flaking flint tools or for a tanning industry, among other purposes (Object no. 734, fig. 11c, pl. 6c; 761, fig. 12, pl. 6d; 790, pl. 6e). The large number of animal bones recovered, especially bones of the *Persian fallow deer*, *Dama mesopotamica*, and the proximity to the river may suggest that hides were tanned there. One very large stone vessel (63.5 x 34 x 22 cm) may have served as a trough or large water container for such a local tannery (Object no. 772, pl. 7a).

Some vessels have strange shapes (for example, Object 781). In these cases it seems that the shape of the vessels was determined by the natural contours of the raw material. While some of the objects are definitely querns (Objects no. 735, 754, 771, and 785), others may have been plates (Object no. 798) or platters (Objects no. 739, 758, 759). The more ambiguous quern/platters do seem to have thicker walls. Almost all definitely identifiable querns were made either of coarse gabbro or fine-grained gabbro. Some querns were made of pillow lava, and some of limestone (Object no. 796). The definitely identifiable platters were also manufactured of limestone, as were some of the grinders (Object no. 782, pl. 7b). Two functions may be suggested by the differential use of the raw materials: the limestone for grinding softer material, and the other types of stone for grinding harder materials. A complementary function of both grinders and querns is suggested by the discovery of two types of each category: smooth grinders (Objects no. 747 and 736) and rough grinders (Object no. 782, pl. 7b); smooth querns (Objects no. 735, 771, 785, and 796) and rough querns (Object no. 754). In addition to the objects described above there are over three hundred functionally unidentifiable fragments of stone implements.

Bone Implements

The faunal collection from Dhali-Agridhi is one of the largest, if not the largest, collection ever found in Neolithic Cyprus within such a small concentrated area of excavation. Yet among this collection only three recognizable bone tools have been recovered within the aceramic deposit (table 5). All were found in the workshop of Area 2, 1976 (see fig. 3). Hence the collection is too small to make any quantitative conclusion possible. It is hoped that further excavation will yield further bone implements, thus enabling the construction of a typology.

The Dhali-Agridhi faunal collection includes many long splinters of bone. Although examination by the eye alone does not reveal any sign of wear, it is possible that some of these may have served as tools. It is planned to examine these splinters using microscopic analysis to determine both possible use and the method of manufacture. One grooved pointed bone shaft (Object no. 730, fig. 13a, pl. 8a), may have been used for butchering meat. The function of the groove may have been to allow for blood flow. The pointed shaft may have functioned as a piercer (Object no. 742, fig. 13b, pl. 8b). The pierced tusk of a wild boar may have been used either as a needle or a pendant (Object no. 737, fig. 13c, pl. 8c).

It is not yet clear whether the bone tools were locally made or imported from another area. In order to manufacture bone tools a burin is usually required, and so far no burin has been found at Dhali-Agridhi. While local manufacture cannot be ruled out, the paucity of bone implements recovered to date may indicate that they were made elsewhere.

The faunal collection included a large number of antlers belonging to Persian fallow deer, *Dama mesopotamica*. These antlers may have functioned as hammers in the flint industry. These will be subjected to microscopic analysis to determine wear and possible usage.

The Ceramic Deposit

Dhali-Agridhi Proper

The horizontal stratigraphic separation between the aceramic and ceramic deposits was clearly apparent in Areas 1A and 2 (see figs. 3 and 4). The sherds from both these areas were of the same Dark-faced Burnished Ware as that found in 1972, and it was possible to join many pieces with those found in the previous seasons. The more-or-less circular shape of Concentration A (1972) appeared almost complete. Unfortunately, however, a post-Neolithic pit (dated to the twelfth century B.C.) had been dug into the ceramic deposit in Area 2 at the expense of the total ceramic area. The ceramic deposit of area 1A measured only 1.50 x 0.50 m, with a maximum depth of 0.17 m.

Nearly 800 potsherds were confined to a circular deposit about 4 m in diameter. Most of these sherds were found at the bottom of the Neolithic layer, just above the sterile soil, and would appear to indicate a living area. However no hard-packed living floor was found, although there was evidence of a post that might have supported a roof in the center of the roughly circular area (Lehavy 1974:98). About 50 percent of the sherds came from the lowest layers of the ceramic Neolithic--Loci 027 and 028 of Area 1, Locus 007 of Area 1A, and Locus 024 of Area 2, all in Concentration A. A fairly large number of the sherds were joined, resulting in at least five restorable vessels. Concentration A is thus interpreted as representing one single occupation level. Moreover it appears highly probably that occupation of this site was short-lived, which in turn explains why no living floor was formed here.

Paleobotanical Remains

As in the case of the aceramic deposit, the amount of seeds retrieved by the flotation method was too small to allow any quantitative comparison. Both grape and lentil seeds were identified. The size of the seed is usually the indicator of whether grape or lentil is wild or domesticated. The grape seeds (*Vitis silvestris*) are very small and lack the deep indentations of the large seeds of modern cultivated varieties. Hence, according to Stewart, these are most probably wild specimens. Grape seeds, either *Vitis silvestris* or *Vitis vinifera*, have been found in other Neolithic and Bronze Age sites in Europe, and there is some evidence that wild grapes were utilized in northern Greece before 2000 B.C. (Renfrew 1973:127). In the Near East wild grapes have been found in several archaeological deposits. One of these finds, dating as far back as 7000 B.C., comes from Çayönü in Turkey (Stewart 1976:221).

According to the map of wild vine distribution presented in Renfrew (1973:126), Cyprus does not fall within the wild area. This would imply that the Neolithic vines of Cyprus had been taken out of their natural habitat zone. If so, then, regardless of seed size, we would have evidence of grape cultivation rather than collection. However Stewart is inclined to include Cyprus in the area of natural distribution of *Vitis*, in which case the Dhali-Agridhi grapes probably indicate evidence of fruit collecting activity.[9]

The lentil seeds found in the ceramic deposit are smaller than the cultivated forms and should, like the aceramic lentils, be identified as *Lens orientalis* (see note no. 3).

Ceramics

The ceramic inventory consists of one large deep bowl (fig. 14b, pl. 9b), three high-necked jars (fig. 14a, pl. 9a), at least two medium-sized bowls, and three small bowls. The pottery is handmade, with wavy rims. Some of the vessels are slipped and burnished both outside and, where possible, inside. The high-necked jars have slip and burnish on the outside only. Most of the vessels are Dark-faced Burnished Ware (DFBW), tempered with grit, and most of the sherds are of the same type. The bases are finger-flanged and bear visible finger or thumb impressions. In the case of the bowls, both the outside and inside walls are smooth, while on the high-necked jars, the finger and thumb impressions are not smoothed out on the inside walls. A few sherds of odd shape do not conform to any known vessel geometry. Sherds that are not of the DFBW type are poorly fired coarse ware, tempered with organic material (Lehavy 1974:84-85, pl. I.3).

What had previously been thought to be a large shallow bowl (ibid.) might have been used as an oven. Additional sherds have been mended to form what now seems to be a horseshoe-shaped vessel, at least 50 cm wide at its widest diameter (fig. 15 and pl. 10). Since not all of the sherds have yet been found, it is hard to determine the width of the mouth. In all probability this vessel was made in situ. The walls of the vessel (10.5 cm high) are better fired than the base, which is very friable and poorly fired. Its walls are thicker than the base (which measures only 6 mm). At the bottom, near the base, they measure 10 mm, in the middle 9 mm, and at the rim 6 mm. Both the walls and the base of this coarse-ware vessel are tempered with organic material. The base is crudely finger-pinched and finger-flanged, and is joined to the walls with the aid of fingers and thumb. The oven appears to have been made on a mat: the base is impressed with the pattern of the mat. Consult Munsell coloring: interior color varies from 2.5 YR 4/4 to 10R 4/1, possibly indicating charring. Comparable coarse ware pottery has been found in the excavation of Lemba and described as trays with wide U-shaped openings. The Lemba trays were found in association with ash, and there were indications that some functioned like baking trays (Peltenburg 1980:3 and 2, fig. 17). [Editor's note: No signs of charring were found on this coarse-ware oven(?). It seems more likely that this vessel served as an olive-oil separating vat.]

Of the vessels described above, the large deep bowl is about 35 cm in diameter and about 18 cm deep, and one of the high-necked jars is at least 40 cm high and 32 cm wide at its widest point (fig. 14a, pl. 9a). The large size of these vessels and the oven(?) built in situ suggest sedentism. Hence it would seem safe to suggest that the people of Dhali-Agridhi lived

---

[9] Personal communication, Robert Stewart.

in the vicinity of the site for a long period of time. However any single occupation of the site must have been short-lived--a conclusion to be drawn from the fact that there was no great depth of deposit. It seems, therefore, that the Dhali-Agridhi people must have shifted about in the general area of the upper terrace on the southern bank of the Yalias River.

The Area 2 ceramic deposit also yielded 32 beads about 5 mm in diameter in addition to the 65 found in 1972. The beads were made from the following material: 7 from fossilized (?) fish teeth; 1 from brown limestone; 3 were made from grained ochre (?), 2 were made out of a conch type sea shell; 2 were made out of green serpentine; 3 were made out of black umber (?); 2 were made out of brown umber (?); and 11 were made out of red umber (?).

No stone vessels were found in the ceramic deposit, but there were a number of flints which have been only preliminarily studied (fig. 8).

Conclusions

The stratigraphical and typological separation between the aceramic and ceramic deposits was examined (see fig. 3). In general, the Dhali-Agridhi aceramic assemblage resembles that from Khirokitia, showing numerous parallels, although few of the Dhali-Agridhi stone vessels are of the same type as those found in Khirokitia. The ceramic deposit, on the other hand, is devoid of any stone vessels. The only stone implements found in the ceramic deposit are flints. All vessels found in it are made of clay. It is interesting to note that although there is obviously some difference in the technology represented by the two deposits, the faunal and floral exploitation was basically the same. The only difference noted so far between the two deposits is the introduction in the ceramic areas of wild grapes (*Vitis silvestris*). Obsidian was found only in the aceramic deposits, which is consistent with all other aceramic sites in Cyprus.

New C^{14} samples have been analyzed at the Radiocarbon Laboratories of the University of Pennsylvania (Meulengracht, McGovern, and Lawn 1981). These assays indicate two different cultures that existed at least 1000 years apart. The Dhali-Agridhi aceramic is dated to 5340±465 B.C. (GX, 2848 A, Libby Half-Life 5568) and 5450±60 B.C. (P-2768, 5568 Half-Life), or 5680±60 B.C. (P-2768, 5730 Half-Life). The C^{14} determination would make the Dhali-Agridhi aceramic contemporary with that of Khirokitia. Another C^{14} assay would date aceramic Dhali-Agridhi earlier than Khirokitia, 6040±80 B.C. (P-2775, 5568 Half-Life), or 6280±80 B.C. (P-2775, 5730 Half-Life). However it is not the earliest aceramic date reported from the island (Todd 1977:381). The earlier aceramic date from Dhali-Agridhi places the site within the generally accepted range of the aceramic Neolithic of Cyprus.

The ceramic deposit includes the earliest Neolithic pottery yet found in Cyprus, dated to the fifth millennium B.C. Two C^{14} samples have been analyzed from the ceramic deposit (see table 6). The ceramic deposit dates, according to C^{14} determination, to 4465±310 B.C. (GX 2847 A, Libby Half-Life 5568) and 3750±100 B.C. (P-2769, 5568 Half-Life), or 3920±100 B.C. (P-2769, 5730 Half-Life). P-2769, when recalibrated according to MASCA, yields a date of 4560±110 B.C.; GX 2847 A is even earlier. These dates fall into a period once considered to be an occupational hiatus on the island, a view that is no longer tenable. The earliest pottery on the island has been described as Dark-faced Burnished Ware (DFBW) and typologically compared with the Amuq ceramic sequence (Watkins 1973:50). A fifth millennium date is plausible when compared with the Dhali-Agridhi C^{14} ceramic deposit dates. Although the second C^{14} date (P-2769) is slightly below 4000 B.C. (uncorrected MASCA), the connections with the Amuq DFBW cannot be ruled out. This possible connection between Cyprus and the Levant requires further detailed study. Up to this time the ceramic dates of Dhali-Agridhi constitute the only evidence for human occupation in Cyprus at the turn of and during the fifth millennium B.C.

The faunal and botanical evidence indicates that the exploitation of the environment was basically the same in the aceramic and ceramic phases of settlement. There is little doubt that Dhali-Agridhi was a sedentary settlement during both phases of occupation. The size of the stone vessels, especially the large trough(?) found in the aceramic deposit, and also the size and types of the pottery vessels (including the oven built *in situ*) indicate some permanency of settlement. The botanical remains in both deposits are of wild forms. All four animals (*Dama mesopotamica*, *Ovis*, *Capra*, and *Sus*) were introduced to the island by man (Schwartz 1973 and Stanley Price 1977b). Hence one may conclude that there was domestication, or at least semidomestication.

All of the data, as evident from both deposits, suggest that the Dhali-Agridhi people were intensive collectors of wild plants growing in the area. The glossy sheen on some of the flint tools suggests that harvesting took place and incipient domestication of some wild botanical forms cannot be ruled out. Diet was supplemented by herding some animals and hunting others. One form, *Dama mesopotamica*, apparently reverted to a feral state, only to be hunted to extinction during the Bronze Age (Schwartz 1973:217). The other three genera, *Ovis*, *Capra*, and *Sus*, became fully domesticated.

Apart from its early date, other reasons make Dhali-Agridhi a key site for the study of Neolithic Cyprus. The aceramic deposit of Dhali-Agridhi represents a settlement of quite different type from contemporary Khirokitia. If Khirokitia may be classified as a farming village with complex architecture that resembles that of an early "urban" site, Dhali-Agridhi is perhaps better classified as a rural settlement. Until recently investigation of the Neolithic period in Cyprus has proved to be oriented more toward establishing a linear chronological sequence than to a study of regional and site variation within contemporary periods (Stanley Price 1972). Further excavation at Dhali-Agridhi and a comparison of the findings with those of other settlement types that date to the same time span should make it possible to present a more realistic picture of the economy and pattern of settlement of Cyprus throughout the Neolithic period. Dhali-Agridhi represents at least two different periods of such rural settlement.

Thus, in the future, special attention will be paid to the study of cultural change and continuity from the aceramic to the ceramic periods of Neolithic Cyprus as evident at Dhali-Agridhi. The site provides a good opportunity to conduct such an investigation. It also enables the study of the nature of regional variation, comparing the successive phases at Dhali-Agridhi with those at other Neolithic sites. This will give a picture of the linear development and at the same time extend knowledge of a variety of regional cultures, a study that has so far been largely neglected.

Table 1. Dhali-Agridhi Obsidian Cross Reference Numbers

Sample registration no.	Field registration no.			Sample analysis no.*	Renfrew classification
	Year	Area	Locus		
880	1974	DA 1A	009	478/12	Çiftlik 2b
732	1976	DA 2	015	610/21	Çiftlik 2b
777	1976	DA 31	003	610/22	Çiftlik 2b
855	1976	DA 31	003	610/23	Çiftlik 2b

*Sample analysis numbers are those of Warren's laboratory numbers.

Table 2. Dhali-Agridhi Area Study of Rock Fragments from Cobble Floor that Show Definite Usage by Man*

Rock type	Bowl Fragments	Hand Grinder	Grinding Quern	Percussion Indentation	Spherical, or Nearly So	Plate Shaped	Disc Shaped	Cylindrical	Additional comments	Total
Limestone	10 1-c	1	4 3-c	2		1 1-c			c = charred	18
Coarse igneous rock (gabbro)								1		1
Coarse diabase		1			2		1			4
Fine diabase			1							1
Pillow lava	3				2					5
Total	13	2	4	3	4	1	1	1		29

*The data were obtained from Frank L. Koucky of the College of Wooster, Ohio, the Idalion Expedition geologist. The excavated area of paved cobble floor consisted of 232 cobble stones or fragments. The table accounts for those pieces that show clear evidence of use. Some of the remaining 203 fragments (not represented in the table) also show evidence of use, but not with certainty.

Table 3. Dhali-Agridhi Area Study of Rock Fragments
from Cobble Floor that Do Not Show Definite Usage by Man

Rock type	No Obvious Usage	Possible Grinding	Percussion	Possible Rim or Other Part	Core	Other	Additional comments	Total
Flat limestone fragments	17 / 1-c			9 / 4-c		4 lids	c = charred	30
Irregular limestone fragments (I and C)	17	1					3 are of a type rare in a riverbed	18
White quartz	1							1
Green prase chert (rare)		2 (1)			1 (2)		only 3 pieces in all, 1 of which was first a grinder, then a core	3
Fine-grained sandstone (I and A)		2					flattened with striations, showing use as sandpaper is used today	2
Coarse-grained calcare-sandstone (I and B)	5	2					1 fragment larger than the others (17 cm)	7
Red ochre (I and C)	1							1
Coarse igneous rock (gabbro)	32	11		8				51
Coarse diabase	10	8	1	1	1	1		20
Fine diabase	23	5	1	3		1-s	s = spherical	33
Pillow lava	14	2		1-c			c = charred	17
Very fine diabase or silicified pillow lava	13	5	2					20
Total	133	38	4	22	1	5		203

Table 4. Stone Object Classification Based on Raw Material

Type of object	Limestone	Gabbro	Diabase	Pillow lava	Sandstone	Chert
Bowl	29	1			3	
Mortar	2	1*		4*		
Hammer			5			1
Quern	1	4	4	1		
Grinder	1	2	4	3		
Platter	5		1		2	
Pounder		1	3	1		
Cylinder	1+					
Trough	1					
Total	40	9	17	9	5	1

*Described below as mortar/bowl, all made of igneous stone.
+Cylindrical stone with hole in center, drilled from both ends.

Table 5. Bone and Ivory Implements

Object registry no.	Area	Locus	Brief description	Plate no.
730	DA.2	015	Grooved pointed bone shaft	8a
737	DA.2	023	Pierced tusk of a wild boar; either a needle or a pendant	8c
742	DA.2	020	Shaft graduated to a point	8b

Table 6. Radiocarbon Dates from Dhali-Agridhi[a]

Provenience	Sample no.	5568 Half-Life	5730 Half-Life	MASCA correction
Area 2, 1976 Loci 021, 024 Concentration A Ceramic	P[b]-2769	3750±100	3920±100	4560±110
Area 1, 1972 Locus 028 NE III Concentration A Ceramic	GX[c] 2847 A	4465±310		
Area 1, 1972 Locus 014 NW III Concentration B Aceramic	GX 2848 A	5340±465		
Site E, 1976 Locus 007 Aceramic	P-2768	5450±60	5680±60	*[d]
Area 12, 1976 Locus 008 (a pit) Aceramic	P-2775	6040±80	6280±80	*

[a] All dates are B.C. and the age is with reference to the year A.D. 1950.

[b] P designates University of Pennsylvania Radiocarbon dates.

[c] GX designates Kruger Enterprises, Inc., Geochron Laboratories Division dates.

[d] * = Beyond range of available corrections.

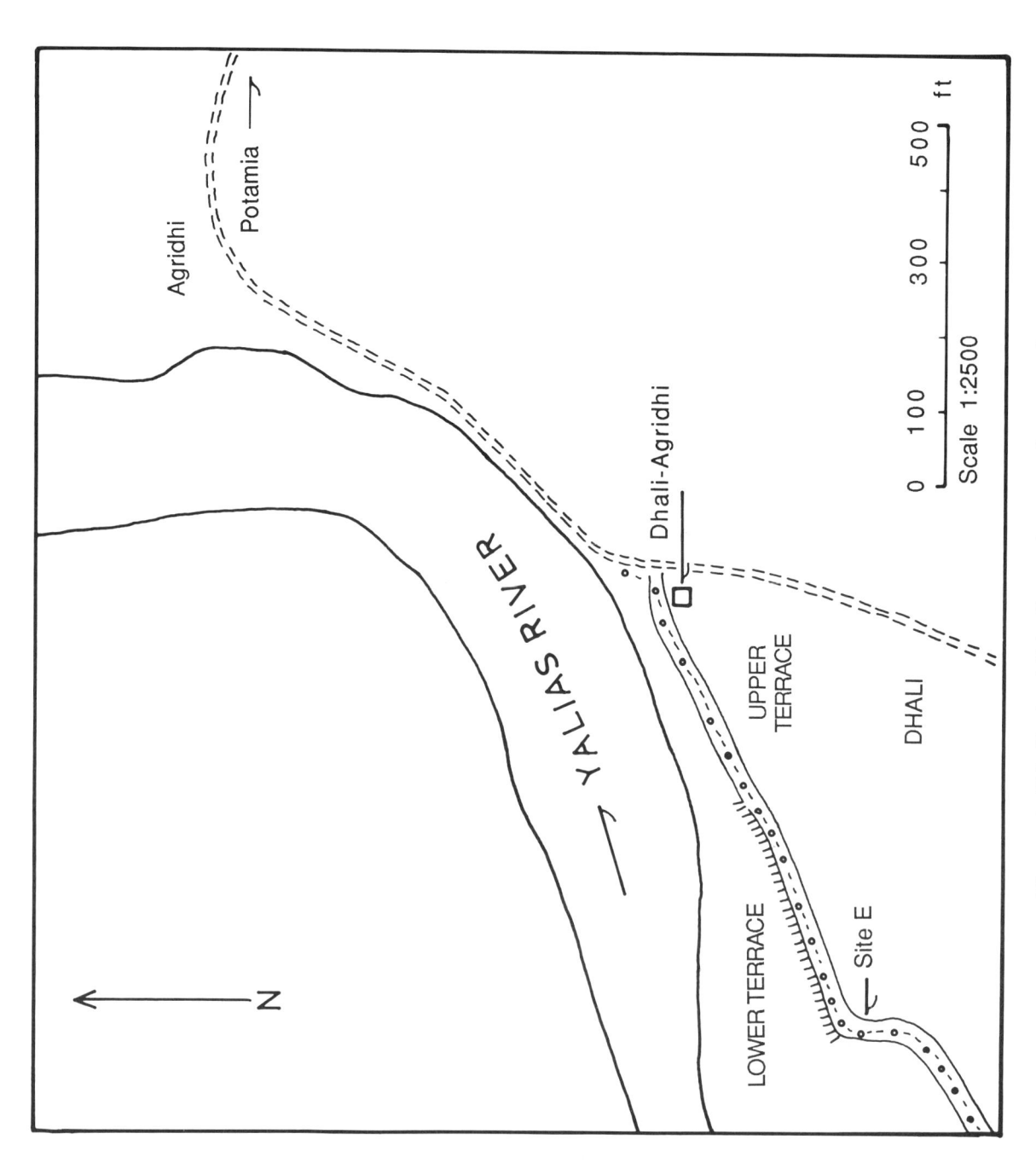

Figure 1. Dhali-Agridhi, General Area of Excavation.

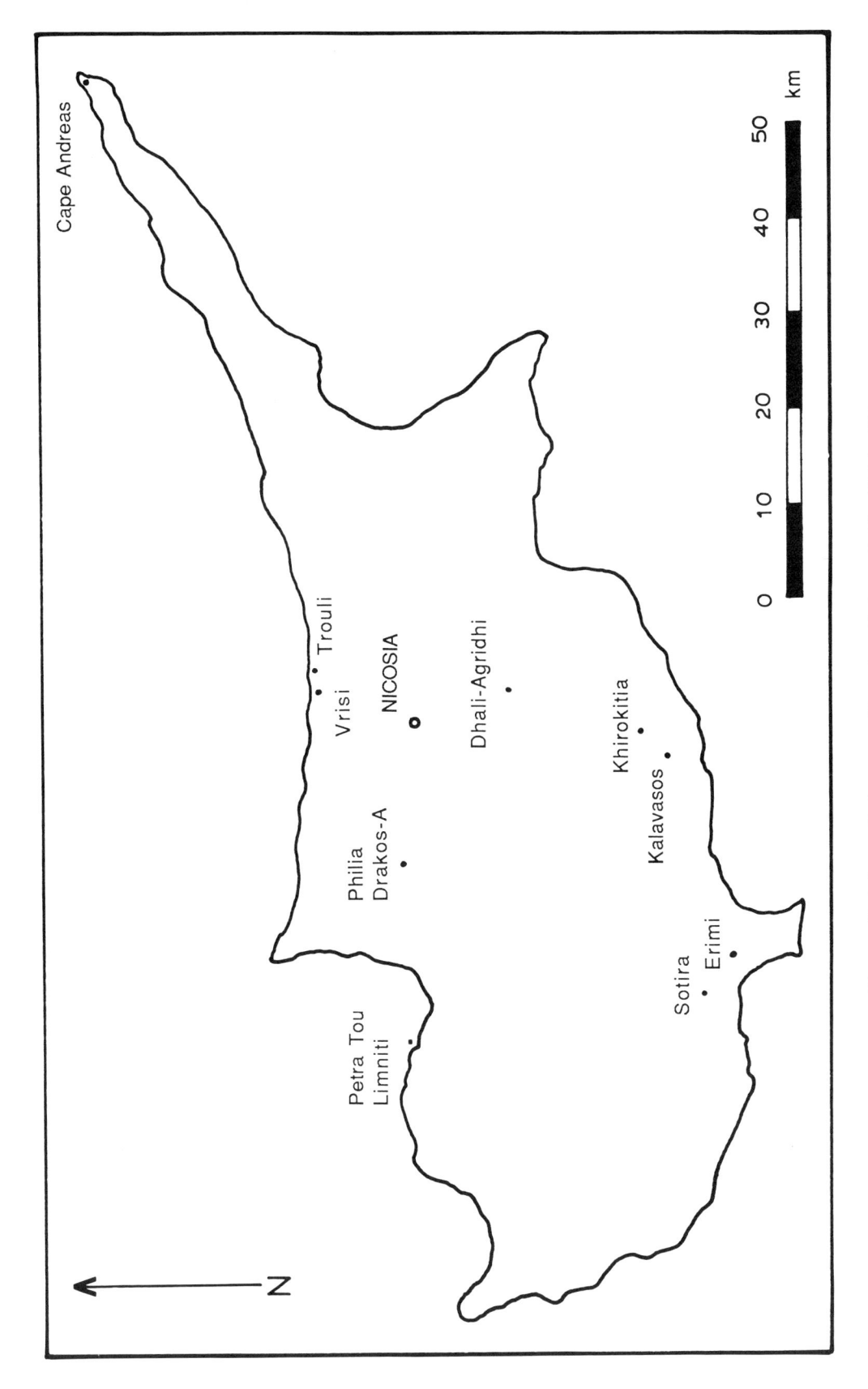

Figure 2. Map of Cyprus, Showing Selected Neolithic Sites.

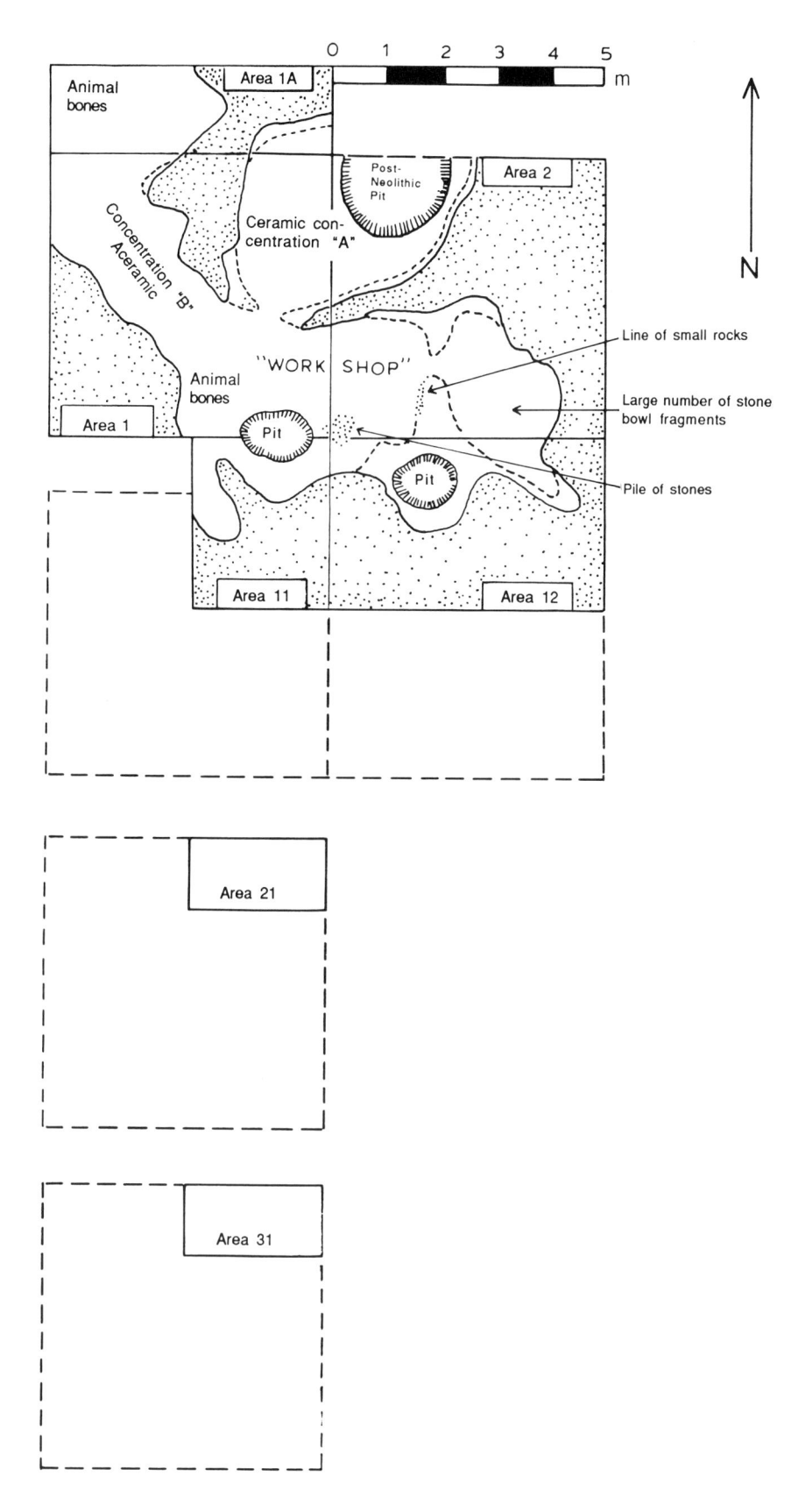

Figure 3. Dhali-Agridhi, Final Top Plan; Seasons 1972, 1974, and 1976. Concentrations A and B, 1972; Areas 1A and 2, 1974; Areas 11, 12, 21, and 31, 1976.

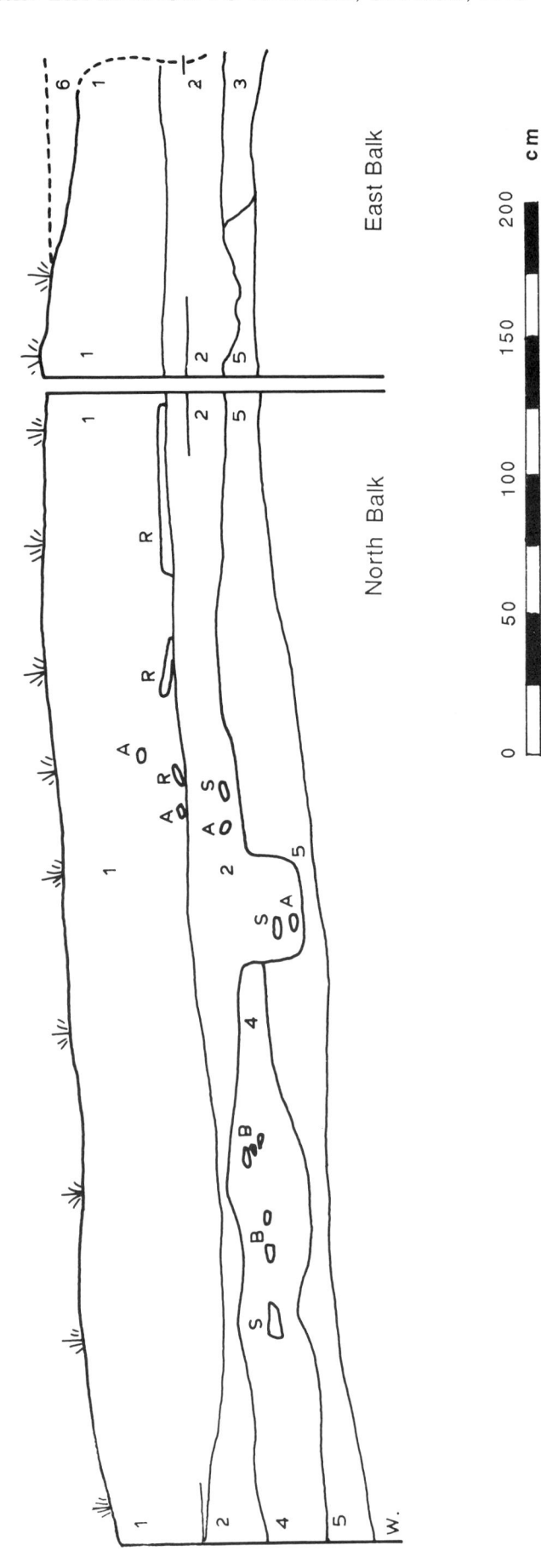

Figure 4. Dhali-Agridhi, Area 1A, North and East Sections. Key: 1. Top soil, 2. Post-Neolithic, 3. Ceramic Neolithic, 4. Aceramic Neolithic, 5. Sterile, 6. Eroded between 1974 and 1976. A. Post-Neolithic sherd, B. Bone, R. Root, S. Stone.

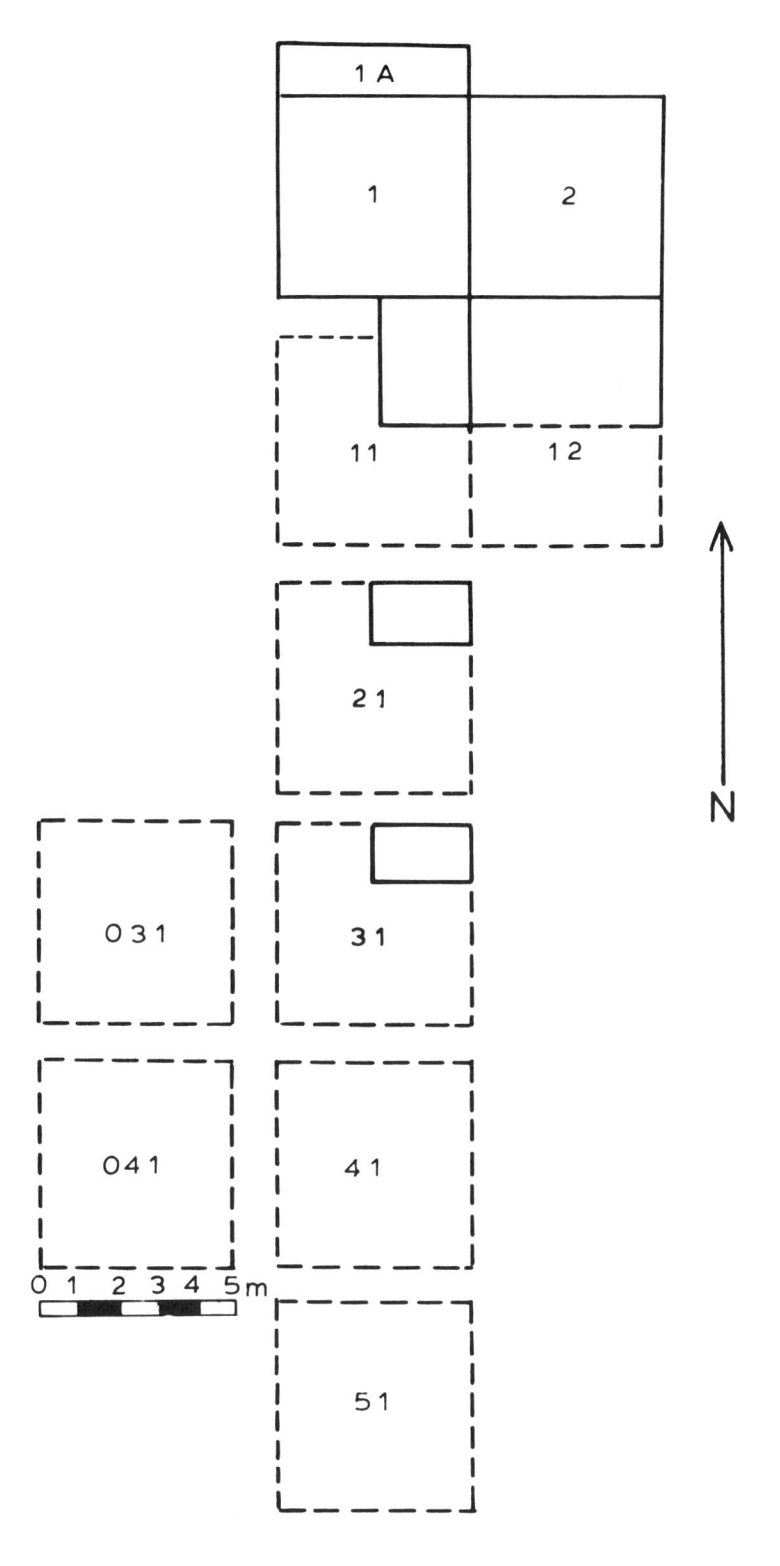

Figure 5. Dhali-Agridhi, Areas of Excavations as of 1976. Key: Solid line indicates areas excavated; dashed line to be excavated.

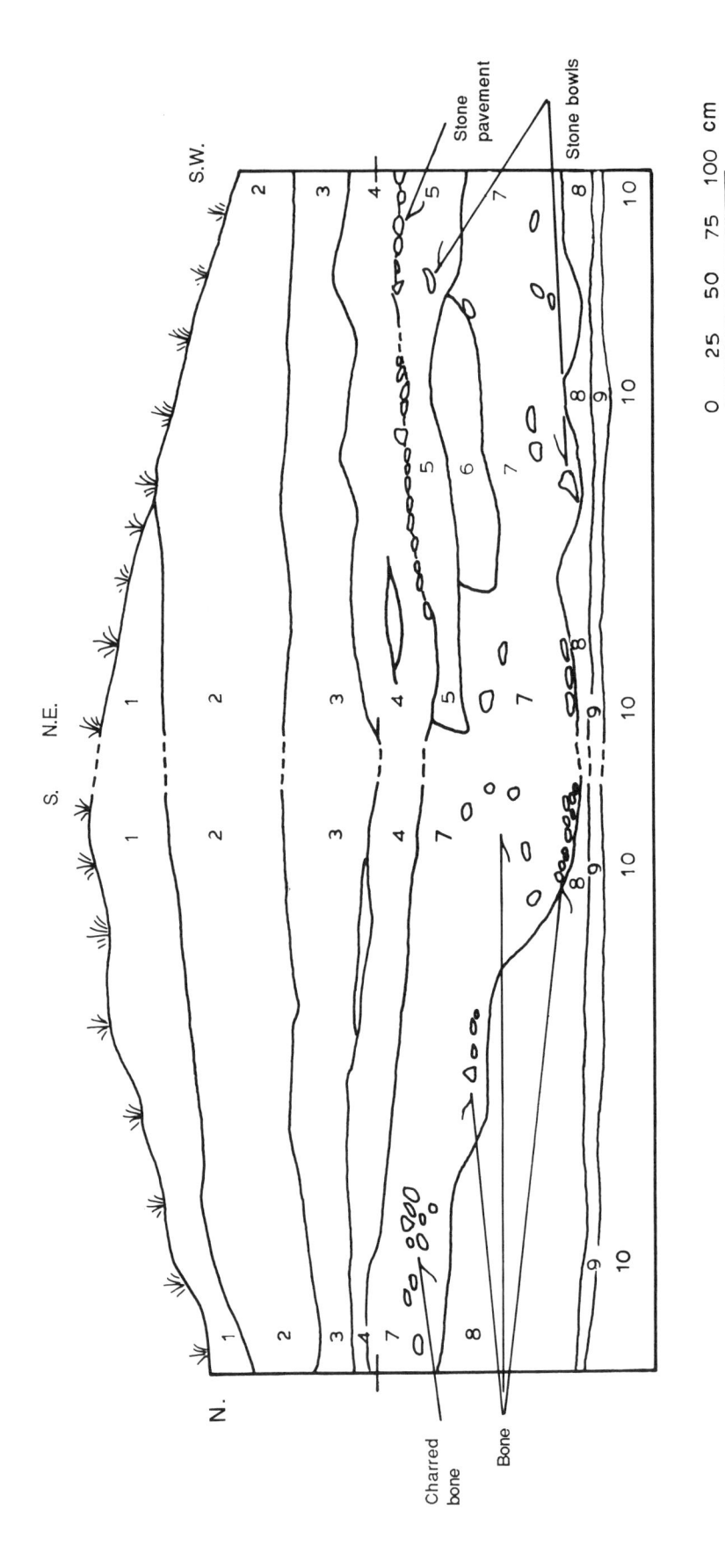

Figure 6. Dhali-Agridhi, Site E, 1976. Sections cut into Upper Terrace from Lower Terrace. Key: 1. Top soil mixed with caliche, 2. Top soil, 3. Soil mixed with gray gravel, 4. Sterile layer, 5. Mud packed below stone pavement–Neolithic, 6. Neolithic layer packed with bone, 7. Neolithic layer, 8. Caliche-sterile layer, 9. Red brown sterile soil, 10. Caliche-sterile layer.

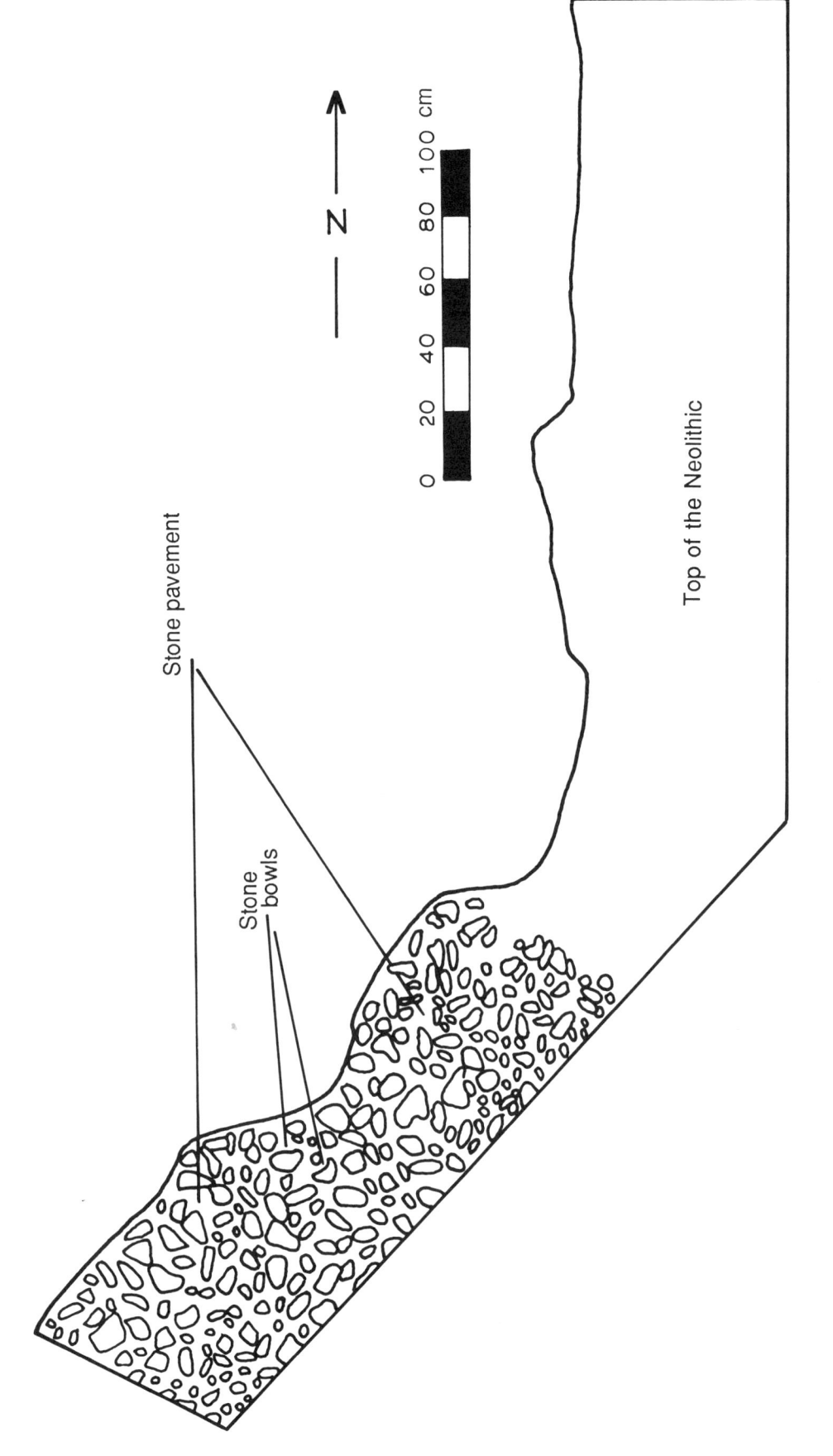

Figure 7. Dhali-Agridhi, Site E, 1976. Plan: top of the Neolithic layer.

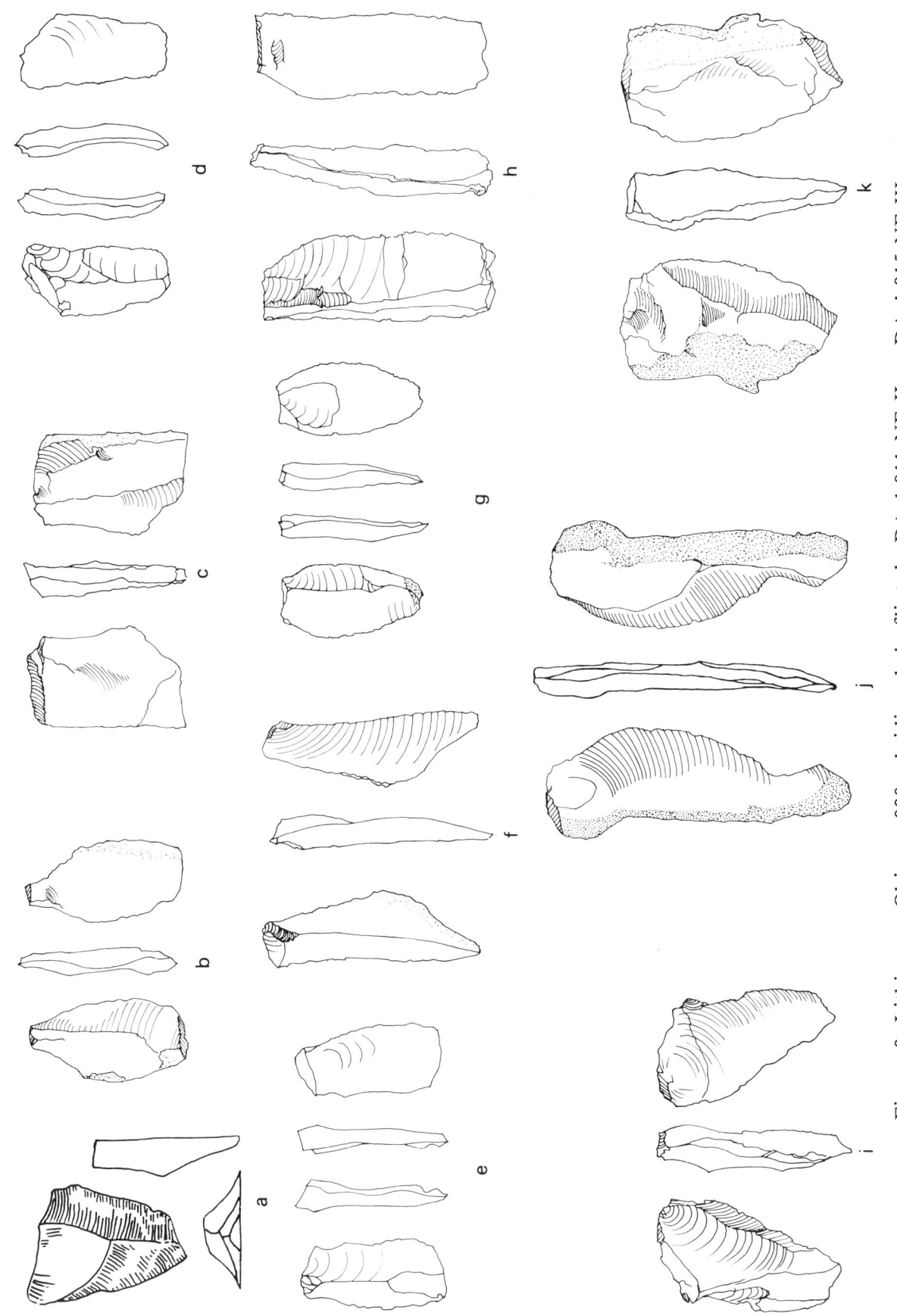

Figure 8. Lithics. a. Obj. no. 880, obsidian, b-k. flint, b. DA 1.011 NE II, c. DA 1.015 NE III, d. DA 1.017 NE II, e. DA 1.017 NE II, f. DA 1.017 NE IV, g. DA 1.018 NE I, h. DA 1.018 NE II, i. DA 1.028 NE II, j. DA 1.028 NE II, k. DA 1.028A NE III. Letters b, d, e, f, g, i, j used for cutting; c and k for scraping; h for cutting and scraping. Scale: a. 1:1, b-k. 2:1.

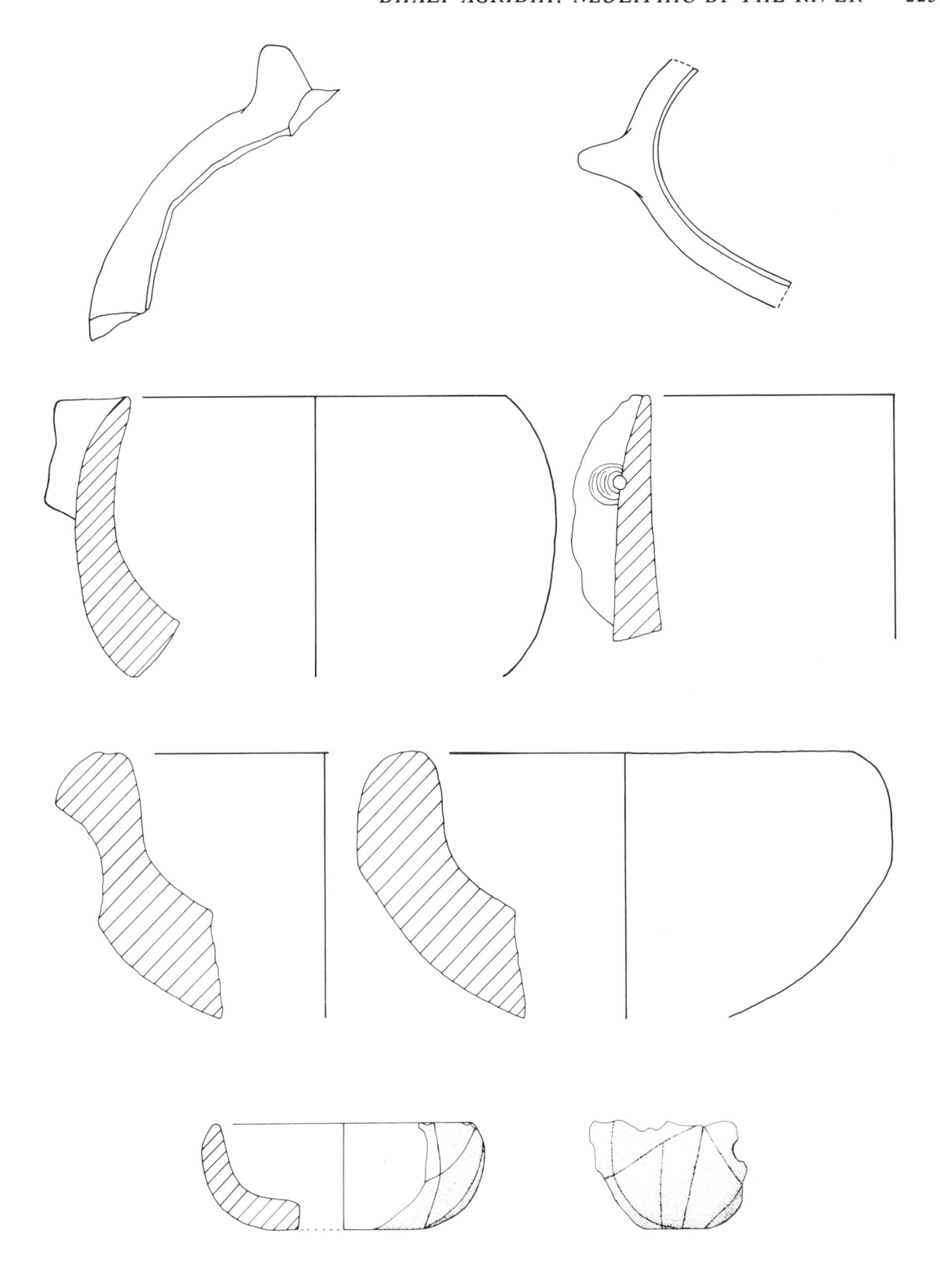

Figure 9. Stone Bowls. a. Obj. no. 724, b. Obj. no. 745, c. Obj. no. 762, d. Obj. no. 774. Scale a-c. 1:2, d. 1:4

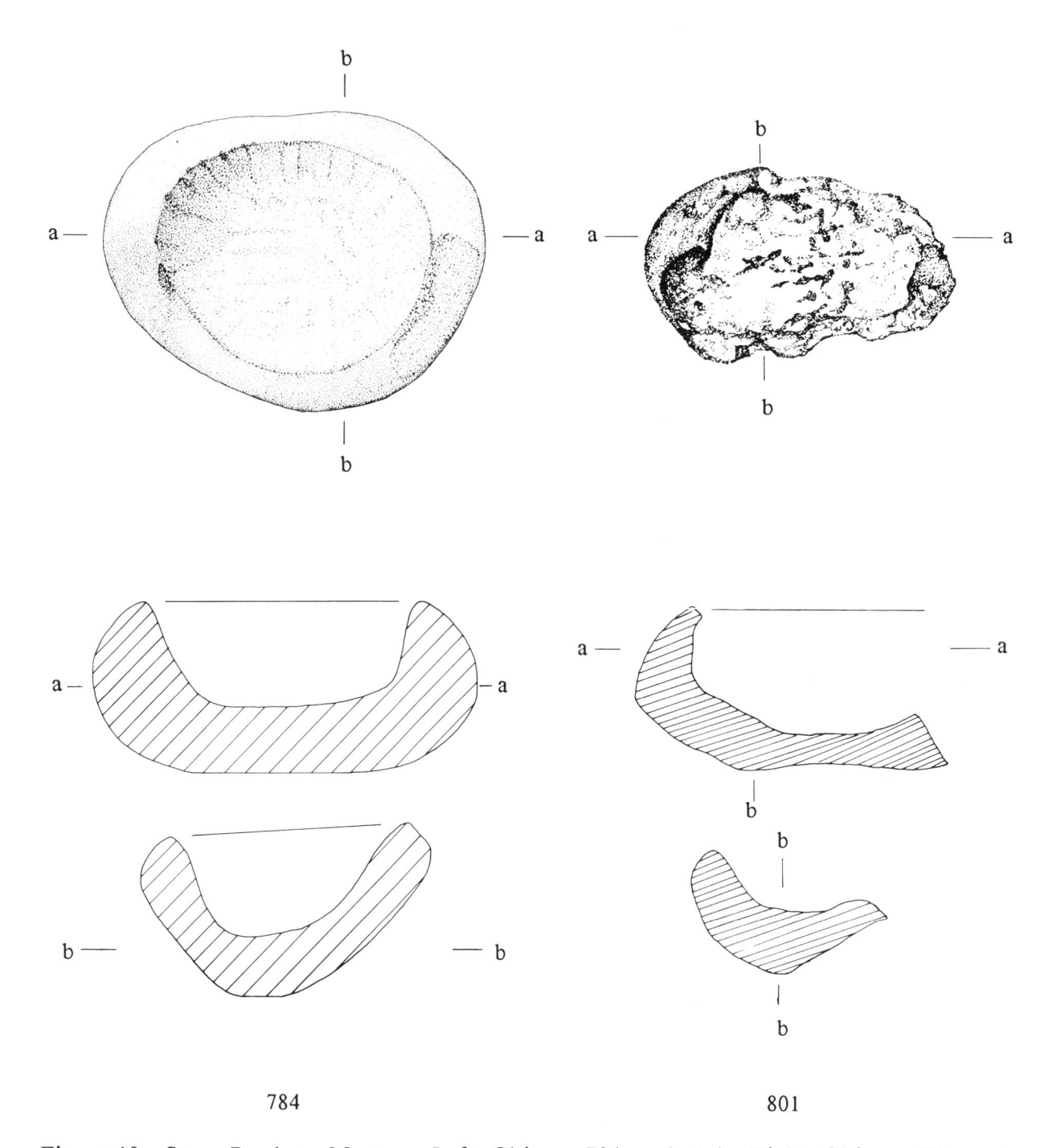

226 AMERICAN EXPEDITION TO IDALION, CYPRUS, 1973-1980

784

801

Figure 10. Stone Bowls or Mortars. Left, Obj. no. 784, scale 1:4. Right, Obj. no. 801, scale 1:3.

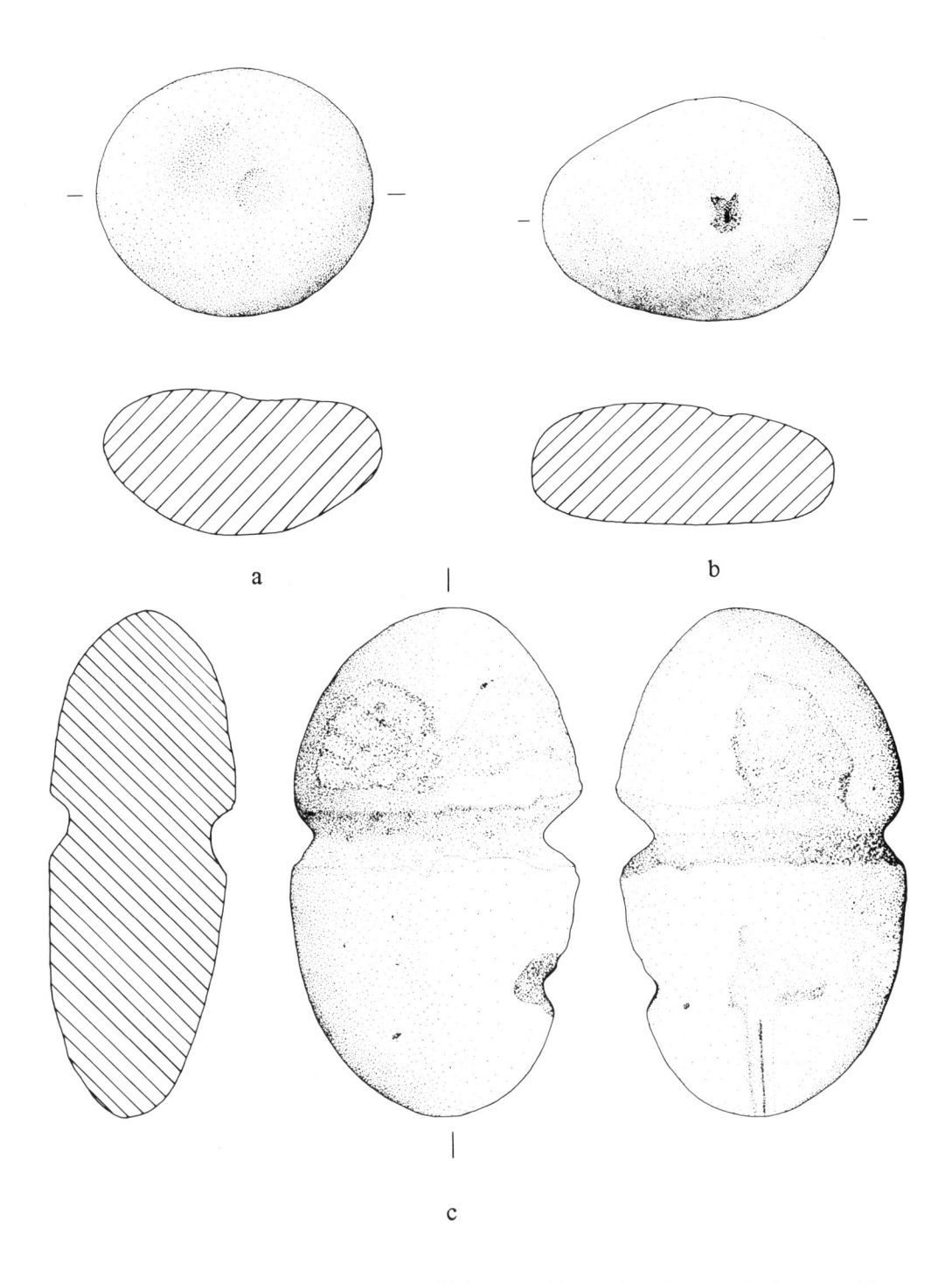

Figure 11. Stone Pounders or Hammers. a. Obj. no. 740, scale 1:2.5; b. Obj. no. 789, scale 1:2; and c. Obj. no. 734, scale 1:2.5.

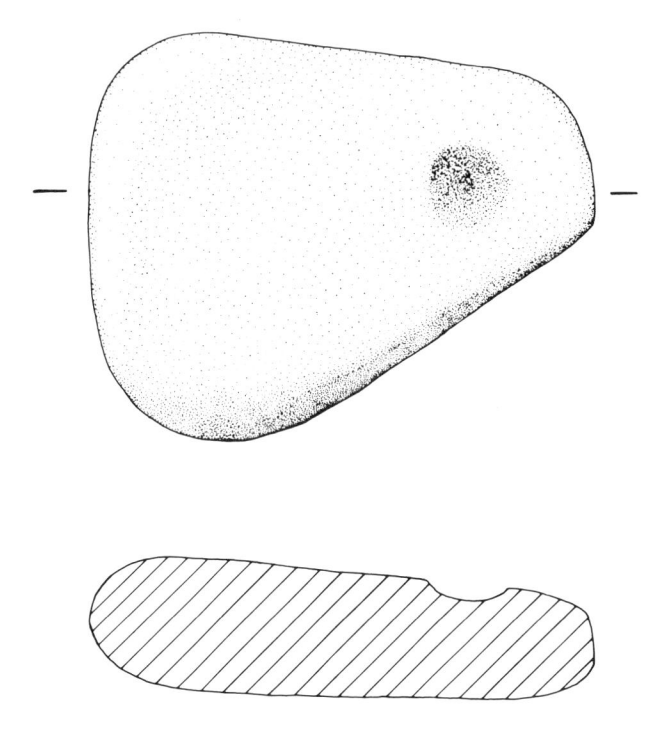

Figure 12. Stone Hammer, Obj. No. 761. Scale 1:1.

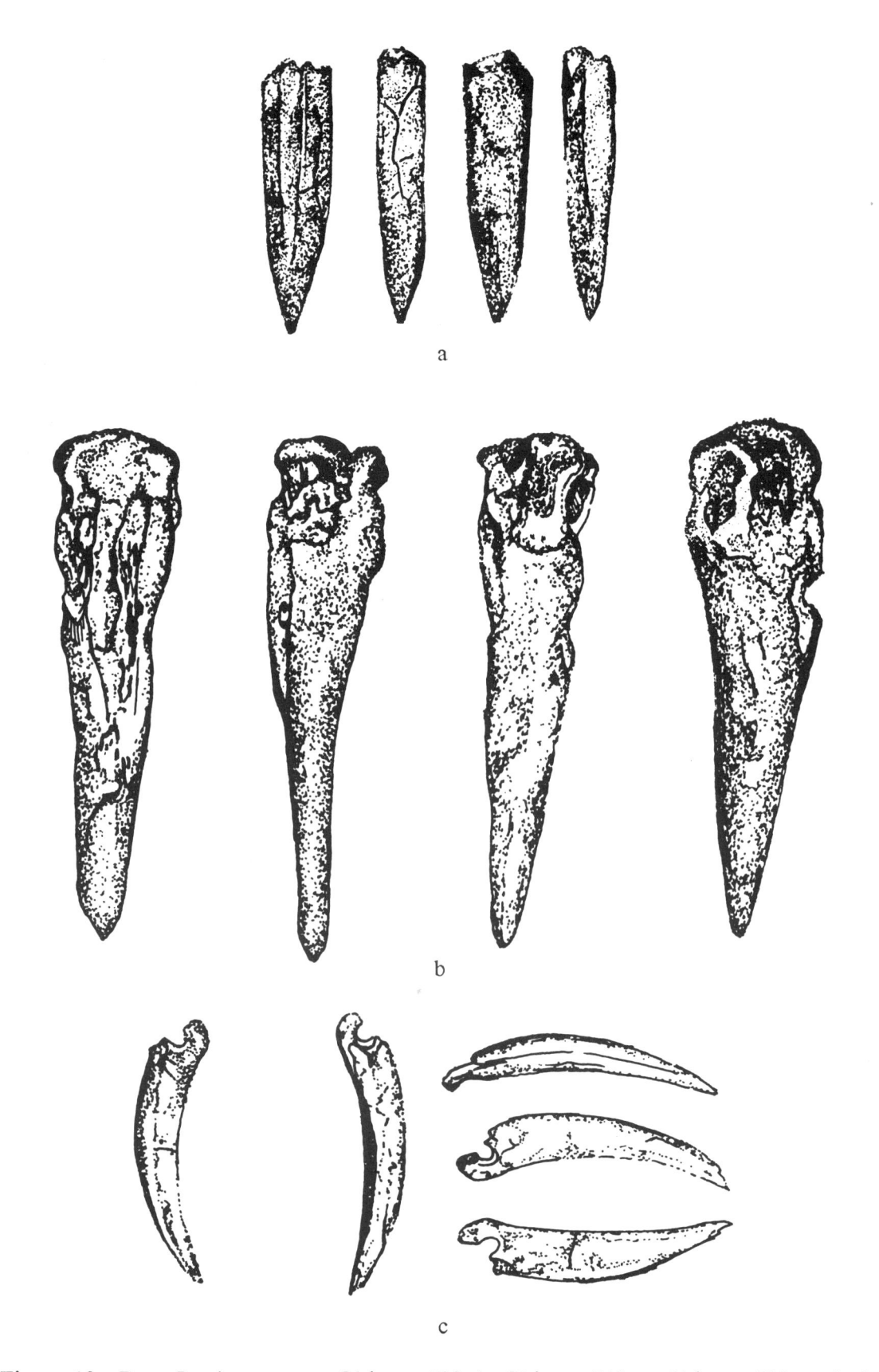

Figure 13. Bone Implements. a. Obj. no. 730, b. Obj. no. 742, c. Obj. no. 737, scale 2:1.

Figure 14. Ceramics, Dark-faced Burnished Ware

Locus	Description
a. Sherds found throughout all Loci of Concentration A Areas DA.1.72, DA.1A.74 and DA.2.76.	High necked jar; assembled from 76 sherds; grit tempered; handmade; wavy rim; slipped and burnished inside (down to shoulder) and outside; surface color varies due to firing from weak red (10 R 4/4) to reddish brown (2.5 YR 5/4) covering most of the exterior with very dark gray (2.5 YR 3/1) to black (5 YR 2/1) covering some parts of the exterior.
b. Sherds found throughout all Loci of Concentration A Areas DA.1.72, DA.1A.74 and DA.2.76	Large deep bowl; assembled from 72 sherds grit tempered; hand made; wavy rim; slipped and burnished inside and outside interior color varies from weak red (2.5 YR 4/2) to red (2.5 YR 5/8); exterior color varies from red (2.5 YR 5/6) to dark red (2.5 YR 3/6) covering most of the exterior and with weak red (2.5 YR 5/2) to dark gray (2.5 YR 4/0) covering some parts of the exterior; exterior color varies due to firing.

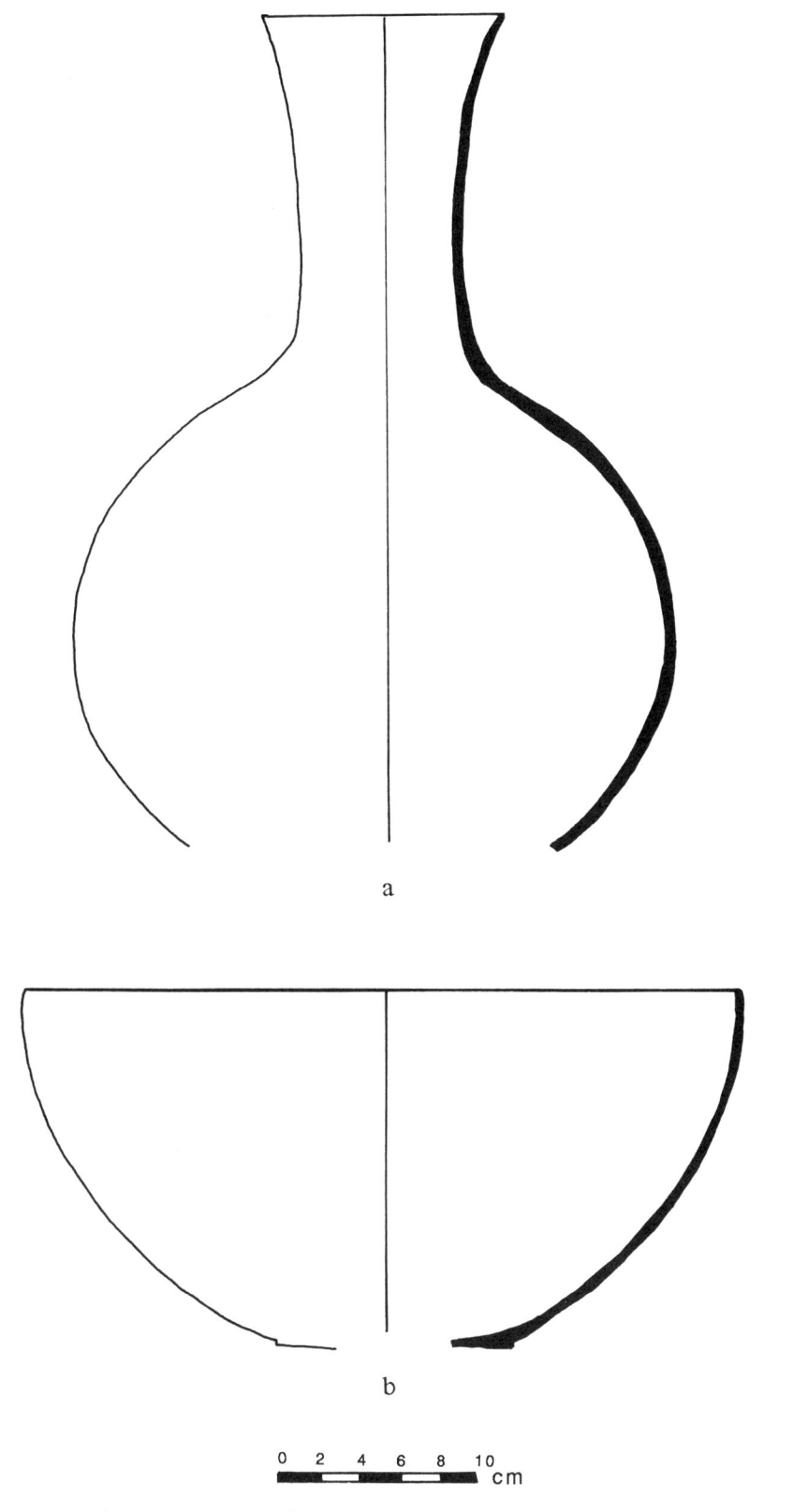

Figure 14. Ceramics, Dark-faced Burnished Ware.

Figure 15. Ceramics, Horseshoe-shaped Vessel.

Locus	Description
Sherds found throughout all Loci of Concentration A Areas DA.1.72, DA.1A.74 and DA.2.76	Horseshoe-shaped vessel; assembled from 10 sherds; tempered with organic material; handmade; wavy rim; mat impression on base; base crudely finger pinched and flanged, base joined with the walls with aid of finger and thumb; slipped inside and outside; interior color reddish brown (2.5 YR 4/4); exterior color varies from reddish brown (2.5 YR 4/4) to dark reddish gray (10 R 4/1); exterior is reddish brown at the upper part of wall but most of wall is dark reddish gray.

DHALI-AGRIDHI: NEOLITHIC BY THE RIVER   233

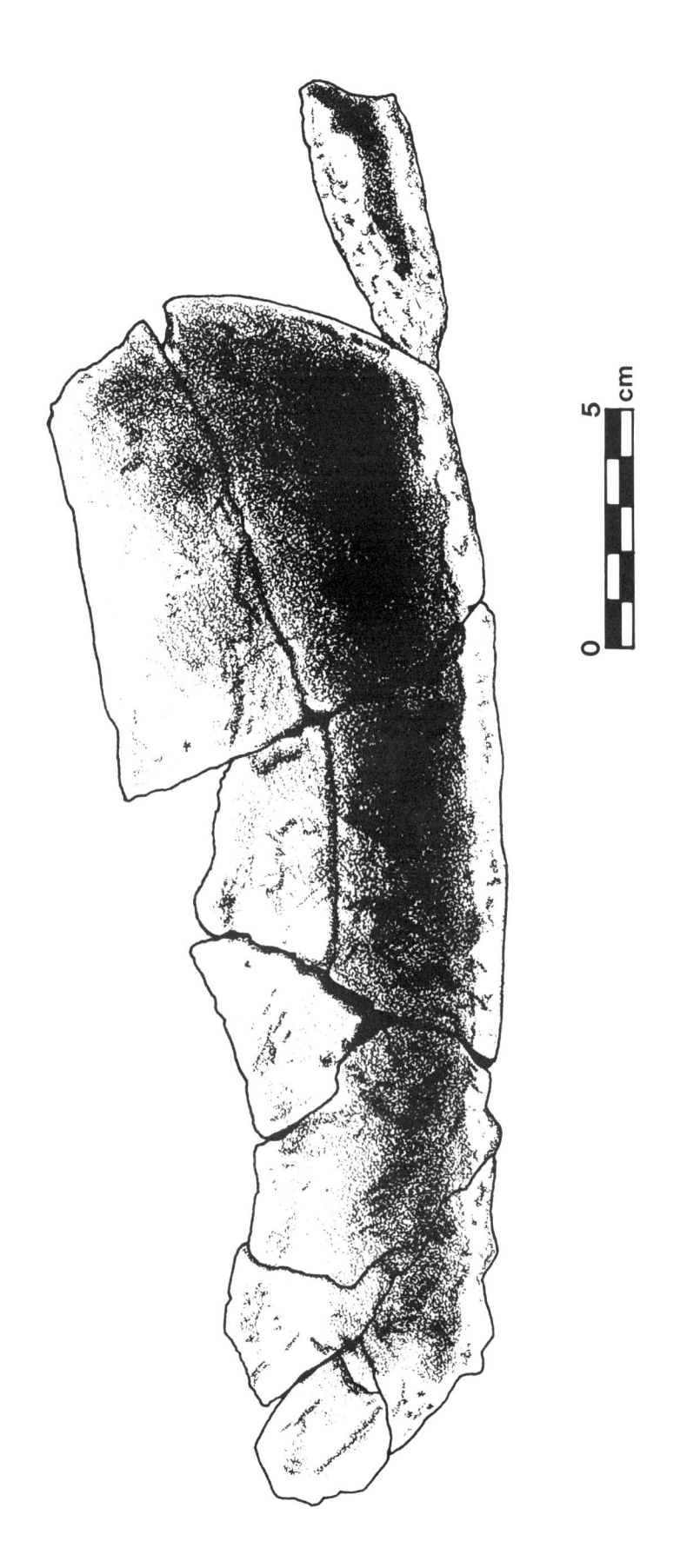

Figure 15. Ceramics, Horseshoe-shaped Vessel.

PLATE 1

a

b

Site before Excavation Started in the Summer of 1972. a. View to north, showing river-bed below the field; b. View to south, from river-bed showing Lower and Upper Terraces. Site is on Upper Terrace.

PLATE 2

Dhali-Agridhi, Area 2 and Site E. a. Area 2, 1976, horizontal separation between the aceramic deposit (on the left) and ceramic deposit (on right); post-Neolithic pit is visible dug into ceramic area; b. Site E, stratigraphy.

PLATE 3

Dhali-Agridhi, Site E. a. and b., looking southwest, showing cobble stone pavement.

PLATE 4

Stone Bowls. a. Obj. no. 724, b. Obj. no. 745, c. Obj. no. 762, d. Obj. no. 774.

PLATE 5

Stone Bowls or Mortars. a. Obj. no. 784, b. Obj. no. 763, c. Obj. no. 801, d. Obj. no. 794, e. Obj. no. 797.

PLATE 6

Stone Pounders or Hammers. a. Obj. no. 740, b. Obj. no. 789, c. Obj. no. 734, d. Obj. no. 761, e. Obj. no. 790.

PLATE 7

a

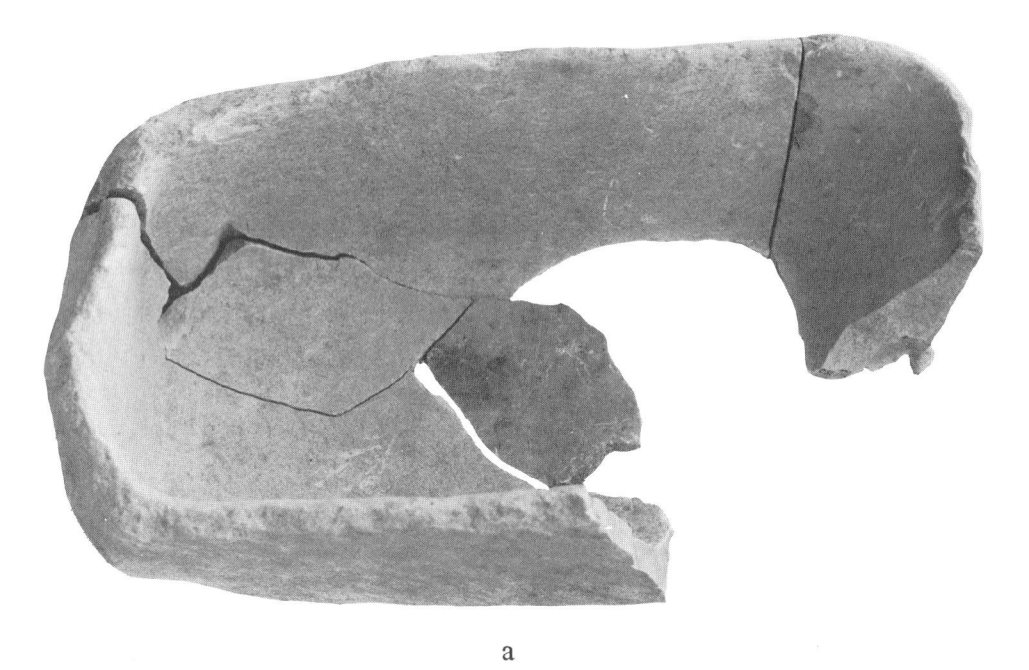

b

Stone Objects. a. Platter, Obj. no. 772; b. Grinder, Obj. no. 782.

PLATE 8

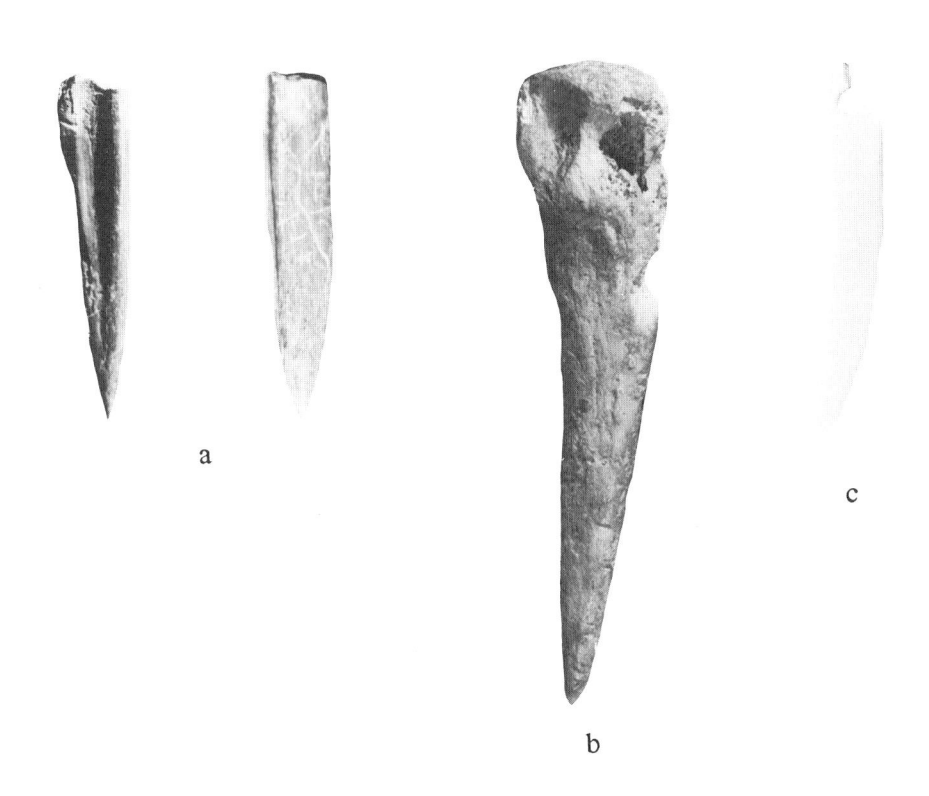

Bone Implements. a. Obj. no. 730, b. Obj. no. 742, c. Obj. no. 737.

PLATE 9

Ceramics, Dark-faced Burnished Ware. a. High-necked jar, b. Large deep bowl.

PLATE 10

a

b

Ceramics, Horseshoe-shaped Vessel. a. Before reconstruction, showing mat impressions on base; b. After reconstruction.

B. FAUNA FROM THE 1976 SEASON

*P. L. Carter**

Since the publication in 1698 by de Bruijn of "Reizen door de vermaardste delen van Klein Asia," in which the presence of Pleistocene animals was first reported, the study of past Cypriot faunas has attracted scholars because of the isolated position of the island and the consequent impoverishment of species. Recently the problems of Cypriot palaeozoology have been discussed in detail by Boekschoten and Sondaar (1972) and Watson, Stanley Price, and Arnold (1977) and their discussion will not be repeated here. It is assumed that the species present on the island before the appearance of man in the sixth millennium B.C. were few in number and limited to *Phanourios minor* (pigmy hippopotamus), *Elaphus cypriotes* (pigmy elephant), the murids *Mus musculus* and *Acomys didimatus* or their immediate ancestors, two species of bats, and a shrew thought by Watson to be *Crosidura russula*.

In view of Watson, Stanley Price, and Arnold's recent paper (1977:246), we must first consider the claim by Schwartz (1973, 1974a and b) that *Cervus elaphus*, *Capreolus capreolus*, *Gazella*, and *Equus* sp. were present during the aceramic at Dhali-Agridhi.

The 1972 material on which Schwartz based his identifications is at present not accessible for study, and the 1974 material has been the subject of a separate unpublished report by K. Basalik and J. Klein under the direction of Dr. J. D. Perkins. The 1976 collection of faunal material was originally examined by Dr. J. S. Aigner, and her preliminary sorting of the material has greatly aided the present study. I have examined in the field the material excavated by Y. M. Lehavy during the 1974 and 1976 seasons, and find no evidence to support the claim that *Capreolus*, *Gazella*, and *Equus* were present. The possible presence of *Cervus* is, however, more complicated, for two reasons. First and most important is that the size range of prehistoric *Dama dama mesopotamica* is poorly documented. Second, since the publication of Schwartz's 1974a paper, the presence of *Cervus* has been claimed for the Neolithic site of Kalavasos-Tenta (I. A. Todd, personal communication), and A. Le Brun has reported the presence of *Bos* sp. at the nearby site of Khirokitia (unpublished workshop paper). Inasmuch as a number of specimens from Dhali-Agridhi could fall outside the upper size range of *Dama dama mesopotamica*, the presence of *Cervus* will be further discussed below, particularly because of the acknowledged difficulty in distinguishing large specimens of *Cervus* from the small species of *Bos* (Reed 1961).

The 1976 Faunal Sample

The problems of sample bias are now well known to most faunal analysts, and, as Payne has shown (1972a, b and 1975), sieving of all excavated material is essential if the study of fauna from any given site is to provide any meaningful information. Specimens excavated in 1976 were therefore collected using a sieving process with a final mesh size of either 1.7 mm or 5 mm. The sieved bone material was then separated into identifiable and unidentifiable groups by Dr. J. S. Aigner. The identifiable fragments were reexamined in 1978. The unidentifiable fragments received no further treatment but have been kept for further study as necessary. The number of identifiable postcranial fragments are listed in tables 1, 2, and 3.

---

*University Museum of Archaeology and Anthropology, Cambridge, England

Dr. A. Walker kindly invited me to study the Dhali-Agridhi fauna. I am most grateful to Dr. F. L. Koucky for several discussions on the subjects of Cypriot palaeogeology and palaeogeography, particularly concerning the age of the Mesaoria. Mr. A. Garrard generously allowed the use of his unpublished data concerning the fauna from Tabun and El Wad. Mr. Y. M. Lehavy, the excavator of Dhali-Agridhi, gave unstinting help during my visit to Cyprus and was a most stimulating sparring partner in discussion.

The following species were recognized in the 1976 material:

Dama dama mesopotamica — Persian fallow deer
Capra hircus — goat
Ovis aries — sheep
Ovis orientalis orientalis — mouflon
Sus scrofa — pig
Pisces — not specifically identified
Crustacea — not specifically identified

Table 1. Number of Identified Postcranial Fragments of Caprovines

	\multicolumn{3}{c}{Proximal Fused}	\multicolumn{3}{c}{Not fused}	\multicolumn{3}{c}{Distal Fused}	\multicolumn{3}{c}{Not fused}	Total
	L	R	I*	L	R	I	L	R	I	L	R	I	
Femur	0	1	2	0	0	0	1	0	0	0	0	0	4
Tibia	1	0	0	0	0	0	0	2	0	0	0	0	3
Humerus	0	0	0	0	0	0	4	6	0	0	0	0	10
Ulna	0	2	0	0	0	0	0	0	0	0	0	0	2
Metapodial	0	0	0	0	0	0	0	0	3	0	0	0	3

	Left	Right	Total
Scapula	1	2	3
Calcaneum	3	2	5
Astragalus	7	5	12

*L = left, R = right, and I = indeterminate

Table 2. Number of Identified Postcranial Fragments of *Sus scrofa*

	\multicolumn{3}{c}{Proximal Fused}	\multicolumn{3}{c}{Not fused}	\multicolumn{3}{c}{Distal Fused}	\multicolumn{3}{c}{Not fused}	Total
	L	R	I*	L	R	I	L	R	I	L	R	I	
Tibia	0	0	0	0	0	0	1	1	0	0	0	0	2
Humerus	0	0	0	0	0	0	2	2	1	0	0	0	5

	Left	Right	Indeterminate	Total
Scapula	1	0	1	2
Calcaneum	0	2	0	2
Astragalus	2	0	0	2

*L = left, R = right, and I = indeterminate

Table 3. Number of Identified Postcranial Fragments of *Dama dama mesopotamica*

| | Proximal | | | | | | Distal | | | | | | Total |
	Fused			Not fused			Fused			Not fused			
	L	R	I*	L	R	I	L	R	I	L	R	I	
Femur	6	2	0	0	0	0	1	1	3	1	0	1	15
Tibia	2	2	0	2	0	0	9	9	0	0	0	0	24
Humerus	2	3	0	0	0	0	12	10	0	0	0	0	27
Radius	1	5	0	0	0	0	3	1	0	0	0	0	10
Ulna	4	0	0	0	0	0	0	0	0	0	0	0	4
Metacarpal	0	0	0	0	0	0	0	0	6	0	0	0	6
Metatarsal	0	2	0	0	0	0	0	0	3	0	0	0	5
Metapodial	0	0	0	0	0	0	0	0	10	0	0	0	10

	Left	Right	Total
Astragalus	6	5	11
Calcaneum	2	1	3
Pelvis	2	5	7
Scapula	11	13	24

*L = left, R = right, and I = indeterminate

The Caprovines

Payne (1972), Higgs (1968), Saxon (1974), and others have discussed the difficulties of distinguishing the fragmentary remains of *Capra*, *Ovis*, and related forms. Such discussion need not be repeated here, but it is evident that in the circum-Mediterranean region extreme caution is necessary in identifying such remains because the size range of sheep, goat, and mouflon, not to mention deer and small antelope, may well overlap at any one prehistoric site.

Of the 63 specimens in the 1976 sample that can be positively identified as caprovine, two (119 and 300) were referred to *Ovis aries*, six (708 [fig. 7], 369, 188, 154, 592, and 691) to *Ovis orientalis orientalis*, and one (715) to *Capra hircus*. Of the remaining 63 specimens three were of the size of *Ovis orientalis orientalis* and the remainder could be either *Ovis* or *Capra*.

All three species have been reported previously in a Cypriot Neolithic context (King 1953; Watson, Stanley Price, and Arnold 1977; and Zeuner 1958). If the sample under consideration here is a true reflection of the respective proportions of animals exploited at Dhali-Agridhi, then mouflon, or a mouflon-sized caprovine, was an important species as compared with other caprovines, even though it numbers only 1.9 percent of the total faunal assemblage, while the dominant species, *Dama dama mesopotamica*, numbers 79.8 percent (table 4).

Table 4. Number of Fragments Identified to the Species Level

Species	Number	Percent
Dama dama mesopotamica	368	79.8
Caprovines	63	13.7
Sus scrofa	30	6.5
Total	461	100.0

Sus scrofa

The number of pig bones identified (30) represents 6.5 percent of the total bones studied. In their description of the fauna from Early Neolithic Knossos, Jarman and Jarman (1968) discuss the relationship between wild and domestic pigs and provide metric data to substantiate the statement that "the available evidence is unequivocally in favour of the Knossos Camp pigs being domesticated." Figures 1 and 2 show the measurements of the Dhali-Agridhi pigs compared with data given in Jarman and Jarman (ibid.) for Knossos and Ducos (1968) for Ain Mallaha. The fact that the Dhali-Agridhi pigs, according to the evidence of M3 and distal humerus measurements, could be either wild or domestic is worthy of comment. It is well known and widely accepted by archaeozoologists that it is difficult to distinguish between wild and domestic animals from the bone remains. What is only slowly being accepted is the fact that the terms wild and domestic may themselves be of limited value when dealing with the economic practices of societies such as Dhali-Agridhi, that appear to be transitional between the ones traditionally called hunting societies and those based on formalized farming. Prehistoric remains from Cyprus provide an excellent opportunity to test the concept of wild and domestic animal exploitation against a background in which the relevant parameters are more closely controlled than is usual under most archaeological conditions. Prior to man's first appearance, the Cypriot fauna was restricted to a very few species, and the modern fauna bears no relationship to this earlier fauna. Both the evidence of the pig remains (the size of the measurable bones, as compared with modern wild and domestic animals) and the high proportion of *Dama dama mesopotamica* present (an animal today considered to be wild) would cause the prehistoric Dhali-Agridhi community to be traditionally interpreted as representing a hunting economy. Since we know, however, that all the animals at Dhali-Agridhi must have been introduced by man, it might be well to avoid the terms wild and domestic altogether--here and in similar situations. It then becomes self-evident that the economic relationship of the early Cypriot inhabitants with *Sus scrofa* and *Dama dama mesopotamica* was more likely to have been a close man/animal relationship than a random hunting relationship. Such a notion is not new, but judging from the literature (Zeuner, Ducos, Higgs) perhaps it deserves more emphasis than it has previously received.

Dama dama mesopotamica

Dama dama mesopotamica represents 79.8 percent of the identifiable bone fragments and clearly was of considerable economic importance to the inhabitants of Dhali-Agridhi.

Antlers

Fifty-one pieces of antler were examined. Specimen 510 showed the palmation typical of this species and Specimen 682 the characteristic low brow tine.

Eleven of the 51 fragments were from basal portions of the antler; nine of the eleven had been cut off or broken from the skull and two had eroded pedicels. These figures would suggest that most of the antler at the site is from unshed heads. As table 5 shows, these figures are in close agreement with Khirokitia, where according to Ducos (1965) 24 out of 26 fragments are of unshed antler.

Table 5. Number of Shed and Unshed Antler Fragments
at Dhali-Agridhi and Khirokitia

Site	Shed	Unshedding	Unshed	Total	Percent unshed
Dhali-Agridhi	0	2	9	11	82
Khirokitia	2	0	24	26	92

Teeth

Sixteen mandibular fragments with teeth were present in the 1976 faunal material and three in the 1974 collection. In nine of these nineteen specimens the third cusp of the permanent lower third molar was fully in wear (65, 90, 150, 166, 241, 247, 370, 425, and 426). In one specimen (378) the cusp was not yet in wear, and in three cases (91, 361, and 586) the deciduous third molar was still present.

Age of animals at death

A detailed study of the fusion patterns in this species remains to be carried out, so that the accurate aging of the animals is not yet possible. Some estimates of the age at which the animals were killed should however be attempted. One hundred and eleven long bone fragments attributed to *Dama dama mesopotamica* contained fusion data (table 6).

Table 6. Number of Fused and Nonfused Bones of *Dama dama mesopotamica*

Sample Size	Fused	Nonfused
111	94	17
100%	84.7%	15.3%

From the evidence of both the fusion patterns (84.7 percent fused bones) and the tooth wear patterns it is clear that mature but not old animals were being preferentially exploited. Such a killing pattern is to be expected when animals are being systematically exploited for meat rather than milk or other secondary products.

It has been suggested above that the economic importance of this species was an integral part of a close man/animal relationship. If so, should we not reconsider the role of *Dama dama mesopotamica* in the economies of sites in the Levant and Anatolia during the millennia prior to the initial colonization of Cyprus? Such a study, however, lies outside the scope of the present work.

Size of Cypriot Dama dama mesopotamica

Figure 3 shows the range and mean value of the epiphyseal width of the proximal radius from sites in the Levant (Tabun, El Wad, Ain Mallaha) and Cyprus (Dhali-Agridhi, Khirokitia) over a time span of some 60,000 years. Figures 4, 5, and 6 show the range and mean value of the astragalus length, distal humerus width, and proximal radius width from Dhali-Agridhi and Ain Mallaha.

The number of Levantine sites with which the Cypriot *Dama dama mesopotamica* can be compared is limited. Tabun, El Wad, and Ain Mallaha have been chosen because they provide comparative measurements over a substantial period of time. These data clearly illustrate two points. First, during the past 60,000 years there has been a measurable decrease in the size of the Levantine *Dama dama mesopotamica*; and second, the decrease in size between 12,000 B.P. (Ain Mallaha) and 7000 B.P. (Dhali-Agridhi) appears to have been greater than between 60,000 B.P. (Tabun) and 12,000 B.P. (Ain Mallaha). Furthermore, when discussing the Cypriot *Dama dama mesopotamica*, Halstead (1977:267) notes that, "a metrical comparison of the Kouklia fallow with those discussed by Ducos (1965:5) suggests a clear diminution of body size in the comparatively short time between the Early Neolithic and the Late Bronze Age."

A similar decrease in size during the Upper Pleistocene in the eastern Mediterranean area is documented for cattle and red deer (Jarman 1969:255). The size decrease in *Dama dama mesopotamica* is most marked at the time that the species was introduced to Cyprus, that is, circa 7000 B.P. It is most marked in the case of cattle at the time when early farming communities can first be recognized in the prehistoric record. Detailed data for red deer (*Cervus elaphus*) are lacking.

Kurten (1959 and 1965) has discussed size change in a number of Upper Pleistocene carnivore species in both Europe and the Levant. He suggests that size changes in the Levantine populations may have resulted from various population density factors, but that clearly the pressure that caused such changes would vary according to the species and the circumstances in each case. How then may we best explain the observed variation in the size of *Dama dama mesopotamica* in the Levant and Cyprus? What is seen is a slow but steady decrease in size between 60,000 B.P. and 10,000 B.P. in the Levant, an accelerated size decrease at the time of introduction to Cyprus, and a continuing size decrease from the initial habitation of the island to the Late Bronze Age.

Decrease in animal body size may be due to any one or a combination of the following factors:

       a) increasing population density
       b) environmental deterioration
       c) Bergmann's rule
       d) selective breeding due to human interference.

The size decrease between 60,000 B.P. and 10,000 B.P. in the Levant could well have been due to a combination of factors a) and b), for, by definition, in Cyprus we are dealing with a new species in a new environment. In their classic work on island biogeography, MacArthur and Wilson (1967:104) write:

> A species that successfully colonises an island has entered a new environment. Not only are physical conditions usually different in some way, but there will always be a different combination of species, or relative abundancies in the species, or both, in the invaded insular environment. As a consequence the colonising species will probably experience one or the other of two kinds of immediate ecological change. Either it will shift its preference, or it will undergo some form of expansion or contraction. These changes might be purely phenotypic at first, reflecting the species' behavioral or morphological plasticity, and be translated into genetic differences later by natural selection, perhaps involving genetic assimilation.

It is highly likely, therefore, that the difference in size changes observed between the Levantine populations represented at Ain Mallaha and the Cypriot populations represented by Dhali-Agridhi and Khirokitia should be interpreted in such terms. Only after further osteological studies have been carried out, however, will we be able to understand the size change between the Early Neolithic and the Later Bronze Age noted by Halstead (1977:276).

Cervus elaphus

The available data are insufficient to establish unequivocally whether *Cervus elaphus* was present at Dhali-Agridhi. It is clear that specimen 88 (proximal ulna, mature) and specimen 181 (distal radius, mature) fall within the range of both *Cervus* and *Dama*, between which there can be an overlap in the size of some bones. Specimen 653 (proximal radius, mature) is also of *Cervus* size. It should be stressed again, however, that the size range of prehistoric *Dama dama mesopotamica* has yet to be adequately established, both in Cyprus and elsewhere.

Several well-documented cases of increase in body and antler weight within a few generations are known where *Cervus elaphus* has been introduced into a new area (Chapman and Chapman 1975:40). It is therefore not surprising to find what are locally large specimens of *Dama dama mesopotamica* in Cyprus, shortly after their introduction to an environment where there can have been few if any competitors.

Like size, the known zoogeographical distribution of *Cervus* and *Dama* in the past is also of little help in deciding whether *Cervus* was present, as both species are known to have occurred in the Levant during the Pleistocene.

It is therefore my opinion that the specimens from Dhali-Agridhi (88 proximal ulna, 181 distal radius, and 653 proximal radius) are more likely to be specimens of *Dama* than specimens of *Cervus*, although one must note that from the sole criterion of size both identifications are equally plausible. It would not therefore be prudent to claim the presence of *Cervus elaphus* at Dhali-Agridhi unless diagnostic specimens such as antler or teeth are excavated.

Discussion

Stanley Price, in an elegantly presented paper (1977a), has argued from an essentially cultural viewpoint that the initial settlement of Cyprus was by Levantine and not Anatolian communities. The faunal remains from Dhali-Agridhi and other Cypriot Neolithic sites are in no way at variance with this hypothesis. In fact, the presence of *Dama dama mesopotamica* and the almost total absence of *Bos taurus* considerably strengthen the case for Levantine origins.[1] In my opinion this cannot be overstressed. What is urgently needed is a comparative study of the faunas from tenth to fifth millennium sites in the Levant, Anatolia, and Cyprus.

Unpublished field work by F. L. Koucky shows convincingly that most of the Mesaoria is of Holocene age. When this fact is taken into account, it becomes clear that Dhali-Agridhi, Khirokitia, and other Neolithic sites were located in similar areas. Each is located beside a radial stream on the edge of the limestone massif, a situation ensuring easy access to both the woodlands of the mountain slopes and the pasture lands of the lowland valleys. Similar catchment basin sites can be expected to result in similar exploitation strategies (Higgs and Vita-Finzi 1972). From the evidence of both the 1974 and 1976 faunal samples there can be little doubt that *Dama dama mesopotamica* was of considerable importance in the economy of Dhali-Agridhi. Although Watson, Stanley Price, and Arnold (1977:245) does not share the views of King (1953) and Ducos (1965), it is highly probably that *Dama* was also of considerable

---

[1] Pliny, in Book VIII of his Natural History, writes of deer swimming from Cilicia to Cyprus, but in view of the questionable authenticity of many of his statements, little credence need be attached to this particular claim. Not only is the open-sea distance far too great for deer to swim, but the statement is in direct opposition to the available osteological evidence.

importance to the economy of Khirokitia. Before the economy of Khirokitia can be fruitfully compared with Dhali-Agridhi, however, a larger sieved faunal sample will be required from Khirokitia.

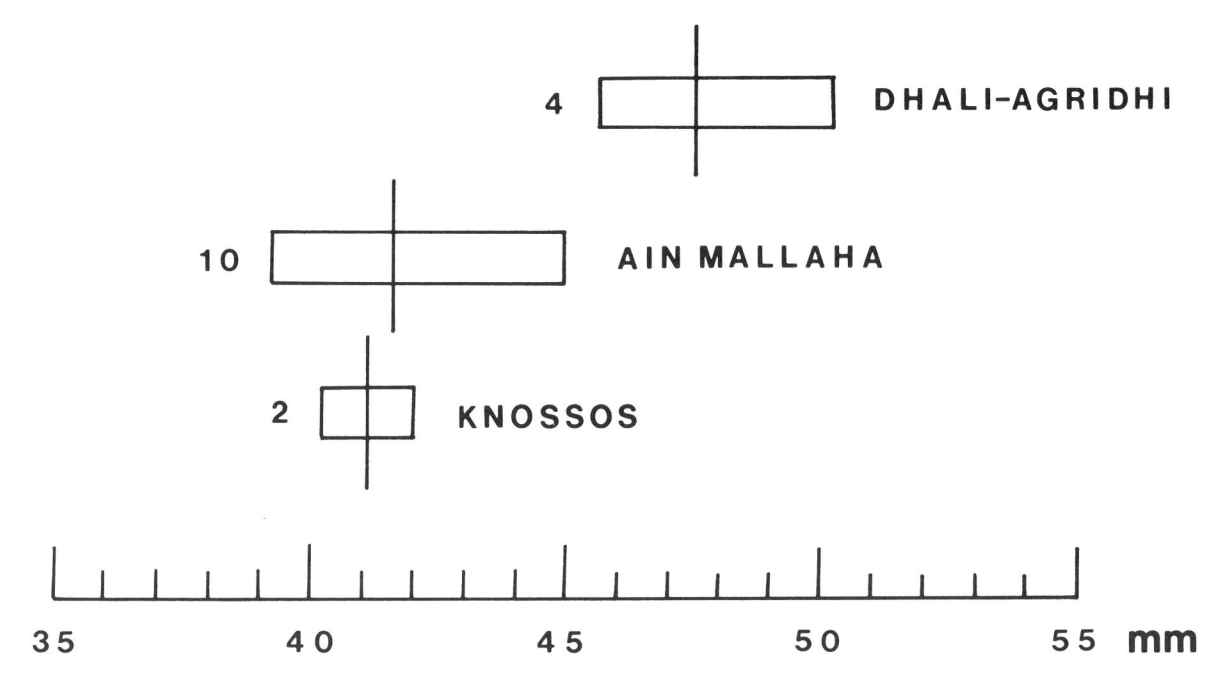

Figure 1. Pig, Maximum Distal Width of Humeri.

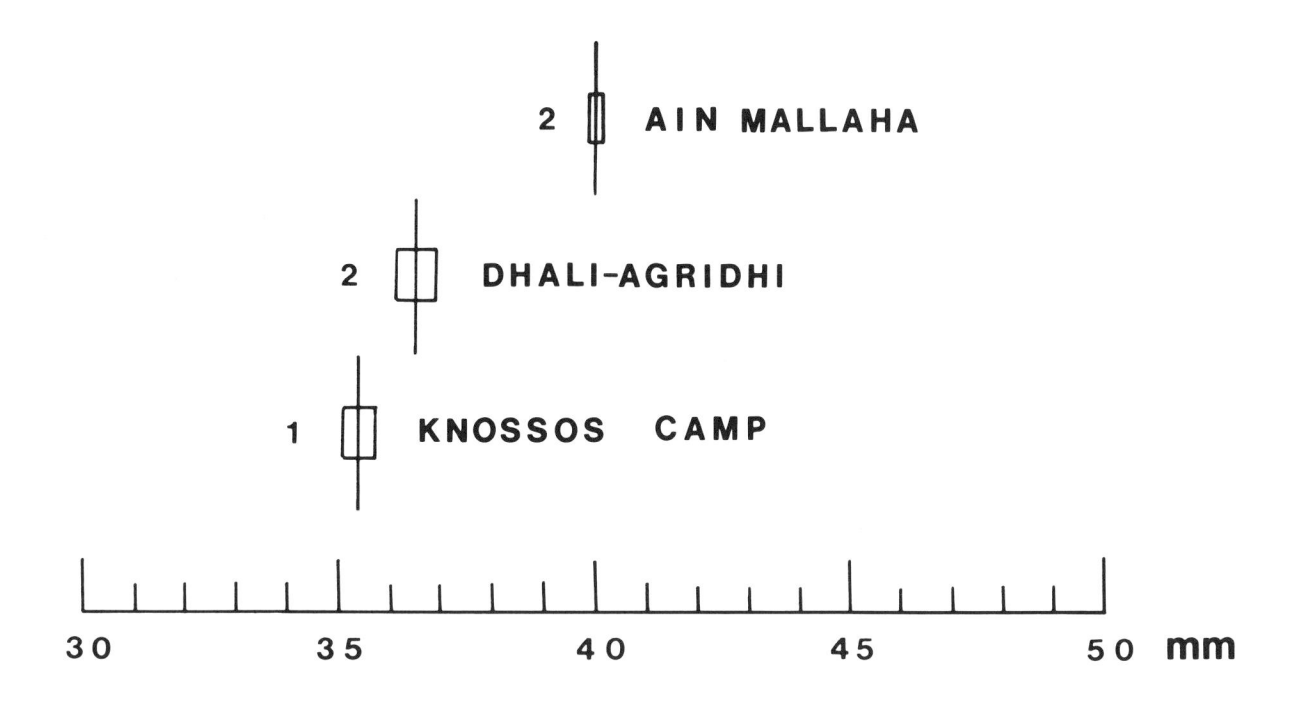

Figure 2. Pig, Length of Third Lower Molar.

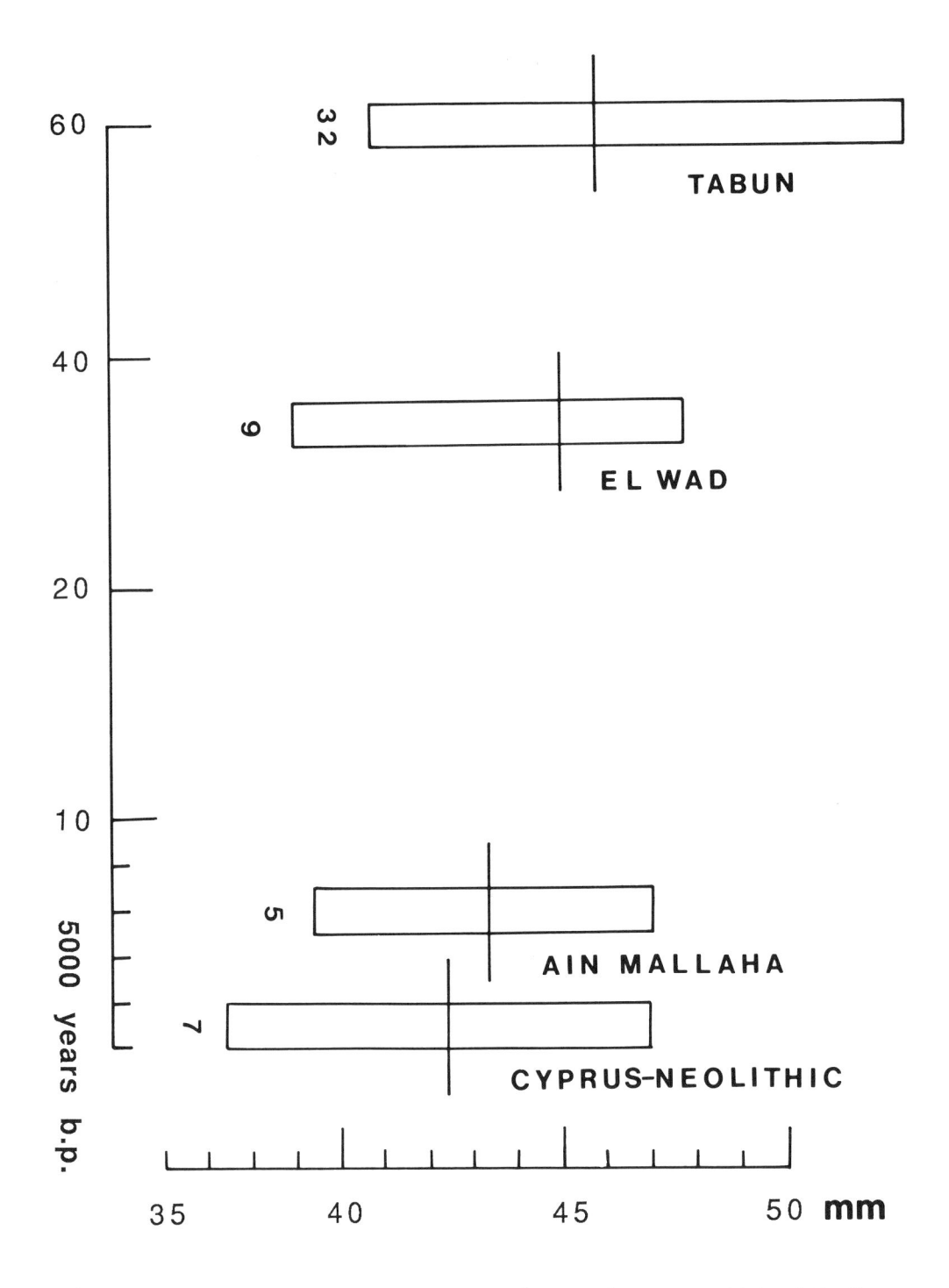

Figure 3. *Dama dama mesopotamica*, Proximal Epiphyseal Width of Radius.

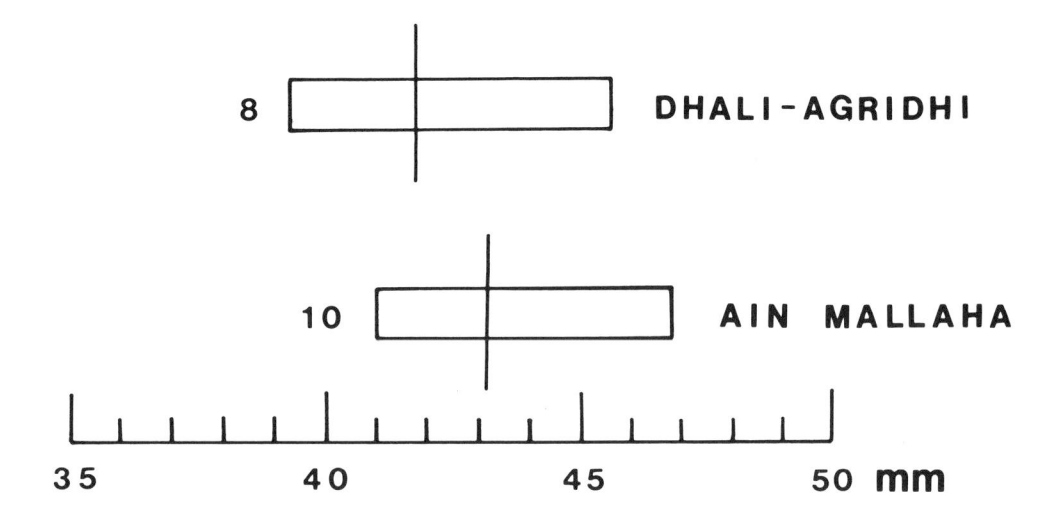

Figure 4. *Dama dama mesopotamica*, Astragalus Length.

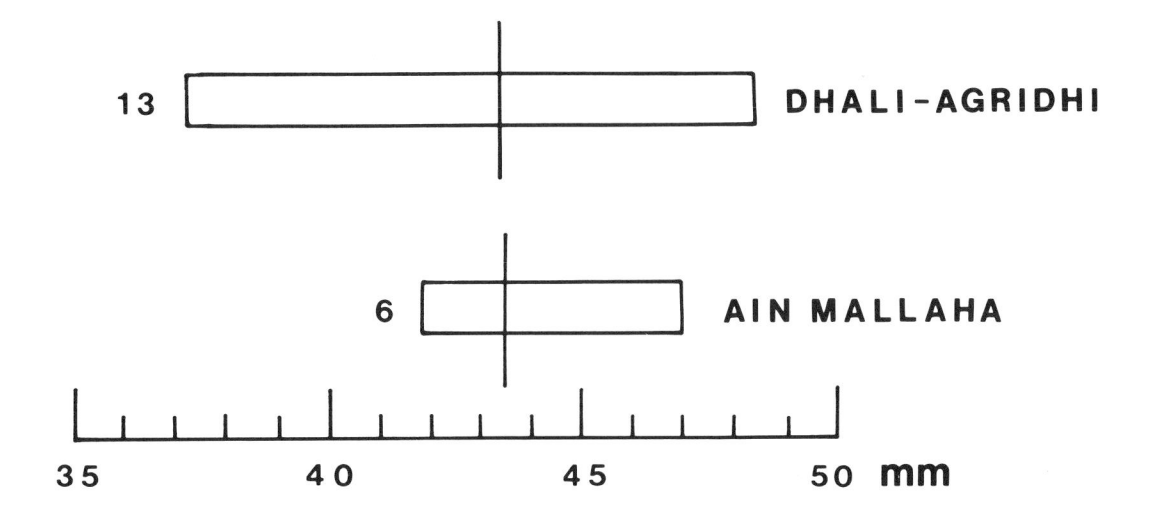

Figure 5. *Dama dama mesopotamica*, Distal Epiphyseal Width of Humerus.

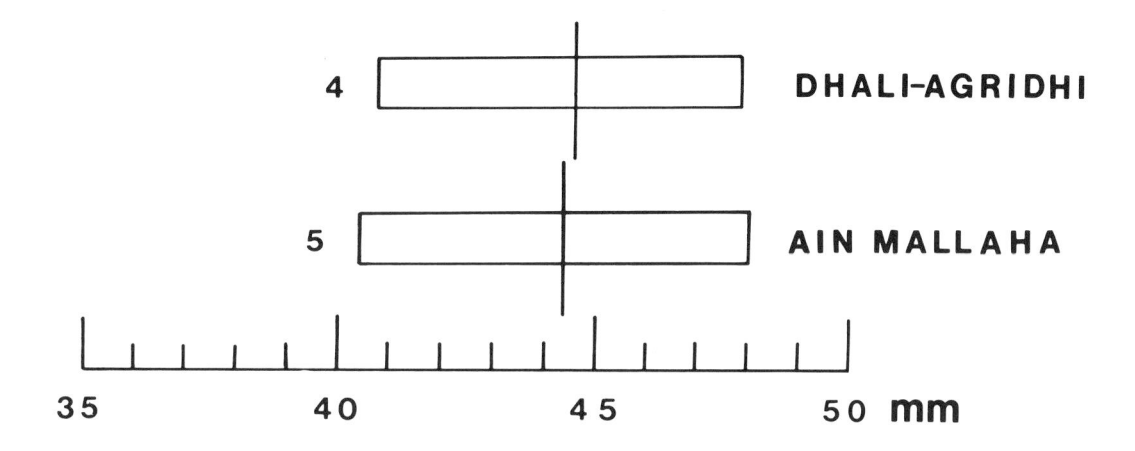

Figure 6. *Dama dama mesopotamica*, Proximal Epiphyseal Width of Radius.

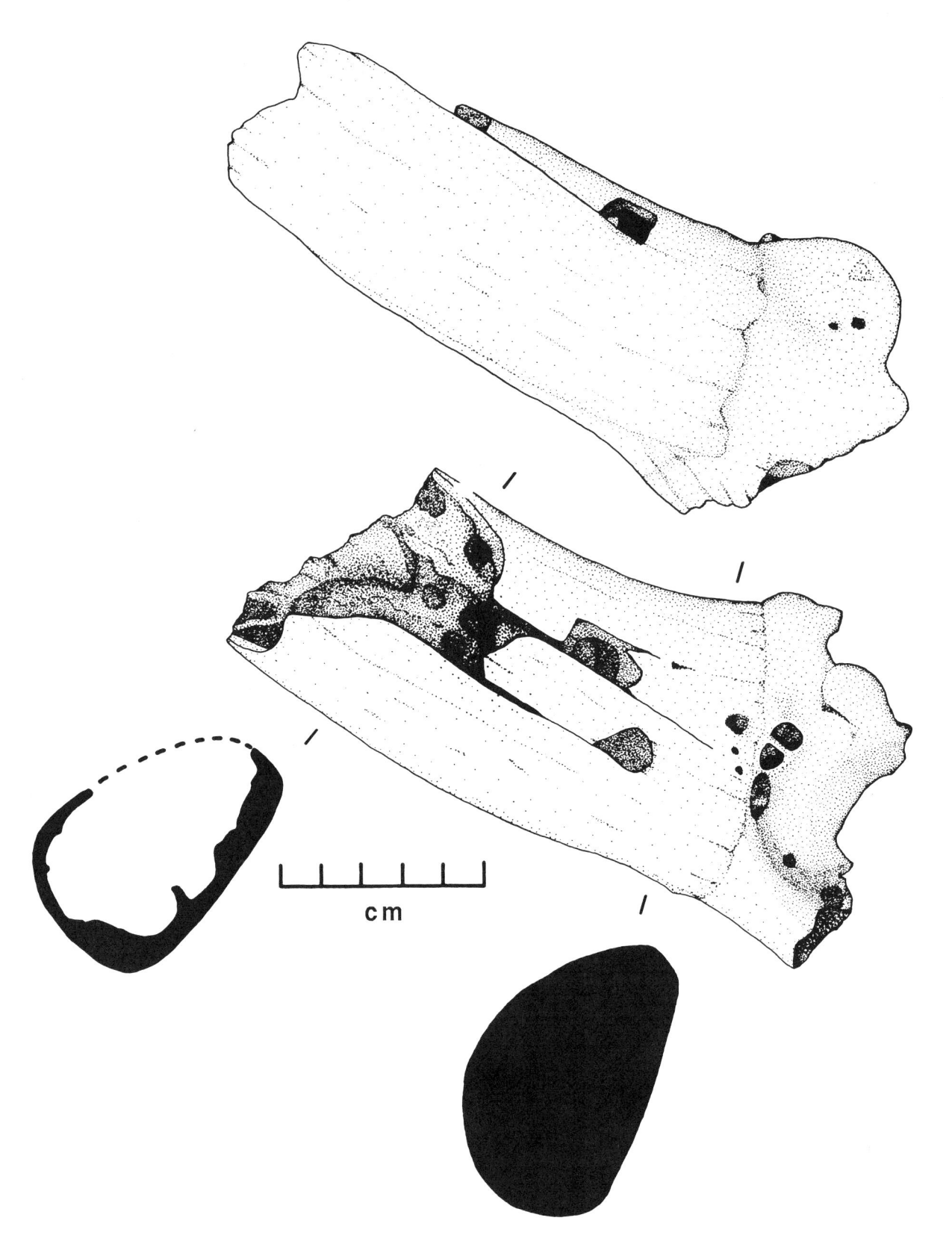

Figure 7. Specimen 708. Horn Core and Section of *Ovis orientalis orientalis*.

C. A RECONSIDERATION OF FAUNA FROM THE 1972 SEASON

Paul Croft [*]

Introduction

The Neolithic site of Dhali-Agridhi (henceforth abbreviated D-A) has yielded a relatively large and well-preserved faunal collection, portions of which have been studied by a variety of analysts.[1] The present report concerns part of the faunal material recovered during the initial 1972 season, and is based on my examination of this material, at the kind invitation of Dr. Anita Walker, in the Cyprus Museum during the winter of 1979-80. The balance of the 1972 faunal remain has been the subject of a separate and independent report by Schwartz (1974a).

General Remarks

The reports by both Carter and Schwartz indicate a predominance in the D-A fauna of deer, followed by caprines and pigs, and the present analysis confirms this pattern. The relative importance of these animals, based on numbers of identified fragments, is indicated in table 1. The remarkably close agreement between Carter's percentage figures and the figures independently derived from the present analysis argues in favor of accurate identifications in both cases, despite the not inconsiderable problems of dealing with fragmentary material and with a range of animals that are, broadly speaking, of the same size.

Table 1. Number of Identified Fragments

	No.	Percent	No.	Percent
Deer	630[a]	77.2	(368)[b]	(79.8)
Caprines	116	14.2	(63)	(13.7)
Pigs	70	8.6	(30)	(6.5)
Total	816	100.0	(461)	(100.0)

[a]Seventy-one fragments of antler, all attributable to <u>Dama mesopotamica</u>, are not included in this total.
[b]Carter's figures are given in parentheses for comparison.

---

[*]Department of Archaeology, University of Cambridge, England

My thanks are due to Dr. P. L. Carter for allowing me to use his unpublished data on the 1976 faunal remains from Dhali-Agridhi, and for helpful discussions of the material. I am also grateful to Dr. A. N. Garrard for permission to use his unpublished metrical data from El Wad and Tabun, and to Mr. P. Halstead for detailed information on the Kouklia faunal remains.

Finally, I am pleased to acknowledge the assistance of the Director of Antiquities, Dr. V. Karageorghis, and members of his staff who facilitated my work in the Cyprus Museum, and in particular Mr. M. Loulloupis, who cheerfully surrendered office space to me and to the bones.

[1] For details see above, P. L. Carter, "Fauna from the 1976 Season."

Table 2 gives a crude assessment of the minimum number of individuals (MNI) represented by the bones of each taxon. The figures are calculated simply on the frequency of the commonest skeletal element, which is given in parentheses. A more rigorous approach to the calculation of the MNI would produce a figure that more closely approximated to the actual number of individuals represented by the bones (which is itself an unknowable quantity), and would involve a far more complex methodology--for example, comparison of all right and left specimens of the same element, and consideration of the aging data provided by the different elements, to determine whether they could derive from the same individual.

This more refined approach has not been adopted here because the material presently under consideration is only a portion of the 1972 season's faunal remains, and consequently an even smaller proportion of the faunal material from the excavated fraction of the site as a whole. The more rigorous approach would thus lend only a spurious accuracy to what is in any case a rather vaguely defined (Grayson 1973) and crude (Uerpmann 1972:31) analytical device. Moreover, apart from their dubious validity, figures thus generated would find no basis for comparison with the results of the other analysts who have reported on D-A faunal material, as none of them have employed this more rigorous technique.

Table 2. Minimum Number of Individuals

	No.	Percent	
Deer	31	68.9	(R* distal scapula)
Caprines	8	17.8	(R distal scapula)
Pigs	6	13.3	(R distal humerus)
Total	45	100.0	

*R = right

As is evident, there are discrepancies in the percentage figures for the relative representations of the different animals as calculated by the two different methods (tables 1 and 2). This may be explained by the well-known tendency of the MNI approach to exaggerate the importance of the less abundantly represented taxa (Uerpmann 1972:311, Payne 1972b:69, Grayson 1978). However, the figures generated by the two techniques are sufficiently similar to justify the conclusion that the animals are represented in the approximate proportions of 75 percent deer, 15 percent caprines, and 10 percent pigs.

It is important to note that all of these faunal remains derive from archaeological contexts that have been firmly attributed by the excavator to the Neolithic period (Lehavy 1974:102). The small quantity of material from other contexts has not been considered. No subdivision of the material according to chronological horizon or cultural stage within the Neolithic has been made, and it should be borne in mind that as a consequence of this, any conclusions drawn regarding human economic behavior at D-A do not elucidate a real situation at any particular point in prehistory, but necessarily provide only a generalized view of subsistence activity over an unspecified but probably considerable period of time. The radiocarbon evidence from the site (Lehavy 1974:98, Stanley Price 1979:47) suggests that the time scale involved may be of the order of a millennium and a half--ample time to accommodate significant changes in man-animal relationships.

The Status of the Animals

It is now generally accepted that all of the mammalian species of significant economic importance to man during the Neolithic and later periods in Cyprus were deliberately introduced by man (Jarman 1976:42; Carter, see his chapter, above). Indeed, in view of the apparently great antiquity of the island's insularity, the suggestion that the populations of pigs, caprines, and deer were indigenous would be rather difficult to support (Watson, Stanley Price, and Arnold 1977:246). One would not, however, be justified in making the glib assumption that all (or any) of the main animals exploited by early prehistoric man on the island were of necessity domestic in the traditionally accepted sense. It is particularly important to consider the possibility of the very early establishment of free-ranging populations of introduced animals on the island. These could have resulted from escapes of animals from populations that were under closer human control (feralization), or could have been initiated through deliberate human policy. The apparently low density of the human population in what was in all probability a far more productive environment than that of present-day Cyprus (Stanley Price 1979:11-15), an environment well suited to supporting free-ranging animal populations with a negligible degree of human control, suggests that purposeful stocking of the landscape with desirable animal resources might have been an extremely attractive low-energy-cost strategy for the early inhabitants of the island. Harvesting of such loosely husbanded animal resources would have depended on some form of hunting. Other conspecific populations could have been maintained under conditions of closer human control, to provide a more accessible, if more expensive, fund of the same resources. In the case of caprines, these latter populations could have supplied additional resources, such as milk and hair wool, not easily harvested from animals unaccustomed to close association with man.

Pigs

The pigs at D-A, as is normal in early prehistoric Cyprus, constitute a significant component in the animal economy. Seventy items were identified as pig remains (table 3). Osteological evidenced does not, however, provide a basis for inference regarding the degree of human control over the exploited population(s), although additional metrical data could ultimately permit the definition of two distinct pig populations, if such existed. As stated above, the overall figure of about 10 percent for the frequency of the pig in the D-A fauna as a whole represents an average over an unknown and possibly lengthy period of time, and could obscure considerable changes in the importance and exploitation of the pig, as has been suggested for other parts of Cyprus. For example a substantial decline in the importance of the pig during the fifth and fourth millennia B.C.[2] has been suggested for the lower Vasilikos Valley in southern Cyprus (Croft 1982:62), but in the northern part of the Ktima lowlands in the extreme west of the island, the third millennium B.C. seems to have witnessed a substantial increase in the importance of this animal (Croft 1981:49).

The limited amount of epiphyseal fusion data in the D-A pig bone sample under consideration is too small for statistical manipulation, but does indicate that a few animals died in their first year, while the majority were dead by the time they were about three and a half years old. It may therefore be suggested that, although the Neolithic inhabitants of D-A had a predilection for very young pork, they more generally killed pigs that were approaching or had attained full body weight.

---

[2] "B.C." means before Christ, the date expressed in uncalibrated radiocarbon years.

Table 3. Number of Identified Fragments of Pig

		Proximal Fused	Proximal Unfused	I[a]	Distal Fused	Distal Unfused	I	Total
Humerus	L[b]	0	0	0	1	0	0	1
	R[c]	1	0	1	4	2	0	8
Radius	L	0	0	0	1	1	0	2
Metacarpal	L	1	0	0	0	1	0	2
Metapodial	I[b]	0	0	0	5	1	0	6
Tibia	L	0	0	0	1	0	0	1
	R	1	0	0	1	0	0	2
Ulna	L	2	1	0	0	0	0	3
	R	1	1	0	0	0	0	2
							Total	27

		Fused	Unfused	I				Total
Calcaneum	L	1	3	0				4
	R	0	1	0				1
Scapula	L	0	0	1				1
							Total	6

		L	R	I				Total
Astragalus		1	3	0				4
Pelvis		4	3	2				9
					Atlas			3
					Sacrum			1
					Phalanges			14
					Head[d]			1
							Total	37
							Grand total	70

[a]I = indeterminate
[b]L = left
[c]R = right
[d]In tables 3, 4 and 5 the term "head" denotes any identifiable cranial fragment excluding isolated teeth which are present to the extent of less than a half, and also excepting pieces of antler, including unshed bases.

Table 4. Number of Identified Fragments of Caprine

		Proximal Fused	Proximal Unfused	I^a	Distal Fused	Distal Unfused	I	Total
Humerus	L[b]	0	0	0	4	0	0	4
	R[c]	0	0	0	4	0	1	5
Femur	L	1	0	0	0	1	0	2
	R	0	0	0	0	1	0	1
Radius	L	0	0	0	1	0	0	1
	R	0	0	0	1	0	0	1
Metacarpal	L	2	0	0	1	0	0	3
	R	1	0	0	0	0	0	1
Metatarsal	L	0	0	0	2	0	0	2
	R	1	0	0	1	0	0	2
Metapodial	I	0	0	0	1	0	0	1
Tibia	L	2	0	0	1	0	0	3
	R	1	0	0	0	0	0	1
Ulna	L	0	1	0	0	0	0	1
							Total	28

		Fused	Unfused	I	
Calcaneum	R	0	2	1	3
Scapula	L	1	0	0	1
	R	6	0	2	8
				Total	12

	L	R		
Astragalus	21			3
Pelvis	12	16		28
Naviculocuboid	0	1		1
			Atlas	3
			Axis	11
			Phalanges	17
			First	6
			Second	7
			Third	4
			Head[d]	13
			Total	76
			Grand total	116

[a] I = indeterminate
[b] L = left
[c] R = right
[d] See note to Table 3.

Caprines

Identified as caprine remains were 116 items, comprising about 15 percent of the analyzed site fauna (table 4). In common with the analyses of Schwartz (1974a) and Carter (see his chapter, above), where bones were attributable to sheep or goat in particular, they more often appeared to derive from the former. Thirty postcranial items were assigned to sheep, compared with nine to goat. Additionally, two horn-core fragments were identified as goat.

I did not find, as did Carter, that there was sufficient variability in the sheep material to justify a claim for the presence of two separate species of sheep; sexual dimorphism could adequately account for the range of metrical and morphological variation in the present sample.

A small quantity of caprine material with appropriate fusion data (table 4) may reflect the mortality pattern. No unfused caprine bone in the present sample indicates death before 28 months (using the aging data of Silver 1969), whereas almost half of the caprines were apparently dead by the age of three and a half years. Incorporation of Carter's information on caprine epiphyseal fusion strongly reinforces the impression that culling began after 28 months and that a substantial number of animals were dead by the age of three and a half.

Such a pattern of caprine mortality, in which young males surplus to breeding requirements do not appear to have been culled at a very young age, suggests that caprines were exploited primarily for meat and that milk production was of little or no importance (see also Halstead 1977:265).

The half of the caprines which were slaughtered between about two and a half and three and a half years of age probably included the majority of males, which had by this time attained their adult body weight. Females, on the other hand, would more profitably have been kept longer, until they ceased to reproduce regularly.

Deer

All of the identified cervid material (701 fragments, if the 71 pieces of antler are included) was attributed to *Dama mesopotamica* (Persian fallow deer) (table 5), which is preeminent in the D-A faunal collection. Neither this analysis nor that of Carter has yielded any indication of the presence of *Cervus* (red deer) or *Capreolus* (roe deer), nor, incidentally, of *Gazella* or *Equus* sp. (Schwartz 1974a). The possible existence of *Cervus* in early prehistoric Cyprus is debatable, but in the continued absence of convincing evidence for its presence I would favor the attribution of the larger cervid remains to a population of *Dama* which possesses a high degree of variability.

I was able to derive useful fusion data from 260 deer bone fragments, of which 74 percent were fused, supporting Carter's observation that "mature but not old animals were being preferentially exploited" (table 6). This larger sample permits some refinement of Carter's statement.

The epiphyseal fusion evidence indicates that something under half of the deer were dead before all of the epiphyses were fused, which probably occurs during the fourth year of life. Half of these preadult deaths were of animals of less than about 18 months in age. Just over half of the deer apparently lived to about 4 years of age or older.

Considering that young male fallow deer grow rapidly for the first three years and more slowly thereafter (fig. 1; Chaplin 1977:132), and that, as with caprines, the majority of males are not required to maintain the breeding potential of the herd, a rational meat-oriented exploitation strategy would involve culling a large number of males at the subadult stage. In fact only about 20 percent of the deer (presumably males) were slaughtered at the optimal subadult stage, a further 20 percent or thereabouts (also presumably males) having been killed at a younger age, during the period of their rapid growth. That the meat-maximizing culling policy was apparently not strictly adhered to by the people of D-A suggests an abundance of available deer meat--Neolithic affluence, epitomized by an "expensive" dietary preference for young venison. Females, on the other hand, would have been allowed to live on to a greater age in order to maintain a high reproductive rate within the population. It is probable that the 60 percent or so of animals that lived to maturity consisted largely of breeding does, with a far smaller number of mature bucks.

Antler, presumably for industrial usage, was normally acquired by removing it from the heads of culled deer rather than gathering it from the countryside in a shed state. The basal portions of 6 antlers were reasonably well preserved, and of these, 3 were certainly and 2 were probably unshed, while one was certainly shed. Three out of 4 well-preserved pedicles bore obvious signs of having been hacked with a heavy chopper, suggesting the removal of unshed antlers, and a further specimen had ambiguous damage that would be consistent with such hacking. Carter (see his chapter above, table 5) has similarly noted that of 11 determinable antler fragments none were shed.

The use of antler as a raw material for artifact manufacture is well attested in Cyprus, for example at Erimi (Dikaios 1936:50), Khirokitia (idem 1953:259, pl. XCIV), Sotira (idem 1961:204, pl. 106), and Kissonerga-Mylouthkia (Croft 1979:40 and n.d.). Far more common than the artifacts themselves, however, is the debris, in the form of hacked pedicles, chopped and cut antler fragments, and grooved and snapped tines, which result from the manufacturing process. Thus, there is reason to believe that not only meat and presumably skins, but also antlers were a resource for which deer were valued.

Plotted on figure 2 are two measurements taken on distal humeri of Dama from D-A. Figure 3 shows a frequency distribution for one of these measurements taken on material from D-A (n = 14), Kissonerga-Mylouthkia (n = 29), and Lemba-Lakkous Area II (n = 7). The latter two sites are dated to the early third and the later third-early second millennia B.C. respectively, and the figures are drawn from my own unpublished data. These metrical data provide a starting point for the discussion of several topics.

1. *Patterning within the Distal Humerus Sample*

The distribution of distal humerus measurements from D-A, shown in figure 2, suggests the presence of two distinct groups within the deer population. This conclusion is strongly reinforced by the bimodal distribution, shown in figure 3, of distal breadth measurements taken on a pooled sample of 50 humeri from three Early Prehistoric sites, and I would suggest that the situation may be accounted for in terms of sexual dimorphism. Note that in both cases the numbers of specimens that fall into each group on the diagram are approximately equal. Equal culling of the sexes is consistent with a pattern of intensive human exploitation (though not necessarily close control), in which all members of the animal population are sooner or later culled. Such a system should not produce the sexually biased mortality pattern (unless preservational or other external factors intervene) that might be expected to result from a less thorough exploitation, in which only some of the animals were killed by man while the remainder died from other causes. The crucial importance of deer in the local economies of D-A and other sites in Cyprus extending from the sixth to the second millennia B.C. also argues in favor of the efficient and intensive exploitation of this animal. In the absence of such a strategy over this long period of prehistory, which undoubtedly witnessed considerable expansion of the human population, it is certain that deer would very rapidly have been culled to extinction.

2. *The Size-Range of Cypriot* Dama

The only published indications of the size range of prehistoric Cypriot Dama are to be found in Ducos' (1965:6-8) measurements of small samples. His 23 distal humeri (one of his larger samples) have a range of width of 38.8 - 49.8 mm. However 27 measurements taken by

Table 5. Number of Identified Fragments of *Dama mesopotamica*

		Proximal Fused	Proximal Unfused	I[a]	Distal Fused	Distal Unfused	I	Medial	Total
Humerus	L[b]	5	2	0	10	1	0	1	19
	R[c]	5	1	0	16	2	1	0	25
Femur	L	6	2	0	13	9	0	0	30
	R	3	5	0	10	6	0	1	25
	I	0	0	0	0	2	0	0	2
Radius	L	5	0	0	4	6	0	0	15
	R	12	0	0	5	2	0	0	19
	I	1	0	0	0	0	0	0	1
Metacarpal	L	2	0	0	4	1	0	0	7
	R	3	0	0	4	3	0	0	10
	I	0	0	0	2	1	0	1	4
Metatarsal	L	3	0	0	2	0	0	0	5
	R	5	0	0	3	0	0	0	8
	I	1	0	0	3	2	0	1	7
Metapodial	I	0	0	0	2	0	0	2	4
Tibia	L	13	0	0	7	0	0	0	20
	R	4	4	0	7	1	0	1	17
Ulna	L	4	10	0	1	0	0	2	17
	R	4	3	0	0	0	0	2	9
								Total	244

		Fused	Unfused	I	
Calcaneum	L	2	1	3	6
	R	6	1	3	10
Scapula	L	9	2	5	16
	R	20	1	10	31
				Total	63

	L	R	I	
Astragalus	10	11	0	21
Pelvis	37	53	4	94
Patella	4	1	1	6
Naviculocuboid	3	3	0	6
Atlas				14
Axis				12
Sacrum				15
Phalanges				59
First				28
Second				16
Third				15
Head[d]				96
Total				323
Grand total				630

[a] I = indeterminate   [b] L = left   [c] R = right   [d] See note to table 3.

Table 6. *Dama mesopotamica* Epiphyseal Fusion Data and Age Structure

	Fused	Unfused	Mortality pattern

Infant (less than ca. 1 year)
    D* scapula + P** radius +
    D humerus
	73	6	8% dead as infants

Juvenile (less than ca.
    1 1/2 years)
    D tibia + D metapodial
	34	8	19% dead as infants or juveniles

Subadult (less than ca. 4 years)
    P and D ulna + calcaneum +
    P and D femur + D radius +
    P tibia + P humerus
	85	54	39% dead before adulthood

Total Percent	192 (74%)	68 (26%)	

*D = distal
**P = proximal

Dr. P. L. Carter and me on D-A material increase the known range of variation for this dimension by about one third--to 37.2-51.4. It is my experience that an increase in sample size results in a considerable increase in the range of variation for many other skeletal elements as well, and one must therefore conclude that Ducos' small number of measurements do not adequately represent the metrical variability of prehistoric Cypriot *Dama*. It should be stressed that even for individual sites, including the relatively short-lived Cypriot ones, the degree of size variation in the *Dama* population may be considerable (fig. 4; see also Bate 1937:210).

3. *Late Pleistocene-Early Holocene Size Reduction of* Dama mesopotamica?

The absolute size of the D-A material represented in figure 2 does not provide support for the model, outlined by Carter, of progressively decreasing body size of *D. mesopotamica* throughout the period ca. 60,000 to 5000 B.C. The range of widths of distal humerus (41.8-47.0 mm; 6 specimens) from the earlier site of Ain Mallaha, Israel (ca. 10,000 B.C.) (Ducos 1968:162) would fit comfortably into the middle of the ranges encountered at both D-A (ca. 5500-4000 B.C.) and Kissonerga-Mylouthkia (ca. 2800 B.C.) (table 7 and fig. 4).

Small samples certainly render the problem of size change difficult to approach, and this is illustrated by the following example. Carter (see his chapter above, fig. 3) shows that a sample of 7 proximal radii from Neolithic Cyprus have a lower mean width than 5 from Ain Mallaha, and this is a strong supporting strut in his argument for size diminution through time. However he also shows (see his chapter above, fig. 6) that the mean of the 4 of these Neolithic Cypriot measurements taken by him on D-A material is marginally higher than that for Ain Mallaha. Furthermore, the mean of 6 width measurements taken by me (45.5 mm) on D-A proximal radii is appreciably greater than that for Ain Mallaha (44.3 mm) (table 7), and slightly greater than the mean figure for the Pleistocene site of El Wad (45.0 mm). Indeed, the mean width of these 6 D-A proximal radii closely approaches that from the very much earlier (ca. 60,000 B.C.) site of Tabun (45.6 mm). If my own and Carter's measurements of D-A proximal radius widths are amalgamated to give a larger sample (10 specimens, mean 44.8 mm) , we still

Table 7. A Metrical Comparison of Selected Skeletal Elements of
Dama mesopotamica from Dhali-Agridhi (D-A) 1972 (ca. 5500-4000 B.C.)
and Ain Mallaha (A-M) (ca. 10,000 B.C.)

			n=	mean	range
Astragalus	Greatest length	D-A	15	42.0	38.3-45.5
		A-M	10	43.2	41.0-46.8
Humerus	Distal breadth	D-A	14	44.8	39.5-51.4
		A-M	6	43.5	41.8-47.0
Radius	Proximal breadth	D-A	6	45.4	41.5-49.5
		A-M	5	44.3	40.4-48.0
Radius	Distal breadth	D-A	11	39.1	34.0-44.8
		A-M	3	40.4	37.0-42.2
Scapula	Greatest length	D-A	22	46.9	41.4-52.4
	of distal end	A-M	4	44.7	42.0-47.0

find that the mean width for this Neolithic Cypriot material is greater than that for Ain Mallaha, and little short of that for El Wad.

This discussion could be repeated with regard to other skeletal elements, and suggests that the unidirectional model of progressive size decrease of *Dama mesopotamica*, in parallel with the size decreases documented in the East Mediterranean for cattle (Jarman 1969:255) and other animals (Kurten 1968:248), requires a more secure basis in the data if its validity is actually to be demonstrated. The lack of clear evidence for the small size of D-A Dama as compared with *Dama* from Ain Mallaha (table 7), albeit on the basis of small samples, calls into question Carter's statement that "the decrease in size between 12,000 B.P. (Ain Mallaha) and 7000 B.P. (Dhali-Agridhi) appears to have been greater than between 60,000 B.P. (Tabun) and 12,000 B.P. (Ain Mallaha)."

The most important point that emerges from the above discussion, which is underscored by the ambiguous results of the comparison presented in table 7, is that we must exercise great caution in drawing conclusions from such small samples.

4. *Later Holocene Size Reduction of Cypriot* Dama mesopotamica?

Consideration of figure 4 urges a discussion of Halstead's suggestion (1977:267, note 1) that there is "a clear diminution of body size [of *Dama*] in the comparatively short time between the Early Neolithic and the Late Bronze Age." Halstead bases this statement on a metrical comparison between a small measured sample of Late Cypriot fallow deer from Kouklia (Halstead, personal communication) and the comparably small sample published by Ducos (1965), in which many elements have somewhat larger mean sizes.

It is assumed by Halstead that the material measured by Ducos is of Early Neolithic date, but in fact Ducos gives no specific provenience or date for it. Proveniences are given for antler fragments mentioned by Ducos, and these come mostly from a variety of Stone Age contexts spanning the sixth to fourth millennia B.C. (Khirokitia, Sotira, and Erimi), but also include specimens from the Late Bronze (Enkomi and Angastina). There would thus seem to be no justification for the assumption that Ducos' measurements refer specifically to Early Neolithic *Dama*, although it seems likely that they do represent bones that come on the whole from Neolithic contexts. I would follow the more cautious approach of Nobis (1977:288), who concedes only that Ducos' material derives from Neolithic and Bronze Age contexts. Thus, leaving aside the argument advanced above, that Ducos' sample is too small to characterize the metrical attributes of Cypriot *Dama* during the Early Neolithic, uncertainty regarding the origin of this material would render questionable its use for such a purpose.

Table 8. Comparison of Mean Values of Three Measured Dimensions
of Some Prehistoric Cypriot *Dama*

		Dhali-Agridhi	Kissonerga-Mylouthkia	Lemba-Lakkous Area II	Ducos' "Daim de Chypre"
Date (millennium B.C.)		6th/5th	3rd	3rd/2nd	6th-2nd(?)
Distal breadth of humerus (mm)	No.	14	29	7	23
	Mean	44.8	46.0	44.6	43.0
Proximal breadth of radius (mm)	No.	6	8	5	3
	Mean	45.4	44.3	44.4	42.3
Distal breadth of tibia (mm)	No.	15	25	4	4
	Mean	38.8	38.6	39.8	38.9

Presented in table 8 is a selection of metrical data for *Dama* from three prehistoric sites in Cyprus, as well as for Ducos' insecurely dated "Daim de Chypre." These sites probably span the entire Early Prehistoric[3] period, but nevertheless the body size of Dama remains constant throughout. This is confirmed by further metrical data not quoted here, both from these and also from other sites. It thus appears that a diminution in body size as suggested by Halstead did not occur within the Early Prehistoric period itself.

If at some point a general diminution in the size of Cypriot Dama did really occur, then it seems that it must have taken place in the millennium or so between the end of the Early Prehistoric period and the Late Cypriot, following a period of some three or four millennia during which there had been no discernible size change. It is certain that the economic importance of deer to the Stone Age inhabitants of Cyprus was far greater than to their metal-using, cattle-keeping successors. Such a change in the economic status of deer denotes a change in their management, which would bring about some modification in the selective pressures operating upon them. This, in turn, could have favored some adaptive alteration in body size.

Another possibility, which I believe to have better foundation in the evidence presently available, is that there was no size diminution. Sexual size dimorphism of *Dama* is observable on a number of skeletal elements, and has been illustrated for the distal humerus in figures 2 and 3. A metrical comparison of the Kouklia *Dama* bones (details of which were kindly furnished by Mr. P. Halstead) with those of D-A and other prehistoric Cypriot sites indicates that while a few of the Late Cypriot bones fall within the larger, male end of the size distribution, a far larger proportion falls within the range of values that I would ascribe to females. It therefore seems probable that the Kouklia sample is, for whatever reason, sexually biased, containing a preponderance of female deer. If this is indeed the case, then a comparison of mean values for measurements taken on this sample with those from a sample that is sexually unbiased, drawn from an identical population, is bound to give the misleading impression that significantly smaller body size characterized the Kouklia population.

On balance, then, there seems to be no firm evidence for any general later Holocene reduction in the size of Cypriot *Dama*. It has been shown that such a size diminution did not occur during the Early Prehistoric period, but that it was perhaps more likely, in theoretical terms, to have occurred at the end of this period, corresponding with a major change in the

---

[3] The term "Early Prehistoric" is used as defined by Stanley Price (1979:xi) to designate that period occupied by the Neolithic and Chalcolithic.

economic status of deer. Nevertheless a consideration, in the light of sexual size dimorphism, of the Kouklia bone measurements, upon which is based the argument for size diminution, suggests that the whole idea of a change in the body size of Cypriot deer could be an illusion arising from a sexually biased sample.[4]

---

[4] A small quantity of bone from smaller creatures than those discussed above was brought to Britain for identification. This material included the femoral shaft of a member of the tortoise family and the distal portion of the femur of a fox. A further four encrusted fragmentary metacarpals, found together in the correct anatomical order, were tentatively identified as cat, but in view of their poor condition the possibility that they are from fox cannot be discounted.

According to the excavator (Lehavy, personal communication) the loci in which were found the tortoise femur and the possible cat metacarpals were aceramic, while the fox femur came from an ambiguous context which could date from the aceramic or the ceramic Neolithic. Other miscellaneous items not attributable to deer, caprines, or pig were examined in Cyprus and could not be specifically identified. These comprised a fish vertebra (diameter 16.5 mm), the claw of a crab, and the fragmentary distal portion of the humerus of a bird, possibly around the size of a pigeon. The former item derived from an ambiguous Neolithic context, while the latter two were from aceramic loci.

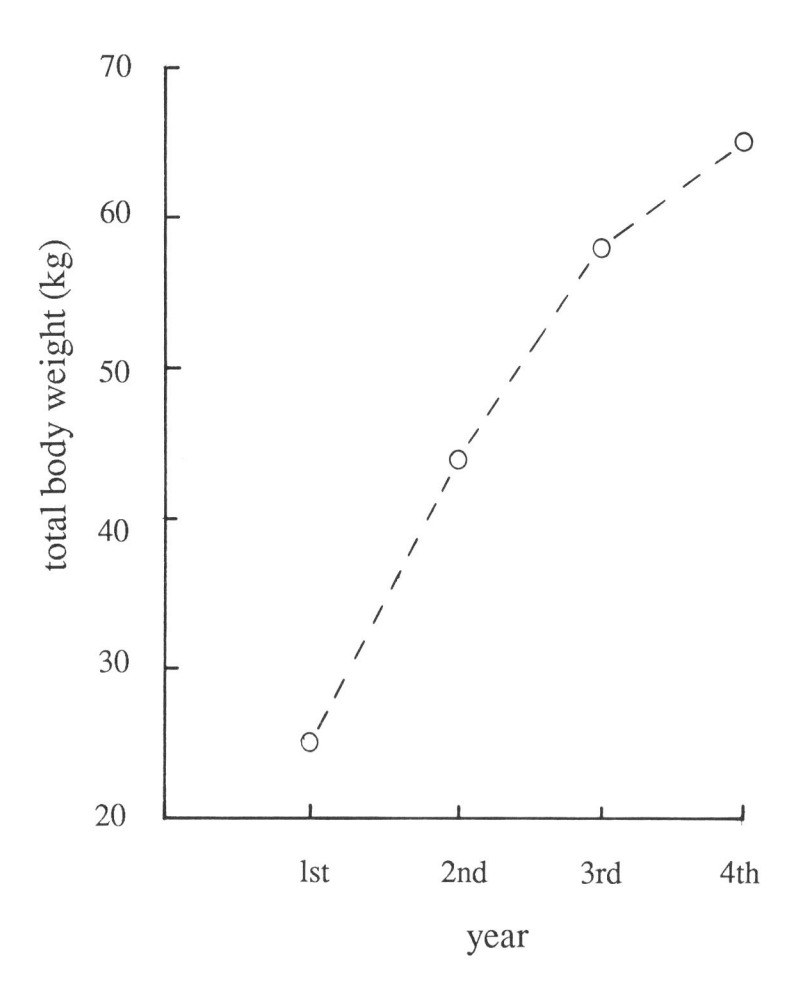

Figure 1. Graph Showing Mean Total Body Weights of Southern English Male Fallow Deer (*Dama dama*) Killed during their First through Fourth Years of Life (adapted from Chaplin and White 1969: 130, fig. 1).

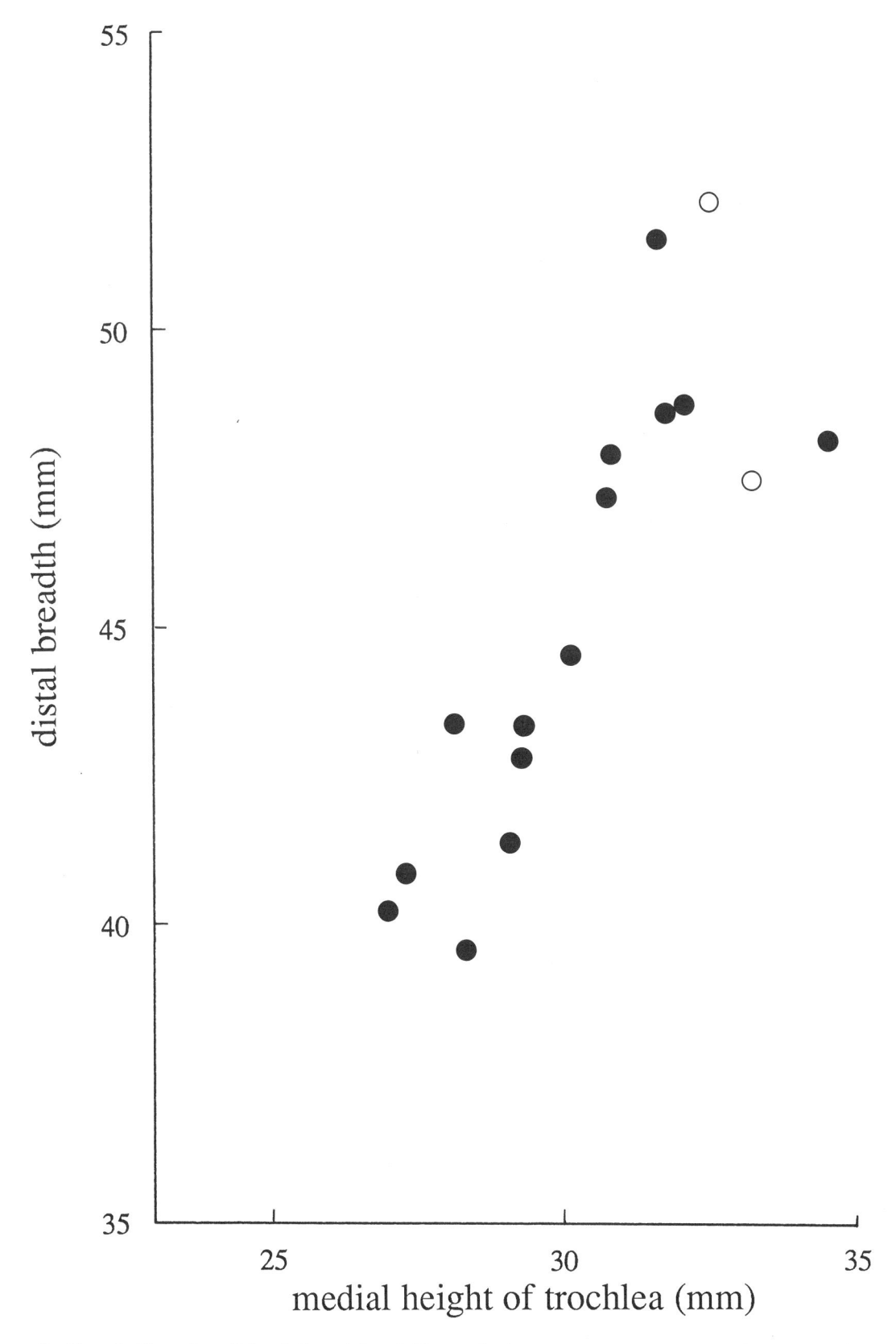

Figure 2. Graph Showing Distal Breadth of Humeri of *Dama mesopotamica* from Dhali-Agridhi Plotted against Medial Height of Trochlea. Open circles indicate specimens for which the distal breadth was estimated.

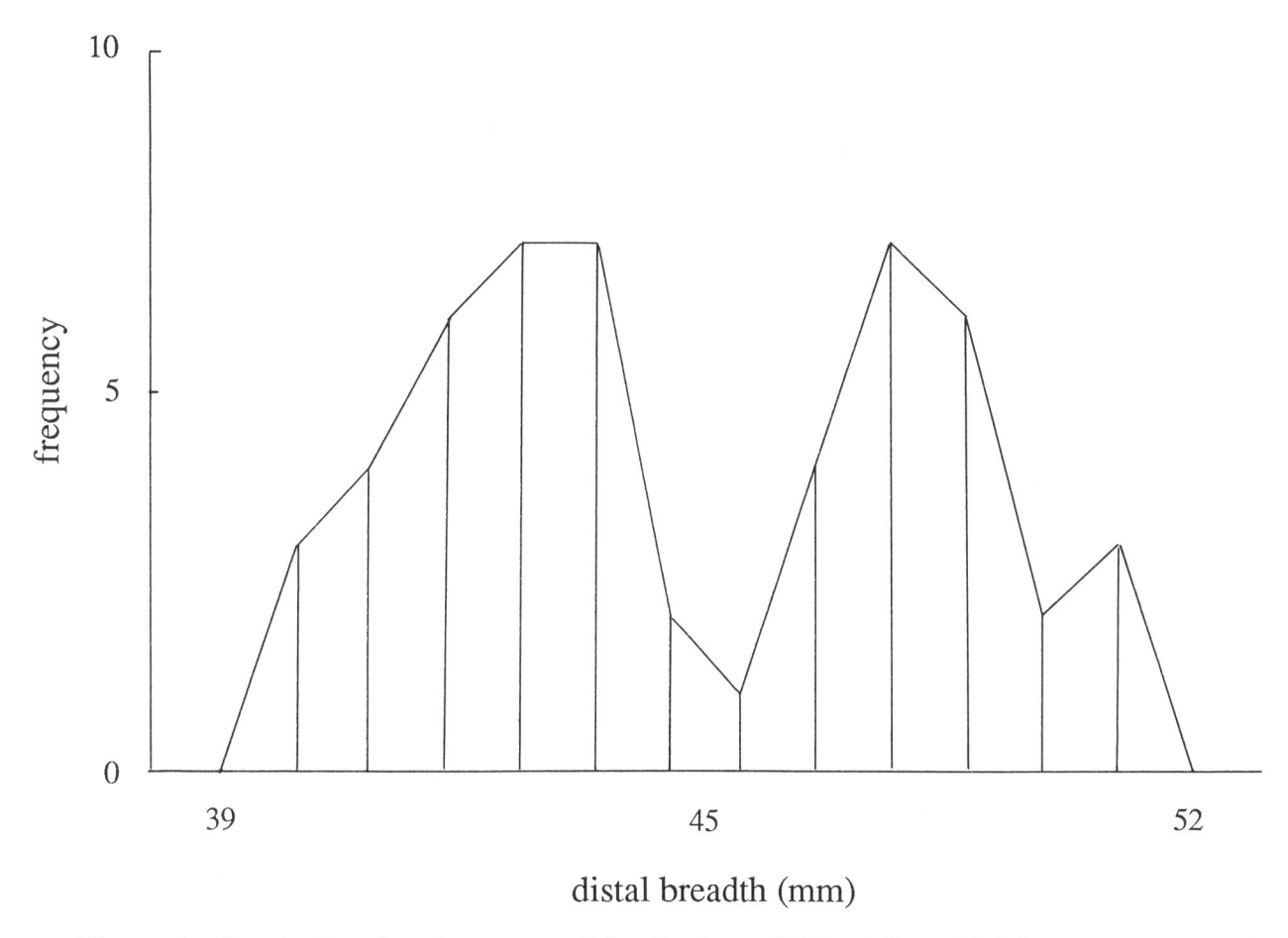

Figure 3. Graph Showing Frequency Distribution of Distal Breadth Measurements on the Humerus of *Dama mesopotamica* from Dhali-Agridhi, Kissonerga-Mylouthkia, and Lemba-Lakkous Area II.

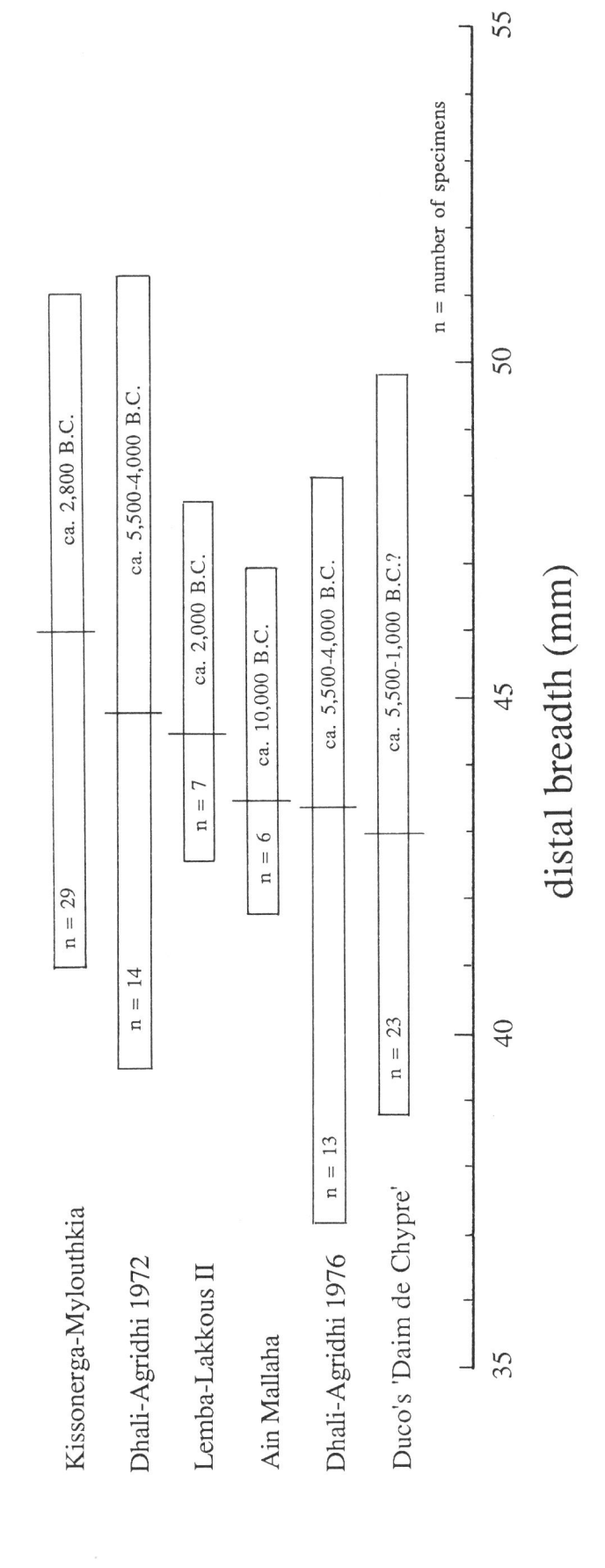

Figure 4. Diagram Showing Ranges and Means of Breadth of *Dama mesopotamica* Distal Humerus.

III. METALLURGICAL STUDIES
A. ANCIENT MINING AND MINERAL DRESSING ON CYPRUS

Frank L. Koucky[*]
Arthur Steinberg[**]

Part 1. INTRODUCTION AND PRELIMINARY IDEAS ON CYPRIOT MINING AND METALLURGY

Introduction

The copper mining industry of Cyprus is located in a great ellipse around the Troodos Mountains in the southwestern portion of the island. It follows the outcrop pattern of the pillow lavas. Only here have there been found massive sulfide mineral deposits capable of exploitation (fig. 1).

It is also along this pattern of pillow lavas that the slag heaps which represent ancient mineral exploitation can be found. The size and distribution of these heaps are highly variable, but clearly the deposits nearest the sea were exploited to a greater degree than those farther inland.

It is unfortunate that these slag heaps have not been treated as important antiquities, for surely they record an effort by man greater than the building of pyramids or the construction of many great cities of the past. Instead they are being rapidly destroyed, used as a source of inexpensive road metal, even in areas where more suitable materials are readily available. Once these heaps are removed, the stratigraphy needed for reconstructing the technical changes in ancient metallurgy will have disappeared (pl. 1).

This study began in 1972 as part of the American Expedition to Idalion. Idalion, like Tamassos, was an important ancient inland city whose prosperity was related to the copper industry. The Idalion project was an attempt not only to excavate an ancient city but also to gain an understanding of the cultural ecology as related to the economic exploitation of the environment of this city and nearby mines. The project was an interdisciplinary venture of the archaeologists and other scientific specialists.

The first Idalion report (*Idalion* 1) gives some hints of the importance of this site and region, and some ideas about ancient Cypriot metallurgy, but work done at the site since this first report forms the background for this study.

---

[*]Department of Geology, College of Wooster, Wooster, Ohio

[**]Department of Humanities, Massachusetts Institute of Technology, Cambridge, Massachusetts

An earlier version of this paper appeared in Wertime and Wertime 1982:149-180.

It would be impossible to acknowledge all who have contributed support and aid to this manuscript. We can single out only a few whose help has been considerable. Dr. Vassos Karageorghis, Director of the Department of Antiquities of Cyprus, suggested and encouraged this study. Dr. George Maliotis and Mr. Nicolas Adamides of the Hellenic Mining Company, Ltd., gave cooperation, field time, and discussion that was invaluable. Dr. Anita Walker of the University of Connecticut took part in the field study and gave vital support to this work. The authors extend special thanks to Dr. Fred Cropp of the College of Wooster for reading and discussing the manuscript.

Previous Studies

It is not the purpose here to summarize the numerous previous studies of ancient mining and metallurgy on Cyprus; this was the subject of a previous paper (Steinberg and Koucky 1974). This earlier paper presented analytical data from some one hundred slag samples from twenty different localities. Ancient Cypriot slags were separated into two chemical types: A) silica-rich slag, and B) iron-rich (silica-poor) slag (fig. 2). These chemical types do not follow the traditional slag classification in general use on Cyprus at the present time: black "Roman" slags and red "Phoenician" slags. All of the silica-rich slags (type A) are called "Roman" but the iron-rich slags (type B) are a mixture of those called "Roman" and "Phoenician."

The two chemical types of slags indicate that two different smelting technologies had been used on Cyprus in the past. Figure 3 shows that the melting points of the two slag types are essentially identical so that there is no temperature advantage of one technique over the other. There are distinct differences in the physical properties between slags when molten, however, and thus they present different smelting problems for copper separation from the slag; these will be discussed later in this paper. Only one such smelting problem will be mentioned here: It should be noted that the iron-rich slag (type B) when molten has a high density, which allows separation of copper metal, but its density is so similar to that of copper matte that the copper matte will not separate readily but remains suspended.

Preliminary Discussion

In order to develop a discussion of the copper technology of ancient civilizations on Cyprus, many ideas need to be clarified or corrected beforehand. The following eight points will serve as background to the arguments presented in the text. They are outlined here, with supportive evidence.

1. Native copper can be found on Cyprus.
2. Gold and silver can be found in moderate abundance on Cyprus.
3. The finding of copper or iron sulfide minerals in a slag or in metallic copper ingots does not necessarily imply that copper sulfides were being smelted.
4. There is no record of Phoenician pottery at the mines or at any slag heap on Cyprus.
5. Mining on Cyprus did not cease with the Romans, but continued into medieval times.
6. Cypriot slags are of many types, not just two ("Roman" and "Phoenician"); these various types of slag can be distinguished in the field.
7. Only a small amount of Cypriot slag is manganese rich.
8. There are no published reports of smelting furnaces on Cyprus except for one mentioned in an abstract of Walker and Koucky (1976).

1. *Native copper can be found on Cyprus.*

Native copper was probably the first form mined in Cyprus, since specimens of Cypriot metal are of great purity (Rickard 1930:13).

The story of copper technology on Cyprus should start with the use of native copper. Unfortunately somehow the idea has been accepted that native copper is not to be found on Cyprus and that copper must therefore have been imported. While native copper is not abundant, certainly there are references to its existence.

In one of the first geologic surveys of Cypriot copper ore districts, Cullis and Edge (1927:43) report finding native copper at Monagroulli (11 miles ENE of Limassol), about a mile above Moni in the Monis River Valley.

In our survey of the Yalias River Valley we have found wire copper in amygdaloidal cavities in the pillow lavas just west of the North Mathiati Mine. This is in a region near

Neolithic sites reported in the Cyprus Archaeological Survey and is not far from the large Neolithic site at Kataliondas (K. Nicolaou 1967). Bear (1963) also reports finding copper in amygdaloidal cavities in the pillow lavas.

Bruce (1949) reports native copper in the mines at Skouriotissa and Mavrovouni in alteration zones marginal to the ore: "Limonite frequently occurs at the hanging wall of the ore bodies. This occasionally carries sheets and stringers of metallic copper (p. 9)."

While thus far no copper has been reported from Neolithic sites, Peltenburg (1978) has found copper tools at the Chalcolithic site he is now excavating (Lemba-Lakkous). It is not known yet whether these were made from native copper or even whether they are of Cypriot origin.

Unfortunately there are no published analyses of native copper from any of the above sources that can be used for comparison with archaeological finds.

2. *Gold and silver can be found in moderate abundance on Cyprus.*

> Where did Cyprus obtain all of this gold? Even Hittite texts include gold as one of the tributes from Cyprus; there are only a few poor gold deposits known on this island (Holmes 1975:94).

The modern discovery of gold on Cyprus is credited to Charles Godfrey Gunther, whose prospecting on Cyprus was responsible for the development of the modern Skouriotissa and Mavrovouni mines. In 1919 the miners at Skouriotissa discovered a "seam of soft, sticky, puttylike clay that looked dry but when squeezed in a man's hand turned to liquid slime (Lavender 1962:124)." The miners named the material "Devil's Mud" because of its acidic, corrosive nature. Gunther immediately suspected that this material was similar to a material he had seen at the Rio Tinto Mines in Spain, where underlying the gossan was a jarosite-rich bed 4 to 8 inches thick that carried 10 to 20 dollars a ton in gold and 40 oz per ton of silver. His first assays gave higher gold values and lower silver values than the Spanish material.

It was recognized that the origin of this type of Devil's Mud deposit was related to the weathering of the massive sulfide ore under the Mediterranean type climate (fig. 4). Rain waters percolating down through the massive sulfide ore oxidize that portion of the ore above the water table. The iron pyrite rusts to a red iron oxide, while most of the silica remains as jasper or chalcedony. This bright red residue, called "gossan," marks the remains of the oxidized ore body.

The sulfur freed by oxidizing sulfide minerals reacts to form a strong acid environment that mobilizes most elements (except iron and silicon) that are washed down to the water table, where the acid is diluted or neutralized. This process allows the precipitation of some of the dissolved elements that form the zone of secondary enrichment. The oxidized zone of secondary enrichment contains the material called Devil's Mud. While the primary massive sulfide ore has gold and silver values too low to allow economic recovery, this highly enriched thin natrojarosite zone contains concentrations of great economic value.

Bruce (1949:8) states that the ratio of gold to silver in the Devil's Mud is generally in the range of 1 to 8 to 1 to 10. The gold is so very fine that little can be seen in gravity concentrates; also, it is associated with dark-colored heavy minerals that tend to make it difficult to find. The Devil's Mud is also often enriched in lead sulfate, often containing up to 1 percent lead, and selenium.

During the depression of the 1930s, when copper and pyrite ore had no market, the Cyprus Mines Corporation turned its effort toward recovering gold, rather than closing down altogether. Other companies followed suit, and Cypriot gold production reached a peak in 1938, when 29,245 oz. of fine gold and 199,719 oz of silver were shipped (Bear 1963:185-89). The recovery of the copper market caused a decrease in gold production, which has never again reached the 1938 level.

There can be no question that minable quantities of gold exist on Cyprus, but since they occur only in the very fine state, with no known nuggets, there is a question whether the gold was known to the ancient miners. Bruce (1949) felt it was not, but later studies at many mines have found the overlying gold-bearing Devil's Mud stripped off. Pantazis (1967), in describing the Platies Mine of the Kalavasos District, states:

> At Platies there are large occurrences of slag and scattered waste dumps. The ore deposits appear to have been extensively mined by the ancients, particularly by the Romans, so that modern work found little ore *in situ*. Most of the ore extracted consisted of sorted and rejected ancient [Roman] residues which average about two per cent copper and 45 per cent sulfur. The Platies ore deposit was under gossan which had originally been mined for gold and silver (p. 144, fig. 5).

Hills (1928a:6), in describing the Skouriotissa Mine, states:

> The ancients, in several places, worked on top of the present pyrite body, and probably they extracted oxidized ores from the entire top area, the concentration of gold and silver there contributing to the known ancient output of these metals from Cyprus.

It should be noted that the gold and silver are found in a similar geologic occurrence at Rio Tinto, Spain. One can find many references to ancient gold and silver mining there (Healy 1977:92).

Thus considerable evidence exists that the mines on Cyprus in antiquity produced not only copper but considerable silver and gold.

3. *The finding of copper or iron sulfide minerals in a slag or in metallic copper ingots does not necessarily imply that copper sulfides were being smelted.*

> The Romans were certainly the first to work sulfide ores generally . Most Roman copper in trade or refinery hoards consists of copper which, by the peculiar structure and the surface of the bars and cakes, together with the sulphur content, can be shown to belong to copper prepared from sulfides (Forbes 1972:25).

Zwicker, Grembler, and Röllig (1977), in their study of Cypriot slags, reach the following conclusion, also on the basis of the copper sulfide content of the slags: "In all other places (660 B.C. to 350 A.D.) from which copper slag was investigated, sulfidic ores were smelted (p. 312)."

We should note that copper and iron are strongly chalcophilic and will combine readily with any sulfur that is available. Thus if pure copper carbonate ores (malachite or azurite) were smelted and the ancient metallurgist added sulfur-bearing flux, it is very likely that copper and/or iron sulfides would appear in the slag and in the separated copper. When we consider the list of typical fluxes that were used in medieval times according to Agricola (1556, book 7, pp. 219-65), we can see that this might well be the case. Typical sulfur-bearing fluxes mentioned by Agricola include alum, vitriol, slag, and pyrite.

It was pointed out earlier (see fig. 4), that sulfated minerals are available and abundant on Cyprus. The smelting of any of these minerals either as a flux or as the ore mineral would tend to produce some sulfides in the slag or separated copper. The total removal of sulfides by smelting was probably possible only by a multiple series of fusions during the refining of the copper.

Clearly the finding of sulfides in the slag or copper can not be used as evidence that there was direct smelting of sulfide ores. This point was well stated by Coghlan (1951):

Small proportions of sulfur have been found in the composition of prehistoric implements, but as long ago as 1899 Gowland (Early Metallurgy of Copper, *Archaeologia*, vol. lvi, p. 275) showed that this did not by any means prove the case [that sulfide ores were smelted]; in his opinion most simple oxide ores contain small portions of iron and copper sulfides, and such is the affinity of copper for sulfur that when these are reduced the copper obtained will contain quite as much of the sulfur as shown in the analyses under discussion (p. 15).

4. *There is no record of Phoenician pottery at the Cypriot mines or at any of the major slag piles.*

Only negative evidence can be presented on this point and thus there is no need for a long discussion. No Phoenician pottery has been found during this investigation of the mines and slag piles; furthermore no reference has been found to Phoenician materials by any other observer of the mines and slags.[1]

It is very likely that the Phoenicians were not involved in the mining and smelting on Cyprus. These activities were undertaken by local populations who traded raw copper ingots to the Phoenicians at major trading centers such as Kition. The Phoenicians then refined, alloyed, and manufactured this trade material.

It is difficult to determine how the name "Phoenician" became associated with the red slags found on Cyprus (pl. 2). Cullis and Edge use the term in their 1922 survey of the island. Rickard (1930) credits it to Victor Bérard,[2] but even earlier the older slags in Spain had been called "Phoenician" by Kennedy (1894).

5. *Mining on Cyprus did not cease with the Romans, but continued into medieval times.*

In 1975 and 1976 excavations were made at a site suspected to be a Roman smelting site at Teredhia, northwest of Lythrodonda. This site proved to be a surprise since all evidence from the excavations indicates that this was a late medieval smelting site (Walker and Koucky 1976).

The work at Teredhia prompted a reinvestigation of the long-held concept that copper mining ended on Cyprus in Roman times.[3] Abundant medieval sherds had been noted in

---

[1] Many authors have been careful in their terminology and thus Davies (1929) and Schaeffer (1936) speak of "Roman" and "pre-Roman" slags.

[2] In Les Phéniciens et l'Odyssée, vol. 1 (Paris, 1902), p. 457.

[3] Bruce (1949) and Rickard (1930) both point to C. D. Cobham for the idea that copper mining ceased on Cyprus with the Romans. Cobham argues that there is no mention of copper mining on Cyprus in the preserved literature. Yet in the short translations he presents in his book, Excerpta Cypria, there are many mentions of blue vitriol ($CuSO_4$). Vitriol can be gained only from mining, since it tends to disappear from the surface after a few years (this is discussed further in part 3 of this paper). It is interesting to note that after Roman times the mines are called vitriol and gold mines.

The following authors in Cobham mention gold and vitriol of Cyprus:
Bordone (1528), p. 61
Porcacchi da Castiglione (1576), p. 162
Lilio (1551), p. 67
Possot (1532), p. 63
Cotovicus (1598), p. 99
Della Valle (1625), p. 215
Lithgow (1609-1621), p. 216
Heyman (1700-1709), p. 248
Pococke (1738) mentions passing abandoned mines and slag piles in his travels (the Soli and Lythrodonda mines).

association with many slag heaps in the survey of slag heaps on the island, but these sherds had been passed over as the debris of medieval picnickers. Reinvestigation now indicates that only medieval sherds are to be found in some slag heaps (e.g., Teredhia, Spilli in the Kalavasos District [pl. 4a], and some heaps along the road east of Mitsero). Other slag heaps, such as those at South Mathiati and Skouriotissa [pl. 4b], prove to be stratified, with medieval slags overlying Roman slags. Davies (1929:79) noted:

> At Lythrodonda, however, there is much slag, and associated with it a site which contains later pottery; among the pieces I picked up were a jug handle which looks fresh and fairly recent, a sherd with bands of fine parallel incisions, which are certainly not used earlier than late Byzantine times and I suspect are later, and a piece of blue-glazed ware which does not look modern but rather Turkish. We may perhaps connect this with the notice of Buffon (*Histoire Naturelle des Mineraux*) that in 1785 Cyprus was producing gold.

It is possible that Davies is describing the Teredhia site.

There is evidence that even by Roman times timber had become rare and precious, with the consequence that not all the copper ore mined was made into copper metal because charcoal was in short supply. Galen's visit to the Cypriot mines in 166 A.D. (described in detail in part 4 of this paper) provides evidence of vitriol production on a large scale. Thus, when one searches for evidence of copper mining in later times, the evidence may appear not as copper smelting, which was a greatly reduced activity, but in the production of copper vitriol and gold and silver. Vitriol has to be manufactured from copper ore.

Biringuccio (1540) describes vitriol production in Venice in the early 16th century. Throughout the chapter in question he continually compares other vitriol to that from Cyprus:

> The Cyprian and Babylonian [vitriol] are greatly praised by alchemists (p. 97).... Roman vitriol is mined in the region of Bagnores. Although it is not well vitrified and clear it is not of the lovely blue-green color like the Cyprian, it still serves very well (p. 97).... That which I have told you is mined at Massa in Tuscany is as powerful and beautiful as the Cyprian (p. 98). As far as I know the alchemists willingly use the Cyprian and the Roman [vitriol] to make their oils and strong corrosive acids (p. 98).... Some say that wherever vitriol is found it is an indication of gold ore.

Clearly the Cypriot vitriol was a desirable and available product in Venice. Alchemists' writings make many references to Cypriot vitriol in their receipts (Partington 1970).

If vitriol was being manufactured on Cyprus and shipped around the Mediterranean, it might be expected to appear on shipping lists. It is of interest that "spices" in Pegolotti's *The Practice of Commerce* (Florence, 1340) includes not only metals but also "vitriol of Cyprus" (Lopez and Raymond 1965).

Porcacchi[4] (1576) wrote that the island contains an abundance of copper mines and gold seams. The mines of gold near Chryssoco (modern Polis) kept workmen continuously employed. Most of the gold probably did not leave the island in raw form, for at this time Cyprus was the center for the manufacture of cloth embroidered with gold thread, which became known as "*or de Chypre*" (Heyd 1879). Lusignano (1580), writing of his visit to Cyprus in 1573 shortly after the Turkish conquest of the island, visited Tamassos and tells of the mines where "one extracted in ancient times powerful vitriol of chrysocolla which are sure indicators that there was an

---

[4]Tommaso Porcacchi (1576), also known as Thomas Porcachi and Porcacchi-da-Castiglione. Although Cobham gives a short quote from the original reference, the whole article could not be obtained, and the information given is from Sonniti, Travels in Greece and Turkey (1801). Brongniart also wrote about the copper sulfate mines of Cyprus in this same period.

abundance of gold," but at the time of his visit the town was abandoned. Accame or Acchamatide was another ancient village where there was "abundant metal, principally gold, and where there are deep shafts containing vitriol or chrysocolla, which is nothing but the waste-product of gold." But most important are Lusignano's comments:

> The Venecians were afraid to extract gold because of the Turks, because they no longer had a single fortress on the island; nevertheless the gold was left hidden as it came from the earth, and it was shipped to Venice as Coupe-rofe (blue vitriol) (p. 225).

There can be little doubt that the Venetians were mining both copper and gold on Cyprus and that this activity was allowed to continue for a while after the Turkish conquest of the island in 1570.

Mas Latrie (1855) presents many documents concerning plans to reconquer Cyprus from the Turks and stating the advantages of doing so. These papers indicate the great economic loss of raw materials the Venetians had suffered, among them the loss of copper, gold, silver, vitriol, and other salts (e.g., halite and soda niter).

There can be little doubt that mining continued on Cyprus into the Middle Ages, even though smelting became less important. Cypriot products were traded through Genoese and Venetian port cities, except for metallic copper and wood which probably went directly to Alexandria to be traded for spices.

6. Cypriot slags are of many types, not just two ("Roman" and "Phoenician"): these various types of slag can be distinguished in the field.

Detailed data on the physical properties of Cypriot slags that form the basis of their classification will be published elsewhere at a later date. A summary is introduced here, however, because the terminology is needed for the present discussion.

The classification results from a comparison of slags from many localities. Before the classification was formulated, chemical data, polished sections, thin sections, and x-ray diffraction data for these samples were studied. The slags were first described in terms of ten properties:

1. Shape of units or fragments
2. Alteration and surface color
3. Surface structures
4. Character of the fragment base
5. Internal color and luster (fresh break)
6. Vesicle abundance, distribution, and shape
7. Internal structure
8. Internal textures
9. Bulk chemistry
10. Special features

Many classifications could be established on the basis of the above data. Our goal was to choose broad simple classification units that could be used easily in the field and would not require laboratory study.

The classification we chose for slags (presented in detail in fig. 5) is the following:

I. Nodular shaped (N)
II. Crucible shaped (C)
III. Blocky shaped--highly oxidized (P, previously called "Phoenician")
IV. Blocky shaped--slightly oxidized (B, pl. 3a)
V. Ropy surface--irregular shaped (R, pl. 3b)

VI. Collapsed ropy--Mn-rich (M, pl. 4a)
VII. Glassy--blocky--conchoidal fracture (G)

Often a single piece of slag may not show enough of the properties to permit a clear classification, but in general a group of pieces should provide the required information. It should be noted that several slag heaps contain more than one of the above slag types. Also, "remelted slags," used for building smelting furnaces, have not been included in the classification. in sampling slag heaps one should choose samples that show the type of structures that develop at both the top and the bottom of the slag.

The time of formation of the various slag types is open to question, since only a limited amount of sherd material has been collected from the slag localities. Slag heaps were clearly refuse piles that contained a variety of waste material, including sherds. Unfortunately much of the ceramic material is furnace liner and nondiagnostic coarse-ware sherds. Larger collections of sherds from most slag areas are needed for study, before the commercial use of these piles in road building and in the cement industry destroy the slag remains completely.

A tentative time classification for the various slag types in presented in table 1.

7. Only a small amount of Cypriot slag is manganese rich.

The high manganese content is noteworthy in all of the ancient slags of Cyprus. It is less in the Phoenician than in the Roman. It seems to indicate a peculiarity in the ancient smelting practice (Cullis and Edge 1927:22).

Unfortunately Cullis and Edge's statement from 1927 has been widely accepted. In 1963 Bear (1963:190) published twenty-one slag analyses from various localities that show only four to be manganese rich; nonetheless he makes the following statement: "Most Roman slags are manganiferous."

In Steinberg and Koucky (1974) 105 slag analyses were published. From the results of these analyses it is clear that manganese slags were not common, and that those found were from restricted locations.

We have since checked some twenty samples from the Teredhia slag heap near Lythrodonda, all of which are manganese rich. We have concluded that all the slag in this heap is of the same type. Five samples from the Spilli slag heap near the Petra Mine in the Kalavasos District show that this heap is also composed entirely of the manganese type (pl. 4a). At both of these slag heaps the sherds collected are medieval, indicating that the copper operations were medieval rather than modern.

At many of the larger slag heaps the slags appear to be stratified, with a veneer of the manganese-rich slag overlying a silica-rich low-manganese-content slag that includes Roman sherds. In the Skouriotissa heap there appears to be an uncomformity near the base, and the base of the heap is most probably Hellenistic in age (see pl. 4b).

Although the stratification of the large slag heap at South Mathiati is now badly disturbed by bulldozing for road metal, this heap seems to have been stratified with a veneer of both glassy slags and Mn-rich slag over silica-rich Roman slag and Cypro-Archaic blocky slags at the base.

Thus only a few slag heaps are composed completely of manganiferous slag, but in some sites a veneer of manganiferous slag covers the heap. The total amount of this manganese-rich slag is small and many heaps are composed of slags where manganese is present only in trace amounts.

Table 1. Tentative Dating of Cypriot Slag Types

N	Nodular	Bronze Age
C	Crucible	Late Bronze through Hellenistic[a]
P	Oxidized blocky	Cypro-Geometric[b]
B	Blocky	Cypro-Archaic through Hellenistic[c]
R	Ropy	Roman and medieval[d]
M	Mn-rich	Medieval
G	Glassy	Roman and medieval[e]

[a]Believed to be in most cases a refining slag and not a primary smelting slag.

[b]Cypro-Geometric pottery sherds were associated with these slags at the Agrokipia Mine. Early Cypro-Archaic pottery was found associated with these slags at Platies. No sherds were found at other sites but pottery often underlies Cypro-Archaic slags.

[c]May have started in Cypro-Geometric, but to date the earliest sherds found in association are Cypro-Archaic.

[d]Mainly Roman sherds found in association.

[e]Probably medieval, but the South Mathiati heaps are disturbed and Roman sherds are present.

The massive sulfide ores on Cyprus are all low in manganese, so the manganese must have been added during the smelting operation. It has been suggested that the black manganese-rich umbers that overlie the pillow lavas are the source of the manganese that was added to the slag. However these umbers generally are not rich enough in manganese to generate the high percentage of manganese found in some of the slags (over 40 percent MnO). The most probably source is the pyrolusite concretions or nodules that are found distributed sporadically in the black umbers. Where these umbers are exposed to weathering, concentrations of these concretions are found on the surface. They are also found as cobbles and pebbles washing down rivers that drain the Troodos Mountains. A report on the manganese deposits of Cyprus can be found in Bear (1963:120-25).

The manganese concretions are easily mistaken for slag because of their black semimetallic luster, high density (near 4.5 g/cm^3), and sometimes porous character. They were probably collected often in ancient times, and thus our survey found a large number in association with the Late Bronze Age forts on Ayios Sozomenos. The concretions are of a size that might have served as slingstones.

8. *There are no published reports of smelting furnaces on Cyprus except for one reported in an abstract of Walker and Koucky (1976).*

A search of the literature has not disclosed any description of a Cypriot smelting furnace.[5] Tylecote (1972) published a report on how a furnace might have been constructed, but it must be stressed that he did not see a furnace.

Thus the furnace excavated at Teredhia (Walker and Koucky 1976) is important for understanding Cypriot metallurgy. After learning the details of the construction of this furnace we were easily able to locate the sites of many other furnaces.

In 1972 we sampled Teredhia slag heaps north of Lythrodonda. At that time stone foundations were visible between the slag heaps, and a cave had been cut into a dike near the site. In 1973 a plane table map of this site was prepared by Koucky and Yarus (figs. 6 and 7). In 1975, when excavations at the Idalion site were impossible, a field party of six members started the Teredhia excavations. We hoped to discover a relationship between the slag heap and the buildings by excavating a trench from the buildings into the slag heap.

---

[5]The Apliki furnace was probably a copper-refining furnace (Taylor 1952).

Not only was it possible to prove that the slags dated from a time contemporaneous with or later than the foundations, but the partial remains of a furnace were found at the base of the slag heap. While most of the furnace had been destroyed, its northwest corner was still fairly well preserved.

The furnace described here was on leveled bedrock of pillow lava, but it was probably not among the first furnaces built at the site, since it was at the side of the slag heap. We assume that the slag heap grew with time, and that the furnaces toward the outside of the heap are of later date than those suspected to underlie the center. There are three slag heaps at the site, and the pottery sherds contained in each are similar. The heaps are therefore assumed to be nearly contemporaneous. We suggest that this furnace, probably typical, is not the first attempt at smelting at the site.

The slag contains copper prills, and pieces of the slag are copper stained, giving every indication that this was a copper-smelting site and that metallic copper was being prepared.

The furnace is oval (nearly rectangular) with rounded corners, and is quite small (outside dimensions: 75 x 125 cm). The outline of the base is made primarily of fragments of slag, with only a few rounded boulders of diabase. The basal course of the furnace is completely preserved, but the second course is discontinuous. The total height of the furnace is unknown, but the thickness of the walls would not have supported much height.

The remains of a clay liner were found inside the furnace. The center portion of the liner is missing, but fragments of the rim are preserved in several areas; the best preserved is the northwest portion. This liner is supported on coarse sherds and pieces of roof tile. Since the liner and sherds are not joined together, it is likely that the clay liner was dry when put in place. Thus we believe the liner was first put in place and leveled with sherds, and then the furnace was built around it.

The liner had a rounded rim and was about 4 cm thick. The grass-filled clay of the liner had oxidized unevenly to a bright red, and in places the inner surface was fused, which suggests that the heat had been applied from the inside. The ceramic liner was in the shape of a large concave platter that sloped to a minimum elevation in the center. The rim of the platter generally fitted tightly against the furnace wall, but in places in the northwest corner the fit was so poor as to allow charcoal fragments to collect under the ceramic platter.

The outer wall of the furnace was usually two rocks thick, and the basal layer was locked in place by "bent" spilled slag. We judge that the "bent" slag was formed by overflow of the platter in some places, but the larger pieces may have formed where the rim was broken deliberately to allow the slag to escape. The furnace wall was not fitted together tightly, and was rather poorly constructed. No tuyeres have been found at this site, nor have they been found near any of the slag heaps on Cyprus. It must be assumed that this was a furnace fanned by wind blowing through the loose rock wall openings.

The homogeneity and fine-grained character of the slag found in association with this furnace suggest that the slag was stirred often (probably with an iron rod) and that it had cooled very rapidly.

We see the furnace as a small open-hearth Catalan type (fig. 7). Since the furnace was open at the top, the charge could be added continuously and more charcoal could be added as needed. The open top allowed stirring, which resulted in homogenization of the slag and better copper separation. The furnace could operate until the bottom ceramic platter was filled with copper and slag, at which time the excess slag would start forming "bent" slags around the furnace. At this time the smelting would be halted and the ceramic rim could be broken to allow most of the slag to run out of the furnace, leaving a copper bun ingot in the furnace. When cooled, the furnace would be destroyed to recover the planoconvex-shaped ingot.

Bun ingots of the size expected from this size furnace have been found in slag heaps in several mining districts, and two are on display at a small museum at the Hellenic Mining Company offices in Nicosia.

There is no known mine at the Teredhia site. The transportation of heavy sulfide ore in large amounts to this site would probably have been difficult, and no oxidized pieces of ore have been found. The problem of the nature of the furnace charge is the concern of the next portions of this paper.

The furnace described, with the ceramic liner, seems to have been typical of medieval and Roman smelting operations. Hellenistic and earlier furnaces seem to have been similar but lacked the ceramic liner.

Part 2. ANCIENT MINING ON CYPRUS

The modern copper mines of Cyprus have been developed primarily on the sites of ancient workings. A few exceptions are the North Mathiati Mine and some of the Kalavasos ore bodies, but even these are in districts discovered by ancient miners. Thus during more recent mining much evidence of ancient mining has been exposed and in most cases destroyed. Fortunately a few studies have preserved records of ancient gallery positions and sizes, and some of the articles found in these ancient workings. The most useful descriptions of these ancient mines are those of J. L. Bruce, who was Director of Cyprus Mines Operations for the Cyprus Mines Corporation,[6] and many references will be made to his works in this paper.

While the large ancient mines have been destroyed by open-pit operations, there still exist many ancient workings that are in deposits too small for modern mining operations. Accordingly Cyprus remains an outstanding place to study ancient technology. This situation may not last too long, however, because in 1980 a large sulfuric acid plant will begin operation on the south coast of Cyprus. This plant will create an enormous demand for high-grade sulfur ore, and even small deposits will soon be consumed.

Studies of modern mining practices around the Mediterranean are exciting, but in most cases the practices differ greatly from those that would have been used in antiquity. Modern research in the last hundred years has introduced such techniques as flotation, cementation, reverberatory smelting, electrolytic refining, and the combined mechanized operations of blasting, crushing, milling, and so forth that have changed both the scale and method of gaining and extracting the ore. In studying modern practices one may be tempted to try to scale them down, substitute simple tools, and assume that the ancient miner or smelter attempted or used the same techniques. Not enough effort has been made to find industrial archaeological evidence through field investigations. But even in gaining field evidence we must remember that the background of the observer will prejudice what he chooses to see and note in the field. We can only hope that enough of the data are faithfully and accurately recorded to allow a reasonable interpretation to develop eventually. Thus we should realize that many of the observations and conclusions presented in this paper are preliminary and are presented merely to encourage discussion and new observations in the study of ancient technology.

A. Nature of the Cypriot Copper Deposits

The copper mines of Cyprus are similar to those of Rio Tinto, Spain, and Ergani-Maden, Turkey, in that they are classified by geologists as massive sulfide deposits.[7] In these

---

[6]He later became Vice-President of Cyprus Mines Corporation.

[7]It is important to contrast these massive sulfide deposits with those mined in ancient times in southern Palestine. The Palestinian ores of the Aqaba and Sinai regions are described by Bender (1974) and Rothenberg (1972). Clearly these are nodular ores in sandstone. The nodules are partially oxidized so that minerals such as malachite, chrysocolla, plachenite, and chalcocite have developed, leaving only minor remnant cores of the primary minerals, pyrite and chal-

mines the predominant ore mineral now being mined is iron pyrite (FeS_2), with little gangue and only a few other ore minerals. In this type of primary ore the copper values vary between 0.5 percent and 3.0 percent copper, and are generally in the 1 to 2 percent range; the primary copper mineral is chalcopyrite ($CuFeS_2$).

The ore bodies are generally lenticular and concordant with the surrounding host rock, which on Cyprus is pillow lava. Copper values are highest near the top of the deposit. The geology of this type of massive sulfide deposit has a long history of study, but only recently, with the new knowledge of plate tectonics, has the volcanogenic origin of these deposits been recognized, and the fact that they form at the ocean-floor-sea-water interfaces.[8] A sketch of a typical unaltered massive sulfide deposit such as is found in Cyprus is shown in figure 8.

When the massive sulfide deposit is brought near the surface by erosion, oxygen-rich water can start to alter the deposit (fig. 9). Through this alteration copper-sulfide-enriched zones form near the margins and along fractures or faults in the massive sulfide (pl. 5a). This alteration develops as two different types of zones, usually separated by a rather sharp boundary (see fig. 4). The outer zone is the thin oxidized secondary enrichment zone; the inner one (closest to the unaltered ore) is dark colored and variable in thickness and is known as the secondary sulfide enrichment zone. The high copper values are found in the secondary sulfide enrichment zone, where the copper occurs in the minerals chalcocite (Cu_2S), bornite (Cu_5FeS_4), chalcopyrite ($CuFeS_2$), and covellite (CuS). This zone still contains pyrite, usually in the form of large distorted cubic crystals.

The thin oxidized secondary enrichment zone is usually composed of a weakly consolidated fine-grained yellow material that may be semistratified with dark bands. It is in this oxidized zone that the Devil's Mud[9] bands, enriched in gold, silver, and anglesite ($PbSO_4$), are found. Many colorful sulfate minerals develop in this zone. The yellow material of this zone is rich in natrojarosite (differing from Rio Tinto, Spain, where the rocks are potassium rich and pure jarosite can form). The local people still think of this material as sulfur and use it for medicinal purposes.

When erosion proceeds far enough to remove the overlying deposits and weather the massive sulfide ore (fig. 10), a thick red hematite-rich gossan develops, overlying the zone of secondary enrichment. The division between the two types of zones of secondary enrichment

---

copyrite. Unlike the silica-poor ores, these ores are associated with abundant silica occurring in the white Nubian sandstone.

The oxidized nodular ores and the associated silica gangue require only fluxing with iron oxide that is locally available. These are smelted directly with charcoal to black copper, without matte formation.

[8]A long list of references relating to recent geologic studies of massive sulfide deposits could be offered, but only a few, relating to Cyprus, are presented here:

G. Constantinou and G. Govett, Genesis of Sulfide Deposits, Ochre and Umber of Cyprus, Transactions of the Institute of Mining and Metallurgy, vol. 81 (London 1972), sec. B, pp. 34-36.

_____, Geology, Geochemistry and Genesis of Cyprus Sulfide Deposits, Economic Geology 68 (1973):843-48.

Robertson, A. H. F., Metallogenesis along a Fossil Oceanic Fracture Zone: Arakapas Fault Belt, Troodos Massif, Cyprus. Earth Planet Science Letters, vol. 41, pp. 317-29 (1978).

[9]Devils Mud: "The name has been applied by miners to a peculiar soft crumbling material. The peculiar property of this substance of passing into liquid slime when pressed between the fingers accounts for its name. The material consists of up to 30% of soluble salts, principally of iron and copper, the remainder being fine slime and siliceous grit. Silver and gold concentrate because it is 'leached out by acid solutions carrying ferric sulphate' to where acidity is reduced and precipitates precious metals" (Cullis and Edge 1927:20). This zone is one to two feet in thickness.

usually marks a stabilized level of the water table of the region at the time of alteration.[10] In addition to hematite and limonite, the red and yellow gossan often contains such minerals as jasper, white chalcedony, green chert (varieties known as plasma and prase), and selenite (gypsum crystals).

B. The Ancient Mines on Cyprus

Davies has suggested that the early miners sought highly colored oxidized minerals such as green malachite ($Cu_2CO_3(OH)_2$), which served as their main ore in smelting (1929:75). These minerals are quite rare on Cyprus. In this warm Mediterranean climate, with prolonged wet and dry periods, a rather complex mineralogy of highly colored sulfates forms.[11] The colored sulfates, like the carbonates, smelt easily and directly to black copper (impure metallic copper) in charcoal fire. They do so without the formation of copper matte and thus can be used in the same manner as the carbonates.

Observations of the ancient galleries exposed in the modern open-pit mines reveal that these galleries were located to gain access to the secondary enrichment zones (pl. 5b). The observations of J. L. Bruce (1937), in which he describes the mines of the Soli area, are confirmed:

> I suspect that the considerably sulphated ores were more easily smelted by the ancients. The theory that they were looking for rich sulfated copper ore affords a better explanation of their extensive meanderings through a large, badly ventilated, and gaseous orebody than does the theory that they were looking for rich copper ore.

Here the term "rich copper ore" is used as in modern mining, and refers to areas enriched in chalcopyrite, such as are found occasionally in the primary massive sulfide ore.

In the Kalavasos District the only mine that is not worked by modern open-pit mining is the Petra Mine. At this mine a large depression overlies the ore body. Mr. George Kavazis, the storeman at the Kalavasos Mines, who has been working in this district for more than thirty years, has stated that the depression existed before modern mining started. It is very likely that this was an open-pit mine in antiquity. Galleries were driven off a large opening in the side of the hill at a lower level. There are extensive slag piles around the Petra Mine, and they contain sherds that can be dated from Cypro-Archaic to Hellenistic (with Cypro-Archaic sherds most abundant). There is no evidence of Roman activity at this mine.

It is likely that the large open pit was operated to recover the "Devil's Mud" for its gold and silver, and that the lower galleries were carved into the sulfide secondary enrichment zone to obtain copper ore.

Additional evidence of ancient open-pit mining is offered by Trennery and Pocock (1972):

> Evidence uncovered by present-day operations (at the Limni Mines) shows that the Romans worked the outcropping Limni deposit by open-cast methods, followed by underground mining; although the underground workings have collapsed over the centuries, sections of timbering that have been preserved show the ancient miners to have sound knowledge of ground support (p. A-1).

---

[10] Rapid sea-level fluctuations during the Pleistocene prevented the levels of secondary enrichment from adjusting to the modern water table, so that the zones reflect a water-table level of the past; perhaps the fluctuations are associated with the last interglacial period (Eemiann or Sangamon interglacial).

[11] The colored copper-bearing sulfate minerals resemble the copper carbonate minerals in color and the two are easily confused.

The collapse of the underground workings caused a depression some four hundred feet in diameter.

Ancient underground galleries discovered at the Skouriotissa and Mavrovouni mines have been described in detail by Hills (1928a, b) and Bruce (1937, 1949). The size and shape of the galleries and the methods of timbering described in the above reports are very similar to the operations summarized by Healy (1977) for the ancient workings at Rio Tinto, Spain.

From the location of the galleries there can be little doubt that the ore taken from the underground mines was from the sulfide secondary enrichment zone. This ore would be rich in the sulfide minerals--chalcopyrite, bornite, chalcocite, covellite, and pyrite. In some cases the minerals had started to convert to sulfate ores before they were mined. Bruce (1949) describes the nature of sulfated ores:

> At Skouriotissa Mine almost all of the ore body is above the natural water table. It is intensely sulphated and impregnated with sulphates of copper, iron, and zinc, including chalcanthite, brochantite, melanterite, and various ferrous and ferric sulphates such as romerite, coquimbite, fibroferrite, copiopite, raimondite, jarosite and others. In places there are occurrences of alunogen and a leathery form of asbestos (p. 212). The pyrite is hygroscopic, automatically absorbing moisture from the air (p. 216). On exposure to the air the ore oxidizes by sulphating with unusual rapidity until protected by the sulphated coating which forms on faces. The amount of heat generated by oxidizing in the Skouriotissa Mine is remarkable. The exhaust fans discharge air ranging from 106 to 110° F. In mining it is necessary to avoid air pockets, such as dead-end entries, in which the air will become impoverished of its oxygen, making the area unsafe. At an early date, it was recognized that the oxidation progressed quickly in piles of broken ore until the oxygen was exhausted from the entrained air (p. 219).

Thus new ore has to be removed quickly from the mine and there could have been no underground stockpiling of ore. Fires by spontaneous combustion of the ore where a continuous danger both in the mines and in the mill. Lavender (1962) describes several fires that took place before large-scale open-pit mining began.

The dating of the pits and galleries is difficult because most artifacts are in poor condition and much of the material recovered is not diagnostic. The highly acidic nature of the mine waters tends to destroy both metal and ceramic materials. If removed from place, sherds often crumble to dust, and moist sherds must be kept moist until studied. Several radiocarbon dates have been obtained from wood samples taken from the mines: a) Zwicker, Grembler, and Röllig (1977) reported the date of a wood implement taken from the galleries of the Kambia Mine to be 600±110 B.C.; b) Cyprus Mines Corporation had an ancient mining timber from Mavrovouni Mine dated to 300 B.C. Bruce (1937) states that such timbers were made of young trees generally under sixty years old; thus this also is a pre-Roman date.

In summary, the data presented on ancient mining on Cyprus indicate several things:

a) Ancient miners were extracting both gold- and silver-bearing ores from the oxidized secondary enrichment zone, as well as from the copper-rich sulfide secondary enrichment zone. They were not extracting the massive pyrite-rich sulfide ore that is the main economic product of the mines today.
b) Mining was both open-pit (often for the gold ore) and gallery mining (often for the copper ore).
c) Many of the galleries were developed in pre-Roman times. A very active mining period was the late Cypro-Archaic to Hellenistic interval.
d) While great quantities of sulfated ore were mined, there is no evidence to contradict that copper-sulfide-rich ores were also mined in great quantities in pre-Roman times.

Part 3. ANCIENT MINERAL DRESSING ON CYPRUS

First of all I will explain the method of preparing the ore; for Nature usually creates metals in an impure state, mixed with earth, stones and solidified juices, it is necessary to separate most of these impurities from the ore as far as can be before they are smelted, and therefore I will now describe the methods by which the ores are sorted, broken with hammers, burnt, crushed with stamps, ground into powder, sifted, washed, roasted and calcined [Agricola 1556:267, part of the introduction to book 8 which deals with mineral dressing, pp. 267-351].

Generally the ore from the mine is not ready for smelting and must be processed through several steps of preparation. Ore that is coarse and blocky will react too slowly in the furnace and in most cases will not react completely. Ore that is too fine often blows away on heating, or oxidizes too easily. At most mines the ore from the mine is too low grade or contains too many undesirable minerals to feed directly into the furnace without upgrading. The preparation of the mine products into material suitable for smelting furnaces is called mineral dressing.

A typical ore mill handling massive sulfide primary ore today is likely to separate it into three parts:

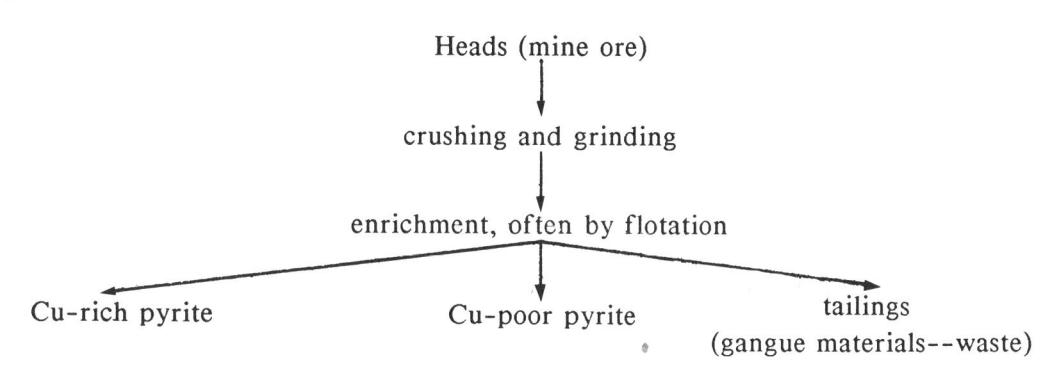

```
                    Heads (mine ore)
                           ↓
                  crushing and grinding
                           ↓
                enrichment, often by flotation
              ↙            ↓             ↘
      Cu-rich pyrite   Cu-poor pyrite    tailings
                                    (gangue materials--waste)
```

The Cu-rich pyrite is used for iron ore after the copper has been separated; the Cu-poor pyrite is sold to make sulfuric acid (in the course of making which the copper may be recovered); and the tailings are dumped near the mill, except when they can be used for fill, fertilizers, or other products.

The ancient copper workers must have used some process of mineral dressing such as hand cobbing, that is, the selection of high-grade pieces of ore and rejection of the waste material by hand picking.[12]

The next step for the ancient worker would probably have been crushing and grinding of the high-grade ore, with a continuation of the hand cobbing process. There would be waste piles associated with each of these steps. Unfortunately if this work was done near the mines, the waste materials would have been similar to the mine waste, and thus work areas for these processes might not be recognizable. Bruce (1949) identified areas of ancient mine waste and a possible work area at the Mavrovouni Mine. He also mentions that there may have been a workshop at the South Mathiati Mine (Bruce 1937).

The first section of this paper concluded that enriched sulfide ores had been mined since early times. If the hand cobbed and high-graded ore composed of copper sulfides intermixed with iron pyrite was fed directly to the smelting furnace, the extractive result would have been

---

[12]Agricola devotes book 8 to mineral dressing. This book has many excellent woodcuts showing entire families involved in hand picking the ore in medieval times. Other woodcuts show crushing and other steps used at that time.

very poor, giving a very low copper yield. Copper-sulfide-rich ores must first be roasted before smelting in order to produce economical yields.

The goal of a partially oxidizing roast of pyritic ore is to decrease the sulfur content and to oxidize the iron while retaining the copper in a sulfide form. During the roast, minerals such as pyrite (FeS_2) and chalcopyrite ($CuFeS_2$) are converted to chalcocite (Cu_2S) and wustite (FeO). There is great danger of overheating the roast pile, since iron-oxidizing reactions are highly exothermic. If the heating is not carefully controlled, the high temperatures will cause the roast pile to sinter and the copper to oxidize. Both the copper oxides and the sintered charge are extremely difficult to reduce to copper metal.

The roasting is usually performed in roast piles where the ore is mixed with brushwood. Once started with a small fire, the pile will continue to react because of the exothermic nature of the oxidizing reactions. The best treated piles are those that "burn" slowly for a month or so; the optimum time is a function of the size of the pile.

The roasted ore is either crushed and fed directly into the smelting furnace, or crushed and mixed with a flux to form the furnace charge. Even at this point the charge, when heated to a high temperature, will not smelt directly to copper metal. Instead the copper-sulfide phase will separate from the iron oxide by sinking to the bottom of the furnace to form what is known as copper matte. This matte must be recrushed to form what is known as copper matte. This matte must be recrushed and resmelted to gain impure copper metal (black copper). A flow diagram for the processing of sulfide-rich ore into copper metal is presented in figure 11.

We have searched carefully both in and near many slag piles on Cyprus for samples of copper matte. Any suspicious fragment was collected and analyzed in the laboratory, but in each case the result was negative. We have also asked at the mines for such fragments as might have been found. While copper ingots have been found (as well as copper fragments), there is no record of any copper matte.

In 1975 we had a chance to visit the Rio Tinto Mines in Spain. Here, too, we searched the enormous slag piles left by ancient smelting for matte, and made special searches near what appeared to be the remains of ancient furnaces. The result of this search was the same as on Cyprus; no matte or tuyeres were found.[13]

While observing the modern ore processing at the Rio Tinto we began to wonder whether sulfide ores might not have been processed into metallic copper without matte formation. Almost all of the slags examined on Cyprus contain metallic copper prills and strongly suggest that the goal of smelting was to gain impure copper directly rather than a copper matte. This being the case, a closer examination of the Rio Tinto processes is warranted.

For a long time the Rio Tinto massive sulfide ore has been processed by hydrometallurgical methods prior to smelting.[14] While only five percent of the copper ore in the United States is now processed by this method, hydrometallurgy is receiving renewed study because of its low pollution and low fuel consumption.

---

[13]Samples thought to be copper matte have proven to be oxidized copper fragments.

[14]According to D. Williams (1934), Rio Tinto, Spain, has been using the leaching process since at least the 1750s. Ancient mine practices are also discussed in M. L. De Launay, Mémoire sur l'industrie du cuivre dans la region d'Huelva, Annales de Mines 16 (1889):427-515. C. Smith reports that recovery of metallic copper from cupriferous mine waters by a cementation with iron was done on a commercial scale in central Europe from the sixteenth century on (The Beginnings of Industrial Electrochemistry, History of Electrochemistry, ed. G. Dubberrell and J. H. Westbrook [New York: Electrochemical Society, 1978], pp. 360-99).

The primary hydrometallurgical process is the leaching of the ore. The ore is stacked on an impervious drainage floor and wetted with a leaching agent or water. The heap is allowed to react for many months. With pyrite-rich ores such as those found on Cyprus and Rio Tinto, the oxidation of the pyrite produces both sulfuric acid and iron sulfates. The combination of ferric sulfate and sulfuric acid produces one of the most corrosive solutions known, and readily attacks other minerals in the ore. Much of the iron in the leach pile is converted into red iron oxides, but most of the other elements are carried away in the solutions that drain from under the pile.

At Rio Tinto the leach solutions from many piles are directed to a dammed river valley where the leach water slowly flows through wooden troughs filled with scrap iron. The copper ions in the solution react with the iron metal, and by an exchange reaction copper metal is precipitated and iron ions are released. This exchange process to produce impure metallic copper is known as cementation (pl. 6a). The copper produced is usually about 70 percent pure and is mixed mainly with iron oxides.[15]

The iron solution that passes through the scrap-iron pile slowly hydrolyzes into iron oxides and forms a fine red precipitate downstream for many miles. It is not unlikely that the flow of such solutions in the past led to the naming of the Rio Tinto River.

While copper cementation can be practiced profitably today because scrap iron is both abundant and inexpensive, this was not the case in medieval times. Both Agricola (1556, book 12) and Biringuccio (1540, chap. 5) reported in detail how to prepare copper vitriol from leach solutions. Lusignano (1580) told of the Venetians shipping both gold and copper vitriol to Venice from Cyprus even after the Turkish conquest; thus Biringuccio's account of the Venetian practices probably describes the way vitriol was actually produced on Cyprus at this time. Biringuccio wrote:

> After you have excavated and sorted out the quantity you wish, the ore must be put in a heap in open airy places before vitriol can be extracted from this soil or ore, however you wish to call it. And it is left thus exposed to the weathering of the rains, the cold, and the sun for five or six months. It must be turned several times in order to bring to the surface that which was underneath; and always when this is done it is broken small with the eye of a mattock, so that it is better heated and baked throughout. When it has been brought to this point it is covered over by a shed built above it or it is carried under a hut that has already been made. Here it is left to stand for another six or eight months before it is worked (p. 95).[16]

The description goes on to tell how the ore was first washed in a large wooden bath, then allowed to settle and the solution decanted off. The solution was then concentrated by heating in large vats until it began to congeal. Finally the thickened salt solution was poured off and allowed to solidify in loaves, which were used in commerce. The fourth method of making vitriol described by Agricola was so similar to the above that one might assume he had read Biringuccio or visited the same plants.

Agricola tells of an additional method, in which crushed ore was placed on the floor of the mine during rainy seasons to give dry footing to the miners. The mine drainage washed through the ore and broke it down. During the dry season this ore from the mine floor was gathered and vitriol was made from it by the process described above. Alum (called alumen in

---

[15] Both Agricola and Biringuccio said the pile must be put "under roof" for six to eight months. Perhaps it was placed in a man-made cavern rather than a hut.

[16] This same process has also been practiced on Cyprus, where mine drainage water is passed through scrap iron to form copper by cementation. Hills (1928a, b) reported 2,000 lbs of 65% copper produced each month. In 1966 the production of cement copper had increased to 14,545 tons (60% Cu) per year (Stavrinou 1970:6).

early works) was also made by leaching pyritic ores in a process similar to that for making vitriol, but with additional processing steps to separate these salts.

The solidified vitriol salt formed by this process would be an impure crystallized sulfate containing iron, sodium, magnesium, copper, and other elements. This vitriol could be smelted directly with charcoal to form impure copper metal, with no intermediate step of matte formation. The flow chart for the hydrometallurgical treatment of copper ore is shown in figure 12.

A careful examination of the area near the ancient mines and smelting areas would probably disclose evidence that a hydrometallurgical process was practiced in ancient times. Bruce (1949:10) provides some evidence that might suggest a leaching process was being used:

> Close investigation of some of the most promising outcrops [ore-bearing surface exposures] demonstrated that they were artificial. An interesting example of this at Mavrovouni mine was a very puzzling iron gossan "outcrop" on the ridge of a hill which appeared to consist principally of Pleistocene clay. . . . Further study led to the conclusion that the outcrop, which covered an area of something like an acre, was actually the thoroughly oxidized remains of a Roman or Phoenician stock pile of pyrite ore, or of low-grade material cobbled off and rejected before smelting. This was several hundred feet from smelter slag heaps.

It is very unlikely that Bruce was correct in concluding that this "outcrop" was a stockpile, for he has already pointed out that ore can not be stockpiled in uncovered piles because it oxidizes very rapidly at the surface and loses its copper values through leaching. It is more likely that what Bruce has described is a large ancient leach pile. He also states (1937):

> At several other points on the island [Cyprus] I have observed superficial iron oxide deposits and the staining of pillow lavas, together with slight indications of oxidized copper, beneath which have been found ancient galleries showing no evidence of having produced commercial ores. In two places beneath iron stained outcroppings we have discovered uniform sized pieces of unmineralized stone forming a porous bed having a large percentage of voids. The pieces have been cemented together by iron oxides carried down from the overlying [man-made] "outcropping" (p. 648).

The above descriptions could easily be those of leach piles. A sketch is offered in figure 13 to show our interpretation of the relations described.

Bruce describes another man-made outcrop: "Subsequent investigation, however, disclosed that there had been ancient galleries in the sedimentary formation running only a few feet beneath the 'outcrop' (ibid.)." Figure 14 is a sketch to illustrate what Bruce is describing.

At the Skouriotissa Mine, near a large ancient cavern entrance to the underground galleries, Bruce found thousands of broken pithoi or amphorae (ibid., p. 663; also a photograph of the pottery dump).[17] A possible use of these pithoi is shown in figure 14. The figure illustrates the use of the pithoi to collect the leach solutions and then to transfer the solutions to the thickening vats.

---

[17]There has been a great deal of speculation about why the ancient miners would have needed so many large pithoi at the mines. Lavender (1962:351) offers the following story:

> More famous was Stebbings' theory about the source of the huge pottery dump. Mixed with the shards he found numerous small black objects that he decided were olive pits. From this he concluded that the slaves had used the amphorae for carrying their lunches into the mines. Tim Sides, who recognized the "pits," suggested that Stebbings bite into a few to see if they tasted like olives. The Englishman found them very bitter and of a flavor he could not pin down. They were dry sheep droppings. Within days the story spread throughout Cyprus.

The field evidence one might expect to find, to indicate ancient use of the leaching process, would be remnant leach piles. It should be noted that roast piles would not be found, since the roasted ore is used in smelting. Through their mapping activities geologists have found outcrops similar to those Bruce described and have called them "false gossans" without recognizing their purpose.

Adamides (1978) mapped a group of "false gossans" in the Kalavasos mining district (pl. 7). In the summer of 1978 these man-made leach piles were examined by us and only medieval sherds were found associated with them. The copper had long ago leached out of these piles and thus they remain as stratified layers of coarse gossan very similar to the piles described by Bruce. There was field evidence to suggest that leach piles had been constructed closer to the mines, but in most cases the leach piles have been disturbed and covered with the spoil piles formed during modern open-pit mining.

In summary, this section has presented evidence concerning the ancient methods of pretreating copper ore before smelting. The following points have been stressed:

a) Copper sulfide ore was not roasted but was treated by hydrometallurgical processing.
b) Heap leaching in the Mediterranean climate is a rapid and efficient means of concentrating copper into a product that allows direct smelting to impure metallic copper.
c) The record of ancient heap leaching is found in numerous ancient leach piles called "false gossans."
d) The large ancient cavern-type gallery with associated abundant amphora sherds was involved in the processing of leach solutions.

Part 4. THE CASE FOR ANCIENT CYPRIOT HYDRO-METALLURGICAL PRACTICES

Previous investigators of the Cypriot slag and mining areas have been misled by the preconception that the ancient technology treated the ore prior to smelting through a series of processes that included roasting (summarized in the flow chart, fig. 11). This supposed manifold operation would have required a great deal of manpower for mining, hauling, crushing, grinding, preparation of charcoal, and other operations. One would therefore expect that large living and working areas would be found close to the mines and slag heaps, which in most cases are in close proximity to each other. Thus in the field we examined not only the slag heaps but also the surrounding area.

A series of inconsistencies was discovered as we attempted to reconcile our observations at the mines with the notion that the sulfide ores were mined and roasted previous to smelting. In view of these apparent contradictions, a few of which are summarized in table 2, we sought possible alternative processes for treating sulfide ores that would explain the data better.

The hydrometallurgical process of treating the ore offers a simple alternative. The advantages of this process are outlined below:

1) All ore mined (massive sulfide, enriched secondary sulfides, and oxidized ores) can be leached.
2) The ore does not have to be hand cobbed or finely ground before being placed in the leach pile. The ore is used just as it comes from the mine. Thus grinding equipment is not needed and no waste piles are created.
3) There is no danger of pile spoilage in leaching, such as might occur by overroasting.
4) Collection of leachate requires very simple equipment, often only amphorae.
5) The impure thickened sulfate salt can be smelted directly to impure metallic copper, or the salt can be further processed to separate white vitriol (aluminum-

rich sulphate), green vitriol (iron-rich sulphate), and blue vitriol (copper-rich sulphate). These salts form important commercial products.

6) The whole process of mining and leaching can be operated on a small scale at a small mine. The solidified sulfate salt can be transported easily to a smelting site.
7) Less charcoal is needed to smelt a sulfate salt than would be needed to smelt roasted copper ore.
8) There would be no failures in the smelting process since the copper sulfate decomposes at a relatively low temperature (approximately 750° C). A spongy copper mass[18] is formed if the temperature is not high enough (above 1083° C) to form a copper ingot. This spongy copper could be processed to gain a mass of copper in the same manner as that used to manufacture wrought iron.

Table 2. Contradictions between Current Metallurgical Concepts and Field Observations

Current concept	Field observation
1. Sulfide ores must be passed through a complex metallurgical process involving roasting and matte smelting to obtain impure copper metal. This process may have been beyond the ability of ancient technology until at least Roman times.	1. Pre-Roman mining extracted sulfide-rich ores for copper production purposes.
2. Ancient furnaces cannot reach high enough temperatures (without the use of tuyeres) to smelt sulfide ores.	2. No tuyeres have been found in or near slag heaps, yet a great deal of copper was smelted.
3. Sulfide ores will smelt only if crushed and roasted. The roasted product must be finely ground and mixed with a flux before smelting.	3. No areas of crushing and grinding equipment have been found. Instead, areas of abundant amphora sherds have been noted.
4. The smelting of roasted sulfide ore should produce abundant copper matte.[a]	4. No copper matte has been discovered, but planoconvex metal copper ingots have been found. Slags contain abundant copper prills suggesting smelting to metallic copper.
5. Oxidized sulfide ore should be found in association with furnaces and slag heaps, because of spillage and preparation of the charge.	5. Slag heaps and furnace areas are notably free of oxidized sulfide ore.

[a]In part 1 it was noted that the iron-rich slag types would not permit matte to separate readily; thus pre-Roman slags could not have used roasted sulfide ore efficiently.

[18]Impure metallic copper dispersed through charcoal and iron-rich material. The copper would be somewhat ductile and the other impurities brittle, so that a separation could be made by crushing.

The impure solidified leachate from the leach piles might be expected to form the blue green mineral called pisanite (a Cu-rich melanterite), $(Fe,Cu)SO_4 \cdot 7H_2O$. Solidified purified blue vitriol is known chemically today as copper sulfate pentahydrate ($CuSO_4 \cdot 5H_2O$). This material occasionally forms in nature by the evaporation of mine water or from sulfating copper sulfide minerals; the material is fairly abundant in the Skouriotissa Mine. The modern mineral name is chalcanthite.[19] Some of the physical properties of this mineral are summarized in table 3. It is unlikely that these minerals were differentiated in ancient times. Probably any blue green sulfate mineral was called blue vitriol.

In medieval times the soluble sulfates had many commercial uses and served as important medicines (see table 3). Both Pliny and Dioscorides mention the use of copper sulfate salts as medicines in Roman times, but the most interesting record is that of the visit of Galen of Pergamon to the Cyprus mines to collect medicines.

The physician Galen of Pergamon made several visits to Cyprus during his lifetime; the visit described in his preserved writings was made about 166 A.D. The purpose of the visit was to study the flora and minerals and to acquire the celebrated copper and iron salts, since these were the finest available. (Galen also believed these were the first copper mines in the world to be operated.) Galen carried away enough material to last him more than thirty years.

Copper sulfate is the basic starting chemical for making many other industrial chemicals. The sulfates would prove a suitable coloring agent for blue and green glass frit and faience. These compounds impart a strong blue green color to flames.

Since Galen was a friend of the supervisor of mines on Cyprus, he had little trouble arranging for a personally escorted tour of the Soli mines. From Galen's description of the three mines he visited, Seeley Mudd[20] (Walsh 1929:107) had little difficulty recognizing two of the mines as those at Skouriotissa and Mavrovouni. The location of the third mine is still uncertain.

Galen describes the mine believed to be at Skouriotissa as follows:

There was a large low house sheltering the ingress into the mine. It was dug into the hill like a cave, in width so that three men touched, in height so that the tallest could walk upright, and on a slight incline. At the bottom, about 600 feet from the entrance, there was a lake of tepid, thick, green, greasy water. Throughout the descent the temperature was about the same as that in the first room of the bath ordinarily called the promalacterion.
   The water dripping from the porous hill drop by drop is collected throughout the twenty-four hours in Roman amphorae. Slaves carried it out and poured it into square earthenware troughs located at the entrance of the house, where after a few days it thickened and chalcanthos was made. At the bottom of the mine the brassy odor is suffocating, and is tolerated with difficulty. The water has a similar taste. The nude slaves carried the jars with the greatest haste in order not to remain long in the mine. There were lights at moderate intervals, but they extinguished frequently. The mine was excavated little by little by the slaves over many years. When the dripping water begins to lessen the slaves dig further into the hill (Walsh 1929:103-4).

---

[19]Bruce (1949) states that brochantite, $Cu_4(SO_4)(OH)_6$, first forms when copper sulfides are sulfated; in time brochantite converts to chalcanthite.

[20]Colonel Seeley Wintersmith Mudd and Philip Wiseman, both mining engineers, founded the Cyprus Mines Corporation. Colonel Mudd was the first president of the corporation.

Table 3. Nature and Properties of Blue Vitriol,* $CuSO_4 \cdot 5H_2O$

Mineral:	chalcanthite	pisanite (Cu-melanterite)
Formula:	$CuSO_4 \cdot 5H_2O$	$(Fe,Cu)SO_4 \cdot 7H_2O$
Color:	sky blue	bluish green

Both minerals form prismatic crystals, less commonly tabular crystals, also found as stalactites, reniform, massive.

Both minerals are members of hydration series:

750° C
$CuSO_4$ —chalcocyanite $FeSO_4$

258° C
$CuSO_4 \cdot 3H_2O$ —poitevinite $(Fe,Cu)SO_4 \cdot 7H_2O$
  —Cu-szomolnokite

177° C
$CuSO_4 \cdot 3H_2O$ —bonattite $(FeSO_4 \cdot 4H_2O$
  —rozenite)

105° C
$CuSO_4 \cdot 5H_2O$ —chalcanthite $(Fe,Cu)SO_4 \cdot 5H_2O$
  —sidotile
  $(FeSO_4 \cdot 6H_2O$
  —ferrohexahydrate

$(CuSO_4 \cdot 7H_2O$ —boothite) $(Fe,Cu)SO_4 \cdot 7H_2O$
  —pisanite
  $Fe_2(SO_4)_3 \cdot 7H_2O$
  —kornelite

(Higher ferric hydrates include quenstedtite, coquimbite, roemerite, and bilinite, but these rapidly dehydrate to melanterite.)

*It is very likely that several modern mineral species were referred to by ancient writers as "blue vitriol" or atramentum sutorium caeruleum, which had water soluble and astringent qualities. "There is no substance of an equally miraculous nature"; description of blue chalcanthum by Pliny (Natural History 34. 32).

Agricola (1546) reports the following uses: Dissolved in water, used to dye hides and wool; also used to dye hair and blacken beards. The dense blue heavy transparent variety is preferred for medicines because it is the most astringent and will heal the body most. If sprinkled on a severed vein it will check profuse bleeding. It expels pus from ulcers and dries excrement. When mixed with honey and wine (or olive oil) and taken internally, it acts as an emetic. The white variety (Mg-Zn) is used in eye salves. Bates (1954) reports that copper sulfate is still commonly used as an insecticide, a weed killer, a bactericide (0.1 ppm destroys algae growth), and a fungicide. It was used much more frequently in the past, but is now being replaced by more powerful and selective chemicals.

Table 4. Interpretation of Ancient Mineralogy Based on
Agricola's *De Natura Fossilium* (1546)

All of the following are water soluble; all are astringent and acrid; all have a natural odor (like that after a bolt of lightning); all may be light and porous and usually occur in rounded masses.

The first four materials are found only as natural minerals, while the fifth is found both as a mineral and in artificial form.

---

misy	yellow golden	forms as an efflorescence on all of the minerals listed below; most tenuous; may be dust; sometimes massive
chalcitis	red or copper colored (Pliny says honey colored)	intermediate properties; sometimes massive
sory	gray when dried, often black when wet	smells more like melanteria; may be hard as stone; porous
melanteria	same color as sory	often foamlike, like plant down; has slightly salty taste
atramentum: sutorium (transparent variety called vitriolum)	various colors, commonly pale to deep green or blue, rarely white	forms naturally as hairs, fibers, or icicles, or as crystals in grapelike bunches

---

M. C. Bandy and J. A. Bandy, who translated the above book, are well-known mineralogists. They have offered the following modern equivalents, on the basis of minerals in the Harz District that would have been available to Agricola:

misy	copiapite $Fe_5(SO_4)_6(OH)_2 \cdot 20H_2O$
	metavoltine $(K,Na,Fe)_5Fe_3(SO_4)_6(OH) \cdot 7H_2O$
chalcitis	romerite $(Fe,Cu)_3(SO_4)_4 \cdot 14H_2O$
	botryogen $MgFe(SO_4)_2(OH) \cdot 7H_2O$
sory	melanterite with $(Fe,Cu,Zn)SO_4 \cdot 7H_2O$
	fine pyrite FeS_2
melanteria	melanterite $(Fe,Cu)SO_4 \cdot 7H_2O$
atramentum: sutorium caeruleum*	chalcanthite $CuSO_4 \cdot 5H_2O$
atramentum sutorium candidum	goslarite $ZnSO_4 \cdot 7H_2O$
atramentum sutorium virida	melanterite $FeSO_4 \cdot 7H_2O$

---

*Also known as blue vitriol or chalcanthum.

At the time of Galen's visit there were no ore-smelting furnaces operating. Galen wished for some volatile material, so a furnace was set up for the purpose. This suggests that during the wet season most of the effort was probably directed toward gathering the copper water and that smelting was done at another season.

Galen describes one place in the Skouriotissa Mine where he collected samples from three layers--the lowest of sory, the next of chalcitis, and the highest of misy. When he examined some of the chalcitis twenty years later it had formed an excrustation of misy (32. 226). Galen also mentions that after twenty years the chalcanthos he collected had changed on the outside to chalcitis.

The misy, chalcitis, sory, and chalcanthos are all caustic and astringent. If Galen's observations are correct, the misy, chalcitis, and chalcanthos are all water soluble.

The interpretation of these minerals--misy, chalcitis, and sory--has caused much difficulty because in the past interpreters were not familiar with the mineralogy of the secondary enrichment zones that developed over massive sulfide mines in the Mediterranean climate. A possible modern interpretation that is based on descriptions of the minerals given by Agricola (1556) is presented in table 4. Minor changes in the list would probably be made if someone were to carry out a modern study of the mineralogy of Cypriot mines.

Ancient accounts of metallurgical processes suffered greatly because the writers lacked the technical vocabulary to describe their observations. Where an ancient writer does use a technical term, it is often difficult to translate accurately. A greater difficulty that has hampered the usefulness of the ancient reports has been a lack of knowledge on the part of translators not only of the technology but also of the geography, climate, and geology of the regions under consideration. Thus a translator has often used a poor equivalent. Or, even worse, the translator has concluded that the ancient writer had made a mistake, and has substituted his own ill-formed concept for the actual historical description.

As we have said, chalcitis is a soluble astringent salt. It is now almost universally agreed that this is an impure iron and copper sulfate, and that "chalcanthon" is a purified copper sulfate. Assuming this interpretation to be correct, the following ancient authors tell us about the early practice of hydrometallurgy:

Aristotle:	Copper is made from chalcitis on Cyprus (*Historia Animalium* 5. 19. 55. 2b. 10-13).
Poseidonius:	The copper of Cyprus is the only copper which produces calamine and chalcanthum and spodium (Strabo, *Geography* 15. 3-4).
Strabo:	At Tamassos there are abundant mines of copper in which is found chalcanthum and also the flowers of copper (Strabo, *Geography* 14. 6-5).
Dioscorides:	Chalcanthum appears as a concretion of liquids that filter drop by drop through the roof of mines. It is for this reason called "stalacton" by those who work in the mines of Cyprus (*De Materia Medica* 5. 98).
Pliny:	Chalcitis is the name given to another mineral from which copper is extracted by heat on Cyprus (*Natural Hist.* 33. 98).

A very unusual statement about the mines is credited to Aristotle:

> In Cyprus copper (χαλκός) is cut into small pieces and sown in the ground, when the rain comes it grows and puts out shoots (αὐξάνεται) and is collected (*On Marvellous Things Heard*, Hett, 43. 833 a-b).

As the statement stands it makes little sense. But if one word, "ore," is added, or if can mean "copper ore," the statement becomes a beautiful nontechnical description of the leaching processes at the mines. Almost anyone with a nontechnical vocabulary would probably describe the growth of the sulfates on the ores in much the same manner: "In Cyprus copper ore is broken into small pieces and placed on the ground; when it rains it grows and puts out shoots and is collected."

Various sulfate minerals seem to grow on the ore like new grass after a rain. These are tiny hairlike crystals at first; after a time they grow into coatings or crusts. Pliny describes chalcitis as resembling matted wool (*Natural History* 34. 117-23). Many different sulfates can grow; thus Pliny describes trichitis (hairy alum): "This is produced from the same ore as copper known as chalcitis. A sort of sweat from that mineral coagulated in foam" (ibid., 52. 186).

The above can be interpreted only to mean that copper ores were being leached and that leach products were being collected in Hellenistic times.

A very puzzling statement by Aristotle has aroused a great deal of discussion, and books have been written concerning it. To us, however, it seems very enlightening:

ἐν δὲ Κύπρῳ, οὗ ἡ χαλκῖτις λίθος καίεται, ἐπὶ πολλὰς ἡμέρας ἐμβαλλόντων, ἐνταῦθα γίγνεται θηρία ἐν τῷ πυρί, τῶν μεγάλων μυιῶν μικρόν τι μείζονα, ὑπόπτερα, ἃ διὰ τοῦ πυρὸς πηδᾷ καὶ βαδίζει.

> In Cyprus, where copper ore is smelted and the ore is piled on the furnace for many successive days, certain creatures are engendered in the fire, slightly larger than flies, and winged, these jump and crawl through the fire.
>
> Source: (*Historia Animalium* 5. 19. 55. 2b. 10-13).

A better translation might be:

> In Cyprus where chalcitis stone is burned and piled up for many successive days, certain creatures are engendered in the fire, slightly larger than flies and winged: these jump and crawl through the fire.

This unusual statement has always caused confusion, but it clearly cannot refer to copper smelting, which would not take many days. Furthermore, in smelting, the ore is not piled. Thus the statement must refer to either a roast pile or a leaching heap. It was and still is common practice in Rio Tinto to cover the pile or heap of coarse ore with an outside layer of finely crushed ore or earth. This outside coating is necessary to control the temperature of the heap, since the ore reacts spontaneously with oxygen and the exothermic reaction generates a great deal of heat--enough heat to cause spontaneous combustion of the pile. Spontaneous combustion must be avoided because it would cause oxidation of the copper minerals to oxides, which would make them nearly impossible to smelt to copper metal. In roasting, the pile must be kept below 700° C, and in leaching the pile should be kept below 100° C.

Since the pile operates for "many successive days" (actually a matter of months), it is not unlikely that the eggs of many insects (especially flies) would hatch out of season in the dirt covering the pile or ore. In the cold winter months a leach pile would give off steam and appear to be burning when the insects were emerging. During these cold months the insects would perish if they left the pile; they would thus remain near it and even crawl back into it. A roast pile, however, would probably operate at too high a temperature, kill the insect eggs, and thus not behave this way. In either case (leaching or roasting), the phenomenon described would be evidence that there had been sulfide-rich ores under treatment in pre-Roman times.

In Egypt the tablets listing tribute paid to Tutmose III include copper associated with "blue stone" that Breasted consistently interpreted as lapis lazuli. We suggest that the "blue stone" may actually have been blue vitriol, which would have been a logical and valuable gift. If such an interpretation is valid, it suggests that hydrometallurgical practices at the mines started very early.

One more speculation we might offer is that Neolithic and Chalcolithic peoples visited gossans to gather soft hematite for pigment. They would occasionally gather the blue and green sulfate minerals. It should not have taken them long to discover the medicinal qualities of these minerals and the ability of these minerals to produce a brilliant blue green flame. If these sulfates were often thrown into ceremonial fires, occasional beads or fragments of spongy copper would have resulted. One wonders whether this might have been the start of copper smelting.

Part 5. THE EFFECTS OF HYDROMETALLURGY ON THE CHEMICAL COMPOSITION OF SLAG

If sulfide ores were processed by ancient technicians by either roasting or leaching, the bulk composition of the smelting slag would probably be the same since in either case the best results would be gained by obtaining minimum melting compositions (fig. 3). The major differences caused by the presmelting treatment would appear in the minor and trace-element composition of the smelting slag.

An effective oxidizing roast of sulfide ores requires, on the one hand, that the temperature be kept below the point at which copper oxides form or where the roast charge sinters, but, on the other hand, that the temperature still be high enough to allow breakdown of pyrite to form iron oxides. Extensive studies indicate that the best temperature range is 540 to 620° C. Important reactions in the roasting process are:

a) above 200° C: Pyrite (FeS_2) begins to oxidize;
b) 250-290° C: $FeS_2 + 3O_2 \rightarrow FeSO_4 + SO_2 \uparrow$;
c) 290-500° C: $4FeS_2 + 11O_2 \rightarrow Fe_2O_3 + 8SO_2 \uparrow$;
d) 500-600° C: $FeS_2 + 5Fe_2O_3 \rightarrow 11FeO + SO_2 \uparrow$;
e) above 750° C: The charge sinters and is difficult to melt.

The roasting of the ore at the optimum temperatures only slightly enriches the final charge because of the loss of volatiles. Not only will sulfur be lost as a volatile gas but volatile elements such as arsenic, antimony, and selenium will also be removed. The original ratio among various nonvolatile metals should remain essentially that of the ore.

The above roasting reactions are all exothermic, and great care must be taken to control the roasting temperature so the piles do not overheat. If such a roasting process was used in ancient times, occasional overroasted piles should be found, but correctly roasted piles would not be found, because the charge would have been consumed in smelting.

Normally roasting is performed in heaps that are allowed to "burn" for several months. Ideally, pyrite (FeS_2), chalcopyrite ($CuFeS_2$), and bornite (Cu_5FeS_4) are converted in the roast pile to a porous, weakly consolidated mixture of wustite (FeO) and "chalcocite" (Cu_2S). This mixture might be fed directly into the smelting furnace, but in most cases the roasted material would be pulverized and mixed with a flux to form the smelting charge.

This brief outline of the roasting process indicates that the smelting charge should not differ chemically from the ore except for those elements added as flux. The composition of a generalized Cypriot massive sulfide ore is given in table 5. Unfortunately very few trace-element data have been published for such ores.

If, prior to smelting, the sulfide ore had been processed by hydrometallurgy instead of roasting, one would expect that the minor-element composition would differ greatly from the composition of the original ore. This would result from the selective leaching of specific ions and the retention of volatiles in the low-temperature processing. The essential chemistry of the hydrometallurgical process explains what elements might become enriched in the smelting change and ultimately appear in the slags.

The heap leaching of the pyritic ore, as in roasting, is an exothermic oxidizing reaction, but the reactions take place in solution. The reactions should be similar to those that took place in nature to form the gossan and underlying natrojarosite-rich layers associated with the Devil's Mud. In nature the reaction is generally slow, since little mineral surface area is exposed to react, and reaction products that form on the mineral surfaces protect the internal mineral from further reaction (pl. 6b). In a crushed-ore pile a large amount of mineral surface will be exposed, and since the reaction generates a great deal of heat, great care must be taken to prevent the leach piles from "burning." If the crushed ore should catch fire, the results would be similar to roasting or overroasting.

The basic chemical reactions desired in the leach pile are:

a) $4FeS_2 + 14O_2 + 4H_2O \rightarrow 4FeSO_4 + 4H_2SO_4$
b) $CuFeS_2 + 4O_2 \rightarrow CuSO_4$
c) $4FeS_2 + 15O_2 + 2H_2O \rightarrow 2Fe_2(SO_4)_3 + 2H_2SO_4$

Table 5. Generalized Composition of Cypriot Massive Sulfide Ore*

Minerals	Percent
S	48.0 - 51.0
Fe	43.0 - 45.0
Cu	0.5 - 4.0
Zn	0.2 - 1.0
SiO_2	0.3 - 3.0
MgO	0.1 - 0.5
Al_2O_3	0.1 - 1.0
CaO	0.1 - 0.5
MnO	0.01 - 0.05
TiO_2	0.01 - 0.06

ppm		ppm	
As	100	Ni	20
Ba	150	P_2O_5	50
Cd	20	Pb	200
Co	40	Sb	100
Mo	50	Ag	10
		Au	3

*Median of reported values.

The amount of ferric sulfate (reaction c) is variable, but $CuSO_4$ in solution increases the rate of formation of ferric sulfate. In dilute solutions ferric sulfate is hydrolyzed to form hematite (Fe_2O_3) or goethite ($9Fe_2O_3 \cdot nH_2O$):

$$Fe_2(SO_4)_3 + 4H_2O \rightarrow Fe_2O_3\ H_2O + 3H_2SO_4$$

The ferric sulfate in sulfuric acid solution forms a powerful lixiviant that can react with most other minerals to cause solution of their contained metals, and thus most metal ions are mobilized.

The copper sulfate solution formed by leaching will react by an exchange reaction with most other sulfides:

$$CuSO_4 + ZnS \rightarrow ZnSO_4 + CuS$$
$$CuSO_4 + FeS \rightarrow FeSO_4 + CuS$$
$$CuSO_4 + PbS \rightarrow PbSO84 + CuS$$

The ferric sulfate present reacts to redissolve the copper sulfides:

$$CuS + Fe_2(SO_4)_3 \rightarrow CuSO_4 + FeSO_4 + S$$

Many of the leaching reactions performed under sterile conditions in the laboratory are extremely slow. It is a fairly recent discovery that the rates of these reactions are increased more than a hundredfold by specialized bacteria, aerobic bacteria called thiobacilli, whose metabolism is based on oxidation of sulfur or sulfide to sulfuric acid. These bacteria are ubiquitous and become established whenever the conditions are correct. Optimum conditions[21] require a warm moist environment with temperatures not exceeding 100° C. The bacterial activity in a leach pile is summarized in figure 15. The warm Mediterranean climate is ideal for bacterial activity during at least nine months of the year. Bacteria are known to be important in aiding the breakdown of the Rio Tinto ores in the leach area. The results in the leaching operations depend largely on the nature and purity of the ore. If pillow lava fragments are introduced with the ore, they will readily alter in the acid environment to free such elements as Mg, Na, and Al to the leachate. These elements are common in the waters of the mines. The calcium of the pillow lava precipitates as gypsum crystals, $CaSO_4 \cdot 2H_2O$; the silica forms chalcedony or jasper.

We believe that the ancient miners primarily excavated the secondary sulfide enrichment ores that were introduced into the leach piles. Such secondary ores will deviate greatly in composition from the primary massive sulfide ore now being mined, the composition of which is presented in table 5. Published analyses of these ores have not been found, since the ores are not mined separately. Judging from their mineralogy these enriched ores should contain from 4 to 30 percent Cu, with a median probably near 12 percent. Since these copper-rich ores form at the expense of the iron sulfides, the iron value is expected to be between 30 and 35 percent. The sulfur value should be 40 to 45 percent.

Estimating the trace-element content of the secondary enrichment ores is more difficult. The enrichment of some elements in these zones has been noted in the literature (fig. 16). Geologists have noted the similarity of the weathering of sulfide deposits to the formation of sedimentary uranium "roll front" deposits, and thus the element-enrichment pattern for these deposits is included in the same diagram. While the uranium, vanadium, and beryllium content of the massive sulfide ore is extremely low, and these are therefore not important elements even with enrichment, the case is different for molybdenum. On the basis of the uranium deposits it

---

[21] Optimum pyrite decay takes place at pH 1.8 but optimum pH for bacterial growth is 3.5. Ferric iron hydrolyzes at higher pH and forms ferric coatings on pyrite that suppress microbiological attack. Maximum bacterial growth takes place below 50° C (Malouf 1971).

might be expected that the molybdenum content of the top of the secondary sulfide-enrichment zone might be increased two to three times over that of the primary ore. Thus one might expect to find 200 to 300 ppm of molybdenum in the top of the secondary sulfide-enrichment zone.

Other elements expected to be enriched in these secondary sulfide ores are zinc and silver. The zinc content, probably appearing as the mineral sphalerite, should be in the 1 to 4 percent range, and silver in the 50 to 100 ppm range. A modern study of the secondary enrichment zones is needed to understand better the nature of the material the ancients introduced into the leaching pile.

Once the secondary sulfide-enrichment ore is mined and placed in a leaching pile, the enrichment cycle is repeated a second time, but now the mobile ions do not move downward to react with pyrite. The mobile ions are removed from the leach pile in solution. It is known from studies in other areas such as Rio Tinto, that zinc is one of the first ions to be mobilized and one of the most completely leached. Thus zinc should be enriched further in the leachate. The solution that exits from the piles will also contain copper and iron sulfates. Molybdenum, while still in the trace range, should be present in the leachate also.

We have mentioned that Na ions may be available from the breakdown of pillow lava.[22] It is also important to note that since all points on Cyprus are near the sea, the rainwater that falls on Cyprus contains sodium chloride. Recent leaching studies indicate that the addition in small quantities of sodium chloride to the leach pile greatly speeds the breakdown of sulfide minerals through the formation of natrojarosite at temperatures of about 70° C. The natrojarosite formed removes from the solution ions that normally form a protective coating and thereby inhibit the breakdown of pyrite and chalcopyrite. Thus the slight addition of sodium chloride increases the reaction rate. One can speculate that the ancient metallurgists may have discovered this through experience, and added halite, which is available on Cyprus.

If zinc were present in the original furnace charge, one would anticipate that it would be lost early in the smelting, and that it would escape as volatile zinc oxide (ancient pompholyx and spodos). Galen, Pliny, and Dioscorides mention that this material was collected for medicines above the copper smelting furnaces of Cyprus. Even though most of the zinc can be expected to escape, some would partition to the copper metal and some would substitute for iron in the fayalite of the slag.

It has also been suggested that molybdenum is enriched through leaching. This element would convert to a ferromolybdate early in smelting and thus would not be volatile. Molybdenum is unusual in that it has no affinity toward partitioning into the copper metal phase. Thus one might expect the total content of molybdenum to remain in the slag. Even if all of the molybdenum remains in the slag, one cannot predict its amount without knowing the amount of dilution of the charge created by the addition of fluxing agents. To reach minimum melting compositions, a silica-rich flux must be added to any charge that might be made from massive sulfide ores.

Zwicker, Grembler, and Röllig (1977:310) mention finding molybdenum as a trace element in several fragments of Enkomi slag, but state: "The origin of the ore which contains molybdenum could not yet be located." Dahl (1979) analyzed the heavier trace elements in 27 slag fragments from 22 different slag heaps and ancient cities on Cyprus, and 17 massive sulfide ore samples from 5 mines. Molybdenum was below his detection limit in all of the massive ore samples, but it was detected in more than half of the slag samples in the 30 to 300 ppm range. In this same study zinc was present in all of the ore samples, varying from 140 to 16,500 ppm. Zinc was in the detectable range in 22 of the 27 slag samples. It was absent in three high-

---

[22]The Cypriot pillow lavas are very low in potassium, and thus this element is not present to form jarosite, such as is found in Spain. Instead of jarosite, abundant natrojarosite forms on Cyprus.

manganese slags--one from Kokkinoya[23] and two Idalion crucible slags.[24] The zinc in the slags varied from 100 to 6100 ppm, with most of the slags in the range of 500 to 2000 ppm Zn.

Dahl also notes that strontium is detectable only in the high-manganese slags and thus must be contained in the manganese fluxing agent added to the charge, since it is not detectable in his ore analyses.

For the sake of brevity, discussion of trace-element enrichment has been limited in this paper to the two elements, molybdenum and zinc. Clearly Dahl's study suggests high enrichment factors for these two elements that are beyond the range that can be expected from roasting of Cypriot sulfide ores. The ancient hydrometallurgical processing of the ores prior to smelting provides a possible simple copper technology that would result in a direct smelting-furnace charge. Such a charge would be consistent with the slag chemistry.

---

[23] The Kokkinoya sample was a deeply weathered red Phoenician slag (type P) that was a surface find. It is possible that all the zinc had leached from it.

[24] The Idalion slags were crucible types (type C), and most probably were copper-refining slags.

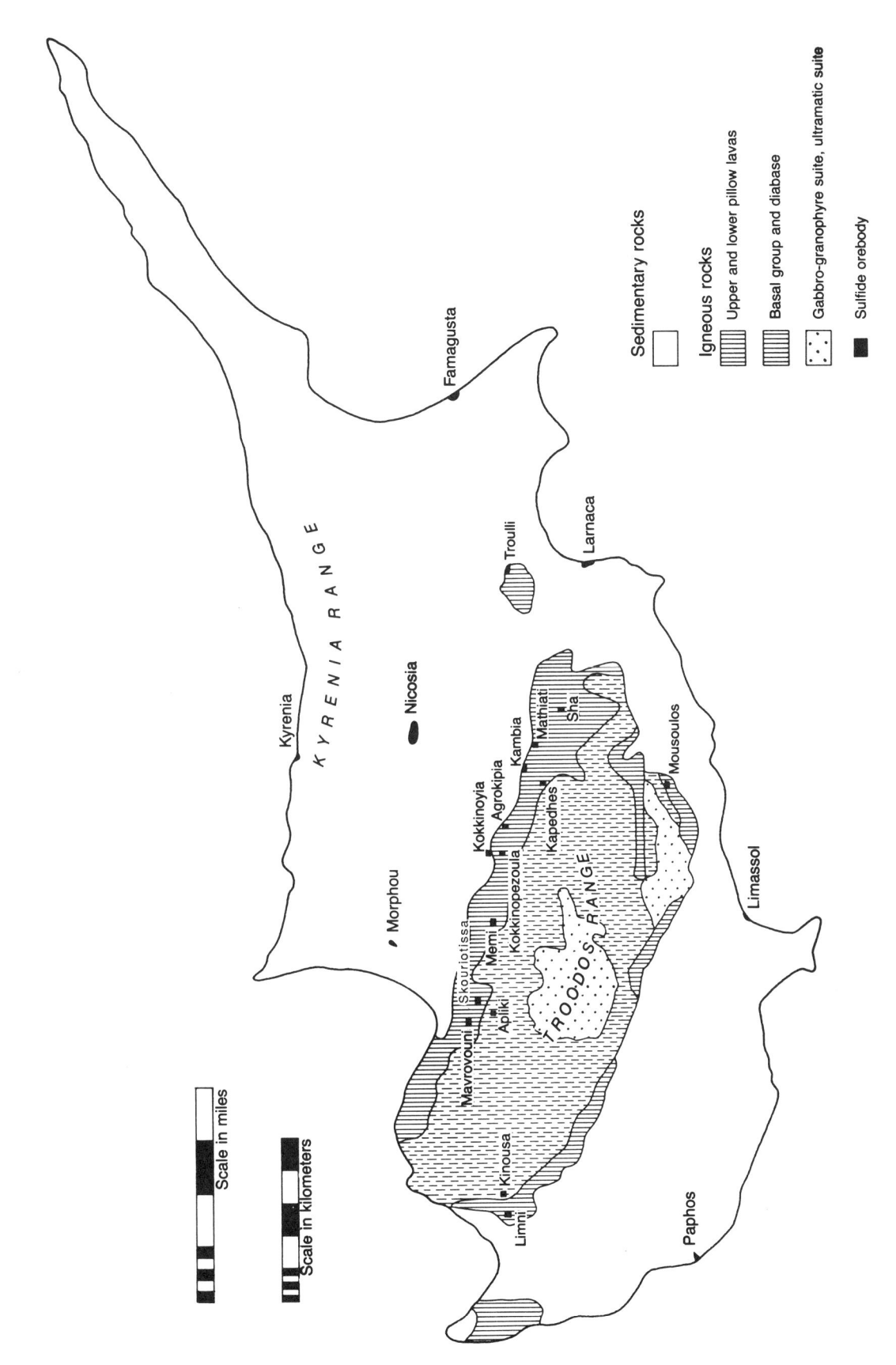

Figure 1. Mine Location Map for Cyprus.

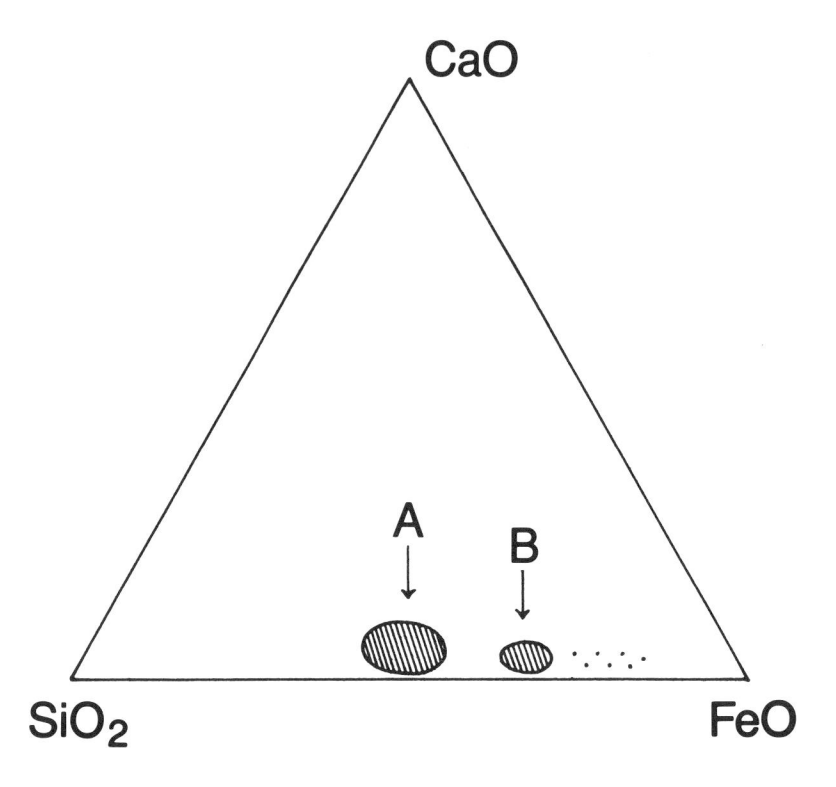

Figure 2. Bulk Analyses of Cypriot Slags (Cu metal excluded and system recalculated as a three-component system): Type A--Grouping of "Roman Slag" analyses; Type B--Grouping of "Roman" and "Phoenician" slag analyses; . . . . . --Isolated "Phoenician Slag" analyses. Slags with greater than 10% MnO excluded; lower MnO included in FeO (after Steinberg and Koucky 1974).

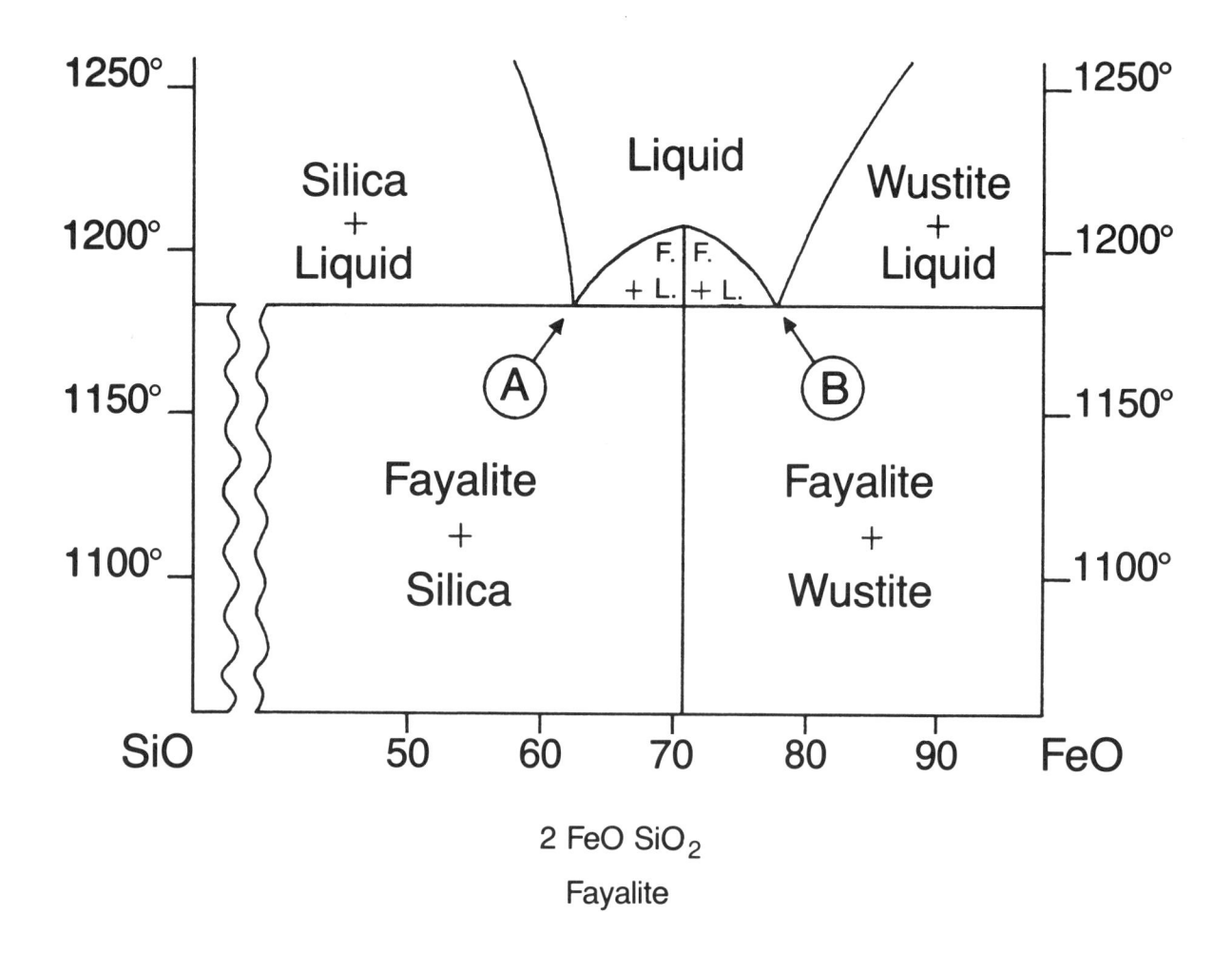

Figure 3. Temperature-composition Diagram for the System: SiO_2-FeO. Note the two compositional groupings of figure 2 cluster near the minimum melting compositions (eutectic temperatures) of this diagram (after Bowen and Schairer 1932).

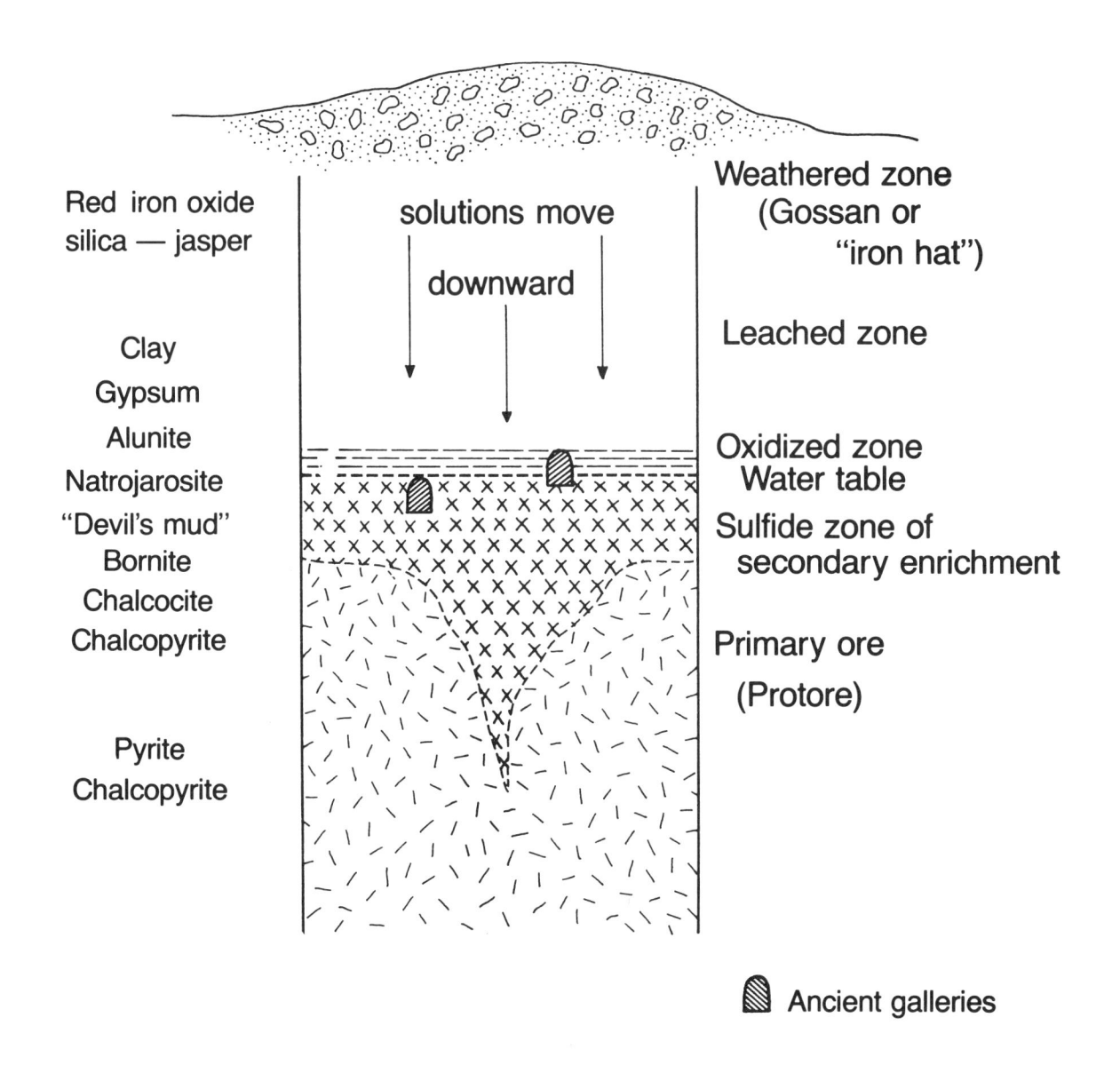

Figure 4. Diagram of Mineral Deposit Being Altered by Weathering. On Cyprus, the bright blue chalcanthite and the green brochantite tend to form in the secondary enrichment zones. These sulfate minerals are often mistaken for azurite and malachite, which are rare on Cyprus (modified from Healy 1977, p. 25).

	**Nodular shaped (N)** semi ovaloid Highly oxidized. Manganese concretions closely resemble this type of slag. "Votive" slags from Athienou
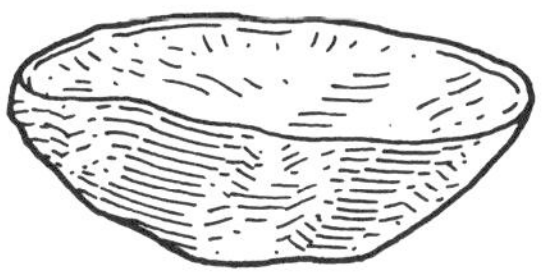	**Crucible shaped (C)** variable interior Many are heterogeneous, multicolored. Interior has charcoal impressions, Cu-prills, prills of Cu-sulfide. Surface oxidized, brown. Enkomi, Kition, Idalion
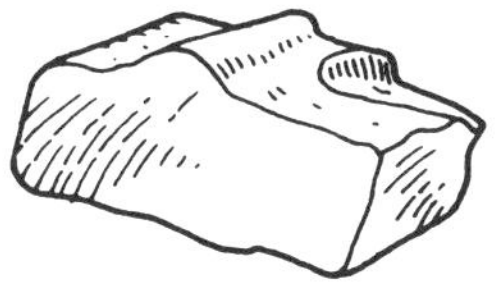 Flat surface with ridges and/or holes	**Highly oxidized blocky (P)** Red slags, formerly called "Phoenician". Interior usually dark brown. Skouriotissa, Platies, Kokkinoyia
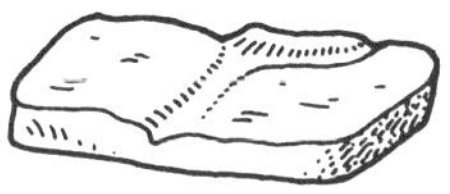 Flat with shallow v-indentations	**Slightly oxidized blocky (B)** Most fragments have flat surface. Exterior dark brown interior black. Similar to (P). Platies, Petra, Sha
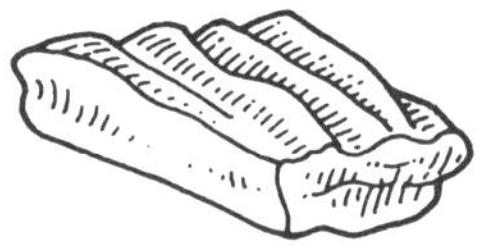	**Slightly oxidized ropy irregular-shaped (R)** Slightly oxidized surface, dull black. Interior black. Many fragments show stratification. Skouriotissa, S. Mathiati
	**Nonoxidized collapsed ropy Mn-rich (M)** Fresh, nearly unaltered. Silver black color. Surface flow structure subdued compared to (R) type. Surface often knobby. Spilli, Teredhia, Skouriotissa
	**Glassy blocky conchoidal fracture (G)** Black, resembles obsidian. Gray weathered surface. S. Mathiati

Figure 5. Classification of Cypriot Slags. Type (P) was previously called "Phoenician," and types (B), (R), (M), and (G) were called "Roman."

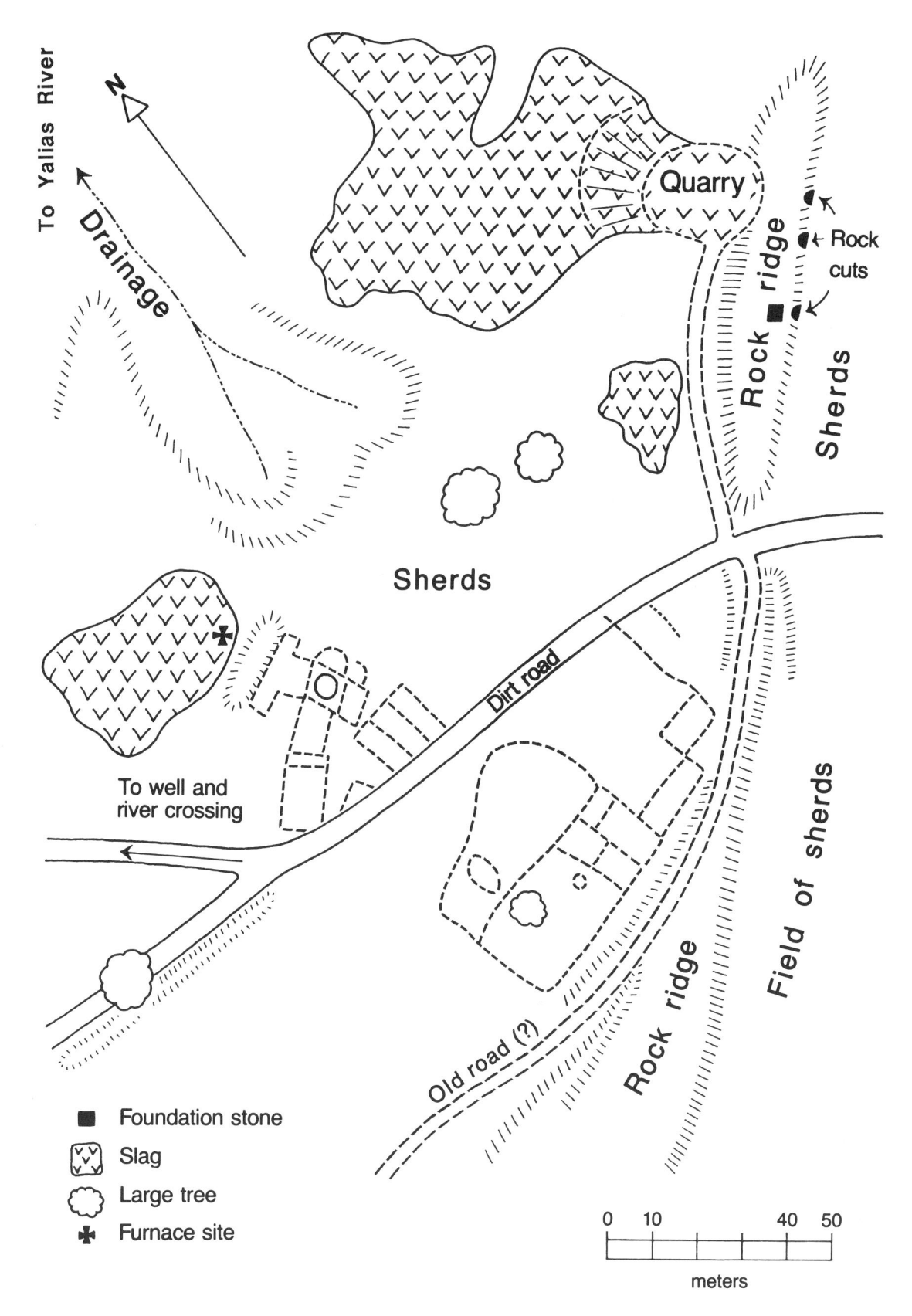

Figure 6. Map of Teredhia Area (after Koucky and Yarus 1973).

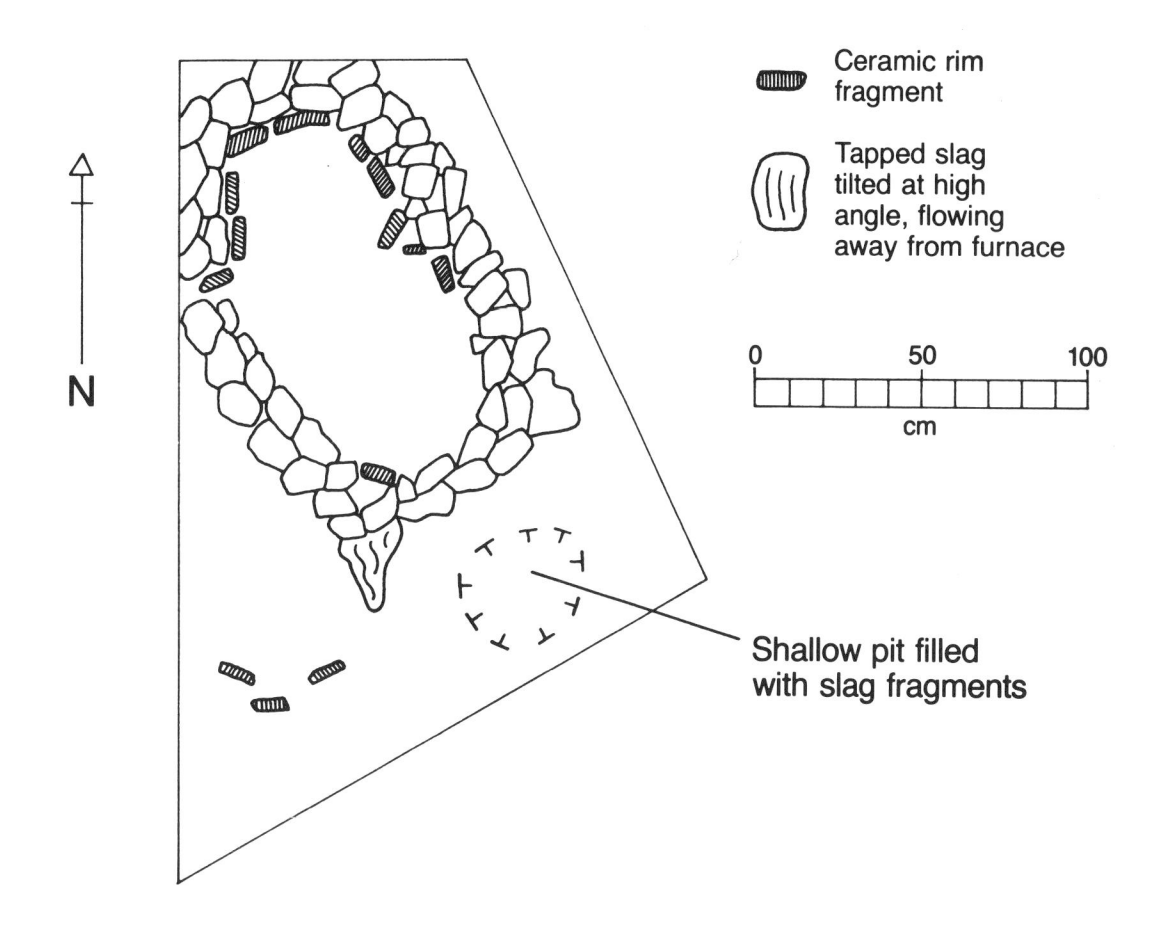

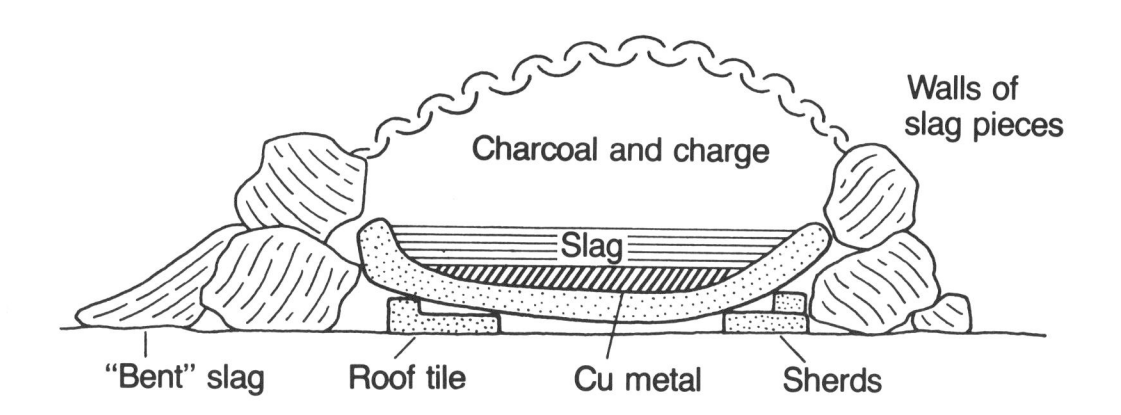

Figure 7. The Teredhia Furnace. At the top is a plan of the furnace excavated in area SW-1/1 at Teredhia. The lower sketch is a reconstruction of the copper-smelting furnace.

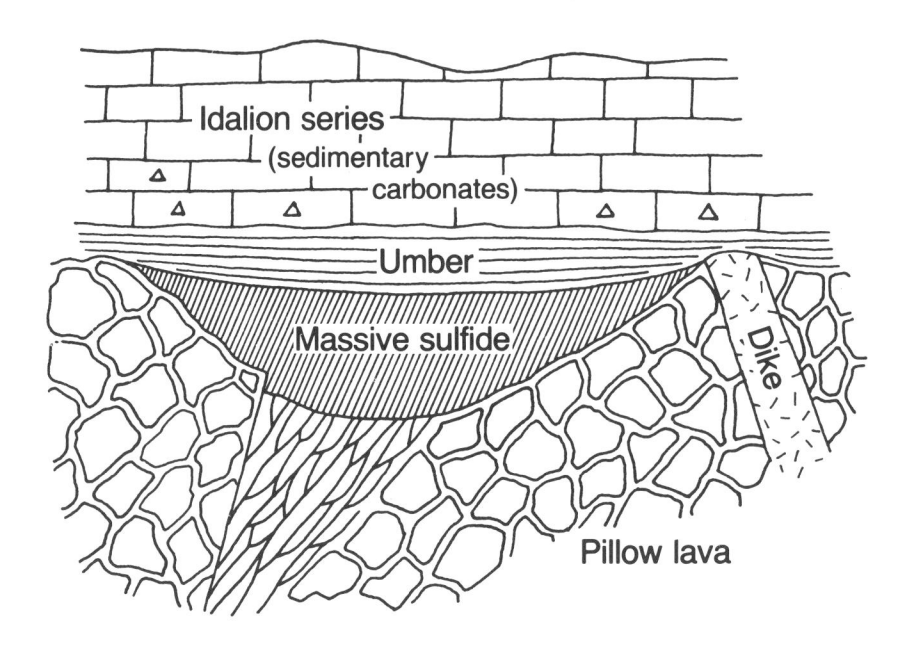

Figure 8. Deeply Buried Massive Sulfide Deposits Having Very Little Alteration or Secondary Enrichment Mineralization. Deposits of this type were unknown to ancient miners.

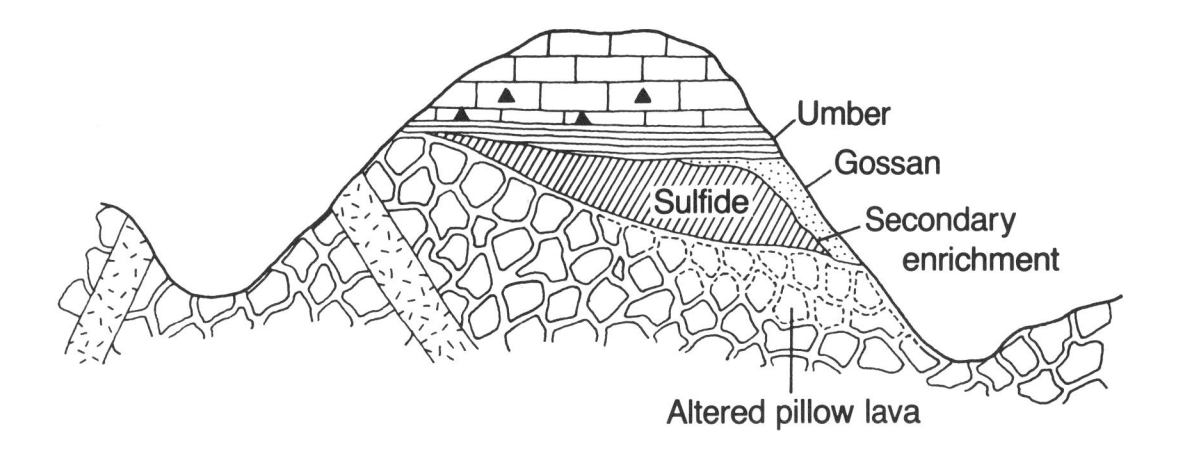

Figure 9. Massive Sulfide Deposit Exposed by Erosion. Secondary enrichment zones may be found both above and below the ore and along fractures. This situation is typical of some mines on Cyprus; such mines do not have serious water elimination problems.

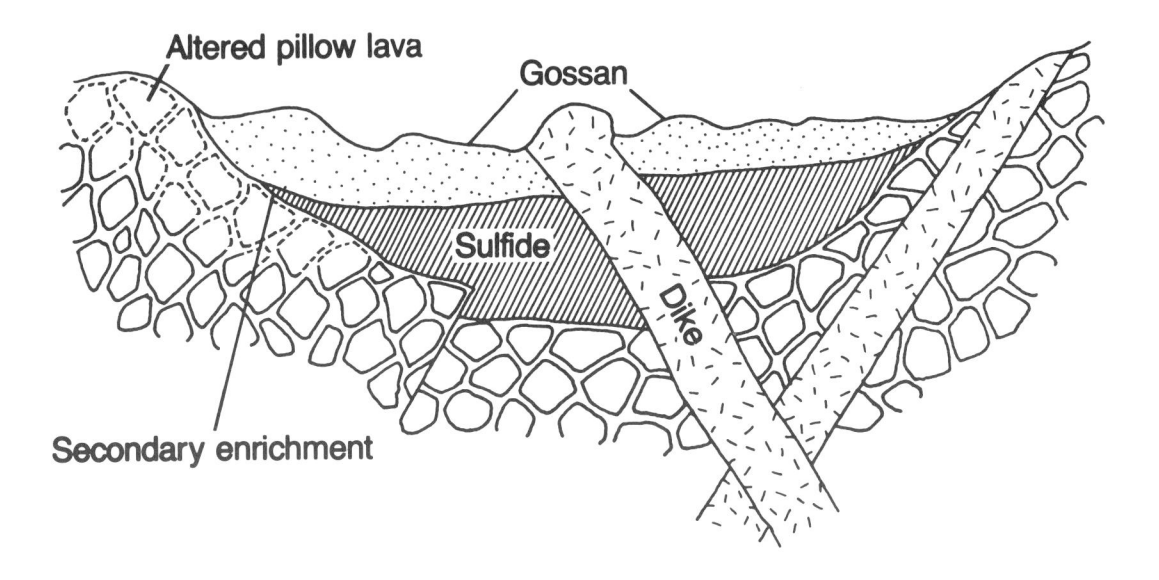

Figure 10. Deeply Weathered Massive Sulfide Ore Deposit. Where overlying rocks have eroded from the massive sulfide ore body, a thick, widespread gossan develops, and considerable secondary enrichment occurs. Mines of this type are apt to have problems with water elimination.

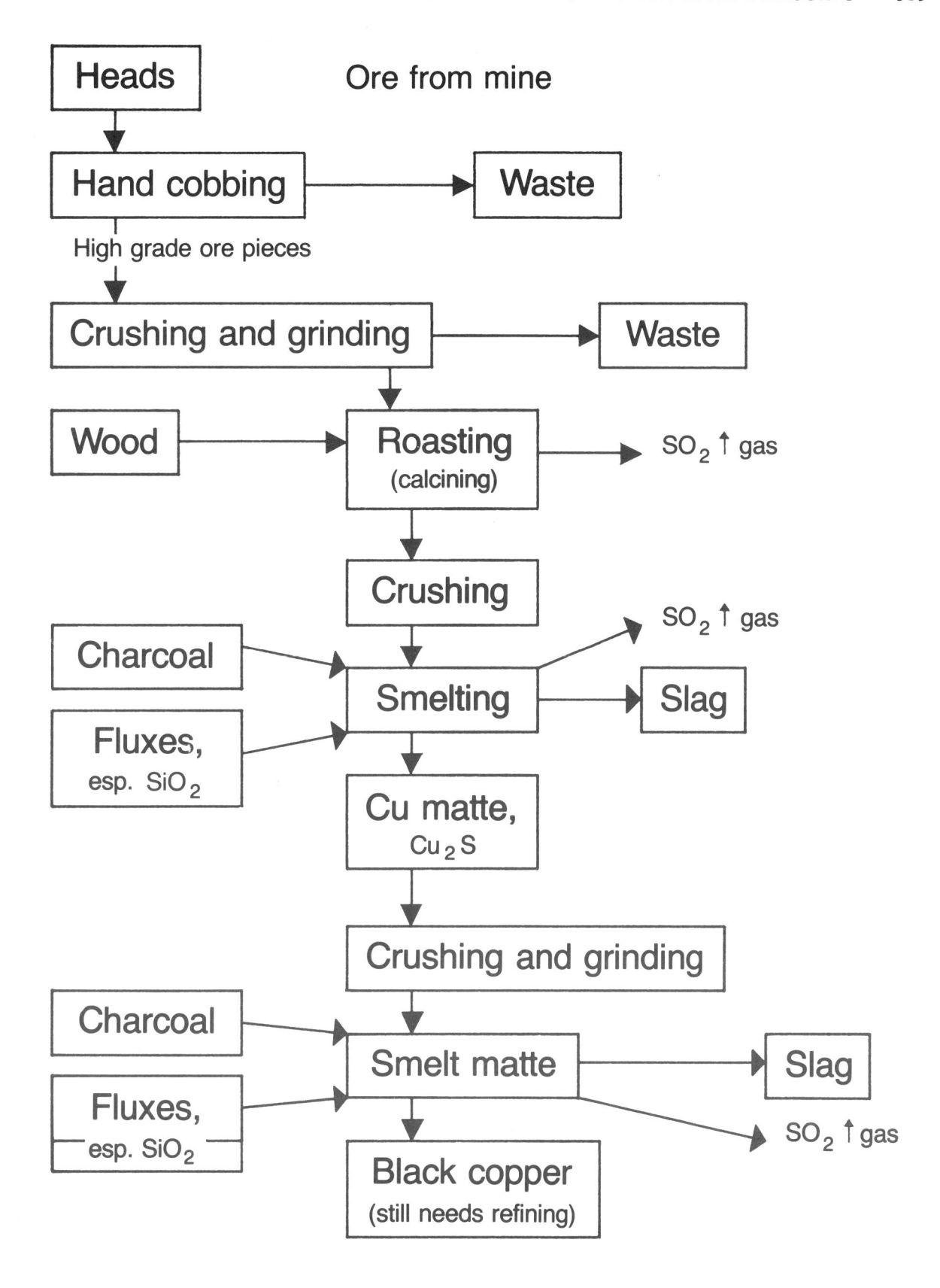

Figure 11. Possible Flow Chart for Obtaining Copper from Sulfide Ores by Roasting.

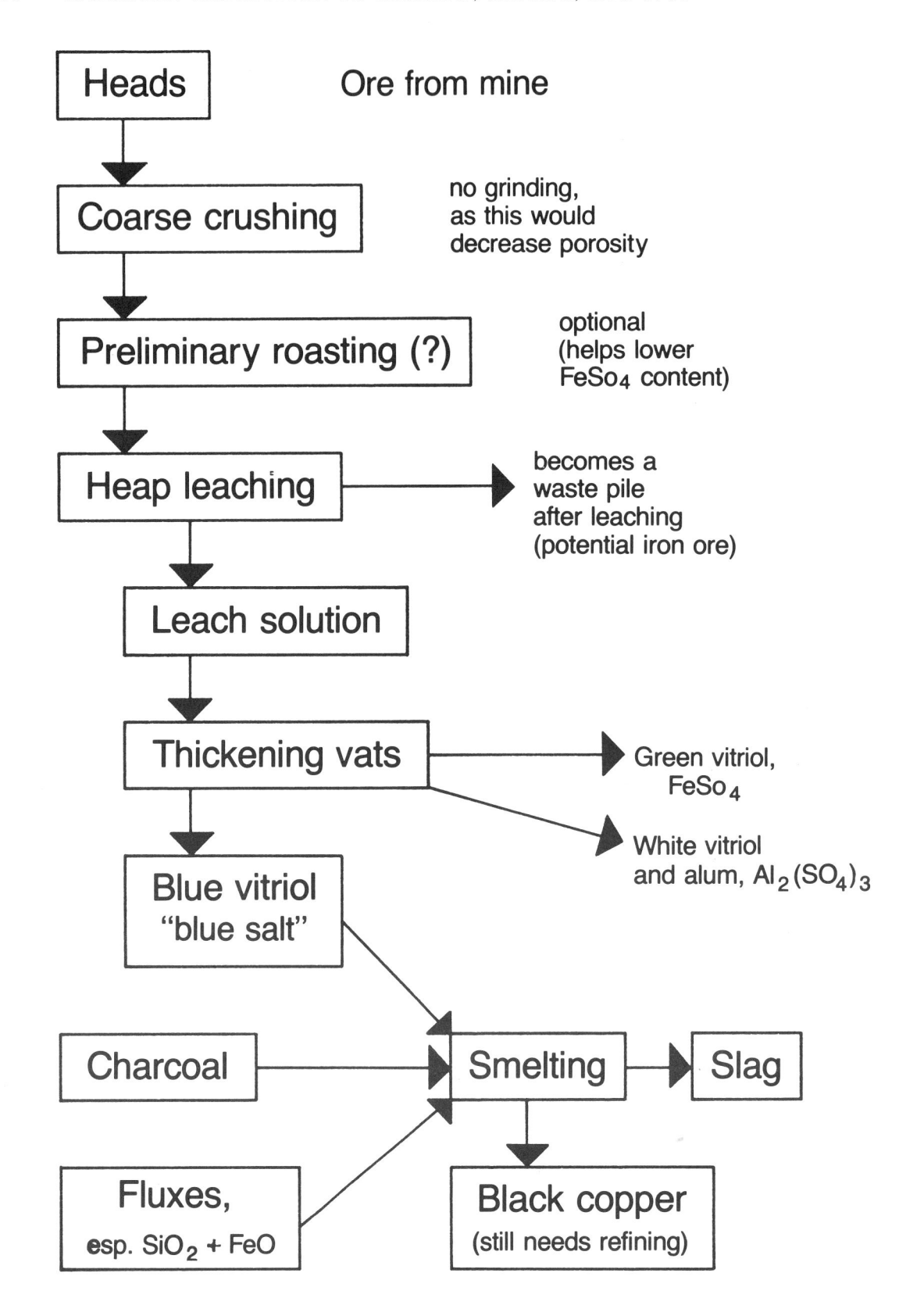

Figure 12. Possible Flow Chart for Obtaining Copper from Sulfide Ores by Hydrometallurgy.

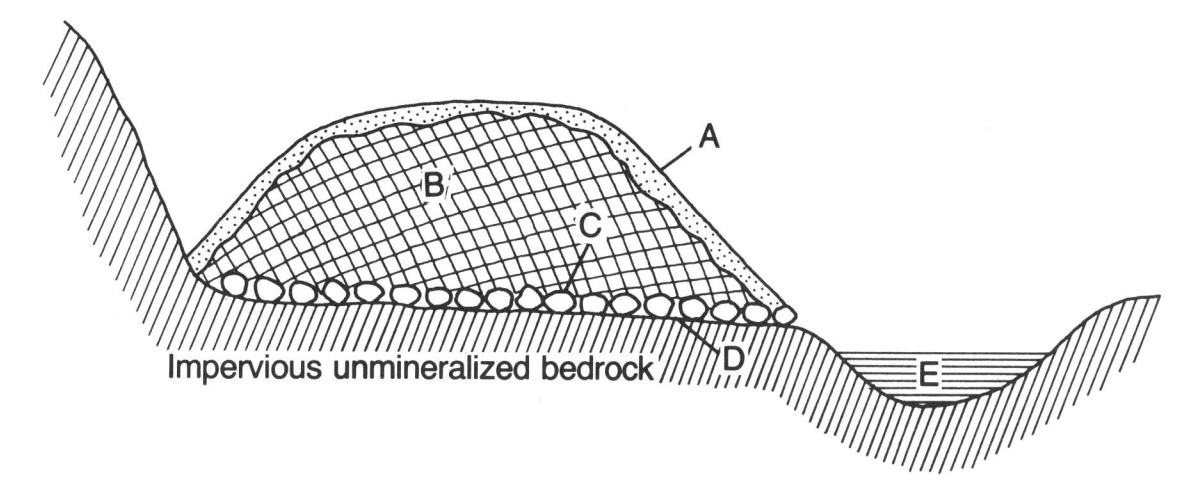

Figure 13. Sketch of an Ancient Heap Leaching Pile: A--Leach pile may have been covered with fine dirt to retain moisture and to prevent too rapid oxidation; B--Ore pile (coarse crushed ore, stratified); C--Floor of uniform coarse gravel; D--Surface of low gradient, draining to (E), the underlying material of which is impervious, unmineralized bedrock; E--Soluble salts collect in vat (based on description by Bruce 1937).

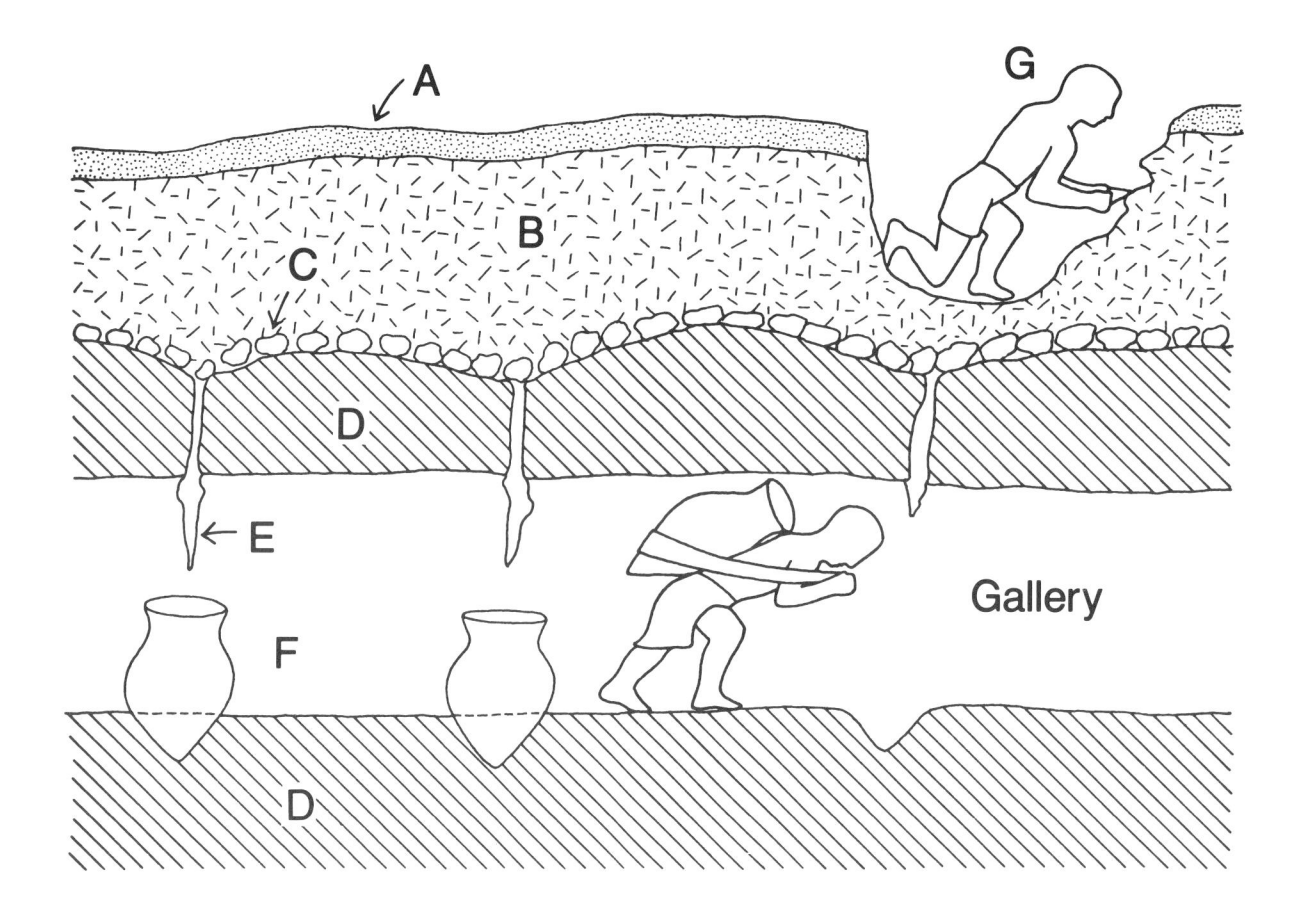

Figure 14. Sketch of Ancient Heap Leaching Galleries. Vitriol-bearing solutions might be caught in pithos and form stalactites: A--Possible dirt cover; B--Crushed ore forming a leach pile; C--Cobbles at base of leach pile forming a permeable and porous bed; D--Gallery roof and floor of impervious nonmineralized rock. Holes were made to allow drainage into gallery; E--Vitriol stalactities; F--Pithos to collect dripping solutions; G--Man turning over the ore pile and breaking lumps (based on description by Bruce 1937).

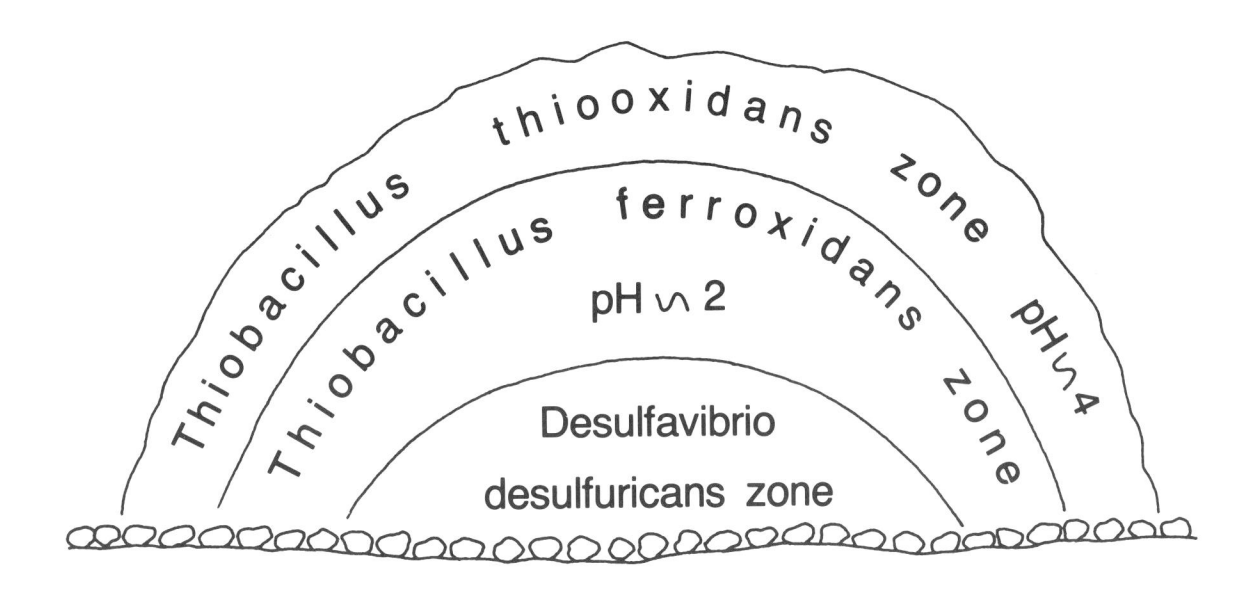

Figure 15. Sketch of Active Leach Pile Showing Biological Leaching Zones. A leach pile of sulfide ore containing pyrite, undergoing active leaching reactions:

Thiobacillus thiooxidans zone: pH approximately 4; *thiooxidans* oxidizes metal sulfides, resulting in both ferrous sulfate and the formation of sulfuric acid. This zone overlaps with species of ferroxidans but thiooxidans cannot survive in a pH much below 4. Ferric iron hydrolyzes in this zone.

Thiobacillus ferroxidans zone: pH 4 to 1.5; *ferroxidans* oxidizes ferrous iron to ferric iron and thus ferric sulfate and sulfuric acid is produced from pyrite. This mixture is a powerful lixiviant that accelerates mineral alteration.

Desulfovibrio desulfuricans zone: anaerobic conditions and low pH favor sulfate reducing bacteria which temporarily hold metals in the form of sulfides. This zone will slowly disappear as the pile reacts, and thus the metals in the pile are released as soluble sulfates or retained as oxides.

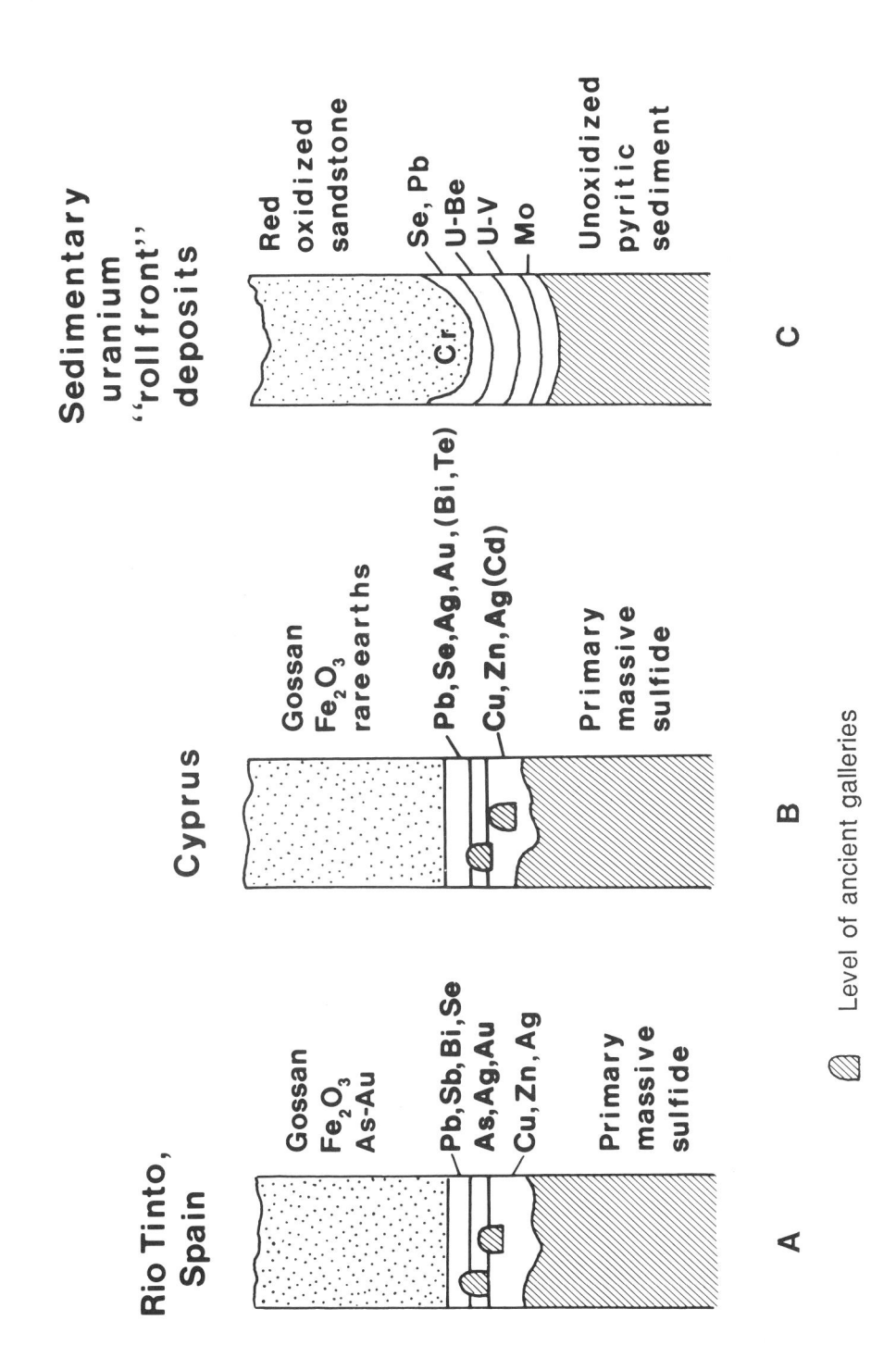

Figure 16. Elements Enriched in Secondary Zones (A, after Williams 1934; B, after Bruce 1949; and C, after Harshman 1967).

PLATE 1

Slag Heap North of Polis.

PLATE 2

West Wall of the Platies Mine, Kalavasos District. Ancient black slags (Cypro-Archaic, type B) underlie the tree in the surface layer. Stratified layers below contain red "Phoenician" slags (type P), which overlie the gossan.

PLATE 3

Slags from Petra and Skouriotissa Slag Piles. a. Ancient Slag in the Petra slag pile, Kalavasos District. This is an example of the dark brown, blocky-shaped, slightly oxidized slag (B). b. A large "bent" slag from the Skouriotissa slag pile. This is an example of the black, ropy-surfaced, irregular-shaped (R) slag.

PLATE 4

a

b

Slags from Spilli and the Skouriotissa Slag Pile. a. Ancient slag in the Spilli slag pile, Kalavasos District. This is an example of the silver-black, collapsed, ropy, manganese-rich slag (type M). b. The large slag pile at Skouriotissa. This has a veneer of the manganese-rich slag (type M), but most of the pile is the black type (type R) shown in plate 3b. A thin layer at the base is the brown, blocky slag similar to that in plate 3a (type B).

PLATE 5

Pits of the Skouriotissa and South Mathiati Mines. a. The main pit of the Skouriotissa Mine. This mine, which resembles that diagrammed in figure 9, is operating in the massive sulfide ore, with enriched, sulfated ore developed along fractures and faults. b. The South Mathiati pit, which was last worked for gold in the 1930s. Ancient galleries follow both the Devil's Mud (oxidized, secondary-enrichment zone) along the bench, and the top of the sulfide, secondary-enrichment zone just above the present lake level.

PLATE 6

a

b

Rio Tinto and Mavri Sykia Mines. a. The hydrometallurgical processing area at Rio Tinto, Spain: a view to the northeast over some of the leach piles and cementation dams at Rio Tinto Mines. b. The Mavri Sykia open-pit mine, Kalavasos District.

PLATE 7

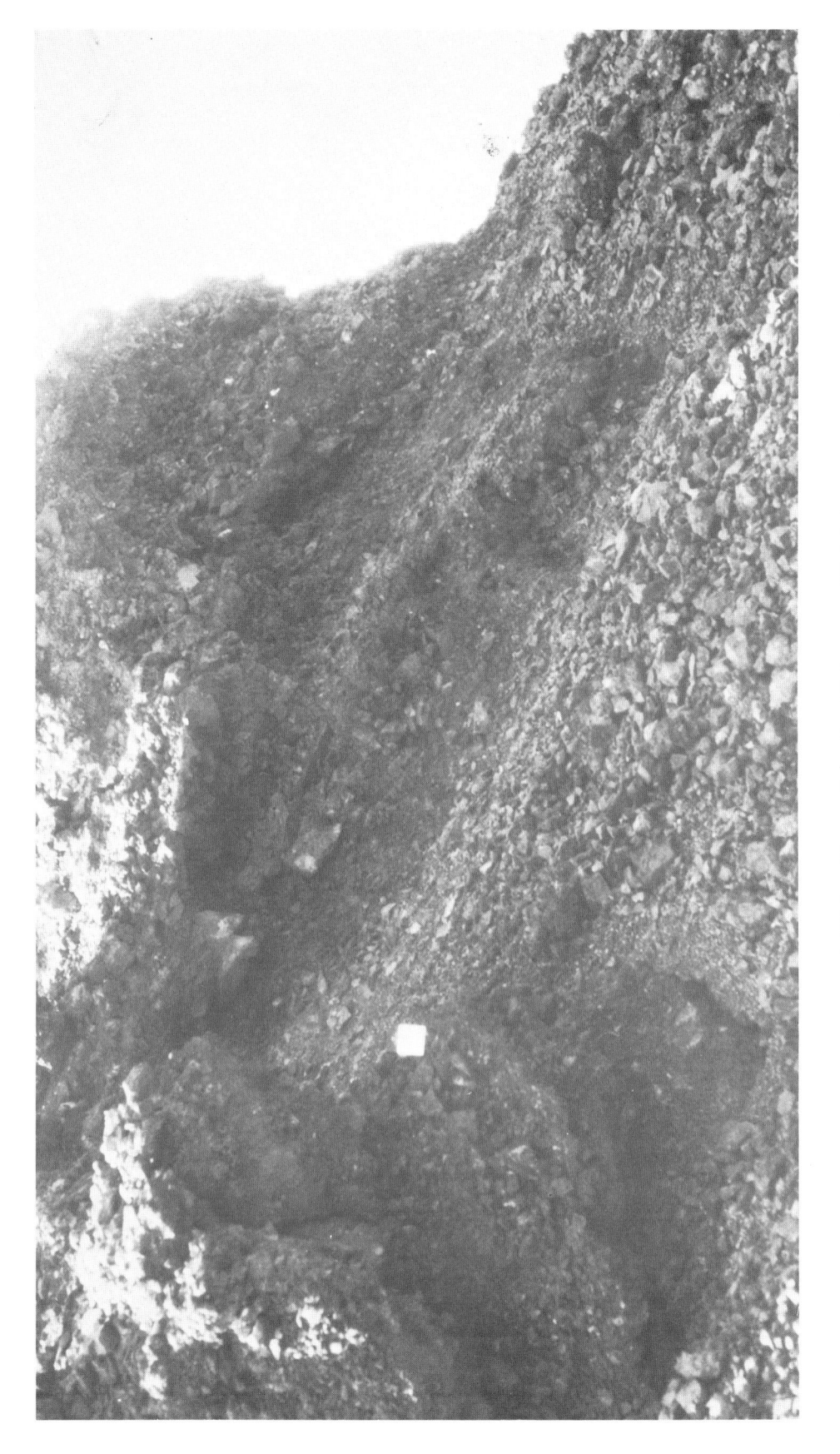

A "False Gossan" in the Kalavasos District.

B. METALWORK FROM IDALION, 1971-1980

*Jane C. Waldbaum**

INTRODUCTION

One of the major objectives of the American Expedition to Idalion was the elucidation of the metal industry on the site and the "relationship between the exploitation of metals and the process of urbanization and deurbanization within the region" (Stager, Walker, and Wright 1974:1, 3-4). On the whole, however, the quantity and range of metal objects and evidence for metalworking so far found at Idalion by the current expedition are relatively sparse. Indeed, given the amount and variety of material found by Gjerstad (e.g., Gjerstad et al. 1935:599-616, pls. CLXXI-CLXXXI), and the expectations of ancient industrial activity raised by the quantities of slag picked up in surface survey (Stager, Walker, and Wright 1974:30, 152), the results can only be described as disappointing.

While installations for copper smelting in the fourth century B.C. were excavated on the West Terrace (Stager, Walker, and Wright 1974:50-56, 152) there is so far no evidence for continuous metallurgical activity at the site although slags have been found in the earliest strata. Furthermore, although objects of metal have been found in most areas excavated by the American Expedition, there is little or no evidence for ongoing manufacture of significant classes of metalwork, nor were specific types of metal objects concentrated in locations that might suggest a functional association.

It is in fact ironic that the largest proportion of metal objects found (some 25 of 86 catalogued objects and many fragments) came from Gjerstad's dump on the West Acropolis and thus have no significant relationship with any of the other material excavated.

Nevertheless, in the interest of completeness, and in the hopes that this body of material will be added to in the future, a brief discussion and catalogue of the metal objects found between 1971 and 1980 are included.[1]

The objects found are of all the major metals utilized by the ancients: copper alloy,[2] iron, lead, gold, and silver, with the majority in copper alloy and iron, and very few of precious metal.

Most of the objects found could be categorized as weapons (primarily arrowheads and sling bullets), defensive armor (only a helmet cheekpiece and a single armor scale belong here),

---

*Department of Art History, University of Wisconsin-Milwaukee, Milwaukee, Wisconsin 53201

[1] I am grateful to Professors Lawrence E. Stager and Anita M. Walker for proposing the study of the metal objects from Idalion to me and for allowing me access to excavation records. Study of the objects in the field and in the Cyprus Museum, Nicosia, where the catalogued objects are housed, was begun in the summer of 1977 and completed in the summer of 1981. All photographs of the metal objects discussed were taken by me. Dr. Vassos Karageorghis kindly permitted me to examine the Idalion material that had been deposited in the Cyprus Museum; Mrs. Ino Nicolaou was most helpful in arranging access to the objects. My transportation to Cyprus in 1977 and 1981 was paid for by the Graduate School, the College of Letters and Science and the Department of Art History of the University of Wisconsin-Milwaukee.

[2] The term "copper alloy" is used in preference to "bronze" for several reasons. First, none of the catalogued copper-based objects from Idalion has been analyzed scientifically to determine its constituents, and it is virtually impossible to know the actual composition of an alloy without proper analysis. Second, analyses of objects of various dates from other sites have shown that it is not wise to assume that most ancient copper-based objects were in fact alloyed with tin to make true bronze (see e.g., Waldbaum 1983:154-77).

utilitarian (miscellaneous domestic and "industrial" implements), jewelry (primarily simple rings and earrings; very few more elaborate objects).

Catalogue entries include material, dimensions in meters, findspot, information on date when available and a brief description. Table 1 provides a concordance of metal objects by findspot. Unless otherwise mentioned objects are complete. Most entries are accompanied by a photograph and where feasible, a drawing. Drawings of objects found in 1971 and 1972 are by Nan Arghyros.

Weapons and Armor

Arrowheads

Thirteen arrowheads were found at Idalion by the current expedition. They fall into two major classes: tanged and socketed. Within each class there are several types.

I. Tanged: Most of the arrowheads found are tanged. There are three types of tanged arrowhead represented.

a) Elongated, straight, narrow head with square section, tapering to a pyramidal point at one end. The tang is long and narrow in proportion to the head and is also foursided. All examples found by the current excavation are of copper alloy, though Gjerstad found specimens in both copper alloy and iron at Idalion and elsewhere on Cyprus ranging in date from Cypro-Archaic I well into Cypro-Classical. Those of our examples that can be dated appear to be Cypro-Classical, though one (no. 1) is possibly Hellenistic.

The type is apparently Cypriot in origin as it is found in numerous sites on the island (e.g., Gjerstad et al. 1935:575, 578, 614-15, pls. CLXXI.14, CLXXIV.18, Idalion periods 5, 6, Type 4 in iron, Type 5 in bronze; Gjerstad et al. 1937:105, pl. XLV.7, Vouni Type 2a; Karageorghis 1970:188, pl. XXXIV.4, Salamis pyre Z, late fourth century B.C.; Karageorghis 1977:192, pls. LXXII, LXXIII, bronze no. 136c, iron no. 137a, b, Kakopetria, ca. 500-425 B.C.), and only rarely outside it (e.g., Woolley 1939:147, fig. 25.A1, MN 222, 164-65, Al Mina Level 3, Late Classical).

Gjerstad (1948:375) ascribes rather far-flung foreign relations to this type. However, he somewhat indiscriminately lumps it with other forms of foursided arrowhead (e.g., our Types Ib and Ic) which appear to have somewhat different distributions.

1. 71/6/F2   Pl. 1, Fig. 1a

    Copper alloy. M.L. 0.073, L. head: 0.040, M.W. head: 0.005, Th. tang: 0.003
    West Acropolis, East of Hellenistic Wall, Id W SE 11/36 Loc. 004.
    Date: Late Classical-Early Hellenistic.
    Complete. Head and tang somewhat pitted from corrosion.

2. 72/424/F304   Pl. 1, Fig. 1b

    Copper alloy. M.P.L. 0.055, L. head: 0.042, W. head: 0.006, Th. tang: 0.004.
    West Acropolis, Gjerstad's dump. Id W SE 7/50 Loc. 014.
    Tang broken; completely oxidized.

3. 72/397/F296   Pl. 1, Fig. 1c

    Copper alloy. M.P.L. 0.055, L. head: 0.0275, W. head: 0.007; Th. tang: 0.0045.
    West Terrace, Area D. Id W SW 11/16 Loc. 014.
    Date: Cypro-Classical.
    Tang tapers to point; sides of head constricted. Surface corroded.

b) These arrowheads are similar to those of Ia in that the lower part of the head is long and narrow with square to lozenge-shaped section. The upper part, however, broadens above center, then tapers to a flatter point than that of the preceding type. There is a sharp longitudinal midridge running from the point to the base of the head. The sides vary from straight and tapered (as in nos. 4, 5, 6, 7), to constricted or double curved (nos. 8, 9). This type appears in the current excavations exclusively in copper alloy. Gjerstad also found numerous examples at Idalion in copper alloy as well as a few in iron (Gjerstad et al. 1935:575, 578, 614-15, pls. CLXXI.13, 15, CLXXIV.19, Types 3 and 5 in iron, Type 6 in bronze).

This type is very common in Cyprus, being found at many sites; and its dating seems to be similar to that of Ia. (See e.g., Gjerstad et al. 1935:302-3, pl. LV.31, 54c, Marion Tomb 43, Cypro-Classical II; 792, 814, pl. CCXLI.6, Ayia Irini, Type 3, uncertain date; Gjerstad et al. 1937:105, 271, pls. XLV.8-10, LXXXVII.8, Vouni, Type 2b; 577, pl. CLXXXII.8, Soli, Type 1, uncertain date; Karageorghis 1970:187, pl. XXXIII, Salamis pyre X nos. 6, 22; 188, pl. XXXIV, pyre Z, no. 3; 193, pl. XXXV, pyre K, no. 7; 194, pl. XXXVI, pyre M, no. 10, fourth century; Karageorghis 1977:192, pls. LXXII, LXXIII no. 136a, b, Kakopetria, ca. 500-425 B.C.). Like Type Ia, this type is not found often outside Cyprus (see e.g. Woolley 1939:25-26, 147, fig. 25.A2, MN 221, 165, Al Mina Level 3, Late Classical).

4.   71/35a/F46   Pl. 1

Copper alloy. M.P.L. 0.055, L. head: 0.038, M.W. head: 0.008, Th. tang: 0.003.
West Acropolis, Gjerstad's dump. Id W SE 11/45 Loc. 003.
Tip of tang broken.

5.   71/35b/F46   Pl. 1, Fig. 1d

Copper alloy. M.P.L. 0.045, L. head: 0.036, M.W. head: 0.0075, Th. tang: 0.003.
West Acropolis, Gjerstad's dump. Id W SE 11/45 Loc. 003.
Tang broken.

6.   71/14/F10   Pl. 1, Fig. 1e

Copper alloy. M.P.L. 0.050, M.W. head: 0.009, Th. tang: 0.003.
West Acropolis, Gjerstad's dump. Id W SE 11/45 Loc. 003.
Some bronze disease. Tang bent.

7.   72/458/F314   Pl. 1, Fig. 1f

Copper alloy. M.P.L. 0.0525, L. head: 0.038, M.W. head: 0.008, Th. tang: 0.004.
West Acropolis, Gjerstad's dump. Id W SE 7/50 Loc. 002.
Short tapered tang.

8.   72/430/F310   Pl. 1, Fig. 1g

Copper alloy. M.P.L. 0.045, M.W. head: 0.008, Th. tang: 0.004.
West Acropolis, Gjerstad's dump. Id W SE 7/50 Loc. 012.
Point and end of tang broken and missing.

9.   72/423/F303   Pl. 1, Fig. 1h

Copper alloy. M.L. 0.068, L. head: 0.029, M.W. head: 0.009, Th. head: 0.0065, Th. tang: 0.003.
East Terrace, Area F. Id E NW 7/8 Loc. 009.
Date: Hellenistic or earlier.
Surfaced corroded. Sides very constricted. Tang has round section and is quite long in proportion to head.
Publ. Stager, Walker, and Wright 1974:65.

c) This type was not distinguished by Gjerstad from arrowheads of our Type Ia, but was instead subsumed into his Type 2 (Gjerstad 1948:375). Instead of being straight-sided with pyramidal tip, however, this type differs from Ia in having a completely pyramidal head that tapers gradually from base to point. It also appears primarily in iron.

Only one certain, and possibly a second example, was found by the current Idalion expedition. At least some of the iron arrowheads of Gjerstad's Type 4 from the first Idalion expedition probably belong to this category (Gjerstad et al. 1935:575, 614, pl. CLXXI.14). The type is common elsewhere in Cyprus as well as abroad (e.g., Gjerstad et al. 1935:301-3, pl. LV.2, nos. 14b, 18, 21, 31, 32, 54b, Marion Tomb 43, Cypro-Classical II, all in bronze; 792, 814, pl. CCXLI.2 (iron), 5 (bronze), Ayia Irini Type 2, period 6, Cypro-Archaic II and uncertain date; Gjerstad et al. 1937:271, 290, pl. LXXXVII.2, Vouni; Karageorghis 1970:193, pl. XXXVI, Salamis pyre M, no. 1, fourth century B.C.; for Palestine: Petrie 1934:10, pl. 30.367, Gaza, stray find; Petrie 1928:15, pl. 28.13-20, Gerar (Tell Jemmeh); Macalister 1912, II:373, III, pl. CCXV.67, Gezer, "Fourth Semitic" and Hellenistic periods; for Greece: Carapanos 1878:102, pl. 58.13, 14, Dodona; Robinson 1941:392-397, pls. CXXIII-CXXIV nos. 1972-2026, Type E, Olynthus, associated with siege of 348 B.C.). Robinson (1941:392) suggests this type is "Cyprian" in origin, although he admits "it is hard to believe that all of the specimens from Olynthus were imported."

Petrie (1928:15 and 1934:10) suggests that such heavy solid arrowheads were used for piercing armor.

10. 80/936/F620 Pl. 1

Iron. M.P.L. 0.0905, M.W. head: 0.014, Th. tang: 0.0055.
West Terrace, Area of Wall. Id 80 CW Loc. 008.
Date: Cypro-Archaic to Hellenistic.
Two joining fragments. Heavily corroded. Tang has round section.

11. 80/950/F630 Pl. 1

Iron. M.P.L. 0.0725, M.W. head: 0.018, M.W. tang: 0.006.
West Terrace. Area C, Loc. 028.
Two fragments, not joining. Identity uncertain. Heavily encrusted and corroded.

II. Socketed: Only two arrowheads found by the current expedition were socketed. Both are different in type.

a) Three-flanged point with short external socket. Only one example of this type was found, and that in Gjerstad's dump. Gjerstad, however, found several of them at Idalion in his periods 5 and 6, as well as variants with internal sockets (Gjerstad et al. 1935:578, 615, pl. CLXXIV.21-22,1 Type 8).

The type is widely distributed in Cyprus (e.g., Gjerstad et al. 1937:105, 271, pls. XLV.12, LXXXVII.9, Vouni; 389, pl. CXLIX.4, 5, Mersinaki; 414, pl. CLXXX.2, 3, CLXXXII.10, Soli; Karageorghis 1970:193, pl. XXXV, Salamis, pyre K, no. 6; Karageorghis 1974, pls. CLXIV, CCLXXXIII, Salamis Tumulus 77, sixth-late fourth century B.C.). It is, however, not a local Cypriot type, but the quintessential Achaemenid Persian type, being found in large numbers at Persepolis (Schmidt 1957:97, 99, pl. 76.7, 8, over 3600 examples) and Pasargadae (Stronach 1978:180-81, 218-19, fig. 94.1-16, pl. 165). It is also found at numerous sites in Greece and the Near East with which the Persians were in contact, either through conquest or administration (see Waldbaum 1983:35 and Snodgrass 1964:151-53 for discussion and refs.).

In Iran, its use dates from late seventh century to at least the early second century B.C. and possibly later (Stronach 1978:181). Elsewhere, it is primarily associated with the period of Persian occupation from the mid-sixth to late fourth centuries B.C.

12. 72/426/F306   Pl. 1, Fig. 1i

   Copper alloy. M.L. 0.036, M.W. 0.013, Diam. socket: 0.007.
   West Acropolis, Gjerstad's dump. Id W SE 7/50 Loc. 010.
   Date: Achaemenid (late sixth-fourth centuries B.C.).
   Short exterior socket. Small hole through one flange.

   b) Apparently triangular head with two edges, a sharp midridge, a lozenge-shaped section and a small, round internal socket. The base of the head possibly once had barbs that had broken off.

   The question of classification rests on whether or not the specimen was once barbed. If not, the arrowhead bears some resemblance to a type in iron found by Gjerstad at Idalion (Gjerstad et al. 1935:575, 614, pl. CLXXI.12, Type 2, periods 4, 5, 6) although these were tanged rather than socketed. If barbed, it is perhaps close to Snodgrass' Type 3A3, apparently a somewhat unusual archaic Greek type which occurs occasionally also in Cyprus, Egypt, northern Europe, and South Russia (Snodgrass 1964:151-52).

13. 71/11/F7   Pl. 1

   Copper alloy. M.P.L. 0.041, M.W. 0.014, Diam. socket: 0.003.
   West Acropolis, Area of Hellenistic Wall. Id W SE 11/36 Loc. 001 (surface).

   Under surface of the base roughened, perhaps indicating breaks. Thin tang once fitted into socket.

   Another arrowhead, in iron, 77/F586, described as a "flat triangular head with barbs and a long tang with round section" was found on the West Terrace, Area D, Id W SW 8/15 Loc. 026. The object was not seen by the writer and no photograph was taken, so it cannot be compared.

Spear or Javelin Heads

   Only two objects were found that possibly fall into this category. They do not appear to belong to distinctive, readily identifiable types.

14. 72/75/F137   Pl. 1

   Iron. M.P.L. 0.122, M.W. 0.024, Th. 0.013.
   West Acropolis, Gjerstad's dump. Id W SE 7/50 Loc. 001.

   Elongated, lanceolate blade tapering to a point. Blade widest below center. Point bent. Slightly sloping shoulders; round socket (broken). Heavy corrosion obscures details, but there was apparently no midrib. Possibly similar to Gjerstad et al. 1935:574, 614, pl. CLXXI.2 or 3 (Types 1 and 2), though these are ribbed.

15. 71/33/F36   Pl. 1

   Iron. M.P.L. 0.076, Diam. base: 0.011.
   West Acropolis, East of Hellenistic Wall. Id W SE 11/36 Loc. 004.
   Date: Late Classical-Hellenistic?

Long slender point with irregular round to lozenge-shaped section. The base is broken and missing so it is not possible to tell if it were once tanged or socketed. It possibly had a low midrib, though this is mostly obscured by corrosion.

Sling Bullets

Nine lead sling bullets were found, ranging in shape from a plump ovoid to a rather elongated amygdaloid. All have plain surfaces; none is inscribed, although three (nos. 19, 20, 23) have an incised pair of diagonal lines coming together to form an open triangle, or perhaps a letter *lambda*. Some also have longitudinal raised ridges (nos. 16, 21, 24).

The use and distribution of sling bullets in Cyprus is best described by I. Nicolaou (Michaelidou-Nicolaou 1969-70:359-69, the main study with refs., parallels, and ancient sources; see also Nicolaou 1968:82-3, pls. XVIII.17a, b, XIX.17c-e; 1972:263, pl. XLVII.25; 1977:211-16 [includes a discussion of manufacturing technique]; 1979:348-50; 1980:261-62; Åström and Nicolaou 1980:29-33 for Late Bronze Age examples).

Nicolaou's inscribed sling bullets generally have raised inscriptions cast directly into the bullet during manufacture, and most inscriptions comprise complete names or phrases. None parallels the kind of incised markings, or single letter, seen in some of these. The closest parallel seems to be two examples from Olynthus, inscribed with the single letters *theta* and *gamma*, which Robinson suggests "might indicate the number of the company" of the user (Robinson 1941:438-39, nos. 2270, 2271, and ref. n. 203 to two others from Greece with *beta* and *alpha* respectively). If this interpretation is correct the Idalion examples, if inscribed with *lambda*s, might stand for the eleventh company.

16. 71/37a/F56   Pl. 1, Fig. 1j

   Lead. L. 0.028, M.W. 0.0165, hole: 0.010 x 0.001.
   West Acropolis, East of Hellenistic Wall. Id W SE 11/36 Loc. 004.
   Date: Late Classical-Early Hellenistic.
   Ovoid with ovoid dent in one side; longitudinal ridge.
   Publ. Stager, Walker, and Wright 1974:61 fig. 50; Nicolaou 1977:215.

17. 71/37b/F56   Pl. 1, Fig. 1k

   Lead. L. 0.033, M.W. 0.015.
   West Acropolis, East of Hellenistic Wall. Id W SE 11/36 Loc. 004.
   Date: Late Classical-Early Hellenistic.
   Amygdaloid. No markings or ridges.
   Publ. Stager, Walker, and Wright 1974:61 fig. 50; Nicolaou 1977:215.

18. 71/37c/F56   Pl. 1, Fig. 1l

   Lead. L. 0.032, M.W. 0.017.
   West Acropolis, East of Hellenistic Wall. Id W SE 11/36 Loc. 004.
   Date: Late Classical-Early Hellenistic.
   Amygdaloid. No markings or ridges.
   Publ. Stager, Walker, and Wright 1974:61 fig. 50; Nicolaou 1977:215.

19. 71/26/F21   Pl. 1, Fig. 1m

   Lead. L. 0.035, M.W. 0.0165.
   West Acropolis, West of Hellenistic Wall. Id W SE 11/36 Loc. 007.
   Date: Late Classical-Early Hellenistic.
   Amygdaloid. Some gashes on surface; two strokes on diagonal coming together as a ∧.
   Publ. Stager, Walker, and Wright 1974:92-93 pl. V.18; Nicolaou 1977:215.

20. 71/36a/F55   Pl. 1, Fig. 1n

    Lead. L. 0.0265, M.W. 0.016.
    West Acropolis, West of Hellenistic Wall, embedded in subfloor fill of phase 2. Id W SE 11/36 Loc. 010.
    Date: Late Classical-Early Hellenistic.
    Flattened ovoid. Two strokes incised on diagonal, coming together as a
    Publ. Stager, Walker, and Wright 1974:59, 61 fig. 50; Nicolaou 1977:215.

21. 71/36b/F55   Pl. 1, Fig. 1o

    Lead. L. 0.029, M.W. 0.017.
    West Acropolis, West of Hellenistic Wall, embedded in subfloor fill of phase 2. Id W SE 11/36 Loc. 010.
    Date: Late Classical-Early Hellenistic.
    Amygdaloid with blunt ends; longitudinal ridge along one side.
    Publ. Stager, Walker, and Wright 1974:59, 61 fig. 50; Nicolaou 1977:215.

22. 72 (not inventoried)   (not figured)

    Lead. Dimensions unknown.
    West Terrace, Area D, copper smelting industrial area. Id W SW 9/16 phase 4 Loc. 012.
    Date: Early Hellenistic.
    Amygdaloid.
    Publ. Stager, Walker, and Wright 1974:56.

23. 71/9/F5   Pl. 1, Fig. 1p

    Lead. L. 0.037, M.W. 0.017.
    West Acropolis, Gjerstad's dump. Id W SE 13/50 Loc. 002.
    Amygdaloid with sharply pointed ends. Two strokes on diagonal near one end coming together as a $\wedge$.
    Publ. Nicolaou 1977:215.

24. 72/253/F206   Pl. 1

    Lead. L. 0.031, M.W. 0.017, Th. 0.014.
    West Acropolis, Gjerstad's dump. Id W SE 7/50 Loc. 004.
    Amygdaloid with pointed ends. Sharp longitudinal ridge; gash on one side near end.

<u>Helmet Cheekpiece</u>

25. 80/929/F618   Pl. 1

    Copper alloy. M.L. (including hinges): 0.141, M.W. 0.095, Diam. tie hole: 0.004, Diam arrow hole: 0.0115.
    West Terrace, Area C Loc. 009.
    Cypro-Classical.

    The cheekpiece, from the right side of a helmet, is rather broad in proportion to its length and is completely without decoration. Its sides are nearly straight, curving slightly inward on the front edge and outward and down on the rear edge to a convex lower edge. The upper edge is slightly convex with the remains of three hinge attachments. A small, regular, round hole at the center of the lower edge was no doubt to hold a leather thong or string for tying the helmet under the chin of the wearer. There are no other holes around the edges to suggest that the cheekpiece was lined with another material such as leather or cloth.

In addition to a large, irregular tear down the center of the object (recently repaired and filled in), there is a jagged but nearly round hole 0.0115 m in diameter, somewhat to the rear of center, possibly formed by the penetration of an arrow or other projectile point. The torn edges of the hole are slightly everted.

The maximum widths of the different types of arrowheads found at Idalion (see above) were compared with the size of the hole to see which type (if any) could have made the hole. Both types Ia and Ib are small enough to have passed completely through the hole, but are perhaps too small to have made it (largest only 0.009 m). The Persian three-flanged type (IIa) is too large to have completely penetrated the hole (max. W. 013 m); however, a similar one could have partly pierced it, stuck there, and been forceably pulled out, thus accounting for the everted edges of the hole. Since the repertoire of arrow types found so far is small, it is of course possible that an entirely different type of point was responsible for the damage.

The problem of finding close parallels for this cheekpiece, and of determining its origin is a difficult one. While helmets with cheekpieces were known in Europe, the eastern Mediterranean, and Near East since the Bronze Age (Borchhardt 1972:15-61, Beilage E, F; Hencken 1971:11), remains of metal helmets and helmet parts are relatively rare, especially in Cyprus.

Gjerstad originally identified several "sole shaped" copper alloy plates from Idalion periods 5 and 6 as cheekpieces (Gjerstad et al. 1935:579, pl. CLXXVI.1-4). He later, however, correctly redefined them as horse blinkers (Gjerstad 1948:148, fig. 26.25-29 and cf. Karageorghis 1967:14, pl. XIV Tomb 2 nos. 49-50; 35, 36, 38, pl. XLVII Tomb 3 nos. 20, 26, 27, 115; 84, pl. LXXX Tomb 47 nos. 112, 113, 115, 116, 118 for the identical blinkers found in horse burials, and cf. also Snodgrass 1964:33-4). On the other hand, two very different objects from Idalion originally lumped by Gjerstad into his "mountings" category (Gjerstad et al. 1935:582, pl. CLXXVIII.15 no. 1071 and pl. CLXXIX.2 no. 315) were later identified respectively as an iron cheekpiece with bronze decoration and a bronze mounting for a "cap-shaped leather helmet with a hinged neck-cover" (Gjerstad 1948:132-33, fig. 20.8 and 140, 141, fig. 24.5). The cheekpiece is similar to ours in shape though it differs in material and in the elaborate decoration of applied bronze strips and bosses. The published photograph (*SCE* II, pl. CLXXVIII) shows slight projections on the top that may be the remains of hinges. These are omitted, however, from the later drawing (*SCE* IV.2 fig. 20.8), and may simply reflect the irregularities of iron corrosion. Gjerstad (1948:132-33) asserts that is it "from a spiked helmet of Assyrian type" (see e.g., Barnett n.d., pls. 48, 77, 108, 110, 111, 120, 129) but Snodgrass (1964:33) points out its resemblance to the cheekpieces of the Greek *kegelhelm*.

According to Gjerstad (1948:378) "Cypriote helmets were usually of leather. . . . For a study of the different varieties and their cultural relations we are therefore mainly confined to representations of them in stone and terracotta sculpture." Indeed, a number of Cypriot statues and statuettes, from Ayia Irini in particular, show male figures wearing different kinds of headgear, often with cheekpieces or flaps (see e.g., Gjerstad et al. 1935, pls. CXC, CXCI, CXCII.1, 2, CXCIII.1-3, CXCIV.1, 3-6, CCXI, CCXV.1, 2, CCXXXVII.2, 3, 7, 8, CCXXVIII.7, 8). In most of these representations the cheekpieces or flaps are rather more elongated and triangular in shape than ours. Most are also lifted up off the ears and tied or rested against the upper sides of the helmet like the flaps on a hunting cap. This mobility of position suggests either hinged metal cheekpieces or flaps of a flexible material such as leather. Gjerstad, indeed, says that the entire helmet is of soft material (1935:778), and the drooping, turned-back peaks on the headgear of several of the Ayia Irini statues (e.g. Gjerstad et al. 1935, pls. CXC.2, CXCII.1, CCXI.2) seem to confirm this conclusion.

Closer in shape, though more remote in date, are several cheekpieces and representations of cheekpieces from Bronze Age contexts. One is a bronze cheekpiece from a Mycenaean context at Ialysos, Rhodes, the second, also bronze, is from Pass Lueg in Austria, dated to the thirteenth century B.C., and the third is a relief of a Hittite warrior, the so-called Guardian of the Gate, from Bogazköy dated ca. 1400 B.C. (Hencken 1971, fig. 9b, Ialysos, figs. 11a, 31, Pass

Lueg, fig. 10a, Bogazköy). Neither of the bronze examples is hinged and it is not possible to tell how the Hittite one was attached. Furthermore, the Pass Lueg specimen is attached to the helmet by heavy loops that Hencken (p. 58) thinks are modern, and is ornamented with elaborate embossed designs. There is no obvious line of development between these and the Idalion piece.

Snodgrass (1964:13-35) has discussed the typology and development of Greek helmets in the Dark Ages and early Archaic period. Although several types have cheekpieces, notably the *kegelhelm* of the late eighth through early seventh centuries B.C., the so-called Illyrian helmet of the seventh century B.C. and later, and the Ionian helmet from the late seventh century on, none of these provides a really close parallel to the Idalion specimen. The cheekpieces of the first two types are fixed--those of the *kegelhelm* riveted, of the Illyrian type hammered in one piece with the cap--and those of the Ionian type, while hinged, are of a more complex shape than ours (Snodgrass 1964:15-6, pls. 5, 9, *kegelhelm*; 18, pl. 10, Illyrian; 31-2, pl. 17, Ionian). The distribution and chronology of the Ionian type, however, does come closer, since it is attested in representations on works of art from mainland Greece to Ionia, Phrygia, and Cyprus (Snodgrass 1964:31-2).

In general, though various types of Greek helmets with cheekpieces continue into the Classical period (see e.g., Snodgrass 1967, figs. 23-25, 47-49, 53), none is really close in form to the Idalion piece.

On the Near Eastern side, the closest parallels seem to be the "cheekpieces" seen on Assyrian helmets in stone reliefs of the ninth through seventh centuries B.C. (as e.g., Barnett n.d., pls. 48, 77, 108, 110, 111, 120, 129). These are somewhat similar in shape, though most appear rather small, hanging straight down from the helmet and apparently intended to cover primarily the ears, rather than curving forward to protect the cheeks and jaw. It is not possible to tell from the carved representations whether or not the Assyrian examples were hinged, although one at least (Barnett n.d., pl. 48) seems to be. None is shown tied under the chin, which would in any case have been difficult given the heavy beards worn by most Assyrian warriors depicted. At any rate, they are too early to be more than distant antecedents to the Idalion cheekpiece.

On the whole, I am inclined to believe that the Idalion cheekpiece is of local Cypriot manufacture, perhaps a variant in metal of those seen on the Ayia Irini statues, and possibly distantly related to certain Greek helmets in the west or to the Assyrian types in the east. More must be learned about native Cypriot armor types before any firm conclusions may be drawn.

Armor Scale

26. 72/75/F137   Pl. 1

Iron. M.L. 0.025, M.W. 0.012, Th. 0.0015.
West Acropolis, Gjerstad's dump. Id W SE 7/50 Loc. 001.
Small rectangular scale with curved lower edge. No visible attachment holes.

Since this is the only example of scale armor found by the current expedition, and since it was not found in a good context, it is not possible to attach much significance to it.

Gjerstad did find quantities of armor scales in both copper alloy and iron dating to period 6A at Idalion; presumably this piece is one he overlooked (cf. Gjerstad et al. 1935:538 no. 236, 575, pl. CLXXII). Scale armor of this general type was utilized by the Achaemenid Persians and was found in abundance at Persepolis and Pasargadae (see Schmidt 1957:97, 100, pl. 77.1-16; Stronach 1978:181, 222-23, fig. 96.1-5), and Herodotus (VII.61, IX.22) describes Persian soldiers wearing scale armor of iron and gold. Perhaps the specimens found at Idalion are remnants of encounters with the Persians such as the attack on Idalion by the "Medes and Kitians" in the reign of Stasikypros, dated by M. Marvin to the mid-fifth century B.C. (Stager, Walker, and Wright 1974, xxv-xxvi).

Utilitarian Objects

A number of objects that functioned as domestic, agricultural or industrial tools and implements were found in a variety of contexts. In most cases, no more than two or three examples of a given class or type were found, thus precluding a discussion of their typological significance or development.

Needles

27. 72/270/F213   Pl. 2

   Copper alloy. M.L. 0.109, W. at eye: 0.004, Th. shaft: 0.003.
   East Terrace, Area F. Id E NW 7/9 Loc. 005.
   Date: Hellenistic or earlier.
   Long shaft with round section tapering to a point. Other end flattened, rounded and pierced through to form the eye.
   Publ. Stager, Walker, and Wright 1974:65.

   Cf. Gjerstad et al. 1935:580, pl. CLXXVI.9. Gjerstad asserts that all the Idalion needles found were of the same type. In fact, however, some, such as our no. 27 and his no. 1051 have pierced eyes; others have the eyes formed by folding over the end of the shaft as in his no. 875 (pl. CLXXVI.10).

28. 73/592/F456   Pl. 2

   Copper alloy. M.P.L. 0.003, Th. 0.0015.
   Lower City, Area B, Building C. Id W NW 8/18 Loc. 015.

   Found together with locket no. 85 and remains of iron nails, part of an iron blade, and other fragments of iron. Completely corroded; head and eye missing; could be a pin. Shaft tapers to a point and is round in section.

Cotter Pins

29. 71/12/F8   Pl. 2

   Copper alloy. M.P.L. 0.0265, W. 0.007, Th. 0.002.
   West Acropolis, Area of Hellenistic Wall. Id W SE 11/36 Loc. 002.
   Ends missing. Small piece of metal bent to form a hairpin-shaped loop; ends bend slightly outward.

   Cf. Gjerstad et al. 1935:582, 616, pl. CLXXVIII.5 "mountings" type 3, periods 5 and 6.

30. 71/10/F6   Pl. 2

   Copper alloy. M.L. 0.032, L. head: 0.010, Th. legs: 0.001, W. head: 0.003.
   West Acropolis, Area of Hellenistic Wall. Id W SE 11/36 Loc. 002.
   Single piece of metal with square section flattened in the middle and folded to form a "head." The legs are pinched together under the head; one is straight, the other bent outward, then in. Somewhat similar to "mountings" in Gjerstad et al. 1935:582, 616, pl. CLXXVIII.5, 8, 9, 10.

Knife

31. 76/845/F556   Pl. 2

   Iron. M.P.L. ca. 0.123, M.W. 0.0275, Th. 0.006.
   Lower City, Area B, Building A. Id W NW 10/18. N balk removal.
   Heavily corroded. Tang and tip broken. Curved blade with convex back, concave edge, tapering to a point at one end. The tang or haft is broken away but the possible remains of a rivet hole are in the butt end.
   Cf. Gjerstad et al. 1935:576, pl. CLXXIII.7, Idalion, iron type 4, period 6; Gjerstad 1948:132, 135, fig. 21.11, Type 1d.

Blade of a knife or dagger

32. 73/S405/F370   Pl. 2

   Iron. M.P.L. 0.064, M.W. 0.0325, Th. at center: 0.009.
   Surface survey, E25/S60 Unit 1.
   Heavily corroded; both ends missing. Apparently part of a straight blade from a knife or dagger. Seems to have an edge on one side.

Trident

33. 71/8/F4   Pl. 2

   Iron. M.P.L. 0.064, span tines at base: 0.038, diam. shaft: 0.016, diam. tines: 0.009, 0.010.
   West Acropolis or Terrace, Id W SE no area given.
   Shaft and ends of tines broken. Shaft and tines have round sections. Base of fork is flattened.

Hooks

34. 71/19/F17   Pl. 2

   Iron. M.P.L. 0.040, Th. 0.006.
   West Acropolis, Hellenistic Wall. Id W SE 11/36 Loc. 005.
   Small hook with square section. Surface corroded.

35. 71/47/F127   Pl. 2

   Copper alloy. M.P.L. 0.037, Th. 0.005.
   East Terrace, Area F. Id E NW 7/7, atop soil dump.
   Both ends missing. Small hook with square section.

36. 71/31/F26   Pl. 2

   Copper alloy. M.L. 0.047, W. shaft: 0.003, Th. hook: 0.004.
   West Acropolis, Gjerstad's dump. Id W SE 11/45 Loc. 003.
   Flat, vertical shaft widening at base to form a curved hook with round section which is flattened and curves outward at the outer end.

Repair Clamp

37. 73/F435   Pl. 2

   Lead. M.P.L. 0.049, Th. long bar: 0.007, Th. cross bar: 0.007.
   Lower City, Area B, Building C. Id W NW 8/18 Loc. 003. Round with several fragments of iron and lead.
   Date: Archaic?
   Two long bars, originally joined by two short bars. The object is of a type used in antiquity to repair pottery and other materials.
   Cf. Waldbaum 1983:67-68 for discussion and refs.; Robinson 1941, pls. XCVIII, XCIX.

Bowl

38. 72/425/F305   Pl. 2

   Copper alloy. M. diam: 0.034, Th. rim: 0.002, H. 0.015.
   West Acropolis, Gjerstad's dump. Id W SE 7/50 Loc. 020.

   Small plain bowl with broken base originally either rounded or flattened. Flaring walls, plain straight rim. Similar to Gjerstad et al. 1935:583, pl. CLXXX.2, Idalion Type 2, periods 5 and 6; Gjerstad 1948:150, 151 fig. 28.5, Type 2a lasting from CG I-CC II.

Ring attachments

39. 71/27/F22   Pl. 2

   Copper alloy. M. diam. ext.: 0.020, int. diam.: 0.013, Th. 0.003.
   West Acropolis, Gjerstad's dump. Id W SE 11/45 locus unavailable.
   Small ring, apparently with open ends. Around the join of the ends is a small flat strip broken off another object to which the ring was attached.

   For possible use see Gjerstad et al. 1935:582, 616, pl. CLXXVIII.9, 10 "mountings"; Karageorghis 1967:82-84, 87, pls. LXXXV, CXLII-CXLIII, Tomb 47 nos. 66-69, 98-102 chariot fittings: yoke rings, CA I.

40. 71/13/F9   Pl. 2

   Copper alloy. Ext. diam. base: 0.0255, ext. diam. top: 0.0235, W. band: 0.011, Th. 0.0015.
   West Acropolis, Gjerstad's dump. Id W SE 13/50 Loc. 003.
   Broad band flaring from top to bottom, flattened or beveled on top; thin edge on bottom; open ends. Probably was attached to another object.

41. 71/34/F45   Fig. 2a

   Copper alloy. Ext. diam.: 0.010, int. diam.: 0.007, Th. 0.0015, W. 0.0055.
   West Acropolis, Gjerstad's dump. Id W SE 11/45 Loc. 003.
   Small, wide ring, apparently from another object, possibly part of a chain or vessel. May be ridged.

Handles

42. 72/429/F309   Pl. 2

   Copper alloy. W. 0.046, H. 0.044, Th. 0.006-0.007, L. rivet: 0.006, diam. ends: 0.010.
   West Acropolis, Gjerstad's dump. Id W SE 7/50 Loc. 017.

Semicircular loop with round section; ends flattened. A rivet passes through each end. Heavily corroded. Probably a swinging handle from a vessel or possibly a box attachment (see Waldbaum 1983:96-97, 141-142).

43.   71/46/F125   Pl. 2

Iron. M.P.L. 0.075, L. rivet: 0.021, W. blade: 0.0355.
West Terrace, Area C. Id W SW 11/9 Loc. 003.
Fragmentary and heavily corroded so difficult to ascertain the original form. Blade or handle apparently flat and rectangular, held to two to three other pieces by a heavy rivet. Half of another rivet hole preserved in broken edge.
Date: Hellenistic or earlier.

Ingot?

44.   72/169/F182   Pl. 3

Copper (alloy?). L. 0.170, W. 0.150, Th. 0.022-0.013.
Surface Survey. Id E NW 19/2.

Apparently complete. Very heavy (though not weighed), flat, rectangular plaque of solid metal. Edges preserved on all sides. On one side the surface is rough and "runny" looking with some black and scoriated patches. The other side is somewhat smoother, though still uneven. The thickness is uneven, being thicker to one side and thinning towards the other. These features all suggest an unworked ingot left as it was poured from the smelting furnace.

Hinge or clasp

45.   72/428/F308   Pl. 3

Copper alloy. M.P.L. 0.068, W. flat end: 0.034, Th. 0.002, Diam. swivel: 0.008.
West Acropolis, Gjerstad's dump. Id W SE 7/50 Loc. 017.
Broad, triangular flat piece tapering to one side which is folded over to form a tubular socket. Through this can be seen the remains of a pin. Two square pieces of metal hold the folded parts together.

Chisels

46.   71/43/F124   Pl. 3, Fig. 2b

Copper alloy. M.L. 0.084, W. edge: 0.013, Th. edge: 0.0015, Th. end: 0.0065.
Lower City, "Well House" Building 5. Id W NW 39/21 Loc. 021.
Date: Cypro-Classical?
Vertical shaft with square section flattened and splayed on one end to a thin working edge. The top of the shaft shows signs of working.
Publ. Stager, Walker, and Wright 1974:50.

47.   72/427/F307   Pl. 3

Copper alloy. M.P.L. 0.102, W. 0.006-0.007.
West Acropolis, Gjerstad's dump. Id W SE 7/50 Loc. 017.
A once straight rod with square to rectangular section flattened and splayed at one end to form an edge. The edge is now bent and curled around. The other end is flattened, possibly from working.

Nails

Most of the nails found were of the same general type: relatively small with tapered shafts, square in section and rounded flat or slightly domed heads. Two or three have shafts with round sections, which is unusual for ancient handmade nails (see Waldbaum 1983:68 for discussion and refs.). Unfortunately, none was found in a context that shed much light on its original function. Most of the nails found are in poor shape, being heavily corroded and broken. Therefore, dimensions given are only approximate. In addition to the nails catalogued here numbers of fragmentary and corroded iron rods that could be parts of nail shafts were found in many loci during excavation.

48.   71/32/F27   Pl. 3

Iron. M.P.L. 0.047, Diam. head: 0.021, Th. shaft: 0.009.
East Terrace, Area F. Id E NW 7/10 Loc. 002.
Tapered shaft with square section widest just under the head; round flat head.

49.   71/16/F12   Pl. 3

Iron. M.P.L. 0.044, Diam. head: 0.013, Th. shaft: 0.006.
West Terrace. Id W SW 6/23 Loc. 002.
Tapered shaft with square section; small, round flat head.

50.   74/701/F522   Pl. 3

Copper alloy? M.P.L. 0.022, Diam. head: 0.016, Th. shaft: 0.006.
West Terrace, Area D. Id W SW 11/17 Balk trim.
Shaft broken and corroded but apparently round in section. The head is round and flat to slightly domed.

51.   71/59/F23   Fig. 2c

Copper alloy. L. 0.0165, Diam. head: 0.010, Th. shaft: 0.0035.
West Terrace. Id W SW 6/23 Loc. 003.
Short tapered shaft with square section. Flat, round to irregular head.

52.   73/F419   Pl. 3

Iron. M.P.L. 0.060, Diam. head: ca. 0.020, shaft too swollen to measure.
Lower City, Area B. Id W NW 8/18 Loc. 005.
Thickly swollen shaft, tapering to a point. Broad, irregular head.

53.   73/F409   Pl. 3

Iron. M.P.L. 0.040, Diam. head: 0.017, Th. shaft: 0.007.
Lower City, Area B. Id W NW 10/17 Loc. 002, plough soil.
Shaft with square section tapers to a point. Round to irregular, slightly domed head.

54-8. 73/F462   Pl. 3

Iron. M.P.L.: 0.054, 0.055, 0.023, Diam. heads: 0.025, 0.018, 0.020; shafts too swollen to measure.
Lower City, Area B, Building C. Id W NW 8/18 Loc. 015. Found with other fragments of iron and lead.
Four to five fragmentary nails with thick, swollen shafts, square in section. Preserved heads apparently found.

59. 73/F434   Pl. 3

   Iron. M.P.L. 0.026, Diam. head: 0.025; shaft too swollen to measure.
   Lower City, Area B. Id W NW 8/19 Loc. 008.
   Shaft broken but has round section; head broad and round.

60. 72/75/F137   Pl. 3
   Iron. M.P.L. 0.021, Diam. shaft: 0.006.
   West Acropolis, Gjerstad's dump. Id W SE 7/50 Loc. 001.
   Shaft broken but round in section; head apparently flat and round, but it too is broken.

Tacks

61. 80/945/F626   Pl. 3

   Copper alloy. M.P.L. 0.015, Diam. head: 0.0065.
   West Terrace, Area C. Loc. 024.
   Short, bent, tapered shaft; round head.

62. 80/946/F627   Pl. 3

   Copper alloy. M.P.L. 0.010, Diam. head: 0.012.
   West Terrace. Area C. Loc. 024.
   Short, tapered shaft; round flat head.

Jewelry

With few exceptions, the jewelry found by the American Expedition to Idalion consists of simple types of rings, earrings, and pins, primarily in copper alloy. Only one fibula fragment and two or three small gold and silver ornaments are of special interest.

Rings

Gjerstad (Gjerstad et al. 1935:580-81) identified five types of rings from Idalion. Of these, all but the fifth, a plain ring with spirally twisted bezel, have also been found by the current expedition.

I. Plain hoop, round or flat in section; no openings in the hoop. This is a common type in Cyprus and elsewhere from the Bronze Age on (see Gjerstad et al. 1935:580, 616, pl. CLXXVI.25, periods 2-3 through 6; Gjerstad 1948:144, 147 fig. 26.10, 217 and p. 389 where he correctly notes that the type is "too widely diffused . . . to be used as a criterion of cultural relations.").

63. 72/454/F311   Pl. 3

   Copper alloy. Ext. diam.: 0.023, Th. 0.003.
   West Acropolis, Gjerstad's dump. Id W SE 7/50 Loc. 002.
   Heavily corroded.

64. 72/454/F311   Pl. 3

   Copper alloy. Est. ext. diam.: 0.019, Th. 0.003.
   West Acropolis, Gjerstad's dump. Id W SE 7/50 Loc. 002.
   Similar to preceding but only half preserved.

II. Plain hoop with open, overlapping ends. Again, this is a common type in use from the Bronze Age on, and cannot be used as a dating criterion. Gjerstad also classified objects similar to this as his Type 1 earring (see Gjerstad et al. 1935:580, 615, pl. CLXXVI.21, found in periods 1, 2, 5, 6; Gjerstad 1948:144, 147 fig. 26.5, 6, 216, CG I-CA II and continuing into CC). It is, of course, possible that so simple an object could function as either a finger ring or earring.

65.   76/846/F557   Pl. 3

   Copper alloy. Est. diam.: ca. 0.018, Th. 0.003.
   Tomb 1, Loc. 004.
   Date: Late Cypriot II C.
   Part of a small spiral with at least two turns. Hoop round in section.

   This is included in C. Adelman's catalogue of objects from Tomb 1 as no. 47, pl. 15, fig. 15 (this volume).

66.   73/F411   Pl. 4

   Copper alloy. Diam. 0.019, Th. 0.004.
   Lower City, Area B. Id W NW 8/18 Loc. 010. Found with many fragments of iron and lead.
   Hoop has round section.

67.   72/459/F315   Pl. 4, Fig. 2d

   Silver? Ext. diam.: 0.020, Th. 0.003.
   West Acropolis, Gjerstad's dump. Id W SE 7/50 Loc. 002.
   Grey patina. Hoop has round section.

68.   71/15/F11   Pl. 4

   Copper alloy. Ext. diam.: 0.019, Th. 0.001.
   West Acropolis, Hellenistic Wall. Id W SE 11/36 Loc. 005.
   Date: Hellenistic or earlier.
   Hoop has round section.

   III. Plain hoop with small gap between the ends. This seems to correspond to Gjerstad's Idalion Type 3, found in periods 3-6 (see Gjerstad et al. 1935:580-81, 616, pl. CLXXVI.27).

69.   74/662/F516   Pl. 4

   Copper alloy. Ext. diam.: 0.014, Th. 0.002.
   West Terrace. Id W SW 6/17 Loc. 001.1, surface.
   Hoop has square section. It is possible that the opening in the hoop is the result of a break and is not intentional.

   IV. Plain hoop with open or closed ends. The center of the hoop is flattened to form a plain oval bezel. The type corresponds to Gjerstad's Idalion Type 4 found in his periods 5-6 and 6 (see Gjerstad et al. 1935:581, 616, pl. CLXXVI.28; Gjerstad 1948:146, 147 fig. 26.15, Type 5, 217, and p. 390 where he notes that the type is found as early as the Bronze Age).

70.   72/456/F312   Pl. 4, Fig. 2e

   Copper alloy. W. hoop: 0.001, Th. 0.001, M.W. bezel: 0.005.
   East Terrace, Area F. Id E NW 7/9 Loc. 001, surface.
   Hoop broken and twisted.

71. 71/5/F1   Pl. 4

   Copper alloy. M. diam.: 0.017, Th. 0.002, M.W. bezel: 0.005.
   West Acropolis, Gjerstad's dump. Id W Se 11/45 Loc. 002.
   Hoop has round section and open ends.

72. 72/212/F167   Pl. 4

   Silver? Ext. diam.: 0.013, Th. 0.002, W. bezel: 0.005.
   West Acropolis, Gjerstad's dump. Id W SE 7/50 Loc. 005.
   Hoop has round section and is closed.

Earrings

   Only three were found. Each is different.

73. 71/7/F3   Pl. 4

   Silver. M.L. 0.015, M.W. 0.012, Th. 0.004.
   West Acropolis, East of Hellenistic Wall. Id W Se 11/36 Loc. 004.
   Date: Hellenistic or earlier.
   Small, plain "leech-shaped" earring, thickened on one side. The thinner end comes to a point.

   This is a very common earring type in Cyprus, the Near East, and the Aegean, and has a long history. For Idalion see Gjerstad et al. 1935:580, 615, pl. CLXXVI.24 in copper alloy, periods 2-6, 583, 616, pl. CLXXX.21, silver, periods 2-3 and 6; Gjerstad 1948:156, 157; fig. 31.13, silver, 219, 385 where he cites Near Eastern examples going back to Sumerian times. Similar ones were also found more recently at Salamis in CA and CC contexts (see Karageorghis 1970:34, pl. XLIX Tomb 16.1a, 2a; 58, pls. XLIX, CXI, Tomb 29.12, 13, 15; 59, pl. CXIII, Tomb 30 no. 3; 62-63, pl. CXVI nos. Dr. 6, Ch. 8, 9, Tomb 33; 87, pl. CXXXVI.13, 16, 17, Tomb 55; 123, pl. CLVII, Tomb 82 nos. 15, 16, 17 in bronze and silver; 168 pl. XLIX, Tomb 115 no. 4).

74. 77/848/F582   (Not figured)

   Copper alloy. Diam. 0.013, Th. 0.002.
   Lower City, Area B. Id W NW 9/20 Loc. 002.
   Small hoop with open, tapered ends. Hoop has round section. Possibly a finger ring?

75. 72/223/F192   Pl. 4

   Gold. Diam. rosette: 0.010, Th. 0.001.
   West Acropolis, Gjerstad's dump. Id W SE 7/50 Loc. 016.
   Small circle of gold foil forms the pendant of an earring. The front of the disk is slightly convex with individual loops of gold wire applied to the convex side to form a rosette pattern. Attached to the center of the back or concave side is a length of wire that probably attached to the actual earring or perhaps to some other kind of object.
   Publ. Stager, Walker, and Wright 1974, fig. 52.

   Nothing similar to this was found by Gjerstad at Idalion. Several somewhat similar objects were found by Cesnola in tombs at Idalion (see Cesnola 1903, pl. XXII.30-42). Most of Cesnola's examples are openwork disks in rosette patterns and most have stones set in the center. The area of closest similarity is in the use of applied wire filigree on some examples (see also Vessberg and Westholm 1956:116 fig. 34.19, 119 Type 9).

Bracelets

76. 71/30/F25   Pl. 4, Fig. 2f

    Copper alloy. M.P.L. 0.064, W. 0.0055, L. rivet: 0.004.
    West Acropolis, over Hellenistic Wall. Id W SE 11/36 Loc. 003.
    Curved strip of metal with upper surface molded in bead and reel pattern. The shape and decoration suggest a fragment of a bracelet, but the fact that two rivets pass through the band, one near each preserved end, may indicate that the object was an attachment of some kind, perhaps for a small box or casket.

    For box attachments see e.g., Waldbaum 1983:76-78.

77. 72/457/F313   Fig. 2g

    Copper alloy. M.P.L. 0.033, Th. 0.0035.
    Surface Survey. Id E NW 25/10.
    Part of a thin curved band with round section. No decoration.

Button or stud

78. 71/48/F129   Pl. 4

    Silver? Diam.: 0.0115, Th. 0.0035.
    West Terrace, Area C.   Id W SW 11/9 Loc. 006.
    Round, disk-like object with possible relief on one flat side (now illegible). In profile there appear to be three disks sandwiched together.

Straight pins

79. 71/39/F113   Pl. 4, Fig. 2h

    Copper alloy. M.P.L. 0.0565, Diam. head: 0.005.
    West Terrace, Area D. Id W SW 10/16 Loc. 011.
    Date: Early Hellenistic?
    Narrow shaft with round section tapering to point. At opposite end is a small globular head. Heavily corroded and shaft bent.
    For date and phasing see Stager, Walker, and Wright 1974:50ff.

    For similar simple pin types from Idalion see Gjerstad et al. 1935:580, 615, pl. CLXXVI.12, periods 2, 3, 6; Gjerstad 1948:143, 145 fig. 25.24, 215.

80. 74/663/F517   Pl. 4

    Copper alloy. M.P.L. 0.010, Diam. head: 0.0025, Th. shaft: 0.002.
    West Terrace. Id W SW 6/17 Loc. 001.1, surface.
    Point and part of shaft broken; small, round, flat head.

81. 80/947/F628   Pl. 4

    Copper alloy. M.P.L. 0.034, Th. 0.004.
    West Terrace, Area C. Loc. 024.
    Two fragments of a pin shaft with flat to round section. Heavily corroded.

Fibula

82.   73/548/F449   Pl. 4

Copper alloy. M.P.L. 0.043, Th. rod of bow: 0.005, Diam. bead: 0.011, Diam. central disk: 0.0115.
Lower City, Area A, City Wall. Id W NW 42/22 Loc. 011 Layer 9, phase 3B.
Date: Archaic.

This fibula is fully described by S. Brown (this volume). In addition to the parallels cited by Brown this fibula seems to have affinities with some archaic Phrygian fibula types in certain of its details. These may be seen in examples of Blinkenberg's Type XII.14 found at Gordion and published by Muscarella (1967:24-25, pls. XI.58, XII.67, XIII.70, 71, XIV.75). Muscarella describes the type as a variant of Type XII.13 having a semicircular bow or arc with oval to round section, a molding at the center of the arc, moldings at each end of the arc and "an additional molding on each arm of the arc between the central and end molding making a total of five moldings. The additional moldings usually consist of sharp disks . . . " (Muscarella 1967:24). This type of fibula is very popular and is found at many sites in Anatolia, Greece, and the Near East, though not so far on Cyprus, in contexts dating from the eighth and seventh centuries B.C. through the sixth century B.C. and later. The main difference between these and the Idalion example is that the Phrygian ones are more regularly semicircular while ours has a somewhat lower curvature to the bow, more typical of the rather asymmetrical bows characteristic of Cypriot fibulae (e.g. Blinkenberg 1926:238-39, figs. 277-79). Another major difference seems to be in the treatment of the catchplate which in the Phrygian types is generally narrower and is usually horned (Muscarella 1967:37), unlike the handcatch seen on the Idalion piece. On the other hand, the clearly articulated and separated beads and disks of the Idalion piece, as well as their five-part division, are unusual for Cypriot and Near Eastern fibulae (cf. Brown, this volume), while they are normal for Phrygian ones (see e.g. Muscarella 1967, pls. XI.58, XII.67, XIII.70, 71, and especially Boehmer 1972:62, 64, pl. VII.125 and 1979:6, pl. IV.2549-552 for examples from Bogazköy with disks on the apex of the bows).

Because of the differences noted, it is unlikely that the Idalion fibula is an Anatolian import. Rather, as Brown suggests, it represents a local type showing strong foreign influence in its design, including, perhaps, some Phrygian elements.

Beads

83.   71/20/F18   Pl. 4, Fig. 2i

Copper alloy. Ext. diam.: 0.005, W. 0.008.
West Acropolis, Hellenistic Wall. Id W SE 11/36 Loc. 005.
Date: Hellenistic or earlier.
Small cylindrical wire spiral with seven turns tightly coiled. Possibly used as a spacer.

84.   72/202/F184   Pl. 4

Gold. M.L. 0.004, diam.: 0.002.
West Acropolis, Gjerstad's dump. Id W SE 7/50 Loc. 002.
Flat strip of sheet gold rolled to form a tiny, tubular bead. Outer surface decorated with four horizontal grooves.

Locket?

85.   73/562/F452   Pl. 4

Copper alloy. Diam. disk: 0.0245, H. sides: 0.004, L. loops: 0.003.

Lower City, Area B, Building C. Id W NW 8/18 Loc. 015. Found with needle no. 28 and fragments of iron and lead objects.

Thin disk with raised edges punctured slightly below center with round hole. On one side are two loops for suspension. Possibly forms half of an object such as a locket.

Disk

86.   74/611/F509   Pl. 4

Copper alloy. M.P.W. 0.039, Th. 0.010, Diam. inner circle: 0.016.
Surface Find. Lower City W NW 13/29.
Amorphous flat piece of metal, once apparently circular. Part of edge preserved on one side. Incised concentric circles on both sides, two near the edge, one at the center.

Table 1. Concordance of Metal Objects by Find Spot

Area	Locus	Cat. no.	Object type
Lower City			
Area B W NW 8/18	003	37	repair clamp
	005	52	nail
	010	66	ring
	015	28	needle
	015	54-58	nails
	015	85	locket?
Area B W NW 8/19	008	59	nail
Area B W NW 9/20	002	74	earring
Area B W NW 10/17	002	53	nail
Area B W NW 10/18	---	31	knife
Well House, Building 5, W NW 39/21	021	46	chisel
Area A, City Wall W NW 42/22	011	82	fibula
East Terrace			
Area F E NW 7/7	soil dump	35	hook
Area F E NW 7/8	009	9	arrowhead
Area F E NW 7/9	001	70	ring
	005	27	needle
Area F E NW 7/10	002	48	nail
West Terrace			
Area C W SW 11/9	003	43	handle
	006	78	button or stud
Area C ---	009	25	cheekpiece
Area C ---	024	61, 62	tacks
Area C ---	024	81	straight pin?
Area C ---	028	11	arrowhead
Area D W SW 9/16	012	22	sling bullet
Area D W SW 10/16	011	79	straight pin
Area D W SW 11/16	014	3	arrowhead
Area D W SW 11/17	balk trim	50	nail
Area D W SW 6/17	001.1	69	ring
Area D	001.1	80	straight pin
Area D	002	49	nail
Area D	003	51	nail
Area of City Wall	008	10	arrowhead
West Terrace or Acropolis			
W SE ---	---	33	trident

Table 1. Concordance of Metal Objects by Find Spot (*cont.*)

Area	Locus	Cat. no.	Object type
West Acropolis			
Area of Hellenistic			
Wall W SE 11/36	001	13	arrowhead
	002	29, 30	cotter pins
	003	76	bracelet?
	004	1	arrowhead
	004	15	spearhead
	004	16–18	sling bullets
	004	73	earring
	005	34	hook
	005	68	ring
	005	83	bead
	007	19	sling bullet
	010	20, 21	sling bullets
West Acropolis			
Gjerstad's Dump			
W SE 7/50	001	14	spearhead
	001	26	armor scale
	001	60	nail
	002	7	arrowhead
	002	63, 64, 67	rings
	002	84	bead
	004	24	sling bullet
	005	72	ring
	010	12	arrowhead
	012	8	arrowhead
	014	2	arrowhead
	016	75	earring pendant
	017	42	handle
	017	45	hinge or clasp
	017	47	chisel
	020	38	bowl
W SE 11/45	002	71	ring
	003	4–6	arrowheads
	003	36	hook
	003	41	ring attachment
	---	39	ring attachment
W SE 13/50	002	23	sling bullet
	003	40	ring attachment
Tomb 1	004	65	ring
Surface Survey E NW 25/10	---	77	bracelet frag.
Surface Survey W NW 13/29	---	86	disk
Surface Survey E NW 19/2	---	44	ingot
Surface Survey E 25/S60			
Unit 1	---	32	blade frag.

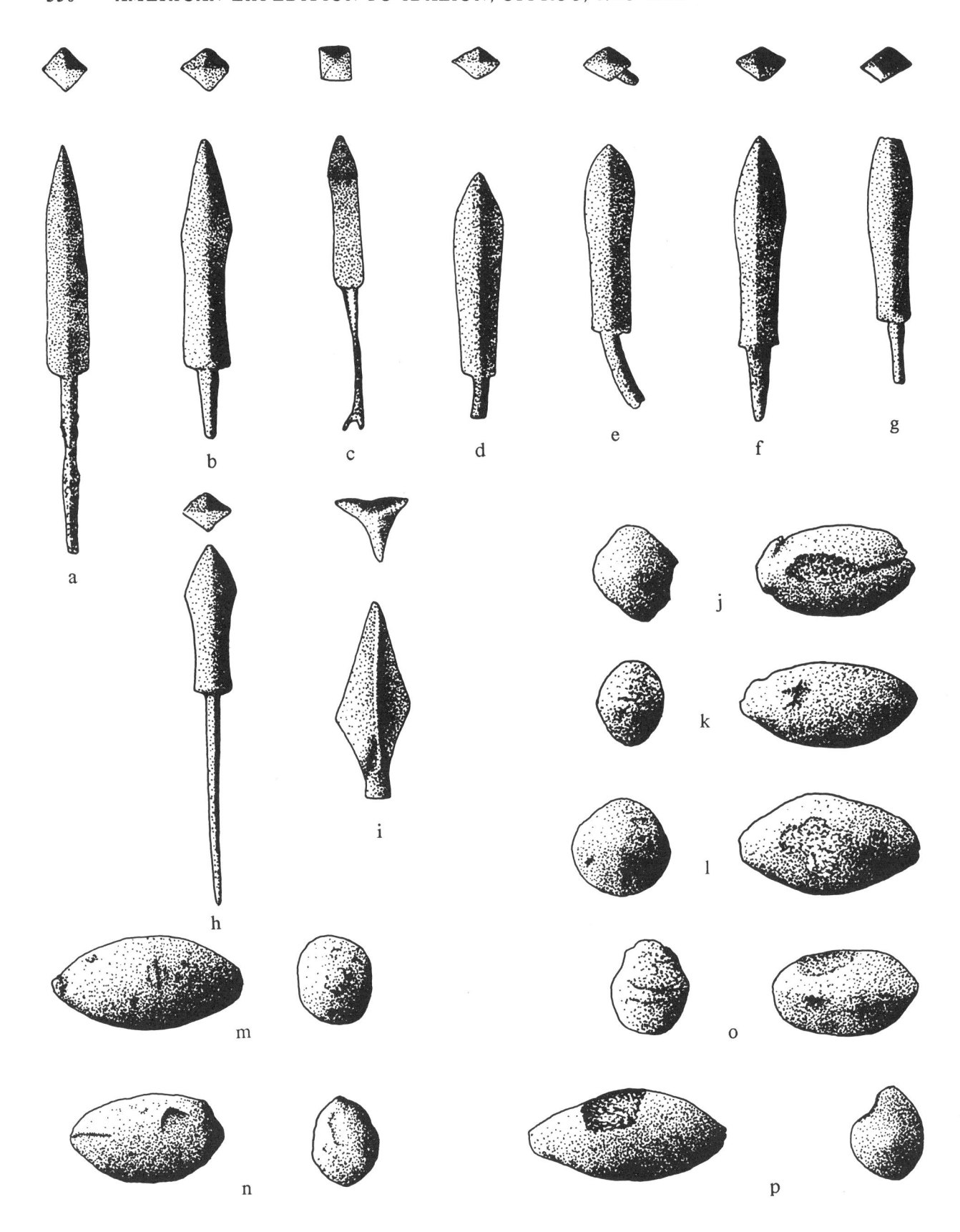

Figure 1. Arrowheads (a-i) and Sling Bullets (j-p). Scale 1:1.

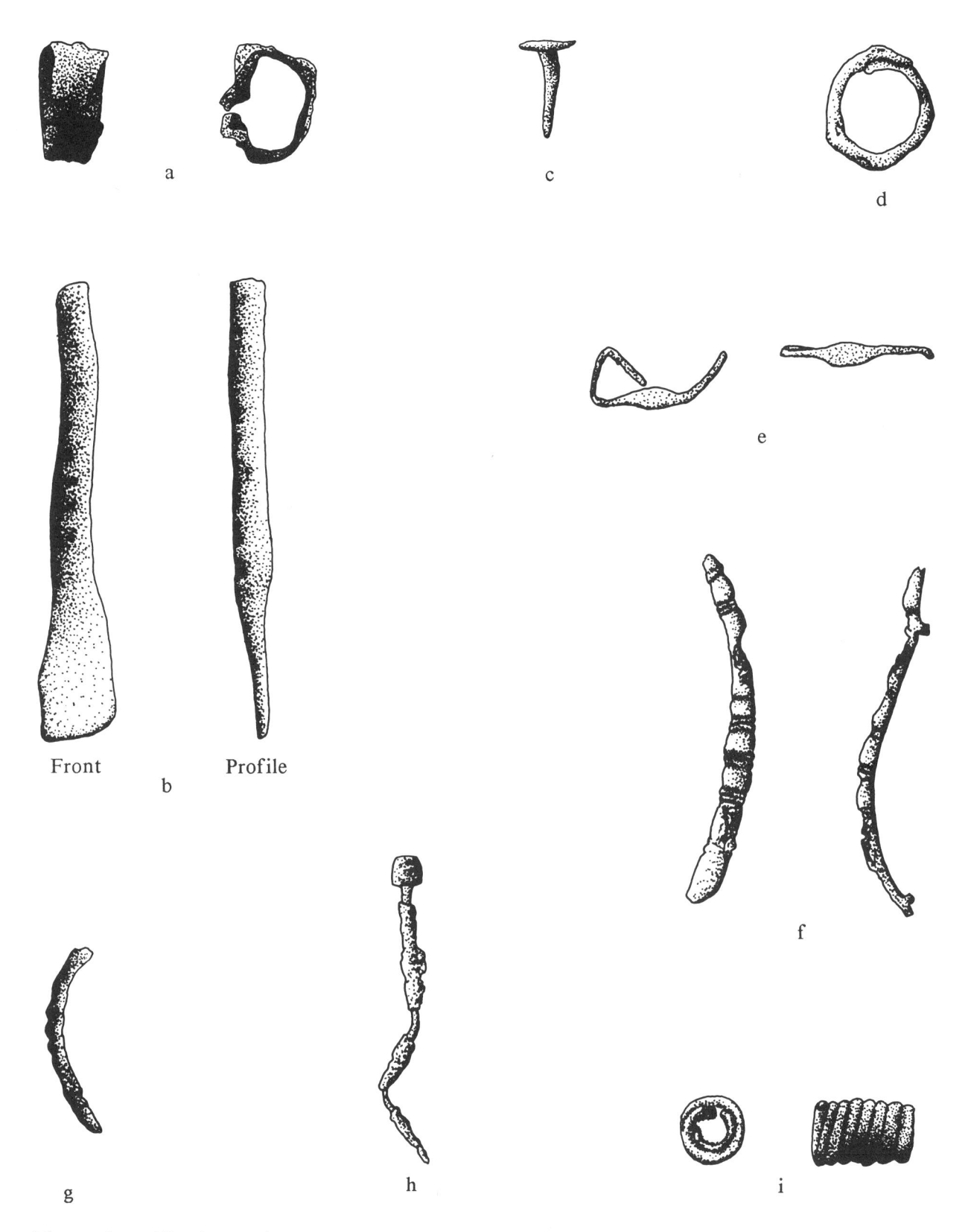

Figure 2. Utilitarian Objects and Jewelry. a. Ring attachment (Cat. no. 41); b. Chisel (Cat. no. 46); c. Nail (Cat. no. 51); d-e. Hoops (Cat. nos. 67-70); f-g. Bracelets (Cat. nos. 76, 77); h. Straight pin (Cat. no. 79); i. Bead (Cat. no. 83). Scale 1:1 (a-h); 2:1 (i).

PLATE 1

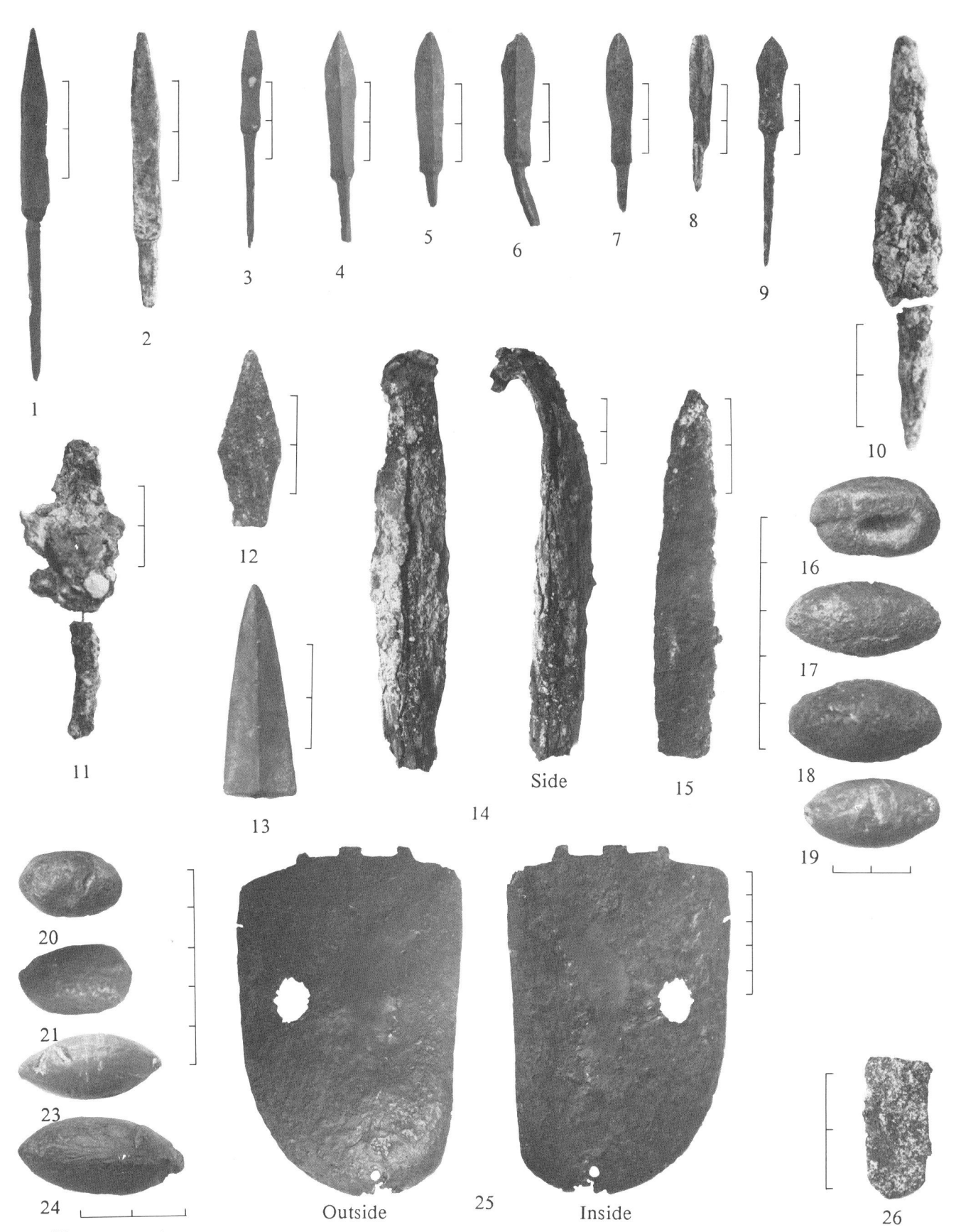

Weapons and Armor (Cat. nos. 1-21 and 23-26). Each scale division represents one centimeter.

PLATE 2

Utilitarian Objects (Cat. nos. 27–40, 42, and 43). Each scale division represents one centimeter.

PLATE 3

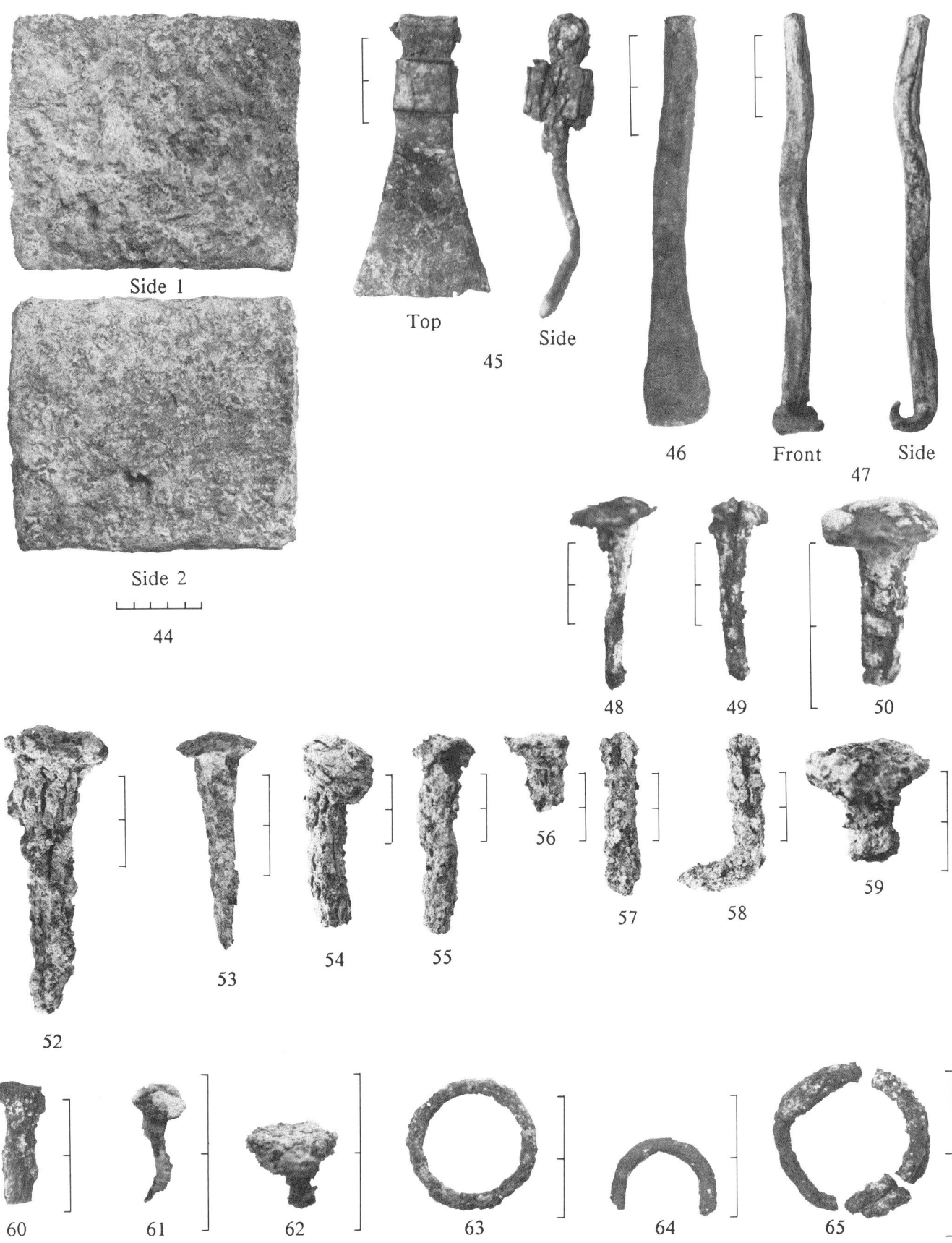

Utilitarian Objects (Cat. nos. 44-50 and 52-62) and Jewelry (Cat. nos. 63-65). Each scale division represents one centimeter.

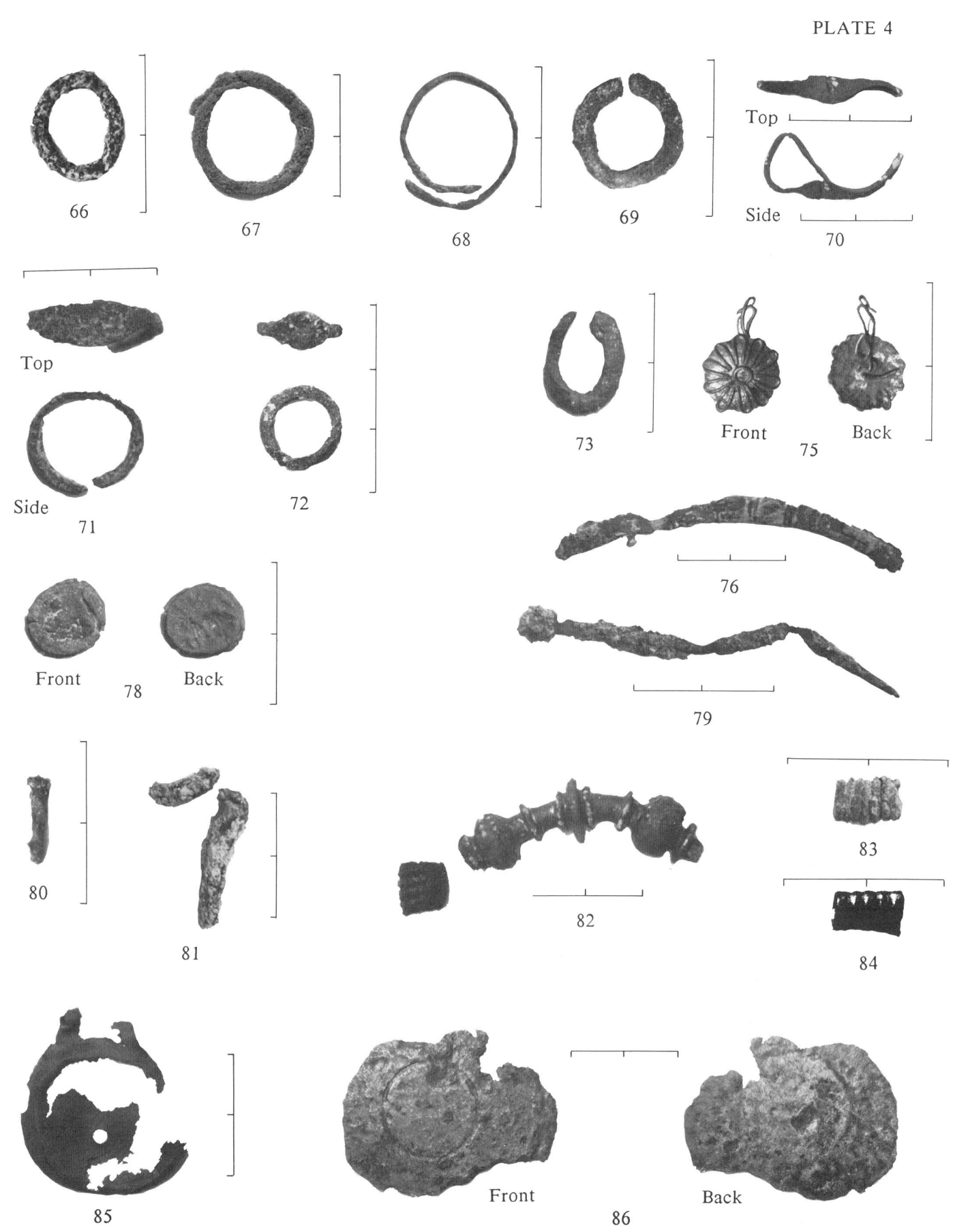

PLATE 4

Jewelry (Cat. nos. 66-73, 75, 76, and 78-86). Each scale division represents one centimeter.

IV. REGIONAL STUDIES
A. NEUTRON ACTIVATION ANALYSIS OF CYPRIOT POTTERY

Alan M. Bieber, Jr.[*]

This study includes analyses of nearly 500 specimens, a substantial body of data. Before the details of neutron activation analysis as used here are presented, a brief discussion of the technique and its history in archaeological applications is in order.

Neutron activation analysis is a way of determining the chemical composition of a material. It has the advantages of requiring only very small amounts of material (in the case of pottery, less than 100 mg), and of being quite sensitive. For many elements it allows routine determination of concentrations in the part-per-million (ppm) range, and it also permits simultaneous determination of the concentrations of many elements in one sample. The technique is based upon the fact that many elements, when bombarded with neutrons, produce radioisotopes that emit gamma rays of known, unique energies. Thus, by counting the number of gamma rays of a given energy emitted by a sample of unknown composition, it is possible to determine the amount of each radioisotope present, and by comparison with an identically bombarded and identically counted sample of known composition, to calculate the concentration of the elements that produced the radioisotopes.

The history of neutron activation analysis in archaeology goes back barely twenty years. Some of the earliest work dealt with Mediterranean ceramics (see Emeleus 1960; Sayre and Dodson 1957; Sayre, Murrenhof, and Weick 1958, inter alia), and there has been a continuing interest in analysis of Near Eastern and Mediterranean ceramics (see, for example, Artzy 1972; Asaro, Perlman, and Dothan, 1971; Perlman and Asaro 1969). Most of these studies, however, have dealt with relatively small numbers of samples that could be compared easily with little or no use of statistics or other numerical techniques, and little attention was paid to the problem of statistical verification of the conclusions.

Recently there has been increasing interest in the use of statistical and numerical techniques for dealing with activation analysis data (see, for example, Ward 1974; Bieber et al. 1976a, 1976b). The large body of data necessary for tests of the hypotheses considered here led to two basic methodological problems:

1. Finding the most practical and most fruitful way of dealing with and summarizing the results of the analysis of a large body of numerical data such as that generated by neutron activation analysis.

2. Choosing between different statistical and taxonomic interpretations of the results.

It is axiomatic in science in general that in order for the results of a procedure to be completely valid one must be able to reproduce them. Given this, some objective procedure must be used to generate the compositional categories of the specimens analyzed and test the

---

[*]Department of Nuclear Energy, Brookhaven National Laboratory, Upton, New York

This research was supported by National Science Foundation grant number SOC 7305582 (GS 40215), and by grants from the National Endowment for the Humanities, the University of Connecticut Research Foundation, and the American Schools of Oriental Research. This work was performed under the auspices of the United States Atomic Energy Commission.

validity of these categories by neutron activation. Statistical methods, being well established, objective, repeatable, and based on a well-developed body of theory, provide one possible means of generating, testing, and comparing groups. In cases where the data do not allow the use of statistical methods, however (due to insufficient sample size, possible nonrandom sampling, or non-normal distributions, for example), the methods of numerical taxonomy, in particular cluster analysis, appear to provide a good alternative. The problem is to decide which statistical and/or taxonomic methods are most applicable, provide the most easily interpretable results, and require the smallest expenditure of time for the most objective, repeatable, and archaeologically interpretable results.

The chemical and archaeological conclusions reached, and a detailed comparison and discussion of various methods of data analysis are presented below.

Selection of Specimens for Analysis

One major problem facing a researcher is the selection of a manageable number of specimens for analysis from the astronomically large number of excavated sherds and vessels. There is also the practical difficulty of making this selection while an excavation is under way, or while in a museum for a limited period of time. Such complications may force certain compromises. One is faced with the problem of selecting a representative group of specimens, both of a practical size and useful for testing the hypotheses. One does this, moreover, without any way of knowing in advance the total size and composition of the statistical universe of specimens from which the group is selected.

Ideally, the selection of specimens for a study such as this should be made on the basis of statistical sampling procedures that maximize the probability that the group will be truly representative of the overall body of material under consideration. In this study, however, practical problems made the use of such techniques impossible, so other means of selection had to be used. Basically, it relies upon the writer's own intuitive judgment and the judgment of other members of the staff of the Idalion excavations (principally Prof. Per Ålin) who were thoroughly familiar with both the pottery excavated at Idalion and Cypriot Iron Age pottery in general. On this basis selected specimens were chosen that would fit the criteria for sherds necessary for this study.

Three categories of specimens were chosen for inclusion. The first consists of sherds excavated at Idalion, dated stylistically to periods that span the Iron Age and judged to be stylistically representative of Idalion ceramics. This category forms the basic comparison group for determining whether samples were manufactured at Idalion or imported from elsewhere. The second category is composed of sets of Iron Age sherds excavated at sites in other parts of Cyprus judged to be stylistically typical of ceramics from those sites. This category provides the basic comparison group for determining the probable origins of imported sherds found at Idalion. The third category is the set of sherds found at Idalion that appear stylistically anomalous and may therefore have been imported. Each of these categories is intended to include specimens from periods and of types appropriate for testing each of the hypotheses outlined below.

In addition, a variety of clay sources were selected for analysis that might have been used around Cyprus in antiquity. The clays were selected with several aims in mind: first, to study a representative collection of clays to aid the geological and ceramic studies that are an integral part of the Idalion project; second, to determine from samples of clays collected in the immediate vicinity of Idalion which types and sources might have been used in antiquity. In addition, a group was chosen for inclusion in this study that provided examples of clays from all parts of the island. These clays provide additional comparative material for determining the sources of imports and for verifying the geographic origins of sherds produced at sites other than Idalion.

Where possible, sherds were taken to Brookhaven National Laboratory for analysis. All such sherds were numbered (if not already numbered), and the number, full provenience information, and a brief description of each sherd were entered in notes. In many cases, however, sherds or vessels had to be sampled in the field, using the procedures outlined elsewhere by the author (Bieber 1977:72-81). In these cases, the sample number, the sherd number, provenience information, and a brief description of the sherd were entered in field notes as each piece was sampled. Where the specimens had been mentioned in the literature (as in the case of the Swedish Cyprus Expedition pottery sampled), the literature reference for each piece was also noted. Full information on each sample included in this study is presented in the tables.

Data Handling and Statistical Analysis

After analyzing a large collection of specimens such as that included in this study, one faces the problem of sorting the data into groups of samples that are similar in composition. In order for such a classification to be useful, each group must be both relatively homogeneous in chemical composition and at the same time sufficiently distinct from all other groups that most samples may be unambiguously assigned to a specific group.

The total spread expected in a group of sherds made from a particular clay is a combination of analytical error, sampling error (that is, error introduced due to nonrepresentative sampling of specimens), and the spread due to the natural compositional variation in the clay(s) used. Mathematically

$$S_T^2 = S_A^2 + S_S^2 + S_N^2,$$

where

S_T^2 is the total variance of a group for a particular element

S_A^2 is the squared analytical error

S_S^2 is the variance due to nonrepresentative sampling, and

S_N^2 is the variance due to compositional variation in the clay(s) used to manufacture the specimens.

S_A^2 can be estimated. $(S_S^2 + S_N^2)$ can be estimated for a particular group and can be minimized by proper sampling, but S_N^2 is of course a function of the characteristics of each specific clay source, and is difficult and impractical to estimate. Experience with groups of sherds from various areas that are archaeologically known to have been made from one source of clay has shown that a group of sherds will have an average spread of 10 to 20%, and that a spread of 5% for any element is about the best that can be expected (see Bieber et al. 1976b; Brooks et al. 1974).

Given the characteristics of these groups, one can proceed to identify within the total collection of samples the groups that appear by inspection to be compositionally similar. Group means and standard deviations may then be calculated, and the groups may be further refined by reshuffling individual samples until a satisfactory classification is produced. This process can be speeded up and made somewhat easier by comparing plots or other graphical representations of the compositions of individual samples, rather than just using lists of numbers. In fact this was the procedure used until fairly recently at Brookhaven National Laboratory (Abascal, Harbottle, and Sayre 1974).

While this procedure is reasonably satisfactory when applied to a relatively small body of data (e.g., fewer than about fifty samples), it has several disadvantages. First of all, no provision is included for multivariate statistical testing of either the separability of the groups generated or of the probability that a given sample belongs to a particular group. Moreover the procedure becomes very time consuming and extremely unwieldy as the number of samples under consideration increases. Finally, the whole procedure is somewhat subjective; ideally, of course, a classificatory procedure should be such that anyone applying it to a given body of data will come out with the same results.

Working with E. V. Sayre at Brookhaven, the author had developed a classification system that can not only deal very readily and rather quickly with large bodies of data objectively, but also includes multivariate statistical tests of group separability and probability of group membership. This system, which combines methods from numerical taxonomy and multivariate statistics, is discussed in detail by Bieber (1977:82-118), with a discussion of the relative merits of several alternative approaches and some of the problems inherent in the basic procedure. Here, it suffices to say that the system allows specimens to be sorted into compositional groups that are meaningful both chemically and archaeologically. Briefly, the system consists of the following steps:

1) Compute matrices of various measures of distance or similarity between all specimens.

2) Run cluster analyses on each of the distance matrices.

3) Pick out those specimens that consistently form clusters, and consider them preliminary groups.

4) Compute group means, standard deviations, and 95% limits for each element in each group. Check whether the preliminary groups are acceptably compact, and provisionally eliminate loose groups and extreme specimens. Also check for unacceptable skewness or kurtosis.

5) Compare one- and two-dimensional plots of groups and determine which elements best discriminate between groups. Also compute correlation matrices, and see which groups of elements are intercorrelated. Be sure to include all elements of a correlated set in the subset chosen for discrimination.

6) Compute Mahalanobis distances and probabilities using sets of discriminating elements, and include or exclude specimens as appropriate.

7) Repeat steps 4) and 6) as necessary, until all groups include all specimens with significant probabilities, all groups have acceptably low standard deviations on all elements, and no groups show excessive skewness or kurtosis.

In the case of groups that have too few members to allow practical multivariate tests, step 6) is skipped. The validity of these groups can be tested by using one- or two-element methods.

Although the procedure outlined is fairly complex, past research and the results discussed below demonstrate that it produces groups that make both chemical and archaeological sense, and at the same time, by including statistical tests of the validity of the results, remain objective and reproducible. The writer believes this procedure to be an optimal combination of the classification techniques presently available.

Compositional Groups

When the numerical analysis techniques just discussed were applied to the chemical data on the sherds selected for solution of the archaeological problems under consideration, there resulted fifteen distinct compositional groups of sherds. Although in most cases twenty-two elements (listed in table 1) were determined in each specimen, the final grouping was made on the basis of only seventeen elements. It was decided not to use the data for tantalum, antimony, uranium, and calcium because they are among the least precisely determined elements. Moreover, for many specimens data on these elements are missing, due to the physical properties (such as thermal neutron capture cross section, half-life, or energy of gamma ray line) and/or low average concentrations of these elements. Therefore it was decided not to take the data for these elements into account in forming groups, to avoid confusing an already complex picture by including samples with many missing data, which might lead to results of questionable validity.

The writer also decided to ignore barium values. Previous research has shown that Black Glazed Ware sherds from Idalion and from Tell el-Hesi, Israel, were identical in chemical composition except for barium, of which the Idalion sherds had on the average twice as high a concentration as the Hesi sherds (Bieber et al. 1976a). Sherds excavated at Idalion are frequently encrusted with a thin coating of limestone due to the highly alkaline soil of the site. This suggested that the higher barium content of the Idalion sherds might be due to barium having been deposited in the sherds after burial, rather than to an actual compositional difference in the clay used. A simple experiment (described fully in Bieber 1977:120) demonstrated conclusively that this was the case, further validating exclusion of this element.

Cluster Analysis

There are many different measures of distance and similarity and many types of cluster analysis. Each combination of a similarity or distance measure with a clustering procedure proceeds in a slightly different way to present a varying picture of the structure of the data. To arrive at the "true" structure of the data, and to control as much as possible for results due to differences in the procedures that might give an erroneous idea of the data structure, three rather different kinds of cluster analysis were performed:

1) clustering on a matrix of Squared Mean Euclidian distances between specimens;

2) average-linkage cluster analysis on a matrix of Cosine Theta coefficients of similarity between specimens; and

3) maximum within-group correlation clustering on a matrix of Pearson product-moment correlations between specimens.

Inspection of the dendograms that resulted from these analyses (Bieber 1977:figs. 1-3) shows that several groups of specimens cluster in all three.

After selecting these obvious groups and removing the specimens from the samples, another set of three cluster analyses was undertaken on the remaining data. Several more clusters that had been obscured by the obvious groups became apparent in this second analysis.

The sets of specimens that consistently appeared together as a result of all three types of clustering formed the basic preliminary groups, which were further refined using the statistical methods described (Bieber 1977).

Univariate Statistics

Following the procedure described above, the preliminary groups resulting from the cluster analyses were tested by calculating the mean and group standard deviation for each chemical element in each group. In some cases the preliminary groups were found to have unacceptably large spreads, and were therefore rejected as valid groups. Also, certain specimens were rejected as being sufficiently dissimilar to the group as a whole (on the basis of univariate 95% confidence intervals) to be valid group members.

Table 1. Chemical Elements Determined By Neutron Activation Analysis in This Study, with the Isotope Produced, Its Half-life, and the Approximate Energy of the Gamma Rays Used

Element	Symbol	Isotope produced	Half-life		Approximate energy of gamma rays used (in keV)
Sodium	Na	Na-24	15.0	hrs	1368.5
Potassium	K	K-42	12.4	hrs	1524.7
Rubidium	Rb	Rb-86	18.7	days	1076.8
Cesium	Cs	Cs-134	2.05	yrs	795.7
Barium	Ba	Ba-131	12.0	days	496.5
Scandium	Sc	Sc-46	83.9	days	889.2, 1120.4
Lanthanum	La	La-140	40.2	hrs	1596.7
Cerium	Ce	Ce-141	32.5	days	145.4
Europium	Eu	Eu-152	12.7	yrs	1408.0
Lutecium	Lu	Lu-177	6.74	days	208.3
Hafnium	Hf	Hf-181	42.5	days	482.3
Thorium	Th	Pa-233	27.0	days	311.9
Tantalum	Ta	Ta-182	115.0	days	1221.4
Chromium	Cr	Cr-51	27.8	days	320.1
Manganese	Mn	Mn-56	155.0	mins	846.9
Iron	Fe	Fe-59	45.6	days	1099.2, 1291.5
Cobalt	Co	Co-60	5.26	yrs	1173.2, 1332.5
Antimony	Sb	Sb-124	60.3	days	1691.0
Uranium	U	Np-239	56.3	hrs	277.5
Calcium	Ca	Ca-47	4.54	days	1296.6
Samarium	Sm	Sm-153	46.8	hrs	103.2
Ytterbium	Yb	Yb-175	42.1	days	396.2

After the univariate tests had been applied, fifteen groups were left. Of these, eight were composed of seven specimens or fewer, so that no further refinement was possible due to the limitations of the multivariate tests and to the fact that tests of skewness and kurtosis are useful only for groups of eleven or more (see Geary 1936).

Multivariate Statistics

The remaining seven groups were sufficiently large that the Mahalanobis distance procedure could be used for further refinement. As some of the groups were initially composed of as few as eight specimens, it was necessary to pick some subset of the seventeen original chemical elements to use in the testing. By comparison of univariate plots, examination of two-element plots and three-element displays, and study of correlation matrices calculated for each group, sufficiently small sets of elements were chosen so that Mahalanobis distances could be calculated for each group versus all other specimens.

The procedure was refined by calculating Mahalanobis distances and eliminating from each group any specimen with a significantly low probability and/or including in the group any specimen with significantly high probability. These calculations were repeated until no more specimens could be either rejected or included. In some cases several different sets of elements were used in order to take into account all elements that allowed discrimination between groups or between group members and ungrouped specimens. In all cases, either the elements used proved to be uncorrelated or all of a set of correlated elements was included.

Two levels of statistical significance were used. It follows from the nature of the Mahalanobis distance technique that if there are relatively few specimens, compared to the number of elements used, the 95% probability volume becomes very large relative to the standard deviation of the group. Thus, where there were fewer than twice as many specimens as elements, 10% were chosen as the minimum probability at which a specimen was acceptable as a group member. In other cases the usual 5% limit was used.

Due to the phenomenon of expansion of probability volumes, a final check was made on each group. The specimen with the lowest probability out of the group was taken and the Mahalanobis distances were recalculated without it, to ensure that the low probability specimen still had a significant probability of belonging and that no other specimens could be included.

For groups that included sufficient samples, measures of skewness and kurtosis were also calculated. A few elements in a few groups were significantly skewed or kurtosic, but just barely, and the departure from normality was not sufficient to cast serious doubt on the results of the Mahalanobis distance refinement procedure.

Full chemical and statistical data on the fifteen compositional groups that resulted from the data analysis are presented by Bieber (1977, tables 7-11). The group to which each specimen was assigned is listed in table 3 below, and the specimens are listed by group with archaeological data in table 4.

Clay Samples

Table 2 gives chemical and provenience data on the clay samples included in this study. These clays were chosen for analysis because it was assumed on the basis of their origins that they were the clays most likely to have been used in antiquity.

All of the groups of sherds were compared using both cluster analysis and Mahalanobis distance to all clays, both raw and treated. The results of the comparisons are discussed below.

Chemical Characteristics of the Groups

For several technical reasons all statistics and clustering done in this study were on the logarithms of the actual chemical concentrations. Thus the group means are actually the geometric means of the concentrations, and the percent standard deviations are actually the factor by which the (geometric) mean is multiplied or divided for the one standard deviation limits (e.g., a 12% standard deviation means that one standard deviation below the mean is the mean divided by 1.12). Skewness and kurtosis are also actually calculated on the logarithms of the concentrations.

Group I is the largest and in many ways the most satisfactory group. Of the seventeen elements used for grouping, only cesium and hafnium have standard deviations greater than 20%, and most are close to 10%. The large hafnium standard deviation is due to the anomalous high concentration in IE7; if IE7 is ignored, the standard deviation is only 11.8%. On close checking, the high hafnium concentration in IE7 does not appear to be due to any analytical error, so it is possible that this specimen should not really be part of this group. In view of its excellent agreement on all other elements, however, it has been included. Cesium has a rather poor analytical precision, so the wide spread for cesium is understandable. None of the clay samples analyzed matched this group, but given its large size and the fact that all of the specimens in it were excavated at Idalion, this group is considered to be representative of a composition of pottery made at Idalion.

Group II is another, smaller, group composed primarily of specimens excavated at Idalion. Sodium, cesium, europium, and lutecium have standard deviations greater than 20%, but most other elements are below 10%. Sodium can be affected by burial conditions (in the same way that barium is), and neither cesium nor lutecium is determined very precisely, so the relatively wide spreads for these elements are probably insignificant. The europium spread is due to the low concentration in MM16, which may indicate that MM16 is not really a member of this group. In this particular case, however, because of problems during the counting of this sample, europium was poorly determined (the counting error alone was greater than 20%), so the specimen was included. If MM16 were ignored, the group standard deviation for europium would be only 10.8%.

The average values of Group II match those of clay RD52 quite closely (see table 2). RD52 is a sample from a mudbrick excavated at Idalion in 1972, so Group II is considered as another group probably manufactured at Idalion.

Group III is a very interesting one because it is composed of sherds with extremely high chromium content, averaging over 6000 ppm (0.6%), as opposed to the more usual average chromium concentration of only 198 ppm of Group I. Group III is a rather good group; only potassium has a standard deviation greater than 20%. Since potassium is not very precisely determined, this is not a problem.

Although no clays matched this group, its high chromium content is an indication of its probable origin. The center of the Troodos massif is an outcrop of ultrabasic enstatite-olivinite and bastite-serpentinite, which are high in chromium. There is a modern chrome mine near the summit of Mt. Olympus. There is also a large outcrop of ultrabasics about 6 km north of Limassol. The origin of Group III is probably in one of these two areas.

Group IV is compositionally related to Group III in that Group IV sherds also have unusually high chromium content. Whereas, Group III sherds are all from one clay source (or at most from a few sources in a very restricted geographical area), Group IV sherds are probably from several geologically related but distinct sources. Group IV is not a tight compositional group, but rather is composed of a number of sherds with similar distinctive but not really identical compositional patterns. The characteristics of this group suggest that it represents pottery made from clay sources located in the areas through which the rivers that drain the ultrabasic outcrops flow, such as the area north and west of Limassol.

Group V is a small group composed of sherds all excavated at Kition. In this group, imprecisely determined cesium is the only element with a standard deviation greater than 20%. Specimen CM10 does not fit the general group pattern as well as the other specimens in the group, but statistically it could not be excluded, so it was retained. Given the provenience of the sherds in this group, it probably represents a compositional pattern of pottery manufactured at Kition.

Group VI includes seven sherds excavated at Tamassos and one from Idalion. It is an excellent group except for its manganese concentrations. Four of the sherds have manganese values greater than 2100 ppm, and four have values below 1800 ppm, which suggests that this group may actually be two groups distinguished by their average manganese values. Until more specimens are analyzed, however, these specimens can be considered one group, probably representative of one compositional pattern of pottery manufactured at Tamassos.

Group VII is a poorly defined group of four specimens from Tamassos. Due to its small size and large standard deviations, no firm conclusions can be drawn concerning this group.

Most of the sherds in Group VIII are of Late Cypriot I date and were excavated at Phlamoudhi on the northeast coast of Cyprus. The fourteen sherds included form a highly homogeneous compositional group, which probably represents a compositional pattern of pottery manufactured at or near Phlamoudhi.

Groups IX and X are also composed mostly of specimens from Phlamoudhi, but both are quite different chemically from Group VIII. Groups IX and X are rather similar, and if there were more data might perhaps be combined into a single group. At present they represent two slightly different but related clay sources, both probably also in the northeast coast area.

Group XI is a small group of sherds of varied provenience and unknown origin.

Group XII includes four sherds excavated at Tyre, Lebanon, and two from Cyprus, one each from Kition and Amathus. This group may have its origins in Syria-Palestine, but without a matching clay, no definite conclusion can be reached. The group is certainly of a very different composition from any of the Cypriot groups.

Groups XIII and XIV are both composed of samples from tombs excavated by the Swedish Cyprus Expedition. Group XIII is a rather loose group, sherds of vessels from Marion; and Group XIV, a somewhat better but still not exceptional group, sherds of vessels from Vouni. Both XIII and XIV are chemically quite distinct from all other groups, and probably represent locally manufactured pottery from Marion and Vouni respectively.

Group XV is composed of four disparate specimens that are rather distinctive in their overall compositional pattern. No indication of the possible origins of the group has been found.

BASIC ASSUMPTIONS

Although the archaeological and historical data available concerning the Cypriot Iron Age are far from complete, enough exist to permit the generation of certain hypotheses concerning the nature of trade at Idalion during this period. These hypotheses are formulated in such a way as to be testable using the results of neutron activation analysis of pottery found at Idalion and of comparative samples of pottery and clay from elsewhere, both on and off Cyprus. The analytical results should permit one to determine the geographical origins of the pottery and should therefore indicate the direction of trade.

Two basic assumptions have been made. First, pottery, identified as part of the material-culture subsystem of the total culture system, is seen as an indicator of overall cultural trajectories. This assumption is necessary to justify the study of pottery within the framework of the basic objective of "New Archaeology," namely, the development of explanatory models for culture change. Second, if it can be demonstrated that pottery manufactured in one place is found in another, this implies that there was trade in pottery or trade with pottery as container (for who knows what) between the two places. Given the archaeologically and historically known characteristics of the overall economy of the eastern Mediterranean region in the first millennium B.C., this should be a reasonable assumption.

Four additional assumptions are necessary if one is to use neutron activation analysis of pottery to test hypotheses concerning trade:

1) That the pottery was manufactured at or near the source of the clay used. That is, that clay itself was not an object of long-distance trade. Ethnographic evidence in general supports this assumption (e.g., Matson 1965:210-11, 1973:121, 123).

2) That the majority of sherds found at any site came from vessels that were manufactured locally. This is true for Idalion, and other research has shown that it is true elsewhere.

3) That the chemical composition of a sherd and a clay, or of two sherds, is the same to within certain statistically defined limits they have the same geographical origin. For this assumption to be valid, there must be sufficient compositional variation in materials from the area of interest so that different localities produce chemically different clays. Previous research has shown that there is considerable variation within rather limited geographical areas (Bieber et al. 1976a; 1976b; Brooks et al. 1974; Asaro, Perlman, and Dothan 1971; Bishop 1975, inter alia). The preliminary study of sherds from Cyprus has confirmed that there is substantial variety in the composition of Cypriot materials. The island is sufficiently diverse in geological terms that one may expect such significant variation to manifest itself in sherd compositions analyzed from different localities (Bieber 1974).

4) That even when pottery is tempered or is made of otherwise modified clay the chemical composition pattern is distinctive enough to allow matching of sherds and clays. Again, previous research supports this assumption (Brooks et al. 1974).

HYPOTHESES

On the basis of available archaeological and historical data, four hypotheses concerning trade have been formulated. These hypotheses are amenable to testing using the results of neutron activation analysis, and provide the framework for archaeological interpretation of these results. After the presentation of each hypothesis, a discussion follows as to whether the evidence supports or fails to support the hypothesis. Those archaeological aspects of the analyses that were not anticipated in the hypotheses are discussed in the section "Implications."

The first hypothesis is concerned with the general place of Idalion vis-à-vis the other stylistic regions of Cyprus; the second, with the relationship between trade and historically documented political events; the third, more narrowly focused, with the interaction between parts of the economic system, specifically, with the nature of the documented copper industry; the fourth, with the origins of Black-on-Red Ware found on Cyprus. Each of these hypotheses is significant for the archaeology and history of Iron Age Cyprus. Inasmuch as the general objective of this study is to place Idalion in perspective in the overall culture system of Cyprus, an understanding of its economic relations with the rest of the island is essential. Each of the four hypotheses addresses a different facet of these relations.

It is appropriate to point out here that lack of evidence in support of a hypothesis (or lack of evidence in clear contradiction of a hypothesis) cannot be construed as disproof of it entirely, for this study has dealt with only a very small proportion of the total number of sherds excavated. Lack of evidence should rather be regarded as a qualified piece of negative information, and one should consider performing other tests that might give less ambiguous results (e.g., analysis of very many more sherds). Similarly, evidence that supports a hypothesis can at best be considered only just that--evidence that suggests that the hypothesis may be correct, not proof positive that the hypothesis is in fact correct.

Hypothesis 1

Idalion had trade relations with all parts of Cyprus during the Cypro-Geometric and Cypro-Archaic periods.

Documentary evidence and the results of the several excavations at the site show that Idalion was a widely known cult center. Consequently, it may be suggested that its importance would have transcended geographical distance and overridden political disputes, and that there would have been extensive trade between Idalion and most or all other parts of Cyprus. Given its location between the areas of the Western and Eastern styles of pottery and sculpture that were present in the Cypro-Geometric III and the Cypro-Archaic periods, Idalion should have pottery stylistically intermediate between the regions of Cyprus, showing influences from all of them and possibly in turn influencing all of them. The pottery from Idalion from these periods does include wares and decorative styles that are characteristic of both the Western and Eastern regions (*SCE* II, pp. 571-73). (Fibulae from Idalion also include forms characteristic of several of the regions of the island, e.g., those listed by Birmingham [1963a:94, 99, 101, 105, 108]). Great compositional diversity in the pottery found at Idalion would be evidence of trade.

Test: If the hypothesis is supported, pottery of types I-IV found at Idalion will vary widely in composition and will include a significant number of specimens with compositional patterns characteristic of several areas of Cyprus. If the hypothesis is incorrect, then pottery found at Idalion will be predominantly from local clay sources.

The results of the analysis support the hypothesis. (See table 4 for archaeological data on the compositional groups.) Sherds excavated at Idalion fall into eight different compositional groups: Groups I and II, probably manufactured at Idalion; Groups III and IV, probably representing sources in or around the Troodos; 1 sherd in Group VI, probably from Tamassos; Groups VIII and X, probably from the Phlamoudhi area on the northeast coast; and 1 sherd in Group XI and 2 sherds in Group XV of unknown origin. Of 164 sherds and vessels found at Idalion, 63 could not be assigned to any of the 15 compositional groups distinguished. This great compositional diversity among the specimens from Idalion supports the hypothesis of widespread contacts.

Hypothesis 2

(a) There was little or no trade between Idalion and Kition at the end of the Cypro-Archaic period (i.e., before the conquest of Idalion by Kition).

(b) There was a significant increase in trade between Idalion and Kition after the conquest, in the early Cypro-Classical period.

(c) There was a major reorientation of Idalion's overall trade pattern after the conquest.

Since there was historically documented hostility between Cypro-Greek Idalion and Cypro-Phoenician Kition during the 5th century B.C., one may postulate that there would have been a major reorientation of Idalion's trade relations after Kition's conquest of Idalion (ca. 450 B.C.). This reorientation would be reflected in a consistent difference between the origins of pottery dating from before and after the conquest, that is, between Cypro-Archaic and Cypro-Classical pottery. The earlier (preconquest) Cypro-Archaic pottery at Idalion should contain a relatively smaller proportion of pottery from Kition; the later, Cypro-Classical pottery, a greater proportion. In any case, the origins (reflected in the composition) of the Cypro-Archaic pottery should be different from those of the Cypro-Classical.

Supporting evidence for part (a) of this three-part hypothesis includes the fact that at the end of the Cypro-Archaic period the city of Kition was Cypro-Phoenician, while Idalion (given the evidence, among other things, of personal names and the names of the deities worshipped there) was Cypro-Greek. Gjerstad emphasized the emotional nature of the conflict between Cypro-Greeks and Cypro-Phoenicians (*SCE* IV:2, pp. 480-81); moreover at that time Kition was at least intermittently at war with Idalion, and ultimately captured the city in the reign of 'Oziba'al (450-425 B.C.).

If it can be demonstrated that political changes are reflected in changes in trading patterns, archaeologists will have both an additional tool for tracing and documenting political change, and additional data for constructing models to explain relationships between component parts of the culture system of Cyprus. Confirmation of this hypothesis would also provide information necessary for reconstructing and understanding the place of Idalion in the culture of Iron Age Cyprus.

Test: The hypothesis will be confirmed if there is little or no pottery of type V found at Idalion that was manufactured at Kition, and a much greater amount of types VI and VII. There should also be a marked difference in the origins of imported type V versus imported Types VI and VII pottery at Idalion. There will be no evidence to support the hypothesis if there is found to be little difference in the origins of imported type V pottery compared with imports of types VI and VII.

The analytical results tend to support this hypothesis. The bulk of the Cypro-Archaic pottery excavated at Idalion was assigned to Group I (probably from Idalion) and groups III and IV (both probably representing sources in or near the Troodos). Much of the Cypro-Classical Idalion pottery could not be assigned to any group, and only Group II (probably from Idalion) contains any significant number of Idalion Cypro-Classical specimens. There is no evidence for direct trade between Kition and Idalion in the composition of either the Cypro-Archaic or the Cypro-Classical pottery. The fact that the Idalion Cypro-Archaic pottery appears in Group I and the Cypro-Classical pottery in Group II is not really germane here, since both groups probably represent clay sources local to Idalion. What is significant is that during the Cypro-Archaic period there appeared at Idalion a large number of pieces probably from the Troodos area, while in the Cypro-Classical period, after the conquest by Kition, none appeared from this area. This suggests a major reorientation of trade, possibly as a result of the conquest.

Hypothesis 3

There was a trading network in which copper ore was mined in the Tamassos region, shipped to Idalion for smelting, and the smelted product shipped to Kition for export.

The excavations have demonstrated that copper processing was an important industry at Idalion, at least during the fourth century B.C. On the basis of the locations of copper ore known to have been exploited in antiquity (these are well known; see Muhly 1969:74-77; Bruce 1937:665, fig. 375 and passim; Steinberg and Koucky 1974:149-50), the excavators have suggested the existence of the hypothesized copper network. Again, confirmation of the hypothesis would provide both general and theoretical data useful for understanding the structure of the culture system of Iron Age Cyprus, and specific information on the place of Idalion in this system.

Test: If, as may be posited, Tamassos was the ore supplier and Kition the shipper of the smelted product, there should be pottery from both Tamassos and Kition found in association with the evidence of copper processing at Idalion--in particular, in Loci 007, 009, and 015 of Square WSW 11/16 (see Stager 1974:50-56). If not, pottery from other ore sources and/or shipping points should be found.

A basic assumption in the test of this hypothesis is that the pottery most likely to be found in the areas of Idalion in which there was evidence of copper processing (that is, in the above-mentioned loci) would be pottery from the areas from which the copper ore came and to which the smelted (or partially smelted--see *Idalion* 1, chap. 9) copper was shipped. This assumption is based on the idea that the ore and smelted product would have to be carried in something, most likely pottery. Accordingly twelve sherds (samples IE52-IE65) from this area at Idalion were analyzed. Of these IE52, IE57, and IE64 were assigned to Group II, suggesting that they were manufactured at Idalion. IE61 and IE62 were assigned to Group IV, the source of which is probably somewhere in the area through which the Troodos are drained (possibly the south coast region). The remaining seven sherds could not be assigned to any compositional group.

These analytical results neither support nor rule out the hypothesis of a Tamassos-Idalion-Kition copper network. In retrospect, it seems probable that a better test of the hypothesis would have sought evidence in the relative proportions of sherds from the site of Idalion as a whole, during the late Cypro-Classical period. However, it is unfortunate that the specimens required for such a test were not included among the samples analyzed here.

Hypothesis 4

The earliest Black-on-Red pottery was imported from somewhere in Anatolia or Syria-Palestine, while examples of later date (types I [III] and later) were made on Cyprus, mostly in the northwestern part of the island. This is the hypothesis put forward by Gjerstad to explain the appearance and changes in distribution, with time, of Black-on-Red and Red Slip wares.

The problem addressed in this hypothesis is significant because many conclusions concerning the general archaeology and history of Iron Age Cyprus are based largely on relationships inferred from stylistic judgments. If we can find a tool that will allow these relationships to be tested objectively, the data will provide a much firmer base on which to build explanatory models. The nature of relations between Cyprus and Syria-Palestine is particularly unclear (see, for example, Birmingham 1963b, Van Beek 1951, and Wright and

Gjerstad 1953 on chronological problems); if trade in pottery between the regions can be documented, the relationships may be better understood.

Test: The hypothesis will be confirmed if the earliest Black-on-Red sherds have a chemical composition that does not match any known Cypriot clay, while later examples have Cypriot compositions. The hypothesis will not be confirmed if early examples of Black-on-Red are found that were manufactured from Cypriot clays, and/or if non-Cypriot examples of later date occur.

The results pertain particularly to the later Black-on-Red pottery. The data tend to refute the writer's hypothesis and that of Gjerstad, and carry implications for the reconstruction of Cypriot Iron Age cultural history.

The majority of the Black-on-Red sherds analyzed fall into Groups III, IV, V, and XII. Groups II, IV, and V are almost certainly of Cypriot origin, probably from the Troodos area, its watershed, and Kition. Group XII, on the other hand, includes four sherds of Black-on-Red Ware excavated at Tyre, Lebanon, in what the excavator describes as a pottery manufacture area (Bikai 1978). These four sherds are stylistically indistinguishable from Cypriot Black-on-Red and all four are nearly identical in composition. Since the compositional pattern of Group XII is sufficiently different from Cypriot ceramics, it is unlikely that this group was made on Cyprus. Although this compositional profile does not exactly match any of the four clay samples from Tyre, its very general overall similarity in compositional pattern to Palestinian ceramics (cf. Brooks et al. 1974) suggests that this group may be of Syro-Palestinian origin.

Thus it seems, in contrast to Gjerstad's conclusions and the hypothesis presented here, that even as late as the Cypro-Archaic period (to which all the Black-on-Red sherds analyzed are dated on stylistic grounds) Black-on-Red pottery continued to be both imported from Syria-Palestine and made on Cyprus.

IMPLICATIONS

Having examined the results of the neutron activation analyses in light of the specific archaeological hypotheses presented, a few general comments are in order.

The results tend to bear out the assumption that a substantial proportion of the pottery found at any given site was locally manufactured. Each site, from which a reasonably large number of sherds were analyzed (more than twenty), was characterized by a group of sherds of distinctive chemical composition (e.g., Idalion by Group I, Kition by Group V, and Tamassos by Group VI).

From the fact that sherds of several different wares may have the same composition, it is also apparent that chemical composition does not necessarily coincide with pottery type, at least not in Cyprus. One might assume a priori that each different pottery type might have a different characteristic compositional pattern because of differences in manufacturing technique and/or the physical requirements of clays used for different shapes and sizes of vessels designed for different purposes. The results show, however, that this is not the case. Rather, the compositional pattern tends to reflect the geographical origin of the pottery, regardless of the stylistic characteristics.

The fact that Group III is probably of Troodos origin has important implications for Idalion. The size of the group suggests that fairly substantial amounts of pottery were imported from this area, which in turn suggests rather well-established trade. What would Idalion seek in the Troodos? Copper ore is a likely answer. The volume of trade (inferred from the number of specimens from Idalion in Group III) and the postulated importance of copper processing in the overall economic system of Idalion suggest that Idalion was trading relatively heavily with an as yet undiscovered center or centers in the Troodos area. Bruce (1937) reported finds of various ancient mining tools and apparatus in mines in the Troodos. It would be extremely interesting to analyze Cypro-Archaic pottery from these ancient mining sites for comparison with my Group III. In particular, Amiantos, Mitsero, and Pedoulas (see Bruce 1937:665, fig. 375) are in the area from which it is postulated that Group III may have come, and these sites might be prime candidates for further investigation. If it could be substantiated that there had been trade (or at least contact) between Idalion and a proven copper source in the Troodos, this would also lend support to the hypothesis that copper processing was a significant part of Idalion's economic system.

Much has been written about both the political history of Cyprus during the Iron Age and possible interactions between the political and economic subsystems in the culture system as a whole. The fact that there appears to have been a major change in Idalion's economic system (a reorientation of trade as reflected in pottery) roughly at the same time there was a major change in the political history of Idalion (the conquest by Kition) has important implications for both. Not only does this suggest that there are close causal links between politics and trade in Iron Age Cyprus (and thus that evidence for political change might be sought by examination of changes in trading patterns), but it also supports the idea that the division between Cypro-Greek and Cypro-Phoenician elements in Cyprus was, as Gjerstad suggests (see above), an important factor in the trajectory of the whole culture system of Iron Age Cyprus.

One of the attractions of Cyprus as an area for archaeological research is the fact that it is on the one hand an island, and thus has easily defined geographical limits and bounds on its culture system, and on the other hand lies at the boundary of the Near East and the Classical world, and thus shows influences from both. In order to understand Cypriot culture history, however, one must be able to document these outside influences. As mentioned above, much has been made of Syro-Palestinian stylistic influence on Cypriot pottery, even to the point of postulating movements of people, on the basis of stylistic traits (such as concentric circle decoration) seen in Cypriot pottery. The conclusion that Black-on-Red pottery continued to be imported to Cyprus (probably from Syria-Palestine) well into the Cypro-Archaic period suggests that movements of people may well have been far less common than suggested in many older reconstructions of Cypriot Iron Age culture history. Rather, the results suggest that trade in artifacts may account for much of the "cultural influence" seen in Cypriot artifact styles. Explanation of the trajectory of the Cypriot Iron Age culture system in future research might well bear this in mind, rather than positing movements of people in the absence of hard evidence for such movements.

These then are the implications drawn from neutron activation analysis of the specific sherds included in this study. The data are of sufficient value and quality (particularly in the light of previous research on the Cypriot Iron Age) to have more than justified the effort required to produce them.

SUGGESTED FUTURE RESEARCH

The above discussion suggests several possible areas for future research in the study of Idalion and the Cypriot Iron Age.

First of all, a larger selection of sherds from Idalion and of clays from possible clay sources should be analyzed, with the aim of pinpointing the geographical origins of the groups that have been distinguished. Such research could provide additional validation for the division of the sherds into fifteen groups, and might allow the classification of some of the sherds that could not be assigned to any group. This research might necessitate further studies (such as more levigation experiments on clays, or petrographic analysis of clays and sherds) in order to be able to match clays with sherds.

The results of such a project should afford a more complete knowledge of the areas with which Idalion traded during the Iron Age. This, in turn, would provide the data base for construction of detailed explanatory hypotheses concerning Idalion's economic base and the relationships between changes in the economy and changes in other parts of Idalion's culture system.

Another problem area that deserves further attention is that of distinguishing between pottery imported into Cyprus and pottery made locally. The implications of the discovery that Black-on-Red pottery continued to be imported well into the Cypro-Archaic period have been discussed above. More work should be done to validate the results published here and to pinpoint the origins of the imported Black-on-Red. The problem of the origin of the quantities of Mycenaean pottery found on Cyprus, touched on briefly, is also worthy of further study.

It has been pointed out that the evidence did not support the attempt to establish the existence of a Tamassos-Idalion-Kition copper-trading network. Further work focusing on this problem might succeed where the present study has failed. Such work should include an investigation of the origins of Group III (Troodos?) pottery, since is seems likely that the source of this pottery is a copper-mining area.

These are only a few of the more obvious areas in which further work is needed in connection with Idalion and its place in Cypriot Iron Age culture. Since much of the work in this area to date has been lacking in explicitly explanatory aims and objective scientific methods, the field is open, and there remain many opportunities to make a significant contribution to the study of Iron Age Cyprus.

Table 2. Chemical and Geographic Data on Clay Specimens*

Sample	Na$_2$O pct	K$_2$O pct	Rb$_2$O ppm	Cs$_2$O ppm	BaO ppm	Sc$_2$O$_3$ ppm
CP 1A	1.160	1.950	64.600	4.730	227.000	32.000
CP 1B	1.040	1.830	68.000	3.620	165.000	34.000
CP 1C	1.070	1.770	60.200	4.080	132.000	34.200
CP 2	0.366	1.990	97.400	4.520	238.000	37.500
CP 5	0.387	0.694	34.900	1.630	95.800	76.000
CP 6	1.170	1.460	50.300	2.550	203.000	39.100
CP 13	0.191	6.260	51.900	0.853	1470.000	5.400
CP 18	1.930	1.860	65.100	2.190	406.000	22.900
CP 19	1.420	1.790	64.500	3.520	248.000	32.900
CP 21	0.210	0.456	52.400	1.290		11.400
CC 1	0.212	0.640	30.700	1.500	353.000	9.540
CC 2	3.260	1.370		0.300		68.400
CC 3	0.264	1.240	39.300	2.650	1020.000	15.500
CC 4	0.251	1.130	45.900	2.400	174.000	15.200
CC 5	0.374					61.000
CC 6	1.460	1.710	69.600	3.220	96.600	33.300
CC 11	1.580	1.590	49.700	2.590	209.000	31.900
CC 14	2.050		6.780			67.400
CC 15	1.880		17.100	0.736	116.000	59.900
CC 16	2.460	0.428				59.700
CC 21	0.338	0.842	34.300	1.780	242.000	10.600
CC 22	0.696	1.260	44.400	2.900	125.000	18.100
CC 23	0.254	0.589	23.800	1.710	89.100	88.100
CC 24	0.811	1.900	66.700	4.400	269.000	21.600
CC 28	0.303	0.816	29.300	1.500	533.000	12.000
CC 31	1.630	1.070	23.300	1.550	395.000	12.100
CC 32	0.145	0.451	18.500	0.893		15.500
CC 33	0.321	0.965		1.640	1640.000	13.400
RD 35	0.254	1.240	38.600	3.340	175.000	14.100
RD 37	1.410	1.080	23.000	1.750	142.000	12.500
RD 42	0.916	1.060	21.800	1.150	509.000	26.800
RD 45	1.010	0.997	25.300	1.190	480.000	29.900
RD 46	0.112	0.425	16.100	1.080	265.000	6.310
RD 52	0.522	0.894	27.500	1.860	280.000	17.800
TC 17			21.200	2.740		24.200
TC 18	2.690		92.700	5.400	242.000	20.000
TC 19			19.200	1.320	231.000	12.000
TC 20			61.400	2.130	300.000	14.800

*Clays Analyzed Without Further Treatment

Table 2. Chemical and Geographic Data on Clay Specimens (*cont.*)

Sample	La$_2$O$_3$ ppm	CeO ppm	Eu$_2$O$_3$ ppm	Lu$_2$O$_3$ ppm	HfO$_2$ ppm	ThO$_2$ ppm
CP 1A	20.400	43.100	1.130	0.355	2.260	6.760
CP 1B	17.200	36.700	1.060	0.355	1.990	5.310
CP 1C	17.400	39.900	0.947	0.349	2.120	5.430
CP 2	59.500	86.500	2.680	0.607	4.760	11.900
CP 5	18.900	37.200	0.981	0.374	2.850	4.910
CP 6	32.500	63.500	2.030	0.633	4.750	7.870
CP 13	8.330	14.900	0.444	0.193	0.920	1.580
CP 18	24.200	44.100	1.660	0.413	3.920	5.490
CP 19	19.400	39.900	1.290	0.370	2.260	5.540
CP 21	114.000	46.500	6.690	1.630	35.200	2.510
CC 1	31.600	54.800	0.806	0.250	1.300	2.680
CC 2	5.510	13.800	0.777	0.615	1.580	0.931
CC 3	15.100	27.000	0.869	0.299	1.740	3.580
CC 4	22.400	38.300	1.020	0.267	2.460	5.750
CC 5	4.190	5.680	0.403	0.198		0.700
CC 6	38.700	73.800	2.180	0.561	3.000	8.140
CC 11	17.400	36.200	1.150	0.379	2.440	4.600
CC 14	7.230	16.500	0.600	0.409	1.160	1.800
CC 15	11.500	25.700	0.924	0.479	1.570	2.680
CC 16	9.280	19.200	0.917	0.690	1.220	0.601
CC 21	20.200	32.600	0.944	0.247	2.060	3.820
CC 22	15.900	35.900	0.740	0.319	1.750	4.030
CC 23	22.400	55.100	0.687	0.424	2.320	4.360
CC 24	23.600	51.200	1.110	0.361	2.900	7.730
CC 28	15.300	26.700	0.883	0.270	1.520	3.010
CC 31	11.200	29.600	0.463	0.186	1.460	3.180
CC 32	116.000	32.300	8.270	1.770	1.350	2.480
CC 33	190.000	55.700	9.740	1.790	2.230	2.630
RD 35	14.500	31.600	0.858	0.204	1.410	4.050
RD 37	12.100	24.100	0.672	0.186	1.350	3.130
RD 42	13.700	26.100	1.030	0.360	1.700	2.480
RD 45	12.800	26.900	1.020	0.349	1.990	2.530
RD 46	11.400	20.000	0.621	0.211	0.845	1.900
RD 52	11.800	22.500	0.660	0.264	1.870	2.550
TC 17	60.100	85.000	2.390	0.615	6.150	10.000
TC 18	59.100	90.800	1.930	0.535	4.190	11.500
TC 19	20.900	47.200	1.230	0.310	3.500	5.200
TC 20	36.200	62.000	1.290	0.351	4.310	6.280

Table 2. Chemical and Geographic Data on Clay Specimens (*cont.*)

Sample	Ta₂O₅ ppm	Cr₂O₃ ppm	MnO ppm	Fe₂O₃ pct	CoO ppm
CP 1A	1.050	303.000	939.000	6.790	28.400
CP 1B	0.804	233.000	948.000	7.280	27.200
CP 1C	0.841	238.000	1040.000	7.410	28.000
CP 2	1.590	1030.000	733.000	9.640	26.400
CP 5	0.662	434.000	1310.000	9.770	66.300
CP 6	1.120	156.000	1220.000	9.220	28.700
CP 13	0.177	40.200	502.000	31.400	8.770
CP 18	0.649	447.000	882.000	5.130	19.900
CP 19	0.738	258.000	1280.000	6.790	33.400
CP 21		47.200	29800.000	51.200	74.200
CC 1	0.371	63.300	913.000	2.200	13.400
CC 2		146.000	2690.000	11.400	45.300
CC 3	0.521	107.000	502.000	3.260	22.000
CC 4	0.636	267.000	474.000	3.870	13.400
CC 5	0.136	122.000	2190.000	8.300	50.300
CC 6	0.928	211.000	617.000	6.550	34.400
CC 11	0.701	311.000	1280.000	6.820	32.400
CC 14	0.364	534.000	1510.000	9.860	46.400
CC 15	0.470	238.000	1690.000	10.400	36.800
CC 16		49.300	1770.000	11.300	46.200
CC 21	0.463	470.000	791.000	2.590	14.900
CC 22	0.788	414.000	587.000	3.870	11.100
CC 23	0.627	707.000	2120.000	9.820	94.600
CC 24	0.631	720.000	1250.000	.5.420	28.000
CC 28	0.290	89.300	948.000	2.700	17.100
CC 31		571.000	576.000	2.980	18.300
CC 32		53.300		61.400	106.000
CC 33		43.700	1900.000	53.200	209.000
RD 35	0.447	169.000	1370.000	3.250	16.300
RD 37	0.439	430.000	598.000	2.930	21.300
RD 42	0.106	132.000	1710.000	5.200	25.000
RD 45	0.512	158.000	1340.000	5.680	26.800
RD 46	0.268	46.700	824.000	1.400	13.100
RD 52	0.321	131.000	689.000	3.790	15.900
TC 17	1.960	197.000	1080.000	5.890	26.400
TC 18	0.955	147.000	258.000	4.200	11.400
TC 19	0.372	72.700	479.000	3.310	11.700
TC 20	1.070	103.000	555.000	3.870	13.800

Table 2. Chemical and Geographic Data on Clay Specimens (*cont.*)

Sample	Sb$_2$O$_3$ ppm	UO$_3$ ppm	Sm$_2$O$_3$ ppm	Yb$_2$O$_3$ pct	CaO ppm
CP 1A					
CP 1B	0.458				
CP 1C	0.819				
CP 2	0.798	1.500	9.960	4.400	
CP 5		1.780	3.540	1.820	3.570
CP 6	0.223	1.770	6.580	3.650	5.120
CP 13	3.390	2.210	1.700	0.868	10.500
CP 18	0.523		4.670	2.820	1.770
CP 19	0.569	1.750	4.130	2.770	11.900
CP 21	7.430	2.460	21.800	9.420	
CC 1	0.595	2.020	3.140	1.540	37.200
CC 2			2.130	2.110	4.190
CC 3	1.000	2.800	3.480	1.560	30.500
CC 4	1.100	1.140	3.830	1.560	28.700
CC 5			1.120	0.813	4.150
CC 6	0.508	2.850	7.800	3.500	1.680
CC 11	0.496	1.390	3.930	2.470	12.800
CC 14	0.246		1.860	1.480	
CC 15	0.457		2.680	1.980	1.920
CC 16			1.830	2.430	4.370
CC 21	0.380	0.862	3.450	1.540	31.000
CC 22	0.684				
CC 23	0.156	0.978	2.650	1.280	5.250
CC 24	0.936	1.870	4.140	2.100	15.800
CC 28					
CC 31		1.580	2.330	1.160	34.800
CC 32		2.520	31.000	12.700	3.590
CC 33		2.080	33.400	14.600	
RD 35					
RD 37					
RD 42					
RD 45					
RD 46					
RD 52					
TC 17	0.796		9.580	2.520	
TC 18	0.647		7.480	3.020	
TC 19	0.895		6.270		
TC 20			5.480	1.870	

Table 2. Chemical and Geographic Data on Clay Specimens (*cont.*)

Geographical Origins of Clay Samples Analyzed

Sample	Geographical origin
CP 1A	Umber samples from mine near Larnaca
CP 1B	Umber samples from mine near Larnaca
CP 1C	Umber samples from mine near Larnaca
CP 2	Phrenaros
CP 5	Phini
CP 6	20 km. west of Nicosia
CP 13	Idalion
CP 18	Famagusta
CP 19	Famagusta
CP 21	Troulli
CC 1	Idalion
CC 2	Mathiati
CC 3	Idalion
CC 4	North of Kythrea
CC 5	40.5 milepost on the road from Nicosia to Troodos
CC 6	Troulli
CC 11	Palekythro
CC 14	Kornos
CC 15	Kornos
CC 16	Apliki
CC 21	Athalassa formation south of Lefkoniko
CC 22	"X" clay from mushroom cave near Kornos
CC 23	Phini
CC 24	Panagra
CC 28	Idalion
CC 31	Angaramenos clay from Phlamoudhi
CC 32	Kataliondas
CC 33	Kataliondas
RD 35	Konos clay from Phlamoudhi
RD 37	Angaramenos clay from Phlamoudhi
RD 42	Idalion: surface soil from field near Neolithic site
RD 45	Roadside midway between Dhali and Potamia
RD 46	Idalion: 3 ft boring in square WNW 5/32
RD 52	Mudbrick sample from Idalion
TC 17	Clay sample from Tyre IC-6 C, Area 8, Stratum III
TC 18	Clay sample from Tyre IC-6 C, Area 8, Stratum III
TC 19	Clay sample from Tyre IC-6 C, Area 8, Stratum III
TC 20	Clay sample from Tyre IC-6 C, Area 8, Stratum III

Table 3. Archaeological Data on Samples Analyzed

Sample	Provenience	Ware	Period	Registry no./ Reference	Compositional group

Site--AMATHUS SURFACE   Source--Surface Collection by Bieber

Sample	Provenience	Ware	Period	Registry no./ Reference	Compositional group
AS 1	Amathus Surface	?	?		Idalion Red/Blk Lust
AS 2	Amathus Surface	White Painted	Cypro-Archaic?		Unassigned Cypriot
AS 3	Amathus Surface	Bichrome			Unassigned Cypriot
AS 4	Amathus Surface	White Painted	Cypro-Archaic?		Unassigned Cypriot
AS 5	Amathus Surface	White Painted			IV--Troodos Area?
AS 6	Amathus Surface	White Painted			IV--Troodos Area?
AS 7	Amathus Surface	White Painted			IV--Troodos Area?

Site--KITION   Source--Dr. Vassos Karageorghis, Cyprus Museum

Sample	Provenience	Ware	Period	Registry no./ Reference	Compositional group
CM 1	Area I Psi 11 350-385	White Painted	Cypro-Classical	Kition 1973	XI--Unknown
CM 2	Area II Omega 9 250-292	Bichrome	Cypro-Classical	Kition 1973	V--Kition
CM 3	Area II Psi 9 284-300	Black-on-Red	Cypro-Archaic	Kition 1973	IV--Troodos Area?
CM 4	Area II Chi 10 90-230	Black-on-Red	Cypro-Classical	Kition 1973	XII--Tyre?
CM 5	Area II Chi 10 90-230	White Painted	Cypro-Classical	Kition 1973	Unassigned Cypriot
CM 6	Area II Chi 11 280-300	White Painted	Cypro-Archaic?	Kition 1973	Unassigned Cypriot
CM 7	Area II Chi 11 280-300	Black-on-Red	Cypro-Archaic?	Kition 1973	V--Kition
CM 8	Area II Chi 11 280-300	Bichrome	Cypro-Archaic?	Kition 1973	V--Kition
CM 9	Area II Chi 11 90-130	Bichrome	Cypro-Classical	Kition 1973	IV--Troodos Area?
CM10	Area II Chi 11 90-130	Black-on-Red	Cypro-Classical	Kition 1973	V--Kition
CM11	Area II Chi 11 90-130	White Painted	Cypro-Classical	Kition 1973	Unassigned Cypriot
CM12	Area II Psi 11 250-277	White Painted	Cypro-Classical	Kition 1973	Unassigned Cypriot
CM13	Area II Psi 11 250-277	Bichrome	Cypro-Classical	Kition 1973	V--Kition
CM14	Area II Psi 11 250-277	Black-on-Red	Cypro-Classical	Kition 1973	V--Kition
CM15	Area II Psi 11 250-277	Bichrome	Cypro-Classical	Kition 1973	IV--Troodos Area?
CM16	Area II Psi 11 115-130	Black-on-Red	Cypro-Classical	Kition 1973	IV--Troodos Area?
CM17	Area II Psi 11 115-130	White Painted	Cypro-Classical	Kition 1973	IV--Troodos Area?
CM18	Area II Psi 11 115-130	White Painted	Cypro-Classical	Kition 1973	IV--Troodos Area?
CM19	Area II Psi 11 115-130	White Painted	Cypro-Classical	Kition 1973	Unassigned Cypriot
CM20	Area II Chi 11 260-285	White Painted	Cypro-Archaic?	Kition 1973	V--Kition
CM21	Area II Chi 11 260-285	White Painted	Cypro-Archaic?	Kition 1973	V--Kition
CM22	Area II Chi 11 260-285	Black-on-Red	Cypro-Archaic?	Kition 1973	V--Kition
CM23	Area II Chi 11 260-285	Bichrome	Cypro-Archaic?	Kition 1973	Unassigned Cypriot
CM24	Area II Chi 10 320-335	White Painted	Cypro-Archaic?	Kition 1973	Unassigned Cypriot
CM25	Area II Chi 10 320-335	White Painted	Cypro-Archaic?	Kition 1973	V--Kition

Site--SALAMIS NECROPOLEIS   Source--Dr. Vassos Karageorghis, Cyprus Museum

Sample	Provenience	Ware	Period	Registry no./ Reference	Compositional group
CM42	Epsilon-Zeta 14-16 0-40	Bichrome	Cypro-Archaic?	Salamis "Koufomeros" 1967	XV--Unknown
CM43	Epsilon-Zeta 14-16 0-40	Bichrome	Cypro-Archaic?	Salamis "Koufomeros" 1967	Unassigned Cypriot

Table 3. Archaeological Data on Samples Analyzed (*cont.*)

Sample	Provenience	Ware	Period	Registry no./Reference	Compositional group
CM44	Epsilon-Zeta 14-16 0-40	Bichrome	Cypro-Archaic?	Salamis "Koufomeros" 1967	Unassigned Cypriot
CM45	Epsilon-Zeta 14-16 0-40	White Painted	Cypro-Archaic?	Salamis "Koufomeros" 1967	Unassigned Cypriot
CM46	Epsilon-Zeta 14-16 0-40	White Painted	Cypro-Archaic?	Salamis "Koufomeros" 1967	Unassigned Cypriot
CM47	Epsilon-Zeta 14-16 0-40	White Painted	Cypro-Archaic?	Salamis "Koufomeros" 1967	Unassigned Cypriot
CM48	Beta-Gamma 48,57 0-50	Bichrome	Cypro-Archaic?	Salamis "Tjiellarka" 1967	Idalion Black Glazed
CM49	Beta-Gamma 48,57 0-50	Bichrome	Cypro-Archaic?	Salamis "Tjiellarka" 1967	Unassigned Cypriot
CM50	Beta-Gamma 48,57 0-50	Bichrome	Cypro-Archaic?	Salamis "Tjiellarka" 1967	Unassigned Cypriot
CM51	Epsilon-Zeta 14-6 Dromos Fill	White Painted	Cypro-Archaic?	Salamis "Koufomeros" 1967	II--Idalion?
CM52	Epsilon-Zeta 14-6 Dromos Fill	White Painted	Cypro-Archaic?	Salamis "Koufomeros" 1967	Unassigned Cypriot

Site--IDALION   Source--American Expedition to Idalion

Sample	Provenience	Ware	Period	Registry no./Reference	Compositional group
ID 1	Idalion Surface	Terra Sigillata	Roman	D72.169	VIII-Phlamoudhi
ID 2	Idalion Surface	White Painted	Cypro-Archaic	D72.403	III--Troodos?
ID 3	Idalion Surface	White Painted	Cypro-Archaic	D72.363	Unassigned Idalion
ID 4	Idalion Surface	White Painted	Cypro-Archaic	D72.404	III--Troodos?
ID 5	Idalion Surface	White Painted	Cypro-Archaic	D72.370	IV--Troodos Area?
ID 6	Idalion Surface	White Painted	Cypro-Archaic	D72.793	XV--Unknown
ID 7	Idalion Surface	White Painted	Cypro-Archaic	D72.345	VI--Tamassos?
ID 8	Idalion Surface	White Painted	Cypro-Archaic	D72.100	I--Idalion
ID 9	Idalion Surface	Bichrome	Cypro-Archaic	D72.733	I--Idalion
ID10	Idalion Surface	Bichrome	Cypro-Archaic		XV--Unknown
ID11	Idalion Surface	Bichrome	Cypro-Archaic	D72.350	Unassigned Idalion
ID12	Idalion Surface	Terra Sigillata?	Roman		Idalion Terra Sigillata
ID13	Idalion Surface	Terra Sigillata	Roman	D72.602	Idalion Terra Sigillata
ID14	Idalion Surface	Terra Sigillata	Roman		Idalion Terra Sigillata

Table 3. Archaeological Data on Samples Analyzed (*cont.*)

Sample	Provenience	Ware	Period	Registry no./ Reference	Compositional group
ID15	Idalion Surface	Terra Sigillata	Roman	D72.723	Idalion Terra Sigillata
ID16	Idalion Surface	Terra Sigillata?	Roman	D72.103	Idalion Black Glazed
ID17	Idalion Surface	Red Bichrome	Cypro-Archaic	D72.434	Unassigned Idalion
ID18	Idalion Surface	Painted Ware	Hellenistic		Idalion Red/Blk Lust
ID19	Idalion Surface	Red Lustrous	Hellenistic		Idalion Terra Sigillata
ID20	Idalion Surface	Red Lustrous	Hellenistic		Idalion Red/Blk Lust
ID21	Idalion Surface	Red Lustrous	Hellenistic	D72.170	Unassigned Idalion
ID22	Idalion Surface	Black Lustrous	Hellenistic	D72.372	Unassigned Idalion
ID23	Idalion Surface	Black Lustrous	Hellenistic		Unassigned Idalion
ID24	Idalion Surface	Black Lustrous	Hellenistic	D72.583	Idalion Red/Blk Lust
ID25	Idalion Surface	Black Lustrous	Hellenistic		VIII--Phlamoudhi
ID26	Idalion Surface	Black Lustous?	Hellenistic?		Idalion Black Glazed
ID27	Idalion Surface	Black Glazed	Cypro-Classical	D72.137	Idalion Black Glazed
ID28	Idalion Surface	Black Glazed	Cypro-Classical	D72.29	Unassigned Idalion
ID29	Idalion Surface	Black Glazed	Cypro-Classical	D72.595	Idalion Black Glazed
ID30	Idalion Surface	Black Glazed	Cypro-Classical	D72.401	Idalion Black Glazed
ID31	ID.ENW 8/10.003 #12	Terra Sigillata	Roman	D72.1082	Idalion Terra Sigillata
ID32	ID.ENW 8/10.003 #12	Terra Sigillata	Roman	D72.1083	Unassigned Idalion
ID33	ID.ENW 7/8.005 #25	Red Lustrous?	Hellenistic?	D72.15777	Idalion Black Glazed
ID38	Idalion Surface	Red Lustrous?	Hellenistic?	D72.15783	Unassigned Idalion
ID35	ID.ENW 8/10.003 #12	Black Lustrous	Hellenistic	D72.15779	Idalion Red/Blk Lust
ID36	ID.ENW 7/8.003 #29	Black Lustrous	Hellenistic	D72.15778	Unassigned Idalion
ID37	Idalion Surface	Black Lustrous	Hellenistic	D72.15782	VIII--Phlamoudhi
ID38	ID.ENW 7/8.005 #16	Black Lustrous	Hellenistic	D72.15781	Unassigned Idalion
ID39	Idalion Surface	Black Glazed	Cypro-Classical	D72.15785	Idalion Black Glazed
ID40	Idalion Surface	Black Glazed	Cypro-Classical	D72.15784	Idalion Black Glazed
ID41	ID.ENW 7/8.003 #29	Black Glazed	Cypro-Classical	D72.15776	Idalion Black Glazed
ID42	ID.ENW 28/9.002 #2	Red-Figured	5th Century BC	D72.4957	Idalion Black Glazed
ID43	ID.ENW 8/10.004 #30	Red-Figured	5th Century BC	D72.15780	Idalion Black Glazed
ID44	ID.WSE 7/50.017 #101	Black-Figured	6th Century BC	D72.13350	Idalion Black Glazed
ID45	ID.WNW 43/23.002:1 #2	White Slip	Late Cypriot	D72.1030	Unassigned Idalion
ID46	ID.WSE 7/50.017 #99	White Slip	Late Cypriot	D72.12561	Unassigned Idalion
ID50	ID.WSW 11/45.Test #12	Mycenaean IIIC1B	Late Cypriot		Unassigned Idalion
ID51	ID.WNW 43/22.022 #59	Geometric	Geometric		Unassigned Idalion
ID52	ID.WNW 9/18.035.2 #67	Bichrome IV	Cypro-Archaic I	D73.2806	III--Troodos?
ID53	ID.WNW 9/18.035.2 #67	Bichrome IV	Cypro-Archaic I	D73.2816	II--Idalion?
ID54	ID.WNW 9/18.035.2 #67	White Painted IV	Cypro-Archaic I	D73.2826	I--Idalion
ID55	ID.WNW 9/18.035.2 #67	Coarse Gray	Cypro-Archaic?	D73.2840	Unassigned Idalion
ID56	ID.WNW 9/18.035.3 #67	White Painted IV	Cypro-Archaic I	D73.2815	I--Idalion
ID57	ID.WNW 9/18.035.2 #67	Black-on-Red II(IV)	Cypro-Archaic I	D73.2841	I--Idalion
ID58	ID.WNW 9/18.035.2 #67	Red Slip II(IV)	Cypro-Archaic I	D73.2814	Unassigned Idalion

Table 3. Archaeological Data on Samples Analyzed (*cont.*)

Sample	Provenience	Ware	Period	Registry no./Reference	Compositional group
ID59	ID.WNW 9/18.035.2 #67	Bichrome IV	Cypro-Archaic I	D73.2812	II--Idalion?
ID60	ID.WNW 8/18.015 #61	Black Lustrous	Hellenistic	D73.3006	Unassigned Idalion
ID61	ID.WNW 8/18.015 #61	Black Lustrous	Hellenistic	D73.3004	Idalion Red/Blk Lust
ID62	ID.WNW 8/18.015 #61	Black Lustrous	Hellenistic	D73.3015	Unassigned Idalion
ID63	ID.WNW 8/18.011 #41	White Painted VII?	Cypro-Classical II?	D73.2630	Unassigned Idalion
ID64	ID.WNW 8/18.011 #41	Lamp Fragment	Early Hellenistic	D73.2631	Idalion Red/Blk Lust
ID65	ID.WNW 8/18.011 #41	Plain White VII	Cypro-Classical II	D73.2623	II--Idalion?
ID66	ID.WNW 8/18.011 #41	Coarse Gray	Early Hellenistic?	D73.2619	Unassigned Idalion
ID67	ID.WNW 8/18.011 #41	Plain White V	Cypro-Classical II	D73.1648	II--Idalion?
ID68	ID.WNW 8/18.011 #41	Plain White V	Cypro-Classical II	D73.2635	III--Troodos?
ID69	ID.WNW 8/17.002 #5	Plain White VII	Cypro-Classical II	D73.2418	Unassigned Idalion
ID70	ID.WNW 8/17.002 #5	Plain White VI	Cypro-Classical I	D73.2427	Unassigned Idalion
ID71	ID.WNW 8/17.002 #5	Plain White VII	Cypro-Classical II	D73.2434	Unassigned Idalion
ID72	ID.WNW 8/17.002 #5	Plain White VII	Cypro-Classical II	D73.2439	Unassigned Idalion
ID73	ID.WNW 8/17.002 #5	Plain White VI	Cypro-Classical I	D73.2452	Unassigned Idalion
ID74	ID.WNW 8/17.002 #5	Plain White VI	Cypro-Classical I	D73.2456	Unassigned Idalion
ID75	ID.WNW 8/17.002 #5	Plain White V	Cypro-Archaic II	D.73.2460	Unassigned Idalion
ID76	ID.WNW 8/19.002 #7	Plain White VI	Cypro-Classical I	D73.1826	Unassigned Idalion
ID77	ID.WNW 8/19.002 #7	Plain White VI	Cypro-Classical I	D73.1827	Unassigned Idalion
ID78	ID.WNW 8/19.002 #7	Plain White VI	Cypro-Classical I	D73.1831	Idalion Black Glazed
ID79	ID.WNW 8/19.002 #7	Plain White VI	Cypro-Classical I	D73.1833	Unassigned Idalion
ID80	ID.WNW 8/19.002 #7	Plain White V	Cypro-Archaic II	D73.1835	Unassigned Idalion
ID81	ID.WNW 8/19.002 #7	White Painted II/III?	Cypro-Geom. II/III?	D73.1840	Unassigned Idalion
ID82	ID.WNW 8/18.006 Flot	?	Cypro-Geom. II/III?	D73.2461	I--Idalion
ID83	ID.WNW 9/17.007 #33	Black Glazed	Hellenistic	D73.5071	Idalion Black Glazed
ID84	ID.WNW 9/17.007 #33	White Painted IV	Cypro-Archaic I	D73.5072	IV--Troodos Area?
ID85	ID.WNW 9/17.007 #33	Plain White VI	Cypro-Classical I	D73.5073	I--Idalion
ID86	ID.WNW 9/17.007 #33	Black-on-Red II(IV)	Cypro-Archaic I	D73.5074	III--Troodos?
ID87	ID.WNW 9/17.007 #33	?	Early Cypriot?	D73.5075	IV--Troodos Area?
ID88	ID.WNW 9/17.007 #33	Coarse Ware	Cypro-Archaic II?	D73.5076	Unassigned Idalion
ID89	ID.WSE 11/36.006	White Painted W.-M. II	Late Cypriot II	51.1?	Unassigned Idalion
ID90	ID.WSE 11/36.006	Mycenaean IIIB	Late Cypriot II	5.5?	Unassigned Idalion
ID91	ID.WSE 11/36.006	Base-Ring	Late Cypriot II	51.2?	Idalion Red/Blk Lust
ID92	ID.WNW 9/18.035 #60	Plain White IV?	Cypro-Archaic I?	D73.5263	I--Idalion
ID93	ID.WNW 9/18.035 #60	Plain White IV	Cypro-Archaic I	D73.5264	I--Idalion
ID94	ID.WNW 9/18.035 #60	White Painted IV	Cypro-Archaic I	D73.5265	X--Phlamoudhi
ID95	ID.WNW 9/18.035 #60	Plain White IV	Cypro-Archaic I	D73.5266	Unassigned Idalion
ID96	ID.WNW 9/18.035 #60	White Painted IV	Cypro-Archaic I	D73.5267	I--Idalion

Table 3. Archaeological Data on Samples Analyzed (*cont.*)

Sample	Provenience	Ware	Period	Registry no./ Reference	Compositional group
ID97	ID.WNW 9/18.035 #60	White Painted IV	Cypro-Archaic I	D73.5268	Unassigned Idalion
ID98	ID.WNW 10/17.003.2 #58	White Painted V	Cypro-Archaic II	D73.6091	I--Idalion
ID99	ID.WNW 10/17.003.2 #58	White Painted V	Cypro-Archaic II	D73.6096	I--Idalion
IE 1	ID.WNW 10/17.003.2 #58	White Painted V	Cypro-Archaic II	D73.6101	I--Idalion
IE 2	ID.WNW 10/17.003.2 #58	Black-on-Red II(IV)	Cypro-Archaic I	D73.6122	III--Troodos?
IE 3	ID.WNW 10/17.003.2 #58	Bichrome V	Cypro-Archaic II	D73.6123	II--Idalion?
IE 4	ID.WNW 10/17.003.2 #58	Bichrome IV	Cypro-Archaic I	D73.6125	I--Idalion
IE 5	ID.WNW 10/17.003.2 #58	Black Slip IV	Cypro-Archaic I	D73.6129	IV--Troodos Area?
IE 6	ID.WNW 10/17.003.2 #58	Black Polished II(IV)	Cypro-Archaic I	D73.6130	II--Idalion?
IE 7	ID.WNW 10/17.003.2 #58	White Painted IV	Cypro-Archaic I	D73.6132	I--Idalion
IE 8	ID.WNW 10/17.003.2 #58	Black-on-Red II(IV)	Cypro-Archaic I	D73.6133	IV--Troodos Area?
IE 9	ID.WNW 10/17.003.2 #58	Bichrome IV	Cypro-Archaic I	D73.6134	I--Idalion
IE10	ID.WNW 9/17.020 #61	Black-on-Red		D73.4175	III--Troodos?
IE11	ID.WNW 9/17.020 #61	Black-on-Red		D73.4174	III--Troodos?
IE12	ID.WNW 9/17.020 #61	White Painted		D73.4177	IV--Troodos Area?
IE13	ID.WNW 9/17.020 #61	White Painted		D73.4179	I--Idalion
IE14	ID.WNW 9/17.020 #61	White Painted		D73.4187	I--Idalion
IE15	ID.WNW 9/17.020 #61	Bichrome		D73.4196	Unassigned Idalion
IE16	ID.WNW 9/17.020 #61	White Painted		D73.4199	I--Idalion
IE17	ID.WNW 9/17.020 #61	Bichrome		D73.6002	IV--Troodos Area?
IE18	ID.WNW 9/17.020 #61	White Painted		D73.6008	I--Idalion
IE19	ID.WNW 9/17.020 #61	White Painted		D73.6009	I--Idalion
IE20	ID.WNW 9/17.020 #61	Black-on-Red		D73.6017	III--Troodos?
IE21	ID.WNW 9/17.020 #61	White Painted		D73.6018	IV--Troodos Area?
IE22	ID.WNW 9/17.020 #61	Black-on-Red		D73.6020	III--Troodos?
IE23	ID.WNW 10/17.031.2 #103	Bichrome		D73.6527	IV--Troodos Area?
IE24	ID.WNW 10/17.031.2 #103	Black-on-Red		D73.6528	I--Idalion
IE25	ID.WNW 10/17.031.2 #103	Bichrome		D73.6525	II--Idalion?
IE26	ID.WNW 42/22.009 Lay 6 #24	Black Slip		D73.1008	I--Idalion
IE27	ID.WNW 43/22.014 #53	Bichrome		D73.726	Unassigned Idalion
IE28	ID.WNW 43/23.022 Lay 7 #68	Black-on-Red		D73.1048	Unassigned Idalion
IE29	ID.WNW 43/23/022 Lay 7 #68	White Painted		D73.1046	Unassigned Idalion
IE30	ID.WNW 43/23.021 Lay 3 #27	Black-on-Red		D73.1011	Unassigned Idalion
IE31	ID.WNW 42/22.009 Lay 5 #25	Black-on-Red		D73.1036	Unassigned Idalion
IE32	ID.WNW 42/22.009 Lay 5 #25	White Painted		D73.1035	Unassigned Idalion
IE33	ID.WNW 43/23.021 Lay 3 #28	Bichrome		D73.1021	I--Idalion

Table 3. Archaeological Data on Samples Analyzed (*cont.*)

Sample	Provenience	Ware	Period	Registry no./Reference	Compositional group
IE34	ID.WNW 43/22.015 Lay 2 #30	White Painted		D73.1014	IV--Troodos Area?
IE35	ID.WNW 43/22.015 Lay 2 #30	White Painted		D73.1015	Unassigned Idalion

Site--IDALION   Source--Mediterranean Museum, Stockholm, Sweden

Sample	Provenience	Ware	Period	Registry no./Reference	Compositional group
IE36	ID.H7 (Deposit)	Red Slip III(V)	Cypro-Archaic II	I.599 (SCE II:548)	Unassigned Idalion
IE37	ID.H7 (Deposit)	White Painted IV	Cypro-Archaic I	I.622 (SCE II:550)	I--Idalion
IE38	ID.H7 (Deposit)	Bichrome V	Cypro-Archaic II	I.747 (SCE II:552)	I--Idalion
IE39	ID.H7 (Deposit)	White Painted IV	Cypro-Archaic I	I.765 (SCE II:553)	I--Idalion
IE40	ID.H7 (Deposit)	"Foreign Ware"	Cypro-Archaic?	I.988 (SCE II:557)	Unassigned Idalion
IE41	ID.G-H.6-7 (Deposit)	Bichrome IV	Cypro-Archaic I	I.1535 (SCE II:570)	IV--Troodos Area?
IE42	ID.G-H.6-7 (Deposit)	Bichrome IV	Cypro-Archaic I	I.1537 (SCE II:570)	Unassigned Idalion
IE43	ID.G-H.6-7 (Deposit)	Bichrome V	Cypro-Archaic II	I.1538 (SCE II:570)	Unassigned Idalion
IE44	ID.G-H.6-7 (Deposit)	Bichrome IV	Cypro-Archaic I	I.1539 (SCE II:570)	Unassigned Idalion
IE45	ID.H7 (Deposit)	Black-on-Red II(IV)	Cypro-Archaic I	I.631 (SCE II:549)	Unassigned Idalion
IE46	ID.H7 (Deposit)	Black-on-Red III(V)	Cypro-Archaic II	I.760 (SCE II:553)	Unassigned Idalion
IE47	ID.H6 (Deposit)	Gray Polished	Cypro-Archaic	I.568 (SCE II:547)	Unassigned Idalion
IE48	ID.H7 (Deposit)	Black-on-Red II(IV)	Cypro-Archaic I	I.613 (SCE II:549)	Unassigned Idalion
IE49	ID.K7.93.4	Black Bucchero W.-M.	Cypro-Archaic	D.423 (SCE II:543)	XI--Unknown
IE50	ID.K7.91.5	Black Slip W.-M.	Cypro-Archaic	I.451 (SCE II:544)	Unassigned Idalion
IE51	ID.K7.90.0	Black Bucchero H.-M.	Cypro-Archaic	D.475 (SCE II:545)	Unassigned Idalion

Site--IDALION   Source--American Expedition to Idalion

Sample	Provenience	Ware	Period	Registry no./Reference	Compositional group
IE52	ID.WSW 11/16.006 #21	Plain White VII	Cypro-Classical II	D72.3763	II--Idalion?
IE53	ID.WSW 11/16.007.1 #50	Plain White VI	Cypro-Classical I	D72.6552	Unassigned Idalion
IE54	ID.WSW 11/16.007.1 #50	Plain White VI	Cypro-Classical I	D72.6566	Unassigned Idalion
IE55	ID.WSW 11/16.007.1 #50	Plain White VI	Cypro-Classical I	D72.6557	Unassigned Idalion
IE56	ID.WSW 11/16.010 #42	Bichrome Red III(VI)	Cypro-Classical I	D72.4107	Idalion Black Glazed
IE57	ID.WSW 11/16.010 #47	Plain White VI	Cypro-Classical I	D72.4104	II--Idalion?

Table 3. Archaeological Data on Samples Analyzed (*cont.*)

Sample Provenience		Ware	Period	Registry no./ Reference	Compositional group
IE58	ID.WSW 11/16.013 #51	Plain White?	Cypro-Classical?	D72.7863	Unassigned Idalion
IE59	ID.WSW 11/16.013 #51	Plain White VII	Cypro-Classical II	D72.7861	Unassigned Idalion
IE60	ID.WSW 11/16.006 #21.22	Bichrome?	Cypro-Classical?	D72.5044	Unassigned Idalion
IE61	ID.WSW 11/16.014 #56.57	White Painted V	Cypro-Archaic II	D72.6588	IV--Troodos Area?
IE62	ID.WSW 11/16.014 #56.57	Black-on-Red III(V)	Cypro-Archaic II	D72.7025	IV--Troodos Area?
IE63	ID.WSW 11/16.014 #56.57	White Painted V	Cypro-Archaic II	D72.7023	Unassigned Idalion
IE64	ID.WSW 11/16.014 #62	Plain White VI	Cypro-Classical I	D72.8330	II--Idalion?
IE65	ID.WSW 11/16.014 #62	White Painted IV	Cypro-Archaic I	D72.8340	Unassigned Idalion
IE66	ID.WNW 10/18.009 #18	Red Slip II(IV)	Cypro-Archaic I	D72.5285	Unassigned Idalion
IE67	ID.WNW 10/18.009 #18	? (VI or later)	Cypro-Classical?		Unassigned Idalion
IE68	ID.WNW 10/18.009 #18	Gray and Blk. Pol. V	Cypro-Archaic II	D72.14527	Unassigned Idalion

Site--KYTHREA Source--Cyprus Museum, Nicosia

KG 1	Kythrea Geometric Tomb 2	White Painted	Cypro-Geometric		Unassigned Cypriot
KG 2	Kythrea Geometric Tomb 2	Gray/Blk Pol	Cypro-Geometric		Unassigned Cypriot
KG 3	Kythrea Geometric Tomb 2	White Painted	Cypro-Geometric		Unassigned Cypriot
KG 4	Kythrea Geometric Tomb 2	White Painted	Cypro-Geometric		Unassigned Cypriot
KG 5	Kythrea Geometric Tomb 2	White Painted	Cypro-Geometric		Unassigned Cypriot
KG 6	Kythrea Geometric Tomb 2	White Painted	Cypro-Geometric		Unassigned Cypriot
KG 7	Kythrea Geometric Tomb 2	White Painted	Cypro-Geometric		Unassigned Cypriot
KG 8	Kythrea Geometric Tomb 2	White Painted	Cypro-Geometric		Unassigned Cypriot
KG 9	Kythrea Geometric Tomb 2	White Painted	Cypro-Geometric		Unassigned Cypriot

Site--VOUNI Source--Mediterranean Museum, Stockholm, Sweden

MM 1	Vouni Tomb 7	Plain White VI	Cypro-Classical II	Bowl, #1 (SCE III:314)	XIV--Vouni
MM 2	Vouni Tomb 7	Plain White VI	Cypro-Classical II	Jug, #7 (SCE III:314)	Unassigned Cypriot
MM 3	Vouni Tomb 7	White Painted VI	Cypro-Classical II	Jug, #5 (SCE III:314)	XIV--Vouni
MM 4	Vouni Tomb 7	Plain White VII	Cypro-Classical II	Pithos, #3 (SCE III:314)	Unassigned Cypriot
MM 5	Vouni Tomb 7	Bichrome VII	Cypro-Classical II	Lid, #19 (SCE III:314)	XIV--Vouni
MM 6	Vouni Tomb 8	Plain White VII	Cypro-Classical II	Jug, #4 (SCE III:317)	Unassigned Cypriot

Table 3. Archaeological Data on Samples Analyzed (*cont.*)

Sample Provenience	Ware	Period	Registry no./ Reference	Compositional group
MM 7 Vouni Tomb 8	White Painted VII	Cypro-Classical II	Amphoriskos, #5, (SCE III:317)	XIV--Vouni
MM 8 Vouni Tomb 8	Bichrome VII	Cypro-Classical II	Jug, #13 (SCE III:317)	Unassigned Cypriot
MM 9 Vouni Tomb 1	White Painted VI	Cypro-Classical I	Jug, #4 (SCE III:301)	Unassigned Cypriot
MM10 Vouni Tomb 1	Plain White VII	Cypro-Classical I	Jug, #8 (SCE III:301)	XIV--Vouni
MM11 Vouni Tomb 1	White Painted VI	Cypro-Classical I	Jug, #43 (SCE III:301)	Unassigned Cypriot
MM12 Vouni Tomb 1	White Painted VI	Cypro-Classical I	Jug, #24 (SCE III:301)	XIV--Vouni
MM13 Vouni Tomb 1	Plain White VI	Cypro-Classical I	Jug, #22 (SCE III:301)	Unassigned Cypriot
MM14 Vouni Tomb 1	White Painted VI	Cypro-Classical I	Hydria, #2 (SCE III:301)	XIV--Vouni

Site--STYLLI   Source--Mediterranean Museum, Stockholm, Sweden

Sample Provenience	Ware	Period	Registry no./ Reference	Compositional group
MM15 Stylli Tomb 6	Bichrome IV	Cypro-Archaic I	Amphora, #14 (SCE II:155)	Unassigned Cypriot
MM16 Stylli Tomb 3	Bichrome IV	Cypro-Archaic I	Jug, #1 (SCE II:148)	II--Idalion?
MM17 Stylli Tomb 2	Bichrome IV	Cypro-Archaic I	Jug, #12 (SCE II:146)	Unassigned Cypriot
MM18 Stylli Tomb 6	White Painted III	Cypro-Archaic I	Bowl, #8 (SCE II:154)	Unassigned Cypriot
MM19 Stylli Tomb 3	White Painted III	Cypro-Archaic I	Jug, #4 (SCE II:149)	Unassigned Cypriot
MM20 Stylli Tomb 6	White Painted III	Cypro-Archaic I	Jug, #16 (SCE II:155)	Unassigned Cypriot
MM21 Stylli Tomb 8	Black-on-Red I(III)	Cypro-Geometric III	Jug, #7 (SCE II:159)	Unassigned Cypriot
MM22 Stylli Tomb 5	Black-on-Red I(III)	Cypro-Archaic I	Bottle, #1 (SCE II:152)	Unassigned Cypriot
MM23 Stylli Tomb 4	Black-on-Red I(III)	Cypro-Archaic I	Bottle, #2 (SCE II:151)	Unassigned Cypriot

Site--AYIOS JAKAVOS   Source--Mediterranean Museum, Stockholm, Sweden

Sample Provenience	Ware	Period	Registry no./ Reference	Compositional group
MM24 Iron Age Sanctuary	White Painted	Cypro-Archaic	Sherd 185-205 KI	Unassigned Cypriot
MM25 Iron Age Sanctuary	White Painted	Cypro-Archaic	Sherd 185-205 KI	Unassigned Cypriot
MM26 Iron Age Sanctuary	White Painted	Cypro-Archaic	Sherd 185-205 KI	XV--Unknown
MM27 Iron Age Sanctuary	White Painted	Cypro-Archaic	Sherd E1 250-280	Unassigned Cypriot
MM28 Iron Age Sanctuary	Bichrome	Cypro-Archaic	Sherd E1 250-280	Unassigned Cypriot
MM29 Iron Age Sanctuary	Bichrome	Cypro-Archaic	Sherd E1 250-280	Unassigned Cypriot

Table 3. Archaeological Data on Samples Analyzed (*cont.*)

Sample Provenience	Ware	Period	Registry no./ Reference	Compositional group
Site--AYIA IRINI	Source--Mediterranean Museum, Stockholm, Sweden			
MM30 L.11, 94.7	White Painted V	Cypro-Archaic I	Jug A.I. 581 (SCE II:691)	IX--Phlamoudhi
MM31 M.11, 95.3	White Painted V	Cypro-Archaic I	Jug A.I. 967 (SCE II:702)	Unassigned Cypriot
MM32 M.9, 94.0	Bichrome IV	Cypro-Archaic I	Jug A.I. 1974 (SCE II:747)	Unassigned Cypriot
MM33 M.11, 95.3	Bichrome IV	Cypro-Archaic I	Bowl A.I. 952 (SCE II:702)	Unassigned Cypriot
MM34 K.8, 94.9	Bichrome IV	Cypro-Archaic I	Jug A.I. 1768 (SCE II:740)	Unassigned Cypriot
MM35 M.9, 94.0	White Painted IV	Cypro-Archaic I	Jug A.I 1972 (SCE II:747)	IV--Troodos Area?
Site--MARION	Source--Mediterranean Museum, Stockholm, Sweden			
MM36 Marion Tomb 69	White Painted IV	Cypro-Archaic II	Jug, #33 (SCE II:389)	Unassigned Cypriot
MM37 Marion Tomb 72	Plain White V	Cypro-Archaic II	Jug, #1 (SCE II:395)	Unassigned Cypriot
MM38 Marion Tomb 72 Dromos #2	Bichrome Red II(IV)	Cypro-Archaic II	Jug (SCE II:395)	XIII--Marion
MM39 Marion Tomb 84	Plain White V	Cypro-Archaic II	Jug, #22 (SCE II:426)	XIII--Marion
MM40 Marion Tomb 84	White Painted V	Cypro-Archaic II	Jug, #3 (SCE II:425)	Unassigned Cypriot
MM41 Marion Tomb 4	White Painted IV	Cypro-Archaic I	Jug, #1 (Marked P.4.1) (SCE II:1)	XIII--Marion
MM42 Marion Tomb 10	Bichrome IV	Cypro-Archaic I	Jug, #7 (SCE II:212-3)	XIII--Marion
MM43 Marion Tomb 10	Bichrome IV	Cypro-Archaic I	Jug, #19 (SCE II:213)	XIII--Marion
MM44 Marion Tomb 13	Bichrome IV	Cypro-Archaic I	Jug, #2 (SCE II:218)	XIII--Marion
Site--AMATHUS	Source--Mediterranean Museum, Stockholm, Sweden			
MM45 Amathus Tomb 7	Black-on-Red II(IV)	Cypro-Archaic I	Jug A7.278 (SCE III:42)	XII--Tyre?
MM46 Amathus Tomb 10	Bichrome Red II(V)	Cypro-Archaic II	Jug A10.13 (SCE II:65-6)	Unassigned Cypriot
MM47 Amathus Tomb 16	Black-on-Red I(III)	Cypro-Geometric III	Bowl A16.99 (SCE II:98)	IV--Troodos Area?

Table 3. Archaeological Data on Samples Analyzed (*cont.*)

Sample Provenience	Ware	Period	Registry no./ Reference	Compositional group
MM48 Amathus Tomb 10	Black-on-Red III(V)	Cypro-Archaic II	Jug A10.14 (SCE II:66)	Unassigned Cypriot
MM49 Amathus Tomb 9	Bichrome V	Cypro-Archaic II	Amphora A9.177 (SCE II:63)	III--Troodos?
MM50 Amathus Tomb 19	Bichrome II	Cypro-Geometric II	Jug A19.20 (SCE II:112)	Unassigned Cypriot
MM51 Amathus Tomb 21	Bichrome II	Cypro-Geometric II	Jug A21.2 (SCE II:116)	III--Troodos?
MM52 Amathus Tomb 24	Bichrome I	Cypro-Geometric I	Jug A24.9 (SCE II:132)	Unassigned Cypriot
MM53 Amathus Tomb 7	White Painted III	Cypro-Geometric III	Jug A7.5 (SCE III:32)	IV--Troodos Area?
MM54 Amathus Tomb 9	White Painted V	Cypro-Archaic II	Jug A9.108 (SCE II:611)	Unassigned Cypriot

Site--LAPITHOS   Source--Mediterranean Museum, Stockholm, Sweden

Sample Provenience	Ware	Period	Registry no./ Reference	Compositional group
MM55 Lapithos Tomb 411	White Painted I	Cypro-Geometric I	Jug L.411.15 (SCE I:215)	Unassigned Cypriot
MM56 Lapithos Tomb 420	White Painted I	Cypro-Geometric I	Askos L.420.65 (SCE I:239)	Unassigned Cypriot
MM57 Lapithos Tomb 421	Black-on-Red I(III)	Cypro-Geometric III	Jug L.421.3 (SCE I:241)	Unassigned Cypriot

Site--PHLAMOUDHI "MELISSA"   Source--Columbia University Excavations

Sample Provenience	Ware	Period	Registry no./ Reference	Compositional group
MS 1 Phlamoudhi "Melissa"	Red-on-Black	Late Cypriot I	2PH M T 37	VIII--Phlamoudhi
MS 2 Phlamoudhi "Melissa"	W.M. Black Slip	Late Cypriot I (II?)	2PH M T1-3 4	IX--Phlamoudhi
MS 3 Phlamoudhi "Melissa"	Monochrome	Late Cypriot IB	2PH M T4 15	VIII--Phlamoudhi
MS 4 Phlamoudhi "Melissa"	Monochrome	Late Cypriot IB	2PH M T2 22	VIII--Phlamoudhi
MS 5 Phlamoudhi "Melissa"	Brown-Slip Monochrome	Late Cypriot IB	2PH M T5 9	VIII--Phlamoudhi

Site--TYRE, LEBANON   Source--Dr. Patricia Bikai, Tyre Excavations

Sample Provenience	Ware	Period	Registry no./ Reference	Compositional group
TC 1 IC-11 A, Bin 11, Str XVII	Red-on-Black	See Bikai 1978	Bikai 1978	VIII--Phlamoudhi
TC 2 IC-6 A, Area 10, Str XVI	Monochrome	See Bikai 1978	Bikai 1978	VIII--Phlamoudhi
TC 3 IC-6 D, Area 1, Str XIV	Milk Bowl--Local?	See Bikai 1978	Bikai 1978	Unassigned Cypriot
TC 4 IC-11 C, Area 7, Str XV	Milk Bowl--LC II	See Bikai 1978	Bikai 1978	Unassigned Cypriot
TC 5 (B, C) IC-6C, Area 16, Str X-2	Black Slip	See Bikai 1978	Bikai 1978	XI--Unknown

Table 3. Archaeological Data on Samples Analyzed (*cont.*)

Sample	Provenience	Ware	Period	Registry no./Reference	Compositional group
TC 6	IC-6 C, Area 16, Str X-2	White Painted	See Bikai 1978	Bikai 1978	Unassigned Cypriot
TC 7	IC-6 C, Area 5, Str II	Black-on-Red	See Bikai 1978	Bikai 1978	XII--Tyre?
TC 8	IC-6 C, Area 2, Str IX	Black-on-Red	See Bikai 1978	Bikai 1978	XII--Tyre?
TC 9	IC-6 D, Area 1, Str VII	Black-on-Red	See Bikai 1978	Bikai 1978	XII--Tyre?
TC10	IC-6 D, Area 1, Unstratified	Black-on-Red	See Bikai 1978	Bikai 1978	XII--Tyre?
TC11	IC-6 C, Area 8, Str II	Black-on-Red	See Bikai 1978	Bikai 1978	III--Troodos?
TC12	IC-6 C, Area 8, Str II	Bichrome	See Bikai 1978	Bikai 1978	IV--Troodos Area?
TC13	IC-6 C, Area 8, Str II	Black-on-Red	See Bikai 1978	Bikai 1978	Unassigned Cypriot
TC14	IC-6 C, Area 8, Str III	Plate Type 2	See Bikai 1978	Bikai 1978	Unassigned Cypriot
TC15	IC-6 C, Area 8, Str III	Fine Ware Plate T.2	See Bikai 1978	Bikai 1978	Unassigned Cypriot
TC16	IC-6 C, Area 8, Str III	Crisp Ware Store Jar	See Bikai 1978	Bikai 1978	Unassigned Cypriot

Site--TAMASSOS   Source--Prof. H-G Buchholz, Tamassos Excavations

Sample	Provenience	Ware	Period	Registry no./Reference	Compositional group
TM 1		"Meniko Ware"	6th Century?	TA I/A1 -50CM	Unassigned Cypriot
TM 2		"Meniko Ware"	6th Century?	TA I/A1 -50CM	Unassigned Cypriot
Tm 3	Aphrodite/Ashtarte Sanctuary	Bichrome	Cypro-Archaic	TA III Gamma/Delta 3 -40Cm	Unassigned Cypriot
TM 4	"Kouphos" Tomb Aug. 1972	Bucchero Ware	Cypro-Geometric		VII--Tamassos?
TM 5	"Kouphos" Tomb Aug. 1972	Bucchero Ware	Cypro-Geometric		VII--Tamassos?
TM 6	"Kouphos" Tomb Aug. 1972	White Painted (III?)	Cypro-Geometric III?		VII--Tamassos?
TM 7	"Kouphos" Tomb Aug. 1972	White Painted (III?)			VII--Tamassos?
TM 8	Aphrodite/Ashtarte Sanctuary	Bichrome	Cypro-Archaic	TA III Gamma/Delta 4 18/8/72	VI--Tamassos?
TM 9	E. Part of Sanctuary A4	White Painted IV	Cypro-Archaic	TA I A4 (1970)	VI--Tamassos?
TM10	E. Part of Sanctuary A4	White Painted IV	Cypro-Archaic	TA I A4 (1970)	Unassigned Cypriot
TM11	Aphrodite/Ashtarte Sanctuary	White Painted	Cypro-Archaic	TA III Delta 6 -00 7/9/72	VI--Tamassos?
TM12	E. Part of Sanctuary A4	"Meniko Ware"	Ca 500 BC	TA I A4 (1970)	Unassigned Cypriot
TM13	Aphrodite/Ashtarte Sanctuary	White Painted V	Cypro-Archaic II	TA III Beta 4 -1.00M 23/8/72	Unassigned Cypriot Unassigned Cypriot
TM14	Aphrodite/Ashtarte Sanctuary	Bichrome IV	Cypro-Archaic I	TA III Alpha-Alpha 3/4 -1.10M	Unassigned Cypriot
TM15	Aphrodite/Ashtarte Sanctuary	White Painted IV	Cypro-Archaic I	TA III Alpha Alpha 3/4 -1.10M	IV--Troodos Area?
TM16	Aphrodite/Ashtarte Sanctuary	Plain White IV	Cypro-Archaic I	TA III Beta 4 -1.10M 22/8/72	II--Idalion?
TM17	Aphrodite/Ashtarte Sanctuary	Plain White IV	Cypro-Archaic I	TA III Beta 4 -1.10M 22/8/72	Unassigned Cypriot Unassigned Cypriot
TM18	Aphrodite/Ashtarte Sanctuary	White Painted IV	Cypro-Archaic I	TA III Beta 4 -1.10M 22/8/72	Unassigned Cypriot Unassigned Cypriot

Table 3. Archaeological Data on Samples Analyzed (*cont.*)

Sample Provenience	Ware	Period	Registry no./Reference	Compositional group
TM19 Aphrodite/Ashtarte Sanctuary	White Painted IV	Cypro-Archaic I	TA III Beta 4 -1.10M 22/8/72	VI--Tamassos?
TM20 Aphrodite/Ashtarte Sanctuary	White Painted IV	Cypro-Archaic I	TA III Beta 4 -1.10M 22/8/72	VI--Tamassos?
TM21 Aphrodite/Ashtarte Sanctuary	Plain White IV	Cypro-Archaic I	TA III Beta 4 -1.10M 22/8/72	III--Troodos?
Tm22 Aphrodite/Ashtarte Sanctuary	White Painted IV	Cypro-Archaic I	TA III Beta 4 -1.10M 22/8/72	VI--Tamassos?
TM23 Aphrodite/Ashtarte Sanctuary	White Painted IV	Cypro-Archaic I	TA III Beta- Beta 4 Deepest Level	VI--Tamassos? VI--Tamassos?
TM24	White Painted V	Cypro-Archaic II	TA III Gamma/ Delta 3 -20 to 40	Unassigned Cypriot Unassigned Cypriot

Site--PHLAMOUDHI "VOUNARI"   Source--Columbia University Excavations

VN 1	Phlamoudhi "Vounari"	Red-on-Black	Late Cypriot I	PH V 1970	VIII--Phlamoudhi
VN 2	Phlamoudhi "Vounari"	Red-on-Black	Late Cypriot I	2PH V E4A 20 1	VIII--Phlamoudhi
VN 3	Phlamoudhi "Vounari"	Red-on-Black	Late Cypriot I	PH V 1970	Unassigned Cypriot
VN 4	Phlamoudhi "Vounari"	Red-on-Black	Late Cypriot I(A?)	W-1 Fill of NS Section	VIII--Phlamoudhi
VN 5	Phlamoudhi "Vounari"	Black Slip	Late Cypriot I	PH V 1970 24-8-70 S3	IX--Phlamoudhi
VN 6	Phlamoudhi "Vounari"	Black Slip, Red Var.	Late Cypriot I	PH V W1 LF 12-8-1970	IX--Phlamoudhi
VN 7	Phlamoudhi "Vounari"	Black Slip	Late Cypriot I	PH V 1970 10-8-70 S1 T-S	X--Phlamoudhi
VN 8	Phlamoudhi "Vounari"	Black Slip	Late Cypriot I	PH V 10-8-70 S1 T-S	X--Phlamoudhi
VN 9	Phlamoudhi "Vounari"	Black Slip?	Late Cypriot I	PH V S2C Red Soil 1/9-1970	Unassigned Cypriot
VN10	Phlamoudhi "Vounari"	Red-on-Black	Late Cypriot I	PH V 1970 W1 17.8	VIII--Phlamoudhi
VN11	Phlamoudhi "Vounari"	Red-on-Black	Late Cypriot I	PH V 1970 S3B RS-TF 25.8	VIII--Phlamoudhi
VN12	Phlamoudhi "Vounari"	Red-on-Black	Late Cypriot I	PH V 1970 10-8-70 S1-T-S	Unassigned Cypriot

Table 4. Archaeological Data on Compositional Groups

Sample	Excavated/Collected	Ware	Period
Group I--IDALION			
ID 8	Idalion	White Painted	Cypro-Archaic
ID 9	Idalion	Bichrome	Cypro-Archaic
ID54	Idalion	White Painted IV	Cypro-Archaic I
ID56	Idalion	White Painted IV	Cypro-Archaic I
ID57	Idalion	Black-on-Red II(IV)	Cypro-Archaic I
ID82	Idalion	?	Cypro-Geometric II/III?
ID85	Idalion	Plain White VI	Cypro-Classical I
ID92	Idalion	Plain White IV?	Cypro-Archaic I?
ID93	Idalion	Plain White IV	Cypro-Archaic I
ID96	Idalion	White Painted IV	Cypro-Archaic I
ID98	Idalion	White Painted V	Cypro-Archaic II
ID99	Idalion	White Painted V	Cypro-Archaic II
IE 1	Idalion	White Painted V	Cypro-Archaic II
IE 4	Idalion	Bichrome IV	Cypro-Archaic I
IE 7	Idalion	White Painted IV	Cypro-Archaic I
IE 9	Idalion	Bichrome IV	Cypro-Archaic I
IE13	Idalion	White Painted	
IE14	Idalion	White Painted	
IE16	Idalion	White Painted	
IE18	Idalion	White Painted	
IE19	Idalion	White Painted	
IE24	Idalion	Black-on-Red	
IE26	Idalion	Black Slip	
IE33	Idalion	Bichrome	
IE37	Idalion	White Painted IV	Cypro-Archaic I
IE38	Idalion	Bichrome V	Cypro-Archaic II
IE39	Idalion	White Painted IV	Cypro-Archaic I
Group II--IDALION?			
CM51	Salamis Necropoleis	White Painted	Cypro-Archaic?
ID53	Idalion	Bichrome IV	Cypro-Archaic I
ID59	Idalion	Bichrome IV	Cypro-Archaic I
ID65	Idalion	Plain White VII	Cypro-Classical II
ID67	Idalion	Plain White V	Cypro-Archaic II
IE 3	Idalion	Bichrome V	Cypro-Archaic II
IE 6	Idalion	Black Polished II(IV)	Cypro-Archaic I
IE25	Idalion	Bichrome	
IE52	Idalion	Plain White VII	Cypro-Classical II
IE57	Idalion	Plain White VI	Cypro-Classical I
IE64	Idalion	Plain White VI	Cypro-Classical I
MM16	Stylli	Bichrome IV	Cypro-Archaic I
TM16	Tamassos	Plain White IV	Cypro-Archaic I

Table 4. Archaeological Data on Compositional Groups (*cont.*)

Sample	Excavated/Collected	Ware	Period
Group III--TROODOS?			
ID 2	Idalion	White Painted	Cypro-Archaic
ID 4	Idalion	White Painted	Cypro-Archaic
ID52	Idalion	Bichrome IV	Cypro-Archaic I
ID68	Idalion	Plain White V	Cypro-Archaic II
ID86	Idalion	Black-on-Red II(IV)	Cypro-Archaic I
IE 2	Idalion	Black-on-Red II(IV)	Cypro-Archaic I
IE10	Idalion	Black-on-Red	
IE11	Idalion	Black-on-Red	
IE20	Idalion	Black-on-Red	
IE22	Idalion	Black-on-Red	
MM49	Amathus	Bichrome V	Cypro-Archaic II
MM51	Amathus	Bichrome II	Cypro-Geometric II
TC11	Tyre, Lebanon	Black-on-Red	Bikai
TM21	Tamassos	Plain White IV	Cypro-Archaic I
Group IV--TROODOS AREA?			
AS 5	Amathus Surface	White Painted	
AS 6	Amathus Surface	White Painted	
AS 7	Amathus Surface	White Painted	
CM 3	Kition	Black-on-Red	Cypro-Archaic
CM 9	Kition	Bichrome	Cypro-Classical
CM15	Kition	Bichrome	Cypro-Classical
CM16	Kition	Black-on-Red	Cypro-Classical
CM17	Kition	White Painted	Cypro-Classical
CM18	Kition	White Painted	Cypro-Classical
ID 5	Idalion	White Painted	Cypro-Archaic
ID84	Idalion	White Painted IV	Cypro-Archaic I
ID87	Idalion	?	Early Cypriot?
IE 5	Idalion	Black Slip IV	Cypro-Archaic I
IE 8	Idalion	Black-on-Red II(IV)	Cypro-Archaic I
IE12	Idalion	White Painted	
IE17	Idalion	Bichrome	
IE21	Idalion	White Painted	
IE23	Idalion	Bichrome	
IE34	Idalion	White Painted	
IE41	Idalion	Bichrome IV	Cypro-Archaic I
IE61	Idalion	White Painted V	Cypro-Archaic II
IE62	Idalion	Black-on-Red III(V)	Cypro-Archaic II
MM35	Ayia Irini	White Painted IV	Cypro-Archaic I
MM47	Amathus	Black-on-Red I(III)	Cypro-Geometric III
MM53	Amathus	White Painted III	Cypro-Geometric III
TC12	Tyre, Lebanon	Bichrome	Bikai
TM15	Tamassos	White Painted IV	Cypro-Archaic I

Table 4. Archaeological Data on Compositional Groups (*cont.*)

Sample	Excavated/Collected	Ware	Period
Group V--KITION			
CM 2	Kition	Bichrome	Cypro-Classical
CM 7	Kition	Black-on-Red	Cypro-Archaic?
CM 8	Kition	Bichrome	Cypro-Archaic?
CM10	Kition	Black-on-Red	Cypro-Classical
CM13	Kition	Bichrome	Cypro-Classical
CM14	Kition	Black-on-Red	Cypro-Classical
CM20	Kition	White Painted	Cypro-Archaic?
CM21	Kition	White Painted	Cypro-Archaic?
CM22	Kition	Black-on-Red	Cypro-Archaic?
CM25	Kition	White Painted	Cypro-Archaic?
Group VI--TAMASSOS?			
ID 7	Idalion	White Painted	Cypro-Archaic
TM 8	Tamassos	Bichrome	Cypro-Archaic
TM 9	Tamassos	White Painted IV	Cypro-Archaic
TM11	Tamassos	White Painted	Cypro-Archaic
TM19	Tamassos	White Painted IV	Cypro-Archaic I
TM20	Tamassos	White Painted IV	Cypro-Archaic I
TM22	Tamassos	White Painted IV	Cypro-Archaic I
TM23	Tamassos	White Painted IV	Cypro-Archaic I
Group VII--TAMASSOS?			
TM 4	Tamassos	Bucchero Ware	Cypro-Geometric
TM 5	Tamassos	Bucchero Ware	Cypro-Geometric
TM 6	Tamassos	White Painted (III?)	Cypro-Geometric III?
TM 7	Tamassos	White Painted (III?)	Cypro-Geometric III?
Group VIII--PHLAMOUDHI			
ID 1	Idalion	Terra Sigillata	Roman
ID25	Idalion	Black Lustrous	Hellenistic
ID37	Idalion	Black Lustrous	Hellenistic
MS 1	Phlamoudhi "Melissa"	Red-on-Black	Late Cypriot I
MS 3	Phlamoudhi "Melissa"	Monochrome	Late Cypriot IB
MS 4	Phlamoudhi "Melissa"	Monochrome	Late Cypriot IB
MS 5	Phlamoudhi "Melissa"	Brown-Slip Monochrome	Late Cypriot IB
TC 1	Tyre, Lebanon	Red-on-Black	Bikai
TC 2	Tyre, Lebanon	Monochrome	Bikai
VN 1	Phlamoudhi "Vounari"	Red-on-Black	Late Cypriot I
VN 2	Phlamoudhi "Vounari"	Red-on-Black	Late Cypriot I

Table 4. Archaeological Data on Compositional Groups (*cont.*)

Sample	Excavated/Collected	Ware	Period
VN 4	Phlamoudhi "Vounari"	Red-on-Black	Late Cypriot I(A?)
VN10	Phlamoudhi "Vounari"	Red-on-Black	Late Cypriot I
VN11	Phlamoudhi "Vounari"	Red-on-Black	Late Cypriot I

Group IX--PHLAMOUDHI

Sample	Excavated/Collected	Ware	Period
MM30	Ayia Irini	White Painted V	Cypro-Archaic I
MS 2	Phlamoudhi "Melissa"	W.M. Black Slip	Late Cypriot I (II?)
VN 5	Phlamoudhi "Vounari"	Black Slip	Late Cypriot I
VN 6	Phlamoudhi "Vounari"	Black Slip, Red Var.	Late Cypriot I

Group X--PHLAMOUDHI

Sample	Excavated/Collected	Ware	Period
ID94	Idalion	White Painted IV	Cypro-Archaic I
VN 7	Phlamoudhi "Vounari"	Black Slip	Late Cypriot I
VN 8	Phlamoudhi "Vounari"	Black Slip	Late Cypriot I

Group XI--UNKNOWN

Sample	Excavated/Collected	Ware	Period
CM 1	Kition	White Painted	Cypro-Classical
IE49	Idalion	Black Bucchero W.-M.	Cypro-Archaic
TC 5	Tyre, Lebanon	Black Slip	Bikai

Group XII--TYRE?

Sample	Excavated/Collected	Ware	Period
CM 4	Kition	Black-on-Red	Cypro-Classical
MM45	Amathus	Black-on-Red II(IV)	Cypro-Archaic I
TC 7	Tyre, Lebanon	Black-on-Red	Bikai
TC 8	Tyre, Lebanon	Black-on-Red	Bikai
TC 9	Tyre, Lebanon	Black-on-Red	Bikai
TC10	Tyre, Lebanon	Black-on-Red	Bikai

Group XIII--MARION

Sample	Excavated/Collected	Ware	Period
MM38	Marion	Bichrome Red II(IV)	Cypro-Archaic II
MM39	Marion	Plain White V	Cypro-Archaic II
MM41	Marion	White Painted IV	Cypro-Archaic I
MM42	Marion	Bichrome IV	Cypro-Archaic I
MM43	Marion	Bichrome IV	Cypro-Archaic I
MM44	Marion	Bichrome IV	Cypro-Archaic I

Table 4. Archaeological Data on Compositional Groups (*cont.*)

Sample	Excavated/Collected	Ware	Period
Group XIV--VOUNI			
MM 1	Vouni	Plain White VI	Cypro-Classical II
MM 3	Vouni	White Painted VI	Cypro-Classical II
MM 5	Vouni	Bichrome VII	Cypro-Classical II
MM 7	Vouni	White Painted VII	Cypro-Classical II
MM10	Vouni	Plain White VII	Cypro-Classical I
MM12	Vouni	White Painted VI	Cypro-Classical I
MM14	Vouni	White Painted VI	Cypro-Classical I
Group XV--UNKNOWN			
CM42	Salamis Necropoleis	Bichrome	Cypro-Archaic?
ID 6	Idalion	White Painted	Cypro-Archaic
ID10	Idalion	Bichrome	Cypro-Archaic
MM26	Ayios Jakavos	White Painted	Cypro-Archaic
Group--IDALION BLACK GLAZED			
CM48	Salamis Necropoleis	Bichrome	Cypro-Archaic?
ID16	Idalion	Terra Sigillata?	Roman
ID26	Idalion	Black Lustrous?	Hellenistic?
ID27	Idalion	Black Glazed	Cypro-Classical
ID29	Idalion	Black Glazed	Cypro-Classical
ID30	Idalion	Black Glazed	Cypro-Classical
ID33	Idalion	Red Lustrous?	Hellenistic?
ID39	Idalion	Black Glazed	Cypro-Classical
ID40	Idalion	Black Glazed	Cypro-Classical
ID41	Idalion	Black Glazed	Cypro-Classical
ID42	Idalion	Red-Figured	5th Century BC
ID43	Idalion	Red-Figured	5th Century BC
ID44	Idalion	Black-Figured	6th Century BC
ID78	Idalion	Plain White VI	Cypro-Classical I
ID83	Idalion	Black Glazed	Hellenistic
ID56	Idalion	Bichrome Red III(VI)	Cypro-Classical I
Group--IDALION TERRA SIGILLATA			
ID12	Idalion	Terra Sigillata?	Roman
ID13	Idalion	Terra Sigillata	Roman
ID14	Idalion	Terra Sigillata	Roman
ID15	Idalion	Terra Sigillata	Roman
ID19	Idalion	Red Lustrous	Hellenistic
ID31	Idalion	Terra Sigillata	Roman

Table 4. Archaeological Data on Compositional Groups (*cont.*)

Sample	Excavated/Collected	Ware	Period
Group--IDALION RED/BLACK LUSTROUS			
AS 1	Amathus Surface	?	?
ID18	Idalion	Painted Ware	Hellenistic
ID20	Idalion	Red Lustrous	Hellenistic
ID24	Idalion	Black Lustrous	Hellenistic
ID35	Idalion	Black Lustrous	Hellenistic
ID61	Idalion	Black Lustrous	Hellenistic
ID64	Idalion	Lamp Fragment	Early Hellenistic
ID91	Idalion	Base-Ring	Late Cypriot II
Group--UNASSIGNED CYPRIOT			
AS 2	Amathus Surface	White Painted	Cypro-Archaic?
AS 3	Amathus Surface	Bichrome	
AS 4	Amathus Surface	White Painted	Cypro-Archaic?
CM 5	Kition	White Painted	Cypro-Classical
CM 6	Kition	White Painted	Cypro-Archaic?
CM11	Kition	White Painted	Cypro-Classical
CM12	Kition	White Painted	Cypro-Classical
CM19	Kition	White Painted	Cypro-Classical
CM23	Kition	Bichrome	Cypro-Archaic?
CM24	Kition	White Painted	Cypro-Archaic?
CM43	Salamis Necropoleis	Bichrome	Cypro-Archaic?
CM44	Salamis Necropoleis	Bichrome	Cypro-Archaic?
CM45	Salamis Necropoleis	White Painted	Cypro-Archaic?
CM46	Salamis Necropoleis	White Painted	Cypro-Archaic?
CM47	Salamis Necropoleis	White Painted	Cypro-Archaic?
CM49	Salamis Necropoleis	Bichrome	Cypro-Archaic?
CM50	Salamis Necropoleis	Bichrome	Cypro-Archaic?
CM52	Salamis Necropoleis	White Painted	Cypro-Archaic?
KG 1	Kythrea	White Painted	Cypro-Geometric
KG 2	Kythrea	Gray/Black Polished	Cypro-Geometric
KG 3	Kythrea	White Painted	Cypro-Geometric
KG 4	Kythrea	White Painted	Cypro-Geometric
KG 5	Kythrea	White Painted	Cypro-Geometric
KG 6	Kythrea	White Painted	Cypro-Geometric
KG 7	Kythrea	White Painted	Cypro-Geometric
KG 8	Kythrea	White Painted	Cypro-Geometric
KG 9	Kythrea	White Painted	Cypro-Geometric
MM 2	Vouni	Plain White VI	Cypro-Classical II
MM 4	Vouni	Plain White VII	Cypro-Classical II
MM 6	Vouni	Plain White VII	Cypro-Classical II
MM 8	Vouni	Bichrome VII	Cypro-Classical II
MM 9	Vouni	White Painted VI	Cypro-Classical I
MM11	Vouni	White Painted VI	Cypro-Classical I
MM13	Vouni	Plain White VI	Cypro-Classical I
MM15	Stylli	Bichrome IV	Cypro-Archaic I
MM17	Stylli	Bichrome IV	Cypro-Archaic I

Table 4. Archaeological Data on Compositional Groups (*cont.*)

Sample	Excavated/Collected	Ware	Period
MM18	Stylli	White Painted III	Cypro-Archaic I
MM19	Stylli	White Painted III	Cypro-Archaic I
MM20	Stylli	White Painted III	Cypro-Archaic I
MM21	Stylli	Black-on-Red I(III)	Cypro-Geometric III
MM22	Stylli	Black-on-Red I(III)	Cypro-Archaic I
MM23	Stylli	Black-on-Red I(III)	Cypro-Archaic I
MM24	Ayios Jakavos	White Painted	Cypro-Archaic
MM25	Ayios Jakavos	White Painted	Cypro-Archaic
MM27	Ayios Jakavos	White Painted	Cypro-Archaic
MM28	Ayios Jakavos	Bichrome	Cypro-Archaic
MM29	Ayios Jakavos	Bichrome	Cypro-Archaic
MM31	Ayia Irini	White Painted V	Cypro-Archaic I
MM32	Ayia Irini	Bichrome IV	Cypro-Archaic I
MM33	Ayia Irini	Bichrome IV	Cypro-Archaic I
MM34	Ayia Irini	Bichrome IV	Cypro-Archaic I
MM36	Marion	White Painted IV	Cypro-Archaic II
MM37	Marion	Plain White V	Cypro-Archaic II
MM40	Marion	White Painted V	Cypro-Archaic II
MM46	Amathus	Bichrome Red II(V)	Cypro-Archaic II
MM48	Amathus	Black-on-Red III(V)	Cypro-Archaic II
MM50	Amathus	Bichrome II	Cypro-Geometric II
MM52	Amathus	Bichrome I	Cypro-Geometric I
MM54	Amathus	White Painted V	Cypro-Archaic II
MM55	Lapithos	White Painted I	Cypro-Geometric I
MM56	Lapithos	White Painted I	Cypro-Geometric I
MM57	Lapithos	Black-on-Red I(III)	Cypro-Geometric III
TC 3	Tyre, Lebanon	Milk Bowl--Local?	Bikai
TC 4	Tyre, Lebanon	Milk Bowl--LC II	Bikai
TC 6	Tyre, Lebanon	White Painted	Bikai
TC13	Tyre, Lebanon	Black-on-Red	Bikai
TC14	Tyre, Lebanon	Plate Type 2	Bikai
TC15	Tyre, Lebanon	Fine Ware Plate T.2	Bikai
TC16	Tyre, Lebanon	Crisp Ware Store Jar	Bikai
TM 1	Tamassos	"Meniko Ware"	6th Century?
TM 2	Tamassos	"Meniko Ware"	6th Century?
TM 3	Tamassos	Bichrome	Cypro-Archaic
TM10	Tamassos	White Painted IV	Cypro-Archaic
TM12	Tamassos	"Meniko Ware"	Ca 500 BC
TM13	Tamassos	White Painted V	Cypro-Archaic II
TM14	Tamassos	Bichrome IV	Cypro-Archaic I
TM17	Tamassos	Plain White IV	Cypro-Archaic I
TM18	Tamassos	White Painted IV	Cypro-Archaic II
TM24	Tamassos	White Painted V	Cypro-Archaic II
VN 3	Phlamoudhi "Vounari"	Red-on-Black	Late Cypriot I
VN 9	Phlamoudhi "Vounari"	Black Slip?	Late Cypriot I
VN12	Phlamoudhi "Vounari"	Red-on-Black	Late Cypriot I

Group--UNASSIGNED IDALION

ID 3	Idalion	White Painted	Cypro-Archaic

Table 4. Archaeological Data on Compositional Groups (*cont.*)

Sample	Excavated/Collected	Ware	Period
ID11	Idalion	Bichrome	Cypro-Archaic
ID17	Idalion	Red Bichrome	Cypro-Archaic
ID21	Idalion	Red Lustrous	Hellenistic
ID22	Idalion	Black Lustrous	Hellenistic
ID23	Idalion	Black Lustrous	Hellenistic
ID28	Idalion	Black Glazed	Cypro-Classical
ID32	Idalion	Terra Sigillata	Roman
ID34	Idalion	Red Lustrous?	Hellenistic?
ID36	Idalion	Black Lustrous	Hellenistic
ID38	Idalion	Black Lustrous	Hellenistic
ID45	Idalion	White Slip	Late Cypriot
ID46	Idalion	White Slip	Late Cypriot
ID50	Idalion	Mycenaean IIIC1B	Late Cypriot
ID51	Idalion	Geometric	Geometric
ID55	Idalion	Coarse Gray	Cypro-Archaic?
ID58	Idalion	Red Slip II(IV)	Cypro-Archaic I
ID60	Idalion	Black Lustrous	Hellenistic
ID62	Idalion	Black Lustrous	Hellenistic
ID63	Idalion	White Painted VII?	Cypro-Classical II?
ID66	Idalion	Coarse Gray	Early Hellenistic?
ID69	Idalion	Plain White VII	Cypro-Classical II
ID70	Idalion	Plain White VI	Cypro-Classical I
ID71	Idalion	Plain White VII	Cypro-Classical II
ID72	Idalion	Plain White VII	Cypro-Classical II
ID72	Idalion	Plain White VI	Cypro-Classical I
ID74	Idalion	Plain White VI	Cypro-Classical I
ID75	Idalion	Plain White V	Cypro-Archaic II
ID76	Idalion	Plain White VI	Cypro-Classical I
ID77	Idalion	Plain White VI	Cypro-Classical I
ID79	Idalion	Plain White VI	Cypro-Classical I
ID80	Idalion	Plain White V	Cypro-Archaic II
ID81	Idalion	White Painted II/III?	Cypro-Geometric II/III?
ID88	Idalion	Coarse Ware	Cypro-Archaic II?
ID89	Idalion	White Painted W.-M. II	Late Cypriot II
ID90	Idalion	Mycenaean IIIB	Late Cypriot II
ID95	Idalion	Plain White IV	Cypro-Archaic I
ID97	Idalion	White Painted IV	Cypro-Archaic I
IE15	Idalion	Bichrome	
IE27	Idalion	Bichrome	
IE28	Idalion	Black-on-Red	
IE29	Idalion	White Painted	
IE30	Idalion	Black-on-Red	
IE31	Idalion	Black-on-Red	
IE32	Idalion	White Painted	
IE35	Idalion	White Painted	
IE36	Idalion	Red Slip III(V)	Cypro-Archaic II
IE40	Idalion	"Foreign Ware"	Cypro-Archaic?
IE42	Idalion	Bichrome IV	Cypro-Archaic I
IE43	Idalion	Bichrome V	Cypro-Archaic II
IE44	Idalion	Bichrome IV	Cypro-Archaic I
IE45	Idalion	Black-on-Red II(IV)	Cypro-Archaic I

Table 4. Archaeological Data on Compositional Groups (*cont.*)

Sample	Excavated/Collected	Ware	Period
IE46	Idalion	Black-on-Red III(V)	Cypro-Archaic II
IE47	Idalion	Gray Polished	Cypro-Archaic
IE48	Idalion	Black-on-Red II(IV)	Cypro-Archaic I
IE50	Idalion	Black Slip W.-M.	Cypro-Archaic
IE51	Idalion	Black Bucchero H.-M.	Cypro-Archaic
IE53	Idalion	Plain White VI	Cypro-Classical I
IE54	Idalion	Plain White VI	Cypro-Classical I
IE55	Idalion	Plain White VI	Cypro-Classical I
IE58	Idalion	Plain White?	Cypro-Classical?
IE59	Idalion	Plain White VII	Cypro-Classical II
IE60	Idalion	Bichrome?	Cypro-Classical?
IE63	Idalion	White Painted V	Cypro-Archaic II
IE65	Idalion	White Painted IV	Cypro-Archaic I
IE66	Idalion	Red Slip II(IV)	Cypro-Archaic I
IE67	Idalion	? (VI or later)	Cypro-Classical?
IE68	Idalion	Gray and Black Polished V	Cypro-Archaic II

B. REGIONAL STYLES
IN CYPRIOT LIMESTONE SCULPTURE

INTRODUCTION

Pamela Gaber

As part of the responsibility of working at a site that had been excavated earlier, it falls to our lot to attempt to integrate previously excavated material with that of the present project. The large corpus of limestone sculpture includes works from R. H. Lang's excavations, M. Ohnefalsch-Richter's excavations, the Swedish Cyprus Expedition, and the American Expedition to Idalion. One advantage of dealing with all of the excavated sculpture is that one is able to ask certain questions of the material that could not be asked of the still small corpus from the latest project alone. Was there a local school of sculptors working at Idalion whose work can be identified? To date, I have examined the sculpture in the Cyprus Museum and in the British Museum in an attempt to answer this question. The British Museum material includes pieces from Lang's and from Ohnefalsch-Richter's excavations; the Cyprus Museum sculpture, pieces from the American Expedition. Already it is possible to suggest that a school of sculpture centering in Idalion is discernible from the life-size and larger stone images of the Late Archaic and Early Classical period.

To provide a chronological framework, this report relies upon the principles originally enunciated by E. Gjerstad (*SCE* IV:2, pp. 207-11, 96-124, pls. II-XVIII) and recently clarified by C. C. Vermeule (1974:287-90). Gathering a large body of excavated sculpture from one site has provided a clearer understanding of regional characteristics, which, when undetected, have complicated the understanding of the chronological sequence of Cypriot styles.

THE SEQUENCE OF SCULPTURE STYLES AT IDALION

Since, as Vermeule states (1974:288) ". . . the bodies of Cypriote limestone statues tend to be decorative vehicles distinguished by costume or quality of carving rather than subtleties of style . . .," it is the heads on which this stylistic study shall concentrate. A head in the British Museum (pl. 1a) exemplifies the characteristics of limestone figures at Idalion from the period 550-520 B.C. The forehead approaches the vertical, and the almond-shaped eyes are relatively small in proportion to the rest of the face. They are fairly narrow, and are set close to the bridge of a nose that is straight in profile and long and slim in frontal appearance. The broad cheekbones are pronounced, although softly modeled, appearing almost like a ledge below the eyes. Typically, the mouth is thin lipped. The upper lip begins with a sharp angle below the nose; its surface is flat, almost beveled in appearance. The patterned beard angles gently forward, unlike the strong forward jut typical of other Cypriot sculptures (although this feature appears to be somewhat more variable than others listed below).

A head that Gjerstad assigned to his "Eastern" Neo-Cypriot style (*SCE* IV:2, pl. VIII), but that belongs to the period 520-480 B.C., exemplifies many of the features which characterize the Idalion School (pl. 1b). The same vertical brow is apparent above eyes that are smaller and more deeply set than those of the previous example. The cheekbones are again broad and prominent, the nose strong and straight. The mouth is small and thick lipped, and still presents a beveled appearance though its edges are somewhat less abrupt than those in the example from the preceding period. The archaic smile is no longer in fashion.

From early in the succeeding Sub-Archaic style (500-450 B.C.) comes another head in the British Museum (pl. 1c) most likely dating close to ca. 480 B.C. The eyebrows below the same straight forehead are modeled in relief here, but this too, is a somewhat variable feature. The eyes of this figure are larger than those of the two preceding examples, but are still relatively narrow in proportion to their length. The cheekbones still broad and pronounced, but the modeling is subtler, just as it is around the nose and mouth. The nose is less prominent than in previous examples, but it is still long, straight, and slender. The characteristically thin-lipped mouth is more naturalistically rendered, but its upper lip retains the beveled appearance we have noted in the earlier heads. This Sub-Archaic piece is unbearded, revealing a broad squarish chin, presented in softly modeled curves. The square chin is typical of unbearded figures in all of the Late Archaic and Early Classical stylistic periods at Idalion.

Also from the early Cypro-Classical period, but perhaps slightly later comes what may be the most famous limestone figure from Idalion (pl. 1d). R. H. Lang found it in the Apollo Amyklos Reshef MKL Temple isolated from the crowd of other sculptures. (Lang 1878:36) It lay next to a base in the center of the room; Lang believed that it was a figure of the god himself or a votive offering from the king. Whatever the case, it is a masterpiece. All of the features suggested here as typical of the Idalion School are apparent in this best example of the local style. The vertical forehead melts into eyebrows rendered in subtle relief. The characteristic eyes now have lids and tearducts. A straight, strong nose divides the familiar prominent cheekbones. A graceful moustache joins the gently stylized curls of the straight-falling beard below. There are many Sub-Archaic heads of this general type from Cyprus, and most can be compared stylistically with this one whose sculptor may have been influential in his time (see below).

The transition from the Sub-Archaic to the Classical sculpture period at Idalion (middle of the fifth century B.C.) is demonstrated by another beardless head (pl. 2a). Most of the traits of the Idalion School noted in earlier examples are also recognizable here. However, a turning away from traditional stylization is becoming apparent. A greater sense of naturalism is evident in the rendering of the lips and in the flesh of the cheeks around the mouth.

This chronological review has touched only large male heads from Idalion. There appear to have been somewhat different canons of taste applied to the rendering of female heads, and these will be examined at a later date. The problems connected with an examination of smaller works will be touched upon below.

SCULPTURE OF OTHER REGIONS

Works of Known Provenience

If we are correct in identifying an Idalion School of sculpture, then it ought to be possible to compare and contrast works from other sites to good advantage. In so doing it becomes clear that other sites also had local sculpture styles, some of which differ greatly from that of the Idalion School and some of which are quite similar.

One of the latter is the style evident at Pyla in the Sub-Archaic period (pls. 2b and c). The two heads illustrated here show obvious similarities to the central figure of Lang's Apollo Temple discussed above (pl. 1d). The straight foreheads and lidded eyes bear a strong resemblance to those of the Idalion piece. The cheekbones of the Pyla figures are more pronounced than those of the Idalion head; in fact they are ledgelike in the Pyla pieces, more in the fashion of earlier Idalion styles (see above). While the mouth of plate 2c appears to be almost a copy of the mouth of the Idalion work, its lower lip is rendered in a fleshier, more rounded fashion. The same could be said of the mouth of plate 2b, and of the nose of plate 2c as well. Perhaps the greatest difference between the Pyla and Idalion styles lies in the rendering of the hair. The facial features and the hair and beard curls are more strongly emphasized than those of the Idalion head. In the Idalion head a fluid sense is retained within the traditionally stylized curls by such devices as the addition of incised lines and separate tendrils of hair (also incised) trailing below the ringlets of the beard. Individual hairs are suggested in the moustache, again by incision. In the Pyla heads the rendering of such details as the curls and moustache is much flatter and more static. Largely because of the lack of incised detail and flowing tendrils, each curl of the Pyla heads retains its individual spiral shape instead of appearing to grow out of those above. This effect of separate shapes is also true of the moustaches of the Pyla figures. The same stylistic contrast could be drawn between the wreaths on the Pyla heads and that of the Idalion figure. Notwithstanding these contrasting features, it might be suggested that the Pyla style is derived from the Idalion style. When one considers the fact that Pyla lies in the geographical sphere of Kition and that Kition conquered Idalion in the fifth century B.C., it is easy to understand how the Pyla sculptors could have come to be familiar with the Idalion statue.

A strong contrast is provided by limestone sculptures from Vouni (pls. 2d and 3a) from the Archaic and Sub-Archaic stylistic periods. A much thinner facial type with a more pointed chin is shared by these examples. While the mouths of the Vouni pieces are thin lipped, they are bowed in a manner that accentuates the overall triangular impression of the face. The difference from the broad square-chinned Idalion faces is marked. Also in the Vouni style is a head from nearby Mersinaki (pl. 3b). It exhibits the same triangular face and bowed mouth noted above in the pieces from Vouni.

Works of Unknown Provenience

In addition to aiding our understanding of the development of Cypriot sculpture as a whole, the further study of regional styles can enable us to discover the origins of works whose provenience is in doubt. One such work where the problem is somewhat limited is the head illustrated in plate 3c. It is labeled in the collection of the British Museum as coming from Idalion, but F. N. Pryce (1931:63) feels that it is more likely to have come from Pyla, and Gjerstad shares his uncertainty (*SCE* IV:2, pl xxv). In view of our above discussion of the differences between the Idalion and the Pyla styles, it may be suggested that this head derives from somewhere near Dhali. The details of the hair and wreath in this figure relate much more closely to the Idalion style (pl. 1d) than to the Pyla works (pls. 2b and c).

The implications for works found outside Cyprus are exciting. By pinpointing the cities of origin of exported works we will gain a much clearer understanding of Cypriot foreign relations.[1]

THE SMALLER SCULPTURES

All of the examples discussed thus far have been near life-size or larger. Smaller stone figures present certain problems. The work illustrated in plate 4a, for example, is 0.74 m in height, or roughly half life-size. It was found at Idalion. Its feet are missing. The facial features of this piece conform in general to characteristics of larger works of the Sub-Archaic style at Idalion discussed above. Half life-size appears to be the critical size below which the problems appear. The figure illustrated in plate 4b is only slightly smaller, standing 0.73 m high with its feet intact. Its mouth and eyes, however, do not conform to the Idalion type. The eyes protrude outward as flat almond shapes, instead of being convex and sunk between lids modeled in relief. The mouth bows sharply upward at the corners, although the lips are thin and beveled. This piece presents the first of the problems with the smaller works: it is of lesser quality. The flat protruding eyes appear in many small stone figures at Idalion. These eyes appear to be a form of "shorthand" rendering. This piece probably belongs with the Idalion School by virtue of the overall face shape, the pronounced cheekbones, and the thinness of the lips already mentioned. But the lopsided impression created by the raising of the left eye and cheek above the right side of the face mark this figure as a piece of poorer workmanship than the preceding example. This impression is supported by a contrast of the drapery modeling of

---

[1] A small head from the Phoenician site of 'Amrit (Marathus) (Klengel 1972:49) closely resembles a head (provenience unknown) from the Sandwith Collection in the British Museum (Pryce 1931:C102). Several heads from Kition now in the Medelhavsmuseet in Stockholm (e.g., K436, K492; SCE III, pls. XXI, 5; XXVI, 6) also closely resemble both these works. This suggests Kition as the place of manufacture for the 'Amrit and the Sandwith heads.

these two pieces, though this does not directly concern the present study. The fact that a smaller votive must have been a less expensive purchase than a life-size figure goes some way toward explaining the lack of uniformity in the quality of the smaller works.

A further complication arises when the votive nature of most of these limestone figures is considered. Most of the British Museum figures were found in Lang's Apollo Temple. It is possible that smaller, more portable votives like that illustrated in plate 4c, for example, were brought from other parts of the island by worshippers at this shrine. It is nearly impossible to discern a regional provenience for this piece, and its overall poor quality of execution must be borne in mind. Still, the portability of smaller figures like this one may compound the problem of assigning them to regional schools of Cypriot sculpture.

CHRONOLOGICAL IMPLICATIONS

The chronological designations applied above to the figures from outside Idalion are taken from E. Gjerstad (*SCE* IV:2, pp. 207-11, 96-124). However, in view of the fact he relies in some measure on facial characteristics for his chronological determinations, these may have to be adjusted somewhat within the progression of each regional style. Until such time as these regional styles can be examined in detail, it is best to recognize that they exist, and, being far more complex than hitherto suspected, may have interfered to some degree with the understanding of the development of Cypriot sculpture. In consequence it is perhaps safest to drop the geographically suggestive elements of stylistic periods such as the "Eastern and Western Neo-Cypriot" styles, and retain only those elements that denote familiar developmental designations. The resulting chronological scheme, for Idalion at least (defining each "style" change somewhat differently from the traditional definitions as discussed above), would be the following:

First Proto-Cypriot style	620-560 B.C.
Second Proto-Cypriot style	560-540 B.C.
Neo-Cypriot style	550-520 B.C.
Cypro-Archaic style	520-480 B.C.
Sub-Archaic style	500-450 B.C.

This retains a general useful stylistic progression[2] which is broad enough to allow for overlap at the beginning and end of each "style." Within this scheme the sculpture of each separate region will no doubt exhibit local variations, and as the study of these regional variations progresses, one will be able to understand the overall chronological sequence better.

CONCLUSIONS

Gathering all the excavated limestone sculptures from the site of Idalion served a number of purposes. It has become possible to outline the traits of the Idalion School of sculpture in the Late Archaic and Early Classical periods. In contrasting the Idalion works with pieces from elsewhere on Cyprus, glimmerings of other regional styles of sculpture have appeared, such as those of Pyla and Vouni. These localized variations of style which are so apparent in the larger figures are more difficult to discern in works of smaller size. In considering the smaller votives, problems of portability and poor quality complicate the picture of regional schools of sculpture. Clarification through further study will refine our understanding of the chronological development of Cypriot sculpture as a whole as it has for the Idalion sequence.[3]

---

[2] As adjusted by C. C. Vermeule (1974:287-90).

[3] Editors' note: For an expanded version of this study, see Gaber-Saletan 1986.

PLATE 1

a

b

c

d

Sculptures from Idalion. a. Ht. 25 cm, b. Ht. 34 cm, c. Ht. 18.8 cm, d. Ht. 1.04 m. Detail. British Museum. (Photos a-c, author; d, E. Gombosi, after *SCE* IV:2, pl. XVI)

PLATE 2

a

b

c

d

Sculptures from Idalion, Pyla, and Vouni. a. From Idalion, ht. 15 cm; b. From Pyla, ht. 33 cm; c. From Pyla, ht. 38 cm; and d. From Vouni, ht. 23.5 cm. a-c. British Museum; d. Medelhavsmuseet. (Photos a-c, author; d, E. Gombosi, after *SCE* IV:2, pl. XIV)

PLATE 3

a

b

c

Sculptures from Vouni, Mersinaki, and Idalion. a. From Vouni, ht. 11 cm; b. From Mersinaki; and c. From Idalion, ht. 33 cm. a-b. Medelhavsmuseet; c. British Museum. (Photos a-b, E. Gombosi, after *SCE* IV:2, pls. XVI, XIV; c, author)

PLATE 4

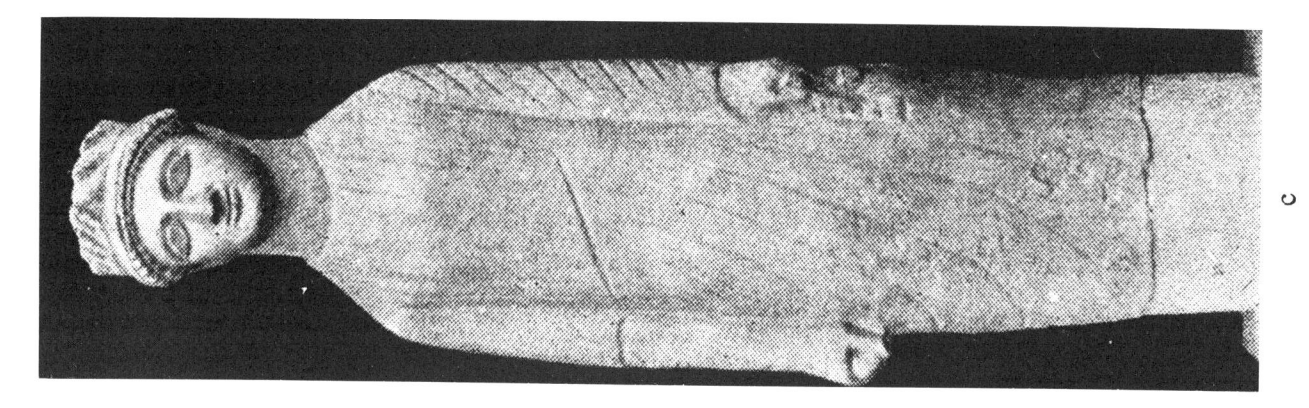

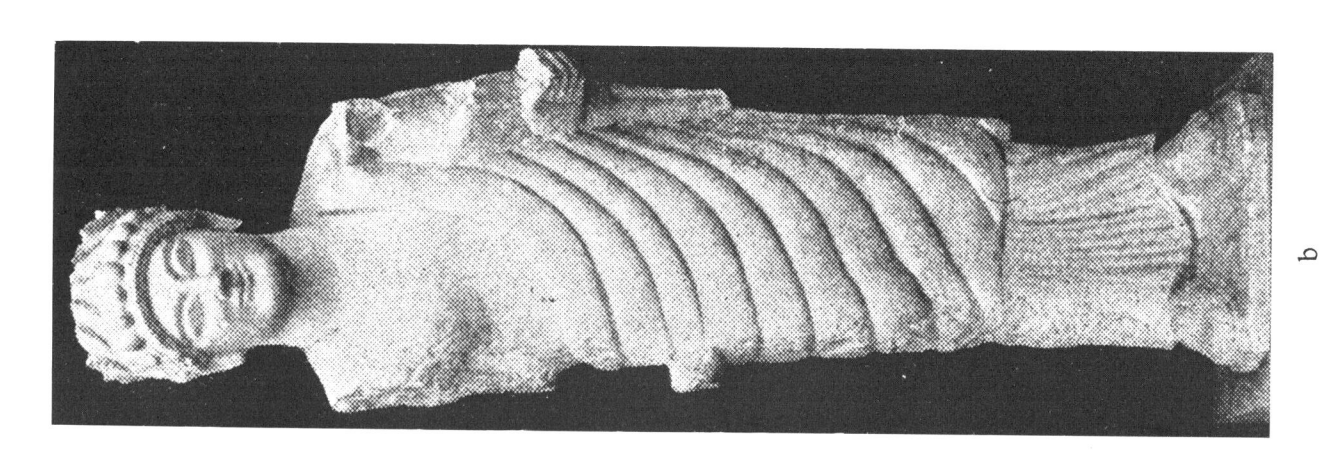

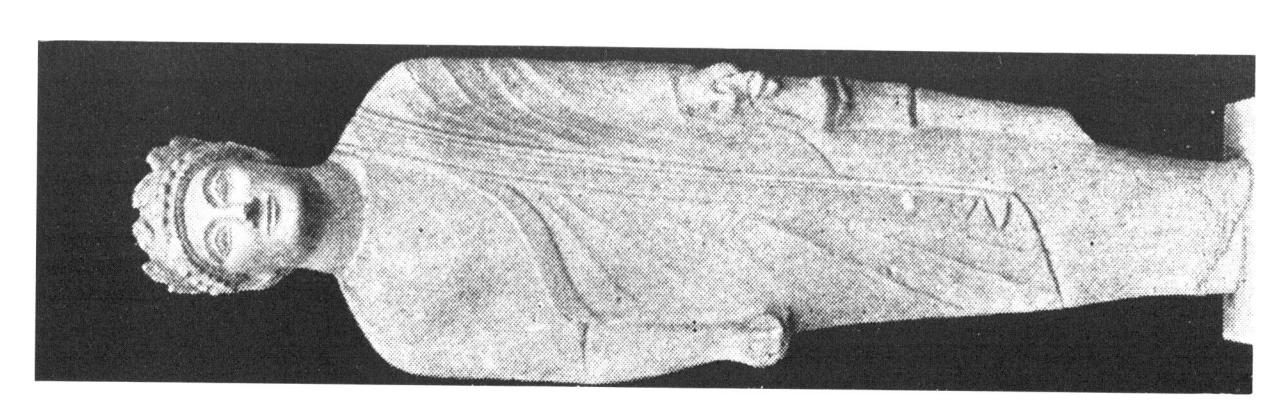

a. Sculptures from Idalion. a. Ht., 74 cm; b. Ht., 73 cm; c. Ht., 56 cm. British Museum. (Photos, author)

V. ETHNOARCHAEOLOGY AND ETHNOGRAPHY
A. ETHNOARCHAEOLOGICAL INVESTIGATIONS, 1976

EVALUATING ASSUMPTIONS CONCERNING SPATIAL PATTERNING
ON THE BASIS OF DATA FROM A CYPRIOT VILLAGE

Jane Katherine Sallade[*]

Introduction

This paper presents an example of the use of ethnographic data to evaluate the assumptions that archaeologists hold about the relationship between past behavior and the spatial arrangement of material remains in the archaeological record. Ethnographic data from a Cypriot village within the general area of Idalion were used to explore the relationship between householders' activity and the association and distribution of objects within a household compound.

The data were recorded and analyzed quantitatively, using methods and techniques comparable to those currently used in the collection and analysis of archaeological data. These ethnographic data can be used to establish regularities of domestic behavior in relation to spatial organization and thereby to improve the predictive value of archaeological inferences.

General Problem

Archaeologists make assumptions about the existence and meaning of spatial patterning in the archaeological record. These assumptions, when used in the collection, integration, and analysis of archaeological data, directly affect interpretations of the interrelationships of objects that compose the archaeological record. This paper examines a number of assumptions that together constitute the view that the spatial patterning of archaeological remains reflects the spatial patterning of past activities.

Archaeologists seek to discern patterns of association in the distribution of the material items that they excavate. They interpret these patterns as indicative of past behavior on the assumption that one can specify a location or locations for particular activities and for objects used together at a site. Objects that were used together are assumed to be found together in the locations in which the activities in which they were used took place. If this assumption is valid, then the spatial analysis of objects in the archaeological record should reveal consistent patterns of association among objects used in different kinds of activities. The composition of "tool kits" can be reconstructed inferentially from these data. It is assumed that the patterns observed in spatially associated objects provide information concerning the organization of associated activity groups (e.g., Binford 1962, 1964, 1968, 1972; Hill 1966; Longacre 1968; cf. Schiffer 1972:156).

---

[*] Ph.D., University of Michigan, Ann Arbor, Michigan; deceased 1979

This fieldwork was financially supported by the Wenner-Gren Foundation for Anthropological Research, Grant #3115. The American Expedition to Idalion, with which the author has been associated since 1973, supplied lab facilities and additional services. Members of the Department of Antiquities and of other offices in the government of the Republic of Cyprus also provided help and encouragement. The author wishes to thank these organizations and the generous people of Alambra for their support.

If these assumptions are not valid, however, then many if not most interpretations of the spatial organization of excavated objects on occupational surfaces are deeply suspect. To date, many of these assumptions remain unexamined. Arguments concerning the validity or applicability of assumptions, methodologies, and analytical techniques will continue until the relevant variables that contribute to the spatial patterning of material objects have been determined. Comparative ethnographic studies should help to delineate the relevant variables that contribute to spatial patterning in contemporary societies at various levels of cultural and economic complexity. Such studies, because they are based on direct observation, are not affected by excavation techniques and postabandonment activity. Therefore if in the analysis of ethnographic data regular spatial patterning does not appear as predicted, this may indicate inadequacies in the assumptions made by archaeologists and in the excavation and/or analytic techniques currently in use and may suggest the need for modifications thereof.

To date, systematic ethnoarchaeological research has focused primarily on hunting and gathering societies (e.g., Gould 1968a, 1968b, 1971; Lee and DeVore 1968; Lee 1969; Wilmsen 1973). Until recently only a small number of analogical and/or unsystematic studies have been attempted on sedentary communities at various levels of cultural complexity (e.g., Stanislawski 1969a, 1969b; Lange and Rydberg 1972; Bonnichen 1973). In only a very few instances (e.g., David 1972; David and Hennig 1972) have the investigators of sedentary communities sought to quantify the observations or relationships on which they report. Several new studies, most of which are now in press, will, I hope, signal a break in the history of such ethnoarchaeological research on sedentary communities (e.g., DeBoer and Lathrap 1976; Kramer 1976).

In 1976 a project was begun in several Cypriot communities to define and examine systematically the variables that contribute to spatial organization in agricultural peasant societies. For five months data were collected by controlled observation on the relationship between behavior and the organization of materials in space in and around the peasant community of Alambra. This paper introduces Alambra as a study area and presents several preliminary statistical analyses as subsequently performed (see below) on data from one household within the community. The analyses investigate two aspects of the relationship between the behavior of persons engaged in an activity and the distribution of material objects within the household compound. The results of these analyses are then discussed in the context of behavioral "models" on which such assumptions are based. The evaluation of these assumptions by methods such as those presented here would encourage increased rigor in the analysis of the archaeological record.

Data Collection

Alambra is in the Nicosia District about seventeen miles south of the capital. The core of the old village, which is located at the end of a short side road that leads west from the main Nicosia-Limassol highway, is effectively bypassed by all major communication. The village is situated on the seasonal Ammos River at the juncture of the central plain with the lower pillow lavas of the Troodos Mountain foothills (fig. 1).

With a population of approximately 600 persons, Alambra is a relatively small village. It is homogeneous in terms of gross socioeconomic statuses and occupations. The residents rely on mixed agriculture and herding for subsistence. Many, but not all, supplement this income with that of part-time wage labor. Within the village, subsistence items are produced, maintained, consumed, and discarded in a variety of activities. The population comprises a full range of age groups. Therefore all spatial associations and spatial patterning of material objects that are dependent on the differential behavior of the sexes and various age cohorts should be present in the composition of activity groups. During the recent conflicts on the island the village suffered no physical damage or abandonment that could have disturbed village activities and spatial organization.

The Lands and Surveys Department of the Cyprus Republic prepares plot maps of all villages. A ten percent random sample of eleven households was drawn from the 108 compounds that appear on the most recent revision of the Alambra plot map. The sample includes families representative of households in different stages of their life cycles, supported by the entire possible range of occupations and activities in the village.

I used the sample households to collect data concerning the relationship between behavior and the organization of activities and objects in space within the household, village, and village field systems. Within the village, the household compound proved to be the most convenient unit of analysis in which controlled observations could be made, since most activities take place within its confines. In each sample household, data were collected on products and materials that entered and left the compound. To evaluate the relationship between activity and the distribution of material objects, data were collected on the objects used in the compounds, their association with other objects in activities, their association with activity groups in a range of activities, and the spatial locales and relations of each of these associations in each of the activities. The pathways over which objects and members of activity groups moved and the time allotted to various activities and stages of activities were included in the record. Collection of such data required the uninterrupted observation of household activities from their initiation in the morning until their cessation after dusk. Maps, catalogues, and photographs were made to record the placement of all objects and to facilitate the collection of data on subsequent changes over time in the associations and location of objects in storage and use.

The analytic tests described in this paper employ data collected within only one of the sample households, Compound 70. The location of this compound and of the other sample households within the village context is presented in figure 2. The extended family that occupies Compound 70 is totally supported by mixed agriculture and animal husbandry. Its members engage in a broad range of subsistence and related domestic activities at least five days a week. During the study period the family consisted of a father and mother, both in their forties; four daughters, aged nine to twenty-five; and the mother's widowed mother, aged seventy-five. The two older girls, besides occasionally helping in the fields, also held jobs in Nicosia. The income from their jobs was reserved for *prika* (dowry) and did not contribute to subsistence (except as it freed some production that might otherwise have been used for *prika*). The father was occupied solely as a farmer. Because of his expertise, he spent some time in the evenings managing the village credit committee, for which he gained some prestige but received no monetary compensation. The family raised its own goats, sheep, chickens, and pigeons. On at least twenty-three widely dispersed plots of land the family produced crops for its own subsistence and a surplus of grain for government sale.

The data used here were collected on 548 movable objects. The locations of these objects at one point in time are mapped in figure 3. The photograph (pl. 1a) was taken from the east side of the compound, looking at the southwest corner of the yard. Another (pl. 1b) was taken from within one of the southern compound entry rooms. The locations of objects at rest are not necessarily the same locations as those at which the objects were used. Only the locations of objects at rest are used in the subsequent analyses, although the locations at which several of the objects were used are considered nonquantitatively in the discussion section. Also, the analyses do not take into account the pathways over which the objects moved. Future analyses will evaluate the relevance of these and many other variables, as well as the effects of differential disposal patterns, and household abandonment and reoccupation activities.

Ten frequently performed activities that took place during the course of thirteen days of observation over a three-week period are used in the analyses presented below. These ten activities took place entirely within the confines of the compound, regardless of the weather. The ten activities are:

1. sweeping and mopping of the interior rooms
2. sweeping the compound yard
3. cleaning the compound yard
4. goat milking
5. animal watering

6. feeding grain or meal to the animals
7. chicken butchering
8. clothes washing
9. bread baking
10. plant watering.

The analyses presented here employ the following coded information for each movable object present within the mapped compound structures and yard:

1) The architectural unit where the object occurred at rest, defined as a building unit or a subcompound surface (such as a smooth mud surface or a cobbled surface)

2) The number of times the object was used in each of the ten activities over the thirteen-day observation period.[1]

The locations of objects on lofts or hanging from walls were coded as if they were to fall directly to the ground in a straight vertical line.

Analysis

This section focuses on several analyses performed on these data. The analyses produced results that can be used to evaluate portions of the above-stated assumptions about spatial patterning and associations of materials. The results of the analyses and additional questions that they raise are presented in this section. A discussion of the relationship between the results and the "models" of behavior on which interpretative assumptions are based forms a subsequent section.

If on a site there are specifiable locations or sets of locations for particular activities and for objects used together in those activities, then one should be able to reconstruct "tool kits" from patterns formed by the spatial associations among the objects. Various statistical techniques are used by archaeologists to delimit such patterns of associations among materials in space (Whallon 1973, 1974, and references therein). If tools that are used together are left together in the locations in which the activities take place, then such associations would likewise be evident in our analyses of ethnographic data. The analytic techniques employed here are the same as those currently and commonly used in analyses of comparably recorded archaeological data. The analyses involve some simple aspects of (1) the co-occurrence of used objects at rest versus the co-occurrence of unused (or infrequently used) objects, and (2) types of rest location of objects in more than one activity. The purpose of my observations was twofold: (1) to determine whether objects used in various activities are distributed in space differently from objects that are not used in these activities, and, if so, then (2) to discover the nature of their aggregation and relate it to behavioral variables.

Aggregation of Used Versus Unused Objects

The first analysis sought to determine whether objects used in an activity were aggregated in any way within the compound. For this purpose, all objects were separated into two categories based on whether or not an object was used at least once in one of the ten given activities during the thirteen-day observation period.

---

[1] Other classes of data, such as the one meter grid square in which the object was located at rest, and the number of times the object was used in each activity per day of the thirteen-day period were coded but not used here. Two-dimensional cartesian coordinates which were recorded for each object, such that every object is located to the north and east of a datum point to the southwest of the compound, will be used in future analyses. Locations of objects were measured to each object's midpoint.

A cross-tabulation of architectural units versus used/unused objects was made to determine whether used objects are distributed differentially in space relative to unused objects, or whether they are merely randomly distributed within the compound. Such a cross-tabulation reveals the difference between the observed number of used objects per spatial observation unit and the number of objects expected under the null hypothesis of a random distribution.

This cross-tabulation of architectural units versus used/unused objects (table not shown) indicated that used objects (in general) are not distributed at random within the compound. Rather, some architectural units have significantly more used objects than one would expect based on the percentage of the total number of objects found in that unit ($X2 = 93.231$; $df = 18$; significance = $p < .0001$). Therefore used movable objects appear to be nonrandomly concentrated in certain locations, and these locations appear to differ from the locations occupied by unused (or infrequently used) movable objects.

Additional questions now arise as to why some units have a disproportionate number of used objects at rest, how and why the used objects are differentially aggregated and in which locations, and whether or not we can expect objects located in certain locations to be frequently used objects. When we can answer these questions, we can begin to answer the question of whether or not we can expect objects located in certain locations to represent "tool kits" from which activities can be inferred. In the discussion section several general and specific suggestions for interpreting these distributions will be made. The remainder of the analysis section describes several relationships between the type of location of objects and object-use frequency.

Types of Rest Location of Objects Versus Use/Nonuse of Objects in Different Activities

The nature of the spatial aggregation of objects used in the ten activities was further examined through an analysis of the locational predictability of objects at rest. For this purpose an "Index of Locational Predictability" was employed, based on the so-called Information Statistic of Shannon and Weaver (1949; cf. Pielou 1967). This index measures the evenness with which a given set of objects is distributed among a given set of classification categories, relative to the maximum condition of evenness possible, given the number of categories involved. The measure can vary between a value of 1.0, indicating maximum evenness, and 0.0, indicating maximum unevenness.[2]

In the present context, three different sets of objects in the compound were analyzed: (1) all objects observed as movable, (2) all used objects, and (3) all objects used in each of the ten coded activities. The interest was in the rest locations of these objects in architectural units. When used as a measurement of the distributional evenness versus unevenness of household objects at rest among architectural units, the index becomes a measure of the inverse probability that the analyzed objects are mutually aggregated in a single unit rather than scattered randomly among many units: the higher the index value, the lower the probability of nonrandom aggregation. The values of the measure, obtained in this present context are presented in table 1.

---

[2] For example, if ten objects are distributed in such a way that an equal number fall into each of five categories, then these objects may be said to be distributed with maximum evenness. If, conversely, these ten objects are distributed in such a way that only one object falls into each of four of the categories while the remainder all fall into the fifth, then this would represent a state of maximum unevenness. In the former situation it can be said that there is a very low level of predictability in the distribution of the ten objects. That is, there is a very low probability that a given object will fall into a particular category. In the latter situation, however, there is a very high probability that a given object will fall into one particular category; there is a high level of predictability in the distribution of the ten objects. The index of evenness, or the index of predictability, used here is known as "H/Hmax" (Pielou 1969:224-34) and is defined as the ratio of the measured evenness of the distribution of objects across classification categories to the maximum level of evenness possible, given the number of categories present.

The results indicate a very low probability (index value = .7395) that all objects (used and unused) are aggregated. The probability that all used objects are aggregated is only slightly greater (index value = .6939). When individual activities are considered, however, two results are notable. The objects used in most of the ten activities tend to be more aggregated by activity than are all movable objects in general. Thus, the rest locations for objects used in the ten coded activities tend to be more predictable, or more highly concentrated in particular spatial units, than the rest locations of all objects in general. Sweeping and mopping of interior rooms and plant watering are exceptions to this statement. Furthermore, when one considers individual activities, the objects used in most of the activities are usually more aggregated by activity than are used movable objects in general. Thus the rest locations of objects used in a given activity tend to be more predictable than the locations of objects used in the ten activities in general. Sweeping and mopping of interior rooms, animal feeding, and plant watering are exceptions to this statement.

There are, therefore, three principal results of this application of the measure of locational predictability. First, frequently used movable objects tend to be mutually more highly aggregated at rest within the household compound than are movable objects in general. Second, objects used in a particular individual activity usually are mutually more highly aggregated at rest than are frequently used objects in general. Third, the objects used in some activities are mutually more highly aggregated at rest than are the objects used in other activities.

I examined the third of these results in further detail. Several possible reasons can be suggested and investigated as to why objects used in some activities are more highly aggregated when at rest than are objects used in other activities. This kind of variability might result from the fact that some activities involve a high proportion of objects used exclusively in those activities, while other activities involve many objects used in at least one additional activity. The use of an object in more than one activity may decrease the probability that it will be found in association with all the other objects with which it is used. To investigate the possibility one has to determine the extent to which the frequency of object use in more than one activity affects aggregation. Therefore the proportion of objects used in one activity exclusively was compared with the index of aggregation for that activity as a whole (table 1).

The results of this comparison can be interpreted to indicate that the greater proportion of objects used exclusively in an activity, the greater will be the aggregation of all objects used in that activity. There is, however, only a slight tendency in this direction. Therefore the variability in the aggregation is only partially to be explained in terms of the variability in the proportion of objects used in more than one activity. For it is also a fact that for some activities the objects used in more than one activity are mutually more highly aggregated at rest than are objects used exclusively in one activity. Objects used in both chicken butchering and in cleaning the compound yard may be cited as examples.

There are, therefore, other factors that affect aggregation beyond simply the frequency of object use in more than one activity.[3] For some activities, objects used in additional activities are just as highly aggregated at rest as objects used in only one activity. For other activities, the objects used exclusively in one activity are more highly aggregated at rest than are objects used in more than one activity. Therefore frequency of object use in multiple activities cannot be said to be the sole factor that determines whether or not an object will be located at rest with other objects with which it is used in a given activity. This observation should lead one to reconsider the interpretations that have been made in the archaeological record concerning associated objects and should encourage further investigation of the variables

---

[3] For example, the frequency with which any object, A, is used with another object, B, may have an effect on whether or not these two objects will be found together at rest. Future analyses should investigate the effect of other factors such as these.

that contribute to the distribution of such objects, using systematically collected ethnographic data.

The purpose of the above analyses was to determine whether frequently used objects are distributed differently in space from infrequently used objects and how their distribution may vary. The analytic results would appear to suggest that frequently used objects are, indeed, distributed differently in space from infrequently used objects and that the former appear to be mutually more highly aggregated than the latter. A great deal of further analysis is needed, however, to determine how behavior is responsible for such differential aggregation of objects. The analyses presented here reveal that while the nature of spatial aggregation of used objects may depend partly on the frequency with which an object is used exclusively in one activity as against several activities, frequency of use is not the sole factor that determines whether or not co-used objects will be found together in locations of rest or use. Therefore further work should examine other variables that could be factors in whether or not objects that are used together are left at rest on the site location in which particular activities take place.

The next section discusses a theoretical framework for the investigation of such additional variables. The results of the analyses presented above and some added observations on the spatial organization of this compound are considered in relation to this framework.

Discussion

Models of human behavior underlie assumptions of spatial patterning. Yet few if any investigations have been undertaken on the relationship between these models and the characteristics of co-used tool aggregations in peasant households. The relationship between a model of human behavior and the specific results of the analyses, the locations of fixed features, and the locations of used objects in the areas where the activity is performed will be discussed in this section to explore the factors that may condition the aggregation of material objects in such space. Although as yet the observations that follow have not been expressed quantitatively, they should be useful in studying the general relationship between behavior and the arrangement of objects used in activities.

Assumptions concerning spatial patterning and association of material objects currently employed in analyzing archaeological data have permitted interpretations of the archaeological record as a "fossilized" picture of past activities (Binford 1964:425). Such interpretations, however, have been based on a simplistic view of how people would behave if they consistently put forth only the least possible effort. Given this viewpoint, objects in the archaeological record have been treated as though they had been discarded where they were used (e.g. Hill 1966; Longacre 1968; Binford et al. 1970).

However recent ethnographic studies of hunter-gatherers, who would be more likely to produce "expedient" tools than groups possessing more complex tool industries, contradict this simple behavioral model and the spatial distribution of material objects that it predicts (e.g., Binford 1974; O'Connell 1977). And certainly in peasant communities many used objects interact with large numbers of other objects in a range of activities that form a network of interactions of associated objects, activity groups, and spatial locales. For example, 38.8 percent of the used objects analyzed in the present study were used in two or more distinct activities. Such tools are retained, transferred between activities, and curated, since the cost of replacing them would be greater than the cost of transferring them from activity to activity. Objects that are curated do not enter the archaeological record with as great frequency as expedient objects. As a result, the collection of assumptions noted earlier may not be valid. But if the assumptions currently made are not valid, then archaeologists remain in need of a model of behavior that can account for the spatial patterning and association of objects that constitute the archaeological record.

Alternative models of behavior can be evaluated using the Alambra ethnographic data. One such model, amenable to testing, is that of George Kingsley Zipf. In his book, *Human*

Behavior and the Principle of Least Effort (1949), Zipf presents a more sophisticated exposition of least effort behavior than that noted above. Zipf argues that human behavior tends toward a minimization of probable rate of work and he predicts the specific spatial organization of "workshops" based on the constant operation of certain least effort principles. If they are valid, the constant operation of these principles can be expected to produce "shop" or activity areas in which the more frequently used tools will tend to be the lighter, smaller, older, more versatile tools. These tools will be more thoroughly integrated with the action of other tools. They will also be located closer to the worker than other co-used tools, whose distance from the worker will increase proportionally as they fail to exhibit the above characteristics (Zipf 1949:158-63).

The remaining discussion attempts to establish the fit between several of Zipf's suggestions, the results of the analyses presented earlier, and additional information on the spatial organization of the compound. First the aggregations of used objects are delineated in space. Then the forms in which the aggregations of used objects occur are examined with respect to (1) the different activities in which the objects were used, (2) the locations in which the activities took place, and (3) the presence or absence of fixed or immovable technological features in association with activities in these locations.

The Areas of Aggregation of Used Objects

Objects used in the ten coded activities were found to be aggregated at rest in the room in the southwest corner of the compound, south of the ovens that are east of this room, in the woodpile area along the northern compound wall, and in one of the metric grid squares of the packed-earth yard. Used objects were also strongly aggregated along the southern compound wall, south of the cement path running east-west across the compound. Used objects were only weakly aggregated atop the ovens. Further delineation of the aggregation of the used objects within these units can be obtained by visually noting which metric grid squares within these units exhibit higher aggregations of used objects than expected. In the southwest room, used objects were highly aggregated in two metric grid squares along the southern and western walls in the southwest corner, opposite the entry to this room. In the cobbled compound area east of this room used objects were highly aggregated in one grid square along the western wall of the yard, just south of the ovens. Aggregated used objects in the area of the woodpile were arranged along its southern, accessible perimeter and at its western edge, where it meets the chicken coop. The photograph that illustrates this latter area (pl. 1b) was taken looking north from an entry room on the southern edge of the compound. South of the cement walk, aggregated used objects were found either within the fixed cement feature surrounding the water source for the compound yard or within a distance of one meter to the east of this feature. These aggregations can be located visually by referring to figure 3, the compound map; plates 1a and 1b, two photographs of the compound; figure 4, a plot of all movable used objects in the compound; and figure 5, a plot of all movable objects in the compound.

The Form of the Aggregations of Co-used Objects

As stated earlier, objects used in several of the ten activities appear highly aggregated, while objects used in other activities do not. This difference in levels of aggregation is related to but is not solely dependent on the relative frequency of object use in only one activity.

The objects used in clothes washing, chicken butchering, goat milking, animal watering, and bread baking are highly aggregated. With the exception of animal watering, these activities also tend to involve a large proportion of objects used exclusively in that one activity. Excluding goat milking, which involves only three objects, the remainder of these activities (bread baking, clothes washing, and chicken butchering) take place in specified areas in association with fixed or immovable technological features. Bread baking takes place in the area south of the ovens of which it makes use (pl. 2). Clothes washing and chicken butchering employ both the objects and the two fixed features in the southwest compound room. The fixed hearth and the gas tank, both located in the southwest corner of this room, are used alternatively for heating the water necessary for these two activities. Depending on the activity, clothes are scrubbed and rinsed in, or chicken feathers plucked into, the limestone basin located along the east wall, north of the doorway to this room. Thus, highly aggregated used objects restricted exclusively to use in one activity tend to be co-used objects, frequently associated at rest with fixed features involved in their use.

The objects used in animal feeding, plant watering, sweeping the compound yard, cleaning the compound yard, and sweeping and mopping of the interior rooms are not highly aggregated. Also, the form of the arrangement of the objects used in these five activities appears to differ from the distributional form of the highly aggregated objects just discussed. The objects used in each of these five activities are also used in a variety of other activities. For example, a bucket used in watering animals is also used in feeding animals and in sweeping and cleaning. The activities in which objects that are not highly aggregated are used also appear to be performed over wider areas than most of the activities discussed in the preceding paragraph. Most of the objects used in the five activities in question appear to be found at rest largely independent from the fixed features with which they may be associated during performance of the activity. Rather they are to be found in a large number of grid squares along the southern wall of the compound and the southern edge of the woodpile. It therefore appears that used objects that are not highly aggregated and that are employed in a variety of activities are arranged in a linear form, independently of most of the fixed features with which they are used.

If the principal location of the person during the performance of the activity is also considered, the spatial distribution of the aggregated objects used in the five activities in question and the relationships between the objects appear to fit several of the expectations suggested by Zipf. For example, the buckets used in these activities tend to be lighter, smaller, and more versatile. They are also kept closer to the worker during a greater portion of the time spent in the activities as a whole than are other used objects. The only way in which these objects do not appear to fit the expectations suggested by Zipf is that they do not appear to be found at rest aggregated with other co-used objects. This divergence seems to result from the fact that the objects are used in more than one activity and that the several activities occur over wide areas of the compound.

The spatial relationships between highly aggregated used objects at rest associated with fixed features have not as yet been analyzed in terms of their fit with the expectations suggested by Zipf. As noted earlier, the objects found in such aggregations generally appear to be co-used objects associated with the given features involved in the performance of the activities. If the objects found in such aggregations do prove to fit Zipf's expectations, then it should be possible to reconstruct the associated activity patterns archaeologically through combined morphological and spatial analyses.

In further analyses the possible presence of unused objects whose rest locations coincide with the location of an activity-specific aggregation must, of course, also be considered. The ability to remove this random spatial "noise," analytically, the possibility of establishing "tool kits" (as co-used objects in these aggregations), and the likelihood of reconstructing activities from them can be investigated by examining other household compounds among which the frequency of performance of individual activities and the range and intensity of the performance of the activity vary. The quantitative measurement and analysis of the operation of these and many other variables[4] are a part of ongoing investigations.

---

[4] Examples of such variables are the frequency with which objects are used in an activity, the frequency with which an activity is performed, the frequency with which an object is used in other activities, and the presence of a permanent feature in the activity.

Summary

Ethnographic data from a village peasant household were used to explore two of the conditions necessary to establish the validity of several currently held archaeological assumptions concerning the relationship between behavior and the spatial association of materials in the archaeological record. Collectively, these assumptions state that objects used together in the past were left together in the locations of use within a site. If so, then archaeological spatial associations among excavated objects, revealed through various kinds of analyses, may be interpreted to indicate activities and the organization of associated activity groups.

If these assumptions are valid, then objects that are used together, ethnographically, must occur together at rest, forming patterns that can be spatially distinguished from those of objects not used together, patterns from which activities can be reasonably inferred. If co-used objects that are also used in multiple activities are not found to occur together at rest, ethnographically, then reconstruction of the range of past activities is further complicated.

Quantitative analyses of ethnographic data collected in Alambra have yielded results that can be used to improve the predictive value of archaeological inferences by modifying the interpretation of analyses, if not the assumptions themselves. Based on this one specific ethnographic test example, it appears that movable objects used in peasant households can be predicted to be nonrandomly aggregated in locations that differ from the locations in which unused (or infrequently used) movable objects are found. Further, it appears that the greater the proportion of objects used exclusively in one activity, the greater will be the aggregation of all objects used in that activity. However, frequency of use cannot be said to be the sole factor that determines whether or not co-used objects will be found together at rest.

The results of the analytic tests, visual inspection of the locations of used objects and fixed features, and additional information on the spatial organization and performance of activities within this compound were used to define further the character of these aggregations and to evaluate the appropriateness of a behavioral model that purports to be associated with the fixed features involved in the performance of the activity. Less highly aggregated used objects, each involved in more than one activity, appeared to be arranged in a linear form and to be associated less frequently with the fixed features involved in more than one activity. Further analyses are necessary to determine whether the relationships between objects in space fit the expectations predicted by the discussed behavioral model. The role of additional variables in observed regularities of domestic behavior in relation to the spatial patterning and association of objects can be delineated through further analyses of such ethnographic data, collected by systematic observation. Thus, ethnoarchaeological studies can contribute to manipulate archaeological data and to the improvement of interpretations of the analytical results.

Table 1. Locational Predictability at Rest and Frequency of Object Use in a Single Activity for Movable Objects in Alambra Compound 70

	A[a]	B[b]	C[c]	D[d]
All movable objects	0.7395	---	---	---
All used movable objects	0.6939	61.2	0.6228	0.6390
Objects used in activity				
01	0.7702	18.2	0.0000	0.7629
02	0.6664	00.0	---	0.6664
03	0.6854	26.3	0.8276	0.6849
04	0.5791	66.7	1.0000	0.0000
05	0.5904	00.0	---	0.5904
06	0.7093	53.8	0.4912	0.7423
07	0.4886	31.3	0.5303	0.4312
08	0.2792	52.9	0.1586	0.4329
09	0.6013	61.1	0.5899	0.6564
10	0.7500	00.0	---	0.7500

[a]Column A: Overall index of locational predictability
[b]Column B: Percentage of objects used exclusively in a single activity
[c]Column C: Index of locational predictability for objects used in a single activity
[d]Column D: Index of locational predictability for objects used in more than one activity

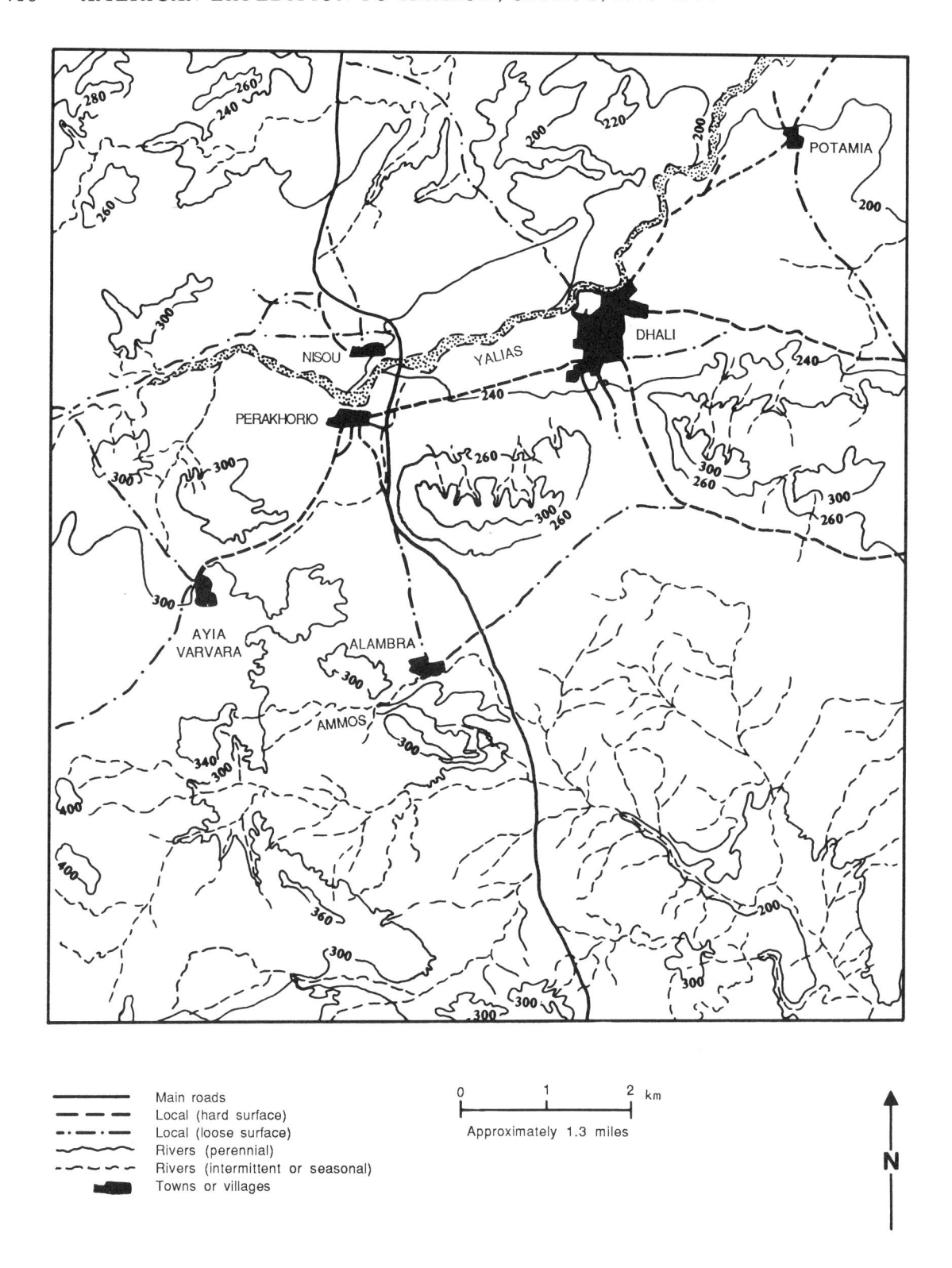

Figure 1. Map of the Alambra Area. This illustrates the surrounding topography, hydrology, road network, and the location of neighboring communities.

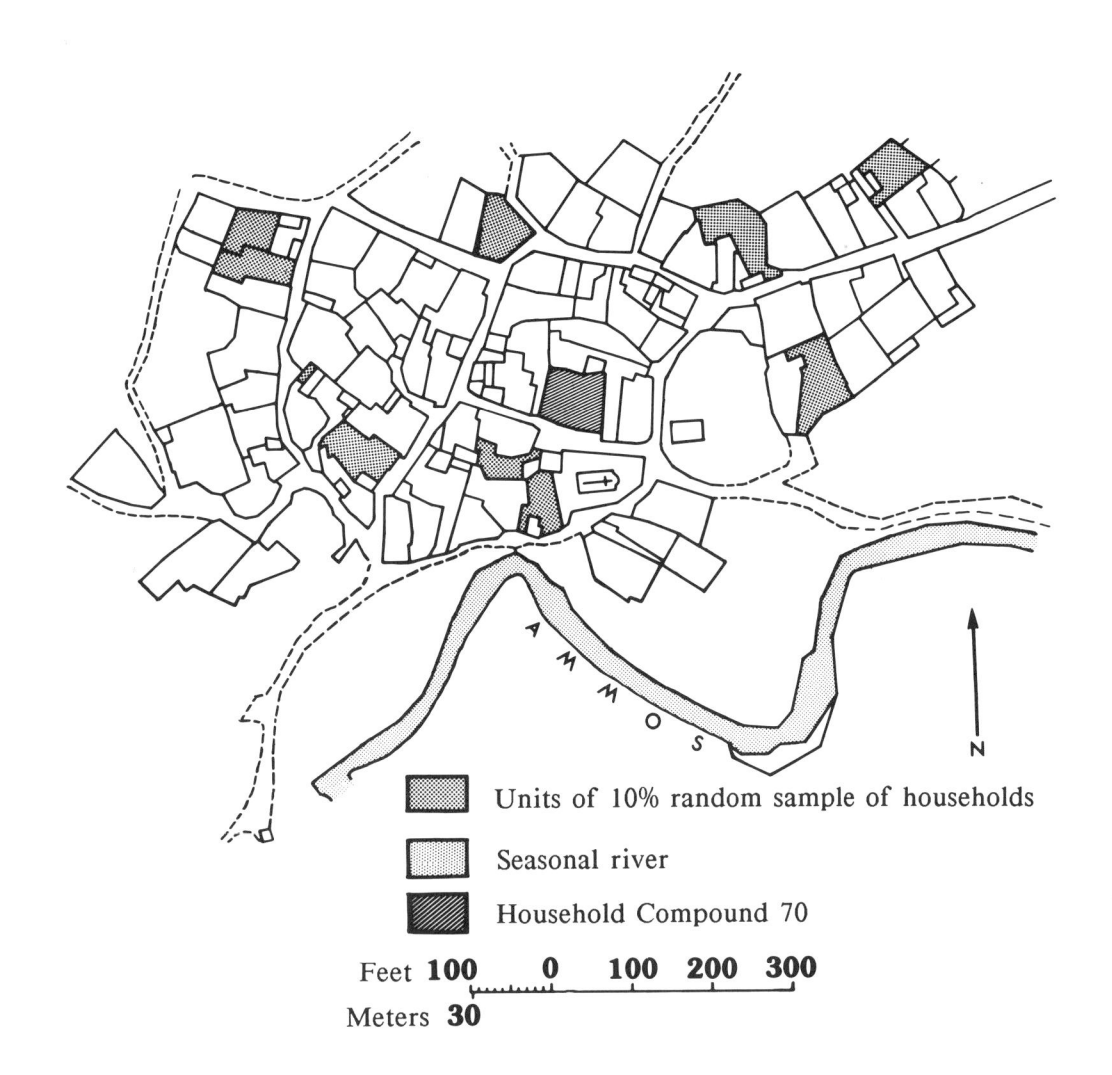

Figure 2. Map of Alambra Village. This illustrates the location of Compound 70 and the other sample households within the village plan and in relation to the Ammos River (after Cyprus Department of Lands and Surveys Plans, February 1967).

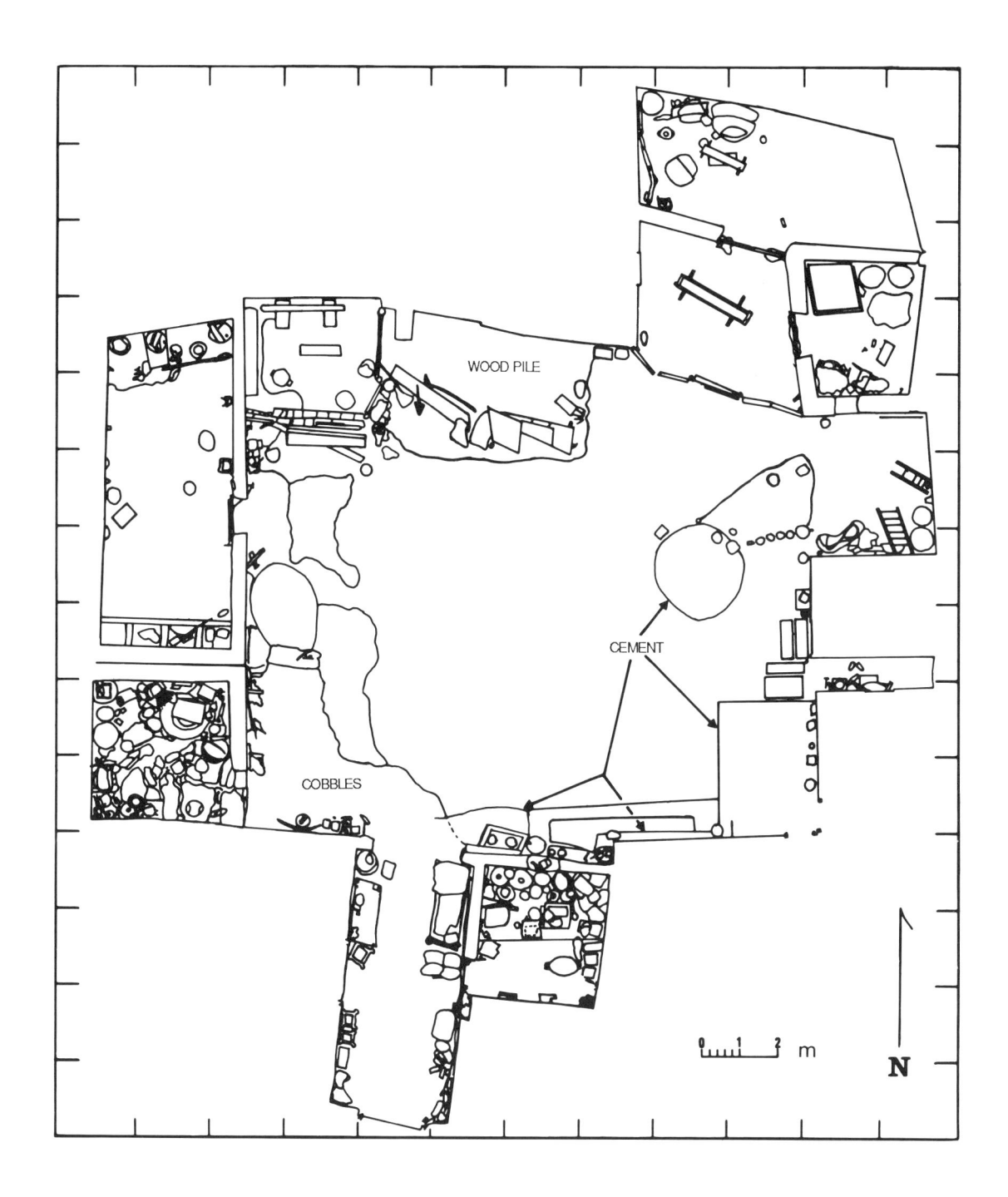

Figure 3. Map of Compound 70, Alambra. This illustrates the locations of movable objects, fixed features, building units, and subcompound surfaces.

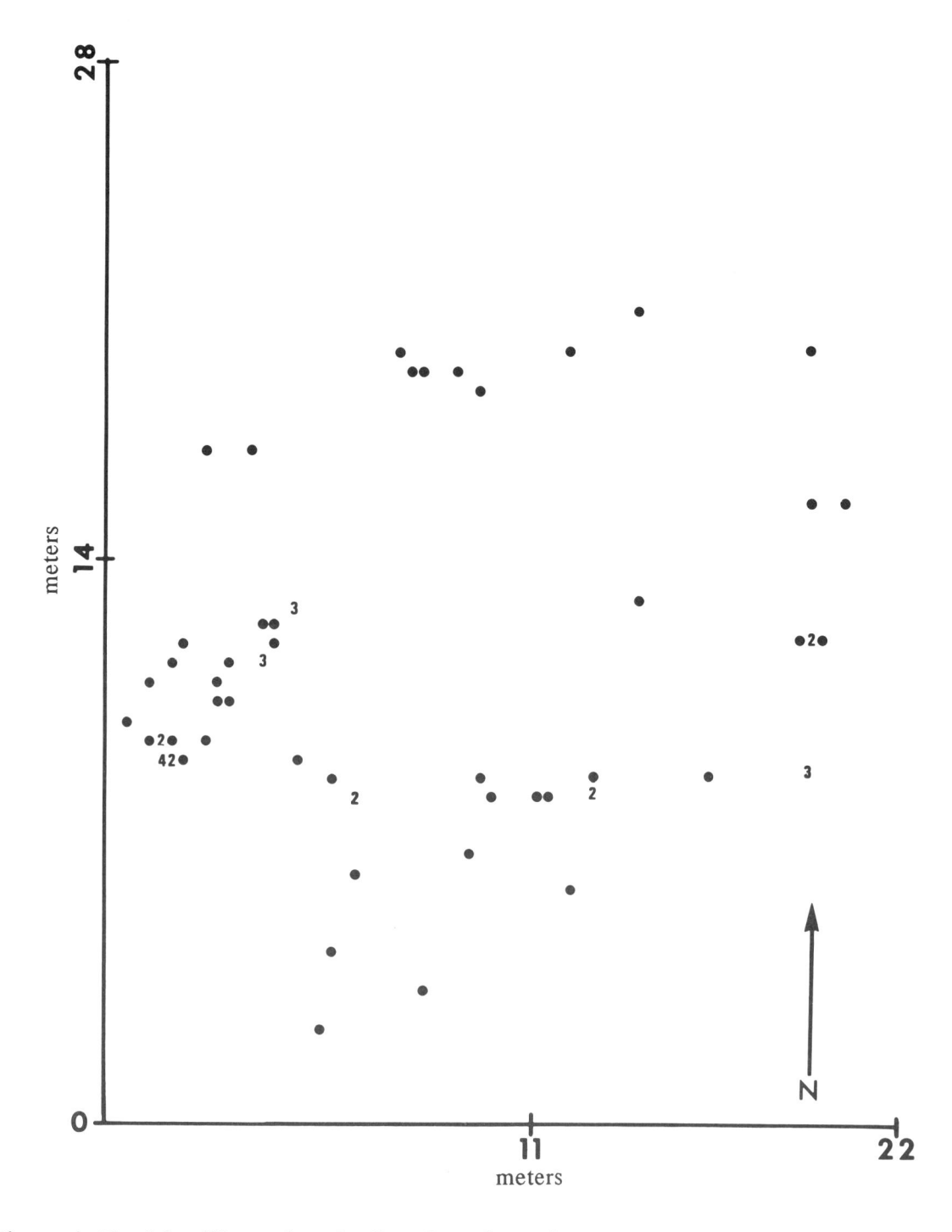

Figure 4. Plot Map Illustrating the Rest Locations of All Movable Objects in Compound 70 that Were Used among the Ten Analyzed Activities. Numbers indicate the total number of separate objects present in a location, given more than one object per location (N = 67).

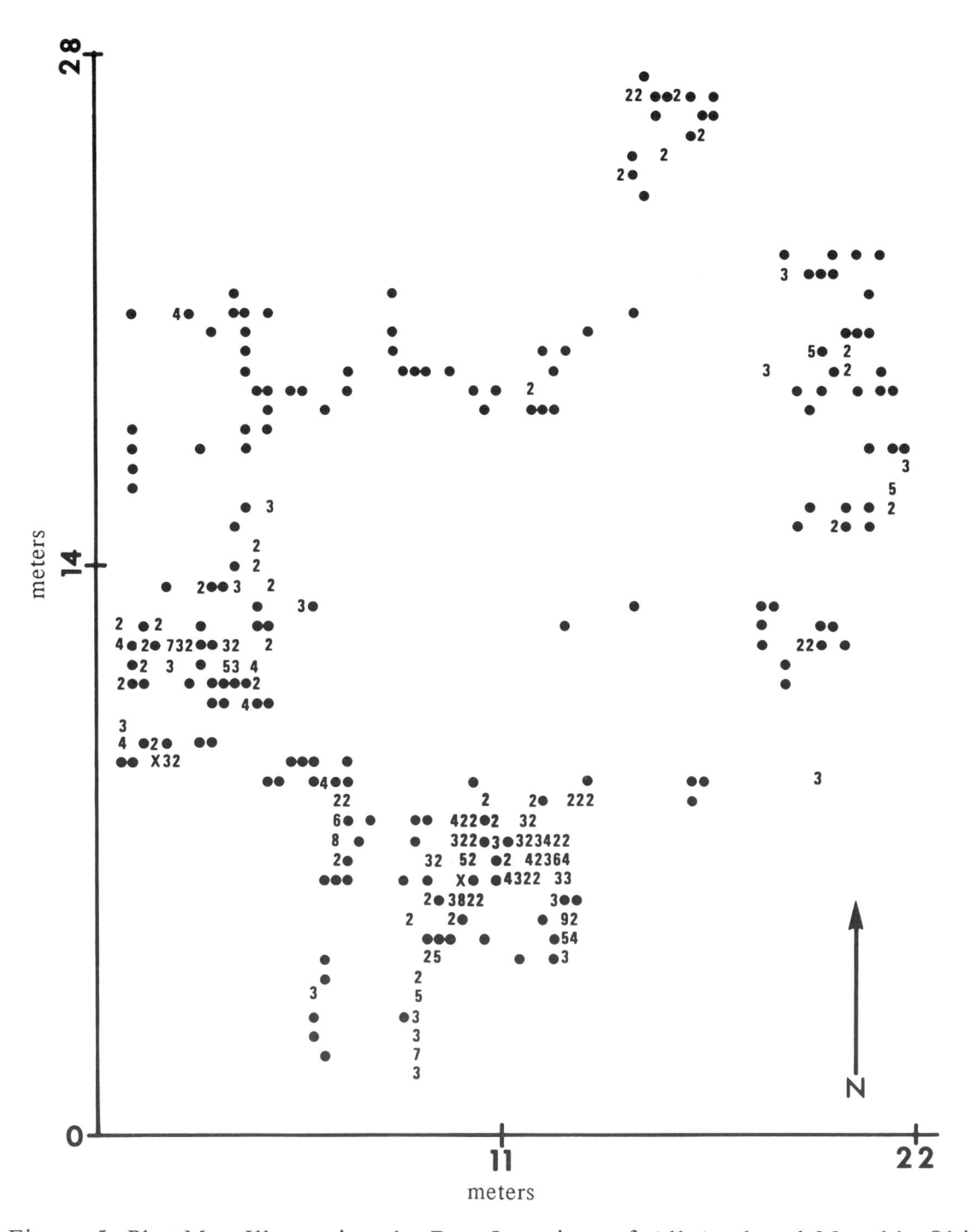

Figure 5. Plot Map Illustrating the Rest Locations of All Analyzed Movable Objects in Compound 70. Numbers indicate the total number of separate objects present in a location, given more than one object per location (X = ten or more objects; N = 548).

PLATE 1

a

b

Compound 70. a. View of the southwest corner, looking southwest from the east side of the compound. Several areas and features mentioned in the text can be identified: the entry to the "southwest room," the cobbled area to the east of this room, and the ovens. b. View of the northern edge of Compound 70, looking north from within one of the southern compound entry rooms. A tile block wall of the chicken coop can be seen to the west of the woodpile. Objects referred to in the text can be seen along the perimeter of the woodpile.

PLATE 2

Compound 70. View of the southwest corner, looking northwest from a southern entry room, during the activity of bread baking. Several of the objects being used in this scene can be located at rest in plate 1.

B. DHALI: A TRADITIONAL COMMUNITY IN TRANSITION

*Peter S. Allen**

The primary goal of ethnographic work in Dhali has been to provide information about select aspects of the culture and society in the modern community that will contribute to the understanding of the social and cultural systems of the inhabitants of ancient Idalion. Information has been collected on those aspects of modern village life which there is good reason to believe have considerable historic (or prehistoric) depth or which show affinities with ancient society and culture. Within this framework emphasis has been placed on aspects of the modern situation that are relevant to the larger objective of the Expedition, that is, to study the relationship between settlement pattern and the exploitation of local resources.

Methodology

In pursuit of the aforementioned goal, two related approaches have been utilized: the study of continuities and ethnographic analogy. Continuities, sometimes called survivals, are those unbroken traditions in material culture and behavior patterns that have persisted unchanged since antiquity. A good example from Dhali is the draft plow and the method of cultivation associated with it (pl. 1a). By all accounts the form and design of this implement have not changed in over 5000 years (Christodoulou 1959:123; Wolf 1966:30-32; Purcell 1968:73). Contemporary usage presumably corresponds closely to ancient usage and thus a modern study can provide insights into the practices of antiquity.

Ethnographic analogy involves extrapolation from a modern situation to an analogous one that existed in the past. Stanley Aschenbrenner, an anthropologist who employed a similar approach in the study of a contemporary community in Messenia, Greece, describes this approach well:

> Some features of the modern village economy may be projected back in time, or can at the least guide such projection. Furthermore, when relationships among factors are being projected backward and when archaeological evidence reveals data for only one (or some) of the factors those without relevant archaeological evidence may be inferred by virtue of the relationship obtaining among them all. Thus, for example, when jars for the storage of olive oil or wine are excavated or when Linear B tablets refer to amounts of these commodities, we may calculate some range of values for the area of land planted in such crops or for labor expended in their production. The basis for the inference is the known relationships in a contemporary community among yield of oil or wine, area cultivated, and labor (1972:47).

Modern demographic data are particularly valuable in establishing such a basis for analogy with the past. At Dhali, for example, this technique can be used to project a rough estimate of the settlement's population in antiquity on the basis of the relationship between the modern population and the local resource base. Moreover, a study of the modern population

---

*Department of Anthropology, Rhode Island College, Providence, Rhode Island

Research was carried out mainly in the summers of 1973 and 1976, with briefer visits in 1974 and 1975. This article has not been revised since it was written in 1977. Support for the research came in part from a Rhode Island College faculty research grant (1976) and from Idalion funds. My greatest debt of gratitude is to the warm and hospitable people of Dhali.

and the factors that affect it can provide insight into the factors and forces that influenced the ancient population.

Cyprus in general is a good place to carry out such a study because the island is in many respects a repository of traditional culture, a fact attributable in part to its insular status and consequent partial isolation.[1] A prominent example of traditionalism on Cyprus is the Cypriot dialect of modern Greek, a form that retains many archaisms and is generally recognized as being closer to ancient Greek than the language spoken today in Greece (Keefe et al. 1971:80). Furthermore the people themselves tend to be conservative and traditional.[2] For example, the ἀλέτρι or wooden plow pictured on plate 1a was still being used in Dhali in 1976 despite the general availability of iron plows and more sophisticated mechanical implements.

At Dhali there are several readily apparent continuities from deep antiquity. Most evident of these is the name of the settlement itself. "Dhali" or "Dali" is simply a modern demotic form of the ancient "Idalion," the name for the settlement dating back to at least the 7th century B.C. (Marvin 1974:pp. XXII-XXIII) and the name for the village that is still used in most formal contexts.

The extraordinary tenacity of traditional life in Cyprus is most noticeable in the material culture of rural areas, where continuities stretching as far back as the Neolithic abound. Stone querns, identical to ones found in Neolithic sites on the island, are still used by many rural Cypriots for a variety of domestic tasks, and beehive-shaped mudbrick ovens like the one shown on plate 1b are known from all periods (Christodoulou 1959:123). Large diamond-shaped pithoi whose form dates back to the Bronze Age were still being made within the past twenty years at Kornos, a small village just southwest of Dhali.

Another material feature with long and apparently unbroken continuity is the vernacular mudbrick architecture of rural Cyprus. Christodoulou sums up the evidence for this architectural continuity:

> As Gjerstad remarks: "modern Cypriot village houses . . . in construction are almost identical with their prehistoric prototypes . . ." The German archaeologist, R. F. von Lichtenberg, has found a close relationship between the ancient Greek μέγαρον and the Cyprus house, while another German student, Madga [sic] F. Ohnefalsch-Richter, has found that not only the ancient Greek house, but also the ancient Aegean house in its purest form has been preserved in Cyprus houses. Descriptions of Byzantine dwellings remind a student of present-day Cyprus houses (1959:64).

Foundations of buildings uncovered at Dhali that date to several early periods are virtually identical with those of modern traditional houses such as those illustrated on plates 2a, b, and 3a.[3]

---

[1] The situation is somewhat paradoxical in light of the veneer of modernism and the high level of development so evident in the cities of Cyprus. Until 1974 the island had the second highest standard of living in the eastern Mediterranean and one of the highest per capita automobile registration rates in the world, yet until recently much of rural Cyprus was little changed from antiquity.

[2] Of course poverty has played an important role in this regard, as Gennadius discovered when he tried to introduce the iron plow to rural villages around the turn of the century (Christodoulou 1959:105), but there has also been a definite reluctance to modernize among the islanders, almost a self-conscious provincialism that cannot be explained easily, although Attalides has made a respectable attempt (1976).

[3] In the early 1970s when excavators at the site of Toumba Tou Skourou near Morphou in northern Cyprus reconstructed portions of mudbrick walls dating to the Late Bronze Age, they discovered that villagers living nearby were still making straw-tempered mud bricks of precisely the same dimensions as those recovered in the excavations.

The material culture of Cyprus is changing rapidly today, however, and the long continuity is finally being broken. Everywhere in Dhali and other villages mudbrick houses are being torn down and replaced by structures of reinforced concrete and brick. In most of the remaining traditional compounds one can still see pottery in shapes that recall Bronze Age forms (Johnston 1974), and implements made of natural materials are still in evidence; but clay pots are rapidly being replaced by plastic containers and traditional material culture is disappearing at an ever increasing rate. In 1973 a woman in Dhali was observed preparing wheat for τραχανᾶς, a cracked-wheat food, in a wooden trough. Three years later the same woman was using a plastic basin for the same task.

More important than specific material continuities, however, are whole aspects of modern life that show affinities with ancient culture. In Dhali critical features of the traditional economy were largely intact until quite recently and are easily recalled and recreated. What follows is a description of the traditional community of Dhali and its inhabitants, followed by a brief discussion of recent changes that are affecting the traditional culture. For the purposes of this essay the traditional period is considered to have lasted until about the middle of the present century, at which time major changes began to take place in the local economy. Throughout, an attempt has been made to establish links with antiquity wherever possible.

The Traditional Community

Adjacent to and partly overlying the site of ancient Idalion is Dhali, a large predominantly Greek Cypriot village. The modern settlement is a nucleated cluster of houses and shops lying mainly on the south bank of the Yalias River in the general vicinity of the Roman and Byzantine settlements (fig. 1). Modern Dhali represents a continuation of human occupation in the region that stretches back almost 8000 years. Although systematic excavations have not yet established a clear record of continuous occupation, materials collected in surveys strongly suggest that there has been some human occupation in the general vicinity of the modern community since Neolithic times. Furthermore, during all periods the inhabitants have undoubtedly derived their subsistence from the cultivation of the same general area as that in which crops are grown today.

The present location of Dhali dates to the late Hellenistic and Roman periods and can be accounted for by the proximity of a reliable source of water along the south bank of the Yalias River bed. Accessibility of water has been a factor of primary importance in determining the site of settlements in this area since the first people settled along the banks of the Yalias in the Neolithic period, and the present location maximizes the exploitation of this vital resource. Koucky and Bullard have posited a correlation between known shifts in settlement location and the desiccation of specific areas within the Dhali region. They suggest that as a portion of the Yalias drainage was progressively depleted of water and the water table on the south and west sides of the acropolis dropped, the ancient city moved eastward, eventually descending from the heights of the acropolis and moving northward toward the bed of the Yalias. By the Roman period the settlement was concentrated heavily along the south banks of the river close to the village's present location (Koucky and Bullard 1974:112-13).

Today the village encompasses a total area of approximately 22,000 dunams (1 dunam equals about one third acre) of which about 15,000 are suitable for cultivation or arboriculture. It is highly probably that this figure corresponds roughly to the amount of land available in antiquity, although some of what is at present farmland may have been wooded during the Bronze Age.[4] The relationship of man to the environment has almost certainly remained

---

[4] The conventional view is that forests originally covered much of the area, but disappeared in the later part of the Bronze Age and in early Classical antiquity as a result of wood being the chief fuel used in firing the furnaces for the smelting of copper. A serious question has been raised, however, as to whether the environment around Dhali was ever able to support forest vegetation (Christodoulou 1959:46, 109). Christodoulou describes the area as "hypothetically forested" in antiquity, noting that there is absolutely no empirical evidence for the existence of these putative forests (ibid., 228-30).

relatively constant. Christodoulou (1959:46) and others maintain that changes in the past 3000 years have not altered the general character of the environment around Dhali to an extent that would have influenced crop selection.

The village itself is a mixture of buildings and building types covering approximately 300 dunams (about 100 acres). The center of Dhali is a cluster of small coffeehouses and shops where men frequently gather and women occasionally shop. Various goods and services are becoming increasingly available (a branch office of the National Bank of Cyprus was opened in 1976), but the majority of villagers continue to make most of their purchases in Nicosia.

Until the early 1960s virtually all buildings in Dhali were one- or two-story mudbrick structures with roofs of clay and wattle overlain with flat stones and red clay tiles (κεραμίδια ; pl. 2a). The interiors, and often also the exteriors, were plastered and painted. Floors were of hard-packed earth or of paving stones of marble (μάρμαρα) or gypsum. Two construction styles predominated--one derived its main support from an arch (καμάρα) (or series of arches) of limestone or sandstone, as seen in plate 3b; the other from a central beam (νεύκα) of oak or, more recently, of eucalyptus wood. In both cases walls were constructed by placing rows of straw-tempered sun-dried mudbrick (πλιθάρια) on low foundations of unmortared fieldstone or river cobbles. Foundation heights vary and there are numerous variations on several basic floor plans, but the techniques and fundamental characteristics are identical to those of vernacular structures of all periods dating back to the Bronze Age (pl. 3a).

The ideal traditional house was, in fact, a compound with an enclosed or semi-enclosed yard (pl. 2b). Outbuildings for stabling animals and storing produce and implements were usually contiguous if not coterminous with human dwellings. In 1960, 37 percent of Dhali's houses had only one or two rooms and 63 percent had three or fewer rooms.[5] Until the 1920s it was common practice to stable draft animals in the human living quarters.[6]

In the past fifteen years reinforced concrete and brick have become the primary building materials used by Dhali villagers. As in the past, interiors and exteriors are plastered and painted, and roofs are either tiled or concrete. Floors are generally made of a stone mosaic. Many villagers still have traditional mudbrick ovens in the yards of their new houses, but these yards are not enclosed with anything more imposing than low fences of decorative cast iron.

The Traditional Economy

Since at least the end of the Bronze Age, most inhabitants of Idalion have undoubtedly been peasant cultivators. Peasants are defined as rural cultivators who are oriented primarily toward family subsistence, but nevertheless usually produce a surplus beyond their immediate needs. They are politically, economically, socially, and culturally subordinate to a city or state, and generally have a distinctive folk culture (Wolf 1966; Foster 1967; Gamst 1974).[7]

---

[5] Island-wide figures for the same year show that 51 percent of all dwellings had one or two rooms and that 58 percent of rural dwellings fell in this category. Apparently families with larger numbers of members tended to have larger houses, so, as in 1946, only 45 percent of the island's population lived in houses of one or two rooms (statistics of this sort were not available for other years).

[6] See pages 67-69 of Christodoulou (1959) for sample floor plans of typical Cypriot rural compounds. Types similar to Christodoulou's figures 47, 48, and 50 have been observed in Dhali.

[7] Land tenure is also an important aspect of peasantry, but most theories concerning peasants maintain that access to land and the means of cultivation are more important distinguishing criteria for peasantry than the particular system of land tenure (e.g., Wolf 1966:61-80). Likewise the theorists stress the fact that political subordination to a form of state is more important than subordination to a specific kind of state (Wolf 1966:10-17; Foster 1967:5-6). All types of land tenure and all political systems in which the people of Idalion have been involved since antiquity fall well within the range of those associated with peasants.

In the Bronze Age the cultivators of Idalion were probably directly subordinate to a local ruling class, although at various times they may have been dominated by outside powers. During much of classical antiquity Idalion was a commercial and cult center ruled by an autonomous or semiautonomous king to whom the local peasants were presumably subject.

Some idea of land tenure during antiquity can be gained from the single most valuable artifact ever unearthed at Idalion, a bilingual bronze tablet of the fifth century B.C. that records an award of land to a physician and his brothers for medical services rendered during a battle.[8] Spyridakis' interpretation of this inscription indicates that the grant was made by the king of Idalion jointly with the city, suggesting that the king was not entirely autocratic. Moreover it firmly establishes the existence at this early date of individual ownership and the conditions thereof (Marvin 1974; pp. XXV-XXVI).[9]

Subsequently control of Cyprus and its inhabitants shifted to alien powers and the residents of Idalion fell subject to the various external states and empires that controlled the island from Roman until modern times. During these years the centers of administrative control lay outside Idalion in the larger towns and cities of Cyprus and ultimately in the urban centers of the imperial powers. The peasants of Idalion toiled not only for the burghers of Nicosia and Larnaca, but also for merchants and administrators in Rome, Constantinople, and London, a situation that prevailed until 1960 when Cyprus was granted full independence from Great Britain, the last foreign power to rule the island.

The pattern of land tenure developed in post-Classical times is described by Christodoulou:

> The early Christian period shows the rural population divided into two classes, the *coloni* and the *ascripticii*, i.e. the free farmers and the slave proprietors. These names in their Greek form of *parici* and *enapographi* continued through the Byzantine era. It appears that the *coloni* were tenants, members of a village society whose lands were probably State property or belonged to very large estates, usually of the church; the village community was taxed as a whole and each *colonus* was obliged to stay in the village to meet his share of the taxation. Judging from the Farmer's Law the village lands were divided into lots, and allocated to members of the community from time to time. Provisions for grazing the stubbles and vineyards remind one of present-day practice (1959:70). (See plate 4a.)

Widespread peasant proprietorship of land in Cyprus dates only to the middle of the nineteenth century, before which time various feudal arrangements prevailed along with limited private ownership. The feudal system was introduced by the Franks in the twelfth and thirteenth centuries A.D. and continued by the Venetians and Ottomans under whom it was substantially modified. There is good evidence that individual peasant proprietorship was practiced during the feudal period, and toward the end of Ottoman rule became the norm (Christodoulou 1959:71-72).

As late as 1946 almost three-fourths of the Dhali household heads were classified as full- or part-time farmers. Unfortunately we do not have comparable statistics for earlier dates, but it is a safe assumption that during the first three decades of this century 80-90 percent of the population was engaged in agriculture, a proportion that in all probability has not varied much since antiquity.

---

[8] For a detailed review of land tenure in Cyprus from prehistory through modern times see Karouzis (1977).

[9] During Classical and Roman times land records were apparently kept in a religious sanctuary or temple (Christodoulou 1959:70). Under the Ottomans, the Orthodox Church was responsible for collecting taxes from the Christian population, and today the church is the largest single landholder on the island. Efkaf, the Muslim religious trust, is the largest Turkish Cypriot landowner.

It would be a mistake to characterize Dhali as not having changed during the past 2000 to 3000 years. The island after all has seen wars, invasions, droughts, plagues, disease, changes in government, and changes in land tenure. The population of Dhali has no doubt fluctuated considerably, and quite possibly the village was abandoned altogether during the extended drought of the fourth century, when Cyprus was virtually deserted. Most of these changes, however, have not been of a type that substantially altered the local economy or lifestyle of village peasant cultivators, the core of the population since the Bronze Age. They have cultivated essentially the same crops, utilizing the same technology as their ancestors. Their daily lives had changed little until the middle of the present century.

Throughout prehistory and history Cypriots have been primarily an agricultural people. Despite the importance of mining on Cyprus, the island has always been more famous for its agricultural produce than for any other commodity.[10] Grains, vines, and olives have been the traditional backbone of Cypriot agriculture, and it is not surprising to learn that during the Classical and later periods the island exported large quantities of grain (Christodoulou 1959:123; Purcell 1968:44, 89, 96). In Roman times Cyprus was famous for its wines, when these along with wheat, olive oil, and dried fruit made up the bulk of its agricultural exports (Purcell 1968:102). Even after the introduction of silkworms, cotton, sugar cane, and other industrial crops, the traditional crops predominated. A visitor in 1579 noted an abundance of "wine, grain, olive oil, and sugar cane" on the island (ibid., p. 108). Today these crops still dominate Cypriot agriculture although they are grown mainly for domestic consumption and have been surpassed in the export market by citrus fruits and potatoes. Agricultural produce constitutes only about one-fifth of the island's current gross domestic product, but accounts for approximately half of all exports (Keefe et al. 1971:202).

Traditional Subsistence

Technology

Until the middle of this century agriculture in Dhali was little changed from the earliest phases of the Bronze Age. The main implement was the ard or Mediterranean scratch plow, a wooden draft plow whose form has not changed since its invention in the Early Bronze Age. Its importance for early agriculture is summed up by Allan:

> With the invention of an efficient plough, civilisation could spread beyond the areas of highly fertile, permanently cultivable, and readily irrigable soils. Plough farming and the production of a reliable surplus became a possibility on soils capable of maintaining their fertility under short periods of cultivation and fallow, using some such system as the alternation of wheat and barley with rest breaks of one, two, or three years, and supplemental irrigation from perennial streams and melting snow. This is still the basis of arable farming in Cyprus and over much of the Middle East, and there is no reason to suppose that it has altered greatly since Bronze Age times (1965:275).

Even today a few Dhali farmers still cultivate with the ard, and less than half a century ago it was virtually the only implement available for preparing the soil.[11]

Planting and weeding of crops were done by hand, as was the collecting of olives and grapes. Cereal grains were harvested with a hand sickle (δρεπάνι). Threshing was carried out on a circular threshing floor (ἀλώνι) over which a wooden sledge (δουκάνι), studded on the

---

[10] Although mining was important in Cyprus from the Bronze Age until late Roman times, mining virtually ceased in the fourth century A.D. and was not revived to any great extent until the nineteenth century (Purcell 1968:106).

[11] By 1946 approximately half of Dhali farmers were using iron plows of a similar form, but none had tractors.

bottom with flints, was dragged by animals. Pitchforks and wooden shovels were used for winnowing. Wine and oil were recovered in manually operated wooden screw presses. All of these implements are known from antiquity, either as artifacts or through representations in ceramic decorations.

Crops and Livestock

Crops grown at Dhali show similar continuity with the past. The climate and soils of Dhali are best suited for the cultivation of cereal grains and legumes, and can support viticulture. Conditions also favor the olive and almond above other crop trees traditionally found in Cyprus.[12] Cereal grains, grapes, and olives, sometimes referred to as the "Mediterranean triad," together account for the overwhelmingly greater part of the traditional agricultural production of Dhali. Modern surveys of land use in Dhali reveal that in the years 1931, 1946, and 1955 wheat accounted for 68 percent, barley for 84 percent, and vines for 86 percent of all nonarboreal cultivation (even in 1971, after dairy farming had become relatively important in Dhali and much land was given over to green fodder, almost 70 percent of land was in wheat and barley.)[13] Olive trees have almost always outnumbered the combined total of all other crop trees in Dhali, accounting for 68 percent in 1931, 47 percent in 1946, and 51 percent in 1955. If we eliminate from this sample citrus and mulberry, trees not cultivated in antiquity, the percentage of olive trees for these three years rises to 80, 70, and 80.[14]

Botanical data from the excavations at Dhali are still quite sparse, but it appears that cereal grains, olives, grapes, and legumes have been cultivated in the vicinity of the village for several millennia (Stewart 1974).[15] Dhali was singled out as an important center of olive production in a report of the late eighteenth century (Christodoulou 1959:171), and in a grain contribution list of 1832 Dhali was the largest contributor in its district and among the largest on the island (Papadopoullos 1965:194). Thus it appears that there has been considerable continuity with respect to the particular crops grown in Dhali since the earliest cultivation there. Given the presumed continuity of ecological conditions, it is quite probably that there has also been continuity in the relative importance of these crops vis-à-vis each other.

A similar picture emerges for livestock raising in Dhali. In the surveys cited above, sheep and goats far outnumbered any other animals in Dhali and continued to do so until 1972, when dairy farming and pig breeding became important activities in the village. Modern animal censuses in Dhali have always indicated the presence not only of sheep and goats, but pigs, cattle, donkeys, and horses as well. Remains of all these animals have also been found in the local archaeological context (Schwartz 1974a).

---

[12] According to Christodoulou (1974:1) Dhali in 1955 was a "typical" Cypriot lowland village exemplifying the "epitome of land use in lowland areas" of the island.

[13] These statistics and others cited in this essay (including population statistics) were provided by the Cyprus Department of Statistics or come from village church records.

[14] Mulberry cultivation goes back to the introduction of sericulture to Cyprus in the sixth century A.D. Silk is no longer produced on the island, however, and mulberry leaves are used only for fodder. Citrus has been raised in Cyprus since medieval times, but in Dhali not on a large scale until this century. As citrus trees require a large initial investment and regular irrigation, they have been cultivated extensively in Dhali only relatively recently, since the advent of cash cropping and investment farming.

[15] Almonds are also known in Dhali from antiquity and quite possibly play a role similar to the one they play today: "the almond trees being usually found in small groves or scattered, occupying the boundaries of vineyards or the edges of terraces, or mixed with other trees like carobs and olives" (Christodoulou 1959:175). This description conforms to the pattern of almond cultivation in Dhali today.

Other Agricultural Practices

Since Neolithic times short-term fallowing has been the primary means by which soil nutrients have been replaced by Cypriot cultivators and it continues to be so today, although alternative methods such as the application of chemical fertilizers and crop rotation are increasingly being employed. Cypriot farmers have also long used animal manure to fertilize fields, but in a way that has been of minimal benefit (Christodoulou 1959:43). Significant gains from the application of chemical fertilizers have been realized only in the past three or four decades.

The Yalias River drainage basin is well watered during the winter and spring by natural irrigation and is well suited for dry cereal cultivation except in the vicinity of the river bed itself, where traditionally horticulture and arboriculture have been practiced. Some form of irrigation undoubtedly has been practiced in the area since the earliest cultivation, but most methods were probably quite crude until the mid-nineteenth century when a chain of wells (λαούμια) several miles in length was constructed along the banks of the Yalias (Christodoulou 1959:120). In good years this system provided water for about 1000 dunams of land in Dhali. Before the drilling of deep wells and the introduction of mechanical pumps about 12 percent of Dhali land was irrigated. At present as much as 35 or 40 percent is within reach of irrigation. Water is still in very short supply, however, and irrigation is severely curtailed in drought years such as 1973, when probably less than 10 percent of the land was irrigated. Thus we can say with some degree of assurance that traditional agricultural practices in Dhali have changed little from those of antiquity.[16]

Yields

Agricultural yields in Cyprus vary a great deal from year to year depending on weather conditions, diseases, and, in the past, plagues of locusts. However there appears to be a kind of pattern to the fluctuations:

> Records for Cyprus, extending over 80 years, show that the wheat growers of the Mesaoria may expect three good seasons, four average seasons, two poor seasons, and one crop failure in each decade (Allan 1965:38).

Undoubtedly Cypriot cultivators have been at least vaguely aware of this cycle and have adjusted their subsistence strategies accordingly. Peasant cultivators, after all, generally produce a surplus, since the size of their populations is necessarily adjusted to the returns of leaner years. Because in Cyprus average or better-than-average years outnumber years of poor yields, peasants there normally grow more than they consume. Moreover, peasants almost always produce more than their own subsistence requirements, for it is they who must produce the food consumed by that element of the larger population not engaged in agriculture.

It is difficult to make accurate estimates of crop yields in antiquity, but with respect to the traditional crops cultivated at Dhali it would appear that returns have not increased significantly over those of antiquity. A scientific study conducted in 1926 revealed that wheat varieties cultivated on the island at that time were virtually unchanged from ancient times (Flaksberger 1927). Christodoulou points out that in the 1950s, return on planted wheat seed was the same as in the sixteenth century--about seven bushels of grain for each bushel of seed planted, or four bushels per dunam (1959:123, 126-27, 219). Furthermore, average yields per dunam for wheat (3.6 bushels) and barley (6.5 bushels) during the period 1949-53 were actually lower than the yields in 1870, when 4.7 bushels per dunam of wheat and 6.7 bushels per dunam of barley were harvested (Christodoulou 1959:123-24).

---

[16] Keefe et al. (1971:151) report that irrigation alone was responsible for a 60% increase in Cypriot agricultural production between 1960 and 1966.

There are no available statistics on the production of grapes and wine in Dhali, but villagers maintain that when vines were cultivated the yields were consistently mediocre. Evidently viticulture was a marginal enterprise in Dhali, and those who practiced it usually produced wines for local consumption only. There is no evidence that vines were ever cultivated scientifically in Dhali and yields were probably no higher than in antiquity.

A similar situation obtains with respect to olive and olive oil yields. Many of the trees in Dhali are hundreds of years old and it is safe to assume that modern olive yields are comparable to those of antiquity.

Summary

The overall picture of traditional agriculture that emerges for Dhali is one in which peasant farmers, equipped with a primitive technology largely unchanged since the Bronze Age and facing an environment virtually identical with that of antiquity, mainly cultivated crops known from the beginnings of agriculture and generally followed practices similar to those of their ancestors. There is no reason to believe that yields in Dhali were significantly greater until the mid-1950s, and after that time only marginally so for the traditional crops.

The Population and the Settlement Pattern

Trying to reconstruct populations is a difficult task and accurate figures for Cyprus are hard to obtain for periods that precede the era of British rule, when systematic censuses were first conducted. There is general agreement, however, that under the Ottomans the island's population never exceeded 200,000 (Papadopoullos 1965; Purcell 1968:180). In earlier periods it rarely ever surpassed 300,000, a figure possibly reached in classical antiquity and medieval times and one that appears to correspond to the upper limits of the island's carrying capacity under traditional methods of cultivation.[17] In modern times this figure was reached around 1920 and the steady growth that has occurred since then can be attributed mainly to improvements in agricultural technology and techniques as well as to growth in industrial and other nonagricultural sectors of the economy in the past two or three decades.

The demographic picture in Dhali has more or less paralleled that of the island as a whole, at least in the past 150 years or so, as indicated in the statistics of table 1. There are no accurate population data available from the Ottoman period, but some documents published by Papadopoullos give us a basis for estimating the population of Dhali in the early part of the nineteenth century. A tax register from 1825 lists 89 Christian taxpayers in "Idalion" (Papadopoullos 1965:129).[18] A figure of four dependents per taxpayer would give a Christian population of 445 for Dhali in 1825. An estimate of the Muslim (Turkish) population of the village can be made on the basis of information provided in a list of grain contributions for purchase dating to 1832 (Papadopoullos 1965:194).[19] That year the Christian population of "Idalion" had an obligation of 82 modii (one modius equaled about 180 kilograms) and the Muslim community 27 modii. If we accept Papadopoullos' interpretation (1965:107-8) that these obligations were more or less equal for both populations, then we can posit a Muslim population

---

[17] Most observers agree that there has been a significant depletion of agricultural potential in Cyprus as a result of deforestation, erosion, and years of destructive agricultural practices, so the carrying capacity has undoubtedly varied (Allan 1965:13).

[18] These 89 taxpayers paid a combined tax of 4519.20 piastres, the largest amount in the Kythrea District and one of the largest contributions of all island villages (Papadopoullos 1965:129).

[19] It appears that each community on the island was obligated to make available for purchase a certain amount of grain at fixed prices to insure an ample supply of food for the nonagricultural population (Papadopoullos 1965:105-8). This grain was above and beyond that required in payment of taxes.

of 147 at this time, giving a total for Dhali of about 592 at the beginning of the second quarter of the nineteenth century. This figure is not at all inconsistent with projections based on later recorded statistics.

As indicated in table 1, the population of Dhali has been growing steadily since the first systematic census was taken in 1881. Growth has been somewhat erratic and has not strictly conformed to the pattern of growth for the island as a whole, although the overall rate of increase in the past century has been about the same. In the past three decades, however, Dhali has grown at a rate 70 percent greater than the island as a whole.

The growth of the village during the two or three decades following the assumption of control by the British in 1878 was probably a result of natural increase as a response to the heavy depopulation of the Ottoman period. The increase may also be partially related to the putative construction of the chain of wells in the middle of the nineteenth century. Population increases resulting from other improvements in agriculture probably did not occur in Dhali until after the turn of the century, when more land came under irrigation and chemical fertilizers were introduced.

The years between 1911 and 1930 were marked by heavy emigration from the village, as reflected in the relatively large number of births and the smaller increase in overall population for this period noted in table 2. Since that time the size of the local population has increased almost exclusively in response to events and forces outside the village. Improvements affecting agriculture have all been introduced from outside, and nonagricultural employment opportunities almost all lie outside the confines of the village.

For Dhali it appears that a figure of about 1500 represents the upper limit for a population engaged mainly in traditional agriculture. This corresponds to the village's population in the early 1930s, just before mechanization and other improvements were introduced to Dhali on a small scale.[20] Meanwhile changes were taking place in the larger economy of the island, and this period marks the beginning of villagers seeking employment outside Dhali.

During the period of traditional subsistence agriculture the configuration and appearance of the village itself changed little; it remained a concentrated nucleus of dwellings and shops. The shape and direction of growth were governed mainly by the accessibility of water and factors of security. Security considerations have been important since Neolithic times and are mainly responsible for the high degree of settlement nucleation. Bronze Age settlements in the Dhali region were probably fortified, and a great wall surrounded the city in Classical and later antiquity.[21] Security continued to be an important consideration long after the threat of external attack was ended, as the open countryside was never fully secure from internal threats, even well into the present century (Christodoulou 1959:63).

---

[20] There were only 27 tractors on the entire island in 1939, and in 1946 only 2% of all olive presses in Cyprus were hydraulically (mechanically) operated (Christodoulou 1959:105, 172).

[21] During the time a wall surrounded the city many people probably lived outside the wall, seeking shelter only in times of crisis, but to my knowledge no evidence of such settlement has been located at Dhali.

Transition: The Modern Community

The real revolution taking place in Dhali today[22] is the transition from a society of traditional peasant cultivators to one composed of individuals receiving wages and salaries for work outside the village. It is a rapid transition and one that is having far-reaching social and cultural effects.[23] The past few decades have been critical, and quite possibly the changes that have taken place in the past three or four decades have had a greater impact on the inhabitants of Dhali than all the changes of the preceding 2500 or more years. Even for those who continue to till the soil there are enormous differences in their approach to farming and in their lifestyles. They are no longer peasants oriented toward family subsistence, but true farmers for whom agriculture is a business that involves capital investment, hired labor, profit margins, and the like. They are no longer constrained by limited resources and the exploitation suffered by their peasant predecessors.

Changes are also taking place in the material culture, as noted earlier. The change in local architecture that began about twenty years ago represents a break with a tradition of vernacular architecture going back perhaps 4000 or more years. Not only have buildings and building materials changed, but the size and function of dwelling units as well. Traditional architecture served the needs of peasant cultivators who grew and raised much of what they consumed. Houses today are larger and designed for a style of living that conforms to the requisites of the modern commuting population.

The Modern Village Economy

The statistics in tables 3 and 4 indicate two distinct trends in Dhali since 1946: a significant increase in the population, and a precipitous decline in the number of full-time farmers (and an even greater decline in their percentage as household heads). Thus, not only can all population growth in Dhali subsequent to 1946 be accounted for by persons not dependent on agriculture, but obviously many individuals who were engaged in farming on a full- or part-time basis have abandoned that occupation in the past three decades. These phenomena can be accounted for by (1) mechanization and other improvements in agriculture and (2) rapid growth of nonagricultural employment opportunities outside the village, coupled with easy access to these jobs.[24]

Peasant agriculture in Dhali has declined in direct relationship to the growth of alternative employment opportunities. Agricultural life has always been a marginal existence fraught with insecurity and hardships (Christodoulou 1959:124-25; Attalides 1976:112-13), even in a relatively prosperous village like Dhali. For centuries Cypriot peasants were subject to oppressive taxation by colonial powers and were at the mercy of unscrupulous moneylenders (Christodoulou 1959:91-96; Karouzis 1977:31-32). Thus it is not surprising that they have readily abandoned cultivation when viable alternatives presented themselves. A study of peasant attitudes toward the land in China revealed a similar tendency among small cultivators there (Gallin 1964).

---

[22] Since the coup d'etat of July 1974 and the subsequent Turkish invasion of Cyprus, the demography of Dhali has been radically altered. Many people left permanently and others spent considerable time away from the village. About 1000 refugees have been relocated in Dhali and hundreds of the Greek Cypriot National Guard are stationed in and around the village inasmuch as the line separating the Greek and Turkish Cypriot sectors is less than two miles from Dhali. Therefore the "ethnographic present" of this essay is preinvasion 1974.

[23] A description and analysis of some of these changes will be presented in a separate publication.

[24] Regular bus service links Dhali with all the cities of Cyprus, and many villagers own automobiles and form car pools for transporting workers to the cities.

Since the late 1930s nonagricultural jobs have become increasingly available in Cyprus, mostly in the rapidly growing cities. Between 1946 and 1974 the urban population of the island more than doubled, growing at a rate five times faster than that of the population as a whole, due mainly to heavy migration from the countryside. As a result many of the small villages have become severely depopulated (Peristiany 1968; Attalides 1976).

In contrast to this general trend, Dhali has thrived during this period and its population has grown steadily, for of the six major cities of Cyprus four are within easy commuting distance of Dhali. As a result the Dhali villagers are able to join the urban labor force without joining the growing ranks of urban migrants.[25] In 1972 more than 70 percent of working male household heads in Dhali were employed outside the village on a regular basis.[26] The village is rapidly becoming a "bedroom community" or "dormitory village," a phenomenon increasingly common in Cyprus since the mid-1950s.

Meanwhile the village economy has been almost totally transformed. Some of the more dramatic changes in the quarter of a century between 1946 and 1970 are reflected in the statistics of table 4. Whereas more than two-thirds of the village household heads in 1946 were full-time farmers, fewer than one-tenth were listed as such in 1970, despite a substantial increase in population. The amount of land under cultivation dropped by one-sixth, yet the average amount of land worked per farmer increased fourfold. In this period there was also a striking increase in the percentage of land leased or sharecropped, a trend entirely consistent with the reduction in the size of the farming population and the expanded area of land cultivated per farmer.

Cultivation, furthermore, has become quite highly mechanized and more and more land is coming under irrigation. It should be borne in mind, however, that most improvements in agricultural technology and techniques, with the exception of the application of fertilizers, have done little to change the yields of traditional crops. Rather these improvements have resulted mostly in enormous savings of time, and have allowed farmers to cultivate new crops. Irrigation, for example, has not only opened up some new areas to cultivation, but has also enabled local farmers to plant new kinds of crops and in some cases to harvest several crops a year, where previously only one crop per year was possible. Newly irrigated fields in which cereal grains had previously been dry-farmed are now planted in green fodder, vegetables for truck, and citrus.[27] Mechanization has not expanded the area of land under cultivation, but the savings in time effected by mechanical threshing (see pl. 4b) and by plowing with tractors has resulted in the availability of thousands of manhours for other tasks.[28]

---

[25] Dhali is less than 15 miles from both Nicosia and Larnaca, and the cities of Famagusta and Limassol are only 35 and 45 miles distant, respectively.

[26] Forty percent of these were involved in some way with the construction industry, and about a third had jobs that could be classified as white collar.

[27] The big leap in agricultural productivity, as noted earlier, came in the 1960s and can be directly linked to increases in the amount of land under irrigation. Notably, however, the expanded productivity did not occur in the traditional crops--grains, vines, and olives--for which irrigation has not resulted in significantly larger yields. The gains have come mainly in the production of citrus and vegetables.

[28] Some idea of the savings effected by mechanization can be gained from the following statistics: Threshing by hand required up to 500 manhours for 1000 okes (1 oke equals about 2.8 pounds) of grain. Today machines such as those shown on plate 4b can thresh the same amount using about 10 manhours. One man and two mules were able to plow an average of three dunams of land per day. Today one man and a tractor can plow an equivalent area of land in less than two hours. A 23-horsepower diesel pump can raise up to 80 tons of water per hour for irrigation compared with less than one-tenth this amount by nonmechanical means.

The net effect of these changes is a transformation of the village economy from one based on subsistence plus cultivation by a basically peasant populace to one of middle-class citizens largely dependent on wage and salaries derived from employment outside the community.

Settlement Pattern

Although the present location of the village core dates back to at least Roman times, when the accessibility of water was the paramount consideration in the siting of human settlements, the accessibility of water no longer plays a significant role in the determination of settlement pattern and the location of new dwellings, because deep wells and (since 1955) piped water have obviated dependence on water from shallow hand-dug wells. Today Dhali is growing rapidly and is expanding in several directions.

One consequence of this expansion is a noticeable decline in the degree of settlement nucleation. Dwellings are more spread out, and several villagers have built houses two or three miles distant from the village center. Of the three factors Christodoulou cites as having been responsible for the high degree of nucleation in the settlement pattern of Cypriot villages—"security, water supply, and the sociability of the people" (1959:63)—the first two no longer play an important role in the location of dwellings. While the "sociability" of rural Cypriots should not be questioned, it does not necessarily account for highly concentrated settlement. In fact, "sociability" may be an adaptation to high rural population density and hence a consequence rather than a cause thereof.

The pattern of recent growth and development in Dhali can be understood in light of several factors. Most important of these is a change in land values that resulted from the wholesale abandonment of subsistence cultivation and the employment of a large number of villagers in Nicosia and other cities. As noted above, since 1946 these changes have contributed to a rate of population increase in Dhali 70 percent greater than the average for all of Cyprus. Housing has therefore become a primary concern of the population. As the value of land for agriculture has declined, the value of land as siting for new houses has increased tremendously.

Although only a small fraction of Dhali's present inhabitants are still farming, virtually all families own land, which today they often measure in building plots (οἰκόπεδα) rather than in dunams, the traditional land measure of cultivated fields (χωράφια).[29] As the villagers become progressively more oriented toward Nicosia and the other urban centers of the island, the value of this land increases according to its proximity to the major roads that lead into and out of the village. Development along these roads, and to a lesser extent along secondary roads, is clearly evident on the map (fig. 1).

This "ribbon" development is common in modern Cyprus and has become a hallmark of the post-subsistence market economy of the island nation. In Dhali it is predictably strongest along the paved road that links the village with the Nicosia-Limassol road in the west. Lesser development has taken place in the east, where only secondary roads lead to small villages, and hence do not draw such heavy settlement. The complete absence of habitation along the main road that leads southeast to Lymbia can be attributed to the fact that land on both sides of this road falls within the confines of ancient Idalion and has "ancient monument" status, a designation bestowed by the Cyprus Department of Antiquities, which prohibits building there. Fortunately this designation came before the explosive growth of the village and the concomitant housing boom.

The road that leads east from the village is likewise devoid of settlement, most probably because it links Dhali with Lourougina, one of the largest Turkish-Cypriot villages in Cyprus.

---

[29] In 1955 a total of 1243 villagers (approximately half the population) owned land in Dhali, yet only 286 persons were listed that year as full-time farmers (Christodoulou 1974:2).

For many years this road has been marked by a sign in Greek, warning that it leads to a Turkish settlement.

Settlement on the north side of the Yalias River has always been minimal because the area is isolated and because ground water there tends to be brackish. In recent years, however, development in that area has increased as communications with the rest of the village are now assured by the existence of a sturdy permanent bridge that is not washed away each winter, and as residents are now able to tap sweet water with deeper wells. Moreover a recent plan to upgrade the dirt road that leads northwest to the Nicosia-Limassol road has resulted in some new construction and a sharp rise in land values there, as villagers anticipate this project.

The construction of a schoolhouse south of the village in 1966 also had a significant effect on development. Although the selection of this site did not involve a conscious effort to direct the course of settlement, the school has acted as a magnet and many villagers have built houses nearby. A map of the settlement dating to 1923 indicates that the other elementary school, on the road leading to Potamia, had a similar effect on the village settlement pattern, when that school was built a few years before the map was made.

Conclusions

The foregoing description of life in traditional Dhali clearly establishes links with the ancient settlement in the key areas of subsistence technology and practices. Substantial continuity from antiquity is evidenced not only in the realm of material culture but also in the entire complex of the peasant agricultural economy and many of its attendant details. Furthermore, demographic and other data have provided a basis for reconstructing significant characteristics of the ancient settlement. For example, it seems highly unlikely that the population of Idalion ever exceeded 1500 in the past, except possibly during the time(s) when a substantial portion of the inhabitants derived their living from nonagricultural employment. The busy center of the metal industry and commerce of late Classical and Hellenistic Idalion may have a partial analogue in the modern community, whose inhabitants are employed mainly outside the village in nonagricultural occupations. Today's population, in excess of 3000, is more than twice the number that can be supported by the agricultural resources of the village. Analogies can also be posited between developmental aspects of the ancient and modern settlement patterns. Perhaps the roads that link the ancient city with the copper mines to the west and with other population centers attracted the sort of ribbon development that is taking place in present-day Dhali.

These are just a few of the insights that ethnographic research in the contemporary community can contribute to historical study. In addition to providing a basis for reconstructing the past, modern ethnographic data can help direct archaeological research by suggesting possible avenues of further inquiry. Moreover, information about the modern community has an ethnographic value apart from its application in the archaeological context, and continued research in Dhali will add to our understanding of modern Cypriot culture and society at the same time that it contributes to our knowledge of the past.

Table 1. Populations of Dhali and Cyprus, 1881-1973

Dhali

		Increase		
Year	Population	Number	Percent	Average annual percent
1881	867	---	---	---
1891	955	88	10	1.0
1901	1109	154	16	1.6
1911	1345	236	21	2.1
1921	1413	68	5	0.5
1931	1486	73	5	0.5
1946	1965	479	33	2.2
1960	2609	644	33	2.2
1973	3056	447	17	1.4

Cyprus

		Increase		
Year	Population	Number	Percent	Average annual percent
1881	186,173	---	---	---
1891	209,286	23,113	12	1.2
1901	237,736	27,736	13	1.3
1911	274,108	37,106	16	1.6
1921	310,715	36,607	13	1.3
1931	347,959	37,244	12	1.2
1946	450,114	75,155	22	1.5
1960	573,566	123,566	27	1.8
1973	631,778	58,212	10	0.8

Table 2. Births and Deaths in Dhali, 1881-1970*

Decade	Births**	Deaths+	Excess of births over deaths	Net population increase
1881-1890	326	180	146	88
1891-1900	340	210	130	154
1901-1910	418	180	238	238
1911-1920	399	210	189	68
1921-1930	343	220	123	73
1931-1940	530	260	270	320
1941-1950	524	250	274	375
1951-1960	594	220	365	430
1961-1970	630	170	460	340

*These figures are based on church records from Dhali and information provided by the Cyprus Department of Statistics.

**Village records were incomplete for some of the early years and some of these figures are estimates based on fragmentary information. No record of Turkish births was available and estimates for these had to be made for each year based on known figures for the size of the Turkish Cypriot population of Dhali.

+No records of village death statistics were available. These figures are calculated on the basis of a crude death rate of 20 up until 1900, 15 between 1901 and 1946, 10 from 1947 until 1960, and 6 thereafter. These rates, and the crude birth rates of 30 between 1901 and 1946 and 23 thereafter, correspond approximately to rates for the island as a whole and agree roughly with those for a Cypriot highland village recorded by Peristiany between 1931 and 1953 (1968:77). In 1972, the only year for which a complete record of village deaths was available, 18 Dhalites died, a crude rate of 6.

Table 3. Population of Dhali, 1881-1973

Year	Rank*	Population+	Males	Females	Households
1881	20	867 (---)	388	479	199
1891	22	955 (139)	445	510	228
1901	28	1109 (110)	542	567	259
1911	23	1345 (124)	661	684	315
1921	26	1413 (138)	696	717	335
1931	27	1486 (131)	710	776	349
1946	31	1965 (206)	...	...	461
1960	22	2609 (206)	1303	1306	623
1973	17	3056 (74)	1527	1529	726

*Rank of Dhali as compared with other population centers in Cyprus.

+Figures in parentheses represent the Turkish Cypriot population of Dhali.

Table 4. A Comparison of Some Critical Statistics
from Dhali for the Years 1946 and 1970

	1946	1970
Population	1965	2989
Households	462	695
Full-time farmers	309	66
Percent of household heads listed as full-time farmers	68	9
Dunams of land under cultivation	7650	6325
Average number of dunams of land cultivated by a full-time farmer	24	96
Percent of land leased or sharecropped	12	60

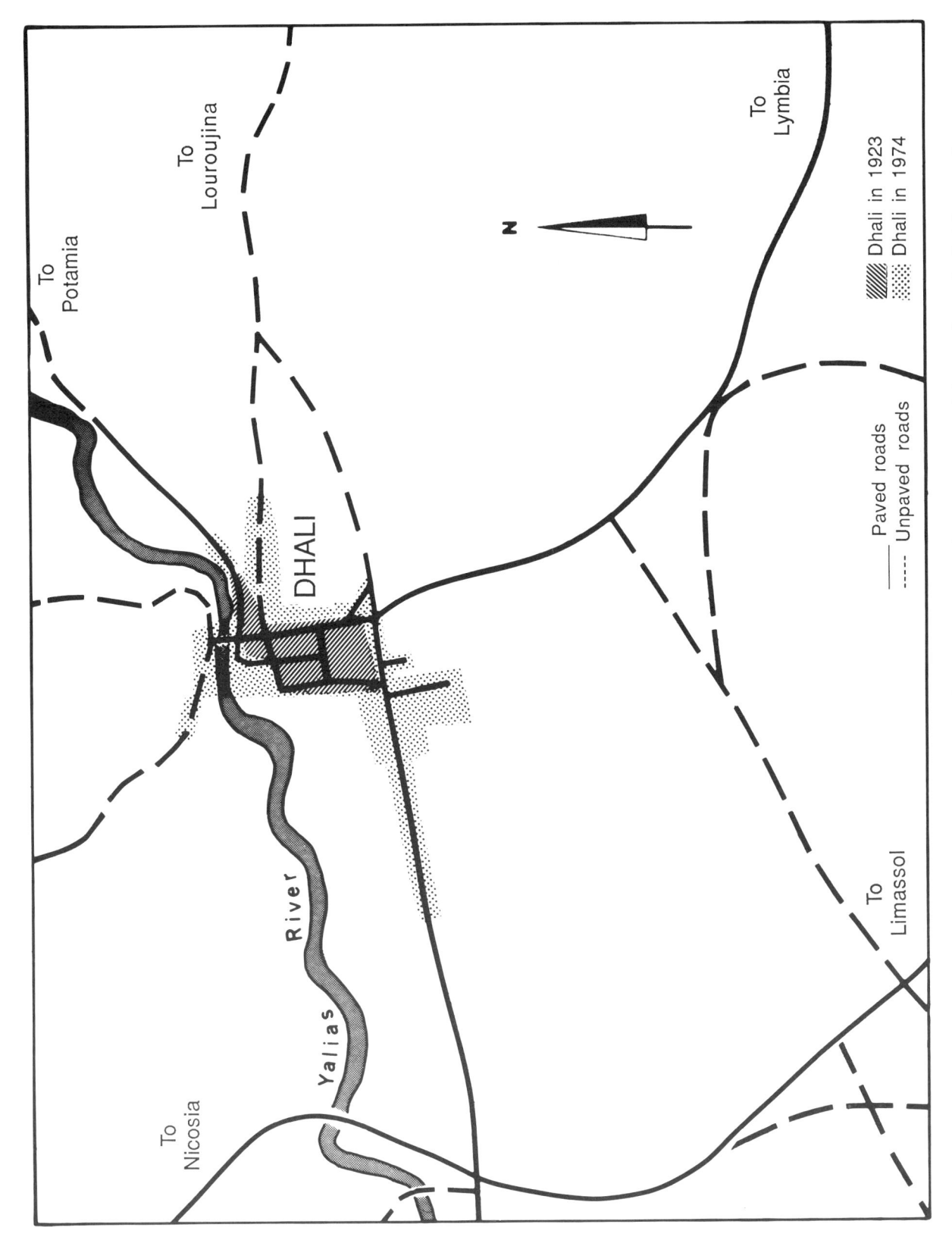

Figure 1. Settlement Expansion in Dhali, 1923–1974. (Map prepared by Robert J. Sullivan of Rhode Island College.)

PLATE 1

Examples of Dhali Continuities. a. Wooden draft plow (with iron share); b. Typical Cypriot "beehive" mudbrick oven.

PLATE 2

Ayios Sozomenos Architecture. a. Two-story mudbrick house; b. Arched entrance to traditional mudbrick compound.

PLATE 3

Architectural Styles from Ayios Sozomenos and Dhali. a. Mudbrick building with high stone foundation, Ayios Sozomenos; b. Stone arch of a ruined house, Dhali.

PLATE 4

Agricultural Activities in Dhali. a. Sheep grazing on grain stubble, b. Modern threshing.

VI. NUMISMATICS
CATALOGUE, IDALION 1970-1977

Ino Nicolaou [*]

Inventory no.	Find spot	Description	Date	Reference
1970				
1) TMB G 64[1]	Surface find	AE. 0.013. obv. Head of Arsinoe III r., wearing stephane, necklace, and earrings, in circle of dots; rev. ribboned double cornucopiae; inscr. ′′′′′ΒΑΣΙΛ′′′ in circle of dots. (pl. 1a)	Ptolemy IV Philopator, 221-204 B.C.	Svoronos, 2, no. 1160, pl. XXXIX:5; cf. SNG Cop., The Ptolemies,[2] pp. 648-50, pl. XXI.
1971				
2) H.1/3	Id WSE 11/36 Loc 003	AE. 0.012. ↑↓ Same type as above but much weathered.	Ptolemy IV Philopator, 221-204 B.C.	Svoronos, 2, no. 1160, pl. XXXIX:5; as above.
3) H.2/17	Id WSE 11/36 Loc 005	AE. 0.018. Evidence of having been cast in a mold; obv. Head of Zeus Ammon, laureate, r., in circle of dots; rev. eagle with closed wings, standing on thunderbolt l, ribboned cornucopiae on shoulder; inscr. ΠΤΟΛΕΜΑΙΟΥ /ΒΑΣΙ′′′ in circle of dots. (pl. 1b)	Ptolemy III Evergetes I, 246-221 B.C.	Svoronos, 2, no. 968, pl. XXIX:23; SNG, pl. VII.
4) H.3/42	Id ENW 7/10 Loc 017	AE. 0.017. obv. As H.2/17 but the edges well filed; rev. as above but without cornucopiae on shoulder; in field l. cornucopiae(?), letter between eagle's legs obscure (Γ or E), aplustre. Inscr. ′′′′′ΛΕΜΑΙΟΥ/ΒΑΣΙΛΕΩΣ in circle of dots. (pl. 1c)	Ptolemy III, Evergetes I, 246-221 B.C.	cf. Svoronos, 2, no. 970, XXIX:25; cf. SNG, pp. 186-87, pl. VII.
5) H.4/49	Id ENW 40/30 Loc 014	AE. 0.015. obv. Lion walking, l., above ram's head l., in circle of dots; rev. horse walking l., above star (much weathered) (cf. pl. 1g)	Evagoras II, 361-351 B.C.	BMC Cyprus, p. 60, pl.XII:6.

[*] Assistant Curator, Cyprus Museum

[1] All of the coins have the dies fixed unless otherwise indicated.

[2] Hereafter *SNG*.

Inventory no.	Find spot	Description	Date	Reference
6) F.129/48	Id WSW 9/11 Loc 006	AE. 0.01. As above but lion walking r. (worn off).	Evagoras II, 361-351 B.C.	Babelon, p. 719, no. 1180, pl. CXXVIII:17; cf. *BMC Cyprus*, p. 60, pl. XII:6.
1972				
7) H.5/66	Id WNW 42/23 Loc 001	AE. 0.016. Unidentifiable, completely worn off.		
8) H.6/69	Id ENW 7/8 Loc 001	AE. 0.018. obv. Head of emperor, laureate, r. (worn); rev. completely worn off.		
9) H.7/70	ID ENW 7/8 Loc 003	AE. 0.012. obv. Head of emperor r., diademed, draped, and cuirassed; inscr. DN THEODO/SIUS PF AVG; rev. Constantinopolis seated, facing front, head r., helmeted, holding globus in in l. hand, spear in r. hand, r. foot on prow(?), in left field O ; inscr. CONCOR/DIA AUGGG; mint mark CONSA. (pl. 1d)	Theodosius, after 379 A.D.	*RIC* 9, p. 227, no. 57(a).
10) H.9/269	Id ENW 7/10 Loc 035	AR. tetradrachm: wt. 16.070 gr.; obv. Head of young Heracles r., wearing lion's skin, in circle of dots; rev. Zeus seated on high-backed throne l., his l. hand resting on a sceptre, holding an eagle in his outstretched r. hand, in field l. ⋈ inscribed in a wreath, beneath the throne H; inscr. ΑΛΕΞΑΝΔΡΟΥ r., ΒΑΣΙΛΕΩΣ below. (Macedonian issue). (pl. 1e)	Alexander the Great, 332-323 B.C.	Müller, pl. XI, no. 714.
11) H.11/490	Id ENW 7/10 Loc 039	AE. 0.012. obv. Bust of Arsinoe III r., wearing stephane, necklace, and earrings, in circle of dots; rev. ribboned double cornucopiae; inscr. ΠΤΟΛΕΜΑΙΟΥ ΒΑΣΙΛΕΩΣ , in circle of dots. (pl. 1f)	Ptolemy IV Philopator, 221-204 B.C.	Svoronos 1, p. 203; 2, no. 1160, pl. XXXIX:4.
12) H.12/491	Id ENW 7/9 Loc 005	AE. 0.013. Unidentifiable (completely worn off).		
13) H.13/492	Id WNW 43/23 Loc 009	AE. 0.015. obv. Lion standing l., above ram's head l., in circle of dots; rev. horse walking l., star of six rays above; ankh in field l., in circle of dots (worn). (pl. 1g)	Evagoras II, 361-351 B.C.	*BMC Cyprus*, p. 60, pl. XII:6.

NUMISMATICS CATALOGUE 449

Inventory no.	Find spot	Description	Date	Reference
14) H.14/493	Id ENW 7/10 Loc 040	AE. 0.015. As above (worn).	Evagoras II, 361-351 B.C.	BMC Cyprus, p. 60, pl. XII:6.
15) H.15/494	Id ENW 7/10 Loc 038	AE. 0.015. As H.13/492.	Evagoras II, 361-351 B.C.	BMC Cyprus, p. 60, pl.XII:6.
16) H.16/495	Id ENW 7/10 Loc 039	AE. 0.012. As H.11/490.	Ptolemy IV, Philopator, 221-204 B.C.	Svoronos, 1, p. 203; 2, no. 1160, pl. XXXIX:4.
17) H.17/496	Id ENW 7/10 Loc 032	AE. 0.015. obv. Macedonian shield with gorgon's head on boss; rev. Macedonian helmet between B-A; below, caduceus on l., on r. $\bigwedge\!\!\!<$ (pl. 1h)	Antigonus I, ca. 316-306 B.C.	CDP, pp. 18-19.
18) H.18/497	Id ENW 7/8 Loc 008	AE. 0.022. obv. Head of Aphrodite r., long hair, wearing polos decorated with rosettes and earrings; rev. eagle standing on thunderbolt l.; in field l., star; inscription worn off, ′′′′′ΛΕΜΑΙ′′′′′ (pl. 1i)	Ptolemy I, 311-306 B.C.	Svoronos, 2, no. 75, pl.VI:23.
19) H.19/498	Id ENW 42/23 Loc 005	AE. 0.018. obv. Head of Heracles r., wearing lion's skin; rev. club r., bow case within bow below, between them; inscr. ′′′′′′′′ ′′′′ΞΑΝ ′′′′′ much worn; (as H.53/557 below).	Alexander the Great, 332-323 B.C.	NC, pp. 298-99, but cf. BMC Cyprus, p. 65, pl.XII:20.
20) H.20/499	Id ENW 7/10 Loc 035.2	AE. 0.01. As H.13/492(?) (very much worn).		
21) H.21/500	Id WSW 9/16 Loc 003	AE. 0.025. obv. Head of Zeus Ammon r.; rev. eagle standing on thunderbolt l., in the field l., aplustre; inscr. ′′′′′′′′′′ / ′′′′ΣΙΛΕ ′′′′′′ (much worn).	Ptolemy, King of Cyprus (?), 81-58 B.C.	BMC Ptolemies, p. 120, nos. 48-51, pl. XXX:2, but cf. Svoronos, 2, no. 1813, pl. LIX:27; SNG, p. 676, pl. XXIII.
22) H.22/501	Id ENW 7/10 Loc 038	AE. 0.012. Unidentifiable (completely worn off).		
23) H.23/502	Id ENW 7/10 Loc 035	AE. 0.014. obv. Head of Zeus Ammon r.; rev. eagle standing on thunderbolt l., (very much worn).	Late Ptolemaic	
24) H.24/503	Id WNW 10/20 Surface find	AE. 0.032. obv. Head of Zeus Ammon r.; rev. two eagles standing on thunderbolt l.; in field l., branch; inscr. ΠΤΟΛΕΜΑΙΟΥ /′′′′′′′′′′′′ in circle of dots. (pl. 1j)	Ptolemy VI Philometor, 180-146/5 B.C.	

450   AMERICAN EXPEDITION TO IDALION, CYPRUS, 1973-1980

Inventory no.	Find spot	Description	Date	Reference
25) H.25/393	Id ENW 7/10 Loc 043	AE. 0.017. ↑↓ Same as H.4/49 (much weathered).	Evagoras II, 361-351 B.C.	See H.4/49.
26) H.26/394	Id WNW 10/18 Loc 009 (= Pit 12)	Silver-plated tetrobol: wt. 2.580 gr.; obv. sphinx seated l. (much worn); rev. lotus flower on two spiral tendrils, ivy leaf on l., astragalus on r. (worn), all in incuse circle. (pl. 1k)	Stasikypros, ca. 460-450 B.C.	Babelon, p. 765, no. 1250, pl. CXXXII:7.
27) H.27/395	Id ENW 29/9 Loc 010, Layer 2	AE. 0.33. obv. Draped bust of emperor Gordian r., laureate; inscr. IMP GORDIANUS PIUS FEL AUG, in beaded circle; rev. nude Jupiter, standing en face, head r., holding thunderbolt in l. hand, long spear in r. hand; in field S/C, inscr. JOVI/STATORI, in circle of dots. (pl. 1l)	Gordianus III, 238-244 A.D.	*RIC* 4:3, pp. 10, 25, no. 84.
28) H.28/396	Id WNW 7/33 Loc 011	AE. 0.01. As TMB G 64 (no. 1 of this catalogue). Inscr. ΒΑΣΙΛ ′′′′′′′′′	Ptolemy IV Philopator, 221-204 B.C.	See TMB G 64.
29) H.29/451	Id ENW 6/6 Loc 001	AE. 0.01. Completely worn off.		
30) H.30/452	Id ENW 7/10 Loc 047	AE. 0.01. ↑↓ obv. Crouching lion l., above star(?) in circle of dots; rev. horse grazing l. (worn). (pl. 1m)	Evagoras II, 361-351 B.C.	Babelon, p. 719, no. 1181, pl. CXXVIII:21.
31) H.31/453	Id ENW 8/10 Loc 006	AE. 0.015. obv. Head of Heracles, completely worn off; rev. club, part of the inscription ′′′′ ΛΕ ′′′′′ and part of the bow are still very faintly visible (very worn); see H.53/557.	Alexander the Great, 332-323 B.C.	See H.53/557.
32) H.32/455	Id WSE 21/4 Loc 008	AE. 0.016. Same as H.4/49(?) (very much worn).		
33) H.33/483	Id ENW 29/9 Loc 024	AE. 0.016. Very much worn.		
34) H.34/484	Id ENW 29/9 Loc 008	AE. 0.015. obv. Cross with a dot at each branch, in circle of dots; inscr. worn off; rev. lion rampant l., in circle of dots; inscr. (worn off), in circle of dots (fragmentary). (pl. 1n)	Henry II, 1310-1324 A.D.	Lambros, p. 25, pl. 4:36.

Inventory no.	Find spot	Description	Date	Reference
1973				
35) H.35/S.8	Sheet XXXIX Plan 8W1, surface find	obv. Bust of emperor, wearing diadem and paludamentum; inscr. DN CONSTANTI/NUS MAX AUG, in circle of dots; rev. camp gate with star above, in exergue SMANT, off.Z (Antioch); inscr. PROVIDEN/TIAE AUGG, in circle of dots. (pl. 1o)	Constantine I, after 327 A.D.	cf. RIC 7, pp. 666-670 and p. 692, no. 84.
36) H.36/S.9	Sheet XXXIX Plan 8W1, Plot 327, surface find	AE. 0.017. obv. Bust of emperor r., wearing diadem and paludamentum; inscr. CONSTANTINUS MAX AUG, in circle of dots; rev. two soldiers standing facing, holding reversed spear and resting hand on shield, with two standards between them; inscr. GLOR/IA EXERC/ITUS, in circle of dots; in exergue mint mark CONS, off. Θ (pl. 1p)	Constantine I, 330-333 A.D.	RIC 7, pp. 567 and 579, no. 59.
37) H.37/S.43	Site B.I. Unit 1 Surface find	AE. 0.017. obv. Macedonian shield with gorgon's head on boss; rev. Macedonian helmet between B-A; below, caduceus on l., NK on r. (cf. pl. 1h)	Antigonus I, 316-306 B.C.	CDP, pp. 18-19.
38) H.38/534	Id WNW 10/17 Loc 002	AE. 0.018. obv. Lion walking l., above ram's head l., in circle of dots; rev. horse walking l., above star of eight rays; in field at front ankh (cf. pl. 1g).	Evagoras II, 361-351 B.C.	BMC Cyprus, p. 60, pl. XII:6.
39) H.39/535	Id WNW 33/1 Surface find	AE. 0.023. ↑↓ obv. Bust of emperor, bearded, en face, holding globus cross in l. hand, cross in r. hand, wearing crown with cross and jeweled robe, in field + Λ/Z, in circle of dots; rev. bust of Christ, bearded, en face, l. hand holding book of Gospels, r. hand raised in benediction, wearing nimbus cross, tunic, and mantle, in field IC/XC, in circle of dots. (pl. 1q)	Alexius I, 1081-1118 A.D.	IBC, 2, p. 548, nos. 39-40, pl. LXV:12.
40) H.40/536	Id WNW 33/1 Surface find	AE. 0.024. ↑↓ obv. Bust of Christ, bearded, en face, l. hand holding book of Gospels, wearing nimbus cross, tunic, and mantle, in field IC/XC, in circle of dots; rev. cross with four rays at center; at each of the extremities three globules, one big and two small; crescent on either side of upper end of cross; flower ornaments at base. (pl. 1r)	Baudouin II of Edessa(?), 1118-1131 A.D.	Schlumberger, p. 22, pl. I:15, but cf. Longuet, p. 136, no. 290.

Inventory no.	Find spot	Description	Date	Reference
41) H.41/537	Id WNW 8/18 Loc 003	AE. 0.017. obv. Head of Aphrodite r., with stephane, in circle of dots; rev. eagle with open wings, standing on thunderbolt l.; inscr. worn. (pl. 1s)	Satrapy of Ptolemy I in Cyprus, 312-310 B.C.	Svoronos, 2, no. 80, pl. VI:25; *SNG*, p. 643, pl. XXI.
42) H.42/538	Id WNW 8/18 Loc 003	AE. 0.026. obv. Head of Zeus Ammon r., (worn); rev. two eagles with closed wings, standing on thunderbolt l.; in field l., headdress of Isis; inscr. worn (fragmentary). (pl. 2a)	Cleopatra VII and Caesarion, after 47 B.C.	Svoronos, 2, no. 1482, pl. LXI:27; cf.*BMC Ptolemies*, p. 121, pl. XXX:4; *SNG*, pp. 683-84, pl. XXII.
43) H.43/539	Id WNW 8/18 Loc 003	AE. 0.017 to 0.022. Still preserves shafts and overflow due to casting in mold; obv. head of Zeus Ammon r., in circle of dots (worn); rev. two eagles standing on thunderbolt l.; in field l., wreath(?); inscr. worn. (pl. 2b)	Ptolemy IX Soter II(?), 116-80 B.C.	Svoronos, 2, no. 1702, pl. LVIII:19.
44) H.45/549	Id WNW 8/18 Loc 003	AE. 0.015. Completely worn off.		
45) H.46/550	Id WNW 8/18 Loc 008	AE. 0.018. Evidence of having been cast in mold, still preserves lateral shafts; obv. head of Zeus Ammon r., laureate, in circle of dots; rev. Zeus, standing en face, head facing l., holding sceptre in l. hand, ears of corn in r. hand, star above. (pl. 2c)	Late Ptolemaic Probably time of Cleopatra VII, 51-30 B.C.	*BMC Cyprus*, p. lxxxi:2.
46) H.47/551	Id WNW 8/18 Loc 010	AE. 0.024. Evidence of having been cast in mold; as H.46/550. (pl. 2d)	Late Ptolemaic Probably time of Cleopatra VII 51-30 B.C.	*BMC Cyprus*, p. lxxxi:2.
47) H.48/552	Id WNW 8/18 Loc 010	AE. 0.025. Evidence of having been cast in mold, still preserves overflow and central boss; obv. head of Zeus Ammon r., laureate, in beaded circle; rev. eagle on thunderbolt standing l. (much worn).	Ptolemaic	
48) H.49/553	Id WNW 10/17 Loc 001	AE. 0.023. As above but very much worn; edges filed.	Ptolemaic	
49) H.51/555	Id WNW 8/18 Loc 010	AE. 0.016. Evidence of having been cast in mold; as H.46/550 but worn.	Late Ptolemaic Probably time of Cleopatra VII, 51-30 B.C.	*BMC Cyprus*, p. lxxxi:2.

Inventory no.	Find spot	Description	Date	Reference
50) H.52/556	Id WNW 8/19 Loc 001	AE. 0.015. obv. Bust of Arsinoe III r., wearing stephane; rev. ribboned double cornucopiae; inscr. worn; see TMB G 64, no. 1 of this catalogue.	Ptolemy IV Philopator, 221-204 B.C.	Svoronos, 1, p. 203; 2, no. 1160, pl. XXXIX:4.
51) H.53/557	Id WNW 42/22 Loc 005	AE. 0.018. obv. Head of young Heracles r., wearing lion's skin, the legs of which are knotted around his neck, beaded border (worn); rev. club r. above, bow case within bow below, between them inscr. ′′′′ NΔP ′′′′′′ (much worn). (pl. 2e)	Alexander the Great 332-323 B.C.	NC, pp. 298-99, but cf. BMC Cyprus, p. 65, pl. XII:20.
52) H.54/558	Id WNW 8/18 Loc 010	AE. 0.01. Evidence of having been cast in mold; as H.52/556.	Ptolemy IV Philopator, 221-204 B.C.	Svoronos, 1, p. 203; 2, no. 1160, pl. XXXIX:4.
53) H.56/560	Id WNW 8/18 Loc 015	AE. 0.018. obv. Head of Roma l., helmeted, surrounded by inscr. URBS ROMA, in circle of dots; rev. she-wolf l., suckling twins, two stars above, in exergue SMK (Cyzicus), in circle of dots; mint mark S. (pl. 2f)	Constantine I, after 330 A.D.	RIC 7, p. 654, pl. 22, nos. 71-72.
54) H.57/561	Id WNW 8/18 Loc 015	AE. 0.025. obv. Head of Zeus diademed r., (worn); rev. eagle with closed wings, standing on thunderbolt l; in field l. Δ , above it star, inscr. ′′′′ ΛΕΜΑΙ / ′′′′′′′ , in circle of dots (fragmentary). (pl. 2g)	Ptolemy X Alexander I, 110 B.C.	Svoronos, 1, pp. 421-22; 2, no. 1706, pl. LVIII,23 but cf. BMC Ptolemies, p. lxxxii, pl. XXX:1.
55) H.58/570	Id WNW 25/3 Surface find	AE. 0.030. ↑↓ obv. Bust of Christ, bearded, en face, wearing nimbus cross, tunic, and mantle, l. hand holding book of Gospels, r. hand raised in benediction (worn); inscr. [+EMMA] / NOYHΛ (worn); rev. cross on two steps, IS-XS above cross, transverse limb below, bAS / ILE bAS / ILE, restruck on coin of John I Zimisces. (pl. 2h)	Michael IV, the Paphlagonian, 1034-1041 A.D.	IBC, 2, p. 497, pl. LVIII:3,4.

454   AMERICAN EXPEDITION TO IDALION, CYPRUS, 1973-1980

Inventory no.	Find spot	Description	Date	Reference
56) H.64/576	Id WNW 25/3 Surface find	AE. 0.028. ↑↓ obv. Figure of Christ, standing en face, wearing nimbus cross, tunic, and mantle (worn); in the field IC-XC; inscr. + [EM MA]/ NOYHΛ (worn), in circle of dots; restruck on the reverse of a coin of Basil II and Constantine VIII(?) (worn); rev. cross consisting of pellets, with a pellet at the end of each limb; in each angle of the cross IC | XC ─|─ | NI | KA . (pl. 2i)	Theodora, 1055-1056 A.D.	*IBC*, 2, p. 507, pl. LX:6.
57) H.66/578	Id WNW 25/3 Surface find	AE. 0.025. ↑↓ obv. Christ, bearded, standing en face, wearing nimbus cross, tunic, and mantle, l. hand holding book of Gospels, r. hand raised in benediction (worn); in field l., IC and eight-petaled rosette (or star), in field r. XC and rosette (worn), in circle of dots; rev. cross with globules at each forked extremity; in center, inscribed in circle, eight-petaled rosette or star; in the field above horizontal limb of cross, l. C, r. Φ , below the limb l. N, r. Δ ; in circle of dots. (pl. 2j)	Nicephoros III Botaniates, 1078-1081 A.D.	*IBC*, 2, p. 538, pl. LXIII:9, 10.
58) H.68/580	Id WNW 25/3 Surface find	AE. 0.025. As H.66/578. (pl. 2k)	Nicephoros III Botaniates, 1078-1081 A.D.	*IBC*,2, p.538, pl. LXIII:9, 10.
59) H.72/584	Id WNW 25/3 Surface find	AE. 0.025. ↑↘ obv. Bust of Christ, bearded, en face, wearing nimbus cross, tunic, and mantle; l. hand holding book of Gospels, r. hand raised in benediction, in circle of dots and border of large pellets (worn); restruck; rev. more than half figure of the Virgin orans, wearing nimbus cross, veil, tunic, and mantle; in field l. M, in field r. Θ , with two circles of large pellets between; restruck on a coin of Basil II and Constantine VIII(?). (pl. 2l)	Constantine IX Monomachos, 1042-1055 A.D.	*IBC*, 2, pl. LIX:9, 11.

Inventory no.	Find spot	Description	Date	Reference
60) H.73/585	Id WNW 25/3 Surface find	AE. 0.027. ↑↓ obv. Bust of Christ, bearded, en face, l. hand holding book of Gospels, wearing nimbus cross, tunic, and mantle; in field IC-XC, in circle of dots; rev. cf. H.40/536; restruck on an earlier type (cf. Schlumberger pl. I,14). (pl. 2m)	Baudouin II of Edessa(?), 1118-1131 A.D.	Schlumberger, p. 22, pl. I:15, but cf. Longuet, p. 136, no. 290.
61) H.74/586	Id WNW 8/18 Loc 018	AE. 0.018. obv. Head of Zeus Ammon r., laureate; rev. eagle with closed wings standing on thunderbolt l.; in field l. lotus(?) bud; inscr. worn off. (pl. 2n)	Ptolemy VIII, 145-116 B.C.	Svoronos, 2, no. 1639, pl. LIV:16.
62) H.75/598	Id WNW 8/17 Loc 002	AE. 0.018. As H.38/534 (worn).	Evagoras II, 361-351 B.C.	BMC Cyprus, p. 60, pl. XII:6.

1974

63) H.87/695	Id WSW 11/9 Loc 037	AE. 0.015. Very worn, unidentifiable.		
64) H.88/698	Id WNW 8/20 Loc 009	AE. 0.018. Very worn, unidentifiable.		

1976

65) H.97/767	Id WNW 8/18 Loc 021	AE. 0.016. ↑↓ obv. Lion walking l., ram's head l. above, in circle of dots (worn); rev. horse walking l. (star and ankh worn) (cf. H.38/534).	Evagoras II, ca. 361-351 B.C.	BMC Cyprus, pp. 60-61, no. 69.
66) H.98/768	Id WNW 8/18 Loc 021	AE. 0.022. obv. Head of Zeus Ammon r. (obliterated); rev. two(?) eagles standing on thunderbolt l.; in field l. wreath(?) (worn). (pl. 2o)	Ptolemy IX Soter II or Ptolemy X Alexander I, 116-80 B.C. or 114-88 B.C.	Svoronos, 2, no. 1702, pl. LVIII:19.
67) H.99/837	LSE 4/3 Loc 006	AE. 0.015. ↑↓ obv. Bust of emperor r., draped, wearing pearled diadem; inscr. DN VALEN //////// (worn off); rev. emperor standing en face, head r., l. hand holding victory on globe, r. hand raising a figure (worn); inscr. worn off; exergual inscr. ANTA (Antioch). (pl. 2p)	Valentinianus II(?), ca. 378-383 A.D.	cf. RIC 9, p. 226, pl. XVI:1.

Inventory no.	Find spot	Description	Date	Reference
1977				
68) H.101/851	Id WNW 10/10 Surface find	Solidus 0.019. obv. Bust of Constantine r., bearded, en face, in robe with dotted lozenge pattern; bust of Romanos II l., beardless, facing front, in robe and mantle, wearing crown with cross; between them they hold patriarchal cross; inscr. CONSTANT CEROMAN AUGG B′R′, in circle of dots; rev. bust of Christ, bearded, en face, wearing nimbus cross, tunic, and mantle, l. hand holding book of Gospels, r. hand raised in benediction; inscr. + INSXPS REX REGNANTIUM, in circle of dots. (pl. 2q)	Constantine VII and Romanos II, 945-959 A.D.	*IBC*, 2, p. 465, pl. LIII:12.

Chart of Coin Frequency

Name	Date	Occurrence
Evagoras II	361-351 B.C.	10
Stasikypros	460-450 B.C.	1
Alexander the Great	332-323 B.C.	4
Antigonus I	316-306 B.C.	2
Ptolemy I	311-306 B.C.	2
Ptolemy III	246-221 B.C.	2
Ptolemy IV	221-204 B.C.	6
Ptolemy VI	180-146/5 B.C.	1
Ptolemy VIII	145-116 B.C.	1
Ptolemy IX	116-80 B.C.	2 (?)
Ptolemy X	114-88 B.C.	1
Ptolemy King of Cyprus	81-58 B.C.	1
Cleopatra VII	51-30 B.C.	4
Ptolemaic--Late Ptolemaic	1st century B.C.	3
Gordianus III	238-244 A.D.	1
Constantine I	330-337 A.D.	3
Valentinianus	378-383 A.D.	1
Theodosius	379-395 A.D.	1
Constantine VII and Romanos II	945-959 A.D.	1
Michael IV	1034-1041 A.D.	1
Constantine IX	1042-1055 A.D.	1
Theodora	1055-1056 A.D.	1
Nicephoros III	1078-1081 A.D.	2
Alexius I	1081-1118 A.D.	1
Baudouin II of Edessa(?)	1118-1131 A.D.	2
Henry II	1310-1324 A.D.	1

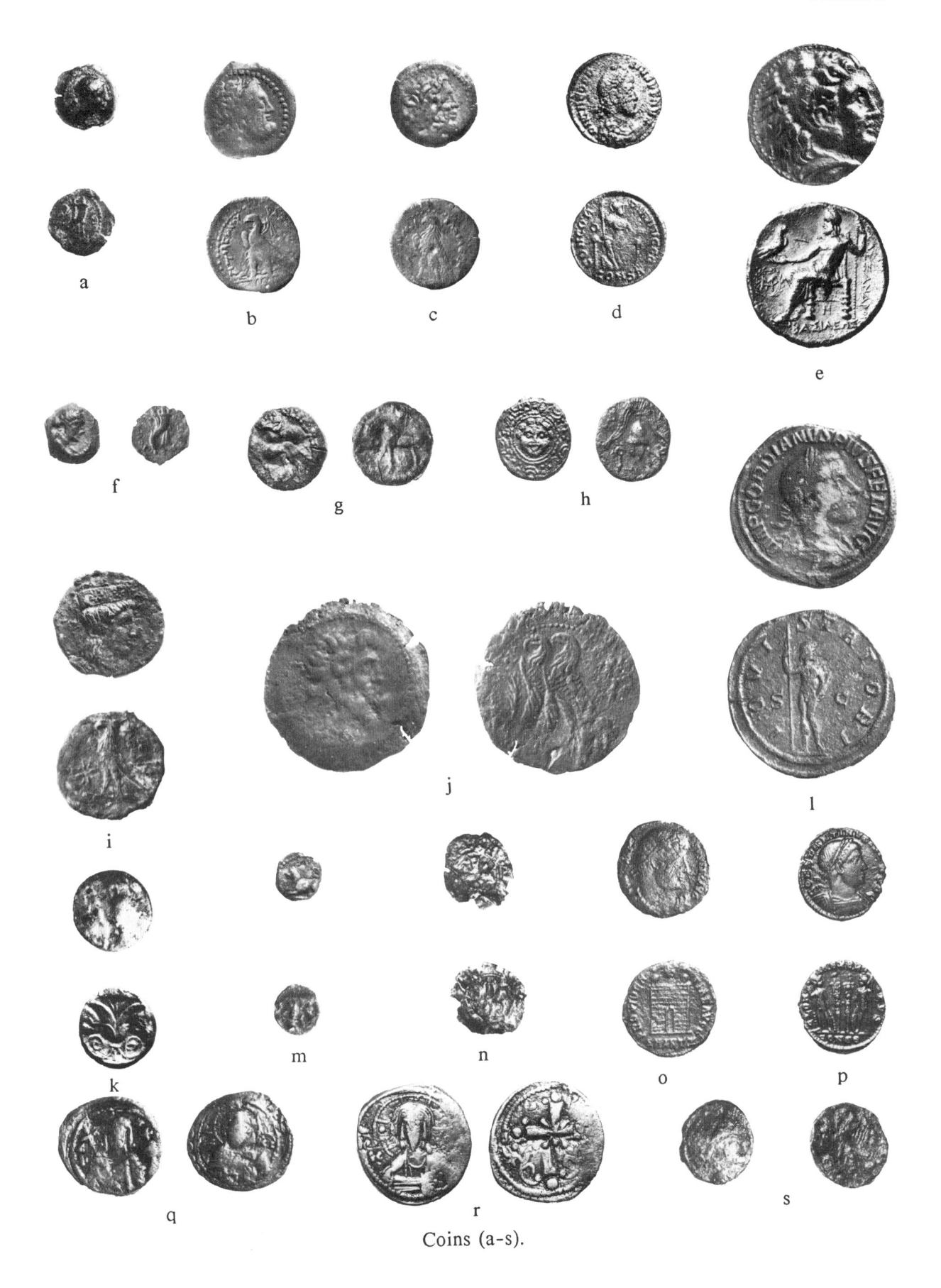

PLATE 1

Coins (a-s).

PLATE 2

Coins (a-q).

VII. SUMMARY

Anita M. Walker

Lawrence E. Stager

Continued excavation and analysis have contributed to our long-range regional objective of studying the relationship between settlement pattern/type and economic system and to our understanding of the larger problem of Cypriot prehistory.

When we began in 1972, Dhali-Agridhi was one of the two known Neolithic sites in the region, the other being Kataliondas, about 8 km farther west up the Yalias River (Catling 1957 and Stanley Price 1972b:15-21). Survey by the Idalion Expedition has not detected other Neolithic sites in the region and Kataliondas has not been excavated (Stanley Price 1979:92). Thus even the limited excavation at Dhali-Agridhi assumes a special importance.

Stanley Price (1977) argued that the original settlers of Cyprus in the aceramic Neolithic came from the Levant in the early sixth millennium, some landing on the east coast of the island and traveling inland along the major river systems. Initial results of the 1972 season at Dhali-Agridhi fitted well into this scenario and excavation in 1974 and 1976 further confirms his hypothesis. The additional C^{14} dates from aceramic Dhali-Agridhi are in line with other aceramic Neolithic sites nearby, such as Khirokitia and Kalavasos-Tenta (Le Brun 1984; Todd 1982). Lehavy sees general parallels between the Dhali-Agridhi and Khirokitia assemblages in the aceramic Neolithic and notes that the origin of the obsidian from Dhali-Agridhi is the same as that from aceramic Khirokitia (Çiftlik 2 B) (Le Brun 1984). The repertoire of fauna present in both Khirokitia and Dhali Agridhi is similar, although the proportions of each species differ, deer being less numerous than sheep/goat in the Khirokitia assemblage (Davis 1984). Carter, in his faunal analysis, argues that the very high proportion of *Dama dama mesopotamica* in the Dhali-Agridhi fauna and the absence of *Bos taurus* also support a Levantine origin.

Stanley Price posited a second wave of immigration to Cyprus with a painted pottery tradition (ceramic Neolithic), which took place in the fourth millennium B.C. after a hiatus in occupation (1977b:39). Here Dhali-Agridhi assumes a critical importance. Lehavy calls the monochrome pottery at Dhali-Agridhi "Dark-Faced Burnished Ware" (DFBW) by analogy to the ware found in Syro-Cilicia. A comparable monochrome ceramic was first found at Philia Drakos Site A, as both Lehavy and Stanley Price have observed. Stanley Price concluded, on the basis of the continuous development of the ceramic from the monochrome to the painted pattern at Philia and on the C^{14} date available from the site, that "the monochrome ware at Philia is no earlier than the early fourth millennium" (1977b:34). He conceded the possibility, on the basis of the 1972 C^{14} data available for the ceramic assemblage at Dhali-Agridhi, that some continuity of occupation was possible from the sixth into the fifth millennium B.C. (1977b:39). Lehavy, on the other hand, concludes on the basis of the two C^{14} dates now available for the ceramic assemblage that two different cultures are represented at Dhali-Agridhi, separated by at least a millennium. He also notes discontinuities between the Dhali-Agridhi aceramic and ceramic assemblages, such as the total absence in the assemblage with ceramics of obsidian blades and stone bowls, which would seem to point towards a reoccupation rather than continued occupation of the site. Nevertheless, such a hypothesis cannot be dismissed. Both Carter and Croft note the continuity in the fauna between the two assemblages. There is also the coincidence of location of settlement in the aceramic and ceramic. According to Stanley Price's model for settlement in the aceramic Neolithic, the first Cypriot settlers in the south and east came up the rivers, settling first at Dhali-Agridhi and secondly at Kataliondas. Dhali-Agridhi shares with Kataliondas, Khirokitia, and Kalavasos-Tenta its location near a major water source. Kataliondas and Khirokitia are located on steep hills and Kalavasos-Tenta is on a small hill; thus these three sites are strategically placed for lookout and defense. Dhali-Agridhi, by contrast, is on a flat terrace of the Yalias River, although there are several defensible hills (like the site of Idalion proper) in the vicinity. Stanley Price's analysis of settlement distribution in the ceramic Neolithic shows that many ceramic Neolithic sites are also located in strategic spots such as headlands (1977b:37). Why then should a second group of immigrants have selected precisely this same flat terrace of the Yalias? Indeed one wonders how they could even have found such an inconspicuous site, unless there was some continuity of occupation. Until a clear stratigraphic succession can be determined one cannot even rule out the possibility that Dhali-Agridhi represents a single period of deposition dating to the end of the aceramic and beginning of the ceramic period on Cyprus, especially in light of the appearance of DFBW in the Levant at the beginning of the sixth millennium. Meanwhile, the C^{14} dates of ceramic Dhali-Agridhi indicate that it must be considerd the earliest ceramic Neolithic occupation on the island.

In addition to the question of continuity between the aceramic and ceramic occupations of the site, Dhali-Agridhi raises some intriguing questions about settlement type and subsistence pattern. Dhali-Agridhi's atypical location on a flat river terrace has already been mentioned. Carter, however, indicates that despite this, Dhali-Agridhi, being situated on an ecotone, shares with other Neolithic sites access to a variety of environments, which would have made it attractive to early settlers less cautious or perhaps more foolhardy than their more strategically located neighbors. Lehavy points out that Dhali-Agridhi is clearly a different kind of settlement from sites like Khirokitia. Although the presence of stone bowls and debitage in the aceramic, and of heavy ceramic pieces in the ceramic assemblages, together with pits and workshop areas, indicate that Dhali-Agridhi was a permanent settlement rather than a hunting-station or other temporary encampment, the round-house architecture typical of other contemporary Neolithic sites is so far conspicuously absent. While this may be a function of limited exposure (the area thus far excavated seems to be on the periphery of the site), it is more likely to indicate, as Lehavy says, regional variation in settlement type.

Analyses by Carter and Croft of the fauna and Stewart's analysis of the scanty plant remains from Dhali-Agridhi contribute to an understanding of man-animal and man-plant relationships in the Cypriot Neolithic. Carter and Croft agree that the animals--*Dama*, caprines, and *Sus*--which form the bulk of the fauna were introduced to the island by man. Carter maintains that the status of the *Sus* is ambiguous according to the criterion of size, while *Dama*, which constituted 79.8% and 77.2% of the fauna, according to Carter and Croft respectively, has traditionally never been considered anything but "wild" on any grounds. Stewart's analysis of the plant remains also indicates that these are morphologically wild. Lehavy concludes that the subsistence pattern at Dhali-Agridhi in both aceramic and ceramic phases was one of intensive collecting of wild plants supplemented by hunting of some animals and herding of others, which were domesticated or semi-domesticated. It is difficult to accept the notion of a pottery-using culture which was still practicing intensive food-collecting. Instead one might posit a situation comparable to that envisaged by Higgs and Jarman for earlier Near Eastern sites, where permanent settlement is associated with morphologically wild animals and plants, and "close man-plant relationships had arisen without concomitant changes in plant or animal morphology" (Higgs and Jarman 1972:8). Croft cautions against an easy acceptance of the idea that the animals first exploited on the island should be seen as "domesticated" in the usual sense. Instead, he sees a complex economic situation involving the purposeful stocking of the environment with some animals, such as *Dama*, which were then culled by hunting, while other animals like caprines were more closely controlled for the exploitation of secondary products like milk and hairwool as well as meat. To refine further our understanding of the early economies on the island, Carter urges the continued collection of large, sieved samples from other comparable sites and a study comparing the island faunal repertoire with those of the Levant and Anatolia.

A major concern of the project has been to understand the processes of urbanization and state formation at Idalion proper. Catling's survey (1963) indicated that at the close of the Bronze Age a number of settlements in the Dhali region were abandoned. From their excavations on the West Acropolis, the Swedish Cyprus Expedition (*SCE* II:460-628) postulated an occupation of this part of Idalion beginning in the Late Cypriot III period and consisting of a fortified settlement with a cult place. For the following Cypro-Geometric I and II periods, however, they found only sherds without associated architectural remains. In the Cypro-Geometric III period they found that the West Acropolis was fortified once more and a new and more elaborate cult place constructed.

In our first two seasons of excavation (Stager, Walker, and Wright 1974) we found a few White Slip II and Mycenaean IIIB sherds in later fills. We thought the first occupation of Idalion was a village or specialized settlement, "emerging in the 12th century as an 'urban' center" (Stager, Walker, and Wright 1974). Subsequent seasons of excavation, however, lead us to modify this original hypothesis. Idalion Tb 1, dating to the Late Cypriot IIC period, is the earliest feature we have found in the vicinity of Idalion proper. Despite its looted state and the fragmentary nature of both the human and artifactual remains, several inferences may be made from this tomb. It is a multiple burial, most probably reflecting several successive interments. The presence of a number of children as well as adults indicates ascribed status and the grave-goods denote an élite burial. All these are consistent with a ranked society at the pre-state level of organization. In addition, both intensive and extensive survey in the vicinity of Idalion and on-site fail to show large-scale, high-density, nucleated settlement in the Late Cypriot period.[1] The only known Late Cypriot occupation at Idalion proper is the fortified settlement found by the Swedish Cyprus Expedition and this appears to be confined to the West Acropolis. This kind of settlement would fit with what Redman describes as one possible archaeological expression of a chiefdom, which consists of "a ceremonial center in which only a few people reside, with neighbouring communities housing the other members of the chiefdom" (Redman 1978).

We may hypothesize that during the Late Bronze Age, while state formation took place elsewhere in Cyprus (notably at nearby Kition), people in the inland region around Dhali remained at a less complex level of organization and in a small-scale, more dispersed pattern of settlement. Perhaps towards the end of the Late Bronze age, when conditions on the island as a whole became politically more unstable, the construction of a fortified settlement on the strategically located West Acropolis provided people in the Dhali region not only with a ceremonial center, but also with a place of refuge.

For the succeeding Cypro-Geometric I and II periods, just as the Swedish Cyprus Expedition found sherds but no architectural remains, so our survey and excavation thus far have shown no evidence of settlement anywhere at Idalion proper in these periods. Instead, excavation has revealed on the West Terrace, beneath the fortification wall in Lower City, and in central Lower City that it was not until the Cypro-Geometric III and early Cypro-Archaic periods that Idalion was extensively settled. Bieber's neutron activation analysis of the Idalion pottery indicates that during the late Cypro-Geometric and Cypro-Archaic periods Idalion had trade relations with all parts of Cyprus and that a large number of the Cypro-Archaic pieces he analyzed came from the Troodos area. This latter information, together with Koucky and Steinberg's observation (based in part on survey of the mine areas in the Dhali region) that the Cypro-Archaic was a very active period for mining on Cyprus, and the presence of small but ubiquitous quantities of slag at Idalion from the Cypro-Archaic onward, all suggest that the impetus to state formation and nucleated settlement was copper mining.[2] Bieber is of the opinion that the source of copper for Idalion was Tamassos, but Koucky and Steinberg think it much more likely that it was the nearest copper source, namely the Sha-Mathiati-Lythrodonda complex. Here, Koucky and Steinberg maintain, the copper ores were not roasted or smelted to

---

[1] Ramesses III recorded dozens of place names on the pylons of Karnak. Five of these names have been identified with towns of Cyprus: srmsk with Salamis, ktn with Kition, 'mr with Marion (?), sr with Soli, and rtr with Idalion (Barnett 1975: 376). None of these identifications is certain, most are uncertain, and rtr with Idalion extremely unlikely.

[2] A recent paper by Rupp suggests that state formation or reformation was taking place at several locations in Cyprus at the end of the Cypro-Geometric, although he does not attribute the impetus for state formation to the exploitation of copper (Rupp 1987).

copper matte but separated by hydro-metallurgical processing. The leached products were smelted directly to impure copper, which was transported to the city site for refining. That Idalion flourished in the Cypro-Archaic is indisputable. It is in this period that the sanctuary of Apollo Amyklos, excavated by Lang, was founded at the base of the East Acropolis. The Greek kantharos found by our expedition in a Cypro-Archaic context below the Lower City part of the fortification wall attests to long-distance trade between Idalion and the Aegean at the end of the Cypro-Geometric and beginning of the Cypro-Archaic I, that is ca. 750 B.C., according to Coldstream (1979:267). One can certainly say that by the first half of the sixth century B.C. Idalion was a city-state and important cult center, governed by a king, and prosperous enough to attract the attentions of Esarhaddon, king of Assyria, who mentions Ekishtura of Edi'il (Idalion) among the ten kings of Cyprus whom he compelled to transport building materials for his palace at Nineveh (Oppenheim 1969:291).

If our hypothesis is incorrect and state formation took place earlier than the end of the Cypro-Geometric, it is on the West Terrace that it can be further tested, since urbanization seems to have taken place there first.

Our soundings to bedrock across the Citadel Wall on the West Terrace revealed two fragments of monumental ashlar walls (Walls 039 and 038) constructed at the beginning of the Cypro-Archaic I period and remaining in use to the Cypro-Archaic II. We infer that one of these walls (039), running along the western perimeter of the West Terrace, constituted the initial fortifications of the citadel area. Soundings and excavation elsewhere on the site do not indicate that Lower City was fortified at this time, although some form of settlement was taking place, indicated by the presence of a series of pits in the West Lower City domestic precinct. The original function of these pits may have been either as underground silos or possibly even as part of semi-subterranean dwellings. Sometime at the beginning of the Cypro-Archaic II period Walls 039 and 038 went out of use. We do not know what replaced them but four meters of occupational debris were deposited in this area of the West Terrace between the destruction of Wall 039 and the construction of the next extant fortification system. Something must have retained this material from slumping down the slope, perhaps a yet undiscovered second fortification wall hidden within the core of the later fortification system. The accumulation of debris, which in Phases 7 and 6 included large molded architectural fragments, attests not only to vigorous building on the West Terrace in the Cypro-Archaic I and II but also represents potentially the richest accumulation of material from this archaeologically little-known period in Cyprus, which would surely reward extensive excavation.

Towards the end of the Cypro-Archaic II (ca. 550-475 B.C., see below) Idalion experienced an expansion and reorganization. It was during the late 6th and first half of the 5th century that Lower City was occupied in its central residential quarters. It is at the end of this period that the fortifications on the West Terrace were radically reorganized and the whole city enclosed with a fortification wall. Sections of the fortification system have been excavated in Lower City and on the West Terrace and traces of the fortifications were also found in soundings on the East Acropolis. The fortification wall was built with a limestone rubble core revetted on its inner and outer faces with ashlar limestone blocks. On the West Terrace there are, however, traces of an ashlar sandstone facing, which in Area CW took the place of the limestone ashlars on the outer face entirely, probably because this part of the fortification system was incorporated into the monumental building complex (see below). Traces of a sandstone facade also exist on the upper levels of the inner face of the fortification system on the West Terrace. There was probably also a mudbrick superstructure which is found only in later detritus. The wall survives to a height of 7.80 m and is 10.75 m wide in our section in Area D on the West Terrace, although in the Lower City it is preserved only 1.60 m high and is 4.25 m wide. However, it may have been designed with rectangular towers or bastions at certain points. Traces of one such bastion were found in Lower City, where the bastion was 8.25 m wide and constructed with a limestone rubble core faced with ashlar blocks, limestone on the inner face and sandstone on the outer. In both West Terrace and Lower City the ashlar blocks were in places consolidated with an identical coarse crushed gypsum mortar.

The location of gates or entrances to Idalion is problematic. No candidate for a gate was found on the West Terrace unless the extraordinary thickness of the wall in our section is interpreted as part of a gate pier. The West Terrace may have been surrounded entirely on the west, south, and east by the massive fortification wall, and accessible only through an aperture within Lower City, as a last line of defense, in the manner of a medieval motte and bailey. Elsewhere, the bastion or pier in Lower City with its sandstone ashlar sheathing quite probably represents one side of a gate (perhaps the Tamassian gate referred to on ostracon T54/308). The main entrance to the city, however, logically lies between the East and West Acropolis, where the main Nicosia-Larnaca road passes today through a deep defile between the two hills. It is outside this gap, south of Idalion, that Koucky discerned the line of an old road leading westward to the area of the mines (see Introduction, fig. 2).

The area enclosed by the walls of Idalion during the period of its use from the early fifth century B.C. to the end of the fourth century B.C. was about 40 hectares. Using Stager's calculation for reconstructing ratio of population to space (Stager 1985:21) we get a population of 8-10,000 inhabitants of Idalion during the Cypro-Classical period. Stewart's analysis of flora from excavation shows that cereal grains, olives, grapes, and legumes were cultivated in the vicinity in this period, while the faunal data indicate that the livestock raised comprised sheep, goats, pigs, cattle, donkeys, and horses. According to Allen's study of recent crop yields using traditional methods of agriculture, the upper limit of population that could be supported in the immediate catchment area of Idalion by such traditional agricultural practice probably did not exceed 1500. The bulk of the city's ancient population must, then, have earned its living from non-agricultural employment and probably also controlled a larger hinterland of arable and pasturage. Koucky and Steinberg's reconstruction of the metal industry at Idalion and the finding of concentrations of Cypro-Archaic and Cypro-Classical sherds in survey of the mine areas nearest to Idalion strongly suggest not only that mining copper was of prime importance to Idalion's economy, but also that the hinterland of Idalion extended at least as far as the Sha-Mathiati-Lythrodonda mine area (ca. 10-15 km from Idalion), where the sherds were collected. Bieber's neutron activation analysis demonstrates that from the Cypro-Archaic through the Cypro-Classical periods there is evidence of well-established trade networks between Idalion and other areas of Cyprus, although he maintains there is a reorientation of that trade from the inland areas in the Cypro-Classical I, a reorientation which he equates with change in the political status of Idalion. The prosperity of Idalion in the 5th century B.C. is further attested by the development of a distinct "Idalion School" of limestone sculpture.

Evidence for town-planning at Idalion comes from our excavations on the West Terrace and in the West Lower City domestic precinct. Traces of monumental architecture in our limited exposures on the West Terrace exhibit alignments suggestive of an overall building plan for the area. Although many of the broad lines of that plan must remain unknown until future excavations, there seems to be little doubt that the ramparts along the western edge of the West Terrace and the buildings to the east were conceived as an organic whole and built at approximately the same time. The location of these buildings between the sacred precincts above, on the West Acropolis, and the domestic precincts below, in the Lower City, suggest that the West Terrace, while a self-contained unit, was nevertheless integrated into the larger city plan through the fortification system built to protect the residential quarters as well. At two distant soundings along the Citadel Wall and the Lower City fortifications, the ceramic evidence converged to suggest a date in the late Cypro-Archaic II (Types IV-V) as a *terminus post quem* for the construction phase of the ramparts, which was then succeeded by use phases of the Cypro-Classical I period. It follows that the West Terrace and Lower City fortifications were built somewhere around 475 B.C., the generally accepted date for the beginning of the Cypro-Classical I period. At the same time the Palace was erected on the West Terrace. Although the founding levels of that structure have not been excavated, the style and techniques of its masonry are so similar to those used in the fortification system that their contemporaneity seems assured. This argument is also buttressed by the Phase 5 occupation in the Area D Building prior to the first appearance of Phoenician inscriptions in Phase 4 of the Area D Room. The key historical question remains: who built the sandstone ashlar buildings and fortifications which the American Expedition has discovered and dated to the Cypro-Classical I period--the Phoenicians or the Greek Cypriots; the kings of Kition or the kings of Idalion?

Using a "high" chronology for the local dynasts of Idalion and contemporary kings of Kition, Gjerstad places the conquest of Idalion by the Phoenicians of Kition during the reign of 'Oziba'al, at ca. 470 B.C. (*SCE* IV:2, p. 497, n. 5; Gjerstad 1979:260, n. 1). Then Idalion ceased to be an independent Greek Cypriot city-state (*polis*), minting its own coins. It was at this time--ca. 470 B.C.--that Gjerstad dates the destruction of the fortified Athena Temple on the West Acropolis to the end of Cypro-Archaic II (Period 6A).

Convinced that the famous Bronze Tablet (purchased by the Duc de Luynes in 1850) was found by peasants reportedly digging on the West Acropolis, Gjerstad was then left to conclude that events recorded on that document must date prior to 470 B.C., the supposed *terminus ante quem* for occupation on the West Acropolis. The Bronze Tablet mentions an unsuccessful siege of Idalion by the "Medes and Kitians" [Persians and Phoenicians] during the reign of King Stasikypros, who has usually been identified with King SA-- who appears on the last independent issues of coins minted at Idalion prior to the takeover by 'Oziba'al. However, rather than accept this identification, Gjerstad prefers to identify King SA-- with a heretofore unattested Stasikypros II and to link Stasikypros of the Bronze Tablet with a king three reigns earlier than SA--; i.e. a king who begins the series of inscribed issues at Idalion before King KI-- (who overstrikes coins of Ba'almilk I). The reading of this earliest monogram remains uncertain except to Gjerstad, who reads SA-- (1979:240, n. 1). Such an identification allows Gjerstad to link the unsuccessful siege of Idalion with troubles in Cyprus following the Ionian Revolt 499/8 B.C. However, since the Palace and fortification system of Idalion were not built until the end of the Cypro-Archaic period, his "high" chronology would also logically imply that this monumental architecture was either built by King SA--, the last king of independent Idalion (his Stasikypros II) and fell at the same time as the Athena Temple to 'Oziba'al almost immediately, or was not, in fact, the work of the rulers of Idalion at all, but of its conquerors.

These hypotheses are possible but not very plausible. If Stasikypros of the Bronze Tablet belongs at the beginning of the inscribed coin series in the opening years of the 5th century B.C., then we must believe that the houses in West Lower City of Idalion successfully withstood a siege unscathed, despite the absence of a fortification system. A similar objection can be raised to the notion that 'Oziba'al was the builder of the Idalion fortification system. Moreover, if King SA-- (Gjerstad's Stasikypros II) built the Palace and fortification system around 475 B.C., then we must assume that all the earlier kings of independent Idalion made do without a palace (so far as we know at present) and with only a fortified citadel. It also supposes a highly compressed sequence of frenzied building activity followed by successful siege. This is likewise the weakness of Masson's dating of the siege to 478 B.C. and the fall of Idalion to 470 B.C., although he identifies King SA-- as Stasikypros of the Bronze Tablet (Masson 1961:235, 238).

The results of our excavations suggest a more plausible scenario for at least a relative sequence of events at Idalion in the 5th century. The Palace and fortification system are constructed around 475 B.C. by one of the early kings of the inscribed coin series. Stasikypros of the Bronze Tablet is the King SA-- of the coin series (Peckham 1968:20-21; see also Nicolaou in this volume). It is he who successfully defends his city against the attack either of Ba'almilk I or 'Oziba'al, from behind his massive walls. It is he who is eventually defeated by 'Oziba'al. In this conquest the houses in the Lower City are laid waste (ca. 450 B.C.). There remain two obstacles to this reconstruction but neither is insurmountable. Although the houses in Lower City are destroyed, the fortification system is not. And what do we do with Gjerstad's dating of the destruction of the Athena Temple to 470 B.C.? As shrewdly noted by Maier, Gjerstad himself provides a possible solution to the latter problem, when he mentions finding post-Archaic coins in the destruction layer, which he dismisses as intrusive (*SCE* 2:617; Maier 1985:34, n. 11). Per Ålin (1978) has examined two loci from Gjerstad's West Acropolis excavations and confirmed a Cypro-Archaic date for the earlier part of Period 6. He noted but has not yet fully studied several loci with a "mixed" range of pottery types from the same area (Ålin, personal communication). The destruction of the Athena Temple should probably be dated later and seen as one with the end of the houses in Lower City. We can explain the absence of damage to the fortification system in two ways. It may be an accident of excavation:

our sample is small and does not include any gate area, the logical place of breakthrough. A successful conqueror who wishes to occupy and subsequently control a city does not destroy its fortification system, except to the extent necessary to take the place. It is not cost effective. However, he may destroy internal structures in the city in a display of *force majeure*. It is likely that this is what happened in the fall of Idalion.

But whether we date the reign of Stasikypros to early 5th or mid-5th century B.C., or whether we date the fall of Idalion to 470 B.C. or 450 B.C., the Bronze Tablet provides important information about the political structure of Idalion in the 5th century, when it was still an independent Greek Cypriot kingdom. The tablet records in Cypro-syllabic a donation of land and money to a group of physicians (Onasilos and his brothers) who tended the wounded of Idalion without fee during the unsuccessful siege. As Spyridakis has emphasized, it is significant that this donation was made by both King Stasikypros and the *polis* to the physicians, suggesting that Idalion was not a pure autocracy but had a mixed constitution in which the City Council (local senate) had a voice (Marvin in *Idalion* I:xxvi).

Gjerstad (*SCE* III:81) has described the spatial relationships between topography and architecture at Vouni in a way that could apply to Idalion as well in the 5th century B.C.:

> Within the ramparts, the space is divided in a very significant way. The area on the very top, to the S., is reserved for the temple of Athena...; on the second largest terrace is situated the palace, surrounded by various minor sanctuaries or chapels. The palace area does not seem to have been separated from the sanctuary of Athena by any kind of wall or other construction. To the N., however, the palace area is delimited by means of a strong, high terraced wall which must have hidden the greater part of the palace from view of anyone standing on the steep northern slope of the hill.

To the north and below Vouni Palace lay a necropolis (cf. Cesnola's predations at Idalion) and beyond that probably the residential area.

Not only does this overall scheme fit almost exactly that which the Swedish and American excavations at Idalion have revealed, but also the "syntactical" patterns of the architectural scheme can be given "semantic" meaning by the contents of the Bronze Tablet, in which money and a parcel of land alienated from city-state property were given to Onasilos and his fellow physicians. Athena enshrined in her Temple (on the West Acropolis) oversaw and guaranteed the agreement reached by King Stasikypros (in his Palace on the West Terrace) in conjunction with the City Council (from Lower City).

Given the Greek Cypriot character of the political structure of Idalion in the early 5th century and its independence from Persian-Phoenician authorities until ca. 450-425 B.C., there is no reason to believe that the layout of the sanctuary of Athena (already in existence for several centuries), the Palace, the fortifications, and the Lower City residences was an "Oriental" or Near Eastern conception imposed upon either Idalion or Vouni by a persophile regime (as Gjerstad has suggested for Palace 1-2 at Vouni, supposedly built under the direction of a persophile regime from Marion [ca. 500-450 B.C.], *SCE* III:286-90).

Throughout the first half of the 5th century B.C. there were various attempts by the Greeks to thwart Persian control of the island (see Hill 1940 and Gjerstad *SCE* III:286ff). As late as 449 B.C. Persian control of Cyprus was still not so complete to discourage another Greek expedition from trying to wrest Cyprus from the Persians. Cimon, admiral of a fleet of 140 ships, sailed to Cyprus in an effort to take Salamis, Kition, and Marion. He died in the assault on Phoenician Kition. The defeat of his naval operation ended a half century of Greek and Persian rivalry for the island, as Cyprus fell completely under Persian rule and that of their clients, the Phoenicians. In the aftermath of Cimon's defeat, the Phoenician ruler ᶜOzibaᶜal incorporated Idalion into the kingdom of Kition, thus reducing Idalion's status from an independent, plucky *polis* to a node along the copper network which the Phoenician dynasty eventually controlled from the mines in the Troodos Mountains to the seaport of Kition.

Sometime after the Phoenician takeover, the Palace on the West Terrace was reorganized (Phase 4) and Phoenician inscriptions began to appear there for the first time (e.g. Area D Room). It probably remained an administrative center during the Phoenician occupation for most of the next century, although this period cannot be detailed archaeologically without further excavations. During this same period (ca. 450/425 - 350/325 B.C.) the residential quarters in central Lower City were deserted.

Shortly before the fall of Idalion in the late 4th century B.C., the southern part of the public precincts on the West Terrace had been converted into an industrial zone for copper metallurgy (Area D Room, Phase 2), and the range of rooms beyond the North Facade and Street (Area C) housed an olive oil factory. Whether parts of the Palace still continued to function as an administrative center remains unclear.

What is clear from archaeology is that a disaster struck Idalion toward the end of the 4th century B.C.; as the West Terrace buildings and industrial areas were buried under an avalanche of stone and mudbrick rubble, the Citadel Wall and Palace remains collapsed almost simultaneously. The nature and date of this massive destruction, which in places reached a depth of 2.00 - 3.00 m, suggest that the agent of destruction was human, probably an invading army. Perhaps we can be more specific. Above the destruction debris of the Citadel Wall, we found a Phoenician ostracon (Obj. No. 669) which has been deciphered by staff epigraphist Frank Moore Cross (publication forthcoming). The text mentions a special kind of sacrifice ($[^c]lt\ smh$), which Cross interprets as a child sacrifice, offered by an inhabitant of Idalion in the fiftieth year of an unnamed Phoenician king. This long-lived Phoenician ruler can only be Pumayyaton (362-312 B.C.), who was beheaded by the Ptolemies in 312 B.C. Perhaps the city was already under siege by the Ptolemies when, according to well-known Phoenician practice, this infant was offered as a sacrifice. Whatever the precise circumstances were, there seems little doubt that Idalion was reduced to rubble by the Ptolemies and never again recovered its former greatness.[3]

---

[3] Table 1 gives a summary of the phasing in the areas excavated in West Lower City and on the West Terrace of Idalion.

Table 1. Summary of Phasing, West Terrace and West Lower City

Period	West Terrace			Lower City	
	Palace		Fortifications	Fortifications	Domestic Precincts
	Area C	Area D			
Modern	1	1	1		1
Hellenistic	2	2	2	1	2
Mid CC I–early Hell I 450–312 B.C.	3	3	3	2	
	4	4	4		
Late CA II–CC I 525/500–450 B.C	5	5	5	2	3
			6		
			6	3	3
CA I–CA II	Unexcavated		7	4	4
CG III–CA I	Unexcavated		8		

BIBLIOGRAPHY

Abascal, M. R.; Harbottle, G.; and Sayre, E. V.

    1974   Correlation between Terra Cotta Figurines and Pottery from the Valley of Mexico and Source Clays by Activation Analysis. In *Archaeological Chemistry*, ed. C. W. Beck, Advances in Chemistry no. 138, pp. 81-99. Washington, D.C.: American Chemical Society.

Adamides, N. G.

    1978   *A Report on the Geology of the Kalavasos Mining Leases.* Unpublished report of the Hellenic Mining Company, Ltd., Nicosia, Cyprus.

Agricola, G.

    1546   *De Natura Fossilium.* Translated by M. C. Bandy and J. A. Bandy. Special Paper 63, Geological Society of America. New York, 1955.

    1556   *De Re Metallica.* Translated by H. C. Hoover and L. H. Hoover, 1912. New York: Dover Publications, 1950.

Ålin, P.

    1978   Idalion Pottery from the Excavations of the Swedish Cyprus Expedition. *Opuscula Atheniensia* 12:91-109. Skrifter Utgivna av Svenska Institutet I Athen 25. Stockholm: Swedish Cyprus Expedition.

Allan, W.

    1965   *The African Husbandman.* Edinburgh and London: Oliver and Boyd.

Angel, J. L.

    1946   Skeletal Change in Ancient Greece. *American Journal of Physical Anthropology* 4:69-97.

    1953   The Human Remains from Khirokitia. In *Khirokitia*, P. Dikaios, appendix II, pp. 416-30. Monographs of the Department of Antiquity of the Government of Cyprus no. 1. London, New York, and Toronto: Oxford University Press.

    1972   Late Bronze Age Cypriots from Bamboula: The Skeletal Remains. In *Bamboula at Kourion*, ed. J. L. Benson, pp. 148-65. Philadelphia: University of Pennsylvania Press.

Artzy, M.

    1972   *The Origin of the Palestinian Bichrome Ware.* Ph.D. dissertation, Brandeis University, Waltham, Massachusetts.

Asaro, F.; Perlman, I.; and Dothan, M.

    1971   An Introductory Study of Mycenaean IIIC1 Ware from Tel Ashdod. *Archaeometry* 13:169-75.

Aschenbrenner, S.

    1972   A Contemporary Community. In *The Minnesota Messenia Expedition: Reconstructing a Bronze Age Regional Environment*, ed. W. A. McDonald and G. R. Rapp, Jr., pp. 47-63. Minneapolis: University of Minnesota Press.

Åström, P.

    1972a   *The Swedish Cyprus Expedition.* Vol. IV, part 1B. *The Middle Cypriot Bronze Age.* Lund: Swedish Cyprus Expedition.

    1972b   *The Swedish Cyprus Expedition.* Vol. IV, part 1C. *The Late Cypriot Bronze Age: Architecture and Pottery.* Lund: Swedish Cyprus Expedition.

Åström, P. and Åström, L.

    1972   *The Swedish Cyprus Expedition.* Vol. IV, part 1D. *The Late Cypriot Bronze Age: Other Arts and Crafts.* Lund: Swedish Cyprus Expedition.

Åström, P. and Nicolaou, I.

    1980   Lead Sling Bullets from Hala Sultan Tekke. *Opuscula Atheniensia* 13:29-33. Skrifter Utgivna av Svenska Institutet I Athen 40. Stockholm.

Attalides, M.

    1976   Social Change and Rural Development in Cyprus. In *Agricultural Science. Proceedings of the 4th Seminar on Agricultural Development (June 3-6, 1974)* 7:109-26.

Babelon, E.

    1910   *Traité des monnaies grecques et romaines* 2. Paris: Leroux.

Barnett, R. D.

    1960   *Assyrian Palace Reliefs and their Influence on the Sculptures of Babylonia and Persia.* London: Batchworth Press.

    1975   The Sea Peoples. In *Cambridge Ancient History*, Vol. II, Part 2, 3rd ed., ed. I. E. S. Edwards, C. J. Gadd, N. G. L. Hammond, and E. Sollberger, pp. 359-78. Cambridge: Cambridge University Press.

Bass, W. M.

    1971   *Human Osteology.* The Missouri Osteological Society, Inc. Columbia, Missouri.

Bate, D. M. A.

    1937   Palaeontology: The Fossil Fauna of the Wady El-Mughara Caves. In *The Stone Age of Mount Carmel*, ed. D. A. E. Garrod and D. M. A. Bate, pp. 135-227. London: Oxford University Press.

Bates, A.

    1954   *Copper*. American Chemical Society Monograph Series. New York: Reinhold.

Bear, L. M.

    1963   The Mineral Resources and Mining Industry of Cyprus. *Geological Survey of Cyprus*, Bulletin 1. Nicosia, Cyprus.

Bender, F. B.

    1974   Geology of the Arabian Peninsula, Jordan. *U.S. Geological Survey Professional Paper* 560-I. Washington, D.C.

Benson, J. L.

    1972   *Bamboula at Kourion*. Museum Monograph of the University Museum. Haney Foundation Series 12. Philadelphia: University of Pennsylvania.

Bérard, V.

    1902   *Les Phéniciens et l'Odyssée*. Vols. 1 and 2. Paris: Colin.

Bieber, A. M., Jr.

    1974   Neutron Activation Analysis. In *Idalion* 1, chap. 8, pp. 141-48.

    1977   *Neutron Activation Analysis of Archaeological Ceramics from Cyprus*. Ph.D. dissertation. University of Connecticut.

Bieber, A. M., Jr.; Brooks, D.; Harbottle, G.; and Sayre, E. V.

    1976a   Compositional Groupings of Some Ancient Aegean and Eastern Mediterranean Pottery. *Applicazione dei metodi nucleari nel campo delle opere d'arte (Rome-Venice, May 24-29, 1973)*. Rome, Atti dei Convegni Lincei, Academia Nazionale dei Lincei.

    1976b   Application of Multivariate Techniques to Analytical Data on Aegean Ceramics. *Archaeometry* 18:59-74.

Bikai, P. M.

    1978   *The Pottery of Tyre*. Warminster: Aris and Phillips.

Binford, L. R.

    1962   Archaeology as Anthropology. *American Antiquity* 28:217-25.

    1964   A Consideration of Archaeological Research Design. *American Antiquity* 29:425-41.

    1968   Archaeological Perspectives. In *New Perspectives in Archaeology*, ed. S. R. Binford and L. R. Binford, pp. 5-32. Chicago: Aldine.

    1972   Directionality in Archaeological Sequences. In *An Archaeological Perspective*, ed. L. R. Binford, pp. 314-26. New York: Seminar Press.

1974   Forty-seven Trips. Manuscript on file, University of New Mexico, Albuquerque.

Binford, L. R.; Binford, S. R.; Whallon, R.; and Hardin, M. A.

1970   Archaeology at Hatchery West. *Society for American Archaeology Memoirs* 24. Washington, D.C.

Biringuccio, V.

1540   *Pirotechnia*. Translated by C. S. Smith and M. T. Gnudi. New York: The American Institute of Mining and Metallurgical Engineers, 1941.

Birmingham, J.

1963a   The Development of the Fibula in Cyprus and the Levant. *Palestine Exploration Quarterly* 95:80-112.

1963b   The Chronology of Some Early and Middle Iron Age Cypriot Sites. *American Journal of Archaeology* 67:15-42.

Bishop, R. L.

1975   *Western Lowland Maya Ceramic Trade: An Archaeological Application of Nuclear Chemical and Geological Data Analysis*. Ph.D. dissertation, Southern Illinois University, Carbondale.

Blinkenberg, Chr.

1926   *Fibules grecques et orientales*. Lindiaka V. Det. Kgl. Danske Videnskabernes Selskab, Historisk-filologiske Meddelelser XIII,I. Copenhagen: Høst.

Blinkenberg, Chr. and Kinch, K. F.

1931   *Lindos* I. *Fouilles et recherches 1902-1914: les petits objets*. Berlin: W. de Gruyter.

Boehmer, R. M.

1972   *Bogazköy-Hattusa VII. Die Kleinfunde von Bogazköy aus den Grabungskampagnen 1931-1939 und 1952-1969*. Wissenschaftliche veröffentlichung der deutschen Orientgesellschaft 87. Berlin: Mann.

1979   *Bogazköy-Hattusa X. Die Kleinfunde aus der Unterstadt von Bogazköy. Grabungskampagnene 1970-1978*. Wissenschaftliche veröffentlichung der deutschen Orientgesellschaft 104. Berlin: Mann.

Boekschoten, G. J. and Sondaar, P. Y.

1972   On the Fossil Mammalia of Cyrprus (sic). *Proceedings of the Koninklijke Nederlanse Akademie voor Wetenschappen*, ser. B. no. 75, pp. 306-38. Amsterdam.

Bökönyi, S.

1969   Archaeological Problems and Methods of Recognizing Animal Domestication. In *The Domestication and Exploitation of Plants and*

Animals, ed. P. J. Ucko and G. W. Dimbleby, pp. 219-29. Chicago: Aldine.

Bonnichen, R.

    1973   Millie's Camp: An Experiment in Archaeology. *World Archaeology* 4:277-91.

Borchhardt, J.

    1972   *Homerische Helme. Helmformen der Ägäis in ihren Beziehungen zu orientalischen und europäischen Helmen in der Bronze- und frühen Eizenzeit*. Römisch-Germanisches Zentralmuseum Mainz. Mainz am Rhein.

Bowen, N. L. and Schairer, J. F.

    1932   The System, $FeO-SiO_2$. *American Journal of Science*, 5th series, 24:177-213.

Brooks, D.; Bieber, A. M., Jr.; Harbottle, G.; and Sayre, E. V.

    1974   Biblical Studies through Activation Analysis of Ancient Pottery. In *Archaeological Chemistry*, ed. C. W. Beck. Advances in Chemistry no. 138, pp. 48-80. Washington, D.C.: American Chemical Society.

Brothwell, D. F.

    1963   *Dental Anthropology*. Vol. 5. Symposium of the Society for the Study of Human Biology. New York: Pergamon Press.

Bruce, J. L.

    1937   Antiquities in the Mines of Cyprus. In *SCE* III, appendix V, pp. 639-71.

    1949   Cyprus Mines Copper Again. *Transactions of the American Institute of Mining and Metallurgical Engineers* 181:205-32.

Calvet, Y. and Yon, M.

    1977   La céramique des îles de l'Egée. In *Greek Geometric and Archaic Pottery Found in Cyprus*, ed. Gjerstad et al., pp. 12-13. Skrifter Utgivna av Svenska Institutet I Athen 26. Lund: Swedish Cyprus Expedition.

Carapanos, C.

    1878   *Dodone et ses ruines*. 2 vols. Paris: n.p.

Catling, H. W.

    1957   Neolithic Settlement Discovered. *Cyprus Pictorial* 1, no. 5.

    1963   Patterns of Settlement in Bronze Age Cyprus. *Opuscula Atheniensia* 4:129-69.

    1982   The Ancient Topography of the Yalias Valley. *RDAC*, pp. 227-36.

Chaplin, R. E.

1971 *The Study of Animal Bones from Archaeological Sites.* New York: Seminar Press.

1977 *Deer.* Poole, Dorset, England: Blandford Press.

Chaplin, R. E. and White, R. W. G.

1969 The Use of Tooth Eruption and Wear, Body Weight, and Antler Characteristics in the Age Estimation of Wild and Park Fallow Deer (*Dama dama*). *Proceedings of the Zoological Society of London* 157:125-32.

Chapman, D. and Chapman, N.

1975 *Fallow Deer: Their History, Distribution and Biology.* Lavenham, England: Terence Dalton.

Christodoulou, D.

1959 *The Evolution of the Rural Land Use Pattern in Cyprus.* World Land Use Survey, monograph 2. Bude (Cornwall), England: Geographical Publications.

1974 *Land Tenure in Cyprus.* Land Tenure Research Papers, no. 1. Land Consolidation Authority, Nicosia, Cyprus.

Cobham, C. D.

1908 *Excerpta Cypria.* New York: Cambridge-Kraus Reprinting Co, 1969.

Coghlan, H. H.

1951 *Notes on Prehistoric Metallurgy of Copper and Bronze in the Old World.* Technical Paper no. 4. Pitt Rivers Museum, Oxford, England.

Coldstream, J. N.

1968 *Greek Geometric Pottery.* London: Methuen and Co., Ltd.

1979 Geometric Skyphoi in Cyprus. *RDAC*, pp. 255-69.

Constantinou, G. and Govett, G.

1972 Genesis of Sulphide Deposits, Ochre and Umber of Cyprus. In *Transactions of the Institute of Mining and Metallurgy* 81:34-36. London.

1973 Geology, Geochemistry and Genesis of Cyprus Sulphide Deposits. *Economic Geology* 68:843-48.

Croft, P. W.

1979 Preliminary Comments on the Faunal Remains from Lemba Project Sites. In Lemba Archaeological Project, Cyprus, 1976-77: Preliminary Report, ed. E. J. Peltenburg. *Levant* 11:9-45.

1981   A Note on the Faunal Remains. In Lemba Archaeological Project, Cyprus, 1979: Preliminary Report, ed. E. J. Peltenburg. *Levant* 13:28-50.

1982   Faunal Remains from Tenta and Ayious. In Vasilikos Valley Project: Fourth Preliminary Report, 1979-1980, ed. I. A. Todd. *Journal of Field Archaeology* 9:36-77.

n.d.   The Antler Industry of Kissonerga-Mylouthkia. Unpublished ms.

Cullis, C. G. and Edge, A. B.

1927   *Cupriferous Deposits of Cyprus.* Crown Agents for the Colonies Report. London: Waterlow & Sons.

Dahl, J.

1979   X-ray Analysis of Trace Elements in Cypriot Copper Slags and Ores for Determination of Ancient Extractive Metallurgical Processes. Undergraduate independent research thesis. College of Wooster, Wooster, OH.

David, N.

1972   On the Life Span of Pottery, Type Frequencies, and Archaeological Inferences. *American Antiquity* 37:141-42.

David, N. and Hennig, H.

1972   *The Ethnography of Pottery: A Fulani Case Seen in Archaeological Perspective.* Addison-Wesley Modular Publications 21. Reading, Massachusetts.

Davies, O.

1929   The Copper Mines of Cyprus. *Annual of the British School of Athens* 29:74-85.

Davis, S. J. M.

1984   Khirokitia and its Mammal Remains. A Neolithic Noah's Ark. In *Fouilles récentes à Khirokitia (Chypre) 1977-1981.* Tomes 1-2, under the direction of A. Le Brun, pp. 147-62. Études néolithiques, Editions Recherche sur les Civilisations, memoire no. 41. Paris.

DeBoer, W. R. and Lathrap, D. W.

1976   The Making and Breaking of Shipibo-Conibo Ceramics. In *Ethnoarchaeology: Implications of Ethnography for Archaeology*, ed. C. Kramer, pp. 102-38. New York: Columbia University Press.

de Bruijn, M.; Korthoven, P. J. M.; van der Steen, A. J.; and Duin, R. P. W.

1974   The Use of Trace Element Concentrations in the Identification of Objects. Paper presented at the Symposium on Archaeometry and Archaeological Prospection, Oxford, March.

de Launay, M. L.

1889 Mémoire sur l'industrie du cuivre dans la région d'Huelva. *Annales de Mines* 16:427-515.

de Mas Latrie, M. L.

1855 *Histoire de l'île de Chypre.* Vol. 3. Documents, pp. 493-98, 528-36. Paris: L'imprimerie impériale.

Deonna, W.

1938 *Exploration archéologique de Délos*, fascicule XVIII. *Le Mobilier délien*, ed. E. de Boccard. Paris: Fontemoing and Cie.

di Cesnola, L. P.

1877 *Cyprus: Its Ancient Cities, Tombs, and Temples.* New York: Harper and Brothers.

1903 *A Descriptive Atlas of the Cesnola Collection of Cypriote Antiquities in the Metropolitan Museum of Art, New York.* Vol. 3, part 1. New York.

Dikaios, P.

1936 The Excavations at Erimi 1933-35. *RDAC*, pp. 1-81.

1953 *Khirokitia: Final Report on the Excavation of a Neolithic Settlement in Cyprus on Behalf of the Department of Antiquities, 1936-1946.* London, New York, and Toronto: Oxford University Press.

1961 *Sotira.* University of Pennsylvania Museum Monographs. Philadelphia.

1963 A "Royal" Tomb at Salamis, Cyprus. *Archäologische Anzeiger* 78, cols. 126-98.

1969a *Enkomi.* Vol. 1. Mainz am Rhein: Philipp von Zabern.

1969b *Enkomi.* Vol. 3a. Mainz am Rhein: Philipp von Zabern.

1971 *Enkomi.* Vol. 2. Mainz am Rhein: Philipp von Zabern.

Dikaios, P. and Stewart, J. R.

1962 *The Swedish Cyprus Expedition.* Vol. IV, part 1A. *The Stone Age and the Early Bronze Age in Cyprus.* Lund: Swedish Cyprus Expedition.

Ducos, P.

1965 Le Daim à Chypre aux époques préhistoriques. *RDAC*, pp. 1-8.

1968 L'Origine des animaux domestiques en Palestine. *Publications de l'Institut de préhistoire de l'Université de Bordeaux*, mémoire 6. Bordeaux: Delmas.

Elayi, J.

1980 Remarques sur un type de mur Phénicien. *Rivista di Studi Fenici* 8:165-80.

Emeleus, V. M.

    1960   Neutron Activation Analysis of Samian Ware Sherds. *Archaeometry* 3:16-19.

Flaksberger, C.

    1927   Wheats on the Island of Cyprus. *Cyprus Agricultural Journal* 22:3-18.

Forbes, R. J.

    1972   *Studies in Ancient Technology.* Vol. 9. *Copper.* Leiden: E. J. Brill.

Foster, G. M.

    1967   Introduction: What Is A Peasant? In *Peasant Society: A Reader*, ed. J. M. Potter, M. N. Diaz, and G. M. Foster, pp. 2-14. Boston: Little, Brown and Co.

French, D. H.

    1971   An Experiment in Water Sieving. *Anatolian Studies* 21:59-64.

Furumark, A.

    1941   *Mycenaean Pottery.* Stockholm: V. Pettersons.

    1965   Excavations at Sinda: Some Historical Results. *Opuscula Atheniensia* 6:99-116. Skrifter Utgivna av Svenska Institutet I Athen 10. Stockholm.

Furumark, A. and Adelman, C. M.

    Forthcoming   *Excavations at Sinda.*

Gaber-Saletan, P.

    1986   *Regional Styles in Cypriote Sculpture: The Sculptures from Idalion.* New York and London: Garland.

Gallin, B.

    1964   Chinese Peasant Values towards the Land. In *Symposium on Community Studies in Anthropology*, ed. V. E. Garfield, pp. 64-71. *Proceedings of the 1963 Annual Meeting of the American Ethnological Society.* Seattle and London: University of Washington Press.

Gamst, F.

    1974   *Peasants in Complex Society.* New York: Holt, Rinehart and Winston.

Geary, R. C.

    1936   Moments of the Ratio of the Mean Deviation in the Standard Deviation for Normal Samples. *Biometrika* 28:295-305.

Gilbert, B. M. and McKern, T. W.

    1973   A Method for Aging the Female Os Pubis. *American Journal of Physical Anthropology* 1:31-38.

Gjerstad, E.

    1948   *The Swedish Cyprus Expedition.* Vol. IV, part 2. *The Cypro-Geometric, Cypro-Archaic and Cypro-Classical Periods.* Stockholm: Swedish Cyprus Expedition.

    1979   The Phoenician Colonization and Expansion in Cyprus. *RDAC*, pp. 230-54.

Gjerstad, E.; Lindros, J.; Sjöqvist, E.; and Westholm, A.

    1934   *The Swedish Cyprus Expedition: Finds and Results of the Excavations in Cyprus 1927-1931.* Vol. I. Stockholm: Swedish Cyprus Expedition.

    1935   *The Swedish Cyprus Expedition: Finds and Results of the Excavations in Cyprus 1927-1931.* Vol. II. Stockholm: Swedish Cyprus Expedition.

    1937   *The Swedish Cyprus Expedition: Finds and Results of the Excavations in Cyprus 1927-1931.* Vol. III. Stockholm: Swedish Cyprus Expedition.

    1977   *Greek Geometric and Archaic Pottery Found in Cyprus.* Skrifter Utgivna av Svenska Institutet I Athen 26. Lund: Swedish Cyprus Expedition.

Gould, R. A.

    1968a   Chipping Stones in the Outback. *Natural History* 77:42-49.

    1968b   Living Archaeology: The Ngatatjara of Western Australia. *Southwestern Journal of Anthropology* 24:101-22.

    1971   The Archaeologist as Ethnographer: A Case Study from the Western Desert of Australia. *World Archaeology* 3:143-77.

Gowland, W.

    1906   Copper and Its Alloys in Prehistoric Times. *Journal of the Anthropological Institute of Great Britain and Ireland* 36:11-38.

Grayson, D. K.

    1973   On the Methodology of Faunal Analysis. *American Antiquity* 38:432-39.

    1978   Minimum Numbers and Sample Size in Vertebrate Faunal Analysis. *American Antiquity* 43:53-65.

Halstead, P.

    1977   A Preliminary Report on the Faunal Remains from Late Bronze Age Kouklia, Paphos. *RDAC*, pp. 261-75.

Harshman, E. N.

 1967 Genetic Implications of Some Elements Associated with Uranium Deposits. *U.S. Geological Survey Professional Paper* 550-C, pp. C167-C173. Washington, D.C.

Healy, J. F.

 1977 *Mining and Metallurgy in the Greek and Roman World*. London: Thames and Hudson.

Helbaek, H.

 1962 Late Cypriot Vegetable Diet at Apliki. *Opuscula Atheniensia* 4:171-86. Skrifter Utgivna av Svenska Institutet I Athen 8. Stockholm.

Hencken, H.

 1971 *The Earliest European Helmets: Bronze Age and Early Iron Age*. Harvard University, American School of Prehistoric Research, Peabody Museum, Bulletin no. 28. Cambridge, Massachusetts.

Hennessy, J. B.

 1963 *Stephania*. London: Colt Archaeological Institute Publications.

Herre, W.

 1969 The Science and History of Domestic Animals. In *Science in Archaeology: A Survey of Progress and Research*, ed. D. Brothwell and E. Higgs, pp. 257-72. Bristol, England: Thames and Hudson.

Heyd, W. T.

 1879 *Geschichte des Levantehandels im Mittelalter*. Vol. 2. Stuttgart: J. G. Cotta.

Higgs, E. S., et al.

 1968 Saliagos Animal Bones. In *Excavations at Saliagos near Antiparos*, ed. J. D. Evans and C. Renfrew. The British School of Archaeology at Athens. London: Thames and Hudson.

Higgs, E. S. and Jarman, M. R.

 1972 Origins of Animal and Plant Husbandry. In *Papers in Economic Prehistory*, ed. E. S. Higgs, pp. 3-13. Cambridge: Cambridge University Press.

Higgs, E. S. and Vita-Finzi, C.

 1972 Prehistoric Economies: A Territorial Approach. In *Papers in Economic Prehistory*, ed. E. S. Higgs, pp. 27-36. Cambridge: Cambridge University Press.

Hill, G. F.

    1904   *A Catalogue of the Greek Coins in the British Museum: Greek Coins of Cyprus.* London: British Museum.

    1940   *A History of Cyprus.* Vol. I. Cambridge: Cambridge University Press.

Hill, J. N.

    1966   A Prehistoric Community in Eastern Arizona. *Southwestern Journal of Anthropology* 22:9-30.

Hills, V. G.

    1928a   The Cyprus Mines Enterprise I. *Engineering and Mining Journal* 126:5-7.

    1928b   The Cyprus Mines Enterprise II. *Engineering and Mining Journal* 126:53-56.

Holmes, Y. L.

    1975   Foreign Trade in Cyprus during the Late Bronze Age. In *The Archaeology of Cyprus*, ed. N. Robertson, pp. 90-110. Park Ridge, New Jersey: Noyes Press.

Hopf, M.

    1969   Plant Remains and Early Farming in Jericho. In *The Domestication and Exploitation of Plants and Animals*, ed. P. J. Ucko and G. W. Dimbleby, pp. 355-59. Chicago: Aldine.

Jarman, M. R.

    1969   The Prehistory of Upper Pleistocene and Recent Cattle, pt. 1: East Mediterranean, with Reference to North-west Europe. *Proceedings of the Prehistoric Society* 35:236-66.

    1976   Animal Husbandry--The Early Stages. In *Origine de l'élevage et de la domestication*, ed. E. S. Higgs, pp. 22-50. Colloque XX de l'IXe Congrès de l'Union Internationale des Sciences Préhistoriques et Protohistoriques, Nice, 14 Septembre 1976.

Jarman, M. R. and Jarman, H. N.

    1968   The Fauna and Economy of Early Neolithic Knossos. *Annual of the British School of Archaeology at Athens* 63, pp. 241-64.

Jarman, H. N.; Legge, A. J.; and Charles, J. A.

    1972   Retrieval of Plant Remains from Archaeological Sites by Froth Flotation. In *Papers in Economic Prehistory*, ed. E. S. Higgs, pp. 39-48. Cambridge: Cambridge University Press.

Johnston, R. H.

    1974   The Cypriot Potter. In *Idalion* 1, chap. 7, pp. 130-39.

Karageorghis, V.

    1965   *Nouveaux documents pour l'étude du bronze récent à Chypre.* Ecole française d'Athènes, Etudes chypriotes 3. Paris.

    1967   *Excavations in the Necropolis of Salamis* I. Nicosia.

    1970   *Excavations in the Necropolis of Salamis* II. Nicosia.

    1974   *Excavations at Kition.* Vol. 1: *The Tombs.* Nicosia: Zavallis Press.

    1976   *Kition: Mycenaean and Phoenician Discoveries in Cyprus. New Aspects of Antiquity.* London: Thames and Hudson.

    1977   A 'Favissa' at Kakopetria. *RDAC*, pp. 178-201.

Karouzis, G.

    1977   *Land Ownership in Cyprus: Past and Present.* Nicosia: Strabo.

Keefe, E. K.; Cover, W. W.; Giloane, W.; Moore, James M., Jr.; Teleki, S.; and White, E. T.

    1971   *Area Handbook for Cyprus.* Washington, D.C.: U.S. Government Printing Office.

Kennedy, N.

    1894   Mining District of Huelva. *Mining Journal* 64, 10 February and 5 May. London.

King, J. E.

    1953   Mammal Bones from Khirokitia and Erimi. In Dikaios, *Khirokitia*, pp. 431-37. London, New York, and Toronto: Oxford University Press.

Klengel, H.

    1972   *The Art of Ancient Syria.* South Brunswick, England, and New York: A. S. Barnes.

Koucky, F. L. and Bullard, R. G.

    1974   The Geology of Idalion. In *Idalion* 1, chap. 2, pp. 11-25.

Kramer, C.

    1979   An Archaeological View of A Contemporary Kurdish Village: Domestic Architecture, Household Size and Wealth. In *Ethnoarchaeology: Implications of Ethnography for Archaeology*, ed. C. Kramer, pp. 139-63. New York: Columbia University Press.

Krogman, W. M.

    1973   *The Human Skeleton in Forensic Medicine.* Springfield, Illinois: Charles C. Thomas.

Kromann, A. and Mørkholm, O.

    1977   *Sylloge Nummorum Graecorum*. The Royal collection of Coins and Medals, Danish National Museum. *Egypt, The Ptolemies*. Copenhagen: 1977.

Kuhn, K. G.

    1821-33   *Claudii Galeni Opera Omnia* (in Greek and Latin). Vol. 12 (3rd chapter of Galen's 9th book). Leipzig: Lipsiae Knoblech.

Kurten, B.

    1959   Rates of Evolution in Fossil Mammals. *Cold Spring Harbor Symposium on Quantitative Biology* 24:205-15.

    1965   The Carnivora of the Palestine Caves. *Acta Zoologica Fennica* 107:1-74.

    1968   *Pleistocene Mammals of Europe*. Chicago: Aldine.

Lambros, P.

    1876   Τα ανέκδοτα νομίσματα τοῦ μεσαιωνικού βασιλείου της Κύπρου. Athens.

Lameere, W.

    1949   Au Temps ou Franz Cumot s'interrogeait sur Aristote. *L'Antiquité classique* 18:279-324.

Lamon, R. S. and Shipton, G. M.

    1939   *Megiddo I. Seasons of 1925-34. Strata I-V*. Oriental Institute Publications 42. Chicago: University of Chicago Press.

Lang, R. H.

    1878   Excavation of a Temple of Apollo at Dali (Idalion), Cyprus. *Transactions of the Royal Society of Literature*, series 2, 11:31-79. London.

Lange, F. W. and Rydberg, C. R.

    1972   Abandonment and Post Abandonment Behavior at a Rural Central American House Site. *American Antiquity* 37:419-34.

Lavender, D.

    1962   *The Story of Cyprus Mines Corporation*. San Marino, California: Huntington Press.

Le Brun, A.

    1984   *Fouilles récentes à Khirokitia (Chypre) 1977-1981*. Tomes 1-2. Études néolithiques, Editions Recherche sur les Civilisations, mémoire 41. Paris.

Lee, R. B.

    1969   !Kung Bushmen Subsistence: An Input-Output Analysis. In *Environment and Cultural Behavior*, ed. a. P. Vayda, pp. 47-79. Garden City, New York: Natural History Press.

Lee, R. B. and DeVore, I., eds.

    1968   *Man the Hunter.* Chicago: Aldine.

Lehavy, Y. M.

    1974   Excavations at Neolithic Dhali-Agridhi: Excavation Report. In *Idalion* 1, chap. 4, pt. 1, pp. 95-102.

Longacre, W. A.

    1968   Some Aspects of Prehistoric Society in East-Central Arizona. In *New Perspectives in Archaeology*, ed. S. R. Binford and L. R. Binford, pp. 89-102. Chicago: Aldine.

Longuet, H.

    1961   *Introduction à la numismatique byzantine.* London: Spink.

Lopez, R. S. and Raymond, I. W.

    1965   *Medieval Trade in the Mediterranean World.* Columbia University Records of Civilization Studies. New York: W. W. Norton & Co.

Lusignano, S.

    1580   *Description de tout l'isle de Chypre et des roys, princes, et seigneurs, tant payens que chrestiens, qui ont command'e en icelle.* Paris: Chez Guillaume Chaudière.

Macalister, R. A. S.

    1912   *The Excavation of Gezer 1902-1905 and 1907-1909.* Vols. 1-3. London: John Murray.

MacArthur, R. H. and Wilson, E. O.

    1967   *The Theory of Island Biogeography.* Princeton, New Jersey: Princeton University Press.

Maier, F. G.

    1985   Factoids in Ancient History: The Case of Fifth-century Cyprus. *Journal of Hellenic Studies* 105:32-39.

Malouf, E. E.

    1971   Role of Microorganisms in Chemical Mining. *Mining Engineering* 23:43-46.

Marvin, M.

    1974   History of the Site of Idalion. In *Idalion* 1, Introduction, pt. 2, pp. XXII-XXVIII.

Masson, O.

    1961   *Les inscriptions chypriotes syllabiques.* Paris: Editions E. de Boccard.

Matson, F. R.

    1965   Ceramic Ecology: An Approach to the Study of the Early Cultures of the Near East. In *Ceramics and Man*, ed. F. R. Matson, pp. 202-17. Viking Fund Publications in Anthropology no. 41, New York. Chicago: Aldine.

    1973   The Potters of Chalkis. In *Classics and the Classical Tradition*, ed. E. N. Borza and R. W. Carruba, pp. 117-42. University Park: Pennsylvania State University.

Mattingly, H.; Sutherland, C.; and Carson, R.

    1951   *The Roman Imperial Coinage in the British Museum.* Vol. 9. London: Spink.

Mattingly, H.; Sydenham, E.; and Sutherland, C.

    1949   *The Roman Imperial Coinage in the British Museum.* Vol. 4, part 3. London: Spink.

McKern, T. W. and Stewart, T. D.

    1957   *Skeletal Age Changes in Young American Males, Analyzed from the Standpoint of Identification.* Technical Report EP-45. Headquarters Quartermaster Research and Development Command. Natick, Massachusetts.

Meulengracht, A.; McGovern, P.; and Lawn, B.

    1981   University of Pennsylvania Radiocarbon Dates XXI. *Radiocarbon* 23:227-40.

Michaelidou-Nicolaou, I.

    1969-1970   Giande Missili di Cipro. *Annuario della R. Scuola Archeologica di Atene*, n.s. 31-32, 359-69.

Muhly, J. D.

    1969   Copper and Tin: The Distribution of Mineral Resources and the Nature of the Metals Trade in the Bronze Age. Ph.D. dissertation, Yale University, New Haven, Connecticut.

Müller, L.

    1855   *Numismatique d'Alexandre le Grand.* Copenhagen: B. Luno. (Reprint, Chicago, 1981, from original edition.)

Muscarella, O. W.

    1967   *Phrygian Fibulae from Gordion.* Colt Archaeological Institute Monograph Series 4. London.

Newell, E. T.

    1915   Some Cypriote "Alexanders." *Numismatic Chronicle*, 4th series, 15:294-322.

1927 *The Coinages of Demetrius Poliorcetes.* London: 1927.

Nicolaou, I.

1968 Inscriptiones Cypriae Alphabeticae VII, 1967. *RDAC*, pp. 72-83

1972 Inscriptiones Cypriae Alphabeticae XI, 1971. *RDAC*, pp. 251-63.

1977 Inscriptiones Cypriae Alphabeticae XVI, 1976. *RDAC*, pp. 209-20.

1979 Inscriptiones Cypriae Alphabeticae XVIII, 1978. *RDAC*, pp. 344-50.

1980 Inscriptiones Cypriae Alphabeticae XIX, 1979. *RDAC*, pp. 260-66.

Nicolaou, K.

1967 The Distribution of Settlements in Stone Age Cyprus. *Kypriakai Spoudai.* Bulletin of the Hetaireia Kypriakon Spoudon. Vol. 31, pp. 37-52. Nicosia.

Nobis, G.

1977 Tierreste aus Tamassos auf Zypern. *Acta Praehistorica et Archaeologica* 7/8, pp. 271-300.

O'Connell, J.

1977 Untitled paper. Presented as part of B. Hayden and J. O'Connell, Ethnoarchaeology in Australia: A review. Paper delivered at the 42nd Annual Meeting of the Society for American Archaeology, New Orleans.

Ohnefalsch-Richter, M.

1893 *Kypros, the Bible, and Homer.* London: Asher and Co.

1899 Neues über die auf Cypern mit Unterstützung seiner Majestät des Kaisers, der Berliner Museen und der Rudolf-Virchow-Stiftung angestellten Ausgrabungen. 25. Die Fibeln und die Haken-Kreuze. *Zeitschrift für Ethnologie* 31:338-45.

Oppenheim, A. L.

1969 Babylonian and Assyrian Historical Texts. In *Ancient Near Eastern Texts Relating to the Old Testament*, ed. J. B. Pritchard, pp. 265-317. Princeton, New Jersey: Princeton University Press.

Pantazis, T. M.

1967 The Geology and Mineral Resources of Pharmakas-Kalavasos Area. *Geological Survey of Cyprus.* Memoir 8. Nicosia, Cyprus.

Papadopoullos, T.

1965 *Social and Historical Data on Population (1570-1881).* Texts and Studies of the History of Cyprus. Vol. 1. Cyprus Research Centre. Nicosia, Cyprus.

Partington, J. R.

1970 *A History of Chemistry*. 3 vols. London: Macmillan and Co.

Payne, S.

1972a Partial Recovery and Sample Bias: The Results of Some Sieving Experiments. In *Papers in Economic Prehistory*, ed. E. S. Higgs, pp. 49-64. Cambridge: Cambridge University Press.

1972b On the Interpretation of Bone Samples from Archaeological Sites. In *Papers in Economic Prehistory*, ed. E. S. Higgs, pp. 65-81. Cambridge: Cambridge University Press.

1975 Partial Recovery and Sample Bias. In *Archaeozoological Studies*, ed. A. T. Clason, pp. 7-17. Amsterdam: North-Holland Publishing Co.

Peckham, J. B.

1968 *The Development of the Late Phoenician Scripts*. Cambridge, Massachusetts: Harvard University Press.

Peltenburg, E. J.

1978 Excavations at Lemba-Lakkous, Cyprus. Lecture presented at Harvard University's Peabody Museum, 27 April; unpublished.

1980 Lemba Archaeological Project, Cyprus, 1978. *Levant* 12:1-21.

Pegolotti, F. B.

1340 *The Practice of Commerce*. Florence. (Reprint, *La practica della mercatura*, ed. A. Evans. Cambridge, Massachusetts, 1936.)

Peristiany, J. G.

1968 Introduction to a Cyprus Highland Village. In *Contributions to Mediterranean Sociology*, ed. J. G. Peristiany, pp. 75-91. Paris and the Hague: Mouton.

Perlman, I. and Asaro, F.

1969 Pottery Analysis by Neutron Activation. *Archaeometry* 11:21-25.

Petrie, W. M. F.

1928 *Gerar*. British School of Archaeology in Egypt, no. 43. London.

1934 *Ancient Gaza* IV. *Tell el 'Ajjul*. British School of Archaeology in Egypt, no. 56. London.

Pielou, E. C.

1967 The Use of Information Theory in the Study of the Diversity of Biological Populations. *Proceedings of the 5th Berkeley Symposium on Mathematical Statistics and Probability* 4:163-77.

1969 *An Introduction to Mathematical Ecology*. New York: John Wiley.

Poole, R. S.

    1883   *A Catalogue of the Greek Coins in the British Museum: The Ptolemies Kings of Egypt.* London.

Porada, E.

    1948   The Cylinder Seals of the Late Cypriote Bronze Age. *American Journal of Archaeology* 52:178-98.

Poursat, J.-C.

    1977   *Catalogue des ivoires mycéniens du Musée national d'Athènes.* Paris: Dépositaire, Diffusion de Boccard.

Pryce, F. N.

    1931   *Catalogue of Sculpture in the Department of Greek and Roman Antiquities.* Vol. 1, pt. 2. London: British Museum.

Purcell, H. D.

    1968   *Cyprus.* New York and Washington: Frederick Praeger.

Redman, C. L.

    1978   *The Rise of Civilization.* San Francisco, California: Freeman.

Reed, C. A.

    1961   Osteological Evidences for Prehistoric Domestication in Southwestern Asia. *Zeitschrift für Tierzüchtung und Züchtungsbiologie* 76:31-38.

Renfrew, J. M.

    1973   *Paleoethnobotany, The Prehistoric Food Plants of the Near East and Europe.* New York: Columbia University Press.

Renfrew, C.; Dixon, J. E.; and Cann, J. R.

    1968   Further Analysis of Near Eastern Obsidian. *Proceedings of the Prehistoric Society* 34:319-31.

Rickard, T. A.

    1930   Copper mining in Cyprus. *Transactions of the Institute of Mining and Metallurgy* 34:285-315. London.

Robertson, A. H. F.

    1978   Metallogenesis along a Fossil Oceanic Fracture Zone: Arakapas Fault Belt, Troodos Massif, Cyprus. *Earth Planet Science Letters* 41:317-29.

Robinson, D. M.

    1941   *Excavations at Olynthus* X. *Metal and Minor Miscellaneous Finds.* Baltimore, Maryland: Johns Hopkins Press.

Rothenberg, B.

 1972 *Timna Valley of the Biblical Copper Mines.* London: Thames & Hudson.

Rupp, D.

 1987 Vive le Roi: The Emergence of the State in Iron Age Cyprus. In *Western Cyprus Connections: An Archaeological Symposium*, ed. D. Rupp, pp. 147-68. Studies in Mediterranean Archaeology. Vol. LXXVII. Göteborg.

Saxon, E. C.; with contributions by Close, A.; Cluzel, C.; Morse, V.; and Shackleton, N. J.

 1974 Results of Recent Investigations at Tamar Hat. *Libyca* 22:49-92.

Sayre, E. V. and Dodson, R. W.

 1957 Neutron Activation Study of Mediterranean Potsherds. *American Journal of Archaeology* 61:35-41.

Sayre, E. V.; Murrenhof, A.; and Weick, C. F.

 1958 The Nondestructive Analysis of Ancient Potsherds through Neutron Activation. Brookhaven National Laboratory, Upton, Long Island, New York.

Schaeffer, C. F. A.

 1936 L'Age des mines de cuivre de Chypre. In *Missions en Chypre, 1932-1935*, chap. 7. Académie des Inscriptions et Belles Lettres. Paris: Librairie Oriental.

Schachermeyr, F.

 1976 *Die ägäische Frühzeit.* Vol. 2: *Die mykenische Zeit und die Gesittung von Thera.* Österreichische Akademie der Wissenschaften, Philosophisch-Historische Klass Sitzungsberichte, vol. 309. Vienna.

Schiffer, M. B.

 1972 Archaeological Context and Systemic Context. *American Antiquity* 37:156-65.

Schlour, H.

 1941 The Development of Human Dentition. *Journal of the American Dental Association* 28:1133-60.

Schlumberger, G. L.

 1954 *Numismatique de l'Orient latin.* Graz, Austria: Akademische Druck- u. Verlagsanstalt.

Schmidt, E. F.

 1957 *Persepolis* II. *Contents of the Treasury and Other Discoveries.* Oriental Institute Publications 69. Chicago: University of Chicago Press.

Schwartz, J. H.

- 1973 The Palaeozoology of Cyprus: A Preliminary Report on Recently Analysed Sites. *World Archaeology* 5:215-20.
- 1974a Excavations at Neolithic Dhali-Agridhi: Faunal List. In *Idalion* 1, chap. 4, pt. 2, pp. 103-18.
- 1974b The Paleo-osteology of Cyprus. In *Idalion* 1, chap. 5, pp. 119-21.
- 1974c The Human Remains from Kition and Hala Sultan Tekke: A Cultural Interpretation. In *Excavations at Kition*. Vol. 1: *The tombs*, V. Karageorghis, pp. 151-62, appendix IV. Nicosia: Zavallis Press.

Shannon, C. E. and Weaver, W.

- 1949 *The Mathematical Theory of Communication*. Urbana, Illinois: University of Illinois Press.

Silver, I. A.

- 1969 The Ageing of Domestic Animals. In *Science in Archaeology: A Survey of Progress and Research*, ed. D. Brothwell and E. Higgs, pp. 283-302. Bristol, England: Thames & Hudson.

Smith, C.

- 1978 The Beginnings of Industrial Electrochemistry. In *History of Electrochemistry*, ed. G. Dubberrell and J. H. Westbrook, pp. 360-99. New York: Electrochemical Society.

Snodgrass, A.

- 1964 *Early Greek Armour and Weapons From the End of the Bronze Age to 600 B. C.* Edinburgh: University Press.
- 1967 *Arms and Armour of the Greeks*. London: Thames and Hudson.

Sonniti, G.

- 1801 *Travels in Greece and Turkey*.

Stager, L. E.

- 1985 The Archaeology of the Family in Ancient Israel. *BASOR* 260:1-35.

Stager, L. E.; Walker, A.; and Wright, G. E.

- 1974 *American Expedition to Idalion, Cyprus. First Preliminary Report: Seasons of 1971 and 1972. BASOR* Supplement 18. Cambridge, Massachusetts: American Schools of Oriental Research.

Stanislawski, M. B.

- 1969a What Good Is A Broken Pot? An Experiment in Hopi-Tewa Ethnoarchaeology. *Southwestern Lore* 35:11-18.
- 1969b The Ethno-archaeology of Hopi Pottery Making. *Plateau* 42:27-33.

Stanley Price, N. P.

 1972a P. Dikaios and the Development of Cypriot Prehistory. *Kypriakai Spoudai*, Bulletin of the Hetaireia Kypriakon Spoudon. Vol. 36, pp. 39-45.

 1972b A Prehistoric Survey of the Analiondas Region. *RDAC*, pp. 15-21.

 1977a Khirokitia and the Initial Settlement of Cyprus. *Levant* 9:66-89.

 1977b Colonization and Continuity in the Early Prehistory of Cyprus. *World Archaeology* 9:27-41.

 1979 *Early Prehistoric Settlement in Cyprus*. British Archaeological Reports, International Series, no. 65. Oxford.

Stavrinou, Y. H.

 1970 *Annual Report of the Geological Survey of Cyprus Department for 1969*. Nicosia.

Steinberg, A. R. and Koucky, F. L.

 1974 Preliminary Metallurgical Research on the Ancient Cypriot Copper Industry. In *Idalion* 1, chap. 9, pp. 149-78.

Stern, E.

 1977 The Excavations at Tell Mevorach and the Later Phoenician Elements in the Architecture of Palestine. *BASOR* 225:17-27.

Stewart, R. T.

 1974 Paleobotanic Investigation: 1972 Season. In *Idalion* 1, chap. 6, pp. 123-29.

 1976 Paleobotanical Report--Cayönü 1972. *Economic Botany* 30:219-25.

Stronach, D.

 1959 The Development of the Fibula in the Near East. *Iraq* 21:181-206.

 1978 *Pasargadae: A Report on the Excavations Conducted by the British Institute of Persian Studies From 1961 to 1963*. New York: Clarendon Press.

Sutherland, C. and Carson, R.

 1966 *The Roman Imperial Coinage in the British Museum*. Vol. 7. London: Spink.

Svoronos, J.

 1904 Τα νομίσματα τοῦ κράτους τῶν πτολεμαίων. Athens.

Taylor, J. du P.

    1952   A Late Bronze Age Settlement at Apliki, Cyprus. *Antiquaries Journal* 32:133-67, pls. XXIV-XXIX.

Todd, I. A.

    1977   Vasilikos Valley Project: First Preliminary Report 1976. *RDAC*, pp. 5-32.

    1982   Radiocarbon Dates for Kalavasos-Tenta and Kalavasos-Ayious. *RDAC*, pp. 8-11.

Trennery, T. C. and Pocock, B. G.

    1972   Mining and Milling Operations at Limni Mines, Cyprus. *Transactions of the Institute of Mining and Metallurgy* 81:A1-A10.

Tylecote, R. F.

    1971   Observations on Cypriotic Copper Smelting. *RDAC*, pp. 53-58.

    1976   *A History of Metallurgy*. London: The Metals Society.

Uerpmann, H.-P.

    1972   Animal Bone Finds and Economic Archaeology: A Critical Study of "Osteoarchaeological" Method. *World Archaeology* 4:307-22.

Van Beek, G. W.

    1951   Cypriote Chronology and the Dating of Iron I Sites in Palestine. *BASOR* 124:26-29.

Van Beek, G. W. and Van Beek, O.

    1981   Canaanite-Phoenician Architecture: The Development of Two Styles. *Eretz-Israel* 15:70-79.

Vermeule, C. C.

    1974   Cypriote Sculpture, the Late Archaic and Early Classical Periods: Towards a More Precise Understanding. *American Journal of Archaeology* 78:287-90.

Vessberg, O. and Westholm, A.

    1956   *The Swedish Cyprus Expedition*. Vol. IV, part 3. *The Hellenistic and Roman Periods in Cyprus*. Lund: Swedish Cyprus Expedition.

Waldbaum, J. C.

    1983   *Metalwork from Sardis: The Finds Through 1974*. Archaeological Exploration of Sardis Monograph 8. Cambridge, Massachusetts: Harvard University Press.

Walker, A. and Koucky, F. L.

    1976   Survey and Excavation in the Idalion Area, Cyprus, Summer 1975. [*Abstracts of Papers Presented at the*] Seventy-seventh General Meeting of the Archaeological Institute of America, p. 27. Washington, D.C.

Walsh, J.

    1929   Galen Visits the Dead Sea and the Copper mines of Cyprus (166 A.D.). *Bulletin of the Geographical Society of Philadelphia* 35:92-110.

Ward, G. K.

    1974   A Systematic Approach to the Definition of Sources of Raw Material. *Archaeometry* 16:41-53.

Watkins, T. F.

    1970   Philia-Drakos Site-A: Pottery, Stratigraphy, Chronology. *RDAC*, pp. 1-9.

    1972   Cypriot Neolithic Chronology and the Pottery from Philia-Drakos A. Praktikon Tou Proto Diethnous Kuprologikou Sunedriou, Tómos A', Leukosia, 1972, pp. 167-174. Nicosia, Cyprus.

    1973   Some Problems of the Neolithic and Chalcolithic Periods in Cyprus. *RDAC*, pp. 34-61.

Watson, J. P. N.; Stanley Price, N. P.; and Arnold, E. N.

    1977   The Vertebrate Fauna from the 1972 Sounding at Khirokitia. *RDAC*, pp. 232-60.

Wertime, T. A. and Wertime, S. F.

    1982   *Early Pyrotechnology: The Evolution of the First Fire-Using Industries.* Washington, D.C.: Smithsonian Institute Press.

Whallon, R., Jr.

    1973   Spatial Analysis of Occupation Floors I: Application of Dimensional Analysis of Variance. *American Antiquity* 38:266-78.

    1974   Spatial Analysis of Occupation Floors II: The Application of Nearest Neighbor Analysis. *American Antiquity* 39:16-34.

Williams, D.

    1934   The Geology of Rio Tinto Mines, Spain. *Transactions of the Institute of Mining and Metallurgy* 43:2-48.

Wilmsen, E. N.

    1973   Interaction, Spacing Behavior, and the Organization of Hunting Bands. *Journal of Anthropological Research* 29:1-31.

Wolf, E.

    1966   *Peasants.* Englewood Cliffs, New Jersey: Prentice Hall.

Woolley, C. L.

1939   The Excavations at Al Mina, Sueidia. I. The Archaeological Report. *Journal of Hellenic Studies* 58:1-30. II. *Journal of Hellenic Studies* 58:133-70.

Wright, G. E. and Gjerstad, E.

1953   Correspondence with Professor Einar Gjerstad on the Chronology of "Cypriote" Pottery from Early Iron Levels in Palestine. *BASOR* 130:22-26.

Wroth, W.

1908   *Imperial Byzantine Coins in the British Museum* 1-2. London.

Zeuner, F. E.

1958   Animal Remains from a Late Bronze Age Sanctuary on Cyprus, and the Problem of the Domestication of Fallow Deer. *Journal of the Palaeontological Society of India* 3:131-35.

Zipf, G. K.

1949   *Human Behavior and the Principle of Least Effort: An Introduction to Human Ecology.* Cambridge, Massachusetts: Addison-Wesley.

Zohary, D., and Hopf, M.

1973   Domestication of Pulses in the Old World. *Science* 182:887-94.

Zwicker, V.; Grembler, E.; and Röllig, H.

1977   Investigations of Copper Slags from Cyprus, Second Report. *RDAC*, pp. 309-16.

GENERAL INDEX

A

aceramic Neolithic, 204, 205, 211, 220, 459
Achaemenid, 331, 332, 336
Acomys didimatus, 244
activity area, 414
agate, 207
agriculture, 408, 409, 430, 432, 433, 434, 435, 437, 463
Alexander I, 453, 455
Alexander the Great, 448, 449, 450, 453, 456
Alexius I, 451, 456
anemia, 129
ankh, 448, 451, 455
Antigonus I, 449, 451, 456
antler(s), 209, 247, 248, 250, 259, 262, 264, 265, 268
Aphrodite, 387, 388, 449, 452
Apollo Amyklos, 400, 462
ard, 430
arrowhead(s), 328, 329, 330, 331, 332, 335, 348, 349, 350
Arsinoe III, 447, 448, 453
ashlar(s), 5, 6, 7, 8, 10, 12, 13, 14, 15, 16, 17, 18, 38, 42, 47, 50, 54, 56, 57, 462, 463
Assyrian, 335, 336
azurite, 278, 308

B

Baᶜalmilk I, 464
Babylonian, 280
Basil II, 454
Bastion, 5, 13, 19, 45, 46, 47, 48, 50, 56, 57, 462, 463
bats, 244
Baudouin II, 451, 455, 456
"bead-and-collar", 62
Bergmann's rule, 249
Biconical, 142
bird(s), 151, 164
blue chalcanthum, 296
blue vitriol, 281, 294, 295, 296, 297, 300
bone tools, 209
Bos, 244
Bos taurus, 250
bronchantite, 295
Bronze Age, 1, 86, 126, 129, 138, 151, 155, 210, 212, 249, 250, 268, 283, 333, 335, 342, 343, 426, 427, 428, 429, 430, 433, 434, 460, 461
Bronze Tablet, 464, 465
Byzantine, 280, 426, 427, 429

C

C^{14}, 203, 204, 206, 211, 459, 460
C-zone soil, 46
caduceus, 449, 451
Caesarion, 452

Canis familiaris, 70
Capra, 212, 246
Capra hircus, 245, 246
Capreolus, 244, 264
Capreolus capreolus, 244
Caprine(s), 220, 260, 263, 264
Carabelli's cusp(s), 126
celadon, 163
cement, 6, 8, 10, 11, 12, 282, 414
cementation, 285, 291, 326
ceramic Neolithic, 204, 205, 209, 220, 459, 460
ceramics:
    Apliki Ware, 157
    Attic Black Glaze, 163, 165
    Attic Middle Geometric, 59
    Base Ring, 139, 140, 145, 146, 147, 149, 150, 157, 162, 173, 203
    Base Ring II, 140, 157, 162, 173, 203
    Base Ring III, 157
    Bichrome, 18, 83, 87, 88, 89, 90, 91, 92, 96, 151, 155, 163, 377, 378, 379, 380, 381, 382, 383, 384, 385, 386, 387, 389, 390, 391, 392, 393, 394, 395, 396, 397
    Bichrome IV, 89, 92, 96, 379, 380, 381, 382, 384, 385, 387, 389, 390, 392, 394, 395, 396
    Bichrome Red, 18, 88, 89, 91, 92, 382, 385, 392, 393, 395
    Bichrome Red III(VI), 88, 393
    Bichrome Red II(V), 89, 395
    Bichrome Red IV, 91
    Bichrome V, 83, 87, 89, 90, 92, 381, 382, 386, 389, 390, 396
    Black Bucchero, 382, 392, 397
    Black Figured, 380, 394
    Black Glazed, 7, 10, 12, 28, 86, 87, 89, 92, 361, 378, 379, 380, 382, 393, 396
    Black Lustrous, 379, 380, 391, 393, 394, 396
    Black Polished, 86, 381, 389, 394, 397
    Black Polished II, 389
    Black Polished III(V), 86
    Black Slip, 90, 138, 150, 156, 169, 203, 381, 382, 386, 388, 389, 390, 392, 395, 397
    Black Slip III-IV, 90
    Black Slip IV, 138, 156, 169, 203, 381, 390
    Black Slip Wheelmade, 162
    Black-on-Red, 18, 87, 88, 89, 91, 92, 96, 155, 163, 366, 368, 369, 370, 371, 377, 379, 380, 381, 382, 383, 384, 385, 386, 387, 389, 390, 391, 392, 395, 396, 397
    Black-on-Red I, 390, 395
    Black-on-Red II, 92, 96, 389, 390, 392, 396, 397
    Black-on-Red III(V), 87, 88, 89, 91, 390, 395, 397
    Brown Slip Monochrome, 387, 392
    Bucchero Handmade, 150, 162, 193, 203
    Bucchero Ware, 162
    Bucchero Wheelmade, 150, 162, 203
    Coarse Gray, 379, 380, 396
    Coarse Monochrome, 139, 156, 157, 169, 203
    Coarse Ware, 85, 86, 87, 88, 89, 90, 91, 92, 94, 95, 146, 159, 210, 380, 396
    Crisp Ware, 387, 395
    Cypro-Mycenaean, 160
    Cypro-Mycenaean IIIA2/IIIB, 160
    Cypro-Mycénienne, 160
    Dark-faced Burnished Ware (DFBW), 203, 209, 210, 211, 230, 231, 242, 459, 460
    East Greek, 163, 165
    Foreign Ware, 382, 396
    Glaze ware, 163

ceramics (cont.):
    Gray and Black, 86, 140, 397
    Gray and Black Polished, 397, 86
    Gray/Black Polished, 394
    Greek Geometric, 46, 47, 58, 60, 61
    Levanto-Mycenaean, 148, 149, 155, 159, 160, 161, 166, 189, 191, 203
    Levanto-/Cypro-Mycenaean, 161
    Meniko Ware, 387, 395
    Milk Bowl, 386, 395
    Monochrome, 139, 155, 156, 157, 169, 171, 203, 386, 391, 459
    Painted Monochrome, 139, 157, 171, 203
    Painted Ware, 93, 379, 394
    Pithos Ware, 159
    Plain White, 10, 12, 18, 85, 86, 87, 88, 89, 90, 91, 92, 93, 95, 96, 141, 142, 143, 144, 145, 155, 156, 158, 159, 160, 163, 166, 175, 177, 179, 181, 183, 203, 380, 383, 384, 385, 387, 388, 389, 390, 392, 393, 394, 395, 396, 397
    Plain White Handmade, 141, 142, 143, 144, 155, 156, 158, 166, 175, 177, 179, 181, 203
    Plain White IV-V, 91
    Plain White V, 18, 85, 86, 87, 88, 89, 90, 91, 92, 95, 380, 385, 389, 390, 392, 395, 396
    Plain White VI, 12, 85, 86, 87, 88, 89, 91, 92, 380, 383, 384, 389, 393, 394, 396, 397
    Plain White VI-VII, 12, 87
    Plain White VII, 389, 393, 394, 396, 397
    Plain White Wheelmade, 145, 158, 159, 160, 166, 183, 203
    Plain White Wheelmade I, 158, 159
    Plain White Wheelmade II, 145, 158, 159, 183, 203
    Red Bichrome, 379, 396
    Red Figured, 10
    Red Lustrous, 379, 393, 394, 396
    Red Slip, 85, 86, 87, 88, 89, 90, 91, 92, 144, 155, 158, 368, 379, 382, 383, 396, 397
    Red Slip II, 89, 90, 91, 396, 397
    Red Slip III(V), 85, 86, 87, 88, 89, 90, 91, 92
    Sinda Ware, 159
    Terra Sigillata, 379, 380, 392, 394, 397
    Wheelmade, 98, 100, 102, 104, 106, 108, 110, 112, 145, 146, 147, 148, 149, 150, 155, 158, 159, 160, 162, 166, 183, 185, 187, 203
    White Handmade, 156
    White Painted, 83, 85, 86, 87, 88, 89, 90, 91, 92, 93, 95, 96, 97, 146, 147, 148, 155, 158, 159, 162, 163, 166, 185, 187, 203, 377, 378, 380, 381, 382, 383, 384, 385, 387, 389, 390, 391, 392, 393, 394, 395, 396, 397
    White Painted III, 92, 97, 390, 395
    White Painted IV, 85, 86, 87, 88, 89, 91, 92, 389, 390, 391, 392, 395, 396, 397
    White Painted V, 83, 85, 86, 87, 88, 89, 90, 91, 92, 95, 385, 389, 390, 392, 395, 397
    White Painted Wheelmade III, 160, 165
    White Shaved, 138, 156
    White Slip, 86, 87, 89, 91, 140, 157, 158, 171, 203, 379, 396, 461
    White Slip II, 140, 157, 158, 171, 203, 461
cereal(s), 208, 431, 432, 436, 463
Cervus, 244, 250, 264
Cervus elaphus, 244, 249, 250
chalcedony, 207, 277, 287, 302
chalcolite, 286
Chalcolithic, 277, 300
chalcopyrite, 286
cheekpiece(s), 10, 328, 334, 335, 336, 348
chert, 11, 98, 100, 204, 207, 208, 214, 215, 287
chrysocolla, 286
Classical, 427

Cleopatra VII, 452, 456
compound(s), 70, 71, 72, 401, 407, 408, 409, 410, 411, 412, 413, 414, 415, 416, 417, 419, 420, 421, 422, 423, 424, 427, 428, 444
concrete, 8, 10, 11, 12, 13, 15, 35, 427, 428
Constantine I, 451, 453, 456
Constantine IX, 454, 456
Constantine VII, 456
Constantine VIII, 454
copper sulfate, 296
crab, 220
cranial deformation, 129
Crosidura russula, 244
Crustacea, 245
curbstone, 6, 7, 32
cylinder seal, 120, 121, 151, 164, 198
Cypro-Archaic, 10, 12, 18, 20, 46, 47, 58, 59, 62, 63, 90, 96, 97, 151, 164, 165, 282, 283, 287, 288, 322, 329, 331, 366, 367, 368, 369, 370, 371, 377, 378, 379, 380, 381, 382, 383, 384, 385, 386, 387, 388, 389, 390, 391, 392, 393, 394, 395, 396, 397, 401, 461, 462, 463, 464
Cypro-Archaic I-II, 20
Cypro-Archaic II, 12, 18, 20, 46, 47, 97, 331, 380, 381, 382, 383, 385, 386, 387, 388, 389, 390, 392, 395, 396, 397, 462, 463, 464
Cypro-Archaic style, 401
Cypro-Classical, 5, 6, 7, 8, 10, 11, 18, 20, 34, 35, 47, 48, 62, 97, 163, 329, 330, 331, 334, 340, 367, 368, 377, 379, 380, 382, 383, 384, 389, 390, 391, 392, 393, 394, 396, 397, 399, 463
Cypro-Classical I, 18, 20, 47, 48, 380, 382, 383, 384, 389, 393, 394, 396, 397, 463
Cypro-Classical II, 7, 10, 330, 331, 380, 382, 383, 384, 389, 393, 394, 396, 397
Cypro-Geometric, 96, 97
Cypro-Geometric I, 386, 395, 461
Cypro-Geometric II, 386, 389, 390, 395, 396
Cypro-Geometric III-Cypro-Archaic I, 17
Cypro-Phoenician, 367, 370
Cypro-syllabic, 11, 12, 13, 37, 465
Cypro-syllabic inscription, 37

D

Dama, 250, 251, 264
Dama dama mesopotamica, 249, 254, 255, 256, 257
Dama mesopotamica, 244, 245, 246, 247, 248, 249, 250, 254, 255, 256, 257, 268, 459
deer, 250
deforestation, 433
Dhali-Agridhi:
    Concentration A, 204, 205, 209, 216, 230, 232
    Concentration B, 204, 205, 206, 216
    Site E, 204, 205, 206, 207, 208, 216, 222, 223, 235, 236
domestic precinct(s), 83, 462, 463
domestication, 212
donkeys, 431, 463
dowry, 409
drafted ashlars, 17

E

Early Classical period, 398
Early Hellenistic, 329, 333, 334, 345, 380, 394, 396
Early Prehistoric, 261, 264, 265, 269

East Acropolis, 1, 13, 462
East Terrace, 1, 330, 337, 338, 341, 343, 348
Elaphus cypriotes, 244
Enkomi, Level IIB, 157, 160, 165
Enkomi, Level IIIA, 159
Equus, 244, 264
Evagoras II, 447, 448, 449, 450, 451, 455, 456

F

fauna, 244, 247, 259, 261, 264, 459, 460
fibula(e), 46, 62, 63, 65, 131, 342, 346, 348, 366
fish, 211
flint(s), 204, 205, 206, 207, 208, 209, 211, 212, 224, 431
fortification system, 18, 45, 46, 47, 48, 462, 463, 464, 465
foundation trench, 10, 15, 16, 17, 18, 31, 40, 46, 47, 54
fox, 220
froth flotation, 204

G

gateway, 48
Gazella, 244, 264
Gjerstad's dump, 328, 329, 330, 331, 332, 334, 336, 338, 339, 340, 342, 343, 344, 346, 349
Glyptic, 151, 156, 198
goat(s), 12, 245, 246, 264, 409, 414, 431, 459, 463
gold, 276, 277, 278, 280, 281, 286, 287, 288, 291, 325, 328, 336, 342, 344, 346
Gordianus III, 450, 456
gorgon's head, 449, 451
grain(s), 8, 100, 409, 410, 430, 431, 432, 433, 436, 446, 463
grape(s), 209, 210, 431, 433, 463
grinder(s), 206, 207, 208, 214, 215, 240, 244, 245
gypsum mortar, 8, 16, 40, 462
gypsum mortar/plaster, 5

H

hammerstones, 207
Handmade, 110, 138, 139, 140, 141, 142, 143, 144, 150, 155, 156, 158, 162, 166, 175, 177, 179, 181, 193, 203, 210, 230, 232, 341
header-stretcher, 16
Hellenistic, 9, 10, 11, 12, 20, 47, 86, 88, 89, 91, 92, 93, 94, 95, 97, 155, 163, 282, 283, 285, 287, 288, 299, 329, 330, 331, 332, 333, 334, 337, 338, 340, 343, 344, 345, 346, 349, 379, 380, 391, 393, 394, 396, 427, 438
Hellenistic I, 10, 12, 88, 89
Hellenistic period, 47, 48, 72
helmet(s), 10, 328, 334, 335, 336, 449, 451
hematite, 286, 287, 300, 302
Henry II, 450, 456
Heracles, 448, 449, 450
Hittite, 277, 335, 336
Holocene, 250, 267, 268, 269
horn-core, 264
horse(s), 90, 151, 335, 431, 447, 448, 450, 451, 455, 463
hunter-gatherers, 413

I

Idalion, Period I, 158
Idalion Deposit, 92
Idalion School, 398, 399, 400, 401, 463
Illyrian helmet, 336
information statistic, 411
inscription(s), 11, 12, 13, 36, 37, 333, 429, 449, 450, 463, 466
Ionian, 336, 464
Ionian Revolt, 462
iron, 286
Iron Age, 93, 138, 155, 163, 165, 195, 358, 365, 366, 367, 368, 369, 370, 371, 384
ivory, 120, 121, 151, 152, 153, 156, 166, 198, 199, 200, 201, 215

J

jarosite, 277, 286, 288
jasper, 277, 287, 302
John I Zimisces, 453

K

kantharos, 46, 58, 59, 60, 61, 462
kegelhelm, 335, 336
King SA--, 462
King KI--, 462
Kitionites, 48
kylix, 160, 161

L

land tenure, 429, 430
lapis lazuli, 300
Late Archaic, 398, 399, 401
Late Bronze Age, 428
Late Classical, 329, 330, 332, 333, 334, 438
Late Cypriot, 119, 121, 163, 164, 165, 166, 268, 269, 343, 364, 379, 380, 386, 388, 391, 392, 394, 395, 396, 460, 461
Late Cypriot I, 364, 386, 388, 391, 392, 395
Late Cypriot II, 119, 343, 380, 394, 396
Late Cypriot IIC, 119, 165, 166, 461
Late Cypriot III, 162
Late Cypriot(e) IIB, 162
Late Minoan, 161
Late Mycenaean, 159
Late Mycenaean IIIB, 159, 160
Late Ptolemaic, 449, 452, 456
LC II, 162
LC IIA-B, 160
LC IIC, 159, 162, 164, 165
LC IIC-III, 162
LC IIIA, 166
LCIIIA1, 162
legumes, 431, 463
Lens culinaris, 206
Lens nigricans, 206
Lens orientalis, 206, 210

lentil(s), 204, 206, 209, 210
lime-cement, 13
lime-mortar, 13
limestone ashlars, 16, 17, 18, 462
Linear B, 425
LM IIA1, 161
LM III, 161
LM IIIA:2, 161
Lower City, general, 1, 2, 5, 7, 8, 12, 13, 14, 18, 19, 62, 74, 75, 340, 341, 343, 344, 461, 462, 463, 464, 465, 466, 467
Lower City structures:
    Building A, 97, 338
    Building B, 84, 85
    Building C, 337, 339, 341, 347
    Building D, 69, 71
    City Wall, 14, 15, 45, 46, 47, 48, 49, 50, 51, 52, 53, 54, 55, 56, 58, 346, 348
    Fortifications, 56, 5, 12, 19, 58, 62, 463
    well(s), 2, 87, 90, 93, 96, 97, 205, 340, 348, 432, 434, 437, 438
    Well House, 340, 348

M

malachite, 278, 287, 308
malaria, 129
Medes and Kitians, 336, 464
medieval, 1, 19, 155, 165, 276, 278, 279, 280, 282, 283, 285, 291, 293, 295, 433, 463
Mediterranean triad, 431
metallurgy:
    ancient gallery, 285
    "bent" slag, 284, 323
    black copper, 287, 290
    bun ingot, 284
    copper, 1, 11, 12, 121, 275, 276, 277, 278, 279, 280, 281, 282, 284, 285, 286, 287, 288, 289, 290, 291, 292, 293, 294, 295, 296, 297, 298, 299, 300, 302, 303, 304, 311, 315, 316, 328, 329, 330, 332, 334, 335, 336, 337, 338, 339, 340, 341, 342, 343, 344, 345, 346, 347, 366, 368, 369, 370, 371, 438, 461, 462, 463, 465, 466
    crucible, 12, 281, 283, 304
    Cyprus Mines Corporation, 277, 285, 288
    Devil's Mud, 277, 278, 286, 287, 301, 325
    false gossan(s), 293, 327
    flux, 278, 290, 294, 300, 303
    furnace(s), 12, 276, 282, 283, 284, 285, 289, 290, 294, 298, 299, 300, 303, 304, 311, 340
    furnace liner, 282
    gallery mining, 288
    gangue, 286, 289
    gossan(s), 277, 278, 286, 287, 292, 293, 300, 301, 314, 322
    hand cobbed, 289, 293
    hand cobbing, 289
    heap leaching, 293, 301, 317, 318
    Hellenic Mining Company, 285
    hydrometallurgy, 290, 298, 300, 301, 316
    leach, 291, 292, 293, 295, 299, 301, 302, 303, 317, 318, 319, 326
    leaching, 291, 292, 293, 294, 299, 300, 301, 302, 303, 319
    massive sulfide, 275, 277, 283, 285, 286, 287, 289, 290, 293, 298, 301, 302, 303, 312, 313, 314, 325
    native copper, 276, 277
    natrojarosite, 277, 286, 301, 303

    open-pit mine(s), 287, 326
    open-pit mining, 287, 288, 293
    ore-smelting, 298
    Phoenician slag, 304
    roast, 290, 293, 299, 300
    roast pile, 290, 299, 300
    roasted, 289, 290, 293, 294, 300, 461
    roasting, 290, 293, 294, 299, 300, 301, 304, 315
    slag(s), 12, 16, 17, 31, 275, 276, 278, 279, 280, 281, 282, 283, 284, 285, 287, 290, 292, 293, 294, 300, 301, 303, 304, 306, 309, 321, 322, 323, 324, 328, 461
    slag heap(s), 12, 31, 275, 276, 280, 282, 283, 284, 285, 293, 294, 303, 321
    slag pile(s), 279, 287, 290, 323, 324
    slag, "bent", 284, 323
    smelted, 461
    smelting, 1, 276, 278, 279, 280, 281, 282, 283, 284, 285, 287, 289, 290, 292, 293, 294, 298, 299, 300, 301, 303, 304, 311, 328, 334, 340, 368
    smelting furnace, 283, 289, 290, 300, 311, 340
    sulfide, 275, 276, 277, 278, 279, 283, 285, 286, 287, 288, 289, 290, 293, 294, 295, 298, 300, 301, 302, 303, 304, 314, 315, 316, 319, 325
    sulfide secondary enrichment zone, 287, 288
    tuyeres, 284, 290, 294
metopism, 129
Michael IV, 453, 456
Minoan, 161
Mitannian, 164
mortar, 5, 6, 8, 10, 16, 40, 41, 208, 215, 462
mouflon, 245, 246
mudbrick, 7, 9, 10, 12, 13, 14, 15, 16, 17, 18, 19, 20, 23, 31, 36, 46, 47, 50, 51, 52, 53, 55, 67, 70, 75, 424, 425, 426, 441, 442, 443, 460, 464
murids, 244
Mus musculus, 244
Mycenaean IIIA:2, 161
Mycenaean IIIA-B, 161
Mycenaean IIIB, 146, 147, 148, 159, 160, 161, 381, 397, 461
Mycenaean IIIC:1b, 166

N

Neo-Cypriot style, 398, 401
Neolithic, 1, 126, 129, 203, 204, 205, 207, 209, 210, 211, 212, 218, 220, 222, 223, 244, 246, 247, 249, 250, 259, 260, 261, 265, 267, 268, 277, 300, 376, 426, 427, 432, 434, 459, 460
Nicephoros III, 454, 456

O

obsidian, 204, 205, 206, 207, 211, 213, 224, 459
olive(s), 8, 34, 110, 210, 296, 425, 430, 431, 433, 463, 466
olive oil, 8, 296, 425, 430, 433, 466
olive press, 8
ostraca, 12, 13
ostracon, 18, 48, 463, 466
oven(s), 210, 212, 414, 423, 426, 428, 443
Ovis, 212, 246
Ovis aries, 245, 246
Ovis orientalis orientalis, 245, 246, 258
ᶜOzibaᶜal, 464

P

Palace, 5, 6, 7, 9, 12, 13, 18, 19, 32, 462, 463, 464, 465, 466
peasant(s), 408, 413, 416, 428, 429, 430, 432, 433, 435, 437, 438, 464
Persian, 6, 209, 264, 331, 332, 335, 336, 465
Persian fallow deer, 208, 209, 245, 264
Phanourios minor, 244
Phoenician, 6, 11, 12, 13, 36, 37, 36, 276, 279, 281, 282, 292, 306, 309, 322, 463, 465, 466
Phoenician inscription, 37
Phrygian, 346
pig(s), 245, 247, 252, 253, 259, 260, 261, 262, 431, 463
pigeons, 220, 409
pigmy elephant, 244
pigmy hippopotamus, 244
Pistacia atlantica, 206
plachenite, 286
Pleistocene, 244, 249, 250, 267, 292
plow(s), 2, 425, 426, 430, 443
potassium, 303
Proto-Corinthian, 58
Proto-Cypriot style, 401
Ptolemaic, 449, 452, 456
Ptolemy, King of Cyprus, 449, 456
Ptolemy I, 449, 452, 456
Ptolemy III, 447, 456
Ptolemy IV, 447, 448, 449, 450, 453, 456
Ptolemy IX, 452, 455, 456
Ptolemy VI, 449, 456
Ptolemy VIII, 455, 456
Ptolemy X, 453, 455, 456
pyrite, 277, 278, 286, 288, 289, 290, 291, 292, 297, 300, 303, 319

Q

quern(s), 208, 215, 244, 245, 426

R

radiocarbon, 211, 216, 260, 288
Ramesses, 461
red deer, 249, 264
red ochre, 9, 207, 214
Reshef MKL, 399
Roman, 11, 276, 278, 279, 280, 281, 282, 283, 285, 287, 292, 294, 295, 306, 309, 378, 379, 391, 393, 396, 427, 429, 430, 437
Romanos II, 456
roof tile, 163, 284
roofing, 9, 35
rubble core, 16, 18, 41, 42, 47, 48, 462

S

sandstone, 5, 6, 7, 9, 10, 12, 15, 16, 17, 18, 23, 24, 38, 40, 43, 47, 48, 208, 214, 215, 428, 462, 463
sandstone ashlar(s), 6, 7, 10, 12, 16, 17, 18, 463
selenite, 287
sexual dimorphism, 133, 264, 265

she-wolf, 453
sheep, 12, 245, 246, 264, 409, 431, 446, 459, 463
shrew, 244
silver, 276, 277, 278, 280, 281, 286, 287, 288, 303, 328, 342, 343, 344, 345, 450
Sinda Period I, 159, 166
Sinda Period I/II, 165
skyphos, 58, 59
sling bullet(s), 328, 348, 349
spatial patterning, 407, 408, 410, 413, 416
Stasikypros, 336, 450, 456, 464, 465
stephane, 447, 448, 452, 453
stone bowl(s), 205, 206, 207, 208, 225, 226, 237, 238, 459, 460
Stone Footing, 7
Sub-Archaic style, 398, 400, 401
subsistence, 260, 408, 409, 427, 428, 430, 432, 434, 435, 437, 460
Sumerian, 344
Sus, 245
Sus scrofa, 245

T

"Tamassian Gate", 48
Temple of Athena, 5, 465
tetrobol, 450
thalassemia, 129
Theodora, 454, 456
Theodosius, 448, 456
Triticum boeoticum var. *aeglopoides*, 206
tortoise, 220
tuck-pointed, 6, 16
tuck-pointing, 7, 16

U

use-surface(s), 14, 16, 46, 47, 48, 54, 68, 69, 84, 85, 90

V

Valentinianus, 455, 456
vines, 436
Virgin orans, 454
viticulture, 431, 433
Vitis silvestris, 209, 210
Vitis vinifera, 210
vitriol, 278, 280, 281, 291, 292, 293, 294, 295, 296, 297, 300, 318
Vouni Palace, 13, 465

W

water-sieving, 204
well(s), 205, 348, 432, 434, 437, 438
West Acropolis, 1, 5, 13, 18, 59, 165, 166, 328, 329, 330, 332, 333, 334, 336, 337, 338, 339, 340, 342, 343, 344, 345, 346, 349, 460, 461, 463, 464, 465
West Lower City, 13, 46, 49, 50, 51, 52, 53, 83, 462, 463, 464, 467
West Terrace, general, 1, 5, 7, 8, 11, 12, 13, 14, 15, 17, 18, 19, 20, 21, 22, 30, 47, 48, 328, 329, 331, 332, 334, 340, 341, 342, 343, 345, 348, 461, 462, 463, 465, 466, 467

West Terrace, structures:
    Area C, 5, 6, 7, 9, 10, 13, 15, 17, 22, 28, 29, 32, 34, 35, 331, 334, 340, 342, 345, 348, 466
    Area C Street, 6
    Area CW, 14, 17, 18, 462
    Area D, 5, 6, 10, 11, 13, 14, 17, 18, 26, 27, 28, 29, 34, 35, 36, 37, 329, 332, 334, 341, 345, 348, 462, 463, 466
    Area D Building, 13, 463
    Area D Room, 6, 34, 35, 36, 37, 463, 466
    Citadel, 6, 7, 8, 10, 12, 13, 14, 15, 16, 17, 18, 19, 20, 30, 31, 38, 39, 40, 41, 42, 43, 462, 463, 464, 466
    Citadel Wall, 6, 7, 8, 10, 12, 13, 14, 15, 16, 17, 18, 19, 30, 31, 38, 39, 40, 41, 42, 43, 462, 463, 466
    city-gate, 14
    Eastern Facade, 5, 6, 7, 32
    fortification wall, 7, 14, 18, 461, 462, 463
    Northern Facade, 5, 7, 8, 13, 33
    pier(s), 6, 7, 8, 9, 19, 32, 463
    stone footing, 7
wild boar, 209, 215
wild einkorn, 206
wild pistachio, 206
wine, 296, 425, 430, 431, 433

Z

Zeus, 447, 448, 449, 452, 453, 455

AUTHOR INDEX

A

Abascal, 359
Adamides, 293
Adelman, 59, 120, 138, 343
Agricola, 157, 159, 165, 166, 278, 289, 291, 296, 297, 298
Aigner, 244
Ålin, 18, 18, 58, 83, 156, 158, 166, 358, 464
Allan, 430, 432, 433
Allen, 425, 463
Angel, 126, 129, 133
Arghyros, 329
Arnold, 244, 246, 250, 261
Artzy, 357
Asaro, 357, 365
Aschenbrenner, 425
Åström, L., 162
Åström, P., 157, 158, 162, 333
Attalides, 435, 436, 426

B

Babelon, 448, 450
Barnett, 335, 336, 461
Basalik, 244
Bass, 126
Bate, 267
Bates, 296
Bear, 277, 282, 283
Bender, 285, 286
Benson, 160, 162, 164
Bérard, 279
Bieber, 357, 359, 360, 361, 363, 365, 377, 461, 463
Bikai, 369, 386, 387, 390, 391, 392, 395
Binford, L. R., 407, 413
Binford, S. R., 413
Biringuccio, 280, 291
Birmingham, 63, 64, 366, 368
Bishop, 365
Blinkenberg, 63, 64, 346
Boehmer, 346
Boekschoten, 244
Bonnichen, 408
Borchhardt, 335
Bowen, 307
Breasted, 300
Brooks, 359, 365, 366, 369
Brothwell, 122
Brown, 62
Bruce, 277, 278, 279, 285, 287, 288, 289, 292, 293, 295, 317, 318, 320, 368, 369, 370
Buchanan, 164
Buffon, 280
Bullard, 427

C

Calvet, 59
Carapanos, 331
Carter, 206, 244, 259, 261, 264, 265, 267, 268, 459, 460
Catling, 459, 460
Chaplin, 264, 271
Chapman, D., 250
Chapman, N., 250
Charles, 2, 59, 204, 277
Christodoulou, 425, 426, 427, 428, 429, 430, 431, 432, 433, 434, 435, 437
Cobham, 279
Coghlan, 278
Coldstream, 58, 59, 462
Constantinou, 286
Croft, 206, 259, 261, 265, 459, 460
Cross, 12, 466
Cullis, 276, 279, 282

D

Dahl, 303, 304
David, 408
Davies, 279, 280
Davis, 459
de Bruijn, 244
DeBoer, 408
de Launay, 290
de Mas Latrie, 281
Deonna, 63, 64
DeVore, 408
di Cesnola, 119, 344, 465
Dikaios, 58, 157, 159, 160, 161, 162, 165, 166, 203, 204, 208, 265
Dodson, 357
Dothan, 357, 365
Ducos, 247, 248, 249, 250, 265, 267, 268, 269

E

Edge, 276, 279, 282
Elayi, 6
Emeleus, 357

F

Flaksberger, 432
Forbes, 278
Foster, 428
French, 204
Furumark, 157, 159, 160, 161, 162, 165, 166

G

Gaber, 1, 5, 398, 401
Galen of Pergamon, 295
Gallin, 435
Gamst, 428

Garrard, 244, 259
Geary, 362
Gilbert, 133
Gjerstad, 5, 6, 12, 19, 5, 6, 12, 19, 58, 59, 63, 328, 329, 330, 331, 332, 334, 335, 336, 337, 338, 339, 340, 342, 343, 344, 345, 346, 349, 367, 368, 369, 370, 398, 400, 401, 426, 464, 465
Gould, 408
Govett, 286
Gowland, 279
Graham, 5
Grayson, 260
Grembler, 278, 288, 303

H

Halstead, 249, 250, 264, 268, 269
Harbottle, 359
Hardin, 411
Harshman, 320
Healy, 278, 288, 308
Hencken, 335, 336
Hennessy, 160, 164
Hennig, 408
Herodotus, 336
Heyd, 280
Higgs, 246, 247, 250, 460
Hill, G. F., 413
Hill, J. N., 407, 465
Hills, 278, 288, 291
Holmes, 277
Hopf, 206

J

Jarman, H. N., 2, 204, 247, 249, 261, 268, 460
Jarman, M. R., 247
Johnston, 427

K

Karageorghis, 119, 120, 159, 160, 162, 163, 164, 165, 166, 329, 330, 331, 335, 339, 344, 377
Karouzis, 429, 435
Kavazis, 287
Keefe, 426, 430, 432
Kennedy, 279
Kinch, 63
King, 246, 250
Klein, 244
Klengel, 400
Koucky, 8, 11, 16, 213, 250, 275, 276, 279, 282, 283, 306, 310, 368, 427, 461, 463
Kramer, 408
Krogman, 132, 133
Kurten, 249, 268

L

Lambros, 450
Lamon, 64

Lang, 398, 399, 401, 462
Lange, 408
Lathrap, 408
Lavender, 277, 288, 292
Lawn, 211
Le Brun, 244, 459
Lee, 408
Legge, 2, 204
Lehavy, 203, 204, 205, 209, 210, 244, 260, 459, 460
Longacre, 407, 413
Longuet, 451, 455
Lopez, 280
Lusignano, 280, 281, 291

M

Macalister, 64, 331
MacArthur, 249
Maier, 464
Maliotis, 275
Malouf, 302
Marvin, 336, 426, 429, 465
Masson, 464
Matson, 365
McGovern, 211
McKern, 133
Meulengracht, 211
Michaelidou-Nicolaou, 333
Mudd, 295
Muhly, 368
Müller, 448
Murrenhof, 357
Muscarella, 346

N

Newell, 449, 453
Nicolaou, I., 72, 333, 334, 447, 464
Nicolaou, K., 277,
Nobis, 268

O

O'Connell, 413
Ohnefalsch-Richter, 63, 64, 119, 398, 426
Oppenheim, 462

P

Pantazis, 278
Papadopoullos, 431, 433
Partington, 280
Payne, 244, 246, 260
Peckham, 464
Pegolotti, 280
Peltenburg, 210, 277
Peristiany, 436, 440

Perkins, 244
Perlman, 357, 365
Petrie, 63, 331
Pielou, 411
Pocock, 287
Porada, 164
Porcacchi, 280
Poursat, 164
Pryce, 400
Purcell, 425, 430, 433

R

Raymond, 280
Redman, 461
Reed, 244
Renfrew, C., 207, 210, 213
Renfrew, J., 206
Rickard, 276, 279
Robertson, 286
Robinson, 331, 333, 339
Röllig, 278, 288, 303
Rothenberg, 285, 286
Rupp, 459, 461
Rydberg, 408

S

Sallade, 407
Saxon, 246
Sayre, 357, 359, 360
Schachermeyr, 160, 166
Schaeffer, 279
Schairer, 307
Schiffer, 407
Schlour, 123
Schlumberger, 451, 455
Schmidt, 331, 336
Schulte-Campbell, 119, 166
Schwartz, 126, 129, 212, 244, 259, 264, 432
Shannon, 411
Shipton, 64
Silver, 264
Sjöqvist, 162
Smith, 290
Snodgrass, 331, 332, 335, 336
Sondaar, 244
Sonniti, 280
Stager, 1, 5, 6, 12, 14, 17, 18, 5, 6, 12, 14, 17, 18, 328, 330, 333, 334, 336, 337, 340, 344, 345, 368, 459, 461, 463
Stanislawski, 408
Stanley Price, 203, 212, 244, 246, 250, 260, 261, 269, 459, 460
Stavrinou, 292
Steinberg, 275, 276, 282, 306, 368, 461, 463
Stern, 6
Stewart, 133, 206, 210, 431, 460, 463
Stronach, 63, 64, 331, 332, 336

Svoronos, 447, 448, 449, 452, 453, 455

T

Taylor, 157, 162, 283
Todd, 211, 244, 459
Trennery, 287
Tylecote, 283

U

Uerpmann, 260

V

Van Beek, G. W., 6, 368
Van Beek, O., 6
Vermeule, 398, 401
Vessberg, 344
Vita-Finzi, 250

W

Waldbaum, 10, 10, 328, 331, 339, 340, 341, 345
Walker, 1, 5, 12, 14, 17, 18, 5, 12, 14, 17, 18, 45, 62, 83, 259, 276, 279, 283, 328, 330, 333, 334, 336, 337, 340, 344, 345, 459, 461
Walsh, 295
Ward, 357
Warren, 213
Watkins, 203, 211
Watson, 244, 246, 250, 261
Weaver, 411
Weick, 357
Wertime, S. F., 275
Wertime, T. A., 275
Westholm, 344
Whallon, 410
White, 271
Williams, 320
Wilmsen, 408
Wilson, 249
Wolf, 425, 428
Woolley, 329, 330
Wright, 1, 5, 12, 14, 17, 18, 5, 12, 14, 17, 18, 328, 330, 333, 334, 336, 337, 340, 344, 345, 368, 461

Y

Yarus, 283, 310
Yon, 59

Z

Zeuner, 246, 247
Zipf, 413, 414, 415
Zohary, 206
Zwicker, 288, 303

PLACE NAME INDEX

A

Aegean, 58, 344, 426, 462
Agrokipia, 283
Ain Mallaha, 247, 249, 250, 267, 268
Akhera, 120, 126, 129
Al Mina, 329, 330
Alambra, 408, 409, 413, 416, 417, 418, 419, 420
Alexandria, 281
Amathus, 366
Ambeleri, 13
Ammos River, 408, 419
Amuq, 203, 211
Anatolia, 207, 248, 250, 346, 368, 460
Angastina, 268
Antioch, 451, 455
Apliki, 157, 376
Aqaba, 286
Assyria, 462
Athena Temple, 464
Ayia Irini, 59, 330, 331, 335, 336, 385, 390, 392, 395
Ayios Sozomenos, 1, 283, 444, 445

B

Bamboula, 126, 129
Bogazköy, 335, 336, 346

C

Carapanos, 331
Çayönü, 210
Çiftlik, 207, 213, 459
Cilicia, 250
Constantinopolis, 448
Crete, 161

D

Delos, 63, 64
Dhali, Neolithic site, 203
Dodona, 331

E

Edessa, 451, 455, 456
Edi'il, 462
Egypt, 300, 332
El Wad, 249, 267, 268
Enkomi, 129, 165, 268, 303
Ergani-Maden, 285
Erimi, 265, 268

F

Famagusta, 59, 376

G

Gaza, 331
Gerar (Tell Jemmeh), 331
Gezer, 64, 331
Gordion, 346

H

Hala Sultan Tekke, 126, 129
Harz District, 297

I

Ialysos, 335
Ionia, 336

K

Kafkalia, 166
Kakopetria, 329, 330
Kalavasos-Tenta, 244, 459
Kambia, 288
Karnak, 461, 469
Kataliondas, 277, 376, 459
Khirokitia, 126, 129, 203, 207, 208, 211, 212, 244, 248, 249, 250, 251, 265, 268, 459, 460
Kissonerga-Mylouthkia, 265, 267, 273
Kition, 126, 129, 159, 161, 164, 165, 279, 364, 365, 367, 368, 369, 370, 377, 390, 391, 392, 394, 400, 461, 463, 464, 465
Knossos, 247
Kokkinoya, 304
Kornos, 376, 426
Kouklia-Mantissa, 159, 162
Kourion, 164
Ktima, 261
Kutrafa Nikitari, 64
Kythrea District, 434

L

Lapithos, 386, 395
Larnaca, 1, 119, 164, 376, 429, 463
Lemba, 210, 265, 269, 273, 277
Lemba-Lakkous, 265
Levant, 63, 211, 248, 249, 250, 459, 460
Limassol, 276, 364, 408, 437, 438
Limni, 287
Louroujina, 1, 437
Lymbia, 437
Lythrodonda, 1, 279, 280, 282, 283, 461, 463

M

Marion, 64, 330, 331, 365, 385, 392, 395, 465
Maroni, 161
Mathiati, 206, 208
Mathiati, 276, 280, 282, 283, 285, 289, 325, 376, 461, 463
Mavrovouni, 277, 288, 289, 292, 295
Mediterranean, 58, 129, 246, 249, 268, 277, 280, 285, 287, 293, 298, 302, 335, 357, 365, 382, 383, 384, 385, 386, 430, 431
Megiddo, 64
Mersinaki, 331, 400, 404
Mesaoria, 250, 432
Messenia, 425
Mitsero, 280, 370
Monagroulli, 276
Moni, 276
Monis River Valley, 276
Morphou, 427, 428

N

Nicosia, 1, 119, 208, 285, 376, 383, 408, 409, 428, 429, 437, 438, 463
Nineveh, 462
North Mathiati, 276, 285

O

Olynthus, 331, 333

P

Palestine, 63, 331, 365, 368, 369, 370
Pasargadae, 331, 336
Pass Lueg, 335, 336
Pendayia, 126, 129
Pergamon, 295
Persepolis, 331, 336
Petra, 282, 287, 323
Philia, 203, 459
Philia-Drakos A, 203, 467
Phlamoudhi, 365
Phrygia, 336
Platies, 278, 283, 322
Potamia, 203, 376, 438
Pyla, 399, 400, 401, 403
Pyla-Verghi, 157, 161

R

Rhodes, 63, 64, 335
Rio Tinto, Spain, 278, 285, 286, 288, 326

S

Salamis, 58, 329, 330, 331, 344, 377, 378, 389, 393, 394, 465
Sha, 206, 208, 461, 463
Sinai, 286

Sinda, 166
Skouriotissa, 277, 278, 280, 282, 288, 292, 295, 298, 323, 324, 325
Soli, 64, 287, 295, 330, 331
Sotira, 265, 268
South Mathiati, 280, 282, 283, 289, 325
South Russia, 332
Spilli, 280, 282, 324
Stephania, 164
Syria, 63, 365, 368, 369, 370
Syro-Cilicia, 459

T

Tabun, 249, 267, 268
Tamassos, 64, 275, 280, 298, 364, 367, 368, 369, 371, 378, 387, 388, 389, 390, 391, 395, 461
Teredhia, 1, 279, 280, 282, 283, 285, 310, 311
Troodos Mountain, 408
Troodos Mountains, 1, 275, 283, 465
Turkey, 210, 285
Tyre, 366

V

Vasilikos Valley, 261
Venice, 280, 281, 291
Vouni, 329, 330, 331, 365, 383, 384, 393, 394, 400, 401, 403, 404, 465

Y

Yalias River, 1, 203, 204, 205, 206, 211, 276, 427, 432, 438, 459